READINGS IN MANAGEMENT ACCOUNTING

Fifth Edition

S. Mark Young

Leventhal School of Accounting
Marshall School of Business
University of Southern California

PRENTICE HALL

Upper Saddle River, New Jersey 07458

This book is dedicated to the memory of Professor John K. Shank – mentor, friend and the best teacher of accounting I have ever encountered.

VP/Editorial Director: Jeff Shelstad
AVP/ Executive Editor: Wendy Craven
Project Manager: Kerri Tomasso
Associate Director, Manufacturing: Vincent Scelta
Production Editor & Buyer: Carol O'Rourke
Printer/Binder: Bind-Rite Graphics, Robbinsville

Pearson Prentice Hall^{TM} *is a trademark of Pearson Education, Inc*

10 9 8 7 6 5 4 3 2 1
ISBN-13: 978-0-13-228022-8
ISBN-10:   0-13-228022-1

Table of Contents

Preface

While this book can be used to supplement any management accounting or cost accounting text, the readings have been tailored to accompany Anthony Atkinson, Robert S. Kaplan, Ella Mae Matsumura and S. Mark Young's textbook, *Management Accounting, 5th Edition* (Prentice Hall, 2007).

To Students

For each textbook chapter there is a corresponding set of readings that complements text material and introduces you to applications of the material in a wide variety of contexts. At the end of each reading, questions test your understanding of what you have read. The readings are taken from many sources including the *Wall Street Journal, Strategic Finance, MIT Sloan Management Review, Harvard Business Review,* and *Accounting Horizons* among others. They represent both classic and current thinking on each of the topics covered in the text.

    The best way to use this book is to read each assigned article in one sitting. Then, read the article a second time taking notes and asking yourself how the article extends your understanding of the text material. In some cases, your instructor may assign specific questions that follow each of the readings. Taking the time to answer these questions thoughtfully will improve your understanding of the material. I hope you find the articles stimulating and thought-provoking.

To Instructors

Readings in Management Accounting, Fifth Edition contains 53 articles representing state-of-the-art thinking and examples on a wide variety of management accounting topics in many types of service and manufacturing contexts. The fifth edition includes most of the readings from fourth and includes ten new articles (1.4, 3.8, 4.5, 5.3, 6.4, 8.4, 8.5, 9.5, 10.6 and 12.4). Please note that several readings have been summarized rather than reprinted in their entirety. Those readings may be accessed by directly contacting the publisher of the article or by going to their Website.

    The suggested solutions to the questions in this book can be found in the *Instructor's Manual* (available online) prepared for *Readings in Management Accounting*. While each of the readings has been listed for a specific chapter, in many cases, a reading may be successfully applied to several chapters. If you have a favorite reading that is not contained in this book, please send me the citation and I will gladly consider it for the next edition and acknowledge your contribution. Thank you very much.

S. Mark Young
Leventhal School of Accounting
Marshall School of Business
University of Southern California
Los Angeles, CA 90089

Acknowledgments

I would like to thank Kerri Tomasso, Linda Albelli, and Jane Avery for their editorial and administrative assistance, and editors, Wendy Craven and Jeff Shelsted for their encouragement and support of the project. Also, I would like to thank Bob Kaplan, Harvard University, Gerald Meyers, Pacific Lutheran University, Mike Shields, Michigan State University and Shannon Anderson, Rice University for readings suggestions. In particular, I am grateful to Ella Mae Matsumura, University of Wisconsin, Madison for her many contributions to this book.

S. Mark Young
University of Southern California

October, 2006

About the Author

S. Mark Young holds the *George Bozanic and Holman G. Hurt Chair in Sports and Entertainment Business* and is also Professor of Accounting, Professor of Management and Organization at the Marshall School of Business, University of Southern California and Professor of Communication at the Annenberg School for Communication at USC. Previously, Dr. Young served as the Associate Dean for Academic Planning and Associate Dean and Academic Director of the Marshall MBA (Full-Time MBA) Program. Professor Young received an A.B. from Oberlin College (Economics), an M. Acc. from the Ohio State University, and a Ph.D. from the University of Pittsburgh.

Professor Young has published research in a variety of journals including *The Accounting Review, Accounting, Organizations and Society*, and the *Journal of Accounting Research*. Currently, he is on the editorial board of several major journals and was past Associate Editor for *The Accounting Review*. In 2006, he was a co-winner of the Notable Contribution to the Accounting Literature (with Shannon Anderson) and has won the *Notable Contributions to the Management Accounting Literature* Award twice—with Frank Selto (1994) and Shannon Anderson (2003). He also received the *Jim Bulloch Award for Innovations in Management Accounting Education* in 2005.

Dr. Young has extensive executive teaching and consulting experience having taught in executive programs for Daimler-Chrysler, Texas Instruments, Shell Oil, AMGEN and British Airways. Most recently, Young has had consulting or research relationships with the First Data Corporation, the Chrysler Corporation, Texas Instruments and Southwest Airlines. He has won four outstanding teaching awards at the undergraduate and graduate levels, including the *Golden Apple Teaching Award* and is a Distinguished Fellow in the Center for Excellence in Teaching at USC. Currently he teaches courses in management accounting and entertainment management, and leads the entertainment management program within the Marshall School at USC. His book, *Entertainment Management – Understanding the Business of Motion Pictures, Television, Music and Games* will soon be published by Prentice-Hall.

Professor Young also maintains an interest in popular culture and his paper "Narcissism and Celebrity" published in the Journal of Research in Personality (with Drew Pinsky) recently received World-Wide attention. Young even appeared on the Howard Stern show to discuss the findings of the research.

Chapter 1

Management Accounting: Information That Creates Value

The readings in Chapter 1 all emphasize the changing role of management accounting information in today's business organizations. Even though Peter Drucker's well-known essay, *Be Data Literate - Know what to Know (Reading 1.1)*, is 15 years old, it is still very relevant today. Drucker argues that there are three informational challenges facing executives. The first is to become information literate to know what information they need, when, and in what form. The second challenge is how to obtain, test, and combine information and integrate it into the existing information system. The final challenge central to the study of management accounting, is that data processing and accounting systems need to be brought together to decrease redundancy and increase compatibility. Drucker discusses the many new roles for accounting information and states: "Accounting has become the most intellectually challenging area in the field of management, and the most turbulent one."

The second article (Reading 1.2) by Bill Ferrara, *Cost/Management Accounting: The 21st Century Paradigm*, traces the development of product costing and pricing through four management accounting eras or paradigms. In Paradigm A – from the early 1900s to the 1940s, standard costing was developed. Prices were determined by taking total cost per unit and adding a desired profit. In Paradigm B, the major advances made were the distinction between fixed and variable costs, the development of direct costing, and greater emphasis on volume and capacity considerations. In the late 1980s and through the early 1990s, Paradigm C arises with the development of activity based costing (ABC) and a new framework for creating greater accuracy in product costing by recognizing product complexity and product diversity as cost drivers. Paradigm D represents the current era and is characterized by the emphasis on target costing. Using this concept, the market determines selling prices, which in turn dictate allowable costs. The author predicts that a combination of Paradigms C and D will be the most useful for the 21st Century.

In Reading 1.3, *Management Accounting in the Era of Electronic Commerce*, A. Kogan, E. F. Sudit and M. A. Vasarhelyi present introductory material on the basics of the Internet, but more importantly tie these fundamental ideas to how companies will conduct part or all of their business from now on. All aspects of the value chain, including idea generation, design, procurement, manufacturing, marketing and distribution will be affected by the Internet. In addition, the vast majority of Fortune 1000 companies are now relying on Electronic Data Interchange (EDI) systems for cost savings and effectiveness. Since small companies cannot afford these private network connections they are turning to EDI-type systems over the Internet. Another key aspect of electronic commerce relates to links being forged between suppliers and subcontractors. Such connections are expected to result in faster turnaround time and huge cost savings. The authors also present material on ERP systems and their implications for management accountants.

Alexander Mersereau argues in Reading 1.4, *Pushing the Art of Management Accounting* that despite the many new advances in management accounting practices that the implementation effectiveness of these new practices has stalled in many organizations. Mersereau suggests that three things have to happen to increase effectiveness: (1) management accountants must know what information the organization needs, how it will be used and how to communicate it to everyone, (2) managers must be trained to understand management accounting information, and (3) managers must be able to act on the information with which they are provided.

Readings
Chapter 1

1.1 Be Data Literate—Know What to Know

by Peter F. Drucker*

Executives have become computer literate. The younger ones, especially, know more about the way the computer works than they know about the mechanics of the automobile or the telephone. But not many executives are information-literature. They know how to get data. But most still have to learn how to use data.

Few executives yet know how to ask: What information do I need to do my job? When do I need it? In what form? And from whom should I be getting it? Fewer still ask: What new tasks can I tackle now that I get all these data? Which old tasks should I abandon? Which tasks should I do differently? Practically no one asks: What information do I owe? To whom? When? In what form?

A "database," no matter how copious, is not information. It is information's ore. For raw material to become information, it must be organized for a task, directed toward specific performance, applied to a decision. Raw material cannot do that itself. Nor can information specialists. They can cajole their customers, the data users. They can advise, demonstrate, and teach. But they can no more manage data for users than a personnel department can take over management of the people who work with an executive.

THE FIRST CHALLENGE

Information specialists are toolmakers. The data users, whether executive or professional, have to decide what information to use, what to use it for and how to use it. They have to make themselves information-literate. This is the first challenge facing information users now that executives have become computer literate.

But the organization also has to become information literature. It also needs to learn to ask: What information do we need in this company? When do we need it? In what form? And where do we get it? So far, such questions are being asked primarily by the military, and even there mainly for tactical, day-to-day decisions. In business such questions have been asked only by a few multinationals, foremost among them the Anglo-Dutch Unilever, a few oil companies such as Shell, and the large Japanese trading companies.

The moment these questions are asked, it becomes clear that the information a business most depends on are available, if at all, only in primitive and disorganized form. For what a business needs the most for its decisions—especially its strategic ones—are data about what goes on outside of it. It is only outside the business where there are results, opportunities and threats.

So far, the only data from the outside that have been integrated into most companies' information systems and into their decision-making process are day-to-day market data: what existing customers buy, where they buy, how they buy. Few businesses have tried to get information about their noncustomers, let alone have integrated such information into their databases. Yet no matter how powerful a company is in its industry or market, noncustomers almost always outnumber customers.

American department stores had a very large customer base, perhaps 30% of the middle-class market, and they had far more information about their own customers than any other industry. Yet their failure to pay attention to the 70% who were not customers largely explains why they are today in a severe crisis. Their noncustomers increasingly were the young affluent, double-earner families who were the growth market of the 1980s.

The commercial banks, for all their copious statistics about their customers, similarly did not realize until very late that more and more of their potential customers had become noncustomers. Many had turned to commercial paper to finance themselves instead of borrowing from the banks.

When it comes to nonmarket information—demographics; the behavior and plans of actual and potential competitors; technology; economics; the shifts signaling foreign-exchange fluctuations to come and capital movements—there are either no data at all or only the broadest of generalizations. Few attempts have been made to think through the bearing that such information has on the company's decisions. How to obtain these data; how to test them; how to put them together with the existing information system to make them effective in a company's decision process—this is the second major challenge facing information users today.

It needs to be tackled soon. Companies today rely for their decisions either on inside data such as costs or on untested assumptions about the outside. In either case they are trying to fly on one wing.

Finally, the most difficult of the new challenges: We will have to bring together the two information systems that businesses now run side by side—computer-based

---

* From P. Drucker, "Be Data Literate—Know What to Know," *Wall Street Journal* (December 1, 1992): 14. Reprinted with permission.

data processing and the accounting system. At least we will have to make the two compatible.

People usually consider accounting to be "financial." But that is valid only for the part, going back 700 years, that deals with assets, liabilities and cash flows; it is only a small part of modern accounting. Most of accounting deals with operations rather than with finance, and for operational accounting money is simply a notation and the language in which to express nonmonetary events. Indeed, accounting is being shaken to its very roots by reform movements—aimed at moving it away from being financial and toward becoming operational.

There is the new "transactional" accounting that attempts to relate operations to their expected results. There are attempts to change asset values from historical cost to estimates of expected future returns. Accounting has become the most intellectually challenging area in the field of management, and the most turbulent one. All these new accounting theories aim at turning accounting data into information for management decision making. In other words, they share the goals of computer-based data processing.

Today these two information systems operate in isolation from each other. They do not even compete, as a rule. In the business schools we keep the two apart with separate departments of accounting and of computer science, and separate degrees in each.

The practitioners have different backgrounds, different values, and different career ladders. They work in different departments and for different bosses. There is a "chief information officer" for computer-based data processing, usually with a background in computer technology. Accounting typically reports to a "chief financial officer," often with a background in financing the company and in managing its money. Neither boss, in other words, is information-focused as a rule.

The two systems increasingly overlap. They also increasingly come up with what look like conflicting—or at least incompatible—data about the same event; for the two look at the same event quite differently. Till now this has created little confusion. Companies tended to pay attention to what their accountants told them and to disregard the data of their information system, at least for top-management decisions. But this is changing as computer-literate executives are moving into decision-making positions.

UP FOR GRABS

One development can be considered highly probable: Managing money—what we now call the "treasury function"—will be divorced from accounting (that is, from its information component) and will be set up, staffed and run separately. How we will otherwise manage the two information systems is up for grabs. But that we will bring them together within the next 10 years, or at least sort out which system does what, can be predicted.

Computer people still are concerned with greater speed and bigger memories. But the challenges increasingly will be not technical, but to convert data into usable information that is actually being used.

Mr. Drucker is professor of social sciences and management at the Claremont Graduate School in California.

QUESTION

1.1 What does Drucker mean when he says: "Be data literate?" understand source + purpose

1.2 Cost/Management Accounting: The Twenty-first Century Paradigm

by William L. Ferrara, CPA*

CERTIFICATE OF MERIT, 1994–95

What will the field of management accounting look like in the twenty-first century? To find out, let's consider four paradigms that cover its recent history. These paradigms provide us with an intriguing review of the current scene from a historical perspective (see Table 1) and an opportunity to focus on unresolved issues. Ultimately, we can consider adjusting and even combining paradigms in anticipation of a new one for the twenty-first century.

For continuity and simplicity, we'll consider each paradigm in the context of both product costing and the determination of selling price. This context is useful especially because the current vogue of activity-based cost analysis emphasizes improved product costing in order to arrive at better pricing decisions.

PARADIGM A: TURN OF THE CENTURY UNTIL THE 1940S—THE ERA OF THE INDUSTRIAL REVOLUTION PLUS

Paradigm A conjures up the image of an early-day industrial engineering type such as Frederick Taylor who was interested in what costs should be, that is, standard costs. These engineering-driven standards were typically a function of product specifications, time and motion studies, and the like. The costs involved were direct

---

* From W. L. Ferrara, "Cost/Management Accounting: The Twenty-first Century Paradigm," *Management Accounting* (December 1995): 30–36. Reprinted with permission.

materials, direct labor, manufacturing overhead, and even marketing and administrative costs, all of which were tied together in a total cost per unit of output.

TABLE 1. A HISTORICAL REVIEW OF COSTING/PRICING ISSUES VIA FOUR PARADIGMS

Cost/Pricing—Paradigm A
Turn of the Century Until 1940s:
The Era of the Industrial Revolution Plus

Direct materials	XX
Direct labor	XX
Manufacturing overhead	XX
Marketing and administrative	XX
Total cost per unit	XX
Desired profit (markup)	XX
Target selling price per unit	XX

Costing/Pricing—Paradigm B
The 1940s Until the 1980s:
The Era of Cost-Volume-Profit Analysis and Direct Costing

Variable costs	XX
Direct materials	XX
Direct labor	XX
Variable manufacturing overhead	XX
Variable marketing and administrative	XX
Total variable cost per unit	XX
Fixed costs	
Fixed manufacturing overhead	XX
Fixed marketing and administrative	XX
Total fixed cost per unit	XX
Grand total cost per unit	XX
Desired profit (markup)	XX
Target selling price per unit	XX

Costing/Pricing—Paradigm C
The late 1980s and Early 1990s:
The Era of Activity-Based Costing

Variable costs	
Direct materials	XX
Direct labor	XX
Variable manufacturing overhead	
Variable with number of units	XX
Variable with product complexity (number of batches)	XX
Variable with product diversity (number of products)	XX
Variable marketing and administrative	XX
Total variance cost per unit	XX
Fixed costs	
Fixed manufacturing overhead	XX
Fixed marketing and administrative	XX
Total fixed cost per unit	XX
Grand total cost per unit	XX
Desired profit (markup)	XX
Target selling price per unit	XX

Costing/Pricing—Paradigm D
The 1990s and Beyond:
The Era of Market-Driven Standard (Allowable) Costs

Selling price (given competitive setting)	XX
Less desired profit	XX
Allowable or target cost per unit	XX

Added to the total cost per unit was a desired profit or markup, and the sum of total cost and desired profit yielded a target selling price per unit. In many instances, the total cost per unit excluded marketing and/or administrative costs, which were included as a factor in the desired profit. The ultimate result was still the target selling price per unit—the price that would yield desired profitability if projected costs per unit could be achieved.

Two issues of contention surface immediately with Paradigm A:

1. What volume of activity should be used to determine unit costs?
2. How should desired profit be determined?

The variety of answers typically offered is amazing even if both questions are put to an audience of practitioners representing various departments of the same company, as I have done over many years.

Table 2 shows possible answers for the "volume of activity" question, which must be addressed to determine total unit costs for Paradigms A, B, and C. Answers usually lean in the direction of expected volume or something referred to as standard or normal volume. A rather difficult aspect of the expected volume answer is its implicit circular reasoning—expected volume assumes a selling price while it is being used to determine unit costs and ultimately a "target" selling price.

The answers for the "desired profit" question typically used to be very subjective or rule-of-thumb oriented. In recent years, however, up-to-date return on investment and cost of capital concepts have been considered in the most prevalent answers.

As we move on to subsequent paradigms, these two questions or issues of contention remain, and others emerge.

PARADIGM B: THE 1940S UNTIL THE 1980S—THE ERA OF COST-VOLUME-PROFIT ANALYSIS AND DIRECT COSTING

Paradigm B introduces the distinction between fixed and variable costs, which ultimately leads to cost-volume-profit analysis and direct costing. The fixed/variable cost dichotomy and its implications encompass the most dynamic developments in management accounting from the 1940s to the 1980s.

On the surface, not much seems to change between Paradigms A and B other than the distinction between fixed and variable costs as part of a total unit cost and a target selling price. However, even a cursory consideration of Tables 1 and 2 reveals a refinement of one of our issues of contention, that is:

1. Variable costs per unit are determined by engineering standards and analytic techniques, which means that the volume of activity issue relates essentially to fixed costs.

TABLE 2. THREE HISTORICAL PARADIGMS RELATIVE TO CALCULATING AND USING UNIT PRODUCT COSTS*

Paradigm A
Calculating and Using Unit Product Costs
Ignoring the Distinction Between Fixed and Variable Costs

Manufacturing costs	
Direct materials	$ 200,000
Direct labor	250,000
Manufacturing overhead	450,000
Marketing and administrative costs	500,000
Total	$1,400,000

Paradigm B
Calculating and Using Unit Product Costs
Using the Distinction Between Fixed and Variable Costs

Variable costs	
Direct materials	1.00 per unit
Direct labor	1.25 per unit
Manufacturing overhead	.50 per unit
Marketing and administrative	.25 per unit
Total	$ 3.00 per unit
Fixed costs	
Manufacturing overhead	350,000
Marketing and administrative	450,000
Total	$ 800,000

Paradigm C
Calculating and Using Unit Product Costs
The New Ideology of Activity-Based Costing

Variable costs	
Direct materials	$ 1.00 per unit
Direct labor	1.25 per unit
Variable manufacturing overhead	
Variable with number of units	.50 per unit
Variable with product complexity (number of batches)	.40 per unit
Variable with product diversity (number of products)	.35 per unit
Variable marketing and administrative	.25 per unit
Total	$ 3.75 per unit
Fixed costs	
Manufacturing overhead	$ 175,000
Marketing and administrative	450,000
Total	$ 625,000

Note: Volume levels to be considered for determining unit costs; actual volume—last period; average actual volume—e.g., past five years; expected volume—next period; average expected volume—e.g., next five years; capacity; other possibilities—standard or normal volume, given that these volume levels can be precisely defined.

* The numbers in the above illustrations are intended only to be illustrative in the broadest sense. They have no other intended purpose.

2. Furthermore, many variable costs have become more fixed over time. Union contracts and labor legislation have affected labor costs in just this fashion.

The issue of how to determine desired profit remains an issue of contention as we move to Paradigms C and D.

Variable costs per unit for direct materials and direct labor are determined easily by the engineering specifications for materials and labor requirements. Similarly, the per-unit amounts of other variable costs can be calculated. Techniques that typically are variations of regression analysis isolate the variable cost per unit as the "b" coefficient in flexible budget formulations.

Deriving variable costs per unit via engineering standards and analytic techniques leaves us with only the fixed costs to consider when determining the volume of activity to divide by in deriving per-unit costs. None of the other issues related to the volume-of-activity question changes from our earlier discussion, except that many variable costs have become more fixed over time. In essence, the issue of volume of activity to divide by has become a larger issue as the relative amount of variable costs has diminished and the relative amount of fixed costs has increased.

PARADIGM C: THE LATE 1980S AND THE EARLY 1990S—THE ERA OF ACTIVITY-BASED COSTING
Much of the recent, exciting revival of interest in cost/management accounting relates to Paradigm C, which embodies activity-based costing (ABC). On the surface, Paradigm C considers only two additional variable costs in the development of a total cost per unit. Recognition of these additional variable costs is designed to improve the accuracy of a total unit cost, which then should improve the determination of selling prices and product mix decisions.

The new or additional variable costs of ABC relate to product complexity and product diversity. As shown in Tables 1 and 2, there are three elements of variable manufacturing cost under ABC:[1]

1. Costs that vary with units of product.
2. Costs that vary with product complexity, such as number of batches.
3. Costs that vary with product diversity, such as number of products.

The implications of the new categories of variable costs initially suggest a decreased number of fixed costs, but *further consideration of ABC leads me to suspect that the supposed additional variable costs are really fixed costs.*

This additional issue of contention could revive the controversy over "direct costing versus absorption costing," a paramount issue of the late 1950s and 1960s. Look at the ABC literature. It doesn't take much to see the possibility that ABC is nothing more than an updated, revised, and, most likely, more accurate version of absorption costing.

It's unfortunate that the advocates of ABC virtually have ignored the significance of Paradigm B's direct costing implications that were put forth so eloquently by J. S. Earley in 1955. According to Earley, the new management accounting "implied basing decisions on their estimated effects on marginal balances and contribution margins rather than upon 'full cost' calculations. It involves consistent references to variable costs and 'specific' fixed costs where these are relevant—and neglect of those costs unaffected by decisions."[2]

Another interesting facet of cost/management accounting virtually ignored by the advocates of ABC is the emergence of Paradigm D. This paradigm, which appears to have hail its origins in Japan (Hiromoto), has the potential to revolutionize cost/management accounting as it implicitly asks ABC enthusiasts, "What do costs have to do with the determination of selling prices? With the exception of cost-based pricing contracts, the market determines the price, and the role of cost is to help determine whether or not it is wise to enter the market or stay in the market."[3]

PARADIGM D: THE 1990S AND BEYOND—THE ERA OF MARKET-DRIVEN STANDARD (ALLOWABLE OR TARGET) COSTS AS OPPOSED TO ENGINEERING-DRIVEN STANDARD COSTS.

Under Paradigm D we no longer look to the development of a total unit cost in order to help determine a selling price. Instead we use the selling price we believe the market will allow to help us determine the cost that the market will allow. Peter Drucker has referred to this concept as price led costing as opposed to cost-led pricing.

The allowable or target cost per unit is a market-driven standard cost that has to be met if desired profits are to be achieved. Paradigm D questions the validity of any paradigm based on engineering-driven standard costs. Perhaps after some 90 years, the engineering-driven standard costs of Frederick Taylor and his contemporaries have been partially or wholly displaced by market-driven standard costs.

We still have the issue of how to determine desired profit with Paradigm D. However, Paradigm D creates a whole series of provocative new issues such as:

1. All that counts is that total cost per unit ultimately must not exceed the allowable or target cost if the desired profit is to be attained. This idea may mean that now the distinction between fixed and variable costs is either irrelevant or considerably less relevant.
2. If we truly believe in continuous improvement, then the allowable or target cost per unit must be reduced over time.
3. The way we work may have to change in order for us to reduce costs. Ultimately, this change can lead to the empowerment of our own workforce for, as we all know, often it is those closest to the action who can lead us on the path of continuous improvement.

This issue of continuous improvement via empowerment involves all people in the workforce—those in the factory, in procurement, in marketing and distribution, and in administrative offices.[4] Continuous improvement even creates the possibility of more positive relationships with suppliers and customers, again to reduce costs and increase quality and performance.[5] Tom Johnson, one of the early enthusiasts of ABC, stated the case for continuous improvement as follows: "Do activity costing if you must. But don't fool yourself into thinking that ABC will help you become a global competitor. For that, get busy with the improvement process!"[6]

REFINING AND FOCUSING ISSUES OF CONTENTION

Look at Paradigm D again. The two questions or issues of contention for Paradigm A concerning desired profit and level of volume remain, but they are easier to deal with in the era of Paradigm D. Given our current knowledge of cost of capital concepts, we can deal effectively with desired profit in terms of the level of profit needed to keep the suppliers of capital (debt and equity) satisfied given a particular profit planning horizon.

In terms of the volume of activity issue, Paradigm D can yield an answer that would have been considered only tentatively under earlier paradigms because of its implicit circular reasoning. For example, given the selling price being considered, one could argue for using the expected volume of activity at that selling price for the time period being considered—whether a month, or a quarter, or a year. The resultant expected cost per unit then could be compared to the allowable or target cost per unit of Paradigm D. An unfavorable comparison should produce a questioning attitude concerning what can be done about costs (fixed, variable, or other) or expected activity via alterations in pricing and promotion strategies that would improve the situation. The answers to such questions could provide the continuous improvements of which Johnson spoke.

When viewing volume of activity after the fact, one should shift to calculating actual costs per unit using the actual volume of activity. The result would be a comparison of allowable (target) costs, expected costs, and actual costs per unit. Especially useful would be the comparison of expected and actual costs per unit in terms of what caused the difference, if any, that is, inability to achieve anticipated continuous cost improvements and/or inability to achieve expected volume for the product promotion and pricing strategies chosen.

THE CURRENT SCENE

Table 3 is designed to point out some remaining issues of contention. The first, concerning the volume of activity to use under Paradigm D, was the one just discussed. The remainder follow.

Diminishing product life cycles. As life cycles for many new products decrease, the reasons for using Paradigm D increase.[7] Some products don't last long enough for engineering-driven standards to be established and utilized. Such products literally must achieve the allowable or target cost of Paradigm D in their design stage if a desired profit is to be realized.

Somewhat related to shorter product life cycles is the notion of idle capacity, which no longer may be as important a costing concept as it used to be. The suggested use of expected and actual volume of activity under Paradigm D surely enhances this thought.

Strategies concerning various product lines. If a company produces both commodity-type products and specialty-type products, it might be able to use both engineering- and market-driven standard costs. Market-driven standards probably would apply more to specialty products with their shorter life cycles. Engineering-driven standards could be more appropriate for the longer life cycles of commodity products. Nevertheless, market-driven standard costs must be determined for any intensely competitive product.

Standard cost variances/responsibility accounting. When we are looking toward a total cost per unit that must meet or better the allowable or target cost, cost variances by individual cost, activity, or department seem to be less relevant. Worker empowerment within a company requires a cooperative spirit rather than a focus on the individual department and cost center. Group or total success is the key today.

TABLE 3. OTHER ISSUES OF POSSIBLE CONTENTION

- Under Paradigm D, what volume of activity should be used when determining actual total cost per unit to compare with allowable or target cost per unit?
- Does the diminishing time frame for the product life cycle have an impact on the movement toward Paradigm D, especially the movement toward market-driven standard (allowable) costs as opposed to engineering-driven standard costs?
- Does a firm's strategic posture by product line allow for a possibility of different paradigms for different product lines?
- Is the old emphasis on cost variances by individual cost categories and departments less or no longer relevant in an era when the total cost from suppliers through to customers is emphasized?
- Where does the "theory of constraints" fit in? It looks like a refinement of the direct costing ideology.
- What method should be used for assigning costs to product lines and individual products within each product line?

The old individual cost and cost center focused control concepts inherent in standard costing and responsibility accounting may be counterproductive in today's world. The need for continuous improvement and forcing a continuous learning curve focused on total cost surely challenges one's training and earlier views.

The theory of constraints. Eli Goldratt, the Israeli physicist turned management consultant, has had an impact in recent years. His concentration on throughput, operating expense, and inventories has intrigued many management accountants. Interestingly, his theory of constraints (TOC) appears to be a refinement of direct costing coupled with linear programming.

TOC concentrates on only three variables: throughput, inventory, and operating expenses. Throughput relates to actual sales minus materials costs. Inventory consists only of purchased items at their purchased cost, and operating expenses are expenses other than materials. The objective is to focus on increasing throughput by eliminating constraints and decreasing both inventory and operating expenses.

In essence, the theory of constraints treats operating expenses as fixed and does not add any value to inventory whether it's in process or a finished state. All operating expenses plus the cost of inventory (materials) used to produce the actual throughput are considered in determining the true profitability of a period's throughput.

There is a direct costing flavor in the theory of constraints. The apparent success of TOC simultaneous with the development of ABC (a form of absorption costing) is worth examining. A detailed comparison of a number of users of both techniques certainly would be useful.

Assigning costs to product lines and within product lines. Ultimately, any cost accounting system has to deal with the twin issues of assigning costs between and within product lines. Activity-based costing may make a real contribution toward resolving both these issues.

ABC's concentration on three categories of variable costs may be especially useful. These three categories relate to the traditional notion of variability with units and the two new ideas of variability with product complexity (such as number of batches) and variability with product diversity (such as number of products). At this point in time, those of us concerned with these product-line issues must be open to alternative points of view.

LOOKING AHEAD—THE TWENTY-FIRST CENTURY PARADIGM

The best hope I see for a new Paradigm for the twenty-first century would be a combination of Paradigms C and D. An alternate variation could combine Paradigms C and D with elements from Paradigm B.

Regarding the first suggestion, in our intensely competitive world marketplace it is difficult to deny the efficacy of Paradigm D. The allowable or target standard cost permitted by our competitors in the marketplace cannot be ignored. Neither can we ignore the necessity for continuous improvement.

Paradigm D, however, is not sufficient. It must be combined with a before-the-fact determination of expected actual cost and an after-the-fact actual cost. The actual costs should be determined using the more precise ABC method, that is, Paradigm C.

The ongoing comparison of a cost per unit allowed by the marketplace (subject to continuous improvement) with the actual and expected actual cost per unit is vital. Such a system of comparison should seek answers to the following questions:

1. What adjustments to product promotion and pricing strategies most likely will yield expected and actual volumes capable of achieving allowable costs?
2. What adjustments to our current cost structure and work procedures will enhance our ability to achieve allowable costs?
3. What adjustments to our current cost structure and the way we cooperate with suppliers and customers will enhance our ability to achieve allowable costs?

What better use could be made of cost/management accounting data than to elicit answers to these questions? The combination of Paradigms C and D provides a meaningful environment in which to use ABC in the determination of product promotion and pricing strategies. Similarly, the combination gives real meaning to ABCs role in forcing consideration of alternative cost structures.

What happens when we add a touch of Paradigm B? Charles Horngren provides the idea for combining B with C and D to develop a new paradigm for the twenty-first century.[8] On numerous occasions he has cautioned us about using per-unit dollar amounts rather than total dollar amounts, especially in the context of fixed costs. By using per-unit amounts, we run the risk of treating fixed costs as variable costs and potentially concentrating too much on parts of the picture rather than the total picture.

Consider a product-line income statement, which has columns for individual products as well as a total column for the sum of individual products. The total column for the product line forces us to keep an eye on "total system" results while simultaneously looking at individual products or pieces of the system.

Shifting from the per-unit concentration of Paradigms C and D can be accomplished easily by multiplying the expected actual and actual volumes for each product by the per-unit amounts at each respective volume level for each product. Then the resulting total dollar amounts can be arranged in the format of a product line income statement as described above.

If we draw the distinction between fixed and variable costs, our product line income statement can include elements from Paradigm B with C and D. For example, if the only variable costs are materials, as assumed in the theory of constraints, we easily can develop contribution margins in the context of our product line income statements. The contribution margin as well as the net income by product and product line yields an opportunity to consider both short- and long-run aspects of profitability simultaneously as individual product and total system profitability are examined.

An intriguing result of combining Paradigm B with C and D is the ability to include, in our analysis of product line income statements, aspects of product life cycles and products that are expected to be cash users vs. cash generators during different stages of their life cycles. The product line income statement in this context looks at individual products and the sum total of a product line over a time frame that encompasses the life cycle of individual products or, at minimum, a three- to five-year period.

LOOKING BACKWARD TO SEE AHEAD

Often it is useful to reconsider where we have been during various stages of our development. Especially helpful would be case studies that could lead to the fine-tuning of a cost/management accounting paradigm for the twenty-first century. Of interest would be:

- A detailed comparison of a number of users of the theory of constraints and ABC.
- Historical analyses of early, prominent, and successful users of Paradigm B and their current status with regard to moving toward Paradigms C and D or combinations thereof.[9]
- Historical analyses of successful companies (defined in some reasonable manner) and their current status in regard to moving toward Paradigms C and D or combinations thereof, with or without elements from Paradigm B.

The suggestions in this article relative to a paradigm for the twenty-first century seem especially useful. There definitely seems to be a place in management accounting for the more refined and exacting calculations of ABC. But that place seems better suited in combination with Paradigm D and perhaps Paradigm B as well, especially as we proceed to the twenty-first century.

ENDNOTES

1. Depending on the product or service offered, one could have the same three elements of variable costs for marketing and administrative activities as well as manufacturing activities.

2. J. S. Earley, "Recent Developments in Cost Accounting and the 'Marginal Analysis'," *Journal of Political Economy*, June 1995, p. 237. The primary source for Earley's comments are the research studies of the Institute of Management Accountants, especially reports 16, 17 and 18 published during 1949 and 1950 on *The Analysis of Cost-Volume-Profit Relationships*.

3. For a discussion of how Paradigm B responds to this comment, see "Profit Planning and Pricing Strategies," Chapter 15 in *Managerial Cost Accounting; Planning and Control* by W. L. Ferrara, et al., Dame Publications, Inc., 1991.

4. See Thomas A. Stewart, "GE Keeps Those Ideas Coming," *Fortune*, August 12, 1991, for one company's approach to continuous improvement and empowerment.

5. See Dave Woodruff and Stephen Phillips, "Ford Has a Better Idea: Let Someone Else Have the Idea," *Business Week*, April 30, 1990.

6. H. T. Johnson, "Let's Set the Record Straight on ABC," *Measurement Systems*, Association for Manufacturing Excellence, March–April 1992.

7. See R. Cooper and P. B. B. Turney, *Hewlett-Packard: Roseville Networks Division*, Harvard Business School Case Study 189–117,1989, for an illustration of diminishing product life cycles and a resultant increase in new products as well as product modifications.

8. C. T. Horngren and G. L. Sundem, *Introduction to Management Accounting*, ninth edition, Prentice Hall, 1993, p. 201.

9. See *Current Applications of Direct Costing*, Institute of Management Accountants, Research Report 37, 1961, for a list of companies from which to choose.

William L. Ferrara, CPA, Ph.D., is the David M. Beights professor of accountancy at Stetson University, DeLand, Fla. He is a member of the Daytona Beach Area Chapter, through which this article was submitted, and can be reached at (904) 822-7421.

QUESTION

1.2 What does Ferrara see as the best combination of Paradigms for the twenty-first century? Explain.

1.3 Management Accounting in the Era of Electronic Commerce

by Alexander Kogan, Ephraim F. Sudit, and Miklos A. Vasarhelyi*

Is management accounting ready for electronic commerce? Recent developments in Internet technology and electronic commerce will have a profound effect on the role of management accounting systems in decision support, internal auditing, and control. Over the next decade we will witness the transformation of traditional commerce into a form of commerce with electronic components if not fully electronic. It will be competitively inconceivable to have some components of the business activity not in the electronic mode. Are management accountants adequately prepared for the impending changes in their power, relevancy, and reach? Our purpose here is to generate a review and discussion of those issues.

What is electronic commerce? In a broad sense, electronic commerce can be understood to encompass any and all business activities and transactions, both internal and external, over the Internet or Internet-type computer networks. These activities can be as straightforward as selling over the Internet or as sophisticated as integrating Internet technologies into all links, functions, and facets of the value chain.

Internet storefronts currently draw considerable attention by being most visible to the public. There are examples of extremely successful Internet selling by both pure Internet-based businesses, such as the bookseller Amazon.com, and traditional companies such as Dell. For example, the June 30, 1997, *USA Today* issue reports (p. B1) that Dell's Web site generates nearly $2 million online sales per day. According to the May 10–16, 1997, issue of *The Economist*, Amazon's virtual bookstore contains more than 2.5 million books, 400,000 of which are kept in stock by Amazon itself, with the rest available from the nearby warehouse of Ingram Book, a large book distributor. In total, this is a much larger collection than is economically feasible to offer in a physical bookstore, and it is serviced by far fewer people. Amazon's lower costs are passed, in part, to its customers in the form of significant discounts (up to 40% of list price on selected bestsellers). At the same time, Amazon provides customers with a range of additional information services about the books it sells including reviews of books by their authors, external reviews, discussions, and interviews.

THE IMPORTANCE OF INTERNET TECHNOLOGY

The revolutionary impact of the Internet technology on the information infrastructure can be seen in the emergence and wide proliferation of new terms. These days "intranets" are known as internal company networks

* From: A. Kogan, E. F. Sudit, and M. A. Vasarhelyi, "Management Accounting in the Era of Electronic Commerce," *Management Accounting* (September 1997): 26–30. Reprinted with permission.

using the Internet technology. "Extranets" refer to secure virtual communication channels established over the Internet among business partners. We progressively are witnessing corporations opening their intranets to trusted partners, suppliers, and clients, sharing applications to improve value-added and to decrease duplication of efforts. The most important common denominator of these nets is the underlying TCP/IP networking, which makes it possible to use basically the same technology in all the links of the modem information infrastructure.

Internet technology is likely to become increasingly more hospitable to electronic commerce. A case in point is an initiative, currently under way, to make Web-based buying and selling smooth and seamless by developing an Internet payment negotiation protocol within the framework of the W3 Consortium and CommerceNet Joint Electronic Payment Initiative (see http://www.w3.org/Payments/). This protocol will allow Internet users to choose from a variety of payment systems such as credit cards, smart cards, or micro-payments.

NOW THE NETS FACILITATE LINKS IN THE VALUE CHAIN

The generic value chain framework encompasses a series of cost/benefit analyses of many sequences of discrete activities that are performed throughout an entire chain of processes spanning conception, planning, design, procurement, production, marketing, and delivery to customers of values in the form of products or services, as well as the service and support of their uses by those customers. Reliable, up-to-date information must flow among the business units in the value chain, their customers, their suppliers, and the environment in which they operate. Internet technology is emerging as the ideal tool for operating these information links. Thus, the Internet, and its recent offspring—extranets and intranets—without doubt will play crucial roles in facilitating essential links in the value chain, thereby supporting electronic commerce.

Value chain activities can be performed by one or many companies. Regardless of their organizational structure, effective management of value chain activities depends, in large part, on the quality of the information links among the business units involved. If, for example, one vertically integrated company controls the whole value chain, it requires, at the very least, external information links to its suppliers and customers, possibly implemented as a mixture of extranets and the public Internet. Internal information links among its own business units can be worked in large measure via intranets. Much of the information to and from the world at large can flow through the Internet. If several firms are in control of separate sectors of the value-added chain, subsets of their operations have to be externally linked, possibly by extranets.

ELECTRONIC DATA INTERCHANGE (EDI) OVER THE INTERNET

Many U.S. and international companies realize significant cost savings and gains in effectiveness by using some form of Electronic Data Interchange (EDI) systems. According to *The Economist*[1] approximately 95% of the Fortune 1000 companies use EDI, but, at the same time, less than 3% of the approximately six million U.S. companies are EDI users. EDI is often the core means of communications of business-to-business transactions.

Small companies cannot afford the setup investments in private network connections, protocol definitions, and software development required for EDI as well as the modifications toward compatible standards between the parties involved. Consequently, companies increasingly are experimenting with EDI-type systems over the Internet. The latter use the standard ubiquitous public Internet and TCP/IP protocol, which may be less reliable or secure than private EDI, but, in return, avoids costly standardization processes and high access setup costs. Conventional EDI systems also tend to be less interactive than Internet EDI.

It is reasonable to expect that, in the foreseeable future a substantive number of EDI transactions will be carried over the Internet or its technological siblings (intranets, extranets, etc.). This expectation is based on serious efforts currently directed at creating a public standard for EDI transactions over the Internet. The Internet Engineering Task Force (IETF)—the main Internet standards-setting body—has established a special working group, "Electronic Data Interchange-Internet Integration (ediint),"[2] for this purpose. Its address is:

http://www.ietf.org/html.charters/ediint-charter.html

The objective of open standards for EDI over the Internet is to ensure the widest range of interoperational capabilities among diverse EDI packages over the Internet. This will allow reliable multivendor service as well as resolve the security issues of Internet-based EDI transactions, such as integrity (transaction cannot be altered by unauthorized parties), privacy (transaction cannot be seen by unauthorized parties), authentication and nonrepudiation (the identity of parties taking part in the transaction can be reliably established without any possibility of repudiation).

ENHANCED ELECTRONIC LINKS TO SUPPLIERS AND SUBCONTRACTORS

The General Electric alternative to EDI over the Internet is an interesting example. GE, a giant that spends about $30 billion a year on supplies, is connected to more than 1,400 of its suppliers through a Web site known as GE's Trading Process Network (TPN):

http://www.tpn.geis.com/

The software on this network is versatile. For example, GE's purchasers use TPN to disseminate requests electronically for bids including instructions as to the type and scope of information required for bidding. In turn, suppliers bid online. The system performs an initial screening of the bids. Processing time is shortened significantly, and a substantially larger number of bids can be solicited and reviewed. GE reports that TPN's online bidding resulted in considerable cost savings. According to the company's Web site, as of March 1997, GE divisions have purchased through the TPN almost $350 million of products, and the company expects to reach $1 billion by the end of 1997. Although this amount will represent less than 4% of the total GE spending on supplies, it is several times higher than the total consumer spending on the Internet.

Even very small suppliers can access GE's TPN system easily. The minimum requirements are a PC, which most firms own, and a $20-a-month access to the Internet. With this minimum investment, the supplier can receive from GE via e-mail all relevant bidding information. GE suppliers also can create their own Web pages, which are stored on the TPN server. As a result, suppliers are likely to get requests for bids from GE business units with which they have never done business. On balance, suppliers face more competitors on TPN, but, at the same time, they are exposed to a larger number of potential GE customers.

At present, most of GE's transactions with suppliers are conducted via non-Internet-based EDI, but the company is in the process of expanding the scope and capabilities of TPN. Other firms are joining. Currently, suppliers do not contact GE business units directly. The longer-term objective is to make the system more interactive by enabling direct suppliers and suppliers of suppliers to negotiate electronically with GE units and among themselves. Eventually, TPN is envisioned to evolve toward a trading community system.

ENTERPRISE-WIDE INFORMATION SYSTEMS AND THE INTERNET

A number of the so-called "enterprise-wide" information systems using Internet technology are available commercially. Basically, they are decision-support systems that initially focused on a company's supply chain but have increasingly broadened their capabilities to include enterprise-wide processes.

Enterprise information systems are fast becoming as essential to the functioning of modern companies as the nerve system is to the functioning of a human being. The leading developers of enterprise information systems are among the largest software companies in the world, and their growth rates have been astounding for years. The best-known systems currently on the market are:

SAP R/3—http:/www.sap.com
Oracle Applications—http://www.oracle.com
PeopleSoft—http://www.peoplesoft.com
BAAN—http://www.baan.com

While, historically, enterprise information systems preceded the World Wide Web and were developed independent of the Internet, all the major players in this field already have released or announced Internet-enabled versions of their systems. Internet enabling is in the eye of the beholder. With the progressive development of Internet technology, more opportunities arise of feature integration. Users must examine the application to understand the level of its Internet usage. The current version (3.1, released in December 1996) of SAP R/3 ships with more than 25 Internet Application Components. On April 22, 1997, Oracle announced the shipping of version 2.0 of Oracle Applications for the Web based on Oracle's Network Computing Architecture. PeopleSoft announced its strategy to make its applications Internet-enabled on March 31, 1997, while BAAN introduced its first Web-enabled applications on March 14, 1997. This race to the Internet is due to the enormous potential and profound impact of the Internet on business processes.

CAPABILITIES OF INTERNET-BASED ENTERPRISE INFORMATION SYSTEMS

To illustrate some of the capabilities of Internet-based information systems that should be of particular interest to management accountants, we use System Applications Products (SAP) as an example. SAP is developed by a multimillion-dollar German company, SAP AG, and has the largest market share. The system is designed to integrate numerous data processes by covering a wide range of customer-to-business, business-to-business, and intranet applications in financial accounting, supply chain management, and human resources functions.

Business Application Programming Interfaces (BAPIs) provide access to the core functions of SAP. The BAPIs set standards for direct communications between suppliers. By providing standard interface capabilities, they enable business enterprises and business units; which may use different system technologies, to exchange transactions directly, such as purchase requisitions and order entries, with little or no human intervention.

Customer-to-business support includes a number of useful components. Easy browsing and graphical display are key features of the Product Catalogue Component of SAP, which provides user-friendly search engines amenable to graphics and text. Customers can place orders for products and specify desired product characteristics and configurations through the use of the Order Entry for Variant Products (Logistics) Component. Once product specifications are confirmed, orders are issued, billed, and immediately posted into production, thereby reducing lead time and providing more timely information at reduced cost. The Electronic Correspondence (Financials) Component enables customers to save costs by mailing automated reminders via the Internet.

Establishment and maintenance of customer-information systems are facilitated by SAPs Interactive Requests (Financials) Component, providing customers with access to self-service, and self-explanatory information related to their transactions, for example, account balances/or status of orders.

Human resource management is streamlined by an Employment Opportunities Component designed to support recruitment by providing vacancies postings. Job applicants respond online or can e-mail unsolicited applications. They are issued unique individual keys for tracing the status of their application.

Using other components, customers can order products specifying desired price and quality features, as well as check electronically on the status of their orders. By using SAP's Service Call (Logistics) Component, customers also can access Web servers of companies to place product service requests directly. Through the use of his or her Internet browser, the customer can identify product problems out of a prespecified list of possible problems, be told how these problems can be handled under the terms of service contracts, and request service.

In the context of business-to-business transactions, Just-in-Time (JIT) systems are facilitated. In SAP, KANBANs and their status are displayed by KANBAN boards. Suppliers access customers' KANBAN boards for which they are responsible to replenish empty boards by initiating shipments to meet just-in-time delivery schedules. SAP's Special Stocks Inquiries (Logistics) Component provides electronic support for important production activities such as management of work-in-process inventory and of consignment stocks, inventory control, job processing, and contrast processing.

For internal business transactions, SAP provides an Ad Hoc Reports Component that accommodates electronic posting via a Web browser interface of activity-based allocations among cost centers by identifying activity types, cost pools, and cost drivers. This capability, usually restricted to intranets, enhances the effectiveness of operating activity-based costing systems throughout the enterprise. Among its other capabilities, the Ad Hoc Reports Component also features multimedia drill-down intranet reporting tools for ad hoc reports and intranet communications modes among employees and business units.

ABOUT INTERNET ARCHITECTURE OF ENTERPRISE INFORMATION SYSTEMS

Although each enterprise information system uses its own proprietary terms, the functionality of these systems is fairly standardized. All these systems are built on the principles of client/server computing. Layered architecture of these systems allows their natural integration with the Internet without drastic changes in the core system architecture.

The main Internet-driven extensions of enterprise systems are happening at the client end. A standard Web browser now can be used to enter orders or track shipments, file expense reports, or review employee records. This capability creates an opportunity for making an enterprise system ubiquitous—it can reach anywhere Internet technology reaches.

A typical approach to enabling this Internet reach is through a special intermediary component introduced between a Web server and the core back-end system. This intermediary accepts information coming from the Web and converts it into the form required by the core system.

This new Internet-based architecture of enterprise information systems reduces the deployment of client software updates to a nonissue: As soon as an update of the client is implemented and installed, the client applet[3] can be downloaded instantly by Web browsers.

IMPLICATIONS FOR MANAGEMENT ACCOUNTANTS

Complex organizations are composed of numerous business units that typically operate their own dedicated and specialized information systems. As a rule, those systems rarely are compatible, and their ability to communicate electronically with each other is tenuous at best. Enterprise-wide information systems like SAP, Oracle Applications, PeopleSoft, and BAAN are specialized enough to meet specific needs of individual business units, but by using Internet technology they can interact freely and integrate diverse components of individual business units. They also can communicate freely with external Internet-based systems and all parties who have access to the World Wide Web. Furthermore, because the introduction of Internet technology is relatively cheap, it affords a drastic expansion in the scope of enterprise information systems at a moderate cost. The use of Internet-enabled functions of enterprise systems requires little training and is easily accessible to the occasional nonexpert user. In contrast, conventional (non-Internet-based) use of enterprise information systems requires well-trained function experts.

Internet-based enterprise-wide information systems provide management accountants with a working set of comprehensive intraorganizational, interorganizational, and global decision/support systems. These systems obtain and organize information horizontally across business units and functions, as well as vertically through drill-down reporting capabilities. The latter relate and summarize data at different hierarchical levels of detail.

Value-chain analysis is facilitated by providing information links throughout the value chain, including utilization of links to suppliers and customers. Standardized classifications of activities, cost pools, and cost drivers make activity-based costing easier to design and implement. Information is available to decision makers and management accountants online and in real time, enhancing the effectiveness of decision support and making possible continuous internal auditing and control.

Internet technology as it stimulates electronic commerce significantly increases the analytical power, relevancy, and reach of management accounting. The profession should be prepared to take advantage of these opportunities.

ENDNOTES

1. *The Economist*, May 10–16, 1997, p. 17 of the Electronic Commerce Survey.
2. The group already has produced a draft of an informational document describing the "Requirements for Inter-operable Internet EDI" (ftp://ftp.ietf.org/internet-drafts/draft-ietf-ediint-req-02.txt).
3. An applet is a small interpreted program (typically written in Java) that is downloaded and executed by a Web browser. This applet is platform-independent (i.e., it will run equally well on a Wintel PC, a UNIX workstation, or a Network Computer).

Alexander Kogan is assistant professor of accounting and information systems, and Ephraim F. Sudit is professor of accounting and information systems and director of the MBA program in professional accounting at Rutgers University. Miklos A. Vasarhelyi, Ph.D., is KPMG Peat Marwick Professor of Accounting Information Systems on the faculty of management, Department of Accounting and Information Systems, Rutgers University, Newark, N. J. He can be reached at (973) 353-5002 or e-mail to: miklosv@andromeda.rutgers.edu.

QUESTIONS

1.3a What is General Electric's Trading Process Network (TPN) and how does it work?

1.3b What are the implications of electronic commerce for management accounting and management accountants?

1.4 Pushing the art of management accounting

Despite the many strides the profession has made over the years, some still believe that management accounting practices haven't taken as strong a hold in organizations as they should. FCMA Alexander Mersereau describes the challenges that are slowing the adoption of critical management accounting tools in broader business

By Alexander Mersereau, CMA, FCMA*

Management accounting practice has developed substantially over the past century, but recent studies suggest that the practice is no longer making the strides that it once did. Unless management accountants take a hard look at the effectiveness of current practice, this situation isn't likely to improve. In some companies, radical changes are needed to the structure of the finance function, the nature of the interactions management accountants have with other managers and the performance metrics used to guide the function itself.

THE GOOD NEWS

The early part of the 20th century was a period of rapid development for the field, when scientific management sought to identify what costs should be and economic organizations began to use budgets and relate returns to levels of investment.

However little development occurred in the following years and, by the early 1980s, management accounting had reached a point of stagnation. H. Thomas Johnson and Robert S. Kaplan, writing in 1987, declared:

Today's management accounting information, driven by the procedures and the cycle of the organization's financial reporting system, is too late, too aggregated and too distorted to be relevant for managers' planning and control decisions.... Management accounting reports are of little help to operating managers as they attempt to reduce costs and improve productivity.[1]

This call for renewal was widely heeded. Their book *Relevance Lost: The Rise and Fall of Management Accounting* became a best seller for the editor of Harvard Business School Press and set off a wave of innovation and interest in the management accounting profession worldwide. Among the numerous technical innovations that came from this period were activity-based cost management, the Balanced Scorecard, benchmarking, life cycle costing, target costing, economic value added measures and strategic cost management. Management

---

* From: A. Mersereau, "Pushing the Art of Management Accounting," *CMA Management* (February 2006): 22–27. Reprinted with Permission.

accounting was also able to build upon innovation in other fields such as Total Quality Management, Six Sigma, Kaizen and Business Process Reengineering. The development was rapid and interest spread well beyond the management accounting community. Peter Drucker, writing in the *Harvard Business Review* in 1990[2], declared that "the most exciting and innovative work in management today is found in accounting."

Fifteen years later, it's a good idea to ask ourselves what has happened to this reform. On one hand, the new tools that came from that period are evidently in use. Advanced management accounting practices such as ABC and non-financial performance measures are included in all major management textbooks. Studies of activity-based cost management (ABC) have reported generally positive user perceptions of benefits. Most of the larger companies appear to have experimented with Balanced Scorecard (BSC) techniques and studies have linked elements of scorecard use to higher profitability. Economic value added (EVA) research has reported positive results. On the other hand, despite these positive results it would appear that the adoption of advanced management accounting practices once again has slowed.

STIPPING STANDARDS
Studies estimate that the use of ABC has fallen and is now below 20%, and the percentage of those considering implementing ABC has also fallen. Of companies that have introduced activity-based techniques, only a minority claim that it is embedded in their organization. Strategic cost management techniques, such as attribute costing, seem little known outside academia. The majority of firms adopting EVA measures apparently don't use them significantly. Balanced Scorecard researchers have concluded that most users make little attempt to link their non-financial performance to strategy and that only a small minority attempt to validate the cause and effect linkages included in their models. Moreover, Balanced Scorecard practice seems to have developed an independent momentum, excluding the finance function altogether in some organizations. There is even pressure for management accountants to do less. In his autobiography, Jack Welch complained: "The budget is the bane of corporate America (and) never should have existed" and research that would enable organizations to move beyond budgeting is underway.

Therefore, it isn't surprising that despite the wave of innovation in management accounting in the late 1980s and early 1990s, a recent study by IBM consulting reported that less than half of managers received role-specific information to support *ad hoc* decisions. Fewer still received frequent operational metrics related to processes under their control and very few could obtain information across functions, processes and geographies. A similar study by Accenture/Economist Intelligence

Unit reported a significant gap between potential and actual practice.[3]

These indications of a slowing pace of management accounting change may be due to a range of factors. In some cases, new management accounting tools aren't adapted to organizational strategy or structure and can't be used. And in some cases, innovation has failed due to implementation-related factors. However, the main problems aren't technical or structural; they lie in the need for a better management of the management accounting process itself.

GETTING INVOLVED
At the heart of the management accounting process is a communications system, or a set of communications systems, that provide information to managers. The ability of management accountants to improve the scope, timeliness or quality of the information they provide depends on how well they understand and manage these systems. There are three main areas in management accounting systems in which communication problems can occur, which are illustrated here using the tale of *The Three Monkeys*.

The three monkeys that most people know are *Speak No Evil, Hear No Evil* and *See No Evil*. In this medieval Japanese illustration, a trio of monkeys is depicted with one having his hands over his mouth, another covering his ears and a third his eyes. The original use of this image seems to have been to illustrate wisdom. The three wise monkeys, as they were referred to, counselled the disciplined avoidance of evil. Conversely in modern times the image of the three monkeys has been used to emphasize stupidity and negligence, or the unwillingness of people to get involved. Here they are used in the latter sense to illustrate the need for management accountants to become more involved in this communications process.

The management accounting communications process begins with a set of inputs to the accounting information system. This data is then encoded into information using a language (accounting) and transmitted to a recipient. Here is our first monkey, the speaking one. The management accountant can't possibly observe, measure and report on everything. She must select from a wide field what to report, how to report it and when. To do this well, she must anticipate how this information ought to be used, have a language at her disposal that succinctly codifies the key data observed, and have a communication medium that reaches the intended audience efficiently and effectively.

The next leg of the communications process is the receipt of the information. Here we confront the second monkey, the hearing one. Managers must be able to correctly decode the reports they receive. They must therefore be familiar with the concepts used in the accounting models that are used to prepare the reports and understand what the variances in the numbers signify.

Finally, managers act on the information received. How they will act depends on how they interpret the message. This is a separate challenge and introduces the third monkey, the seeing one. Individuals interpret and act on information using personal decision rules that they have learned over time. A large part of any manager's decision strategy will be guided by how he views his organization and his role in it, and personal and corporate objectives are never completely aligned.

The actions that a manager takes as a result of receiving information (including actions taken in anticipation) and the consequences of these actions should be of great interest to the management accountant. These consequences become part of the world she must observe. This is the first monkey all over again, and so the cycle continues.

At the heart of the management accounting process is a communications system, or a set of communications systems, that provide information to managers. The ability of management accountants to improve the scope, timeliness or quality of the information they provide depends on how well they understand and manage these systems.

BIG PICTURE PROVIDERS

How do some organizations meet the challenges illustrated by the three monkeys? Let's look again at the first monkey, the speaking one. To be able to communicate to managers, accountants must have a clear picture of the strategic importance of the phenomena they observe, and they must have a clear idea of how operating decisions are made. Some of this can be learned in university but most of it comes from day-to-day experiences within operations. This requires frequent contact between management accountants and other managers.

However, the cycles of monthly, quarterly and annual planning and reporting are punishing and accountants regularly work overtime during these periods. To overcome these barriers, some organizations encourage contact by physically locating accountants with other managers. Some deliberately place accountants on interfunctional working groups and many ensure that management accountants have either dotted or solid line accountability to operating managers. Some organizations have adopted a structure in which some management accountants don't have routine reporting responsibilities.

A complicating factor is how management accountants are themselves received when dealing with operations personnel. Over the years in some quarters accountants have earned a reputation for bringing an unbalanced and overly financial point of view to problem solving, which has diminished their position in the hierarchy. Some managers have characterized financial managers as among those with the least mental flexibility, the most closed minds and the least willingness to take risks.

While some of the blame for this impression can be attributed to poor public relations, the selection and training of accountants remains a significant issue. Management accounting requires practitioners with a "big picture" point of view who are able to challenge operating managers as peers. Formal education may actually have a negative effect on recruitment. Several studies have suggested that accountants may follow a training regime that is too highly oriented to the financial aspects of their work and not sufficiently directed to the behavioural side. Others have observed that the financial bias to the educational component has the regrettable consequence of attracting candidates to the profession who are more comfortable with a formulabased approach to decision making and less at ease with the ambiguities that characterise managerial work.

EDUCATING OTHERS

Let's turn now to the hearing monkey, which refers to the ability of managers to understand the accounting reports they receive. When financial accounts are prepared and distributed externally, accountants are permitted to assume that the reader is trained in accounting. This isn't the case inside the organization, where a vast majority of managers haven't completed any significant formal accounting training, and those who have will have forgotten much of what they learned.

Some organizations are attempting to overcome this problem by supplementing or replacing financial reports with symbols or colours (green for OK, yellow to signal issues and red to announce a real problem). While such systems have the advantage of simplicity, questions need to be asked about the overall content of such communications. What does yellow or green really mean? What about the grey areas in between? And in the political context of organizations, how might these ambiguities be exploited for personal benefit?

Rather than reducing the content of accounting messages to one of three possible states, accountants need to help end users become more proficient in reading accounting reports. Some organizations have built accounting training modules for their managers that help them understand the specific reports they receive. Management accountants have an important role to play in preparing and delivering training materials. In today's complex managerial environment technical functions, especially accounting, need to become more than suppliers of information. They must become a kind of a school where managers can receive training. Yet in many organizations, accountants are too busy to become trainers and internal reward systems likely discourage such activities. Here the training activity itself needs to be repositioned to make it attractive to accountants.

As the scope of management accounting messages widens to include non-financial performance indicators, management accountants acquire an additional challenge.

Many managers have difficulties visualizing the cause and effect relationships that link value drivers to financial returns. Yet this is the key knowledge needed to manage value, and training is often required to help managers understand better the cause and effect relationships that underlie shareholder value.

The third monkey, the seeing one, refers also to the manager, this time to the conflict that exists between shareholder values and the interests of individual managers. Increasing functional specialization means that managers are increasingly disconnected from shareholder values. Many managers are strongly committed to the organization without being committed to the financial goals that drive it. Management accountants have a role to play in instilling financial discipline and conveying financial values to non-financial managers. One method is to require operating managers (rather than accountants) to systematically prepare and present the financial analysis of their business unit. Shareholder value training is also important.

At the same time that the management accounting function must pay greater attention to the effectiveness of its internal communications processes, other demands are arising. There is increasing pressure to reduce the overall cost of the finance function as a percentage of revenues. There are increasingly time consuming demands for more detailed external reporting. While these latter goals are important and must be achieved, putting the priority there only increases the risk that internal accounting communications will fail to achieve their objectives and that management accounting system change will be further delayed.

THE WAY FORWARD

Improving management accounting begins with a commitment to change. For many organizations, this is a huge step. Accountants have been found to be the first to resist accounting change, and the failure of various ABC and scorecard projects has been linked to the unwillingness of accountants themselves to see the project through. Many accountants are afraid that radical change might endanger existing systems and processes. To ensure that change is permanent, commitment to change must come from the top and must be sustained.

As the previous examples illustrate, improving the management accounting function often requires structural reorganization. If everyone is consumed by the routine reporting cycles, there will be no one left to assume emerging roles in areas such as management training. In some organizations bringing in new people will be necessary. Management accounting is more than just accounting, it requires people who understand the behavioural consequences of numbers and who can link controls to strategy.

Last, but not least, the management accounting process requires new metrics. Most accounting functions measure timeliness, in terms of the delay between the end of the reporting cycle and the issuing of the report, and many measure the cost of the finance function relative to revenues. Few organizations measure the use or the usefulness of the management accounting information provided. The absence of such measures guarantees that things will remain the same.

DIAGNOSTIC

Management accountants should conduct frequent analyses of their communications processes. Such a diagnosis would include the following questions:

- What changes to management accounting practice have you initiated in the last two years?
- How many people are committed to real change?
- Do accounting personnel regard themselves as members of the operating team?
- How much time do management accountants spend with non-financial personnel?
- Are management accounting personnel physically located in such a way as to bring them in regular contact with nonfinancial managers?
- Do management accountants have a reporting responsibility to operational managers?
- Do reports to individual managers/units contain a maximum amount of information about that specific unit?
- Are accountants given responsibilities that can only be discharged by working with operational people?
- Do the accountants who have these responsibilities have sufficient status to maintain working relationships on the basis of mutual respect?
- How many accounting personnel do not have significant routine reporting responsibilities?
- How much financial training is provided for operating management?
- Does this training explain the links between financial and operational events?
- Does this training explain why financial goals are important?
- Are operating managers required to systematically prepare and present the financial analysis of their unit?
- Do performance measures other than cost and timeliness exist for the management accounting function?
- What priority is given to these metrics and how are they used?

The more management accountants can respond positively to these questions, the better organizations will become at managing the communications processes that underlie management accounting. This will create a better understanding of the role that management accountants can play in achieving success and it is in this context that significant management accounting change will occur.

Alexander Mersereau, CMA, FCMA, D.Sc., is a professor at HEC Montreal.

ENDNOTES

1. Johnson, H. & Kaplan, R. (1987), *Relevance Lost: The Rise and Fall of Management Accounting*, Boston, Harvard Business School Press, p 269.
2. Drucker, Peter (1990) The Emerging Theory of Manufacturing *Harvard Business Review* May/June pp. 94–102.
3. Accenture Finance Solutions (2004) *Best in Class How Finance Business Process Outsourcing Can Help Create a High Performance Finance Function*.

QUESTION

1.4. According to Mersereau who is often the first to resist accounting change? Why is this the case?

Chapter 2

A Framework for Management Accounting and Control Systems

John Shank and Vijay Govindarajan's article, *Strategic Cost Management and the Value Chain* (Reading 2.1), begins the series of articles for this chapter. The article discusses the value chain concept as the central building block of strategic cost management. Management accounting methods such as activity based costing and other tools can be incorporated into the value chain concept. The authors illustrate their method of developing a value chain within an organization and then use a case study of the paper industry to illustrate their argument. This article could also be used with material in Chapter 9 on managing costs across the value chain.

In *ABC and High Technology: A Story with a Moral*, (Reading 2.2), Frank Selto and Dale Jasinski discuss their case study of a small high technology company's experience in attempting to implement activity based costing. Data-Com, a premier supplier of computer communication links to mainframe computer, original equipment manufacturers (OEM), was a fast growing firm. During the late 1980s, the company lost its major OEM partner, which led to a steady decline in its business. In 1992, the company embarked on a new strategic plan to revitalize itself. The plan included the creation of three decentralized business units from the existing centralized operation. Part of this plan involved the implementation of ABC to better analyze and cost support services to all three units. Unfortunately, as the article chronicles, the ABC effort failed due to the lack of top management support in the form of necessary resources and the failing commitment of the CFO - one of the system's key supporters. Selto and Jasinski conclude that unless ABC is truly integrated and accepted as part of the strategic plan, management accounting will always be relegated to its traditional scorekeeping function.

ABC and Life-Cycle Costing for Environmental Expenditures by Jerry Kreuze and Gale Newell (Reading 2.3) presents an interesting application of ABC and Cooper's activity classification to environmental costing settings. The article addresses issues related to the costs of hazardous waste disposal, cleaning up polluted water, soil, and buildings, and many other issues. The concept of life-cycle costing also is introduced and is extremely pertinent for dealing with products or processes that may ultimately result in environmental problems. For instance, Kreuze and Newell state that responsibility for dealing with hazardous waste essentially lasts forever. The ABC classification of costs is used very effectively to illustrate how environmental costs can be separated and managed.

Readings
Chapter 2

2.1 Strategic Cost Management and the Value Chain

by John K. Shank and Vijay Govindarajan*

Strategic Cost Management (SCM) is organized around the value chain concept. The value chain is the linked set of value-creating activities. In contrast, traditional management accounting uses the value-added perspective.

The value chain framework is a method for breaking down the chain – from suppliers of basic raw materials to end-use customers – into strategically relevant activities in order to understand the behavior of costs and the sources of differentiation. Gaining and sustaining competitive advantage requires the firm to understand the entire value delivery system.

The value-added concept has two big disadvantages – it starts too late and stops too soon. For instance the value added concept begins with payments to suppliers (purchases) and stops with charges to customers (sales). The key is to maximize the difference (the value added) between purchases and sales. Starting cost analysis with purchases misses all of the opportunities for exploiting linkages with the firm's suppliers.

Traditional management accounting relies on a single cost driver – output volume. Cost concepts relate to output volume – fixed versus variable cost, average cost versus marginal cost and others.

In contrast, in the value chain framework, output volume is seen to capture little of the richness of cost behavior. Instead, multiple cost drivers are used based on the various types of activities throughout the value chain. These cost drivers are broken into two types: structural and executional cost drivers.

STRUCTURAL COST DRIVERS INCLUDE:

- Scale – What is the size of investments in manufacturing, R&D and marketing?
- Scope – What is the degree of vertical integration?

- Experience – how many times in the past has the firm done what it is doing again?
- Technology – what process technologies are used in each step of the firm's value chain
- Complexity – how wide a line of products or services is being offered to customers?

EXECUTIONAL COST DRIVERS INCLUDE:

- Workforce involvement – Is the work force committed to continuous improvement?
- Total quality management (TQM) – Is the work force committed to total product quality?
- Capacity utilization – What are the scale choices on maximum plant construction?
- Plant Layout – How efficient, against current norms, is the plant's layout?
- Product Configuration - Is the design or formulation of the produce effective?
- Linkages with suppliers or customers – Is the linage with suppliers or customers exploited, according to the firm's value chain?

Shank and Govindarajan provide several examples to illustrate how to use both structural and executional drivers to derive the most benefit from using a value chain approach.

QUESTIONS

2.1a What is the difference between the value-added and value-chain concepts? Explain.

2.1b What are structural and executional cost drivers and how are they distinguished in Shank and Govindarajan's article?

---

* This article has been summarized from the original article by John K. Shank and Vijay Govindarajan, "Strategic Cost Management and the Value Chain," *Journal of Cost Management* (Winter 1992): 5–21.

2.2 ABC and High Technology: A Story with a Moral

*by Frank H. Selto and Dale W. Jasinski**

Except in some large companies that are well-staffed, well-trained, and well-funded, there is not much evidence that ABC is understood well enough to be designed or implemented successfully as a stand-alone system, let alone one that is integrated with strategy. Even in large firms, widespread success of ABC is not obvious.

Because most job creation and innovative economic activity occur in small firms, we describe here the efforts of an accounting staff to design and implement an activity-based accounting system to support strategic changes in a relatively small, high-technology firm with approximately $100 million in annual sales. The experience has lessons for others who embark on similar tasks.

The company, which chooses to remain anonymous and which we will call DataCom, is an entrepreneurial, privately held, high-technology concern that designs, assembles, and markets computer communication equipment. DataCom has faced challenges of rapid growth and equally rapid changes in both technology and customer needs that beset any high-technology company. Those that survive, and especially those that thrive, must be creative, agile, and quick to the market. DataCom encountered a dramatic change in its business environment that tested its abilities to survive.

Founded in 1985, DataCom quickly built its reputation as a premier supplier of computer communication links to mainframe computer original equipment manufacturers (OEMs) that incorporated DataCom's products without DataCom's name. DataCom enjoyed steady growth and added OEM partners. Founders of the company eagerly anticipated the right opportunity to take the firm public. In 1989, DataCom's primary OEM partner unexpectedly acquired its own mainframe communications technology and did not renew its contract. Sales dropped, but large cash reserves preserved the existence of DataCom.

DataCom's initial response was to redefine its marketing strategy as direct sellers to end users. Lack of name recognition and experience with direct sales, however, prevented significant sales growth. DataCom had no information that would measure the profitability of alternative markets or channels of distribution. DataCom downsized in 1990, primarily by reducing its direct sales force, and it focused on a few key markets. Cost cutting and focused marketing returned profitability in late 1990 and 1991. As a result, the company expanded its direct sales force to seek an increased market share, primarily in Europe where mainframe computing continued to be the technology of choice.

Economic recession in Europe in 1992 and rapid changes in U.S. computing technology to networked personal computers abruptly cut DataCom's already declining sales in half. DataCom had not foreseen the recession and had not expected domestic computing technology to switch so quickly away from mainframes. Although DataCom was not the only myopic firm at this time, in retrospect it was far more dependent on a dominant technology within a single market than was prudent. DataCom, however, never was blind to technological change and had continued to invest heavily in R&D even when sales first dropped in 1989.

By 1992 the combination of high expenditures for R&D, marketing, and administration had all but eliminated the company's sizable cash reserves, dropping its liquidity ratio from 5.0 to 1.0, with more than 50% of the 1992 numerator as receivables. DataCom found itself with a failing marketing strategy and a dependency on an apparently outmoded technology. It had neglected its creativity and agility and was in danger of being an also-ran in the market. During this threatening time, the accounting function continued to play a scorekeeping role—an increasingly unpleasant task.

STRATEGIC RESPONSE

In 1992, DataCom's executive committee began urgent strategic planning. In the process, it affirmed that its comparative advantages were its abilities to:

1. Anticipate emerging communications technology accurately;
2. Create innovative, value-adding solutions to communications problems in the new technology; and
3. Deliver outstanding functional quality.

The executive committee noted that continued investment in R&D had not resulted in significant new products. The causes were identified as diffused engineering efforts directed at putting out fires and making marginal changes to existing products to chase marginal sales. The executive committee sought a structural solution to refocus DataCom's considerable technological talent on its comparative advantages. The solution was to transform the highly centralized company into three distinct business units, each operating within technological boundaries. These business units were to be evaluated individually as profit centers that competed for scarce internal funds for growth.

The three business units were Harvest, Integration, and Network.

---

* From F. H. Selto and D. W. Jasinski, "ABC and High Technology: A Story with a Moral," *Management Accounting* (March 1996): 37–40. Reprinted with permission.

Harvest: The first unit was dedicated to prolonging the original line of business that connected mainframe computers to remote terminals. It would be operated as a harvest unit that generated cash to fund new product development. Technological risks were negligible, but the company expected that this market would disappear—but not, the company hoped, before new products were brought to market.

Integration: The second unit was designed to develop a complementary line of business that integrated communications among different computing technologies. This unit would extend DataCom's current expertise, but it followed previous R&D efforts. The integration problem is a significant barrier to computer communications and DataCom believed it could develop innovative solutions in this large market. Growth in this market could prove to be steady but might level off within a few years.

Network: The third unit was organized to seek communication solutions to the emerging network computing technology. Though related to DataCom's previous efforts, this technology was sufficiently new to represent significant technological risk. If successful, however, solutions to network communication problems had the potential to repeat or outstrip DataCom's original level of success. This unit's performance would be the "home run" the executive committee sought, if its prediction was realized that networks would be the dominant computing technology of the foreseeable future.

ACTIVITY-BASED INFORMATION

The information needs to manage these three business units were somewhat different, requiring innovative solutions. Common to all three divisions was a need to identify and measure the costs of support activities provided to each unit, including design and test engineering. (Figure 1 shows the history of the shifting allocations over four quarters. As new directions were chosen, each unit was dramatically impacted.)

The Harvest business unit primarily required accurate scorekeeping to monitor profitability, cash flow, and marketing effectiveness—a familiar task for accounting. The new technology units, Integration and Network, weren't generating significant sales, but they did require expertise to evaluate the financial impacts of alternative technology and product development scenarios. The accounting staff was less prepared to fill this need.

Top management believed that an activity-based accounting system would enable them to better identify and cost DataCom's value-adding activities. The CEO, an engineer by training, saw that "as you get narrower (level of detail), you can look at the things that really impact your business. One of the things you find out as you do this is that your information systems may not be adequate to break down costs at the level that you need to make these decisions."

Accordingly, the CFO and the accounting department determined to develop an accounting system that would monitor the operations of the three business units as if they were separate entities and, at the same time, support managers' efforts to allocate resources efficiently. Some employees and activities were identified clearly with specific business units, including several financial staff who were to provide financial modeling assistance to unit managers. The majority of the company's employees still provided support activities from centralized service departments. These indirect expenses were and would continue to be a large percentage of total expenses.

The CFO began tracking service activity and costs to the business units. Interestingly, the CFO would not call this process ABC because of the connotation that ABC systems required special financial expertise and software, which at the time DataCom did not have and could not afford. At the same time, however, engineers in the centralized design unit were accustomed to recording their time, activities, and costs to projects and were well aware of the concepts and practices of ABC.

FIGURE 1. INDIRECT EXPENSE ALLOCATIONS—1993

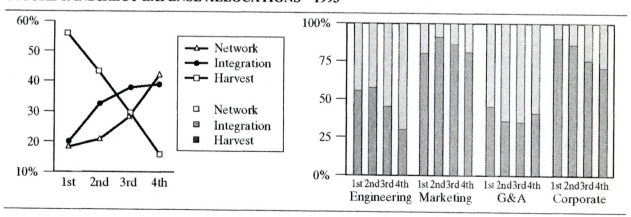

Despite the executive committee's desire to identify activities and to trace them to business units and products, the CFO never received sufficient resources to complete a thorough study. Because of the costs involved, the CFO never directly requested resources for that purpose. The engineers' comfort with ABC was not repeated in other service areas, and unassigned indirect costs averaged 38% of total expenses during 1993. The CFO allocated these expenses on the basis of revenues and hoped that business unit managers would reject these arbitrary allocations and demand more accurate, activity-based cost assignments—and then supply resources to generate the information. In 1993, based on revenue, the Harvest division received the great majority of the allocation, followed by the Integration division, which began to bring products to market. The Network division was shipping no products and was spared any revenue-based allocation.

Perhaps not surprisingly, the vice president of manufacturing and manager of the Integration business unit believed, "The new financial reporting that we have with the separation of the business units is clearly giving us a view of where the winners are and where the losers are. There have been some complaints from those who are spending time putting all these numbers together, saying, 'Where's the benefit? Where's the beef?' but for those of us who have become accustomed to it, it is a good decision-making tool."

Because the Harvest unit could "afford" the expense allocation and the other units saw no advantage to arguing for larger cost assignments, demand for improved activity-based information never materialized. Business unit managers did demand and receive extensive, centralized marketing services, which were traced only partially. Despite their increasing ABC skills, the accounting staff never got beyond their comfortable scorekeeping role, and they complained (somewhat incorrectly as it turned out): "The frustration from a planning point is—and we can do numbers as well as anybody else—that sometimes you still have to make a decision based upon those numbers, and we haven't made any decisions based on the numbers. We would view it [tracing activities and cost] as

sort of a waste of time." (Table 1 displays the different information needs for each unit and the frustrating disparity between the needs of the units and what the accountants were able to provide.)

It was common knowledge that the revenue-based allocations were distorting business-unit profitability and that activity-based information could reveal a different picture: "If you use those [activity-based] numbers, you would discontinue the new products and continue to build the old, because they're making a bundle of money, and the new products are costing you a ton of money. But everyone thinks the future is Network.

"I'm wasting the company's dollars by spending my time tracking it now … they're dumping all the dollars in revenue anyway … and putting it into the Harvest business, which in reality has been taking substantially less of my time."

The accounting staff focused on scorekeeping of existing products rather than supporting the company's primary competencies—anticipating technological change, developing innovative solutions, and delivering high quality. The executive committee, however, did make critical decisions without accurate information about the activities necessary to support alternative product scenarios. Harvest was virtually eliminated, and Integration was divested, despite the facts that both generated positive cash flow and both probably were profitable.

Furthermore, the Integration market was growing more than had been anticipated and was receiving larger revenue-based allocations. Both units were judged to be insufficiently profitable to continue. (Integration is profitable under new ownership.)

The executive committee swung for the fence on Network and did hit the home run, as it turned out, while ignoring the high percentage hit that Integration delivered. This may be a defining difference between entrepreneurial, high-technology firms and more mature firms—the penchant for the home run and disdain for more conservative alternatives. Traditional management accounting's focus on scorekeeping may add relatively little value in this setting.

TABLE 1. BUSINESS UNIT—INFORMATION NEEDS

	Harvest	Integration	Network
Strategic Accounting Need	Scorekeeping: ABC system to monitor profitability, cash flow, and marketing effectiveness.	Problem-solving: ABC system to evaluate financial impacts of alternative technology and product development scenarios.	Problem-solving: ABC system to evaluate financial impacts of alternative technology and product development scenarios.
Accounting Information's Actual Impact on Strategy	Misleading (over) allocations led to its elimination.	Misleading (over) allocations masked real contributions and led to its divestiture.	Misleading (under) allocations enabled it to continue to receive resources until market success achieved.

The CFO was sanguine about the prospects of developing improved, activity-based information, knowing that the future of the company rested on predicting the direction of computing technology accurately. The predisposition of the executive committee to go for the home run had been reinforced by misleading business unit profitability: "We have to go forward with the new development on our new product line [Network], which represents the future of business. Since we are trying to fund Network through the Harvest business unit, which happens to be the declining business, the decisions of how quickly to move forward would be the same [depending on cash flow]. So I am not convinced that we [would] have made different decisions [with better activity-based information]."

This comment probably was both rationalization and statement of fact. It was clear from the initial formation of the business units that Network was the executive committee favorite. Financial investigation of alternatives was limited because the CFO was the only member of the executive committee not given an explicit strategy formulation role. If aggregate scorekeeping was all that accounting could provide accurately it could not bring much of value to the strategy table. Indeed, in the subsequent strategic planning process, the executive committee decided to solicit more input from throughout the organization and formed a planning committee of approximately 25 members. Any member of the executive committee could nominate an employee to serve on the committee. The only functional area not to have a representative was finance and accounting.

It seems likely that lack of accounting input will be repeated when DataCom eventually seeks a new home run technology to replace Network. After the sale of Integration, the accounting staff dropped efforts to trace activities and costs to any specific products or projects. An opportunity to add value to strategic decision making by developing activity-based information was missed, and aggregate scorekeeping is still accounting's primary function.

THE MORAL OF THE STORY
Although ABC holds much promise for organizations, it cannot be implemented or evaluated independently of the organization's strategy. Unless ABC is integral to the company's strategy, it is unlikely that management accountants can break through the high-technology glass ceiling and become important members of the strategic planning team. Absent that input, it is clear that the job security of management accountants depends on providing relevant information to support the organization's decision making, and scorekeeping alone may be inadequate. Formulation and implementation of strategy will proceed with or without the accounting staff's contribution.

This research has been supported by the Institute of Management Accountants and the University of Colorado Hart Fellowship Program. We also gratefully acknowledge and appreciate the virtually unlimited access to personnel and information granted to us by our field hosts.

Frank H. Selto, Ph.D., teaches accounting and is chair of the Accounting and Information Systems Division at the College of Business and Administration, University of Colorado at Boulder. Dale W. Jasinski will join the faculty at Idaho State University, Pocatello. Dr. Selto can be reached at (303) 492-1549, and Mr. Jasinski is at (303) 492-1175. This article was submitted through IMA's Boulder Valley (Colo.) Chapter.

QUESTIONS

2.2a Were the information needs of all three divisions of DataCom the same? Explain.

2.2b According to Selto and Jasinski, why did ABC fail at DataCom?

2.3 ABC and Life-Cycle Costing for Environmental Expenditures
The combination gives companies a more accurate snapshot.

*by Jerry G. Kreuze, CPA, and Gale E. Newell, CMA**

Costs of cleaning up polluted soil, water, buildings, and equipment; related expenditures for equipment record keeping; and monitoring for compliance with government regulations have become significant variables for companies to consider in protecting their financial health. A primary concern is the potential for large losses attributable to environmental problems.

In an earlier article[1] we addressed the role of management accountants in helping their companies deal with hazardous waste problems. We encouraged them to work closely with production personnel in finding cost effective ways to reduce, control, transport, and dispose of hazardous waste. They also should analyze alternative production and disposal methods to reduce the volume or

---

* From J. G. Kreuze and G. E. Newell, "ABC and Life-Cycle Costing for Environmental Expenditures," *Management Accounting* (February 1994): 38–42. Reprinted with permission.

toxicity of hazardous wastes produced and to determine the disposal method(s) that minimizes disposal costs at an acceptable level of risk.

Now we need to determine how environmental expenditures should be allocated to products. Activity-based costing (ABC) and life-cycle costing techniques are the foundation for allocating environmental expenditures to products. By identifying the costs of all activities, a company can attempt to eliminate, or at least minimize, the costs related to those activities that do not add value to the product.

LIFE-CYCLE COSTING FOR ENVIRONMENTAL EXPENDITURES

Life-cycle costing considers the full costs over the product's (system's, operation's) life cycle—from research through disposal, from cradle to grave. Most of the cost of a new product is committed after the design stage, so manufacturing alternatives can influence only a small portion of the total product cost. Life-cycle costing measures the entire 100% of these costs, not just the costs incurred during production, and responsibility for environmental impacts has extended product costs well beyond the life cycle of the product. Responsibility for hazardous waste, for example, lasts forever. Therefore, all costs are discounted to the present to facilitate comparisons with competing products. Life-cycle costing may reveal that a product with low acquisition costs but high operations, maintenance, environmental, or disposal costs may be a less desirable alternative than a competing product with a higher initial cost.

All cost-bearing activities associated with a product throughout its life-cycle time must be identified. The costs of each cost-bearing activity must be accumulated and, in some instances, estimated. In this situation, similar to capital budgeting techniques, future costs are discounted to present-day dollars. Cost estimates, particularly for future environmental expenditures, are unavoidable but are needed for evaluation purposes. All costs throughout a product's life cycle must be considered for a valid comparison of competing products or processes. In light of the potential magnitude of environmental expenditures, it may be better to be vaguely right than precisely wrong.

Paul E. Bailey[2] identified four levels of environmental costs that are important to a full costing analysis: usual capital and operating costs, hidden regulatory costs, contingent liability costs, and less tangible costs.

Usual Costs and Operating Costs. Usual costs are costs associated directly with products, including costs of buildings, equipment, materials, start-up, training, labor, and energy costs. Traditionally these costs have been allocated to products, often using an application rate based on direct labor hours.

Hidden Regulatory Costs. The costs of governmental and regulatory compliance include notification, reporting, permitting, monitoring, testing, training, and inspection expenditures. Proper cost allocation requires these costs to be allocated to those activities causing the expenditures. It is critical because these costs have the potential of being very large. For example, *The Wall Street Journal* reported that the government forms dealing with disposal of dirty cleaning rags at Bernhardt Furniture Company in Lenoir, N.C., created a pile 6 ft 2 in. tall. Moreover, Alex Bernhardt, the company's president, says that his company "could easily spend twice as much on (environmental) compliance in the next five years as on R&D and new machinery and equipment" combined.

Contingent Liability Costs. These costs can include both (a) penalties and fines for noncompliance and (b) legal claims, awards, and settlements for remedial actions, personal injuries, and property damage for future routine and accidental environmental concerns. Often these costs must be estimated, and companies must be careful not to underestimate these amounts or the likelihood of their occurring. All companies that generate and release hazardous waste and materials have future contingent liability costs, so when estimating these costs, they must accept that environmental regulations will tend to converge upward, causing contingent liability costs to increase.

Less Tangible Costs. By reducing or eliminating polution and responding to consumer demands for environmentally friendly products, a company can realize cost savings (less tangible costs) through increased revenues or decreased expenses due to improved consumer satisfaction, employee relations, and corporate image. Given the growing legislative and regulatory pressure and increasing consumer awareness, progressive companies are altering the way they design, make, and market their products so products can be used longer and reused, either in part or whole. If a company makes ecological and economic goals joint objectives its less tangible costs, at least, partially can offset its contingent liability costs. As Exxon's experience in Alaska demonstrated, however, an accidental release can override many corporate efforts in the area of less tangible costs.

ABC AND ENVIRONMENTAL EXPENDITURES

Activity-based costing techniques can provide the means to identify cost-bearing activities effectively and to allocate costs to individual products. The basic premise of ABC is to cost activities, not products. Costs are allocated to products on the basis of the individual product's demand for those activities. The allocation bases—cost drivers—are the quantification of activities performed.

The merging of life-cycle costing and ABC is not a revolutionary concept. Consideration of all costs, from the introduction phases to product maturity, can allow for the development of better design methods, production methodologies, marketing strategies, and disposal options. Environmental expenditures *must* be a major part of those cost considerations.

Traditionally, ABC allocates activities among unit-level, batch-level, product-sustaining, and facility-sustaining activities. Unit-level activities are performed on individual units, batch-level activities allow batches of units to be processed, product-sustaining activities provide the capacity to produce a particular product, and facility-sustaining activities sustain a manufacturing facility's general manufacturing capacity. Environmental expenditures can occur in any of those levels.

Consequently, the four levels of environmental costs for full costing should be identified and included in the appropriate cost activity level. For example, isopropyl alcohol left over from the production of computer monitor screens would be a unit-level activity cost. That same alcohol can be used as a solvent to clean casts for steel products, making it a batch-level activity cost. Many regulatory and governmental compliance costs would be product-sustaining activity costs, such as the costs associated with the reporting of cleaning rag disposal at Bernhardt Furniture Company. Future contingent cleanup costs at waste sites, product-sustaining activities, also should be estimated for a complete full costing analysis. Finally, air pollution devices installed on manufacturing facilities create significant facility-sustaining activity costs.

ABC AND LIFE-CYCLE COSTING: AN ILLUSTRATION

The use of ABC in a life-cycle costing analysis can be seen in the case of a hypothetical manufacturing company, Ready Manufacturing, with two of its products, Product A and Product B. Product A is a high-volume item that is produced through a single production process that does not generate any hazardous waste and requires no governmental and regulatory compliance costs. Product B is a low-volume item that generates sufficient quantities of hazardous waste in the production process to qualify Ready Manufacturing as large-quantity producer. As a result, Ready manufacturing is subject to numerous environmental regulations and reporting requirements.

Annual sales of Products A and B are 200,000 and 50,000 units, respectively. Both products require three direct labor hours for completion, causing the company to operate 750,000 direct labor hours per year (250,000 units of product @ three direct labor hours per product). At a rate of $20 per direct labor hour, the cost of direct labor for products A and B is $60 per product. Direct materials costs are $100 for Product A and $80 for Product B.

As presented in Table 1, Ready Manufacturing's overhead costs total $17,250,000. Although the same amount of direct labor hours is required for each product (three hours), Product B requires more machine setups and more quality inspections than Product A because of its design complexity. Moreover, Product B is produced in smaller lots, thus causing it to require a relatively large number of production orders as compared to Product A. The bill of materials indicates that Products A and B are composed of six and four subcomponents, respectively.

Ready Manufacturing has analyzed its operations and determined that activities act as cost drivers in the incurrence of overhead costs as presented in Table 2. The unit-, batch-, and product-level environmental expenditures are related to Product B exclusively and, as such, should be allocated entirely to Product B. That is, no cost driver, other than Product B itself, is appropriate. The facility-level environmental standards expenditures are assumed to relate to pollution control equipment installed on the manufacturing facility's stacks. The stacks vent the entire factory operation, so they relate equally to Products A and B. Those costs then are allocated to products on the same basis as the remaining facility-level activity costs—on a percent value-added basis.

Table 3 shows the total costs for Products A and B. The allocation of environmental costs, other than facility-level environmental expenditures, partially causes Product B's overhead costs to exceed those of Product A. Environmental costs are allocated to the product(s) causing those expenditures. Given the significance of environmental costs ($3,690,000, or 21% of the total manufacturing overhead costs for Ready Manufacturing) it is imperative that those costs be identified and allocated to products properly.

TABLE 1. READY MANUFACTURING'S OVERHEAD COSTS (CATEGORIZED BY ACTIVITIES)

Activity	Overhead Costs	
Unit-level:		
Machine costs	$2,400,000	
Energy	1,000,000	
Disposal of hazardous waste	400,000	3,800,000
Batch-level:		
Inspection	1,200,000	
Material movements	1,450,000	
Support services	1,800,000	
Disposal of hazardous waste	300,000	
Environmental reporting requirements	200,000	4,950,000
Product-level:		
R&D and parts maintenance	2,110,000	
Environmental reporting requirements	200,000	
Environmental inspections	500,000	
Waste treatment costs on site	1,000,000	
Landfill disposal costs	800,000	4,610,000
Facility-level:		
Plant maintenance	2,000,000	
Buildings and grounds	1,000,000	
Heating and lighting	600,000	
Environmental standards	290,000	3,890,000
Total Overhead Costs		**$17,250,000**

TABLE 2. COST DRIVERS AND OVERHEAD RATES FOR READY MANUFACTURING'S OVERHEAD COSTS

Cost Drivers by Activity

Activity	Cost Driver
Unit-level:	
Machine costs	Machine hours used
Energy	Machine hours used
Disposal of hazardous waste	Product B exclusively
Batch-level:	
Inspection	Number of quality inspections
Material movements	Number of production orders
Support services	Number of machine setups
Disposal of hazardous waste	Product B exclusively
Environmental reporting requirements	Product B exclusively
Product-level:	
R&D and parts maintenance	Number of subcomponents
Environmental reporting requirements	Product B exclusively
Environmental inspections	Product B exclusively
Waste treatment costs on site	Product B exclusively
Landfill disposal costs	Product B exclusively
Facility-level:	
Plant maintenance	% value added
Buildings and grounds	% value added
Heating and lighting	% value added
Environmental standards	% value added

Overhead Rates by Activity

Activity	Cost	Number of Events	Rate per Event
Unit-level:			
Machine costs	$2,400,000	20,000	$120/machine hr.
Energy	$2,400,000	20,000	$50/machine hr.
Batch-level:			
Inspection	1,200,000	2,500	$480/inspection
Material movements	1,450,000	500	$2,900/order
Support services	1,800,000	1,500	$1,200/setup
Product-level:			
R&D and parts maintenance	$2,110,000	10	$211,000/ subcomponent

The importance of using ABC to allocate costs to products is illustrated in Table 4, which presents the product costs for Ready Manufacturing using the traditional direct labor hours method. The manufacturing cost per unit for Products A and B are $229 and $209, respectively. Product A, with direct labor hours as an allocation base, received 68% more overhead cost than under ABC ($69.00 compared to $41.09). Conversely, Product B was allocated 62% fewer overhead costs using direct labor hours as the allocation base ($69.00 compared to $180.65). With direct labor hours, Product A is assigned a greater cost per unit ($229) than is Product B ($209). ABC produces an opposite effect, with the cost/unit for Product A at $201.09 and Product B at $320.65.

Environmental costs related to certain products can cause the traditional direct labor hours cost allocation method to produce faulty product costs. In fact, product-specific environmental costs for many companies may require the use of ABC costing to a greater extent than do differences in volume, machine setups, production orders, quality inspections, and number of subcomponents.

The total manufacturing costs per unit of $201.09 for Product A and $320.65 for Product B were obtained from information contained in the historical-cost-based general ledger system. Life-cycle costing, particularly for environmental expenditures, requires that all costs (past, present, and future) be included in the product's profitability analysis. That is, while the manufacturing costs computed in Table 3 are useful for financial statement preparation and current operating performance measures, a better measure of long-term product performance also should include future environmental expenditures. In particular, the above analysis includes only the first two levels of life-cycle costing, namely usual and operating costs and hidden regulatory costs. The remaining levels, contingent liability costs and less tangible costs, have not been considered yet.

Unfortunately, these costs must be estimated because their expenditures occur in the future. But they should not be ignored when determining the long-term profitability of products, especially considering their potential magnitude. For example, cleanup of the United States' known hazardous waste sites now is estimated to cost $752 billion over 30 years under current environmental standards. In all likelihood, those costs have not been allocated to activities/products causing those expenditures. To the extent possible, these future potential environmental costs should be included in a complete life-cycle costing analysis to properly determine the worth of competing products. Environmental consultants, engineers, and lawyers may be required to interpret the facts and evaluate environmental cost exposure.

In estimating contingent liability costs, Ready Manufacturing has identified three environmental activities that may impose some exposure: waste treatment on site, transportation, and disposal in a landfill. Consultations with environmental experts indicate that Ready Manufacturing will be subject to some potential liability from these activities. The annual liability costs attached to those environmental activities, discounted at its cost-of-capital rate, are assumed to be $250,000 per year. Those costs effectively add $5/unit ($250,000/50,000 units of Product B) to the manufacturing cost of Product B. As Ready Manufacturing is operating under the highest environmental standards, no benefits are possible in the less tangible costs area.

TABLE 3. MANUFACTURING COSTS FOR PRODUCTS A AND B (USING ABC COSTING)

	Product A		Product B	
	Events	Amount	Events	Amount
Overhead costs:				
Unit-level:				
Machine costs at, $120/hour	15,000	$1,800,000	5,000	$600,000
Energy at $50/hour	15,000	750,000	5,000	250,000
Disposal of hazardous waste			—	400,000
Batch-level				
Inspection at $480/inspection	1,000	480,000	1,500	720,000
Material movements at $2,900/order	300	870,000	200	580,000
Support services at $1,200/setup	1,000	1,200,000	500	600,000
Disposal of hazardous waste				300,000
Environmental reporting				200,000
Product-level:				
R&D and parts maintenance at $211,000/subcomponent	6	1,266,000	A	844,000
Environmental reporting		—		200,000
Environmental inspections		—		500,000
Waste treatment costs		—		1,000,000
Landfill disposal costs		—		800,000
Subtotal		$6,366,000		$6,994,000
Facility-level:				
Total costs of $3,890,000, % value added				
A – 47.6%		1,851,640		
8 – 52.4%				2,038,360
Total overhead cost		$8,217,640		$9,032,360
Number of units produced		200,000		50,000
Overhead cost/unit		$ 41.09		$ 180.65
Direct material cost/unit		100.00		80.00
Direct labor cost/unit		60.00		60.00
Overhead cost/unit		41.09		180.65
Total manufacturing cost/unit		$ 201.09		$ 320.65

TABLE 4. MANUFACTURING COSTS FOR PRODUCTS A AND B (USING DIRECT LABOR HOURS)

	Product A	Product B
A. Overhead cost/unit	$69	$69
$17,250,000/750,000 DLH = $23/DLH		
(23 × 3 hours)		
B. Direct material cost/unit	100	80
C. Direct labor cost/unit	60	60
Total manufacturing cost/unit	$209	$209

These Level 4 environmental costs would be applicable if Ready Manufacturing could use another technology for better waste treatment. The higher costs associated with the better method could be partially offset by potential benefits associated with improved community and labor relations, but these benefits often are uncertain and difficult to quantify. Level 4 environmental costs perhaps can be used best to compare treatment methods and/or products.

IMPLICATIONS

The wave of environmental concerns and regulations sweeping the world have increased costs for many companies. Environmental standards probably will rise. The highest standards today may be marginal tomorrow. Given the current costs associated with environmental concerns and the expected future upward trend in those costs, it is imperative that companies allocate environmental costs to products properly.

Activity-based costing can allocate environmental expenditures to products effectively. Care must be taken to uncover hidden regulatory and compliance costs so that proper cost allocation can be obtained. By uncovering these costs, management accountants can produce relevant information for their engineers, production personnel, marketing staff, and others. Environmental activities can be highlighted and the magnitude of their costs identified. If those activities do not add value to the product or process, the goal would be to eliminate, or at least minimize, their necessity.

Life-cycle costing extends the ABC analysis to consider future costs, including contingent liability costs and less tangible costs. With environmental matters, current activities can cause costs to be incurred 10, 20, or even 30 years from today. Consequently, potential future environmental liabilities should, at the very least, be considered in a systematic manner when evaluating the long-term profitability of competing products. Care must be taken not to underestimate these potential expenditures. The acceptance of today's highest environmental standards can be good business. Profit enhancement through less tangible costs is possible for companies that are environmentally concerned. Frequently customers, employees, and the general public view a company's environmental record as a proxy for its quality and reliability.

The combination of ABC and life-cycle costing can provide management with accurate product cost information and therefore a realistic understanding of profitability. Relevant product cost information permits management accountants to identify the costs associated with nonvalue-adding activities. Moreover, by identifying potential contingent environmental liabilities, management accountants, along with environmental consultants, engineers, lawyers, and others have relevant information to evaluate the profitability of competing products.

ENDNOTES

1. G. Newell, J. Kreuze, and S. Newell, "Accounting for Hazardous Waste," MANAGEMENT AC-COUNTING®, May 1990.
2. P. Bailey, "Full Cost Accounting for Life-Cycle Costs —A Guide for Engineers and Financial Analysts," *Environmental Finance*, Spring 1991.

Jerry G. Kreuze, CPA, is professor of accounting at Western Michigan University. He holds a Ph.D. degree in accounting from the University of Missouri-Columbia.

Gale E. Newell, CMA, is professor of accounting at Western Michigan University. He holds a Ph.D. degree in accounting from Michigan State University.

Both authors are members of the Kalamazoo Chapter, through which this article was submitted.

QUESTION

2.3 Describe the four levels of environmental costs that are important to a full costing analysis as discussed in the Kreuze and Newell article. Why are all four levels needed in such an analysis?

Chapter 3

Traditional Cost Management Systems

The first article for this section is Reading 3.1, Robin Cooper and Robert Kaplan's *How Cost Accounting Distorts Product Costs*. In this now classic article, Cooper and Kaplan strongly question the relevance of the traditional cost accounting model and its applicability for product costing. The authors discuss problems with traditional cost accounting including the inadequacy of both variable and full costing methods for accurate product costing and the failure of both marginal and fixed-cost allocations. Other topics, such as understanding the cost of complexity and transaction costing (an early name for activity-based costing), are introduced. This article helped set the stage for a great deal of research on the failings of traditional cost accounting methods.

The linkages among variations in product and cost standards, cost behavior, and quality costs are highlighted in Harold Roth and Tom Albright's article, *What Are the Costs of Variability*, Reading 3.2. To illustrate the cost of variability, the authors cite a number of examples including a study, which sought to understand the sources of variation in the quality of paperboard output. In that study, data was collected on variables such as the shifts, crews, grades of product, grade changes, etc. The company under study was operating in a capacity-constrained environment, and the cost accountants developed a product cost analysis that showed the cost of products that were lost due to variations in the manufacturing process. Their model included the variable cost of materials and overhead, a fixed cost allocation, and the lost contribution margin. Using this model, the company was able to determine that the cost of certain grades of paperboard exceeded their selling price. The strategic implications of manufacturing products with high variation in product quality became much more evident as a result of the study.

Ralph Drtina's article *The Outsourcing Decision*, Reading 3.3, discusses how to determine whether a particular activity should be outsourced. Using a value chain approach, Drtina focuses on outsourcing decisions relating to services. An example used is the decision to outsource fleet maintenance. Three key questions are addressed: (1) Is it possible to purchase the service externally? (2) Does the firm need to control the service activity as would be the case with secret documents or a critical technology? and (3) Is the firm capable of delivering the service at a world-class level of performance? A traditional numerical example that breaks down fixed and variable costs in a make-buy context is provided. Drtina argues that such an analysis ignores qualitative factors and that any outsourcing decision must integrate with the organization's strategy.

Reading 3.4, Robin Cooper's *Does Your Company Need a New Cost System*, poses a critical question for managers: "Do I really know what my products cost?" Answering this question will allow managers to determine whether their costing system is reporting accurate product costs. In order to address this question, Cooper suggests that managers look for symptoms that often point to poor system design. For example, one symptom of a poor system occurs when a firm's customers completely ignore price increases, even though the firm's manufacturing costs haven't changed. In this instance, the cost system may be underestimating product costs, and, thus, the associated markup is still below market. Cooper outlines a number of other design flaws that managers should understand as they attempt to develop more accurate systems.

Consistent with Robin Cooper's article, Norm Raffish argues in *How Much Does That Product Really Co$t* (Reading 3.5), that the business world has changed so much that traditional cost accounting is no longer applicable. For one thing, the relative proportions of what go into product costs have changed significantly with direct labor content dropping to between 5 and 15%, materials content falling between 45% and 55%, and overhead soaring to between 30% and 50%. Raffish builds the case for activity-based costing as a much more accurate method for determining (among other things) more accurate product costs.

William Baker, Timothy Fry and Kirk Karwan's article, Reading 3.6 *The Rise and Fall of Time-Based Manufacturing*, presents a case study of Knussman Corporation's Brice Plant (a fictitious name), an automotive supplier, who established quality and time-based performance measures in order to help them compete more effectively. Unfortunately, the company's managers continued to rely on a traditional cost accounting system that emphasized standard costing and evaluation based on direct labor variances, both of which resulted in manager behavior that obviated the effects of the quality and throughput time measures. The authors suggest alternatives such as just-in-time manufacturing and activity based costing that the company could have used to be more consistent with its new performance quality measures.

Some critics of cost management practices today have suggested that the distinction between direct and indirect costs is no longer relevant for decision making. In Reading 3.7, *Distinguishing between Direct and Indirect Costs Is Crucial for Internet Companies*, L. Gordon and M. Loeb argue that the distinction between direct and indirect costs is still highly salient for e-commerce firms. In addition to using products, services and departments as cost objects the authors state that Internet companies must also treat customers as key cost objects — a notion highly consistent with the current view on the importance of assessing customer profitability.

In *Caution: Fraud Overhead* (Reading 3.8), John MacArthur, Bobby Waldrup and Gary Fane describe a situation in which the "Wapello Manufacturing Inc.", consultants were called in to investigate a potential fraud. Apart from uncovering a number of internal control problems, the analysis of the company's records revealed large overhead accounts. Because overhead contains a wide variety of costs and accounts such as indirect salaries, supplies, taxes, insurance and depreciation, fraudulent expenses can often be hidden in journal entries and in overhead variance calculations. Due to complexity, the management of such large accounts is often left to the controller – someone who clearly understands what is contained in them. In this case, the controller was arrested for embezzlement.

Readings
Chapter 3

3.1 How Cost Accounting Distorts Product Costs

The traditional cost system that defines variable costs as varying in the short-term with production will misclassify these costs as fixed.

by Robin Cooper and Robert S. Kaplan*

In order to make sensible decisions concerning the products they market, managers need to know what their products cost. Product design, new product introduction decisions, and the amount of effort expended on trying to market a given product or product line will be influenced by the anticipated cost and profitability of the product. Conversely, if product profitability appears to drop, the question of discontinuance will be raised. Product costs also can play an important role in setting prices, particularly for customized products with low sales volumes and without readily available market prices.

The cumulative effect of decisions on product design, introduction, support, discontinuance, and pricing helps define a firm's strategy. If the product cost information is distorted, the firm can follow an inappropriate and unprofitable strategy. For example, the low-cost producer often achieves competitive advantage by servicing a broad range of customers. This strategy will be successful if the economies of scale exceed the additional costs, the diseconomies of scope, caused by producing and servicing a more diverse product line. If the cost system does not correctly attribute the additional costs to the products that cause them, then the firm might end up competing in segments where the scope-related costs exceed the benefits from larger scale production.

Similarly, a differentiated producer achieves competitive advantage by meeting specialized customers' needs with products whose costs of differentiation are lower than the price premiums charged for special features and services. If the cost system fails to measure differentiation costs properly, then the firm might choose to compete in segments that are actually unprofitable.

FULL VS. VARIABLE COST
Despite the importance of cost information, disagreement still exists about whether product costs should be measured by full or by variable cost. In a full-cost system, fixed production costs are allocated to products so that reported product costs measure total manufacturing costs. In a variable cost system, the fixed costs are not allocated and product costs reflect only the marginal cost of manufacturing.

Academic accountants, supported by economists, have argued strongly that variable costs are the relevant ones for product decisions. They have demonstrated, using increasingly complex models, that setting marginal revenues equal to marginal costs will produce the highest profit. In contrast, accountants in practice continue to report full costs in their cost accounting systems.

The definition of variable cost used by academic accountants assumes that product decisions have a short-time horizon, typically a month or a quarter. Costs are variable only if they vary directly with monthly or quarterly changes in production volume. Such a definition is appropriate if the volume of production of all products can be changed at will and there is no way to change simultaneously the level of fixed costs.

In practice, managers reject this short-term perspective because the decision to offer a product creates a long-term commitment to manufacture, market, and support that product. Given this perspective, short-term variable cost is an inadequate measure of product cost.

While full cost is meant to be a surrogate for long-run manufacturing costs, in nearly all of the companies we visited, management was not convinced that their full-cost systems were adequate for its product-related decisions. In particular, management did not believe their systems accurately reflected the costs of resources consumed to manufacture products. But they were also unwilling to adopt a variable-cost approach.

Of the more than 20 firms we visited and documented, Mayers Tap, Rockford, and Schrader Bellows provided particularly useful insights on how product costs were systematically distorted.[1] These companies had several significant common characteristics.

They all produced a large number of distinct products in a single facility. The products formed several distinct product lines and were sold through diverse marketing channels. The range in demand volume for products within a product line was high, with sales of high-volume products between 100 and 1,000 times greater than sales of low-volume products. As a consequence, products were manufactured and shipped in highly varied lot sizes. While our findings are based

* From: R. Cooper and R. S. Kaplan, "How Cost Accounting Distorts Product Costs," *Management Accounting* (April 1988): 20–27. Reprinted with permission.

upon these three companies, the same effects were observed at several other sites.

In all three companies, product costs played an important role in the decisions that surrounded the introduction, pricing, and discontinuance of products. Reported product costs also appeared to play a significant role in determining how much effort should be assigned to marketing and selling products.

Typically, the individual responsible for introducing new products also was responsible for setting prices. Cost-plus pricing to achieve a desired level of gross margin predominantly was used for the special products, though substantial modifications to the resulting estimated prices occurred when direct competition existed. Such competition was common for high-volume products but rarely occurred for the low-volume items. Frequently, no obvious market prices existed for low-volume products because they had been designed to meet a particular customer's needs.

ACCURACY OF PRODUCT COSTS
Managers in all three firms expressed serious concerns about the accuracy of their product-costing systems.

For example, Rockford attempted to obtain much higher margins for its low-volume products to compensate, on an ad hoc basis, for the gross underestimates of costs that it believed the cost system produced for these products. But management was not able to justify its decisions on cutoff points to identify low-volume products or the magnitude of the ad hoc margin increases. Further, Rockford's management believed that its faulty cost system explained the ability of small firms to compete effectively against it for high-volume business. These small firms, with no apparent economic or technological advantage, were winning high-volume business with prices that were at or below Rockford's reported costs. And the small firms seemed to be prospering at these prices.

At Schrader Bellows, production managers believed that certain products were not earning their keep because they were so difficult to produce. But the cost system reported that these products were among the most profitable in the line. The managers also were convinced that they could make certain products as efficiently as anybody else. Yet competitors were consistently pricing comparable products considerably lower. Management suspected that the cost system contributed to this problem.

At Mayers Tap, the financial accounting profits were always much lower than those predicted by the cost system, but no one could explain the discrepancy. Also, the senior managers were concerned by their failure to predict which bids they would win or lose. Mayers Tap often won bids that had been overpriced because it did not really want the business, and lost bids it had deliberately underpriced in order to get the business.

TWO-STAGE COST ALLOCATION SYSTEM
The cost systems of all companies we visited had many common characteristics. Most important was the use of a two-stage cost allocation system: in the first stage, costs were assigned to cost pools (often called cost centers), and in the second stage, costs were allocated from the cost pools to the products.

The companies used many different allocation bases in the first stage to allocate costs from plant overhead accounts to cost centers. Despite the variation in allocation bases in the first stage, however, all companies used direct labor hours in the second stage to allocate overhead from the cost pools to the products. Direct labor hours were used in the second allocation stage even when the production process was highly automated so that burden rates exceeded 1,000%. Figure 1 illustrates a typical two-stage allocation process.

Of the three companies we examined in detail, only one had a cost accounting system capable of reporting variable product costs. Variable cost was identified at the budgeting stage in one other site, but this information was not subsequently used for product costing. The inability of the cost system to report variable cost was a common feature of many of the systems we observed. Reporting variable product costs was the exception, not the rule.

Firms used only one cost system even though costs were collected and allocated for several purposes, including product costing, operational control, and inventory valuation. The cost systems seemed to be designed primarily to perform the inventory valuation function for financial reporting because they had serious deficiencies for operational control (too delayed and too aggregate) and for product costing (too aggregate).

THE FAILURE OF MARGINAL COSTING
The extensive use of fixed-cost allocations in all the companies we investigated contrasts sharply with a 65-year history of academics advocating marginal costing for product decisions. If the marginal-cost concept had been adopted by companies' management, then we would have expected to see product-costing systems that explicitly reported variable-cost information. Instead, we observed cost systems that reported variable as well as full costs in only a small minority of companies.

The traditional academic recommendation for marginal costing may have made sense when variable costs (labor, material, and some overhead) were a relatively high proportion of total manufactured cost and when product diversity was sufficiently small that there was not wide variation in the demands made by different products on the firm's production and marketing resources. But these conditions are no longer typical of many of today's organizations. Increasingly, overhead (most of it considered "fixed") is becoming a larger share of total manufacturing costs. In addition, the plants we examined are being asked to produce an increasing variety of products that make quite different demands on equipment and support departments. Thus, even if direct or marginal costing were once a useful recommendation to management, direct costing, even if correctly implemented, is not likely a solution—and may perhaps be a major problem—for product costing in the contemporary manufacturing environment.

THE FAILURE OF FIXED-COST ALLOCATIONS

While we consistently observed managers avoiding the use of variable or marginal costs for their product-related decisions, we observed also their discomfort with the full-cost allocations produced by their existing cost systems. We believe that we have identified the two major sources for the discomfort.

The first problem arises from the use of direct labor hours in the second allocation stage to assign costs from cost centers to products. This procedure may have been adequate many decades ago when direct labor was the principal value-adding activity in the material conversion process. But as firms introduce more automated machinery, direct labor is increasingly engaged in setup and supervisory functions (rather than actually performing the work on the product) and no longer represents a reasonable surrogate for resource demands by product.

In many of the plants we visited, labor's main tasks are to load the machines and to act as troubleshooters. Labor frequently works on several different products at the same time so that it becomes impossible to assign labor hours intelligently to products. Some of the companies we visited had responded to this situation by beginning experiments using machine hours instead of labor hours to allocate costs from cost pools to products (for the second stage of the allocation process). Other companies, particularly those adopting just-in-time or continuous-flow production processes, were moving to material dollars as the basis for distributing costs from pools to products. Material dollars provide a less expensive method for cost allocation than machine hours because, as with labor hours, material dollars are collected by the existing cost system. A move to a machine-hour basis would require the collection of new data for many of these companies.

Shifting from labor hours to machine hours or material dollars provides some relief from the problem of using unrealistic bases for attributing costs to products. In fact, some companies have been experimenting with using all three allocations bases simultaneously: labor hours for those costs that vary with the number of labor hours worked (e.g., supervision—if the amount of labor in a product is high, the amount of supervision related to that product also is likely to be high), machine hours for those costs that vary with the number of hours the machine is running (e.g., power—the longer the machine is running the more power that is consumed by that product), and material dollars for those costs that vary with the value of material in the product (e.g., material handling—the higher the value of the material in the product, the greater the material-handling costs associated with those products are likely to be).

Using multiple allocation bases allows a finer attribution of costs to the products responsible for the incurrence of those costs. In particular, it allows for product diversity where the direct labor, machine hours, and material dollars consumed in the manufacture of different products are not directly proportional to each other.

For reported product costs to be correct, however, the allocation bases used must be capable of accounting for all aspects of product diversity. Such an accounting is not always possible even using all three volume-related allocation bases we described. As the number of product items manufactured increases, so does the number of direct labor hours, machine hours, and material dollars consumed. The designer of the cost system, in adopting these bases, assumes that all allocated costs have the same behavior; namely that they increase in direct relationship to the volume of product items manufactured. But there are many costs that vary with the diversity and complexity of products, not by the number of units produced.

THE COST OF COMPLEXITY

The complexity costs of a full-line producer can be illustrated as follows. Consider two identical plants. One plant produces 1,000,000 units of product A. The second plant produces 100,000 units of product A and 900,000 units of 199 similar products. (The similar products have sales volumes that vary from 100 to 100,000 units.)

The first plant has a simple production environment and requires limited manufacturing-support facilities. Few setups, expediting, and scheduling activities are required.

The other plant presents a much more complex production-management environment. Its 200 products have to be scheduled through the plant, requiring frequent setups, inventory movements, purchases, receipts, and inspections. To handle this complexity, the support departments must be larger and more sophisticated.

The traditional cost accounting system plays an important role in obfuscating the underlying relationship between the range of products produced and the size of the support departments. First, the costs of most support departments are classified as fixed, making it difficult to realize that these costs are systematically varying. Second, the use of volume-related allocation bases makes it difficult to recognize how these support-department costs vary.

FIGURE 1. THE TWO-STAGE PROGRESS

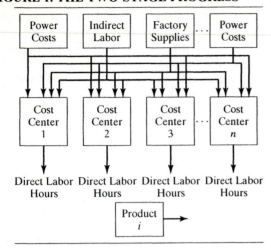

Support-department costs must vary with something because they have been among the fastest growing in the overall cost structure of manufactured products. As the example demonstrates, support-department costs vary not with the volume of product items manufactured, rather they vary with the range of items produced (i.e., the complexity of the production process). The traditional definition of variable cost, with its monthly or quarterly perspective, views such costs as fixed because complexity-related costs do not vary significantly in such a short time frame. Across an extended period of time, however, the increasing complexity of the production process places additional demands on support departments, and their costs eventually and inevitably rise.

The output of a support department consists of the activities its personnel perform. These include such activities as setups, inspections, material handling, and scheduling. The output of the departments can be represented by the number of distinct activities that are performed or the number of transactions handled. Because most of the output of these departments consists of human activities, however, output can increase quite significantly before an immediate deterioration in the quality of service is detected. Eventually, the maximum output of the department is reached and additional personnel are requested. The request typically comes some time after the initial increase in diversity and output. Thus, support departments, while varying with the diversity of the demanded output, grow intermittently. The practice of annually budgeting the size of the departments further hides the underlying relationship between the mix and volume of demand and the size of the department. The support departments often are constrained to grow only when budgeted to do so.

Support-department costs are perhaps best described as "discretionary" because they are budgeted and authorized each year. The questions we must address are: What determines the level of these discretionary fixed costs? Why, if these costs are not affected by the quantity of production, are there eight people in a support department and not one? What generates the work, if not physical quantities of inputs or outputs, that requires large support-department staffs? We believe the answers to these questions on the origins of discretionary overhead costs (i.e., what drives these costs) can be found by analyzing the activities or transactions demanded when producing a full and diverse line of products.

TRANSACTION COSTING

Low-volume products create more transactions per unit manufactured than their high-volume counterparts. The per unit share of these costs should, therefore, be higher for the low-volume products. But when volume-related bases are used exclusively to allocate support-department costs, high-volume and low-volume products receive similar transaction-related costs. When only volume-related bases are used for second-stage allocations, high-volume products receive an excessively high fraction of support-department costs and, therefore, subsidize the low-volume products.

As the range between low-volume and high-volume products increases, the degree of cross-subsidization rises. Support departments expand to cope with the additional complexity of more products, leading to increased overhead charges. The reported product cost of all products consequently increases. The high-volume products appear more expensive to produce than previously, even though they are not responsible for the additional costs. The costs triggered by the introduction of new, low-volume products are systematically shifted to high-volume products that may be placing relatively few demands on the plant's support departments.

Many of the transactions that generate work for production-support departments can be proxied by the number of setups. For example, the movement of material in the plant often occurs at the commencement or completion of a production run. Similarly, the majority of the time spent on parts inspection occurs just after a setup or changeover. Thus, while the support departments are engaged in a broad array of activities, a considerable portion of their costs may be attributed to the number of setups.

Not all of the support-department costs are related (or relatable) to the number of setups. The cost of setup personnel relates more to the quantity of setup hours than to the actual number of setups. The number of inspections of incoming material can be directly related to the number of material receipts, as would be the time spent moving the received material into inventory, The number of outgoing shipments can be used to predict the activity level of the finished-goods and shipping departments. The assignment of all these support costs with a transactions-based approach reinforces the effect of the setup-related costs because the low-sales-volume items tend to trigger more small incoming and outgoing shipments.

Schrader Bellows had recently performed a "strategic cost analysis" that significantly increased the number of bases used to allocate costs to the products; many second-stage allocations used transactions costs to assign support-department costs to products. In particular, the number of setups allocated a sizable percentage of support-department costs to products.

The effect of changing these second-stage allocations from a direct labor to a transaction basis was dramatic. While the support-department costs accounted for about 50% of overhead (or about 25% of total costs), the change in the reported product costs ranged from about minus 10% to plus 1,000%. The significant change in the reported product costs for the low-volume items was due to the substantial cost of the support departments and the low batch size over which the transaction cost was spread.

Table 1 shows the magnitude of the shift in reported product costs for seven representative products. The existing cost system reported gross margins that varied from 26% to 47%, while the strategic analysis showed gross margin that ranged from –258% to +46%. The trends in the two sets of reported product profitabilities were clear: the existing direct-labor-based system had identified the low-volume products as the most profitable, while the strategic cost analysis indicated exactly the reverse.

There are three important messages in the table and in the company's findings in general.

- Traditional systems that assign costs to products using a single volume-related base seriously distort product costs.
- The distortion is systematic. Low-volume products are undercosted, and high-volume products are overcosted.
- Accurate product costs cannot, in general, be achieved by cost systems that rely only on volume-related bases (even multiple bases such as machine hours and material quantities) for second-stage allocations. A different type of allocation base must be used for overhead costs that vary with the number of transactions performed, as opposed to the volume of product produced.

The shift to transaction-related allocation bases is a more fundamental change to the philosophy of cost-systems design than is at first realized. In a traditional cost system that uses volume-related bases, the costing element is always the product. It is the product that

consumes direct labor hours, machine hours, or material dollars. Therefore, it is the product that gets costed.

In a transaction-related system, costs are assigned to the units that caused the transaction to be originated. For example, if the transaction is a setup, then the costing will be the production lot because each production lot requires a single setup. The same is true for purchasing activities, inspections, scheduling, and material movements. The costing element is no longer the product but those elements the transaction affects.

In the transaction-related costing system, the unit cost of a product is determined by dividing the cost of a transaction by the number of units in the costing element. For example, when the costing element is a production lot, the unit cost of a product is determined by dividing the production lot cost by the number of units in the production lot.

This change in the costing element is not trivial. In the Schrader Bellows strategic cost analysis (see Table 1), product seven appears to violate the strong inverse relationship between profits and production-lot size for the other six products. A more detailed analysis of the seven products, however, showed that product seven was assembled with components also used to produce two high-volume products (numbers one and six) and that it was the production-lot size of the components that was the dominant cost driver, not the assembly-lot size, or the shipping-lot size.

In a traditional cost system, the value of commonality of parts is hidden. Low-volume components appear to cost only slightly more than their high-volume counterparts. There is no incentive to design products with common parts. The shift to transaction-related costing identifies the much lower costs that derive from designing products with common (or fewer) parts and the much higher costs generated when large numbers of unique parts are specified for low-volume products. In recognition of this phenomenon, more companies are experimenting with assigning material-related overhead on the basis of the total number of different parts used, and not on the physical or dollar volume of materials used.

LONG-TERM VARIABLE COST

The volume-unrelated support-department costs, unlike traditional variable costs, do not vary with short-term changes in activity levels. Traditional variable costs vary in the short run with production fluctuations because they represent cost elements that require no managerial actions to change the level of expenditure.

TABLE 1. COMPARISON OF REPORTED PRODUCT COSTS AT SCHRADER BELLOWS

Product	Sales Volume	Existing Cost System		Transaction-Based System		Percent of Change	
		Unit Cost[a]	Unit Gross Margin	Unit Cost[a]	Unit Gross Margin	Unit Cost	Unit Gross Margin
1	43,562	7.85	5.52	7.17	6.19	(8.7)	12.3
2	500	8.74	3.76	15.45	(2.95)	76.8	(178.5)
3	53	12.15	10.89	82.49	(59.45)	578.9	(645.9)
4	2,079	13.63	4.91	24.51	(5.97)	79.8	(221.6)
5	5,670	12.40	7.95	19.99	0.36	61.3	(93.4)
6	11,169	8.04	5.49	7.96	5.57	(1.0)	1.5
7	423	8.47	3.74	6.93	5.28	(18.2)	41.2

[a] The sum of total cost (sales volume × unit cost) for all seven products is different under the two systems because the seven products only represent a small fraction of total production.

In contrast, any amount of decrease in overhead costs associated with reducing diversity and complexity in the factory will take many months to realize and will require specific managerial actions. The number of personnel in support departments will have to be reduced, machines may have to be sold off, and some supervisors will become redundant. Actions to accomplish these overhead cost reductions will lag, by months, the complexity-reducing actions in the product line and in the process technology. But this long-term cost response mirrors the way overhead costs were first built up in the factory—as more products with specialized designs were added to the product line, the organization simply muddled through with existing personnel. It was only over time that overworked support departments requested and received additional personnel to handle the increased number of transactions that had been thrust upon them.

The personnel in the support departments are often highly skilled and possess a high degree of firm-specific knowledge. Management is loathe to lay them off when changes in market conditions temporarily reduce the level of production complexity. Consequently, when the work load of these departments drops, surplus capacity exists.

The long-term perspective management had adopted toward its products often made it difficult to use the surplus capacity. When it was used, it was not to make products never to be produced again, but rather to produce inventory of products that were known to disrupt production (typically the very low-volume items) or to produce, under short-term contract, products for other companies. We did not observe or hear about a situation in which this capacity was used to introduce a product that had only a short life expectancy. Some companies justified the acceptance of special orders or incremental business because they "knew" that the income from this business more than covered their variable or incremental costs. They failed to realize that the long-term consequence from accepting such incremental business was a steady rise in the costs of their support departments.

WHEN PRODUCT COSTS ARE NOT KNOWN
The magnitude of the errors in reported product costs and the nature of their bias make it difficult for full-line producers to enact sensible strategies. The existing cost systems clearly identify the low-volume products as the most profitable and the high-volume ones as the least profitable. Focused competitors, on the other hand, will not suffer from the same handicap. Their cost systems, while equally poorly designed, will report more accurate product costs because they are not distorted as much by lot-size diversity.

With access to more accurate product cost data, a focused competitor can sell the high-volume products at a lower price. The full-line producer is then apparently faced with very low margins on these products and is naturally tempted to de-emphasize this business and concentrate on apparently higher-profit, low-volume specialty business. This shift from high-volume to low-volume products, however, does not produce the anticipated higher profitability. The firm, believing in its cost system, chases illusory profits.

The firm has been victimized by diseconomies of scope. In trying to obtain the benefits of economy of scale by expanding its product offerings to better utilize its fixed or capacity resources, the firm does not see the high diseconomies it has introduced by creating a far more complex production environment. The cost accounting system fails to reveal this diseconomy of scope.

A COMPREHENSIVE COST SYSTEM
One message comes through overwhelmingly in our experiences with the three firms, and with the many others we talked and worked with. Almost all product-related decisions—introduction, pricing, and discontinuance—are long-term. Management accounting thinking (and teaching) during the past half-century has concentrated on information for making short-run incremental decisions based on variable, incremental, or relevant costs. It has missed the most important aspect of product decisions.

Invariably, the time period for measuring "variable," "incremental," or "relevant" costs has been about a month (the time period corresponding to the cycle of the firm's internal financial reporting system). While academics admonish that notions of fixed and variable are meaningful only with respect to a particular time period, they immediately discard this warning and teach from the perspective of one-month decision horizons.

This short-term focus for product costing has led all the companies we visited to view a large and growing proportion of their total manufacturing costs as "fixed." In fact, however, what they call "fixed" costs have been the most variable and rapidly increasing costs. This paradox has seemingly eluded most accounting practitioners and scholars. Two fundamental changes in our thinking about cost behavior must be introduced.

First, the allocation of costs from the cost pools to the products should be achieved using bases that reflect cost drivers. Because many overhead costs are driven by the complexity of production, not the volume of production, nonvolume-related bases are required. Second, many of these overhead costs are somewhat discretionary. While they vary with changes in the complexity of the production process, these changes are intermittent. A traditional cost system that defines variable costs as varying in the short term with production volume will misclassify these costs as fixed.

The misclassification also arises from an inadequate understanding of the actual cost drivers for most overhead costs. Many overhead costs vary with transactions: transactions to order, schedule, receive, inspect, and pay for shipments; to move, track, and count inventory; to schedule production work; to set up machines; to perform quality assurance; to implement engineering change orders; and to expedite and ship orders. The cost of these transactions is largely independent of the size of the order being handled; the cost does not vary with the amount of inputs or outputs. It does vary, however, with the need for the transaction itself. If the firm introduces more products, if it needs to expedite more orders, or if it needs to inspect more components, then it will need larger overhead departments to perform these additional transactions.

SUMMARY

Product costs are almost all variable costs. Some of the sources of variability relate to physical volume of items produced. These costs will vary with units produced, or in a varied, multiproduct environment, with surrogate measures such as labor hours, machine hours, material dollars and quantities, or elapsed time of production. Other costs, however, particularly those arising from overhead support and marketing departments, vary with the diversity and complexity in the product line. The variability of these costs is best explained by the

incidence of transactions to initiate the next stage in the production, logistics, or distribution process.

A comprehensive product cost system, incorporating the long-term variable costs of manufacturing and marketing each product or product line, should provide a much better basis for managerial decisions on pricing, introducing, discontinuing, and reengineering product lines. The cost system may even become strategically important for running the business and creating sustainable competitive advantages for the firm.

THE IMPORTANCE OF FIELD RESEARCH
The accompanying article, coauthored with Robin Cooper, is excerpted from *Accounting & Management: Field Study Perspectives* (Boston, Mass., Harvard Business School Press, 1987) William J. Bruns, Jr. and Robert S. Kaplan (eds.). The book contains 13 field studies on management accounting innovations presented at a colloquium at the Harvard Business School in June 1986 by leading academic researchers from the U.S. and Western Europe. The colloquium represents the largest single collection of field research studies on management accounting practices in organizations.

The HBS colloquium had two principal objectives. First, the authors were to understand and document the management accounting practices of actual organizations. Some of the organizations would be captured in a process of transition: attempting, and occasionally succeeding to modify their systems to measure, motivate and evaluate operating performance. Other organizations were studied just to understand the system of measurement and control that had evolved in their particular environment.

A second, and even more important, objective of the colloquium was to begin the process by which field research methods in management accounting could be established as a legitimate method of inquiry. Academic researchers in accounting have extensive experience with deductive, model-building, analytic research with the design and analysis of controlled experiments, usually in a laboratory setting; and with the empirical analysis of large data bases. This experience has yielded research guidance and criteria that, while not always explicit, nevertheless are widely shared and permit research to be conducted and evaluated.

At a time when so many organizations are reexamining the adequacy of their management accounting systems it is especially important that university-based researchers spend more time working directly with innovating organizations. We are pleased that MANAGEMENT ACCOUNTING, through publication of this article, is helping to publicize the existence of the field studies performed to date.

The experiences described in the accompanying article, as well as in the other papers in the colloquium volume, indicate a very different role for management accounting systems in organizations than is currently taught in most of our business schools and accounting departments. We believe that present and future field research and casewriting will lead to major changes in management accounting courses. To facilitate the needed changes in curriculum and research, however, requires extensive cooperation between university faculty and practicing management accountants. As noted by observers at the Harvard colloquium:

> There is a tremendous store of knowledge about management accounting practices and ideas out there in real companies. Academicians as a whole are far too ignorant of that knowledge. When academics begin to see the relevance of this data base, perhaps generations of students will become more aware of its richness. Such awareness must precede any real progress on prescribing good management accounting for any given situation.
>
> To observe is also to discover. The authors have observed interesting phenomena. We do not know how prevalent these phenomena are or under what conditions they exist or do not exist. But the studies suggest possible relationships, causes, effects, and even dynamic process in the sense that Yogi Berra must have had in mind when he said, "Sometimes you can observe a lot just by watching."

With the research support and cooperation of the members of the National Association of Accountants, many university professors are looking forward to watching and also describing the changes now under way so that academics can begin to develop theories, teach, and finally prescribe about the new opportunities for management accounting.

Robert S. Kaplan

ENDNOTES

1. Mayers Tap (disguised name) is described in Harvard Business School, case series 9-185-111. Schrader-Bellows is described in HBS Case Series 9-186-272.

Robin Cooper is an associate professor of business administration at the Harvard Business School and a fellow of the Institute of Chartered Accountants in England and Wales. He writes a column, "Cost Management Principles and Concepts," in the Journal of Cost Management *and has produced research on activity-based costing for the CAM-1 Cost Management System Project.*

Robert S. Kaplan is the Arthur Lowes Dickinson Professor of Accounting at the Harvard Business School and a professor of industrial administration at Carnegie-Mellon University. Currently, Professor Kaplan serves on the Executive Committee of the CAM-1 Cost Management System Project, the Manufacturing Studies Board of the National Research Council, and the Financial Accounting Standards Advisory Committee.

QUESTION

3.1 What does the term "cost of complexity" mean in Cooper and Kaplan's article? Is this concept used in traditional cost-accounting systems?

3.2 What Are the Costs of Variability?

Knowing the answer is key to a company's quest for quality.

by Harold P. Roth, CMA, and Thomas L. Albright, CPA*

CERTIFICATE OF MERIT, 1992–93

Zero defects and robust quality are two quality philosophies used to help U.S. companies compete in the global marketplace. An important measure in any quality philosophy is the cost of product variability.

Although variation among products may affect the consumers' perceptions of quality, the importance of consistency to a producer depends on the quality philosophy it follows. For example, with a zero defects philosophy the only cost attributed to variation occurs when products fall outside the specification limits. Thus, the cost of variation depends on whether the product can be reworked, if there are constraints on production, and the distance between product specification limits.

On the other hand, a robust quality program claims that any variation is undesirable and causes costs to be incurred by the manufacturer, consumer, or society. An estimate of these costs is provided by the quality loss function.

TWO PHILOSOPHIES

The term "quality" has many different meanings depending on the context used. When quality is used to describe products, it may mean "conforming to specifications" or "fitness for use." Although these two definitions may mean the same thing to many people, they have different implications for how quality is evaluated and the importance of product variability.

---

* From: H. P. Roth and T. L. Albright, "What Are the Costs of Variability?" *Management Accounting* (June 1994): 51–55. Reprinted with permission.

38

The philosophy underlying the "conformance to specifications" definition generally leads to a zero defects approach to quality while the "fitness for use" philosophy leads to a robust quality approach.[1]

The role of product variability in evaluating quality depends on whether the company has adopted a zero defects or a robust quality philosophy. With a zero defects philosophy, the allowable variation is defined by specification limits, and any variation within those limits is acceptable. According to the robust quality philosophy, any variation from a target value represents a condition that is less than ideal, with potential economic consequences. Thus, robustness is the result of meeting exact targets consistently—not from always staying within tolerances.

In turn, the cost of variation also depends on the philosophy. Generally, companies that adopt a zero defects philosophy will not attribute any cost to variability if the product is within specification limits. But the robust quality proponent will assign a cost to variability whenever a product varies from a target. Companies following a robust quality philosophy believe any variation from target results in a loss. Furthermore, greater losses will occur as the variation from target becomes larger.

VARIABILITY FROM TARGET

A case study at the Sony Corporation supports the idea that a relationship exists between variability and the zero defects and robust quality philosophies.[2] The study involved the color density of television sets produced in two manufacturing facilities—one in San Diego and the other in Tokyo.

The color density distribution associated with the output of each manufacturing site is illustrated in Figure 1. Three reference points: the lower specification limit, target value, and upper specification limit appear on the horizontal axis of the graph.

Generally, Sony considers any television set with color density measurement less than the lower specification limit or greater than the upper specification limit to be defective. However, the approach to quality differs between the two plants.

FIGURE 1. DISTRIBUTION OF COLOR DENSITY

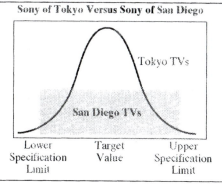

Sony of Tokyo strives to produce at the target value and does not inspect each unit. Thus, some out-of-spec units are shipped to customers, as evidenced by the tails of the distribution that fall outside the specification limits. In contrast, Sony of San Diego uses 100% inspection to ensure that the televisions fall within the specification limits and to prevent the shipment of defective units to distributors.

After studying the output of the plants, Sony discovered that although the number of defective units was similar in both manufacturing plants, the variation around the target specification was not. As shown in Figure 1, there is less variation in the televisions produced in the Tokyo plant because more sets are near the target value. The distribution of color densities from the San Diego plant (which is shown by the rectangular distribution) indicates greater variability than that of the Tokyo plant because more sets fall farther away from the target value.

Customers who purchased television sets manufactured by Sony of Tokyo reported greater satisfaction and filed fewer warranty claims than those who purchased products manufactured by Sony of San Diego. The lesson to Sony was clear—variation from the target specification of a critical component has implications for customer satisfaction and, therefore, costs.

COST OF VARIABILITY

There are many costs associated with variability in product attributes. For example, raw material costs will be higher if products use more materials than specified by engineering standards (for example, the target value). Likewise, variability in material thickness or weight may result in added wear on down-stream machines that cause more maintenance and repair costs.

Also, products that exceed material usage targets may have higher delivery costs because they weigh more than the target weight. However, these costs are not attributed to variability with the zero defects philosophy. Instead, costs of variability are recognized only when a product falls outside the specification limits. When products meet specifications, they are assumed to meet the customers' requirements.

The costs incurred when products fall outside the specification limits depend on three factors: whether the product can be reworked or repaired, production constraints, and where specification limits are set.

When products fall outside the specification limits, it may be less costly to rework or repair them than to discard them. When products are reworked and then sold, there is no loss of the materials and parts that comprise the final product. In addition, disposal costs are reduced or avoided by the producer, so costs are generally lower if rework is possible.

The constraints that exist in the production process also affect the cost. If excess capacity exists and additional units can be produced to replace nonconforming products, the costs incurred because a product fails to meet specifications depend on whether the nonconforming unit is sold or discarded. But if additional units cannot be produced, then the cost of variability includes an opportunity cost for the lost sales. Thus, the economic costs of lost production are higher when there are constraints than if no constraints exist.

A paper manufacturer provides an example of the costs of variability in a capacity-constrained environment.[3] A study was conducted to understand the sources of variation in the quality of paperboard output. The variables studied included crews, shifts, grades of product, rest interval between shifts, and whether a product was produced immediately following a grade change. The variability and cost data that resulted from the study had strategic implications for the company.

Because the company was operating in a capacity-constrained environment, the cost accountants developed a product cost analysis that captured the economic cost of a unit of product that was lost as a result of variability in the manufacturing process. The cost included the variable cost of materials and overhead (less any pulp or chemicals that could be recovered through reworking the product), a fixed cost allocation, and the lost contribution margin (a surrogate for the opportunity cost from producing a defective product in a capacity-constrained environment).

The revised cost numbers had strategic implications for the product mix manufactured by the plant. By analyzing the cost of each grade of product, the company discovered that the cost of certain grades far exceeded the selling price.

For example, the company learned that the production of uncoated paperboard resulted in a much larger proportion of defective units than that of coated paper-board. This knowledge helped the company analyze the strategic implications of manufacturing a product that exhibits extreme variation in the quality of production by attaching a cost to products exhibiting high rates of variability.

CALCULATING THE COSTS
Various costs are incurred when products fall outside the specification limits. These include out-of-pocket costs such as costs of inspection and rework.

If the product can be sold as a first-quality unit after the rework, these out-of-pocket costs are the total costs of variability. If the reworked unit cannot be sold as a first-quality unit, then the cost of variability also may include an opportunity cost. The opportunity cost will be relevant if the second-quality item replaces a sale for a first-quality item. In this case, the opportunity cost of variability is the difference between the contribution margin of the first-quality product and the actual contribution margin.

If a product falls outside the specification limits, cannot be reworked, and must be scrapped, then the cost of variability includes the materials, labor, and other costs incurred in producing the product. In addition, any cost incurred in disposing of the product also is a cost of variability.

To illustrate the computation of costs that are caused by variability, assume a company is producing a product that sells for $50 per unit. The variable production cost is $20, and the unit contribution margin is $30. During the last month, the company manufactured 100,000 units that used all the available machine hours. All units produced are sold.

The weight is a critical dimension for this product. The target value for the weight is 20 kg, and the specification limits are set at plus or minus 2 kg. For the units produced last month, the weights followed a normal distribution with an average of 20 kg and a standard deviation of 0.8 kg. Figure 2 illustrates the distribution of the weights from this production process.

As shown in Figure 2, most of the weights fall between 18 and 22 kg and, therefore, conform to the specifications. However, some of the weights are above the upper specification limit of 22 kg, and some are below the lower specification limits of 18 kg. These units that fall in the tails of the distribution are nonconforming. To determine the number of nonconforming units, a z-value is calculated, and a table for areas under the normal curve is consulted to determine the portion in the tails of the distribution.[4]

For this example, the calculated z-value shows that the specification limit is 2.5 standard normal deviates from the mean (see Figure 2). With z equal to 2.5, a table for the area under the normal curve shows that 0.0062% of the observations exceed 22 kg. Because the distribution is symmetrical, an equal portion falls below the lower specification limit of 18 kg. Thus, the number of nonconforming products manufactured last month was 1,240 [100,000 (2 × 0.0062)].

FIGURE 2. DISTRIBUTION OF PRODUCTS

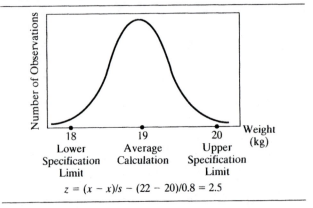

$z = (x - \bar{x})/s - (22 - 20)/0.8 = 2.5$

The cost attributed to the variability of these 1,240 units depends on their disposal. If the units can be reworked[5] for $12 a unit and then sold for the normal sales price of $50, the cost of variability is equal to the rework cost. But if the products only can be sold for $45 a unit, there is also an opportunity cost of $5 per unit, for a total cost of $17. If the product cannot be reworked, then the relevant cost of variability is the variable production cost, the opportunity cost, and any disposal cost.

Table 1 summarizes the cost of variability for various conditions. The total cost of variability for this product can be calculated by multiplying the unit cost by the number of nonconforming units. With 1,240 nonconforming units during the month, the cost of variability could range from a low of $14,880 ($12 × 1,240) if the units are reworked and sold as first-quality units to a high of $68,200 ($55 × 1,240) if the units cannot be reworked and must be disposed of at a cost of $5 per unit.

This example shows how organizations might estimate their costs of variability when they manufacture products that do not conform to specifications. But it ignores any costs incurred because products vary within the specification limits and any costs incurred by consumers because of variability in the products.

Thus, the philosophy of zero defects may understate the total cost of product variability. The quality loss function provides an alternative way to measure the cost of variability that is consistent with the robust quality philosophy.

QUALITY LOSS FUNCTION
The quality loss function (QLF) is a part of the Taguchi quality philosophy.[6] The QLF is based on the idea that any variability from a target value causes a loss to society. Thus, his proponents believe that any variability is costly even if the products still fall within the specification limits.

There are several variations of the quality loss function, and the appropriate one depends on how quality is measured. In the example presented earlier, the quality

characteristic (weight) represents a nominal-is-better function. In other words, the target value of 20 kg is the nominal value, and production should strive to manufacture products weighing 20 kg. Any variation from this value results in a loss under the quality loss function.

The quality loss function is a quadratic function where costs increase as the actual product characteristic deviates from the target value. Figure 3 shows the quality loss function for the nominal-is-better case, and Table 2 presents the formula for measuring the quality loss for an individual unit.

To determine the total loss for a period using the quality loss function, an average loss per unit can be calculated and multiplied by the total number of units. When the average and standard deviation are known, the average loss can be estimated using the formula also shown in Table 2.

With 100,000 units, the quality loss is $192,000 [$1.92 × 100,000] which is much larger than the cost of variability estimated using the conformance to specification model. The reason for the greater cost is that the quality loss function includes a cost for any unit that varies from the target value regardless of whether it falls inside or outside the specification limits.

WHY VARIABILITY IS IMPORTANT
According to research, a lack of product consistency is a major factor in customers' perceptions of poor quality. The relationship between variability and quality is recognized in many quality control techniques such as statistical process control. It is also recognized by companies such as Oregon Cutting Systems where the operational definition of quality is to "reduce variability around the target."[7]

Measuring variability should provide managers with information that can help them improve operations by identifying opportunities for improving product quality. If specific parts of a product can be identified as the source of variability, then managers know where they should focus their quality improvement efforts.

TABLE 1. COST OF VARIABILITY

Sales price per first-quality unit	$50
Sales price per second-quality unit	45
Variable production cost per unit	20
Normal contribution margin per unit	30
Rework cost per unit	12
Disposal cost per unit	5

Condition	Variable Production Cost	Rework Cost	Disposal Cost	Lost Contribution Margin	Total Unit Cost
Unit is reworked and sold for $50		$12			$12
Unit is reworked and sold for $45		12		$5	17
Unit cannot be reworked and has no disposal cost	$20			30	50
Unit cannot be reworked and has a $5 disposal cost	20		$5	30	55

FIGURE 3. QUALITY LOSS FUNCTION

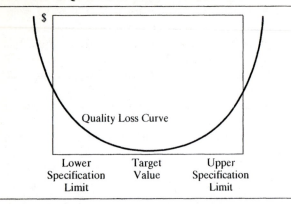

TABLE 2. MEASURING QUALITY LOSS

Quality Loss for an Individual Unit:

$$L = k(Y - T)^2$$

where L = unit loss,

$\qquad Y$ = actual value of characteristic,

$\qquad T$ = target value of characteristic, and

$\qquad k$ = proportionality constant.

The value of k is usually computed by dividing the loss for a product, which falls at the specification limit by the squared distance form the target value to the specification limit, i.e.:

$$k = \frac{c}{d^2}$$

where c = loss associated with a unit produced at the spec. limit, and

$\qquad d$ = distance from target value to spec limit.

In this example, if the loss for a unit at the specification limit is $12, then the proportionality constant is $3:

$$k = \frac{\$12}{(22 - 20)^2} = \frac{\$12}{2^2} = \$3$$

Average Loss per Unit:

$\qquad$ Average loss = $k[s^2 + (Y - T)^2]$

$\qquad$ where s = standard deviation

$\qquad\qquad Y$ = average (mean)

$\qquad\qquad T$ = target value, and

$\qquad\qquad k$ = proportionality constant.

From the data given above, the average loss is $1.92:

$\qquad$ Average loss = $\$3[0.8^2 + (20 - 20)^2] = \$3 \times 0.64 = \$1.92$

These efforts may involve educating and retraining employees, redesigning production processes, investing in equipment, and even redesigning products. If a product can be manufactured using a smaller number of components and parts, there is less likelihood that the sum of the individual variations will result in significant quality problems.

Measuring the cost of variability also should help managers in their quest for quality. If managers do not define quality in terms of variability, they may not be aware of the types of costs associated with variability and of the magnitude of the costs. With an estimate of the cost, managers may be more likely to understand the financial implication of variability and the savings that result from their efforts to reduce it. Unless cost savings are measured, the financial impact of the efforts will not be known.

Although all processes and products will show some variation because it is a law of nature, companies need to measure it and strive to reduce it if they want to be competitive. If they do not reduce variation, it is likely their competitors will, and the consistently performing product may be perceived as higher quality by customers.

ENDNOTES

1. For a discussion of robust quality see Genichi Taguchi and Don Clausing, "Robust Quality," *Harvard Business Review* January–February 1990, pp. 65–75.

2. This case study is discussed by Taguchi and Clausing, pp. 68–69; and by Ranjit Roy, *A Primer on the Taguchi Method*, Van Nostrand Reinhold, New York, 1990, pp. 12–13.

3. For further details on the study see T. L. Albright and J. M. Reeve, "A Case Study on the Impact of Material Yield-Related Cost Drivers on Economic Improvement," *Journal of Management Accounting Research*, Fall 1992, pp. 20–43.

4. Most statistics books provide tables showing Areas under the Normal Curve. For an example, see Eugene L. Grant and Richard S. Leavenworth *Statistics Quality Control*, 5th ed., McGraw-Hill Book Company, New York, 1980, pp. 628–629.

5. Because the example states that production uses all available machinery, this example assumes that the reworking is done by laborers using different machines than used for the initial production.

6. Genichi Taguchi is a Japanese engineer who has developed statistical approaches to improving product and process quality. His approaches are discussed in many books dealing with quality engineering and design. Examples include Ranjit Roy, *A Primer on the Taguchi Method*, Van Nostrand Reinhold, New York, 1990; Philip J. Ross, *Taguchi Techniques for Quality Engineering*, McGraw-Hill Book Company, New York, 1988; and Thomas B. Barker, *Engineering Quality by Design*, Marcel Dekker, Inc., New York, and ASQC Quality Press, Milwaukee, 1990.

7. Jack Bailes, Ilene Kleinsorge, and Larry White, "How Support Services Can Use Process Control," MANAGEMENT ACCOUNTING® October 1992, p. 45.

Harold P. Roth, CMA, CPA, Ph.D., is a professor of accounting at the University of Tennessee, Knoxville. He is past president of IMA's Knoxville Chapter, through which this article was submitted. Dr. Roth can be reached by calling (615) 974-1756.

Thomas L. Albright, CPA, is an assistant professor of accounting in the Culverhouse School of Accountancy at the University of Alabama. He holds a Ph.D. degree from the University of Tennessee. Dr. Albright is a member of IMA's West Alabama Chapter and can be reached at (205) 348–6131.

QUESTIONS

3.2a   Is the "cost of variability" concept applied consistently under the zero defects and robust quality philosophies? Explain.
3.2b   Describe the "quality loss function" in Roth and Albright's article.

3.3 The Outsourcing Decision
Seize the opportunity to focus on activities that give your company the competitive edge.

*by Ralph E. Drtina**

Each business day the number of management accountants affected by massive restructuring and layoffs increases. In their efforts to streamline operations, managers are dismantling bureaucracies and questioning the benefits of vertical integration.

One alternative is a strategy that focuses internal operations on a small set of critical core activities. Nonessential services are then outsourced to external vendors, who can offer advantages such as cost, flexibility, and access to the latest technology.

Firms in high-technology industries, such as computers and biotechnology, have been pioneers in developing partnered relationships and focused strategies. Consider, for example, the case of Sun Microsystems, a leading maker of computer workstations. Sun concentrates on hardware and software design, where it distinguished itself from competitors, and outsources almost everything else in its value chain. It relies so heavily on external manufacturers and distributors that its own employees never touch one of its top selling products. After a vendor assembles the machine, another contract supplier delivers it to the customer.

Firms like Sun have been referred to as "intellectual holding companies." Numerous other companies—Apple, Honda, and Gallo Winery—also bank their success on a limited number of specific core technologies, although perhaps not to the outsourcing extreme exhibited by Sun Microsystems.

Management accountants can play an important role in deciding which activities should be performed within the firm and which should be bought externally.[1] But what is the correct methodology for helping managers make such strategic make-buy decisions?

Accounting educators, for example, normally frame the make-buy discussion within a manufacturing context. These decisions are presented as short term in duration and seek to increase corporate earnings by finding ways to reduce costs.

Management strategists, who initiate outsourcing policy, are more concerned with creating shareholder value. Their policies often zero in on eliminating nonmanufacturing service overhead.

ACTIVITIES TO OUTSOURCE

The first step in preparing an outsourcing study is understanding your firm's value chain and the relationships among its service activities. Figure 1 is an example of typical services in a value chain.

Value is added at each stage beginning with product concept and ending with after-sales service. Corporate staff services—such as legal and accounting—provide the secondary support necessary to maintain the organization and its primary value chain activities. Both services provided by corporate staff and in the value chain can qualify for outsourcing.

Each stage of service delivery can be broken down further into its requisite subcomponent activities. Distribution, for example, is subdivided into four specific service activities. Fleet maintenance, an indirect activity that supports the distribution service, is identified in Figure 1 as being a candidate for external outsourcing.

Some activities are eliminated immediately as candidates for outsourcing, either because the service cannot be contracted outside or because the firm must control the activity to maintain its competitive position. For example, a high-technology research facility would not be able to outsource its typing or photocopying due to the highly classified nature of work. Similarly, Hewlett-Packard carefully controls the software for a laser printer it coproduces with Canon Inc. of Japan, thereby preventing its partner from replicating the laserjet technology for its own benefit.

* From: R. Drtina, "The Outsourcing Decision," *Management Accounting* (March 1994): 56–62. Reprinted with permission.

FIGURE 1. KEY SERVICE ACTIVITIES

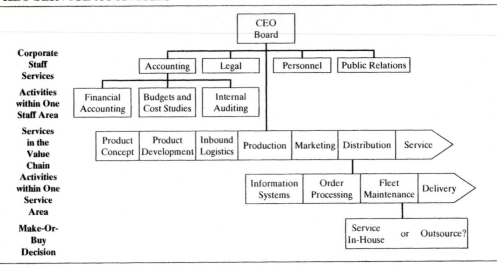

For those activities eligible for outsourcing, the key strategic question to ask is whether the firm can perform a service activity on a level comparable with the best organizations in the world. Productivity measurements should be compiled to capture these critical success factors for the activity: availability, timeliness, flexibility, quality, and cost reduction. Measures are then benchmarked against the results of firms that offer these same services in the marketplace.

Thus, we might find that a firm evaluating its fleet maintenance activity compares performance measures like those listed in Table 1. If the firm's performance does not stand up to the external measures. A determination must be made whether the firm can achieve a world-class level of delivery. If it is not possible to accomplish benchmarked standards of performance, the activity should be outsourced. To reiterate, the firm should concentrate only on those core activities that enhance its unique marketplace advantages.

OUTSOURCING FLEET MAINTENANCE
The service activity in question must pass several hurdles:

- Is it possible to purchase the service externally?
- Does the firm need to control the service activity—as would be the case with secret documents or a critical technology?
- Most important, is the firm capable of delivering the service at a world-class standard of performance?

If the service survives these preliminary cutoffs, the next step is to decide if the service to be outsourced is central to the firm's core strategic activities. Cost analysis plays an important part in the decision to "make" the service activity internally or to "buy" from external sources.

TABLE 1. BENCHMARKING THE FLEET MAINTENANCE ACTIVITY

Critical Success Factors	Measures
Availability	Downtime
	Unscheduled repair
	Vehicle breakdowns
Timeliness	Time needed for repair
	On-time vehicle delivery
Flexibility	Turnaround time for unscheduled repairs
Quality	Rework
	Fuel efficiency
	Internal customer satisfaction
	Frequency of unscheduled repairs
Cost reduction	Cost per service operation
	Demonstrated process improvements
Accuracy	Historical record keeping

Refer once again to the benchmarks for the fleet maintenance activity in Table 1. Information about the present level of maintenance performance is in Table 2.

Assume that the accountants conducted a benchmarking comparison that revealed performance measures for fleet maintenance fell slightly short in several areas. After careful study, however, the accountants expect that maintenance can be brought up to a world-class standard by spending an average of $20 more per year for supplies and parts per vehicle and by investing an additional $6,000 per year in training. Hence, to achieve the benchmarked performance standard, supplies and parts will cost $470 per vehicle, and the combined cost of payroll and training is increased to $102,000 for the year.

The top panel of Table 2 presents the "make" option of servicing vehicles internally. Total costs to attain best-in-the-world maintenance performance are projected for each of the next five years.

TABLE 2. OUTSOURCE FLEET MAINTENANCE DIFFERENTIAL COST ANALYSIS

Panel 1. Make option: Service vehicles in-house

	Planning Horizon*					Total
	Year 1	Year 2	Year 3	Year 4	Year 5	
Vehicles per year	600	625	650	675	700	
Variable cost/vehicle supplies, parts	$470	$470	$470	$470	$470	
	$282,000	$293,750	$305,500	$317,250	$329,000	
Fixed costs/per year						
Payroll and training	102,000	102,000	110,500	110,500	119,000	
Facilities-utilities, maintenance	15,000	15,000	15,000	15,000	15,000	
Facilities-depreciation						
(cost = $900,000, 30 yr. life)	30,000	30,000	30,000	30,000	30,000	
	147,000	147,000	155,500	155,500	164,000	
Total costs	429,000	440,750	461,000	472,750	493,000	
Less tax effect @ 34%	145,860	149,855	156,740	160,735	167,620	
Net cost of servicing vehicles in house	$283,140	$290,895	$304,260	$312,015	$325,380	$1,515,690
Average cost per vehicle	$472	$465	$468	$462	$465	

Panel 2. Buy option: Outsource vehicle service

	Year 1	Year 2	Year 3	Year 4	Year 5	Total
Vehicles per year	600	625	650	675	700	
Service cost per vehicle	$870	$870	$870	$870	$870	
Total contractual costs	$522,000	$543,750	$565,500	$587,250	$609,000	
Facilities-depreciation	30,000	30,000	30,000	30,000	30,000	
Total operating costs	552,000	573,750	595,500	617,250	639,000	
Less opportunity cost: rental revenue†	135,000	135,00	135,000	135,000	135,000	
Total costs	417,000	438,750	460,500	482,250	504,000	
Less tax effect @ 34%	141,780	149,175	156,570	163,965	171,360	
Net cost of outsourcing vehicle maintenance	$275,220	$289,575	$303,930	$318,285	$332,640	$1,519,650
Average cost per vehicle	$459	$463	$468	$472	$475	

	Year 1	Year 2	Year 3	Year 4	Year 5	Total
Panel 3. Differential cost to outsource‡	$7,920	$1,320	$330	($6,270)	($7,260)	($3,960)

* This model is based on a 5-year planning horizon, which represents management's time frame of outsourcing commitment at this stage of strategy formulation.

† In order to focus the illustration on the outsourcing decision process, it is assumed that the maintenance facility will be retained regardless of the decision outcome. If a decision to outsource is accompanied by plant disposal, additional complications arise concerning the amount and timing of disposal proceeds and differences between the planning horizon and the economic life at the facility.

‡ Differential costs increase in years 4 and 5 as the in-house service option enjoys scale efficiencies due to increases in the volume of vehicles serviced.

Management has chosen a five-year planning horizon to allow for a long-term partnering arrangement with the supplying vendor. Also built into the cost schedule is a projection for the expected number of vehicles the firm expects to maintain. The firm's strategic plan calls for an annual increase of 25 fleet vehicles. No adjustments have been made to cost estimates for inflation. That is, all reported numbers are measured in constant year 1 dollars. The only fixed costs expected to change with increased volume are payroll and training, which are adjusted for an addition of a one-half position in year 3 and another one-half position in year 5. Total costs for in-house fleet maintenance are reduced by 34%, the firm's marginal tax rate. Total net-of-tax costs per year and average costs per vehicle per year are reported at the bottom of the panel. Costs per vehicle range from a high of $472 in year 1 to a low of $462 in year 4.

The second panel of Table 2 presents information for the outsourcing buy option. Based on preliminary negotiations, the firm expects to contract out its fleet maintenance service at a cost of $870 per vehicle per year. While the contract calls for annual inflation adjustments to this fee, all costs in the analysis are expected to be affected equally by inflation and thus are ignored.

If the firm chooses to outsource maintenance, it will downsize by eliminating all its current department employees. The only cost it will continue to incur is annual depreciation of $30,000 on the maintenance facility that will be rented for $135,000 per year. Rental revenues represent the opportunity costs of the idled facility and are a deduction to the cost of outsourcing. The tenants will assume all utilities and maintenance fees on the facility as part of the leasing agreement. After adjusting for tax effects, the average annual cost per vehicle ranges from a high of $475 in year 5 to a low of $459 in year 1.

The bottom panel of Table 2 reports the differential cost of servicing in-house versus outsourcing. While there is a cost advantage to outsource of $7,920 in year 1, the total cost effect for the five-year period is ($3,960).

In other words, the firm would show a cumulative decrease to net income of $3,960 if the outsourcing option is chosen. Thus, a conventional make-buy analysis that focuses on income effects for one year would favor the buy option. But a cumulative five-year income analysis supports in-house servicing. Unfortunately, neither of these approaches addresses the time value of invested capital.

The analysis presented in Table 2 concludes with those costs that will change if the firm outsources its fleet maintenance activity as opposed to servicing in-house. Included in the calculation is the opportunity cost of facilities idled by a decision to buy outside.

This format follows the approach normally recommended by accounting educators, who stress the importance of differential costs and opportunity costs in a make-buy calculation. It differs, however, in that it makes explicit the long-term cost effects of a decision to buy outside.

As seen in virtually all cost and management accounting textbooks, the make-buy decision is limited to differential *income effects in the current operating time period alone*. Typically a caveat follows the numeric calculation.

The analyst is encouraged to consider qualitative factors—such as quality of parts, possibility for supply interruptions, and technological innovation—but no examples are given where long-term effects actually become part of the calculation.

Two implicit assumptions seem to explain the short-term emphasis in the accountant's conventional approach to make-buy analysis. First, the underlying decision objective is focused on maximizing the use of available capacity.[2]

This is stated explicitly by authors of two texts: by Horngren and Foster and by Moscove and Wright. This perspective emphasizes alternative ways to use idled facilities, yet it implies that changes in facility use are easily reversible and without cost.

Second, discussions on make-buy are concerned almost exclusively with purchasing parts or subassemblies, with in-frequent attention given to decisions on buying services. The modeling implication is that a firm has no particular loyalties to any one vendor, and, as with idled facilities, changes between vendors are accomplished easily in the short term.

Both these short-term assumptions can be challenged in today's global business environment. Efficient use of facilities is an important factor in building market advantage, but use of facilities should be part of an integrated firm-wide plan on the development of its core competencies.

Similarly, moving from vendor to vendor can minimize short-term costs, but long-term advantages can be surrendered as a result. One of the advantages of outsourcing is that firms have the opportunity to develop alliances with established repeat vendors, whose success becomes tied to that of its customers. Both parties can gain from established linkages.

Consider, for example, a medical supplies vendor who receives information directly from a hospital's information system on daily supplies needs for scheduled surgeries. By shifting inventory control responsibilities to its vendor, the hospital saves inventory carrying costs, and the vendor has guaranteed sales. Conversely, firms that insulate themselves through vertical integration run the risk of being bypassed by technological advancements from vendors.

CREATING SHAREHOLDER WEALTH

Little will be gained in the long term if management seizes short-term cost savings while losing its broader strategic focus. Unlike assumptions about decision reversibility that underlie conventional make-buy analysis, outsourcing analysis must take into account long-term effects.

As with any long-term investment decision, the criterion for acceptance shifts from an income perspective to one that seeks to optimize shareholder wealth. Thus, the foundation for strategic outsourcing analysis is the use of discounted cash flow to measure changes to a firm's value.

One impediment is the difficulty of identifying, estimating, and measuring the effects of relationships. Following my suggested decision path, however, avoids the need to measure these uncertain potential benefits because of the benchmarking process. Management is convinced that the service activity in question will be performed at a world-class standard if it is performed in-house. By establishing that equal benefit will be gained regardless of whether an activity is performed internal or external to the firm, management can ignore differences in value creation—at least for the first round of investigation. Consequently, the outsourcing analysis can focus on a differential cost comparison similar to the one presented earlier for fleet maintenance service.

To illustrate this point, Table 2 also considers the time-value effects of the outsourcing investment decision. The net costs for servicing vehicles in-house and for outsourcing are converted to cash flows by adding back depreciation, a noncash expense.

The difference between the cash outflow to service internally and the cash requirement to outsource is shown on the table as the annual cash difference if outsourced. These annual amounts are the same as the differential costs to outsource. The net cash stream is discounted at an uninflated after-tax rate, assumed as 16%, which is in keeping with the use of uninflated dollars in the illustration.

The result of this analysis—a positive net present value of $1,010—suggests the firm will increase shareholder value if the fleet maintenance service is outsourced. This conclusion conflicts with the five-year cumulative effect to income, ($3,960), which would have supported the in-house service option.

STRATEGIC CONCERNS
Before making a final decision, however, management must consider the less tangible, more uncertain benefits and costs that can accrue from global outsourcing.[3] These qualitative factors may prove significant and may take precedence over results favored in the discounted-cash-flow analysis. The following are among the most important strategic considerations.

Technical supremacy. By outsourcing noncritical activities, a firm can gain by sharing in the vendor's expertise and economies of scale. A world-class service provider would be expected to employ the latest innovations and service delivery systems available. The cost of these state-of-the-art processes then can be shared, thus providing customers with technology they otherwise may not have been able to afford.

Flexibility. Firms that outsource services have the advantage of not being tied to past investments. Particularly in fast-changing industries, a firm's survival may depend on its achieving the best in components and service necessary to compete. If a vendor fails to maintain its position of service supremacy, the buyer has the option to look for a competing source.

Opportunities to coproduce innovation. One of the benefits of developing coalitions with external partners is the potential for the emergence of innovative opportunities. For example, a vendor may find ways to improve the very nature of the activity or its delivery mechanism. In addition, dealings with a specialized vendor may create new market opportunities or partnered ventures.

It is unlikely the analyst can place a reliable dollar number on any of these potential benefits, but their effects should not be overlooked. Bromich and Bhimani suggested a format for scoring intangible benefits related to investments in advanced manufacturing technology.[4] At a minimum, making these benefits explicit, even if not quantified, draws attention to their existence.

Additional intangible costs also might be introduced by outsourcing. One of the greatest potential costs is the damage incurred by a firm that becomes overly dependent on its outsourcing partner. Taken to the extreme, a firm could become so dependent on vendor services that it loses its competitive advantage if the vendor withdraws its service or decides to compete in the same market.

Managers can manage their dependency on vendors by retaining alternative outsourcing options. Further, if a firm's sustainable competitive advantage is threatened by overreliance on the vendor, the service would seem to be an important core activity in the film's value chain. Thus, it may be preferable to perform the service in-house (see Figure 2).

TABLE 3. DISCOUNTED CASH FLOW (UNINFLATED, AFTER-TAX COST OF CAPITAL 16%)

	Year 1	Year 2	Year 3	Year 4	Year 5
Net cost of outsourcing vehicle maintenance*	($275,220)	($289,575)	($303,930)	($318,285)	($332,640)
Add back depreciation	30,000	30,000	30,000	30,000	30,000
Net cash flow to outsource	(245,220)	(259,575)	(273,930)	(288,285)	(302,640)
Less net cost of servicing vehicles in-house†	(283,140)	(290,895)	(304,260)	(312,015)	(325,380)
Add back depreciation	30,000	30,000	30,000	30,000	30,000
Net cost to service in-house	(253,140)	(260,895)	(274,260)	(282,015)	(295,380)
Annual cash differential if outsourced	7,920	1,320	330	(6,270)	(7,260)
Discount factor	0.862	0.743	0.641	0.552	0.476
Discounted cash flows	$6,828	$981	$211	($3,463)	($3,457)
Net Present Value‡	$1,101				

* From Table 2, panel 2.
† From Table 2, panel 1.
‡ Net present value (NPV) should be recalculated to find its sensitivity to changes in the discount rate. Interestingly, in this case a higher discount rate results in a higher NPV advantage for outsourcing. For example, the NPV at 12% is $254 and at 20%, $1,766. Higher rates reduce the negative differential cash effects in later years.

FIGURE 2. STEPS IN THE OUTSOURCING DECISION ANALYSIS

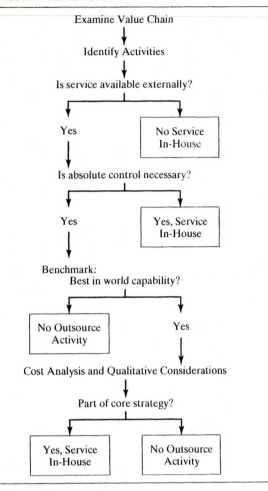

FORMING ALLIANCES

Having completed the computational analysis and considered the qualitative factors, the analyst has laid the foundation for deciding whether to outsource. One critical determination remains: Is this service activity part of the firm's core strategy?

Answering this question will require a strategic analysis on the part of top management—an assignment that calls for a different set of skills than accountants are trained to offer. Understanding the value-added cost impact due to an outsourcing arrangement is, however, a necessary first step toward making these strategic decisions.

Managers embracing a core competency philosophy look to the film's value chain to discover where outsourcing coalitions will offer greatest benefit. Ideally, the firm will capitalize on its own special skills and strengths while forming alliances with other firms to tap into their unique competencies.

This may mean looking outside the firm for such fundamental activities as product design, warehousing, market research, distribution, or after-sale repair and service. The desired result is a leveraging effect in which the firm essentially commands a network of activities that extends its own core competencies into a more sustainable market advantage.

THE CASE OF SEAGATE TECHNOLOGY

Seagate Technology is the world's largest producer of computer hard disk drives and commands about 25% of the world's market. Over the past several years, however, it has found itself battling as a "sluggardly giant" in an industry composed of fast-growing, innovative competitors such as Conner Peripherals, Quantum, and Maxtor.

Seagate initially built its market strength by delivering low-cost products that were designed and manufactured internally, while it outsourced its deliveries. Seagate's approach to owning and operating its own plants differs from that of its competitors, who mainly rely on outside suppliers. Quantum, for example, outsources virtually every piece of its disk drives while building its market position on the strength of its software and design.

Seagate has found its position threatened, some say, due to its overreliance on in-house technologies. The firm's vertically integrated operation, which resulted in cost savings previously, has hampered innovation and the development of new products. Its competitors have been more flexible and have taken advantage of technological advances made in combination with external suppliers. Conner and Quantum, for example, signed rich contracts with computer makers, such as Apple and Compaq, because of their ability to switch faster from 5 1/4-inch to 3 1/2-inch drives.

Seagate also has been hampered during the recent recession by its massive overhead. Its profits fell more than those of its competitors as a result of its high facility fixed costs. The other disk producers proved to be more agile. When demand fell off, they were able to cut costs quickly by simply reducing orders from contractors.

Under the direction of its new CEO, Seagate is making changes. For one, it concedes it may have stuck too long with in-house technologies. It now relies on external vendors to supply 40% of its disks—about twice the percentage of two years ago. The firm also will forego some of its focus on low cost. Current plans are to reduce the time from design to production, even if it means using more expensive materials or a more costly design.

The company still defends its penchant for vertical integration, saying it keeps cost down. Analysts, who do not seem convinced, say the company's long-term outlook depends on its ability to fend off competitors in the high end of the drive market.

ENDNOTES

1. This article builds on strategy concepts from two articles by James Brian Quinn, Thomas L. Doorley,

and Penny C. Pacquette: "Beyond Products: Services-Based Strategy," *Harvard Business Review*, March–April 1990, pp. 58–67; "Technology in Services: Rethinking Strategic Focus," *Sloan Management Review*, Winter 1990, pp. 79–87.

2. This is stated explicitly in the writings of Charles Horngren and George Foster and of Stephen A. Moscove and Arnold Wright.
3. For More Information, see Mark L. Fagan, "A Guide To Global Sourcing," *The Journal of Business Strategy*, March/April 1991, pp. 21–25.
4. Michael Bromwich and Al Bhimani, "Strategic Investment Appraisal," *MANAGEMENT ACCOUNTING®*, March 1991, pp. 45–48.

Adapted from Ken Yamada, "Once-Battered Seagate Gains in Computer Price War," Wall Street Journal, June 1, 1992, p. B3; and G. Pascal Zachary, "High-Tech Firms Find It's Good to Line Up Outside Contractors," Wall Street Journal, July 29, 1992, pp. A1 and A5.

Author's Note: I would like to thank James Targay III, Serge Matulick, and Ted Veit for their helpful comments during my preparation of this article.
Ralph E. Drtina, Ph.D., is professor of accounting and management at the Crummer Graduate School of Business, Rollins College, Winger Park, Fla. He is a member of the Mid-Florida Chapter and can be reached at (407) 646–2344.

QUESTION

3.3 What are the strategic concerns that Drtina contends must be considered before outsourcing occurs? Are these qualitative or quantitative factors? Explain.

3.4 Does Your Company Need a New Cost System?

by Robin Cooper*

Today's cost management systems have to be scrutinized frequently in order to determine if they reporting accurate product costs. If they are not, they need to be overhauled, according to this article by Robin Cooper.

Cooper argues that managers need to ask themselves the following question, "Do I really know what my products cost?" Answering this question requires an often elaborate and detailed study which can be very expensive. Cooper suggests that before undertaking such a study that management look for the following symptoms of a poorly designed or obsolete cost system as well as its design flaws.

SYMPTOMS THAT YOU MAY NEED A NEW COST SYSTEM:

1. *Products that are very difficult to produce are reported to be very profitable even though they are not premium priced.*
   Intuitively products that are hard to produce should cost more to make and should either be selling at a premium or have low margins. If this is not the case there may be a problem with the cost system.
2. *Profits margins cannot be easily explained.*
   Managers should be able to state why some products are more profitable than others. Factors such as market share, quality differences and economies of scale influence profitability. If the cost system is reporting accurately then management should be able to explain the overall pattern of profitability.
3. *The results of bids are difficult to explain.*
   If management cannot predict which bids they think they can win, the cost system may be reporting inaccurate product costs. For instance if management thinks it is bidding too low and wins and bids too high and loses bids then problems probably exist.
4. *The competition's high-volume products are priced at apparently unrealistically low levels.*
   High volume products typically are less expensive to produce than low volume products and many cost systems fail to accurately account for these differences. If a company with no clear competitive advantage is pricing high volume products at very low levels and making a good profit then problems may exist.
5. *Vendor bids for parts are considerably lower than expected.*
   Companies often put parts out to bid as they may be too expensive to produce in-house. If outside vendor bids are much lower than expected the cost system may be at fault.
6. *Customers ignore price increases, even when there is no corresponding increase in cost.*
   When prices go up customers usually react negatively and demand goes down. If there is little to no reaction to a price increase then the cost system may be underestimating product costs.

---

* This article has been summarized from the original article by R. Cooper, "Does Your Company Need a New Cost System?" *Journal of Cost Management* (Spring 1987): 45–49.

FLAWS IN SYSTEM DESIGN:

Costing systems may be flawed in several ways. These flaws can result in severe distortion of product costs.

1. *Only direct labor hours (or dollars) are used to allocate overhead from cost pools (cost centers) to the products.*

    When direct labor was a significant part of the total cost of a product (say 30% to 40%) the use of direct labor as an allocation basis may have been appropriate. In today's environment direct labor is often less than 10% of total product cost and using it as an allocation basis can distort product costs.

2. *Only volume-related allocation bases (e.g. labor hours, machine hours, and material dollars) are used to allocate overhead from cost pools to products.*

    volume vs Batch [handwritten margin note]

    Using volume-related allocation bases assumes that the cost of producing a production lot varies in direct proportion to the number of items in the lot. This assumption may hold for volume related activities such as direct labor, supplies, etc. but does not hold for non-volume related activities such as inspection and setups. Such costs vary with the number of inspections and setups.

need smaller cost centers [handwritten top margin note]

3. *Cost pools are too large and contain machines that have very different overhead structures.*

    Due to enormous increases in automation many cost centers now contain a mix of conventional and automated machinery. As these centers get larger and larger overhead get higher and higher as do overhead rates. Such high rates can lead to a distortion in product costs.

4. *The cost of marketing and delivering the product varies dramatically by distribution channel, and the cost accounting system effectively ignores marketing costs.*

    While we have been discussing production costs primarily in this article, other period costs need to considered when a manager is trying to determine overall product line profitability. Thus, factors such as different distribution channels and differential marketing costs must be considered for each product line. This line of analysis is called customer profitability analysis.

QUESTION

3.4   What are three of the symptoms that Cooper says accompany a poorly designed or obsolete costing system? Do each of these definitely mean that the existing system needs to be abandoned? *No* [handwritten]

3.5 How Much Does That Product Really Co$t?

Finding out may be as easy as ABC.

*by Norm Raffish**

It's not that traditional cost accounting doesn't work—it's that the world it was designed for is rapidly disappearing. Product costs used to consist primarily of direct labor and material; today we have a manufacturing environment in which direct labor usually accounts for a ballpark figure of 5% to 15% of the costs and material accounts for 45% to 55%. That leaves us with a whopping 30% to 50% for overhead (see Figure 1). And the overhead is shifting from variable to fixed as a result of our investments in automation. Given this scenario, it's not difficult to imagine that our current cost accounting systems probably don't reflect the true costs of our products.

What clues do we have that this description is true? An article by Professor Robin Cooper of Harvard University in the *Harvard Business Review*, January–February 1989, was titled "You Need a New Cost System When ...." The article describes several symptoms of problems with existing cost systems. Cooper says it may be time to redesign your cost system if:

FIGURE 1. PRODUCT COST TRENDS

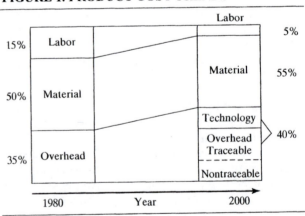

- Functional managers want to drop seemingly profitable lines;
- Hard-to-make products show big profits;

* From: N. Raffish, "How Much Does that Product Really Co$t?" *Management Accounting* (March 1991): 36–39. Reprinted with permission.

- Departments have their own cost systems;
- You have a high-margin niche all to yourself, and
- Competitors' prices are unrealistically low.

We need to recognize that our existing cost systems were meant primarily to value inventory and provide data for the profit and loss statements. They really were never designed to discriminate between product lines or products within those lines. Cost systems were meant to focus on "how much," not "why." It is understanding the "why," however, that permits management to focus on the issues that require action.

INTERORGANIZATIONAL COST PERFORMANCE

Consider the concept of interorganizational cost (intercost) performance. How would your current cost systems deal with the cost of an engineering change or segregating the cost of quality? How would you assign those costs, if you knew them, to a specific product line or product? Just to focus on one example of the intercost problem, let's examine a production schedule change requested by Marketing to meet a customer's needs.

Normally, the various costs of expediting an order are borne by all the orders that pass through the production environment, through the standard technique of absorbing in direct costs into manufacturing overhead. Thus, the expedited order will appear to have a more favorable margin than it should. And, did anyone charge Engineering for total cost of the ECN? How much cost should have been assigned to the particular part or work order? In the long run, Manufacturing's operating results, when compared to budget, will look less favorable, and Marketing's performance actually may improve in the customer satisfaction area (see Figure 2). Do we really know the cost of that order, and did we capture or even understand the intercost effect on performance?

Two other points about traditional costing systems are worth mentioning before we move forward. The first deals with the identification of nonvalue-added activities. Current systems don't have any mechanisms to assist management in this critical area. It's difficult to put a continuous improvement program in place if you can't identify and quantify the nonvalue-added activities.

The second point is more fundamental to costing in general. Our systems today measure that segment of a product's life beginning at the time it enters production. The system is oblivious to the fact that 85% of the cost of a new product is committed after the design phase, and manufacturing can influence only about 10% to 15% or so of the cost (see Figure 3). We are not capturing and allocating research and development costs so that management can determine the true profitability of a product over its life.

Let's consider a different but not necessarily replacement approach. Does this imply two cost systems?

Maybe. More on this subject when we discuss strategic versus tactical approaches to costing.

ACTIVITY-BASED COSTING

Activity-based costing (ABC) has been a concept waiting for the computer and a few innovative people. What is it? A good basic definition was developed by the Computer Aided Manufacturing-International (CAM-I) organization of Arlington, Texas, a nonprofit industry-sponsored consortium that works on contemporary industry problems. Its Cost Management System (CMS) project defines ABC as "the collection of financial and operation performance information tracing the significant activities of the firm to product costs."

CAM-I used cost management as an umbrella for many related issues. This broader definition encompasses activity-based costing, life cycle management, performance management, investment management, and cost planning and control. We will focus on ABC and its relationship to the intercost performance issues.

FIGURE 2. INTERCOST EFFECT

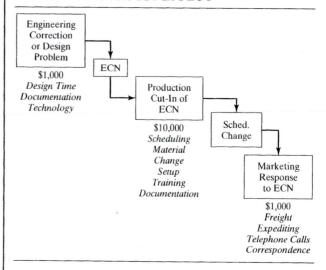

FIGURE 3. PRODUCT LIFE-CYCLE COSTS

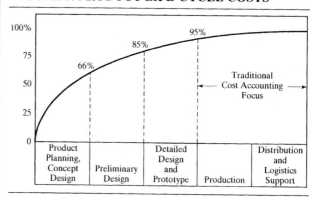

The three key areas of ABC are product cost differentiation, activities and their cost drivers, and identification of nonvalue-added cost improvement opportunities. ABC assigns product costs based on the activities that a product draws upon. An activity may be defined as a particular operation in the production cycle, or it could be defined as the entire material acquisition process. Activities use resources such as support labor, technology cells, or utilities. The agents that cause activities to happen are called cost drivers. An example of a cost driver is an engineering change order (ECO). The issuing of an ECO causes many activities to occur, such as release of the ECO documentation package, changes to the production schedule, acquisition of new material, changes to the process, and new quality instructions.

Figure 4A illustrates the basic ABC Logical Model. The Cost View indicates the general flow of costs. For example, the resources assigned to the inventory control activity will be directly traced or allocated to particular products based on some causal relationship. The Process View indicates the flow of information and transactions. As an example, the receipt of material on the dock triggers the inventory handling activities. In addition, information such as the number of moves, how many times an order was moved, and the cost per move, can be obtained for performance analysis. An expanded example of this model is illustrated in Figure 4B.

The identification, measurement, and control of cost drivers is essential to ABC. Some cost drivers are very inefficient. They may have root causes that have been hidden from management's view for a long time. As an example, one root cause of having too much inventory may be the performance measurement that rewards the buyer for obtaining the lowest unit price of an item. If the buyer is procuring by the truckload to obtain his desired measurement, and the company needs only a few cases, then the result is predictable. One of the more severe and insidious of root causes stems from inappropriate or obsolete policies, procedures, and performance measurements.

FIGURE 4A. ACTIVITY-BASED COSTING LOGICAL MODEL

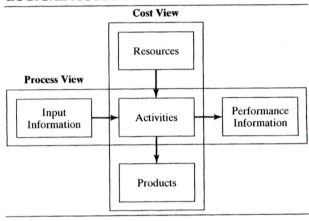

FIGURE 4B. EXPANDED ABC LOGICAL MODEL EXAMPLE

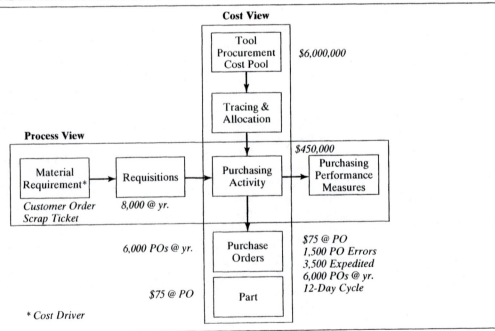

Often policies and procedures have been overcome by events but remain in force through inattention to the new reality of the situation. For example, a vendor's goods might be certified as "source inspected," but, when they arrive, they are routinely moved to receiving inspection—because that is the procedure on the dock for all production goods. Then, of course, when the inspector sees the certification, he calls material handling and has the goods moved to Stores. This policy/procedure adds lead time to the process, causes the cost of a secondary material move, and has taken up the time of the inspector who should be inspecting material that needs his attention.

After we analyze and define activities and are able to isolate and measure their cost drivers, then we will be in a position to determine product cost information as it most closely fits the reality of the manufacturing environment.

Let's revisit the intercost issue to gain a better focus on the subject. We can assume that the engineering change referred to in Figure 2 was proposed and approved based on demonstrated need (the actual cost to propose, prepare, and deliver a complete ECO package will usually be far less than the impact of the change). That change, in this example, will affect Manufacturing and Marketing. Manufacturing will absorb the associated costs of the change into its budget and schedule. Marketing will absorb effects relating to changes in distribution costs and any customer ill will that may have been generated due to possible delays in the shipment. Using the concept of tracing or allocating the cost of activities to products, we can capture and evaluate true product costs as well as understand the intercost impact and its effect on performance measurement. In this case, understanding the root cause of the cost driver may lead us to discover that the product is of poor design and therefore needs constant engineering maintenance. This discovery could lead to redesigning the product or raising the selling price to cover the real product support costs.

How do you capture and allocate costs in an ABC system? It has been said that all you need is lots of cost pools. That statement is somewhat exaggerated, but there is some truth in it. Certainly in order to capture the necessary detail, new activity cost pools would be established. It is the direct cost tracing and allocation schemes that are critical, however. Traditionally we have assigned costs based on three volume-related criteria: direct labor (dollars or hours), material cost, and machine-hours. While these criteria still are valid for certain cost entities, cost assignment bases are needed for many overhead and indirect cost entities. Some of these new bases are number of setups, number of orders, number of times material is handled, and number of part numbers processed. Using such bases as a way to trace or allocate activity costs to a product offers a whole new perspective on product cost assignment.

As an example, the number of purchase orders or line items processed may be a much better way to assign material acquisition costs than the value of the material ordered. A work order may have one purchase order with $100,000 of material assigned to it. Another work order may have 10 purchase orders worth $75,000 assigned to it. Guess which one incurred the most acquisition costs. Under today's methods, guess which one was allocated the most cost.

REAL LIFE

Discussing new concepts can be interesting and even exciting, but if they don't work "in the field," they don't work.

A large industrial electronics firm was dissatisfied with the product costing information it was receiving, especially at the printed circuit board level. Management decided to try a new costing approach based on the work that CAM-I had done on ABC and activity-based performance analysis. In order not to disrupt the division or disturb the current financial systems, it chose a single department that fabricated printed circuit boards.

The division finance department coordinated the pilot project with support from Manufacturing Engineering. In its presentation to management, it explained why it felt the experiment was needed. The controller said that the current system did not provide accurate information for make/buy decisions or for investment opportunities and that the current decision-making process was using distorted information. The major deficiencies of the current system were the inability to recognize unnecessary (nonvalue-added) activities and the lack of adequate traceability of costs and of a way to quantify quality, throughput, and flexibility.

Project objectives as stated by management were:

- Provide a breakout of department costs into activity costs,
- Identify cost drivers and their causal relationships,
- Determine actual costs for each product line, and
- Provide a tool for better decision making.

The process began by defining the activities for the PCB shop based on its actual practices. In the main, most of the activities involved either preparation for production or the actual production of various product families. Next, a survey instrument was constructed. The primary purpose of the survey was to develop a database that defined what people really did and for which product line. For example, the survey disclosed that direct labor operators spent a far greater share of their time in material-handling tasks than had been recognized. In light of their pay scale, the delivery of material to the line is being reviewed for possible reorganization. Further, the analysis showed that support costs that had been allocated on a straight-line basis among products did in fact vary significantly by product family, especially as they related to the number of layers on a PC board.

Cost drivers were defined and quantified. Typical of the types of cost drivers were lack of technical supervision, chemical contamination, schedule change, excessive quality verification, time card audits, and Material Review Board activities. In all, more than 50 cost drivers were isolated. Some, of course, were meaningful while others generated little cost and were not tracked. The exercise of developing the activity and cost driver database was invaluable, however, for future and much larger application of ABC in the company.

In the final analysis, the percentage spread of over-costing to undercosting of the PC board product families ranged from a negative 100% to a positive 80%. The division now plans to expand the ABC activity to other departments.

A second example involves a large multidivisional consumer electronics manufacturer. In this case the manufacturer wanted to understand the impact of allocated costs on the two main product lines in one key division. One line (product line L) is older and has a moderately high labor content. The second line (product line A) is newer and uses more automation.

The initial figures indicated that the average base cost of the product line L (high labor) was about $350 a unit and that of product line A (high automation) was $240 a unit. Keep in mind that product line L was manufactured at about a 7:1 rate over product line A. This will explain the impact of shifting a small percentage of L's dollars to A.

The activity cost analysis showed several interesting points for management to consider. First, after cost based on activities was reallocated and the technology costs of product line A were isolated, the costs were restated to show product line L as $300 and product line A as $450. Second, because most of the technology costs were fixed or semivariable, as production in A was forecasted to increase the base unit cost would be reduced considerably, but in later years.

Third, product line L would have a longer profitable life than originally anticipated, and some price reductions would be in order so that it could remain competitive. Finally, the firm gained some valuable insights on activities and costs drivers with respect to automation. The current allocation schemes had no method for differentiating technology costs, such as the cost of industrial engineering support. The activity analysis revealed that the IE cost allocation for A versus L in actuality ran about 4:1. The current system had indicated that the ratio was about 1:8 because labor had been the basis for the allocation.

WHAT NOW?

Activity-based costing is not a panacea for all the product cost accounting ills or shortcomings in manufacturing. It does not directly address the issues of life cycle costing or performance measurement, for example, although ABC will support those functions with valuable information. ABC is, however, a more relevant method for costing products than some older methods because it forces traceability of costs to products, based on the resources consumed by the activities needed to produce individual products. The key factors are activities and their associated cost drivers. If a product does not use an activity, it should not absorb any of its related costs.

The costing methods commonly used today, for example, may tie allocations of overhead to direct labor so that some products are being charged for resources they never used. Unless we change our allocation methods to recognize the shift in the character of overhead from variable toward fixed, as the use of technology increases, severe product cost distortion will only accelerate.

One final topic—will ABC necessitate another set of accounting records? At this stage of ABC's acceptance and development, many consider it an advanced analytical tool for management as opposed to an official set of records. It certainly may not yet be robust enough to replace our day-to-day systems. Each implementation of ABC at this point probably will be tailored to each user's objectives. There is not yet an "off the shell" solution that has been accepted as the standard. In the last two years we have begun to see the emergence of commercially available software to assist in the implementation process.

Thus, although we currently may view ABC as a significant management tool for issues such as pricing schemes and product abandonment analysis rather than as a tactical accounting system, some firms are evaluating the impact of a conversion to ABC as the accounting system of record. As the ABC "body of knowledge" is expanded and codified, activity-based costing may well eventually replace our current cost accounting systems.

Norm Raffish, CPIM, is a senior manager in the management consulting practice of Ernst & Young. Prior to joining the firm, he spent several years as a consultant and 12 years with the Xerox Corporation's Computer Services Division, engaged in industry and strategic product planning and the design and development of integrated manufacturing systems. He says that in 1991 the CAM-I CMS project will publish a new glossary on activity-based costing. It is hoped that this glossary will be the basis for a future common language in the area of ABC.

QUESTION

3.5 In Norm Raffish's paper, what are the five steps involved in product life-cycle costs? How much of a product's cost is committed after the design phase, and why is this number important?

3.6 The Rise and Fall of Time-Based Manufacturing

A stubborn refusal to abandon traditional performance measures put the brakes on an automotive supplier's efforts to compete.

by William M. Baker, CMA, Timothy D. Fry, and Kirk Karwan*

In the late 1980s, foreign competition—particularly from the Japanese—forced U.S. automotive suppliers to switch from competition based upon (lowest) cost to competition based upon on-time delivery and high quality. In order to meet these objectives, many companies began to implement programs to minimize throughput time and maximize quality.

Companies also realized that traditional standard costing systems, entrenched in direct labor and variance calculations, should be viewed first as financial accounting mechanisms and then used cautiously for the purpose of controlling costs. Knussma`nn Corporation's Brice Plant[1] is an example of an automotive supplier that strived to move away from its emphasis on traditional performance measures but failed.

In January 1988, Knussmann's president established time-based and quality-based goals for its plants located throughout the United States. Each plant, according to the president, was to develop a throughput time of one week (work-in-process inventory was to be turned over 52 times per year) and to reduce scrap to 0.5% of cost of goods sold.[2]

When these objectives were established, work-in-process inventory turnovers averaged approximately 10 per year at the Brice plant. Scrap was about 4.5%.

During 1988, no noticeable changes in inventory ratios or scrap levels occurred. Consequently, in December 1988 Knussmann's president called a meeting with his plant managers. Essentially, his message was: "Meet these objectives or I will get someone who can!"

Prior to 1988, the Brice plant used a traditional costing system similar to systems used in most American manufacturing facilities. Product costs at the Brice plant were direct materials, 30%; direct labor, 8%; factory overhead, 62%. The Brice plant used standard costing and applied factory overhead using direct labor costs.

The emphasis placed upon direct labor costs by the standard cost system permeated the entire plant. Production output from each department was measured by "earned standard dollars," which is a standard measure of actual output.

Monthly variance reports were generated and variances calculated for "controllable" costs such as supplies, indirect labor, maintenance, and machining. The variance for "direct labor" was considered so important as to be calculated and supplied to management in a separate report. Primary emphasis was given to minimizing direct labor variances. Departmental managers had to explain all unfavorable variances in weekly meetings. The reliance on these traditional performance measurements hindered the Brice plant from achieving the two company objectives.

Figure 1 presents the manufacturing performance at the Brice plant. Work-in-process inventory turnovers (turns) for the 24-month period are shown. "Inventory turns this year" results from dividing the monthly standard dollars shipped by the monthly ending inventory in standard dollars and multiplying by 12 to obtain turns per year. Corresponding monthly scrap levels are expressed as a percentage of standard dollars shipped. "Earned standard direct labor dollars," as referred to by the Brice cost accounting system, is shown along with the actual dollars spent on direct labor. The difference between the two, representing a favorable or unfavorable variance, also is shown.

BRICE'S FALL

Brice plant managers responded to the ultimatum given by the company president by stressing inventory reductions and quality improvements in all departments. As a result, the amount of money spent on direct and indirect labor was increased from May 1989 to October 1989 (see Figure 1). Additional labor costs resulted from hiring more workers to operate machinery, move materials, and inspect production. In addition, existing workers were paid overtime.

During this same period, the earned direct labor standards did not increase at a comparable rate because the input of work into the shop was not increased beyond demand levels. This factor resulted in a marked decrease in the level of inventory in the plant over the same time period. As indicated by Figure 1, this drop was from $1,122,000 to $806,000. A comparable increase in the dollars shipped and inventory turns resulted, partly due to the decrease in inventory.

---

* From W. M. Baker, T. D. Fry, and K. Karwan, "The Rise and Fall of Time-Based Manufacturing," *Management Accounting* (June 1994): 56–59. Reprinted with permission.

FIGURE 1. BRICE PLANT MANUFACTURING PERFORMANCE

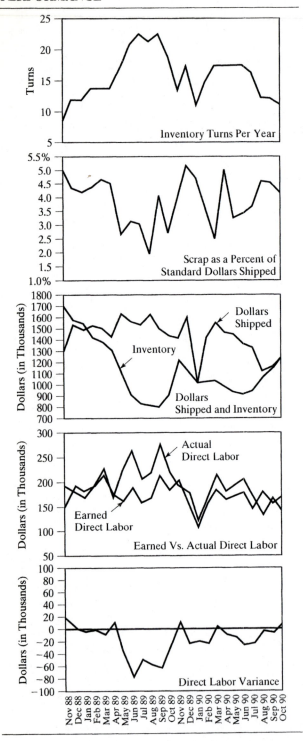

shipped leveling off), the corporate vice president for manufacturing sent a memorandum to the Brice plant manager demanding an explanation.

For a while top management at Knussmann "looked the other way." They accepted the unfavorable variances in May, June, July, and August due to the high increase in dollars shipped. But when the standard dollars shipped leveled off in September and October, they were no longer willing to disregard the unfavorable variances. A memo, stressing a need for the control of direct labor costs, was followed by several phone calls from the corporate controller to the Brice plant manager.

Brice management responded by not allowing any overtime in the plant. As a result, the actual dollars spent on direct labor decreased. Also, more material was input into the plant by starting scheduled orders early. This served to increase inventory, which also increased the earned standard direct labor.

As expected, unfavorable direct labor variances decreased, with a comparable decrease in inventory turns. By the end of 1989, inventory turns had decreased to 18 and inventory had increased from the low of $806,000 in August to $1,108,000.

Throughout the next 12 months, no noticeable change was apparent in inventory or scrap. Inventory turns in October 1990 were 12 per year, which was the lowest level since the beginning of the 24-month period.

A comparison of data on "scrap as a percent of standard dollars shipped" to "dollars shipped and inventory" shows that when inventory levels went down, scrap percentages went down. In December 1988 and January 1989, scrap averaged about 4.4%. In August 1989, when inventory was at its lowest level, scrap was at its lowest level, too—1.9%! From August 1989 until October 1990, dramatic fluctuations in scrap levels occurred. But the scrap levels tended to move upward, and by the end of the 24-month period, scrap averaged 4.1%.

While scrap levels decreased when management spent additional labor dollars to control for scrap, it was clear by the end of the 24-month period that no marked improvement in scrap levels had been realized. This had been one of the two major objectives set forth by the corporation.

Thus, reliance on a traditional, yet improper, set of performance measures not only hinders the implementation of time-based or quality-based manufacturing but actually may halt it. Despite the development of time-based and quality-based corporate objectives at Knussmann—a one-week manufacturing lead time thereby turning work-in-process 52 times per year and a quality objective of 0.5% scrap—the use of standard costing and the concentration on direct labor variances prevented the Brice plant from making long-run progress towards meeting these objectives.

Despite noticeable improvements in turnover and scrap levels during a six-month period in 1989 and for a

Due to the increase in actual dollars spent on direct labor and the lack of an increase in earned standard direct labor dollars, unfavorable direct labor variances for the six-month period (May–October 1989) increased dramatically, as shown in Figure 1. In direct response to these unfavorable variances (and standard dollars very brief period in 1990, top management at Knussmann was unwilling (or unable) to discard a cost-based performance system that had been used for several decades. No performance measures that related to the new company objectives were developed.

Simply setting the new objectives was not enough. Strategic planning would suggest that plans are necessary to achieve the new objectives. Managers at the Brice plant seemingly implemented such plans. Through direct and indirect labor expenditures, they acquired sufficient capacity to achieve the new objectives. But while corporate objectives were communicated, plans were not.

No new performance measures were designed. Knussmann managers set forth new objectives and attempted to measure achievement using the traditional standard cost system. Managers at Brice developed new measures—simple measures such as turnover and scrap percentages. They seemed appropriate. But Knussmann managers were overwhelmed by direct labor variances and reliance upon cost measures.

CHANGE THE COST SYSTEM

Who is the scapegoat now that Brice failed to meet its objectives? Are managers at Knussmann at fault for not adopting a new performance measurement system? Should Brice managers be blamed for not insisting that measures relating to the objectives be used? Perhaps the cost accounting system itself is to blame. Is the cost system wrong, or is it simply being misused? Are variances at fault, or are there better variances?

Today managers realize that some thing must change if companies are to become effective manufacturers. Many alternatives for change, some which can co-exist, some which cannot, should be considered for the Brice plant.

Turn to JIT. Many companies have adopted some type of just-in-time (JIT) philosophy in order to compete on the basis of time. This is more effective for some companies than for others. Certainly, the idea of eliminating waste would be effective at the Brice plant. And just about any company can benefit from the value-added/nonvalue-added ideas offered by some JIT philosophies.

What if the Brice plant had implemented a JIT philosophy? A vast array of nonvalue-added activities would probably be identified. This might be quite effective. Anything might seem effective to a company that has tried for too long to depend on a standard cost system to identify inefficiencies when the standard cost system is obsolete.

Adopt ABC. Similarly, activity-based costing (ABC) might seem effective to a company such as the Brice plant. ABC does not change the financial process to inventory costing materially, so top management may be more willing to adopt ABC than JIT. JIT and other new production philosophies seem "more radical" than ABC.

The costing mechanism inherent in ABC may not provide immediate benefit, but the activity-based management aspects of ABC could help the Brice plant. By identifying the activities that, when reduced, will accomplish Knussmann's objectives, Brice can obtain its goals successfully while using ABC. But ABC may be more than what the Brice plant needs.

Modify the existing cost accounting system. ABC and JIT may be important enough to warrant consideration at the Brice plant. But top managers, especially those entrenched in traditional cost accounting systems, often are reluctant to change the cost accounting system. Typically, any modification to existing systems involves only the overhead allocation approach. This might be enough for the Brice plant!

Hiromoto[3] suggests that the allocation base should be determined by the activity that management wants to minimize. The cost accounting systems in Japan, for example, use allocation bases that will *motivate* management decision making toward long-run objectives rather than to pinpoint short-run costs. American accountants often are accused of being good "pinpointers," carrying calculations to extra decimal places while ignoring the long run.

Managers at Knussmann want the Brice plant to become a time-based manufacturer. In that case, the one activity that must be minimized is the time required from the release of raw materials until the shipment of the finished product to customers (throughput time). Using product throughput time as the allocation base encourages operations managers to strive constantly to reduce throughput time and, in turn, reduces product cost.

At the same time, these efforts improve the company's competitive advantage—time. If throughput time is used as the allocation base, direct labor still could be traced to products. Overhead costs would be allocated using throughput time.

Managers who concentrate on minimizing product cost need to reduce the time required to manufacture each product, if product costs are to decrease. This focus encourages both the production of smaller batch sizes and setup time reductions to minimize a product's queue time at each machine.

It also encourages managers to move materials more quickly and thereby improve the process flow. Quality improvements, the second objective set forth by Knussmann management, would be encouraged (and necessary). As quality improves, quality appraisal time (for example, inspection time) can be reduced and throughput time decreased.

Direct labor cost must be reduced to justify purchasing new inspection equipment to allow workers to inspect their own work. Such direct labor cost reductions could not be shown at the Brice plant. Such expenditures were not made. The beauty of throughput time as an allocation base is that time reductions would *require* such investments. And the cost accounting system's effects on net income calculation will not be altered by the use of throughput time.

As with any standard cost system, if throughput time is used, the standards must be kept accurate and up-to-date. We believe that if standards are up-to-date, throughput time should serve the Brice plant well. Before you know it, managers at Brice would do everything they could to reduce throughput time. They would be searching for activities that do not add value, and they would attempt to eliminate them. They would move inventory out quickly, and inventory levels would go down.

Crude as it seems, we think that such actions sound like activity-based management and JIT philosophies. Even if they are not, such actions should still help the Brice plant. If nothing else, managers at Brice would then have a better chance of convincing managers at Knussmann to consider adopting JIT or ABC.

THE PROBLEM: STUBBORN MANAGERS

Top managers were successful in getting managers at the Brice plant to try to compete on the basis of time and quality, not cost. While the Brice plant had some success in achieving those objectives, it was short-lived.

Who's to blame? Knussmann's management? Brice's management? Lack of goal congruence? Failure to plan?

Even the cost accounting system appears as a potential cause for failure. For whatever reason, managers at Knussmann were unwilling to abandon traditional cost accounting performance measures, and this was the plant's downfall.

When managers are unwilling to abandon traditional cost accounting measures, it may be difficult, or impossible, to compete based upon time and quality. This outcome seems to be especially true when the traditional measures revolve around labor in non-labor-intensive processes.

When traditional cost accounting is that entrenched, the best hope usually is to begin by trying to convince management to try a different allocation base. For the Brice plant, we recommend throughput time as an allocation base. Once a new allocation base is in place, other good things such as JIT and ABC might happen.

ENDNOTES

1. These are not the real names. These names are used to maintain the confidentiality of both the company and the plant.
2. No finished goods inventory is carried by any plant as finished products are either shipped directly to the customer or to a distribution warehouse. Work-in-process is the only inventory that the plant is charged with carrying.
3. Toshiro Hiromoto. "Another Hidden Edge—Japanese Management Accounting," *Harvard Business Review*, July–August 1989, pp. 22–26.

William M. Baker, CMA, Ph.D., CCE, CCA, is an assistant accounting professor at Appalachian State University in Boone, N.C. He is a member of the Catawba Valley Chapter, through which this article was submitted. Timothy D. Fry and Kirk Karwan are associate professors in management science at the University of South Carolina in Columbia.

QUESTION

3.6 In the article "*The Rise and Fall of Time-Based Manufacturing*" the authors state that one traditional measure was so important that management received a separate report on it. What is this measure, and what is its significance to the problems experienced at the Knussmann Company?

3.7 Distinguishing Between Direct and Indirect Costs Is Crucial for Internet Companies

by Lawrence A. Gordon, Ph.D., and Martin P. Loeb, Ph.D. *

EXECUTIVE SUMMARY

People who argue that distinguishing between direct and indirect costs is of no relevance in today's Information Economy are dead wrong! Indeed, the importance of the direct vs. indirect costs dichotomy (as well as with many other management accounting techniques) may be even more crucial to an Internet-based firm's survival than to other companies. The key paradigm shift here is that,

when separating direct from indirect costs, we need to think of customers as a primary cost objective in such an environment.

Cost management is an important aspect of running a corporation successfully. A crucial part of costs management is the proper allocation of costs to various products and services. Indeed, the way costs are allocated plays a key role in determining the reported profitability

_____

* From: L. Gordon and M. Loeb. "Distinguishing Between Direct and Indirect Costs Is Crucial for Internet Companies," *Management Accounting Quaterly* (Summer 2001): 12–17. Reprinted with permission.

of individual products and/or services. In addition, product-line decisions and pricing decisions (of both an internal and external nature) often are affected by cost allocation decisions.

At the heart of cost allocation decisions is the dichotomy between direct and indirect costs. Because a given cost can be direct with respect to one cost objective and indirect with respect to another cost objective, determining the appropriate cost objective is fundamental. This fact not-withstanding, there seems to be a growing concern, if not confusion, on the importance of the distinction between direct and indirect costs for Internet-based businesses. We argue that the distinction between direct and indirect costs is as important for Internet-based companies as it is for other companies. The e-commerce revolution, however, requires many companies to make a fundamental change in the way they consider the notion of a cost objective and, in turn, cost management. In particular, Internet-based companies need to view the *customer* as a primary cost objective for purposes of allocating costs.

DIRECT VS. INDIRECT COSTS: A TRADITIONAL VIEW

Direct costs can easily be traced to the cost objective and can be assigned to the cost objective in a straightforward manner. In contrast, *indirect costs* cannot be easily traced to the cost objective.[1] They need some sort of allocation scheme. Thus, the choice of cost objective is critical to the determination of whether a cost is considered direct or indirect.

A cost objective is the purpose for which a cost is being measured. Further, it is quite common for a given cost to be measured for multiple purposes. Thus, a given cost may be direct with respect to another cost objective and indirect with respect to another cost objective.[2] Traditionally, products, services, and departments have served as key cost objectives in managing the operations of a firm. In manufacturing firms, the primary cost objective is traditionally assumed to be the physical products being produced. A computer manufacturer, for example, would usually consider the need to determine the cost of producing a computer as the primary purpose for which costs (at least manufacturing costs) are being measured. As such, the costs of materials and labor that can easily be traced to the production of individual computers would be considered direct costs. Costs of materials and labor that cannot be directly related to the production of individual computers would be considered indirect costs. In a similar vein, the costs associated with depreciating machinery, utilities, and accident insurance would be additional indirect costs in most manufacturing firms.

Knowing the costs of manufacturing a product is important in determining the product's profitability, even where prices are market driven,[3] because in these markets the costs will determine the desirability of being in the market. In markets where prices are driven more by

costs, knowing the cost of producing a product is all that more important. Further, many new cost management techniques, such as target costing, are focused on controlling product costs. Assessing the contribution of one subunit versus another subunit within a given company also requires a financial manager to determine product costs for transfer pricing purposes. Accordingly, choosing products as the primary cost objective seems quite logical for most manufacturing firms.

Whereas tangible products are logical choices for primary cost objectives in most manufacturing firms, services are logical choices for primary cost objectives in other firms. For example, in the banking industry, the distinction between a direct and an indirect cost is usually considered in terms of whether the cost can or cannot be directly related to a particular service (e.g., processing a loan). Choosing departments as the primary cost objective seems to make sense in other firms. For example, in a retail department store, the distinction between direct and indirect costs is often thought of in terms of whether the cost can or cannot he related to a specific department (e.g., men's clothing). As with measuring the cost of products, measuring the cost of services and departments will facilitate profitability analysis as well as pricing decisions.[4]

Yet a fundamental change in the way many companies do business has taken place over the past five years. This change falls under the rubric of e-commerce (i.e., electronic commerce) and is largely the result of the Internet E-commerce has changed the way companies interact with their suppliers and, even more important, the way they interact with their customers. In fact, Internet commerce has changed the very essence of the way many companies do business. Now, many companies generate a large portion of their revenues via the Internet, and a growing number generate the *majority* of their revenues that way. We refer to these companies as Internet-based because they epitomize the essence of the new Information Economy.[5]

To date, most companies still consider costs as being direct or indirect in terms of products, services, or departments. This is true even for many Internet-based firms. Though the basic nature of doing business has changed for a large segment of our economy, the essence of cost management has not changed. In particular, many Internet-based firms have not abandoned the old way of thinking about cost objectives. Yet the important distinction between direct and indirect costs is becoming fuzzy. Some people even argue that distinguishing between direct and indirect costs is no longer a valid way to look at costs for a company operating in an e-commerce environment where intangible assets (e.g., intellectual capital) are so prevalent. For example, in the popular book *The Blur*, Davis and Myer argue that "direct costs are dead, and diminishing marginal returns died with them, a victim of intangibles." We disagree!

In our opinion, the need to differentiate between direct and indirect costs is as valid today in an e-commerce environment as it is in a traditional (brick-and-mortar) environment. Profitability analysis, product-line decisions, and pricing decisions are still significantly affected by the way costs are classified in terms of direct and indirect. The thing that is often no longer valid, however, is the focus on the old notion of cost objectives for firms that operate in an e-commerce environment. We believe companies actively involved in e-commerce need to view customers, as well as products, services, and departments, as key cost objectives. Nowhere is this need more important than in Internet-based firms.

Direct vs. Indirect Costs in Internet-Based Firms

The number of firms that derive the majority of their sales over the Internet has grown at a rapid rate. The U.S. Bureau of Census conservatively estimated that $5.3 billion (0.64%) of retail sales in the fourth quarter of 1999 was conducted using the Internet.[6] Furthermore, this estimate excludes the huge number of Internet sales from business to business. Clearly, the growth of the Internet is changing all facets of commerce. Understanding the impact of these changes on corporate cost management systems is vital.

The distinguishing feature of an e-commerce environment is that business transactions are handled electronically. The hallmark of such an environment has become the way firms interact with customers via the Internet. A logical way to decide whether to classify a firm as being dominated by an e-commerce environment is to use the percentage of the firm's sales generated from the Internet. For a firm to be eligible for the Dow Jones Internet Composite Index (which is further subdivided into the Dow Jones Internet Commerce Index and the Dow Jones Internet Service Index), the company must generate at least half of its sales via the Internet.[7]

Internet customers, be they households, businesses, or government agencies, can and do conduct quick and inexpensive shopping comparisons. These comparisons take place in a nanosecond, with the click of a mouse, Hence companies are required to continually adjust prices to respond to price changes initiated by competitors. At the same time, their competitors are making similar price adjustments. As a result, companies are required to expend continuous real-time efforts at attracting and tracking customers.

In the e-commerce environment, where information search costs approach zero and competitors match price cuts almost instantaneously, competing only in price is not likely to be the means to attracting and maintaining a loyal customer base. Pricing over the Internet has pushed firms to operate in highly competitive, if not purely competitive, economic markets. Businesses are quickly learning that a comparative advantage in the cyber marketplace (or, as some have called it, the marketspace) can

be secured only by competing effectively in quality customer service to the point of becoming customer-centric. Understanding and managing such services requires the allocation of these costs among customers. The proper allocation, in this regard, requires that customers become a key, if not the primary, cost objective for the purposes of distinguishing between direct and indirect costs.

Most Internet-based firms use business models that are classified as business-to-business (B2B) or business-to-consumer (B2C). As the names of these models indicate, B2B means that the firm is using the Internet to generate sales of goods and services to other businesses, while B2C means that the firm uses the Internet to generate sales directly to consumers (i.e., retail sales). In addition, the business models used by some Internet-based firms would be classified as business-to-government (B2G) or consumer-to-consumer (C2C). B2G means that the firm sells its products and services primarily to government agencies. C2C means that the firm (for example, eBay) facilitates direct trades among consumers by providing a central marketplace in cyberspace. A firm using a C2C business model typically generates revenues from fees and commissions paid by consumers for participating in the electronic marketplace. Of course, many major corporations use more than one of the above business models.

Security analysts and the general investing public commonly use the B2B designation to refer to companies (e.g., Ariba and i2 Technologies) that produce products and services (e.g., software and consulting) to facilitate B2B transactions among businesses via the Internet. The products and services produced by such B2B firms use the Internet to help match sellers of inputs of production with the buyers of these inputs in an efficient manner so firms secure the right inputs at the right time at minimum cost. Such supply chain management benefits sellers by expanding their geographical market to the entire globe and benefits buyers by facilitating the search for low-cost suppliers, reducing the processing costs associated with materials acquisition, and reducing their inventory holding costs.

While the companies designated in the media as B2B firms have often been associated with generating high growth in revenues and profits, the larger effects of the B2B revolution are seen outside the firms given the B2B designation. The larger impact on the economy comes from the rapidly expanding number of firms that have embraced B2B for their supply chain management and for sales of their products to other businesses. Irrespective of whether a firm uses the Internet to sell its products and/or services to other businesses, to consumers, or to government agencies, the environment of electronic commerce requires successful firms to focus data collection on customers or customer classes. Because selling via the Internet empowers customers by reducing their information search costs and their costs of switching from one vendor to another, firms selling via the Internet have strong motivation to treat customers as key cost objectives than do firms that sell through non-Internet sources.

Whether using e-commerce for retail sales or business-to-business sales, companies must devote substantial resources to providing their customers with a user friendly, secure, and hassle-free shopping experience. The development, maintenance, and enhancement of software that keeps track of customer preferences is essential for ensuring such an experience. In essence, Internet-based firms rely much less on traditional infrastructure assets, such as buildings, and more on computers, specialized software, and intellectual capital that cater to customers in cyberspace.

When comparing one seller with another, customers cannot compare the service level that would be provided as easily as they can compare quoted prices. Nevertheless, with the wealth of information on the Web, including the seller's website, websites of consumer groups, bulletin boards, and message boards, customers can gather information about the quality of service at a fraction of the cost of a decade earlier. These comparisons result in diminishing customer loyalty. Moreover, with venture capitalists funding start-up companies on a regular basis and with more brick-and-mortar companies adding e-commerce divisions, new competition is constantly coming to the marketplace. Thus, companies face a dynamic, increasingly competitive environment.

In this new environment, companies that are going to be competitive need to devote substantial resources to attracting customers through advertising on the Internet as well as in traditional media (e.g., newspapers, magazines, and television) that direct customers to the firm's Internet sales site. During the actual sales, it is easier for competitive Internet-based firms than traditional firms to customize the physical product (e.g., specifications of a machine being purchased by one firm from another) or service (e.g., loan agreement) being sold. Internet-based sales provide an easy mechanism for direct and instantaneous contact with customers so companies can quickly modify products to new specifications (e.g., the addition it deletion of a clause in a loan agreement). It is also incumbent upon e-commerce firms to provide a high level of post-sale services to customers because such services are often carried out in an easy, quick, and inexpensive manner. Tracking delivery from the time of sale is a good example of the type of postsale service easily provided in an e-commerce environment.

For all the reasons we have noted, tracing costs to individual customers and/or customer classes is an essential competitive strategy for Internet-based companies. In other words, the customer must be a primary cost objective for them. Furthermore, tracing costs to customers cannot be considered a one-time or even periodic investment. Instead, tracing costs to customers must be done on a continuous basis and requires a real-time cost system. For many Internet-based companies, this requires a major change from the way they accumulate costs.[8] In fact, Internet-based firms that fail to treat customers as a primary cost objective face the danger of being outsmarted by the competition and left with the least profitable customers in the marketplace.[9]

For an Internet-based retailer, the costs of products a customer buys would be classified as direct costs for the customer. For an Internet-based manufacturing firm, the manufacturing cost of products would represent an intermediate cost objective, and the total cost (including costs which are indirect with respect to products) would be traced directly to the customers. Because software can identify the specific Internet advertising that routes a particular customer to the firm's e-store, the cost of this advertising can also be allocated to customers in logical manner. It may even be possible to trace specific software-related costs to particular customers in an e-commerce environment, thereby treating these costs as direct costs in terms of customers.[10] In essence, many of the costs of pre- and post-sale services, as well as the costs for services incurred during the actual sale, could be traced to individual customers and/or customer classes and treated as direct costs for e-commerce firms.[11] Costs that cannot be traced directly to individual customers and/or customer classes, such as the costs associated with computer hardware, would be treated as indirect costs.

By treating the customer as a primary cost objective, effective resource allocation decisions will be enhanced. In addition, effective customer profitability analysis, pricing decisions, and marketing decisions will be greatly facilitated. Finally, and of no small consequence, the use of customers as a primary cost objective will facilitate the very essence of being an Internet-based firm (i.e., an Internet-based cost management system will facilitate e-commerce business).

It is well known, and accepted, that focusing on the needs and desires of customers is fundamental to running a successful business. This is true whether the business is Internet-based or brick-and-mortar. Yet a fundamental cost objective for Internet-based firms needs to be the customer. In other words, in accumulating and allocating costs, Internet-based firms need to adopt a customer focus. Once they recognize this fact, it becomes clear that the distinction between direct and indirect costs is as important for them as it is for other firms.

Of course, the fact that Internet-based firms need to adopt a customer focus in allocating costs in no way mitigates the potential importance of knowing the costs of individual products (or services) as well as departments. Thus, Internet-based firms may well consider other cost objectives in differentiating between direct and indirect costs. To the extent that this is the case, the argument that distinguishes between direct and indirect costs is a relevant and important activity for Internet-based firms is only strengthened.

USE MANAGEMENT ACCOUNTING TECHNIQUES PROPERLY

Cost allocations are fundamental to effective cost management, and, as we have emphasized, a key aspect of cost allocations is the distinction between direct and indirect costs. Nevertheless, the clams that this distinction is not relevant to Internet-based companies have been promulgated lately. We disagree with this claim, for the reasons given above. A fundamental aspect of our argument is the need for Internet-based firms to trace costs to customers. Hence, Internet-based firms need to treat the customer as a primary cost objective in differentiating between direct and indirect costs.

The new Information Economy has important implications for the field of management accounting. Direct vs. indirect costs is only one such implication. Other implications include the way companies need to consider performance measures, profit planning, and the use of cost information for pricing decisions. While the sum of these implications represents a fundamental shift in the management accounting paradigm, it does not represent the demise of management accounting. Indeed, the proper use of management accounting techniques is more relevant to the survival of firms in today's dynamic information economy than ever before in the history of commerce.

Lawrence A. Gordon, Ph.D., is the Ernst & Young Alumni Professor of Managerial Accounting at the Robert H. Smith School of Business, University of Maryland, College Park, Md. He can be reached at (301) 405-2255 or lgordon@rhsmith.umd.edu.

Martin P. Loeb, Ph.D., is professor of accounting and Deloitte & Touche Faculty Fellow at the Robert H. Smith School of Business, University of Maryland, College Park, Md. He can be reached at (301) 405-2209 or mloeb@rhsmith.umd.edu.

1. Indirect costs are often referred to as overhead costs. Because the term overhead is misleading, we will use indirect to refer to such costs.
2. For examples illustrating this point, see Chapter 3 of Gordon. *Managerial Accounting: Concepts and Empirical Evidence*, in Further Reading section.
3. In the extreme case of prices being set by the market-place, we have what economists refer to as a purely competitive market. In a purely competitive market, firms essentially take the market price as given and need to focus on cost management techniques to earn a desirable level of profit.
4. Of course, firms are interested in many cost objectives. Hence, the designation of one cost objective as primary does not preclude the use of other cost objectives.
5. Our definition of what constitutes an Internet-based firm is consistent with the way Dow Jones derives its list of such firms (i.e., for more information, see http://indexes.dowjones.com./djii/djiiabout.html).
6. The U.S. Department of Commerce reports (*Digital Economy 2000*, June 2000, p. 9) "private estimates for consumer e-commerce in the fourth quarter of 1999 ranged from approximately $4 billion to $14 billion."
7. Clearly, the trend is for all firms to increase their Internet-based sales. Accordingly, the distinction between Internet-based firms and non-Internet-based firms is one of degree rather that absoluteness. Over time, it seems logical to expect more and more firms to become Internet-based.
8. Although not the focus of this article, it is equally important for Internet-based firms to identify the revenues of individual customers and/or customer classes.
9. The growing emphasis on linking customers to the production process in the emerging literature on supply chain management is consistent with this argument. For an interesting discussion on the use of "customer-product maps," in the context of supply chain management, see Cloud in the Further Reading section.
10. In a non-e-commerce environment, computer-related costs are traditionally considered to be indirect with respect to a firm's products and services. Given that these assets are an important aspect of an e-commerce firm's assets, this reclassification has nontrivial implications.
11. Recent work in database design has centered on customer focused data models. This work has particular relevance to the arguments presented in this section.

FURTHER READING

R. J. Cloud, "Supply Chain Management: New Role for Finance Professionals," *Strategic Finance*, August 2000. pp. 28–32.

S. Davis and C. Myer, *Blur: The Speed of Change in the Connected Economy*, Addison Wesley, 1998.

Dow Jones Internet Indexes, Dow Jones Company, 2000, http://indexes.dowjones.com./djii/djiiabout.html.

L. A. Gordon, *Managerial Accounting: Concepts and Empirical Evidence*, 5th Edition, McGraw-Hill, 2000.

United States Commerce Dept., *Digital Economy 2000*, June 2000, http://www.esa.doc.gov/de2000.pdf.

QUESTIONS

3.7a Describe the differences between B2B, B2C, B2G and C2C business models within the context of Internet firms.

3.7b Why is there a need among Internet firms to provide such a high level of service to customers? Furthermore, why do the authors state that customers must be considered a primary cost object for these types of firms?

3.8 Caution: Fraud Overhead

Overhead accounts are a breeding ground for fraud. What to do?

by John B. Macarthur, FCCA, Bobby E. Waldrup, CPA, and Gary R. Fane, CMA, CPA*

TABLE 1: SELECTED FRAUD SYMPTOMS

Analytical Symptoms

Ending inventory balances appear too high or are increasing too fast.

Reported cost of goods manufactured/sold (COGS) balances appear too high.

Overhead variances increase in frequency and/or size.

Increasing ratio of ending inventory account balances to ending inventory physical counts.

Accounting/Documentary Symptoms

Inventory and/or COGS transactions aren't recorded in a complete or timely manner.

End-of-period inventory and/or COGS adjustments are high or increasing in frequency.

Control Symptoms

Management overrides internal controls related to inventory or COGS.

Overhead application rates are raised or lowered by management throughout the year.

Behavioral/Verbal Symptoms

Management or employees give inconsistent or vague responses to inventory and/or COGS inquires.

Unusual delays occur in providing requested inventory and/or COGS information.

The behavior or responses of management are suspicious when management is asked about inventory and/or COGS transactions, vendors, or accounts.

Lifestyle Symptoms

Loan covenants benefiting officers have a collateral relationship to reported/physical inventory levels.

Managers or employees have significant personal financial pressures.

Tips/Complaints

Complaints from vendors/customers that relate to inventory.

Complaints from employees and other stakeholders about noninventory cash transactions. Often, a fraud in the overhead accounts can be traced to inappropriate overhead charges deliberately misdirected from operating expense and other accounts.

Source: Adapted from W. Steven Albrecht and Chad Albrecht, *Fraud Examination and Prevention*, Thomson South-Western, Mason, Ohio, 2003, pp. 272–273.

$1 MILLION FOUND

The forensic accountant/consultant investigated Wapello's accounting records, including the executive payroll, and discovered that the controller had been fraudulently issuing additional paychecks to himself. In addition to the payroll discrepancies, the consultant discovered that the controller had destroyed many of the accounting records from prior years. There were missing purchase invoices, which made it necessary for the consultant and Wapello people to reconstruct the payables accounts, especially the company's freight bills.

The consultant also found that the controller was embezzling money through the loans payable account. All the fraudulent transactions were charged to the manufacturing overhead account, mainly as fictitious tool purchases.

How could this fraud have occurred?

"BLACK BOX" OVERHEAD ACCOUNTS

First, any company is likely to be more vulnerable to fraud if it has grown from microsize to midsize. A small company with a single or small group of owners tends to centralize all decision making at the executive management level, with little or no control policies in place. As the company's operations grow, there's a need to implement formal internal control procedures, but the legacy of "small firm" management style may linger through the growth period. And that usually means that putting

* From: J. B. MacArthur, B. E. Waldrup and G. R. Fane, "Caution: Fraud Overhead," *Strategic Finance* (October 2004): 28–32. Reprinted with Permission.

adequate internal controls in place often gets overlooked or deferred because available resources are used to support more "front-line" activities.

Moreover, the potential of fraud is exacerbated at midsize companies when the following types of conditions exist:

- Few—if any—controls over upper management, such as requiring duplicate signatures on payroll checks.
- Accounting record keeping is concentrated in a few hands, with little separation of duties.
- There's a culture of implicit employee trust, especially in long-standing employees and professional accountants.
- There's no external audit.
- Owners have little or no accounting knowledge.
- The company has relatively large overhead accounts where fraudulent expenses can be hidden.

Furthermore, overhead costing in midsize manufacturing companies is particularly susceptible to fraud because the costing is complex, the accounts have relatively large dollar values, and nonaccounting managers don't understand how they work.

To nonaccountants, overhead accounts are a confusing "black box" because accumulating and applying overhead is one of the least understood activities of the costing process. The manufacturing overhead account and associated subsidiary records such as the tooling account are some of the most exploitable accounting records. The manufacturing overhead account is a particularly large "sink" for all the various overhead items, such as plant depreciation, indirect salaries, plant supplies, and plant insurance. Fraudulent expenses can be hidden among the many journal entries that are made to this account that likely won't rise to the audit materiality threshold individually. Also, predetermined overhead rates are typically applied to production, and overhead

variances for underapplied and overapplied overhead are to be expected. These overhead variances could include fraudulent expenses that can be explained as part of the estimating errors.

Because of this, nonaccountant owners/managers may find the whole costing process in general opaque and highly technical, with cost variances in particular difficult to understand. Consequently, they'll often leave the details to a controller or other trusted employee. But sometimes that employee can't be trusted.

A SETTING FOR FRAUD

At Wapello Manufacturing, the outside consulting accountant identified a number of accounting system issues and inadequacies after completing his three-month investigation. Among them were the following:

The use of a predetermined plant-wide overhead allocation method. The company had growing overhead variances because this allocation method tends to result in less accurate overhead cost assignments to products as the number and variety of products expand.

The accounting system lacked adequate separation of duties. The controller had sole control of both the product costing system and payroll preparation. The controller was authorized to prepare journal entries, sign payroll checks, and reconcile bank statements. Because no formal CFO had ever been hired, the controller effectively performed the duties of both positions.

The social characteristics of top management. The executive management displayed social attributes that concerned the consultant. First, the owner/CEO tried to keep executive payroll secret by delegating preparation of it to the controller, facilitating the fraudulent executive-payroll transactions. Next, the controller was uncooperative and resistant, refusing to speak with the consultant unless the president of the firm was present. Finally, both the CEO and president mistakenly trusted the skill level and honesty of the controller unconditionally.

TABLE 2: OCCUPATIONAL FRAUD BY COMPANY SIZE

Firm Type	Median Loss Per Fraud Scheme	Firm Characteristics
Micro/Small	$127,500	1–99 employees.
		Executive management is owner concentrated.
		Has few or no formal accounting controls.
Midsize	$135,000	100–999 employees.
		Specialized nonowner executive management.
		Has minimal separation of accounting duties.
Large	$53,000	1,000–9,999 employees.
		Nonowner executive management.
		Has formal Internal controls and external audit.
Global	$97,000	10,000 or more employees.
		Executive management reports to formal board of directors.
		Has an Internal audit department and structured controls.

Adapted from: The Association of Certified Fraud Examiners, *2002 Report to the Nation: Occupational Fraud and Abuse*, pp. 17–18.

INTERNAL CONTROLS

Robust internal controls of overhead accounts can help prevent fraud.

Wapello's consultant recommended strengthening the company's internal controls over its manufacturing overhead transactions by taking the following measures:

- All adjusting entries to manufacturing overhead and inventory accounts should be reviewed by an independent member of management.
- Significant manufacturing overhead variances should be analyzed both within and across time periods to identify anomalies.
- Nonaccounting management should be told about complaints concerning high product costs.
- The roles of product costing and payroll preparation should be separated.
- An improved overhead allocation system, such as departmental or activity-based costing, should be implemented if it is cost beneficial.

Other recommendations from the consultant included establishing an internal audit function and developing a formal system whereby the outside auditor would report control weaknesses separately to both accounting and nonaccounting management.

To that list, we recommend adding close monitoring of fluctuating cost of goods manufactured, cost of goods sold, inventory balances, and looking out for other symptoms of potential fraud, as shown in Table 1.

MORE MEASURES

Paradoxically, more money is fraudulently stolen from smaller companies, which have less elaborate accounting control systems, than is stolen from large ones, as shown in Table 2.

As companies grow in size and complexity, it's important to review and revise their internal controls to make sure they are adequate to deter fraudulent activity. In particular, as companies grow from micro/small to midsize businesses, owner/managers can no longer monitor all activities by physical observation alone, nor can they trust all new, nonfamily-member employees to be honest.

Among the lessons Wapello's CEO learned from this ordeal is to separate accounting duties; closely monitor accounts that are obvious places to hide fraudulent transactions, such as manufacturing overhead; and make sure proper internal controls are in place.

The authors thank University of North Florida graduate students Jamie D. Collis, Harry I. Eloranta, Melissa J. Gruebel, Aaron Kendrick III, Betty J. Saunders, and Christopher M. Shetzline for their work on the "Wapello" case.

John B. MacArthur, Ph.D., FCCA, is the Kathryn and Richard Kip Professor of Accounting and Cost Management at the Coggin College of Business at the University of North Florida in Jacksonville, Fla. You can reach John at (904) 620-1689 or macarth@unf.edu.

Bobby E. Waldrup, Ph.D., CPA, is an assistant professor of accounting at the Coggin College of Business at the University of North Florida in Jacksonville, Fla. You can reach Bobby at (904) 620-1669 or bwaldrup@unf.edu.

Gary R. Fane, Ph.D., CMA, CPA, is a professor of accounting and interim dean at the Coggin College of Business at the University of North Florida. You can reach Gary at (904) 620-1546 or gfane@unf.edu.

QUESTION

3.8 At Wapello Manufacturing what were some of the major accounting system issues and inadequacies that led to an environment in which fraud could occur?

Chapter 4

Activity Based Cost Management Systems

Six articles on activity-based costing are included in this section. Taken together, the articles highlight the applications of ABC to many different types of organizations.

The first article, T. L. Estrin, J. Kantor, and D. Albers' *Is ABC Suitable for Your Company?* (Reading 4.1), presents a method for determining whether ABC is appropriate for a particular company. The authors develop what they call a contingency grid based on two dimensions: the potential for ABC to provide costing information that is significantly different from what a traditional system would generate, and the propensity for the organization's managers to use the newly generated information. By answering a series of questions, an organization can score and locate itself on the grid. The authors state that while there is subjectivity in how an organization scores itself and that the factors used are not exhaustive, the contingency grid provides some structure that will allow managers to determine whether ABC should even be attempted in their organizations. While the early applications of ABC were developed in manufacturing settings, more recent applications have surfaced in service organizations.

Reading 4.2 is R. Kaplan and V. Narayanan's article, *Measuring and Managing Customer Profitability*. Consistent with Foster and Gupta's article (Reading 4.2), the authors provide a very insightful table (Exhibit 2) that can be used to identify high versus low cost-to-serve customers. Another key contribution of the article is the portrayal of the whale curve of cumulative profitability. This diagram describes the overall contribution of the most profitable and least profitable customers to cumulative profitability. Using the whale curve managers can begin the process of turning unprofitable customers to profitable ones by focusing on three areas: process improvements, pricing decisions and relationship management. The authors close the article with a discussion of barriers to implementation success.

The last two articles in the section are R. B. Sweeny and J. W. Mays', *ABM Lifts Bank's Bottom Line* (Reading 4.3), and Lawrence Carr's, *Unbundling the Cost of Hospitalization* (Reading 4.4), provide examples of how ABC can be applied in other service settings such as banks and hospitals. Sweeny and Mays' article illustrates how ABM was implemented at First Tennessee National Corporation in the late 1980s. The bank attributed an $11 million profit improvement as a result of ABM implementation. ABM was part of a six-step process toward increased profitability. Following ABM, which was the third step, the bank initiated an internal benchmarking study followed by an external benchmarking study and a process reengineering project. The article provides a clear contrast between the application of ABC in manufacturing versus a banking context. It also identifies how banks classify their activities into customer-order-driven activities and ongoing-concern activities. This article may also be a useful supplement for material in Chapter 9 on benchmarking.

Reading 4.4, *Unbundling the Cost of Hospitalization*, by Larry Carr, illustrates the implementation of an ABC system at Braintree Hospital in Boston. This application was designed to tease apart (or unbundle) the fixed cost allocation of nursing services. In the past, nursing costs were simply allocated into the cost per day of a hospital room. However, since nurses have different professional qualifications and skills, and patients require different care and have differential lengths of stay; devising a more accurate costing system would be beneficial to patients and the hospital. Certainly a patient would no longer be charged the average cost of nursing, especially if he or she required little nursing care, and the hospital would have a much more diagnostic system for activity and cost control.

Mitchell Max discusses the resurgence of interest in applying activity based costing in the banking industry in Reading 4.5, *ABC Trends in the Banking Sector: A Practitioner's Perspective*. The resurgence has occurred as banks are finding new ways to leverage cost and profitability information. Some of these include, activity based pricing for Business-to-Business services, linking ABC with performance management scorecards, providing information to support cost improvements and for customer profitability analysis.

Readings
Chapter 4

4.1 Is ABC Suitable for Your Company?

An impartial analysis of overall operations can tell you yes or no.

by T. L. Estrin, CMA, Jeffrey Kantor, and David Albers*

How do you know if activity-based costing (ABC) would be right for your company? There's an objective way to decide before your company takes the plunge. For ABC to be effective, a majority of all costs incurred by a significant unit of a business must be analyzed systematically. These costs include not only most fixed and variable factory burden costs, but also some fixed and variable marketing and administrative costs. Implementation of ABC requires a complex, comprehensive process that is costly and time-consuming, so naturally managers would want to be assured of the advantages before embarking on the implementation of ABC.

The potential benefits of ABC can be analyzed in advance along two separate dimensions. The first is based on the probability that, in a given application, ABC will produce costs or other results that are significantly different from ones that could be generated with more conventional or less costly methods. The ABC-generated costs may or may not be "better" or more accurate, but they are different in amount. The second dimension of the model seeks to establish that, given that cost information generated by ABC is indeed different, management will use it for significant decisions. Managers must regard ABC information as superior, and the nature of the organization and its competitive, legal, and social environments must allow managers to use the information freely.

The factors involved in the first dimension include the number and diversity of products or services produced, the diversity and differential degree of support services used for different products, the extent to which common or joint processes are used, the effectiveness of current cost allocation methods, and the rate of growth of period costs. The factors involved in the second dimension are management's freedom to set prices, the ratio of period costs to total costs, strategic considerations, the climate and culture of cost reduction in the company, and the frequency of analysis that is desirable or necessary.

A CONTINGENCY APPROACH TO IMPLEMENTING ABC

This methodology is based on a company's analysis of itself. It consists of weighting and combining the weights of the above factors and dimensions in order to evaluate the likelihood of success of implementing ABC. The combined weighted scores are plotted as a point on one of the four quadrants of a graph. Meanings are attached to the quadrant and the location of the final score in that quadrant. The methodology is not designed to produce a ratio-scale number indicating the relative benefits of ABC but to structure a systematic analysis by which the managers of a company can discuss the common factors that support or reject implementation.

To start, management must analyze the nature of the company in light of responses to two key questions:

1. For a given organization, is it likely that ABC will produce costs that are significantly different from those that are generated with conventional accounting, and does it seem likely that those costs will be "better"?

2. If information that is considered "better" is generated by the new system, will the new information change the dependent decisions made by the management?

FINDING THE ANSWERS

Ten mediating factors can guide management in determining the answers. The first five address the potential advantages of ABC versus traditional costing methods, and the second five deal with management's need and ability to react to product costing distortions.

Product diversity (PD). Product diversity refers to the quantity or range of distinct products or the variety of product families offered. Minor product variations should not be confused with product diversity. For example, it is unlikely that .20 cm. diameter ball bearings are a different product offering from .21 cm. diameter ball bearings. Differences in the complexity of various products also should be reflected in this analysis. Products that appear relatively homogeneous but that vary greatly in complexity are indicative of high diversity (such as 64K memory chips versus 1024K memory chips). Color variations, if applicable, need to be examined carefully. Does changing the color materially change the product? Is the function color dependent?

---

* From: T. L. Estrin, J. Kantor, and D. Albers, "Is ABC Suitable for Your Company?" *Management Accounting* (April 1994): 40–45. Reprinted with permission.

(For example, contrast red ink versus blue ink pens and red versus blue cars.)

There are numerous considerations in evaluating the extent and degree of product diversity:

- Accounting product classifications. Does the general ledger incorporate different product classifications? Are there internal reports that attempt to split sales, margins, or earnings by product lines?
- Markets served. Are they broken into geographical or industrial groups that purchase different types of products? Is the manufacturing department organized sequentially or in parallel? Sequential organization suggests limited product differentiation; parallel organization can indicate product diversity.
- Stockrooms. Are different stockrooms handling the same inventory classification (for example, raw material, finished goods) for different products?
- Sales. Does the company sell both OEM and manufactured items?
- Advertising. Does the company advertise only its name and/or one product, or does its advertising reflect different products?

Support diversity (SD). Support diversity refers to the range or variation of support overhead given to products. Assumptions can't be based on size. Even if the organization is only a cost center or a production facility, if it has more than one basic product or family of products, diversity in product support requirements probably exists. In this connection, reference to the manufacturing activities required is particularly useful. A superficial look at the organization may indicate little diversity, but a closer examination may reveal that actual activities vary greatly by product.

To determine and evaluate the degree of support diversity, companies should answer the following questions:

- Do departmental titles contain product names, and/or are departmental activities driven by specific products? Are there engineering support departments, and, if so, are their efforts skewed toward specific products?
- Are different manufacturing locations included in the one costing system?
- Are the manufacturing products relatively complex? (As a rule of thumb, complex products require more support, so the likelihood of diversity in support requirements increases.)
- Do different products use different distribution channels, have separate advertising requirements, or go to different markets?
- Is research and development homogeneous or product oriented?

- Is the company organized in (product-focused) modules, or do product task forces exist?
- Do different products require different material handling processes? Do different stockrooms exist?
- Is the organization operating in or moving toward a JIT environment?
- Are there major differences in product volumes or lot sizes?
- Is there a "new product introduction" organization?
- Does the company sell both OEM and manufactured items?

Common process (CP). Common process refers to the degree of commonality of processes among the different product offerings. "Processes" encompass all identifiable activities including manufacturing, engineering, marketing, distribution, accounting, material handling, quality control, research and development, and administration. If there is a high degree of commonality of processes or activities among products, period costs required by each product cannot be separated using conventional management accounting. ABC, by its nature, may be more effective.

Before assigning a common process value, companies should answer the following questions:

- If the organization examines profitability by product, are many expenses captured directly, or are they based on allocation or other arbitrary factors? Direct capture of most expenses may indicate a high degree of process segregation.
- Do different products require different production processes? Do production departments have more than one product to which to charge time?
- Are there distinct material handling processes? Do various products use different stockrooms? Is purchasing organized by product type or by type of material purchased? What degree of commonality exists between suppliers?
- Are engineering or shop support departments organized by product? Do engineers or technicians frequently support different products? Can they charge their time to different products?
- Is more than one distribution channel used?
- Is quality control organized by products?
- Do research and development personnel concentrate on specific products, or is the R&D more general in nature? Are R&D costs captured by product?
- Is administration organized by product?

Period cost allocation (CA). Period cost allocation refers to the existing costing system's conceptual ability to allocate period costs properly. In essence, period cost allocation is an analysis of the allocation methodology to determine if it is capable of mimicking the results of ABC. It is a premise of ABC that, over time, so-called period costs (indirect, variable, and fixed costs) are attributable to the activities required in making various products. Thus, a major focus of ABC analysis is on associating period costs with products. ABC also suggests that many nonmanufacturing costs, such as marketing costs, also are a function of product activity and should be loaded onto the products responsible for their incurrence.

- Is the general ledger set up to capture support expenses by product through the use of product-specific departments, engineering time sheets, indirect labor classifications, and the like?
- To what extent are indirect expenses not identified by product?
- How many concurrent bases of allocation are used?
- Are they consistent with the major cost drivers?
- How many levels are in the allocation hierarchy? If multi-level, are the allocations on a product-specific basis?
- Is the allocation hierarchy riddled with estimates or arbitrary factors?
- How many cost centers exist, and how product-specific are the cost centers?
- If only one allocation basis is used, can it distribute the costs by product accurately despite the probable lack of correlation between output and the consumption of resources? Would the distribution of costs still be accurate if there were significant changes in the nature of the period costs? (Assume that the more allocation bases are used, the more readily changes can be reflected in product costs.)
- Can the allocation bases reflect the impact of product volume fluctuations accurately? (For instance, burden rates are established based upon anticipated product volumes. Will the allocation bases recognize the probable change in support requirements if the product mix changes significantly?)

Rate of growth of period costs (PG). Rate of growth of period costs refers to the growth in period costs as an indicator of the dynamism required by the costing system. One of ABC's strengths is its ability to capture changes in the support requirements of products quickly through its direct measurement of activity levels. If period costs, as a percentage, remain relatively stable over years, management can to some extent adjust implicitly for the distortions produced by a conventional cost system. Also, given period cost stability for several years, a traditional costing system can be structured to provide product costs similar or identical to those calculated by ABC (excluding below-the-line, cost of goods manufactured costs).

HOW DOES MANAGEMENT USE COST INFORMATION IN DECISIONS?

If management agrees that the nature of the products, the productive processes, and the marketing of the products are such that the costs generated by ABC will be significantly different from traditional management accounting costs and that ABC costs reflect true product costs more accurately, it still may not be able to, or may not want to, use this better information. A number of factors will influence management's desire for or ability to use cost information in its deliberations. Among these factors are pricing freedom, period expense ratio, strategic considerations, cost reduction efforts, and analysis frequency.

Pricing freedom (PF). Pricing freedom refers to the company's degree of power and freedom to set prices and therefore establish product profitability. The more freedom a company has, the less important product costs become. Pricing will be set to maximize profits and will depend on market elasticity. Where monopoly conditions apply and demand is inelastic, high prices will be set. Where there are pure competition, many competitors, and good substitute products available, however, prices will be determined entirely by market forces.

Because the vast majority of organizations face situations somewhere between the two extremes, companies should answer the following questions as they evaluate this factor:

- Are all product prices regulated? If so, are the prices based on costs and subject to appeal and revision?
- How competitive is the market? Are price surveys common or available? Does the profitability of the industry appear unusually high or low? Are the competitive aspects based on some factor other than price?
- Are there high barriers to entry?
- Do the company's products occupy a unique position within the market? Can premium prices be justified due to service?
- Where are the products within their life cycle?
- Is the company a price leader or a price follower?
- How dynamic are the products' prices? What are the causes of the changes or lack thereof?

Period expense ratio (FE). Period expense ratio addresses the possible materiality of product cost distortions directly. If possible distortions are so minimal that no management actions would result from their correction, then the distortions become irrelevant. Although the materiality of this factor also should be evaluated from the perspective of percentage change in reported costs, the primary focus should be on the impact upon product profitability. (For example, a reported cost change of 5% may be immaterial to a jeweler operating on 300% markup, but it is extremely significant to a volume-based grocery working with 2%–4% margins.)

Although there is no specific formula for quantifying possible product cost distortions and determining the materiality of those distortions, the following questions may help the appraisal process. When answering these questions, companies should consider only period costs that must be allocated; variable costs that can be loaded directly onto products should be ignored.

- What is/would be the plant average or blanket burden rate? Is it a large multiple of labor? How does it compare to various product or cost center rates?
- Are period costs a "significant" proportion of the total cost structure (including direct costs)? What would be the impact upon total profitability if the percentage of period costs increased 10%? 50%? 100%?
- Are cost reduction activities focused upon product costs (such as reduction of supplier prices) or upon period costs? Is it management's belief that focusing upon direct costs offers greater potential benefits? Is this belief appropriate?

Strategic considerations (SC). Strategic considerations refer to the constraints imposed upon management's decisions by its explicit or implicit strategies—in other words, the degree to which strategies override costs in the decision-making process. These strategies are not limited to marketing strategies; they also include secondary strategies and objectives related to technology, manufacturing, quality, and the like.

- Is a "market niche" strategy being employed? Is the strategy dependent upon product profitability/costs?
- Are capital expenditures for new products, manufacturing changes, or capacity expansions frequently justified explicitly on the basis of "strategic reasons" instead of economic returns?
- Are capital expenditures frequently initiated implicitly and driven by strategic considerations, with the financial benefits of the project being used merely to obtain project approval?
- What type of analysis and justification is necessary for approval of R&D expenditures? Is the true rationale more strategic in nature?
- Does the organization establish customer prices based upon costs or market? If the company sells to related entities using prices based upon costs, would changes in the transfer pricing result in changes in volume or in the receiving location's decisions?
- Are make-versus-buy comparisons performed frequently? Does the organization have this option, or do technological or policy restrictions constrain it?
- Are changes in product design or manufacturing processes driven mainly by costs, or are other sources such as market or product requirements critical?
- Are product discontinuation analyses performed regularly in an attempt to (indirectly) reduce costs or for reasons such as fostering specific market perceptions?

Cost reduction (CR). Cost reduction involves the corporate culture as it affects the relationship between internal cost-related decisions and the indirect component of the total cost of products. It involves the nature of internal cost-related decisions and the degree to which the decisions depend upon accurate allocations of period costs. A number of potential internal decisions depend on accurate costs—manufacturing process changes, product design modifications, make-versus-buy comparisons, product scrubbing, capacity expansion evaluation, and so on. Analysis of these activities will indicate the likelihood of management action resulting from changes in reported product costs due to the elimination of distortions in the period cost allocation.

- How extensive are cost reduction activities within the organization? Do any engineering groups focus exclusively upon cost reduction? Is there an employee suggestion plan?
- Are there numerous or frequent cost-oriented task forces? Are cost reduction metrics tracked internally? Are there frequent changes in head count unrelated to load?
- Are the above cost reduction activities general in nature and not related to specific products? Are cost reduction targets established in total only, or by function/activity, or by product?
- Do the cost reduction activities focus upon nonperiod targets? Are there material or labor variance targets?
- Are make-versus-buy comparisons applicable? If so, how frequent are the analyses? How close are the decisions?
- Are product scrubbing decisions both frequent and dependent upon costs? Are period costs a major factor in the decision?
- Are process modifications focused upon the manufacturing organization? Are period costs relevant?
- Are capacity changes dependent upon costs? Are allocated period costs incorporated into—or even relevant to—the decisions?

Analysis frequency (AF). Analysis frequency refers to the frequency, either routine or special, of product cost analyses and incorporates both the current and the desired frequencies. A measure of dynamism, it also embodies the other management action factors. A discrepancy between the existing and desired frequencies of analysis indicates dissatisfaction with the existing costing system.

- Are product profitability reports issued routinely from the existing costing system? Are they believed, or are "adjustments" made? If believed, are they used fruitfully?

- How frequently are special studies or ad hoc analyses of product costs performed or requested? Is there a lack of credibility in the existing data, or are the existing data insufficient? If studies/analyses are infrequent, why? Is it due to a low requirement or to the difficulty of obtaining "accurate" data?
- What prompts special cost study requests, volume fluctuations, pricing requests, and the like? Do these changes occur often?
- Would management like more frequent or more detailed product cost analyses? For what purpose?

PLOTTING THE ANSWERS

Now let's assign values to the factors listed above and plot them on a chart to provide a focus for a discussion among managers and give them a mechanism for highlighting their differences in order to reach a consensus in a more effective manner.

Figure 1 shows a grid that may be used to plot the situational factors in an evaluation of the potential of ABC for a particular situation. Each of the 10 factors is scored on a –5 to +5 scale, and the scores of each of the two sets of five factors are weighted and combined into the two scores, which are plotted on the grid. A weighted aggregate score of the five factors affecting "product cost distortion," which indicates the potential benefits of ABC for the company, is plotted on the "Y" axis of the grid. A weighted composite score of all the factors affecting management's need and ability to act on better cost information in making decisions is plotted on the "X" axis.

FIGURE 1. THE CONTINGENCY GRID

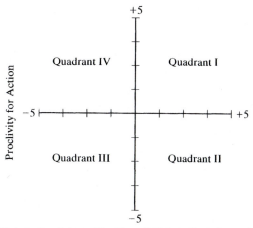

Potential for ABC Due to Product Cost Distortions

"X" Axis, Proclivity to Use Cost Information in Business Decisions	"Y" Axis, Basic Potential for ABC Based on Cost Distortions
PF—Pricing Freedom	PD—Pricing Diversity
FE—Fixed Expense Ratio	SD—Support Diversity
SC—Strategic Considerations	CP—Common Processes
CR—Cost Reduction Effort	CA—Cost Allocation
AF—Analysis Frequency	FG—Growth of Indirect Costs

In order to show the scores from the two sets of factors on the two-dimensional contingency grid, we must combine the scores of each set into a single score on that characteristic. It is necessary to weigh each of the five factors in both classifications to recognize that differences exist in the relative importance of each factor in a given company.

Each of the five factors on each dimension of the grid can be assigned a score depending on management's analysis of its situation. The weighting process begins with the presumption of equal ranking (i.e., weighting of 20%). Then managers examine each factor to determine if the weighting should be changed. This end can be achieved in a "Delphi" process where managers from all pertinent areas submit scores and their reasoning for all factors by mail. Then they receive the high, low, and average scores with rationales and revise their estimates. The first rounds of this process can be on an area-by-area basis (such as accounting or production), and the last rounds of this process can be done with broadly representative members of management meeting to determine the scores.

The examination is based on three main criteria:

1. If this factor had the extreme value of + or –5, to what extent is the main characteristic impacted? For example, without product diversity, will product cost distortions occur? Without material pricing freedom, will management actions occur?
2. If this factor has the extreme value of + or –5, what is the impact upon the other factors?
3. Is this factor extremely subjective or difficult to measure, and should weighting be structured to ameliorate its impact?

INTERPRETING THE RESULTS

Quadrant I. Results that are plotted in Quadrant I (both "X" and "Y" are positive) initially suggest because product cost distortions are likely and management is free to act upon corrected product costs, an ABC system should be implemented. It is possible, and even likely, however, that the source of the cost distortions is included in the category of "below-the-line" (selling and administrative) expenses and that the current traditional allocation technique is providing adequate overhead cost information. Because recommendations differ depending on the source of the distortions (traditional "overhead" or the "below-the-line" category), managers must perform the "potential for ABC due to product cost distortions" section of the analysis again, omitting any consideration of nonoverhead, organizations, activities, or similar expenses.

If the revised composite score remains Quadrant I, it is an indication that the source of the distortions is within the category defined as traditional overhead. In this case, companies should consider implementing a full ABC system or a costing system that incorporates ABC concepts. Product cost distortions probably are occurring, and because those costs are being used extensively within the organization, it is likely that less than optimal decisions are being made.

If the revised composite score shifts to Quadrant II, the source of the distortions is within the category known as "below-the-line" (selling and marketing, administration, and research and development). In this case, implementation of a full ABC system is not warranted—the existing traditional allocation technique is providing adequate cost information for the overhead component of the product costs, and there is no reason to incur the implementation and maintenance costs of a full-blown ABC system. If "below-the-line" expenses for total product cost purposes are the main culprits in reporting incorrect products costs, however, managers should scrutinize the allocation methodology of those analyses for possible errors. A stand-alone system using ABC concepts and addressing only "below-the-line" costs may be appropriate.

Quadrant II. If the results of the analysis are plotted in this quadrant, it indicates that although management is free to utilize product cost information, it is unlikely that those costs contain material distortions. Because there are no direct benefits, implementing ABC at this time is not recommended. The situation should be monitored for changes over time, however, particularly if the "Y" value is relatively small.

Quadrant III. Results plotted in this quadrant clearly indicate that ABC is not recommended. It is unlikely that material product cost distortions are present, and management has limited ability to utilize or react to modified costs.

Quadrant IV. Results occurring in this quadrant suggest that although product cost distortions are likely, management has little ability to modify its decisions that are cost dependent. Management should re-examine its use of product cost information and its freedom to react to changes, including performing the "management action" section of the model analysis again. Although management may be constrained from acting on cost information in the short run, many valuable long-term uses for this information may appear. Only when management is satisfied that it would *not* use corrected product cost information should it reject possible implementation of an ABC system.

THE FINAL DECISION

After reading about ABC, attending ABC seminars, or being approached by ABC consultants, many managers still may be in a quandary as to whether the implementation of this technique will improve the competitiveness of their particular companies. These executives need some method of evaluating whether the potential claimed benefits of ABC would outweigh the certain and substantial costs of its implementation. Our contingency analysis model should help them by matching the characteristics of their company, its products, and the costing system used with the factors that make ABC most effective.

The factors we presented are neither mutually exclusive nor collectively exhaustive. While the scoring system is subjective, it is grounded on factors cited in the ABC literature as being causal in determining the superiority of ABC over traditional costing. Most important, it presents a structure for managers to use in their deliberations and encourages them to arrive at some consensus with regard to the degree to which the factors are present in their company and ultimately to convince themselves as to either the uselessness, the desirability, or the critical necessity for the implementation of ABC.

T. L. Estrin, CMA, Ph.D., is an associate professor of business administration at the University of Windsor, Windsor, Canada, and a director of the Cost Management Group there. He is a member of the Society of Management Accountants of Canada and the Inst. of Mgmt. Accountants. He may be reached at (519) 253-4232, ext. 3457.

Jeffrey Kantor, Ph.D., CA, is a professor of business administration at the University of Windsor and a director of the Cost Management Group.

David C. Albers is the regional support international manager for Multimedia Communication Systems and has done process analysis with Northern Telecom Inc. for several years.

QUESTION

4.1 Using Estrin, Kantor and Albers' contingency grid, if an organization's score puts it in Quadrant III, is ABC implementation recommended? Explain. Is their method "foolproof?"

4.2 Measuring and Managing Customer Profitability

by Robert S. Kaplan and V. G. Narayanan*

In this article R. Kaplan and V. G. Narayanan discuss the issue of customer profitability analysis. They argue that today organizations have invested in enterprise resource planning (ERP) systems and data warehouses to track detailed data about individual customer transactions and relationships and in customer relationship management (CRM) to improve customer satisfaction. Despite these innovations, many companies don't know if they are actually making money from their customers. The difficulty is that in an age of heightened customer demands, companies are customizing products and services but not necessarily linking the costs of doing so on a customer-by-customer basis.

Activity-based costing (ABC) and associated software can be used as the conceptual framework for linking customer transactional data from ERP and CRM systems with financial information.

ABC can be used to calculate individual customer profitability. The output from the ABC analysis is called a whale curve (see Exhibit 1), which plots cumulative profitability against customers. While cumulative sales usually follow the typical 20/80 rule (e.g. 20% of the customers provide 80%) of the sales), the whale curve for cumulative profitability usually reveals that the most profitable 20% of customers generate between 150% and 300% percent of total profits. The middle 70% break even and the least profitable 10% of customers lose from 50% to 200% of total profits, leaving the company with its 100% of total profits.

Many large customers often turn out to be the most unprofitable. Companies cannot afford to lose large sums of money from small customers as they simply do not do enough business with them to incur large losses. Only a large customer can be a large-loss customer. Large customers tend to be either the most profitable or the least profitable in the entire customer base. It is unusual for a large customer to be in the middle of the total profitability ratings.

Exhibit 2 identifies dimensions that help companies identify diversity in their cost of serving individual customers. For service companies, customer profitability is more important than product profitability as the costs of providing service are usually determined by customer behavior.

Once a company studies its whale curve of customer profitability, several actions to transform unprofitable customers to profitable ones can take place. These include improving processes by lowering costs to serve, changing pricing strategies to include menu pricing, and improving customer relationship management and measurement.

EXHIBIT 1. THE WHALE CURVE OF CUMULATIVE PROFITABILITY

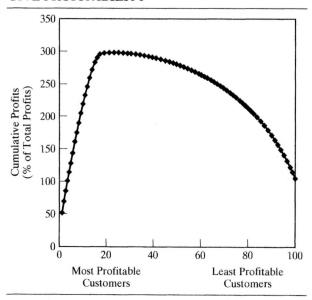

EXHIBIT 2 - IDENTIFYING DIVERSITY IN VARYING COST-TO-SERVE CUSTOMERS

High Cost to Serve Customers	Low Cost to Serve Customers
Order custom products	Order standard products
Order small quantities	Order large quantities
Unpredictable order arrivals	Predictable order arrivals
Frequent changes in delivery requirements	Standard delivery
Manual processing	Electronic processing
Large amount of pre-sales support	Little to no pre-sales support
Large amounts of post-sales support	No post-sales support
Require company to hold inventory	Replenish as produced
Pay slowly (high accounts receivable)	Pay on time

QUESTIONS

4.2a What does the whale curve of cumulative profitability illustrate?

4.2b Describe the characteristics of high-cost-to-serve and low-cost-to-serve customers.

---

* This article has been summarized from the original article by Robert S. Kaplan and V. G. Narayanan, "Measuring and Managing Customer Profitability," *Journal of Cost Management* (September/October 2001): 5–15.

4.3 ABM Lifts Bank's Bottom Line

*by Robert B. Sweeny, CPA, and James W. Mays, CMA**

Activity-based management (ABM) was implemented at First Tennessee National Corporation, a regional bank holding company, eight years ago. The initial profit improvement was $750,000; by the end of 1994, the total profit improvement had risen to almost $11 million and could reach twice that amount annually by the year 2000. (For a look at some of the contributing factors and solutions, see Figure 1.)

For the cost management department at First Tennessee, activity-based management is but one step to increased profitability through cost management. The steps toward increased profitability start with financial accounting, then management reporting, then activity-based cost management, internal and external benchmarking, and, finally, process reengineering. (See Figure 2.)

Step three, activity-based costing (ABC), replaced a sophisticated product costing system at First Tennessee. That system did not provide operating management with the information needed to control costs and increase profitability. Activity-based costing, on the other hand, supports process analysis, design, and, to some extent, reengineering. It focuses attention on productivity by examining product performance and resource consumption. The answer sought by First Tennessee's management accountants was, "Are we receiving adequate revenue for the value-added services we provide our customers?"

Banking is a time-based industry, and its mission is to provide the most value at the lowest cost in the least elapsed time. To achieve this mission, efficiency and effectiveness are paramount. Efficiency (doing things right) controls the pattern of resources consumption; effectiveness (doing the right things) generates profit.

There are two prime inhibitors of efficiency and effectiveness in banking. They are cross-subsidization among customers and cross-functional internal processes. An example of cross-subsidization can be seen when profitable customers pay for unprofitable customers, as in the use of pricing schedules that are unrelated to the cost of services. Fee revenue traditionally has been a secondary source of income, but that is no longer true. The key to increasing return on equity is to make fee income grow without increasing equity. Internal benchmarking is the next step after implementing activity-based costing as shown in Figure 2. It is actually an interactive process. After applying ABC concepts to one operation or process, the results are applied to the same or similar processes at another location. Each location learns from the other, and both processes, the benchmark process and the process to which the benchmark is applied, are improved, further increasing efficiency and profitability.

External benchmarking moves one step closer to increased profitability by extending the process outside the company. While process reengineering may take place at any time, it is the next logical step after external benchmarking. Reengineering processes involving automation, replacing people, and, to some extent, replacing paper with virtual electronic systems represent the final steps toward increased profitability. What were viewed before as temporary changes are more likely to be seen as changes in culture today.

ABC: MANUFACTURING VS. BANKING

As a time-based industry, banking is significantly different from manufacturing, which was one of the first groups to apply activity-based costing concepts. In manufacturing, production generally precedes the sale, modified only slightly by just-in-time (JIT) operations. The cost of manufacturing, therefore, is incurred prior to making a sale, and profit is determined at the point of sale. In banking, the sale precedes the processing. For example, a sale occurs when a potential customer opens a checking account. The major portion of the processing occurs after that. This issue is exacerbated by the fact that profit is determined by customers' activity over time. While the unit cost of maintaining a checking account is basically fixed, the customer's volume of activity determines the total cost and, thus, the profitability. The balance maintained by the customer in a checking account also materially affects profitability. If we have set levels at which monthly service charges are discontinued using traditional costing, we may learn after applying activity-based costing that we are serving some of our customers at a loss. This outcome occurs because the customers did what we told them to do—keep their account balance slightly above a minimum balance level. There is a risk that this minimum balance may produce insufficient revenue.

Another difference between banking and manufacturing is that once products or services are sold, they stay in production for years. Unfortunately, processing is difficult to schedule because the customer determines the usage of various services.

* From: R. B. Sweeny and J. W. Mays, "ABM Lifts Bank's Bottom Line," *Management Accounting* (March 1997): 21–26. Reprinted with permission.

FIGURE 1. PROFIT IMPROVEMENT THROUGH ACTIVITY-BASED MANAGEMENT

Profit Improvement 1989–1994 $10,875,000

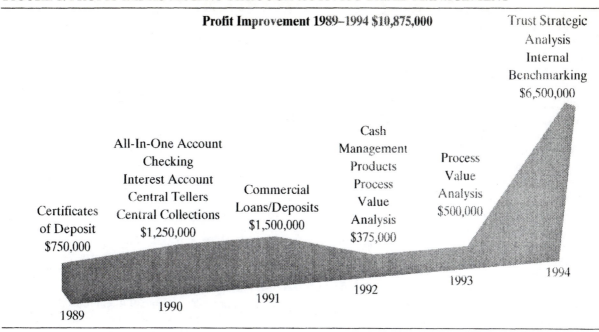

Certificates of Deposit $750,000 (1989)

All-In-One Account Checking Interest Account Central Tellers Central Collections $1,250,000 (1990)

Commercial Loans/Deposits $1,500,000 (1991)

Cash Management Products Process Value Analysis $375,000 (1992)

Process Value Analysis $500,000 (1993)

Trust Strategic Analysis Internal Benchmarking $6,500,000 (1994)

FIGURE 2. STEPS TOWARD INCREASED PROFITABILITY

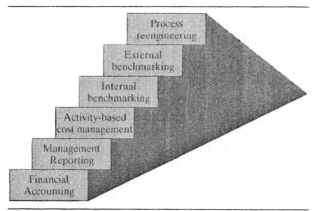

Process reengineering
External benchmarking
Internal benchmarking
Activity-based cost management
Management Reporting
Financial Accounting

Two other realities also are significant. First, banking operates in an overcapacity environment. That is, there are too many banks. Only half of the top 10 most profitable banks in 1984 and 1985 are still in existence. The second reality is that bank revenues are derived in two ways—by charging service fees and by the spread on interest rates, and neither is tied directly to customer usage. For example, people who maintain higher balances may write the same number as or, in many cases, fewer checks than those with smaller balances. The same phenomenon is observed with Automated Teller Machines (ATMs). Those with smaller balances tend to make more numerous, smaller withdrawals; those with larger balances have fewer but larger withdrawals.

MODIFYING ABC FOR BANKING

ABC requires the identification and classification of activities. In banking, activities are classified first as customer order-driven activities and ongoing-concern activities. The customer order-driven activities include such things as sales, services, processing, and administration. The ongoing-concern activities include areas considered as over-head such as accounting and finance, personnel, general counsel, and purchasing among others. A major effort is made to minimize the cost of these activities using the value-added, nonvalue-added activities analysis. These analyses have been renamed mission-related activities and nonmission-related activities analysis. Mission-related activities are defined as the things we do to satisfy the needs of constituents, while nonmission-related activities are those things we do that increase the elapsed time of various processes, such as inspection, movement, storage, and error correction. The objective is to eliminate or at least reduce the amount of nonmission activities. A major reason for using the word mission instead of value in classifying activities is psychological. We do not want to imply that an activity, such as correcting errors, has no value. Rather, we want to convey the idea that by avoiding errors we can achieve our mission and avoid the correction activity.

Activity-based costing. Adopting a new cost system can be a traumatic process. While senior management endorsed the effort to apply activity-based costing to various services and processes within the bank, a degree of skepticism prevailed among operating management. The first product to which activity-based costing was applied was certificates of deposit (CDs). The cost of processing a CD is fixed regardless of the magnitude of the certificate, but the revenue is a function of the dollar amount of the certificate. Thus, a 90-day $500 CD that is reopened four times a year generates only $5 a year on a 1% interest spread, providing considerably less revenue than the processing cost of transactions.

By applying ABC concepts, CDs were put into 10 categories. (See Figure 3.) The graph shows that 30% of our customers were providing 88% of our profit, while another 30% of our customers actually are serviced at a loss of 7%. This situation was corrected through a combination of higher minimum balances, new products, and process redesign.

After the initial success with the CD project, interest among operating management began to build. A subsequent project focused on commercial loans normally handled by bank loan officers. The project involved analyzing loans by amount and amortization period. An analysis of the typical profitability three-year term loans $50,000, $20,000, $3,000 is shown in Figure 4. The sloping lines reflect the revenue generated by each loan over the three-year period. The total cost per loan line is constant over the three years and is the same for all three loans.

Note that the $50,000 loan is profitable for the first 19 months and, therefore, is profitable over the entire life of the loan. Surprisingly, neither the $20,000 nor the $3,000 loan is profitable in any month.

The situation has been addressed by a combination of pricing, product redesign, and processing changes. A profit improvement of at least $1.5 million per year has been the result.

Internal benchmarking. This procedure begins by applying the basic concepts of activity-based costing to a process or operation similar to one reviewed previously. Next, the unit costs of the product components and the cost drivers in the processes are cataloged. Then a root cause analysis is performed, comparing the two operations on the bases of technology, people, methods, and environment. Identifying and sharing best practices at each location results in lower unit costs at both locations.

FIGURE 4. COMMERCIAL LOANS—3-YEAR AMORTIZATION

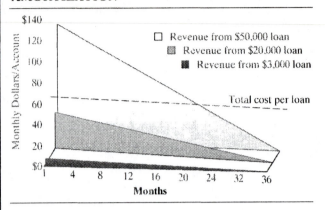

The internal benchmarking of proof operations illustrates this process. Cost management personnel who previously had applied ABC to one operation at Location A studied the second proof function at Location B, interviewing the appropriate personnel to gain insight into the operation. This process ferreted out the unit costs of product components and the applicable cost drivers.

The root cause analysis reflects differences between the benchmark operation in Location A and Location B proof operations. (See Figure 5.) In terms of technology, Location B had older check filing machines and no optical code reader. Concerning the methods employed, Location B had more diverse operations and smaller processing volumes. Additionally, filming was required for security. The environment differed in that there were more widely scattered collection points and poor workspace layout. The operation was in a high-risk downtown location, which impacted employee tenure negatively.

The most significant aspect of the root cause analysis related to people. All of the findings were interrelated. The low pay rates created a high turnover, and the high turnover resulted in an inexperienced staff and the need for more training time. The net result was lower processing efficiency in Location B compared to Location A. Some problems could be remedied easily,

FIGURE 3. CD PROFITABILITY DISTRIBUTION

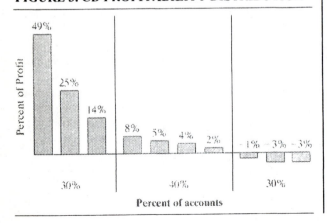

FIGURE 5. INTERNAL BENCHMARKING OF PROOF OPERATIONS—LOCATION B

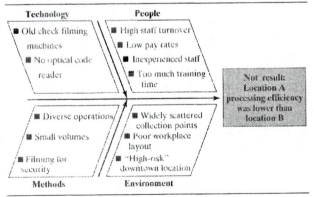

TABLE 1. ROOT CAUSE ANALYSIS

	Location A	Current	Location B With/ Location A Benchmark
Total paid proof operator hours	38,000	24,000	15,770
Less vacation, holidays, sick/personal hours	(4,340)	(2,160)	(1,419)
Total proof operator work hours	33,660	21,840	14,351
Less: Nonproductive proof work hours (breaks, meetings, training, etc.)	(8,580)	(7,450)	(3,658)
Total productive proof operator work hours	25,080	14,390	10,693
Percent of total proof operator work hours	75%	66%	75%
Processing hours per total fields encode	1,870	1,870	1,870
Total proof operator fields encoded	18	12	8
Fields encoded	63,753,360	27,182,170	27,182,170
Fields encoded per productive hour	2,542	1,889	2,542
Total personnel expense (fringe loaded)	$474,240	$271,920	$196,810
Personnel expense savings			$75,110
Total personnel dollars per total fields encoded per hour	$12.48	$11.33	$12.48

such as replacing old check filming machines and changing the workspace. The major problem was staff turnover. Employees were leaving for higher pay after being trained in Location B.

In the root cause analysis in Table 1 the first two columns of numbers represent data collected from operations in both locations. Note that the fields encoded per productive hour in Location B are considerably less than in Location A. While they are offset by lower personnel cost per hour, the inefficiency still results in a much higher cost per field encoded. The Location A cost per 1,000 fields coded is $5.76 compared with the Location B cost of $8.23.

Using the benchmark approach, the management accounting staff adjusted data for Location B to the Location A standards using $12.48 as the cost per hour and 2,542 as the fields encoded per production hour to reflect the anticipated rate from lower turnover. The result is that only eight people were required to perform the proof operation in Location B, which had been using 12 people. The total personnel expense was reduced from $271,920 to $196,810, generating profit improvement of approximately $75,000. Total profit improvement in 1994 resulting from such internal benchmarking was $500,000.

THE FUTURE

As noted earlier, the implementation of ABC concepts has provided First Tennessee with a profit improvement of approximately $11 million. The next major steps are external benchmarking and more extensive reengineering, as all levels of management continue to recognize the positive impact that activity-based management has had on corporate performance. Management now has the tools to increase its productivity, and the result has been increased profitability. Activity-based costing is firmly set as a cornerstone of continuous productivity improvement at First Tennessee.

Robert B. Sweeney, CPA, Ph.D., now deceased, held the Thompson-Hill Chair of Excellency in Accountancy at the University of Memphis, Memphis, Tenn. He was a member of the Memphis Chapter of the IMA, through which this article was submitted.

James W. Mays is vice president and manager of cost management at First Tennessee National Corporation. He is a member of the Memphis Chapter of the IMA, and he can be reached at (901) 523-5606.

QUESTIONS

4.3a According to Sweeny and Mays, how do the manufacturing and banking processes differ?

4.3b What are the differences between (a) customer order-driven activities and ongoing-concern activities, and (b) mission-related and nonmission-related activities at the First Tennessee National Corporation?

4.4 Unbundling the Cost of Hospitalization
ABC can keep health care providers off the critical list.

by Lawrence P. Carr*

In the health care industry, the insurance companies leverage their considerable power by scrutinizing the billing practices of the health care providers. A serious concern of insurers is the cost of hospital nursing care and related services.

Traditionally, the cost of nursing is factored into the daily room charge for a hospital stay. For example, a rate of $500 to $800 per day covers the 24-hour nursing availability for the patient. Nursing expenses, primarily labor costs, are part of the overhead rate comprising the daily $500 to $800 billing to the patient. Charges are aggregate in nature with the same average fixed fee applied to all patients.

The problem with this typical convention is that not all patients use nursing services in equal amounts. Patient utilization of nursing services is individualistic. Fixed charges are not always related to the services rendered. Further, nursing services are available "on call" to handle possible patient emergencies where the value may not be readily quantifiable.

Braintree Hospital is a private rehabilitation hospital providing in-patient and outpatient treatment. It is one of the largest rehabilitation network care providers in the country with 168 beds on site and management contracts covering 200 more beds. Generally patients are referred to Braintree by other hospitals or private physicians.

The patient's average stay is approximately 21 days, during which time the individual progresses through a comprehensive program aimed at restoring and maintaining functional abilities (basic living skills). Patients enter with physical disabilities due to neurological and orthopedic diseases or injury and normally are diagnosed as one of the following: stroke, spinal cord injury, congenital deformity, amputation, major multiple trauma, fracture of femur, brain injury, polyarthritis & joint replacement, neurological disorders, burns and neoplasms.

An activity-based costing system enabled Boston's Braintree Hospital to satisfy, in the near term, the insurance industry's changing approach to reimbursement. In the medium term, it positioned the hospital to enter the 1990s with the shifting payment paradigm of managed care. Knowing the cost of nursing care provided to each individual patient by diagnosis gave management reliable data to negotiate per diem rates.

NURSING SERVICES PROVIDED

Typically, nursing services in the hospital consist of a varied skill mix: professional registered nurses (RNs), licensed practical nurses (LPNs), and ancillary nursing assistants (NAs). These professionals have different levels of education, training, and hospital experience.

For example, the north wing of the second floor of Braintree Hospital has 43 beds. The nursing staff consists of a nurse manager, RNs, LPNs, and NAs who work varying shifts to cover the unit 24 hours, seven days a week. The staff is reduced for the 11 p.m. to 7:30 a.m. shift due to workload distribution.

Teams of nurses perform many different functions. They administer medication, maintain daily patient records, assist the physicians with medical care, monitor medical devices, conduct routine tests, and so on. They are responsible for the routine jobs of feeding the patients, administering to their bodily needs, bathing, ensuring patient safety, and evaluating the care provided. Perhaps most important, they provide personal comfort and care for the patient.

The professional RN is licensed and can perform all of the many nursing functions in the hospital. But he or she concentrates primarily on the more intense and demanding patients and functions. At the same time, RNs are responsible for the delivery of care to a specific group of patients on a floor or ward.

The other nursing team members normally work with the RNs to deliver care to their group of patients. Thus, the array of services is delivered by a team with varying skill levels. There is a hierarchy of nursing from the RN to the NA with the top level capable of doing all of the functions of the levels below. Pay scales vary from $26 per hour to $8 per hour, depending on the personal skill/educational level and specific position.

As you might imagine, there is a wide variation in the amount of nursing services consumed by patients, just as there is a wide variety of patient ailments that require differing degrees of nursing attention. The health care industry has recognized this phenomenon, and third-party payers are pushing very hard to pay only for services used by the patient and at the lowest price.

Patients are becoming more aware of and interested in the distribution of care and the inherent costs, probably

---

* From L. P. Carr, "Unbundling the Cost of Hospitalization," *Management Accounting* (November 1993): 43–48. Reprinted with permission.

due to the economy and media attention focused on health care costs. Such comments as, "Mrs. Smith is getting all of the nursing attention. She needs it and, thankfully, I don't, but I have to pay for it. This doesn't seem fair," are quite common.

NO HARD DATA
Mary-Jean Crockett, the progressive-thinking vice president of nursing, recognized that nursing services delivery needed to be understood better. She felt the growing pressure from the insurance companies that pay for most of Braintree's patient care and heard the "buzz" at national professional conferences. She was determined to find an easy, reliable, and fair method to ascertain the amount, mix, and resulting cost of nursing services consumed by individual patients. She also wanted a more accurate approach to forecasting the skill mix associated with care of the different diagnostic groups. She remained cognizant that she also needed to monitor the high level of quality, comfort, and safety that leads to positive patient outcomes.

Two years ago, Mary-Jean initiated the nursing services analysis project by chairing a project team of nurses and administrators. Team members included the staff development instructor, nursing MIS project manager, and the nursing supervisor/coordinator of quality assurance. All the team members worked as staff members on the nursing care units and were familiar with the actual work flow at Braintree.

After the first organizational meeting and the sharing of the concerns for the nursing service issues, the team realized it had no hard data upon which to make its assessment. Everyone had anecdotal stories with the constant theme of the imbalance between the actual delivered nursing and the fixed single billing rate. Additionally, Mary-Jean was very interested in the efficiency as well as the effectiveness of the current nursing staffing levels and delivery of care system.

THE PILOT STUDY
A literature review and discussion with "experts" in the field did not provide insight into assessing the workflow in the Braintree environment. Then a process analysis was conducted that produced time, motion, and frequency studies of the routine and special medical events on all of the nursing units.

The routine events such as vital sign test, medication, and bed changing were easy to predict and consistent across all units. The percentage of baseline routine nursing time could vary from 5% to 70%, depending on the medical problem and length of hospital stay. For example, a new brain injury patient requires constant care, and routine nursing, may comprise just 5% of the total daily nursing services consumed. On the other hand, a burn patient about to be discharged may be quite self-sufficient, and the routine care would consist of 70% of the total daily nursing care. The team concluded that it needed more data to predict the nonroutine, variable, or special events that consumed considerable nursing, time. It believed the non-routine events were the driving forces behind the varying levels of services needed and provided.

The team, after many additional meetings, developed a simple but quite reliable data gathering instrument to capture variable and unpredictable events and build a database. Figure 1 shows the nursing service classification data form. The established procedure provided that the nurses from each shift simply checked the appropriate boxes for the service rendered for each individual patient. The sheets were collected daily for the previous 24 hours and entered into the database system created for the study. The nursing staff openly accepted the study and, with very few exceptions, completed the form accurately and in a timely manner.

This cooperation reflects the strength of employee empowerment because the nursing staff assisted with the system implementation. The project manager reviewed the input daily and followed up quickly to correct any data collection problems. Currently this system is automated with touch-screen data entry at the locations and automatic download to the database.

The staff became very proficient at completing the form, and the project team members monitored the process. They were very pleased with the data integrity. Table 1 shows a daily summary of the data. Panel A shows the distribution of nursing care by types of activities. The unit in this case is the floor and wing of the hospital (2N-2nd floor North Wing). Panel B shows the distribution of nursing by diagnosis (illness for which the patient was admitted to the hospital). Panels C and D organize the data around the hospital unit.

Table 2 shows an individual patient classification summary of the data over a 44-day period. Using a database system, the team was able to organize the fields of data in an appropriate configuration. Mary-Jean immediately saw how she could use this information for nurse staffing and operational planning. Team members were pleased with the process insight provided by the amassed data, but they were not clear how to use the information in the managed care environment. The missing element was the assignment of the percentage of nursing time used for each skill level.

FIGURE 1. SERVICE CLASSIFICATION FORM

PRIMARY DIAGNOSIS _____ CLASSIFIER'S NAME _____ DATE _____	ADDRESSOGRAPH

PILOT CLASSIFICATION TOOL   DRAFT 3

In each of the following sections, place a check mark in the most appropriate box corresponding to the most complex level of case documented in the past 24 hours.

FEEDING
A1 ☐ Setup
A2 ☐ Enteral Feed
A3 ☐ Distant Supervision
A4 ☐ 1:1 Supervision
A5 ☐ Dependent P.O. Feed

MOBILITY
B1 ☐ Contact Guard, Walker
Independent, Stand Pivot Min-Mod
of 1, Sliding Board Independent or
Assist Min-Mod of 1
B2 ☐ Hoyer Lift/Transiad
B3 ☐ Max of 1, Mod-Max of 2, Stand
Pivot, Squat, Sliding Board Max 1

ADL
C1 ☐ Setup or Min Assist
C2 ☐ Min-Mod Assist
C3 ☐ Mod Assist
C4 ☐ Mod-Max Assist
C5 ☐ Total Dependence
C6 ☐ Dependent Shave
C7 ☐ Dependent Bed Shampoo

MEDICAL
D1 ☐ Routine Medical Supervision
D2 ☐ VS Q VShift
D3 ☐ Assist with M.D. Procedure
D4 ☐ # of Procedures Performed in 24 Hours
D5 ☐ Frequent Vital Signs
(Q 1-2 hrs over 24 hrs)
D6 ☐ Precautions, Respiratory
D7 ☐ Precautions, Wound/Skin, Enteric

MEDICATIONS
E1 ☐ Routine Meds, P.O.
E2 ☐ Meds IM, SC
E3 ☐ Meds PR, Enteral, or Topical
E4 ☐ Meds PRN (any route)
E5 ☐ Receiving Meds and/or Hydration IV

ELIMINATION
F1 ☐ Continent Bowel/Bladder
or Continent of Bowel with
Foley Catheter
F2 ☐ Incontinent Bowel and/or Bladder
F3 ☐ Assist-Dependent Ostomy Care
F4 ☐ Texas Cath
F5 ☐ Straight Cath

ELIMINATION
G1 ☐ Teaching, Psych/Soc Support, Safety Interventions
(Non-Aggitated Patient)
G2 ☐ Q 15 Minute Safety Checks
by M.D. Order
G3 ☐ 1:1 Observation
G4 ☐ # Shifts
G5 ☐ Skill (RN, LPN, RT, NA)
G6 ☐ Frequent Aggressive or
Aggitated Behavior Requiring
Intervantion of Only 1 Staff Member
G7 ☐ Frequent Aggressive or Aggitated
Behavior Requiring Intervention
More Than 1 Staff Member

SKIN CARE
H1 ☐ Routine Skin Care, Includes
Topical Treatments
H2 ☐ Wound Care
H3 ☐ # Treatments in 24 Hrs.
H4 ☐ Central Line

RESPIRATORY
I1 ☐ Routine TCDB, O2 Equipment
I2 ☐ Routine Tracheostomy Care
(include up to one additional
suctioning per shift)
I3 ☐ Requires Suctioning Two or
More Times Per Shift
I4 ☐ Manage Meds by Nebulizer
Incentive Spirometry,
Humidification

TABLE 1. PATIENT CLASSIFICATION SUMMARY (PANELS A AND B)

PANEL A UNIT	CENSUS	NUTR	MOBIL	ADL	MEDICAL	MEDS	ELIM	SAFETY	SKIN	RESP	INDIR	OTHER	HOURS	AVERAGE
					DISTRIBUTION OF CARE ACTIVITIES				CLASSIFICATION DATE				11/05/92	
2N	41	7.0%	8.0%	10.0%	1.0%	5.0%	10.0%	5.0%	3.0%	0.0%	45.0%	5.21%	208.4	5.1
2S	30	11.0%	10.0%	13.0%	1.0%	5.0%	9.0%	4.0%	1.0%	1.0%	40.0%	5.21%	170.4	5.7
3N	40	6.0%	7.0%	10.0%	1.0%	5.0%	8.0%	6.0%	1.0%	0.0%	49.0%	5.21%	187.9	4.7
3S	41	5.0%	5.0%	12.0%	3.0%	5.0%	6.0%	5.0%	2.0%	1.0%	49.0%	5.21%	191.0	4.7
	152	7.2%	7.5%	11.2%	1.7%	5.1%	8.2%	5.3%	2.0%	0.4%	46.1%	5.2%	757.7	5.0

PANEL B CASE MIX	DX	CENSUS	NUTR	MOBIL	ADL	MEDICAL	MEDS	ELIM	SAFETY	SKIN	RESP	INDIR	OTHER	HOURS	AVERAGE
				BY DIAGNOSIS											
32%	1	49	25.1	23.8	30.8	2.6	12.3	23.4	12.3	3.4	0.0	112.7	13.5	259.9	5.3
16%	6	24	3.1	8.3	11.0	1.2	6.0	10.4	6.0	2.9	0.0	55.2	5.7	109.9	4.6
15%	12	23	6.7	6.8	12.6	4.6	5.8	7.8	7.8	3.3	1.5	52.9	6.0	115.7	5.0
11%	8	17	0.9	3.7	7.4	0.9	4.3	3.4	4.3	1.8	0.0	39.1	3.6	69.1	4.1
9%	7	13	9.8	6.3	9.0	0.8	4.0	6.6	3.3	0.9	1.5	29.9	4.0	75.9	5.8
7%	9	11	3.9	3.2	5.3	0.6	2.8	3.8	2.8	0.7	0.0	25.3	2.6	50.8	4.6
4%	4	6	0.3	1.8	2.7	0.3	1.5	2.0	1.5	1.4	0.0	13.8	1.4	26.7	4.4
3%	11	5	3.0	2.5	3.4	1.7	1.3	3.4	1.3	0.8	0.0	11.5	1.6	30.3	6.1
1%	5	2	0.1	0.3	0.8	0.1	0.5	0.4	0.5	0.0	0.0	4.6	0.4	7.8	3.9
1%	2	2	1.8	0.3	1.8	0.1	0.5	1.2	0.5	0.3	0.0	4.6	0.6	11.7	5.8
0%														0.0	0.0
		152												0.0	0.0

TABLE 1. PATIENT CLASSIFICATION SUMMARY (PANEL C)

UNIT	CLASSIFIED HOURS		HOURS WORKED	PRODUCTIVITY CLASSIFIED HAVE	APPROPRIATE STAFFING HAVE CLASSIFIED
2N	208.398		186	112%	89%
	93.779	DAY	85.225	110%	91%
	73.9812	EVE	62	119%	84%
	40.6375	NOC	38.75	105%	95%
2S	170.418		186	92%	109%
	76.688	DAY	77.5	99%	101%
	60.4983	EVE	62	96%	102%
	33.2314	NOC	46.5	71%	140%
3N	187.931		201.5	93%	107%
	84.5688	DAY	85.25	99%	101%
	66.7154	EVE	69.75	98%	105%
	36.6465	NOC	46.5	79%	127%
3S	190.955		178.25	107%	93%
	85.9298	DAY	77.5	111%	90%
	67.789	EVE	69.75	97%	103%
	37.2362	NOC	31	120%	83%
TOTAL	757.701		751.75	101%	99%
	340.965	DAY	325.5	105%	95%
	268.984	EVE	263.5	102%	98%
	147.752	NOC	162.75	91%	110%

WORKLOAD DISTRIBUTION

DAY	45.0%	EVE	35.5%	NOC	19.5%

TABLE 1. PATIENT CLASSIFICATION SUMMARY (PANEL D)

Panel D UNIT	Dx 1	Dx 2	Dx 3	Dx 4	Dx 5	Dx 6	Dx 7	Dx 8	Dx 9	Dx 10	Dx 11	Dx 12
				DIAGNOSTIC DISTRIBUTION BY UNIT								
CENSUS	49	2	0	6	2	24	13	17	11	0	5	23
2N	31%	0%	0%	100%	50%	25%	0%	24%	9%	0%	0%	35%
2S	31%	0%	0%	0%	0%	0%	100%	0%	9%	0%	20%	0%
3N	18%	0%	0%	0%	0%	38%	0%	41%	36%	0%	20%	43%
3S	20%	100%	0%	0%	50%s	38%	0%	35%	45%	0%	60%	22%

TABLE 2. PATIENT CLASSIFICATION SUMMARY

Sample patient listing of a single patient throughout hospitalization

CLASSIFIER	DENUM, M	LAURENCE, J	DENUM, M	BRODERICK, K	GILMORE, J
PATIENT			MYPATHY		
REC#			092131		
UNIT			2S		
ROOM#			217A		
SEX			M		
DATE	12/29/92	01/13/93	01/29/93	02/10/93	02/22/93
ADM	12/24/92	12/24/92	12/24/92	12/24/92	12/24/92
NUTR	1.70	0.33	0.05	0.33	0.05
MOBIL	1.00	0.17	0.17	0.17	0.17
ADL	0.72	0.58	0.72	0.58	0.42
MEDICAL	0.05	0.05	0.05	0.05	0.05
MEDS	0.25	0.25	0.25	0.25	0.25
ELIM	1.00	1.00	1.00	1.00	0.20
SAFETY	0.25	0.25	0.25	0.25	0.25
SKIN	0.02	0.02	0.22	0.02	0.02
RESP	0.00	0.00	0.00	0.00	0.00
INDIR	2.30	2.30	2.30	2.30	2.30
OTHER	0.40	0.27	0.28	0.27	0.20
UNIT	2S	2S	2S	2S	2S
DX	1	1	1	1	1
HOURS	7.68	5.22	5.28	5.22	3.90
DAY	5	21	36	48	60
RN	2.54	2.18	2.32	2.18	1.79
LPN	1.68	1.13	1.19	1.13	0.82
NA RT	3.47	1.91	1.77	1.91	1.30

MODEL OF ACTIVITIES

The pilot team met with a consultant, who explained how to assign the skill mix information by activity. The consultant, using activity-based costing principles, revealed to team members how they had captured the nursing resources consumed by the various patients' diagnosis.

A further analysis of these data also demonstrated that the nursing resource consumption changed with the length of stay of the patient. Most patients have a large consumption of nursing services during the initial period of their stay, and, over time, the consumption declines. Thus, the consumption of nursing services is a function of both the mix of patient diagnosis and the length of hospital stay.

The team reviewed each activity and assigned a percentage of time spent for each skill level of nursing (RN, LPN, and NA). In this manner, a matrix was built where all the activities performed by the various skill levels were determined for each category of patient illness. This relationship was tracked over the length of hospital stay by patient category.

The data were reconfigured to provide the nursing skill level needed to deliver care (based on their activities) for each type of patient. In addition, the total amount of the time each skill level spent in each activity was readily available. The team now had a model of the activities consumed by each patient by classification based on the patient's use of all skill levels as well as the amount of nursing services. The team had developed the nursing resource consumption model for the hospital.

For example, a patient entered the hospital on 12/24 with a traumatic head injury and was released on 2/22 for a total stay of 60 days. As shown in Table 3, the total nonroutine nursing services used on 12/29 were 7.68 hours with RN 2.54 (33%), LPN 1.68 (22%), and NA 3.47 (45%) hours. On 2/22, 57 days later, the total nonroutine nursing is 3.90 hours, 50% less than the initial consumption. The distribution also has changed with RN 1.79 (45%), LPN .82 (21%), and NA 1.30 (34%). This trend over time and composition mix change has economic and staffing implications for the hospital.

As demonstrated, nursing costs by skill level were applied to the data, producing a predictable and reliable cost of nursing service by diagnosis over the length of the patient stay model. This information is invaluable when the hospital contracts with the insurance companies for a fixed daily hospital fee for specific rehabilitation diagnosis.

TABLE 3. PATIENT CARE SUMMARY

MYPATHY	12/29	5	7.68	33%	22%	45%
	1/14	21	5.22	42%	22%	36%
	1/29	36	5.28	44%	22%	34%
	2/10	48	5.22	42%	22%	36%
	2/22	60	3.9	45%	21%	34%

IT WORKS

The system unbundled a previously fixed cost allocation for nursing. The consumption of nursing services based on patient diagnosis and length of stay, coupled with the other cost elements of a hospital stay, enabled the hospital to contract knowledgeably with the third-party payers. Prior to this information, the hospital cost management called for full bed occupancy and hoped for the right mix of patients to allow the hospital to cover its costs. Or, it operated with a more costly, inefficient mix. The new system produced the costs for those nursing services actually used by the patient. This information changes the management economic focus from filling all beds to looking at the nursing skill level and seeking those patients who have a consumption level compatible with the available nursing services. Or, adjust the nursing mix for the forecasted consumption level.

The team was elated with the model and its potential use. To confirm the model's accuracy, extensive validity and reliability tests were performed. These tests showed a 99% accuracy as correlated to actual staffing patterns and standards of practice as established by the nursing department. The model works!

At present the hospital uses these data to structure its contract negotiations with insurance carriers and for management decisions concerning nursing work flow trends and stalling. Mary-Jean Crockett uses the database to aid in the management of the delivery and quality of nursing services. She points out that "the purpose of our patient classification system is to provide quality nursing care by providing a sufficient number and skill mix of staff necessary to do so, based upon actual patient care requirements." She can match the necessary total staff by skill mix with the actual staff by skill mix and make the necessary adjustments to ensure both quality of care and cost effectiveness.

The new data permit the hospital to unbundle the previously fixed single nursing services charge. The effect on patient mix and length of stay by diagnosis on the economic structure of the hospital becomes apparent. In an environment of reduced third-party payments and increased competition, the hospital can use this new information. Jeffrey Goode, vice president-finance, said, "Rates are negotiable depending on circumstance. The third-party payers are very sophisticated today. I use the new information to help negotiate per diem rates with the insurance companies. Rate negotiation is one of the keys to our success. Having this information is critical in today's health care environment."

Financially, the hospital matches the daily revenues with the daily expenses to arrive at a hospital profit. Normally the daily patient stay is 40% of the revenue, with inpatient ancillary services representing 60% of the daily revenue. Wherever possible, ancillary services such as physical therapy, medication, and so on are billed directly. The costs of the ancillary services are captured directly, while the costs of a patient's daily stay are rolled into the fixed daily charge. Nursing services costs are approximately 50% of the total fixed daily charge. With the new activity-based system, 50% of the fixed patient overhead—nursing services—can be allocated based on the direct consumption by the patient.

Armed with this new information, financial forecasting is more reliable. The patient load and mix projections can be translated into a cost behavior model based on resource consumption. More important, the hospital armed with new cost data can negotiate rates and fees more intelligently with the third-party payers.

KEY SUCCESS FACTORS

The ability to understand the nursing services delivery process and to unbundle the nursing tasks was critical to the success of the project. The project team members were nurses with many years of practice. Even the designer and manager of the database was an RN. The project leader, Mary-Jean, understood the balance of delivering quality nursing care in the changing economic structure of our health care delivery system. She was determined to maintain and value appropriately the quality and caring of nursing services.

The hospital senior management fully supported the project. Team members worked well together and they communicated their progress and findings regularly. The output was nonthreatening. The nursing staff viewed this information as an enabler, which permitted better staffing.

The enthusiasm and seriousness of the team sent a clear and positive message to the hospital staff. The data collection was made simple and easy, first the paper form and later the electronic form. It was part of the nursing delivery process. The Braintree nurses shared Mary-Jean's concerns and knew that the data somehow would benefit them and make their job better understood. The high validity of the pilot test was very convincing.

The accounting and finance departments became involved after the consultant showed the team how to add cost data to the operational data. They saw which operational factors drove the costs and arrived at an activity-based costing and management system. This linkage is invaluable for doing business and managing in the new managed care economic health care environment.

HEALTH RESULTS

The success at Braintree Hospital was communicated to the 32 other rehabilitation facilities throughout the parent company. The model has been replicated successfully at many of the network facilities. In fact, the parent company's Big 6 auditing and consulting firm has incorporated the model into the financial program of all of company facilities. Now the activity-based cost model is a key part of the entire company's cost accounting system.

Using basic process analysis and sensible data collection, they developed an activity-based cost management system (ABC-MS). It provided valuable operational information for managing nursing services delivery and the cost consumption data to meet the changing health care reimbursement practices. This information changed the way Braintree Hospital conducts business. By understanding the delivery process, the hospital is compensated for the actual services delivered, and the third-party payers have a feeling of equity. The ideal health care system is where we pay for what we use and we use only what we need. The activity-based cost management system moves us toward this goal.

Lawrence P. Carr, Ph.D., is the Trivisonno term chair and assistant professor, Babson College. He can be reached at (617) 239–5138.

Note:
This work was made possible by the openness and cooperation of the Braintree Hospital staff. A special thanks is extended to the members of the CMS project team (M. DiBlasi, P. Flaherty and K. Sampson) and Mary-Jean Crockett, vice president of nursing.

QUESTION

4.4   In Lawrence Carr's article on the cost of healthcare, the consumption of nursing services is a function of what factors? Did the system work?

4.5 ABC Trends in the Banking Sector–A Practitioner's Perspective

*by Mitchell Max, Managing Partner, The Performax Group**

Ten years ago, in *The Information Executives Truly Need*, Peter Drucker observed that service industries - including banks - "have practically no cost information at all[1]". Today, not only has Activity-Based Costing (ABC) become common in the financial services arena, but it is in the midst of an unprecedented resurgence as organizations move quickly to replace, revise or extend their ABC systems and processes. Organizations that have avoided ABC due to perceptions of it being too complex or not producing enough value relative to initial and ongoing effort are now embracing ABC as a new weapon in their arsenals. Individuals with skills in this area are in high demand. Technology developments and investments are stronger than ever, as the tools have caught up with the aspirations of leaders in the field, enabling them to operate in new ways. What is driving this change? Is this truly an evolution or merely a fad which will pass?

From a practioner's perspective, this change is being driven by a number of critical business needs which are outlined in this paper. Today's implementers are leveraging advanced technologies and approaches in new ways to deliver sustained value for their organizations through Activity-Based Costing information. This paper seeks to present the reader with a compelling justification for advancing their ABC initiatives, and an understanding of how the new technologies and approaches can be effectively leveraged. It draws on direct experience and interaction with organizations that are raising the bar for value from their ABC investments and looks to measure the progress we have made over the past decade, along with some thoughts for the future.

THE NEED FOR ABC INFORMATION
Drucker noted that "Enterprises are paid to create wealth, not control costs.... They have to be managed for ... wealth creation. To do that requires information that enables executives to make informed judgments.[2]" Today's CFO's are responding to an unprecedented need for improved, sustained bank performance to meet growing stakeholder expectations. Sophisticated banks - and their stakeholders - realize that improved performance cannot come from cost-cutting alone. Comprehensive performance management approaches, systematic management of central costs, razor-sharp pricing and customer profitability information are emerging by enlightened banks as the keys to their profitable future.

The demand for actionable, accurate and transparent cost and profitability information is growing. Bank mergers have promised significant savings, but obvious resource duplication is only one source of cost reduction, and scale efficiencies have not materialized to the extent promised. Technology innovation has also been slow to dramatically drive down operating costs. As a result, banks are looking for more comprehensive and deep understanding of cost information as they strive to meet stakeholder expectations.

Banks have traditionally used average costs as part of their profitability analysis. For those banks that do use ABC, it often takes the form of standard unit costs, with some transactional differentiation - for example, using different costs for assisted vs. self-service transactions - applied to channel-specific transaction volumes. While providing directionally correct information at a high

* From: M. Max, "ABC Trends in the Banking Sector – A Practitioner's Perspective," *Journal of Performance Management* (2004): 23–40. Reprinted with permission of the Association for Management Information in Financial Services (AMIfs), www.amifs.org.

level, accurate costing often remains elusive to these banks, particularly when viewed at the detailed level.

As differentiation of service increases in financial institutions, it drives multiple levels of complexity. In turn, complexity drives highly different levels of cost consumption, for example:

- Product customization, which often requires special back-office processing
- Special compliance functions/procedures
- Manual reporting/government filings
- Significant effort to explain product features to clients
- High error rates triggering significant levels of manual adjustments
- Degree of online self-service capability
- Product complexity driving level of sales/advisory effort
- Electronic versus manual transactions
- Straight-through vs. manual processing

Studies have shown unit cost factors, due to differing demand intensity impacting consumption, to be in some cases 5 or 10 times higher or lower than the "average". As a result, *average costs have never been more inappropriate!* In fact, the level of cost differentiation has become so significant that even business unit executives are rejecting the use of average costs as a basis for decision-making. Only when costs are based on actual consumption, and demonstrated in a transparent fashion, will they be truly accepted by all parts of the business. In fact, when presented in a transparent way, cost information forms a powerful tool in dialog with customers.

NEW APPLICATIONS FOR ABC
Today's banks are identifying new and unique ways to leverage cost and profitability information, including:
- Activity-Based Pricing, particularly for Business-to-Business services;
- Linking ABC information into Performance Management scorecards and processes;
- Providing information on a process view of costs, both to support cost improvement needs and to enable ongoing accountability for management by business process; and
- Information on the profitability of discrete customer relationships.

ACTIVITY-BASED PRICING
Financial services organizations are recognizing that significant value can be derived from pricing which leverages ABC information. In situations where pricing is determined solely by reference to the market, organizations can do little but select and nurture customer relationships with high yields and lower cost to serve. There are many situations however, where pricing can

and must be based on an understanding of the cost to serve for each product and customer. In particular, business-to-business services have significant potential for profit optimization when the cost to serve can be transparently calculated, and in many cases discussed with clients during price negotiation. As a result, there is great demand for accurate, transparent and reliable cost information by the customer-facing sides of the business.

In one case, a transaction processing outsourcer has been highly successful in using this information to target specific clients and, through training of its sales force has begun to improve the profitability of client relationships. Previously, discussions could only refer refer subjectively to the level of complexity of their interactions. With new information, specific measures of transaction intensity can be described with clients, and additional opportunities to capture pricing for special "value-added" services become more evident.

INTEGRATING ABC AND PERFORMANCE MANAGEMENT
In their initial work with ABC, most banks focused their implementations narrowly, developing isolated unit costs, product cost data and departmental cost studies, with a focus on understanding specific unit costs - generally focused on product and organizational profitability. Many of these studies were static, and quickly became outdated.

Increasingly, we are witnessing a need to develop more comprehensive cost and profitability information, looking for example at the cost of an entire business process which now encompasses multiple channels and organizational units. Further, organizations recognize the significant value that can be derived from weaving cost and profitability information into more comprehensive and integrated performance management applications across the organization. Cost data now forms an integral part of Balanced Scorecard applications, and internal performance benchmarks are used to identify opportunities for performance improvement. The need for external bench-marking is growing rapidly. Cost and profitability are now critical elements in assessing and managing the *ongoing* performance of branches, channels and customers.

As a result, banks are experiencing the need to develop linkages between ABC tools, data warehouses and Corporate Performance Management (CPM) platforms. IT groups are becoming more directly involved in ABC applications, as they begin to treat cost information as a corporate asset, and identify the way it is foundational to other information - such as CRM data or CPM applications. This technical data integration is expected to continue at an increasing pace as CPM rises in prominence due to a heightened focus by many of the technology analysts. New approaches to Performance Management, such as Beyond Budgeting[3], are reinforcing the need for the integration of these components by demonstrating the need for open and transparent information as the basis for relative performance management and interactive control processes.

THE NEW GOALPOST: TRUE CUSTOMER PROFITABILITY

Studies continue to show that banks that manage the profitability of customer relationships outperform banks managing without this data. Experience has demonstrated that non-profitability-based segmentation (e.g., based on revenue, balances or number of products) can produce behaviors that reward retention of high touch - and generally less profitable - customers. (One retail broker found that over 20% of their "high target" customers were in the lowest two profitability deciles.)

The sheer fact that *customers have multiple channel and process options* for sales and service interaction with banks, means that only by understanding and managing customer demand can cost and profitability be understood and managed. Best practice organizations explicitly measure and manage the true profitability of each customer relationship.

All banks recognize the criticality of customer profitability information. The information is increasingly used in developing and executing customer acquisition and retention strategies, with leading organizations incorporating this information into their customer relationship management (CRM) systems. As the more sophisticated banks divest themselves of low-profitability customers, other banks must be wary of accepting their "hand-me-down" accounts. Banks that market "free checking" models run the risk of being selected by the very low-profitability customers that have "terminated" relationships with other banks. Consequently, profitability analysis at the customer level is no longer optional.

Accurate analysis across multiple dimensions requires cost assignment down to the lowest cost object level-the account. The best way to understand costs across dimensions-including customer, product and channel dimensions-is to actually cost them out at the account level. Understanding that lowest level and then developing rollups of the information across all cost object dimensions results in truly accurate information that can be used across the organization. Traditional applications which cascade costs from one profitability dimension to another (organizational, product, channel, and customer) do not meet the test of accuracy.

Based on these observations, it is anticipated that:

■ *Large banks will continue to refine and extend their customer profitability platforms.* Many of the largest banks calculate standard unit costs for each channel-specific transaction type, and multiply those costs by transaction volumes to determine and store customer profitability information in massive data warehouses.

While these solutions continue to meet many of the profitability analysis needs within those large banks, such as supporting CRM solutions, they do not address operational cost management needs, or the cross functional process costing analysis requirements for these complex organizations. With new, more scalable costing technology offerings becoming available, larger organizations, with tens or hundreds of millions of customers, are looking towards newer solutions in meeting their costing needs. One major brokerage company, for example, recently converted their in-house ABC application to a commercial software product, enabling them to efficiently and effectively prepare and analyze the profitability of each of its 8 million customers on a monthly basis. By integrating their previously separate unit cost and profitability models, they are able to better use more discrete (and hence, more accurate) cost information and "Black Belts", who drive their teams towards more discrete and detailed measures of process performance. This forces a greater level of interest in true qualitative cost drivers (e.g., the level of training) and on process performance measures (e.g., error rates) which in some cases can force additional detail into ABC models. While this is not news to our manufacturing colleagues, this is a clear shift in emphasis as banks realize the degree to which some parts of their organizations resemble factory operations.

This trend creates a number of demands on costing systems and professionals:

■ *Greater need for process costing information and management.* Organizations need more detailed process costing information for management reporting. ABC models need to be able to report on costs both by department and process. As banks begin to appoint process owners, information on the cost of business processes is being increasingly demanded - in addition to traditional departmental cost data.

■ *Need for better, ongoing measures of performance.* When it comes to measuring performance, financial institutions need more granular, rigorous, accurate and timely information. A shift is on to better understand the factors of cost causation, including qualitative cost drivers and the management of demand intensity.

■ *Linkages from ABC foundations to other initiatives.* Scorecards, performance measurements, and other components of the CPM tool sets are linked to ABC and changes in costing- and are thus becoming more critical. Software vendors are becoming increasingly aware of the need to demonstrate integration amongst the various performance management tools.

MANAGING THE BANK AS AN ECONOMIC UNIT

Financial services organizations are clearly becoming more sophisticated about how they manage costs. As banks expand and enhance their costing capabilities, we are witnessing a return to the use of *Activity-Based Management* as a key weapon in the war on costs. Over their history, banks have inadvertently made ABM more difficult to implement, by breaking up their operations into discrete organizational units in the drive for consolidation and efficiency. This has made it difficult to manage activities as an entire process. For example, customer transactions are handled in one area, branch back-offices are often consolidated in a geographic area, major processing is handled in a central unit or outsourced. Understanding and managing total economic costs through process "swim lanes" has become a major undertaking.

Banks are beginning to apply process management techniques. More recently, as they seek innovative ways to reduce costs, banks have begun to organize around processes and look at costs from a customer perspective, including recognition that costs will cross multiple sales and delivery channels. Early analysis here often focuses on the total cost of a process (i.e. mortgage origination cost). Since most banks continue to organize and operate in functional silos, ABM information is increasingly in demand, and ABC software is being utilized increasingly to tag activities by business process regardless of where it resides for organizational convenience.

At the same time, process improvement techniques are becoming more sophisticated, with an increasing prevalence of Six Sigma and other detailed process techniques. The Six Sigma approaches popularized by such companies as Motorola and GE are now being embraced by the financial services sector; back-office processing facilities are starting to introduce Lean Manufacturing techniques. At one large transaction processor, multi-disciplinary ABC project teams include "Black Belts", who drive their teams towards more discrete and concrete action and provide more transparent profitability measures to their business segments.

■ *Mid-size banks and non-retail lines of business in large banks also require scalable customer profitability platforms.* Mid-size banks and non-retail lines of business need access to comparable customer profitability tools scaled to support customer levels in the ten-million range. Newer ABC tools are making this possible.

■ *Need for effective integration of transactional information across the organization.* Pulling data into large data warehouses and understanding how to use and leverage it effectively will ultimately determine the success of the financial institution's customer profitability initiative. As organizations begin to collect and manage a variety of information at the customer level, there is an increasing need to optimize not only the physical storage of this but also the leveraging of this related data amongst all information consumers within the bank.

■ *An end to the separation of cost and profitability information at the customer level.* Increasingly, banks now look to solutions which combine unit cost and customer profitability, along with other profitability measures, in a single product or model. While this was previously not possible, advances in technology have begun to open this solution up to all but the largest banks. One regional bank has retained the use of its A/LM package for Funds Transfer Pricing at a customer level, and is linking it to customer-level cost data from a new ABC system.

■ *Strain between detail required for ABC and causal factors needed for reengineering and Six Sigma programs.* As financial institutions take more strategic approaches to building costing systems, they need to develop ABC information at a level of detail that will support the causal factor requirements of reengineering and Six Sigma programs. This granularity is much lower than that required for strategic (product, channel) cost analysis. Greater care and the use of professional judgment are needed in the development of cost models to meet these often-conflicting scenarios.

NEW CHALLENGES FOR ABC IMPLEMENTATIONS

The new needs presented above are matched with a new set of challenges facing ABC implementers.

While the need for this information is rising, the appetite for spending on ABC systems and supporting infrastructure is clearly waning as finance continually looks to optimize the value it provides to the bank. ABC groups are being constantly challenged to "do more with less":

■ *Need for regular updates and ongoing reporting is driving the need for lower total cost of ownership (TCO).* Early adopters of ABC were plagued by the size of the staff groups that were needed to maintain their systems; without large staff complements, ABC models quickly became outdated. It is not uncommon to find ABC teams with over 20 people, plus a dedicated systems group supporting them. As a result, frustration with the significant maintenance costs associated with ABC has become rampant. As ABC becomes more critical to success and corporations are increasingly in flux, organizations are focusing on how they can develop and maintain accurate costing systems while keeping down costs-particularly ongoing labor costs. Time-baseding down costs-particularly ongoing labor costs. Time-based cost models and strong data automation, discussed later in this paper, are supporting a renewed ABC approach with a lower ongoing cost of ownership.

- *Survey tools falling out of favor.* Surveys have traditionally been used to capture the assignment of resources to activities in ABC models. With variable staffing models on the rise, and the frequency of organizational change, survey information has become increasingly inaccurate and requires significant maintenance resources. Different approaches are needed.

- *Focus on data integrity for external and regular management reporting.* As line-of-business profitability and costing information increasingly finds its way into externally published reports, organizations will need to ensure that the information meets generally accepted accounting principles (GAAP) and regulatory requirements and complies with Sarbanes-Oxley legislation. Tying ABC information to authoritative and certified back-office systems is becoming a new theme in advanced applications. CFO's must demonstrate that the information presented in segmented reporting has the same integrity as that presented under the GAAP statements. The same standards apply to the use of ABC information in supporting decisions made by management or the board. ABC practitioners are now coming to realize that cost systems must be as complete and accurate as the information produced for external and other internal reporting, and that compliance will be fully required. Approximates or estimates are coming under greater scrutiny when used as the basis for cost allocation.

At the same time, changes in the structure of bank operations are presenting new challenges to ABC implements, both for initial design and also for ongoing application maintenance:

- *Use of non-banking concepts in cost modeling.* Banks combine both product "manufacturing" (marketing, operations) and "distribution" (sales and service channels). As they reorganize, banks have increasingly been working to separate these functions, and separate cost information is required to support the accountabilities that management is introducing. The traditional non-banking approach of separating product manufacturing from service fulfillment/delivery allows greater flexibility in costing than the single - model approach which has been historically employed. With separate accountabilities, the organization can discretely flow costs between different parts of the organization. For example, mortgage applications and mortgage processing on the product side would be kept separate from loan distribution. Standard costs at the transfer point can be used to measure the efficiency of each group

separately. This is a new approach to cost modeling which is being addressed. Traceback of costs through these separate models is a requirement of many new systems.

- *Shared Services are here to stay.* Banks are unique in the high levels of common cost base and infrastructure which is used to support its products and customers. When costs are fully allocated to branches, many banks find that the level of indirect costs is over 50% of total non-interest costs. To better measure and manage this high level of common costs, Shared Service approaches are becoming commonplace in banks. IT, HR, financial and customer service applications are being centralized and shared. Accountabilities are created for cost and profitability information at discrete levels in the organization. Best practice execution of shared services methodologies require cost allocation models tuned to the organization's culture - taking it out of the technical implementation approach and relying to a much greater extent on the use of Change Management specialists.

- *The need to reflect a systemic view of costs. A financial institution cannot manage technology without considering operations, and vice versa.* When examining the cost of processing a mortgage application, for example, a bank needs to consider both the technology and labor costs of the activity or process. If a bank wants to know how much it will cost to process an ATM deposit, it needs to look at the technology costs of running the machines, the costs of servicing the machines, and the costs of the courier systems and item processing areas that handle deposit slips. Interestingly, many banks have begun a move to combine organizational responsibility for technology and back-office operations. These new Chief Technology and Operations Officers need new information on the total cost of transaction or service handling if they are to make effective decisions. Costs must therefore flow together to support this ongoing analysis - for example, by helping to analyze the business case for a technology investment in terms of its ability to reduce manual effort - and to track the achievement of benefits post-implementation. This requires a more integrated approach to modeling than is done when the items are treated in distinct models silos.

- *Banks change fast-traditional costing systems can't keep up!* To a greater degree than ever before, change is the only constant.

As a result, banks are seeking ABC platforms that can meet a wide variety of needs - concurrently and over time. No one ABC approach or model design will fit all parts of an organization. The organization must find tools flexible enough to meet a variety of needs and evolve as those needs change. Limitations in software design are tolerated less than ever before, simply because the future is so unknown.

CHANGE MANAGEMENT IMPACTS
In addition to the systems changes that these needs and challenges drive, a number of organizational and "people" impacts are becoming prevalent:

- More widespread use and greater access to ABC models and information. ABC no longer lives predominantly in the realm of finance. Learning that usage and sponsorship are critical to driving value from ABC, Operations, Marketing, HR and IT departments-as well as various lines of business-are increasingly driving the application of ABC - with Finance in a supporting role.
- Need for broad change management and links to regular decision-making. Bringing ABC information more broadly into the organization shifts the focus from costing as an accounting science to costing as a management and behavioral science. ABC departments are beginning to re-tool, building competencies in training and change management to augment the purely technical modeling and analysis skills.
- Centers of excellence approach to ABC support. Centralized costing groups actively encourage the use of ABC information across the organization, changing the way that information is used and deployed. This reinforces the need for improved training, and also for leveraging technologies which support distributed cost modeling and analysis.

CLOSING THE GAP: NEW APPROACHES AND TECHNOLOGIES
ABC approaches and technologies are responding to the challenges presented above. While history doesn't always exactly repeat itself, some concepts do re-emerge when the time is right. Advances in ABC technologies have facilitated a return to original principles in costing in financial services.

Resurfacing of time-based approach. Over the past 10 years, ABC implementation approaches have shifted from the use of time-based standards to the use of periodic (or often continuous) survey tools. The high level of effort associated with maintaining survey information on resource consumption - which frequently changes - is often cited as a reason for abandonment of ABC initiatives. The tide has now turned: in recent implementations, we have begun to see engineering-style estimates for time standards-once the basis for leading banking applications - returning into vogue as part of the ABC lexicon. This approach is consistent with a more rigorous and scientific approach to the use of metrics in operations. In fact, a natural linkage exists between time-based analysis and

productivity standards in back-office operations (e.g., daily applications processed per FTE), which have become stronger as a result of centralization. This approach is only now feasible with the technological innovations that allow for time to be dynamically assigned based on transactional activity in operational areas.

Awareness and management of key capacity drivers. The use of time-based costing is also facilitating a renewed interest in the cost of capacity. More sophisticated than a simple fixed/variable cost analysis, our clients are increasingly looking to better measure and manage capacity, both in order to support more refined pricing, and to find ways to focus the organization on developing more flexible platforms. One major organization, for example, has begun to look at alternatives to internal technology capacity as a result of this newly focused attention, with the potential savings of millions of dollars annually. Similarly, significant capacity exists in fixed staffing models; organizations that are able to create flexible work environments can better respond to dynamically changing business volumes and price more aggressively in the market.

Flexible, less specialized business models require adaptive ABC approaches. In the recent past, organizations focused on fixed, specialized business models. As organizations look to better leverage their investment in human capital in a rapidly changing environment, there is a movement back towards flexibility - particularly with staffing models that must incorporate such trends as job sharing, flexible hours, cross training and seasonality. As staffing needs change daily or even hourly, fixed percentages are increasingly irrelevant in allocating resource costs.

Weights and estimates are arbitrary. ABC practitioners have long used weights and estimates as proxies for average complexity. However, each customer drives distinct consumption levels based on product/channel/service mix. Only systems and approaches based on actual behavior and costs derived from real transactions - using the actual sales or delivery usage by the customer - will give the most accurate, reliable and supportable cost and profitability information.

CONCLUSIONS
Clearly, ABC is becoming the sophisticated foundation for enterprise performance management in the financial services sector. The movement of ABC into the mainstream, the renewal of earlier costing ideas, the emergence of process management and new business models, the intensification of differentiation, and attainable customer profitability - all highlight a renewed need for accurate costing implementations.

We have come a long way from Drucker's original challenge. While it is difficult to predict the future, ABC software vendors and consultants report an increasing level of interest from banks in dramatically advancing their cost and performance management capabilities. As bank mergers continue, and stakeholders' performance expectations continue to rise, the demand for - and investment in - costing resources, processes and technologies will also be sustained.

Improved technologies and new financial leadership are critical in supporting this new evolution. Technology is delivering on the promise of ABC that practitioners have looked forward to for many years. However, technology alone can't completely fulfill ABC's potential. ABC thought leaders and practitioners must continue to use ABC-generated information to capture value that supports more investments in the technology.

The true value of ABC is limited only by the creativity of practitioners and the support of corporate leadership. Thankfully, more CFO's, COO's and CIO's now understand the value of this information. With their support, financial institutions can continue to invest in the technology and human resources that will lead to even more successful ABC initiatives, and ultimately, sustained performance improvement of their organizations.

ENDNOTES

1. Drucker, Peter F., *The Information Executives Truly Need*, Harvard Business Review, January-February 1995
2. Ibid
3. For more information, see Max Mitchell, "Budgeting Revisited: Cracks in the Foundation of Bank Performance Management", Journal of Bank Cost and Management Accounting, Vol. 15 No. 3; and also www.bbrt.org.

QUESTION

4.5   Discuss the challenges faced by banks as they implement activity based costing.

Chapter 5

Management Accounting Information for Activity and Process Decisions

The readings in this section all relate to various aspects of process and activity decisions. Another process that is critical for many firms is reducing costs without adversely affecting the mission and objectives of the organization. In *Effective Long-Term Cost Reduction: A Strategic Perspective* (Reading 5.1), authors Michael D. Shields and S. Mark Young caution against the most expedient, short-term, traditional method for reducing costs - firing employees. This traditional approach has a number of significant ramifications such as reducing employee morale and motivation and losing valuable work-related knowledge as each employee is fired. Both morale and motivation can decline as remaining employees experience greater stress given their greater work load and their constant worry that they will be next. In turn, coordination problems - such as production delays, missed schedules, and decreases in quality and delivery time, - can occur. Shields and Young argue for a much more strategic approach to cost reduction and develop a set of guidelines that firms can use to avoid the "slash and burn" traditional approach. These guidelines focus on reducing costs by improving organizational activities and processes and viewing employees as resources rather than as costs.

Reading 5.2, *GE Takes Six Sigma Beyond the Bottom Line*, by Gregory Lucier and Sridhar Seshadri, describes the evolution of the Six Sigma Program beginning in 1995. The program has been very successful at GE with enormous productivity and profitability gains. Achieving a Six Sigma level of quality means that a process produces only 3.4 defects out of a million opportunities. Since most organizations probably rate their current rate of quality between three and four sigma, achieving six sigma level is a major feat. The article describes how GE implemented the program and how they go about maintaining it through their Master Black Belt mentoring and training program.

Tom Lin's article, *Effective OEC Management Control at China Haier Group*, Reading 5.3, describes a Chinese company that implemented a very clear cultural change based on modern day operations and control principles. The company began as a refrigerator company but expanded into other electronic household items in the 1990s. Today Haier is considered one of the top world-wide brands. The company's cultural change strategy involved developing what they call OEC management. The "O" stands for *Overall*, the E for Everyone, Everything, and Everyday, and the C for Control and Clear. The article details how this management system was successfully implemented.

Readings
Chapter 5

5.1 Effective Long-Term Cost Reduction: A Strategic Perspective

by Michael D. Shields and S. Mark Young*

In the 1970's cost reduction programs relied on the traditional method of simply cutting costs by eliminating jobs and thus reducing payroll. A traditional cost reduction program is usually triggered by an immediate threat to the organization such as poor performance, loss of contracts, or price reductions. Traditional programs tend to be short term in nature and often are ineffective in developing long term sustained change.

While these programs do reduce costs in the short run the associated reduction in the value of human assets sets the stage for potential long-term failure. The five traditional cost reduction programs typically used are:

THE TECHNOLOGY APPROACH
This approach focuses on replacing direct labor with technology to increase operating efficiency and to reduce the influence of unions. This approach is usually adopted or intensified after performance measures indicate poor performance. This approach has not worked in many companies especially those in which labor cost is a small percentage of total product cost.

LEAN AND MEAN
The Lean and Mean approach uses a tough policy to reduce the number of employees. A common approach is to employ across-the-board cuts through layoffs and reductions in pay and benefits. Lean and mean is not effective in the long term, because it attempts to reduce costs by reducing workers, but it does not reduce the work that needs to be done to make and sell products.

OFFSHORE RETREAT
This approach relies on reducing costs by moving to locations such as Asia that offer the promise of lower labor costs. The success of this type of approach is often contingent upon how employees at home are treated and on the vagaries of exchange rates and currency fluctuations. Employee morale at home can be hurt if domestic or local employees are laid off when the firm moves jobs offshore.

MERGERS
Mergers purport to create economies of scale for the merging firms. The idea is to eliminate overlapping employees, products, plants and overhead. Problems arise, however, when the merging firms differ significantly on corporate culture, types of products and technologies. Those who remain in their jobs can suffer motivation and morale loss.

DIVERSIFICATION
Diversification into new industries is an approach that firms often used when they are searching for less expensive operating environments. If a firm expands beyond its core competency, however, it is likely to experience difficulties in developing and implementing new products, technologies, or distribution systems, with the result that costs are higher, rather than lower, than expected.

STRATEGIC COST REDUCTION
Strategic cost reduction as an alternative approach that focuses on a long term approach integrating competitive strategy, technological strategies, human resource strategies and organizational design considerations to provide a focused and coordinated basis for sustaining competitive advantage.

At the core of strategic cost reduction is the idea top management will be clearly involved in developing a sound and humane approach to cost cutting, that employees must be educated in being very cost conscious in the firm, and that employees are the ultimate source of competitive advantage. To this end, the organization must attempt to offer long-term employment to employees in order to gain their trust and support and to increase their motivation.

Organizations must attempt to develop these types of norms before engaging in cost reduction. Since the five approaches mentioned above have not been particularly successful to date, firms need to seriously consider the strategic cost reduction approach.

QUESTION

5.1   What are five of the most frequently used traditional cost reduction programs, and how effective is each one?

---

* This article has been summarized from the original article by Michael D. Shields and S. Mark Young, "Effective Long-Term Cost Reduction: A Strategic Perspective," *Journal of Cost Management* (Spring 1992): 16–30.

5.2 GE Takes Six Sigma Beyond the Bottom Line

Now that its own Six Sigma effort is so successful, GE Medical Systems is taking it to customers to help them improve their operations.

by Gregory T. Lucier and Sridhar Seshadri*

Imagine working for a company where every employee is required to go through two weeks of intensive training in statistical process control. Then at the end of this training, participants are required to demonstrate proficiency by completing two projects that directly improve either company or customer performance.

On top of that, the company's website provides 24/7 access to the tools and methodology required to support the quality improvement efforts of more than 300,000 employees worldwide. The site is constantly and consistently measuring and quantifying thousands upon thousands of active projects.

Has your satellite TV system somehow mingled the contents of the business channel with a late-night science fiction film? No. You're experiencing GE's Six Sigma quality program, one that has netted the corporation such amazing results that now GE's customers are clamoring for help.

GETTING STARTED

Roll back to 1981, when Jack Welch first took the helm at GE and began to transform (or reshape) the company from a $25 billion bureaucratic quagmire into a well-run and highly respected $100 billion giant. Welch understood the "command and control" management approach had run its course and spent the next 20 years resolutely pursuing other options, borrowing best practices, and implementing winning strategies.

Through the remainder of the '80s, GE employed corporate-wide streamlining to get the fat out of its organization while maintaining the muscle. In 1989, as the tumult began to settle, Welch realized the need to empower employees and give them a greater level of participation in the decision-making process. Despite a decade of change, the level of hierarchy and top-down communication had remained an impediment. To solve this, Welch launched an initiative known as Work-Out™, which is designed to facilitate focused decision making, resolve issues, and improve processes. A Work-Out session is generally led by those closest to a process or issue, with the goal toward finding workable solutions and developing action plans. Work-Out can be used to eliminate unnecessary steps and streamline tasks or to remove barriers between different departments or reporting levels. Built into this process are mechanisms for ensuring management buy-in and follow-through.

Some Work-Out session examples are:

- Improving back-office processing with new financial systems,
- Improving internal paperwork flow, and
- Streamlining approval processes.

By the mid-'90s it was time to shake things up again, this time with a focus on quality. Not because GE wasn't performing well, but because feedback from employees convinced the CEO that, despite top- and bottom-line growth, quality wasn't where it should be.

Welch decided Six Sigma was the way to go. He had learned about Six Sigma from Larry Bossidy, a former GE executive who left to take the helm at Allied Signal, a company then implementing the program. Bossidy introduced Welch to Mikel Harry of the Six Sigma Academy and to this breakthrough strategy for statistical process control. Jack Welch had always maintained that GE must look outside itself to identify and adopt best practices wherever they could be found. So in the spring of 1995, Welch asked Bossidy to share his unique Six Sigma philosophy with GE's executive council.

They were impressed. Welch set targets out past five years and proclaimed Six Sigma the largest, most significant initiative ever undertaken at GE. Since that proclamation, Six Sigma has been implemented aggressively and has become deeply ingrained in the corporation's culture. The company has deployed the methodology more extensively than any other to date, and maintaining its vitality continues to be a top priority. Throughout GE, there's a commonly echoed phrase…Six Sigma is "The Way We Work." Acquiring and using Six Sigma skills is considered a core competency for leadership roles, and each year new "stretch" goals and projects are established.

In terms of bottom-line impact, payback, ROI, benefit —whatever you want to call it—GE has achieved it. During the first five years of the program, the company increased annual productivity gains by over 266% and improved operating margins from 14.4% to 18.4% (see Figure 1). The bottom line was enhanced tremendously, and stockholders were rewarded handsomely and consistently.

Six Sigma wasn't invented by GE (Motorola initiated a version of Six Sigma in the later 1980s). But the results

* From: G.T. Lucierr and S. Seshadri, "GE Takes Six Sigma Beyond the Bottom Line," *Strategic Finance* (May 2001): 41–46. Reprinted with permission.

the corporation has achieved from its implementation have attracted attention from several fronts, especially a large segment of the international business community and GE's customers. In response, GE decided to offer customers high-level instruction in Six Sigma. For example, last year our group, GE Medical Systems, began taking Six Sigma to healthcare customers. That first effort resulted in over $94 million in benefits after touching only a fraction of the market. And as recognition grows, so will the numbers.

A CLOSER LOOK AT THE SIX SIGMA APPROACH

The name Six Sigma is derived from a statistical heritage and focus on measuring product or process defects. Sigma is the Greek letter assigned to represent standard deviation. Achieving a Six Sigma level of quality equates to nearly error-free performance—where a given process produces only 3.4 defects out of a million opportunities. Here are some perspectives on levels of Sigma:

SIGMA	DEFECTS PER MILLION OPPORTUNITIES
2	308,537
3	66,807
4	6,210
5	233
6	3.4

Most organizations would probably rate their current quality at between Three and Four Sigma. When Jack Welch challenged GE to become a Six Sigma organization in four years, he was in effect calling for a reduction in defect levels of 84% per year. At stake was an estimated $8–$10 billion in costs consumed by lower levels of quality.

While the measure of quality is the cornerstone of the Six Sigma approach, it's the methodology and tools driving process change that translate to the difference between a simple quality campaign slogan and a rigorous management philosophy based on science. At the heart of the Six Sigma approach is a method summarized by the acronym DMAIC (see Figure 2).

Define. The GE process starts here. Teams work to clearly define problems related to the business or critical to customer satisfaction. CTQ (Critical to Quality) factors essential for customer satisfaction are correlated with the overall business process at issue. Project charters are established, required resources are identified, and leadership approvals are obtained to maximize project outcomes.

In preparation for this phase, employee training includes a review of process mapping techniques and orientation to online tools available to support teams.

Measure. The next stage is to establish base-level measures of defects inherent in the existing process. Customer expectations are defined to determine "out of specification" conditions. Training for this phase consists of basic probability and statistics, statistical analysis software, and measurement analysis.

While this heavy bombardment of statistics causes many participants to run for cover, GE makes it easier for employees to learn. It partners experienced Six Sigma practitioners with employees going through the training for the first time, which helps beginners overcome the challenge of mastering the concepts. And the use of automated tools minimizes the time required for complex calculations.

FIGURE 1. GE'S RESULTS FROM SIX SIGMA

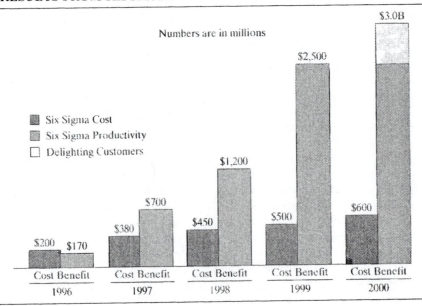

FIGURE 2. DMAIC

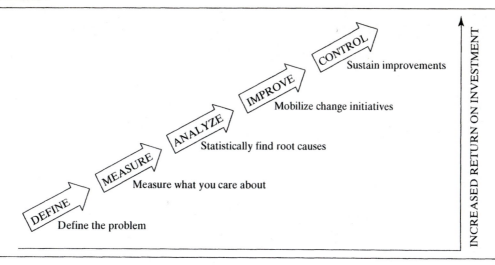

DEFINE — Define the problem

MEASURE — Measure what you care about

ANALYZE — Statistically find root causes

IMPROVE — Mobilize change initiatives

CONTROL — Sustain improvements

INCREASED RETURN ON INVESTMENT

Analyze. In this phase, teams explore underlying reasons for defects. They use statistical analysis to examine potential variables affecting the outcome and seek to identify the most significant root causes. Then they develop a prioritized list of factors influencing the desired outcome.

Tools used for this phase include multivariate analysis, test for normality, ANOVA, correlation, and regression. Again, these tools aren't for those who have difficulty balancing a checkbook, but most participants succeed with help from their mentors.

Improve. During this phase, teams seek the optimal solution and develop and test a plan of action for implementing and confirming the solution. The process is modified and the outcome measured to determine whether the revised method produces results within customer expectations.

Additional statistical methods covering design of experiments and multiple linear regression are reviewed with trainees to support the final analysis of the problem and to test the proposed solutions.

Control. To ensure changes stick, ongoing measures are implemented to keep the problem from recurring. Control charting techniques are used as the basis for developing the ongoing measures.

The concept of control—taking concrete steps to make sure improvements don't unravel over time—has been missing from other process improvement initiatives. It's this phase of Six Sigma that leads to long-term payoffs—both in quality and monetary terms.

IMPLEMENTING THE PROGRAM

Training for GE employees takes about 10 classroom days spread over four sessions and 90 calendar days. Action teams are created in each class to attack an existing business problem. As each aspect of Six Sigma is taught, the team immediately applies the concepts to the chosen problem.

The mentoring structure behind Six Sigma training and the full-time dedication of the Black Belts and Master Black Belts have provided the momentum necessary to complete thousands of projects at GE.

There's a progressions of competency levels beginning with Green Belts—and all employees from clerical staff up are required to reach this level of proficiency. Green Belts must complete the required training and two projects to achieve certification. They must also complete one additional project and eight hours of post-certification training each year. While Green Belts are trained in Six Sigma, they hold non-Six Sigma positions within the company. New employees are expected to obtain Green Belt certification within the first year of employment.

All other "Belts" are 100% Six Sigma assignments and are selected from the top performers in our talent pipeline:

- Black Belts act as technical and cultural change agents for quality. They are leaders of small teams implementing/executing the Six Sigma methodology in business-related projects, and they coach Green Belts on their projects. Today there are more than 4,500 Black Belts within GE.

- Master Black Belts teach, mentor, and develop Six Sigma tools and are full-time teachers of the Six Sigma process. Today there are over 800 Master Black Belts within GE.

- Champions back and promote the Six Sigma initiative and work with executives to help drive initiatives into daily operations and business metrics.

THE PAYBACK

To evaluate the payback of the significant commitment during the initial five-year implementation, we can look at individual projects and the cumulative results of thousands of projects.

One division recently reduced its annual expense for teleconferencing by $1.5 million encompassing a total of 19 million minutes. Another team customer order processing time in half. As a rule of thumb, GE managers expect that each project will save between $50,000 and $150,000.

TAKING SIX SIGMA TO CUSTOMERS
Once we had proof that the system really works, we decided to take Six Sigma beyond internal projects. Our group, GE Medical Systems, is offering its expertise to customers to enhance value and provide additional benefits.

The healthcare industry continues to experience monumental changes and tough challenges. Lower reimbursement, competition, and consolidation have transformed organizations from a 1980s' model—targeting quality at all costs—to today's approach where quality and efficiency must be the driving forces in the delivery of care.

In the 1990s, the industry saw a bevy of quality and reengineering consultants attempt to remedy the situation, but such efforts at cost cutting were quickly canceled by the need to rehire personnel. Old operational habits also died hard for a lack of sustainable change management that should have included—among other elements—skills transfer.

The healthcare industry has quickly responded to the promise of Six Sigma. As of December 2000, GE Medical Systems reported 1,149 active Six Sigma projects for customers. GE even created a service unit expressly dedicated to providing Six Sigma management tools and processes to healthcare organizations requesting more extensive assistance in improving performance.

Is it working? Yes. Commonwealth Health Corporation, a 478-bed medical center in Kentucky, began its journey to implement a Six Sigma improvement culture over three years ago. Results have been overwhelming as the medical center reports a reinvigorated and transformed management culture. Within a mere 18 months, errors in one ordering process were reduced over 90%, overall operating expenses had been reduced by $800,000, and employee survey results had improved by 20%. These results were from a single division within the organization. Now the medical center has realized improvements in excess of $1.5 million and is expanding the program to other areas.

One of the main reasons the program is working is because customers determine project scope, acquire on-site training and tools, and verify the benefits they have received. During last year alone, 466 customer projects were completed that resulted in $91.2 million in customer benefits. Because it relies on rigorous statistical methods and puts control mechanisms in place, Six, Sigma actually connects the dots among quality, cost, process, people, and accountability.

Some customers are using GE's Six Sigma program to achieve even higher measures of success. As part of their Star Initiative, a system-wide performance improvement effort, Virtua Health of Marlton, N.J., saw the Six Sigma program as an opportunity to vault their system to the next level of clinical quality, patient satisfaction, and financial performance. Walter Ettinger, M.D., executive vice president at Virtua, credits the partnership with GE and the use of the Six Sigma program as helping to make vital changes in the organization. "The Six Sigma program has provided everyone in the organization with a common language and toolbox for achieving our objectives. The methodology is sound, and we have begun to get buy-in from our medical staff, who are very results oriented and turned off by initiatives du jour. Our goal is to use Six Sigma to create an outstanding experience for our patients, which is the first priority of our Trustees."

VARIATIONS ON A THEME
There are a couple of variations to the DMAIC process we mentioned. One involves the opportunity to create a Six Sigma process where there are no existing processes in place. In this case, participants use a variation of DMAIC called Design for Six Sigma (DFSS).

Here's an example of an actual DFSS project that author Sridhar Seshadri completed in working toward his Green Belt certification. In this project, one of GE's businesses developed and implemented an entire business plan to provide professional services ranging from project management, systems integration, and consulting services regarding installation of complex medical imaging systems.

Prior to this project, GE typically installed such equipment with value-added services almost being an afterthought. The DFSS team—operating under the notion that the "whole solution" included hardware, software, and professional services—went through a formal DEFINE and MEASURE phase where customer requirements and analyses of the market were rigorously scrutinized.

The team then developed a business plan using a statistical modeling tool called Crystal Ball. The "stakeholders," including business leaders and other participants essential to making the project work, reviewed the business plan. Finally, the process was test-run at a few customer sites, then formalized and implemented.

So how is this different from a traditional rollout of a new project? First, DFSS applies a level of rigor not consistently seen in traditional business plans—consistent being the key word. Second, since Six Sigma is "institutionalized," everyone involved immediately understood the details of the project and could provide meaningful feedback and advice. Third, with project tracking the team was able to review similar projects across all of GE and learn from them. This set of services first implemented in the fall of 1999 is now routinely offered in over 90% of customer projects.

When talking about the payback associated with Six Sigma, think about popcorn. One kernel popping by itself (or one project completed) won't make much of a difference. But if you keep the heat on and thousands of kernels pop, you've multiplied the results exponentially. GE has kept the heat on now for five years, and the results are in. The following is a summary of some key performance measures at GE.

	SIX SIGMA BEGINS: 1995	FIVE YEARS LATER: 2000
Annual Productivity Gain	1.5%	4.0%
Operating Margin	14.4%	18.4%
Inventory Turns	5.8%	9.2%

By internal calculations, the benefits of Six Sigma exceeded $2 billion in 2000. Certainly a four-to-one payback in quality and the associated savings resulting from reduced cycle times and defects would interest many considering similar options for their organizations.

The lesson we learned at GE is that there is definitely a payback. Complete dedication to the program and enterprise-wide implementation is attainable and rewarding in terms of quality, productivity, and the bottom line.

Greg Lucier is president and CEO of GE Medical Systems Information Technologies. With more than 15 years of technology management experience, he joined GE in 1995 as a manager of business and general manager of GE Transportation Systems, GE-Harris Railway Electronics. In 1999 he became vice president and general manager of global services at GE Medical Systems. He was promoted to his current position in August 2000. You can reach Greg at Greg.Lucier@med.ge.com.

Sridhar Seshadri is vice president and general manager of Healthcare Solutions with GE Medical Information Systems Information Technologies. He has held this position since July 2000. Before joining GE Medical Systems in 1998 as business manager, IT Services, he served as lead engineer, imaging systems, with the University of Pennsylvania's Radiology Department and launched the Medical Informatics Group, responsible for developing Picture Archiving and Communication Systems. You can reach Sridhar at Sridhar.Seshadri@med.ge.com.

Both authors hold Green Belts.

QUESTIONS

5.2a Describe the levels of competency within the Six Sigma Program at GE.

5.2b What were the benefits to GE of implementing the Six Sigma Program?

5.3 Effective Oec Mamagement Control at China Haíer Group

The company has become successful through excellent customer service, product quality, operating efficiency, innovation, and speed to market.

by Thomas W. Lin, CMA*

In 1984, Zhang Ruimin took over a nearly bankrupt refrigerator factory in Qingdao, China. In 2003, the company's global sales hit $9.7 billion with a growth rate of 70% during the previous 19 years. Today, Haier Group is recognized as a worldwide brand. On January 31, 2004, the firm ranked 95th after such household names as Coca-Cola, McDonald's, and Nokia, which were the top three on the World Brand Laboratory's list of the 100 most recognizable brands. Haier was the only Chinese brand on the list.

So how did they achieve their success? As one of China's fastest-growing companies, Haier Group fits a 1999 Gallup survey profile for a successful company. Customer service, product quality, operating efficiency, innovation, and speed to market are among the top seven factors for success. Haier excels in all these areas.

To achieve success the company developed its corporate culture, business strategy, and OEC management-control system, which enforces firm work rules and discipline. Haier's Human Resource Management Director Wang Yingmin explains the OEC acronym: "O stands for Overall; E stands for Everyone, Everything, and Everyday; C stands for Control and Clear. OEC means that every employee has to accomplish the target work every day. The OEC management-control system aims at overall control of everything that every employee finishes on his or her job every day, with a 1% increase over what was done the previous day."

Why did Haier choose to implement the OEC system? According to CEO Zhang, "If you observe Chinese people's behaviors at the traffic lights, when the red light is on, people simply ignore it and cross the street anyway. At the workplace, Chinese people also tend to ignore rules and do not pay enough attention to details. We need a tough management system with fair rewards and penalty features to help our workers get things done properly."

* From: T. W. Lin, Effective OEC Management Control at China Haier Group," *Strategic Finance* (May 2005): 39–45. Reprinted with permission.

OEC works. When I visited Haier's air conditioner manufacturing facility in the Haier High Tech Industrial Park at Yellow Island in July 2004, the factory floors were clean, and workers, wearing uniforms with photo ID badges, operated in an orderly manner at the assembly lines. Banners featuring quotes such as "A Product with Defects Is Useless" and "Innovation Is the Soul of Haier Culture" line the factory walls. One large bulletin board says, "Every day is a new day; all activities are completed in the same day by innovations." The OEC management-control system implementation has resulted in satisfied customers, efficient and effective processes, motivated and prepared employees, sustainable revenue, and profit growth.

Let's look at how OEC helped turn the company into one of the world's top brands.

BUSINESS STRATEGY

Haier CEO Zhang Ruimin and President Yang Mianmian say the firm developed three major strategies over three stages: brand building or recognition strategy, expansion or diversification strategy, and globalization strategy (see Figure 1). Called the famous-brand strategy, the first stage lasted from 1984 to 1991. During this period, the company created and built Haier-brand products and set up a quality-assurance system. In April 1985, Zhang gathered all employees and battered the first poor-quality refrigerator with a hammer, and then the employees responsible for these goods battered 76 defective refrigerators. The event woke up the quality awareness of all employees and established the concepts of "defective products are wasters" and "excellent products are produced by talented employees." The thinking shifted from volume as the priority to quality and brand recognition being the priorities.

FIGURE 1: THREE STAGES OF STRATEGY DEVELOPMENT

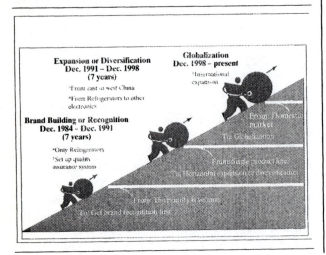

From 1991 to 1998, the second stage featured an expansion or diversification strategy within China. Since the firm bases itself on quality instead of quantity, it decided that if someone bought a Haier Group refrigerator, then maybe they would want to buy something else from the firm. The business was developed primarily through mergers and acquisitions to cover all kinds of household electrical appliances and electronic consumer goods instead of just one product. At this time it also focused on building great distribution channels all over China and improving product development speed and quality.

Since December 1998, the third stage has focused on the globalization strategy. Haier exported its products to Germany first, then to other European countries, the U.S., Southeast Asian countries, Middle Eastern countries, and India. In 2000, the firm opened a $35 million refrigerator factory in Camden, S.C., and started selling products through Wal-Mart and many other national and regional chains. In 2002, Haier opened its American headquarters in New York City.

The firm's international promotion framework encompasses global networks for design, production, distribution, and aftersales services. It established 18 design institutes, 10 industrial complexes, 22 overseas production factories, and 58,800 sales agents worldwide. Haier sells its products in 12 out of 15 European chain supermarkets and 10 of America's chain stores. And it has design, production, and sales facilities in the United States and some European countries with local employees primarily running them. None of the employees at its New York headquarters is Chinese.

Two other key business strategies at Haier relate to winning over consumers: speed and differentiation. Speed means to satisfy the consumer's needs as quickly as possible; differentiation means to introduce brand-new products or products with features to meet different needs. For example, the firm's U.S. president requested that the Haier headquarters design a new refrigerator that has pullout drawers in the freezer chest for the U.S. market, and in 17 hours a micro-freezer prototype was built. This really exemplifies the firm's speed strategy. Another example of the firm's differentiation in action: One employee discovered through visiting rural customers in the western part of China that they frequently used their washing machines not only to launder clothes but to also clean vegetables. Later, the firm marketed the machines as versatile enough to wash both clothing and vegetables for China's rural areas.

Haier differs from other appliance companies in that it will build products to order and it doesn't compete on price. Its philosophy is: "Customer is the king for every Haier salesperson." All employees learn that they have to give customers what they want. For example, if a customer buys a refrigerator, an employee goes to the customer's home to set it up for them.

HOW DOES OEC MANAGEMENT WORK AT HAIER?

For constant business growth, a company needs to continuously raise its goals and quality through innovation. That's where OEC comes in. Based on market competition, OEC management strives to continuously raise the firm's goals and improve management skills to achieve a sustainable competitive advantage. Every employee at Haier attends one month of corporate culture and OEC management training before being put to work.

Haier's OEC management-control system and enterprise culture have the following characteristics:

- Focus on and understand customer value, product quality, operating efficiency, innovation, and speed to market.
- Commit top management and leadership to creating a "new way of management" and a performance culture.
- Involve management and employees in creating the OEC management-control system. Allow them to become familiar with OEC so they feel included and share in ownership of the system.
- Educate management and employees. Use seminars and weekly company newsletters to explain the firm's strategy, customer value, OEC management, and the idea of every employee being a strategic business unit (SBU) to enable them to understand

the concept and appreciate the benefits. (SBU means that each employee is a profit center with the responsibility to make a profit. Each employee generates his or her revenue by providing the best service to the employee in the next step downstream and incurs expense or cost by receiving service from the employee in the previous step upstream and resources from various supporting departments.)

- Create desired incentives, and reassure employees that they will be properly evaluated in accordance with their performance.

The OEC management-control system has three subsystems: target setting; control, checking, and clearance; and incentive mechanism. Here's how these subsystems work.

TARGET SETTING

Every December, Haier headquarters sets the next year's guidelines and goals for each division by considering past performance, market demand forecast, group long-term goals, and each division's input on specific market-development needs (see Table 1).

Each division submits a divisional action program form with respect to its annual guidelines and goals. Also called the divisional management account, it includes specific annual goals, specific targets, and action programs, deadlines, responsible divisions, quality criteria, evaluation method, and frequency (see Table 2).

TABLE 1: DIVISION _____ FISCAL YEAR GUIDELINES AND GOALS

GUIDELINES	X-1 YEAR:		X YEAR:			X+1 YEAR:		
GOALS	**CONTRAST ITEMS**		**CURRENT LEVEL HOME AND ABROAD**		**FACTS OF ____ DIVISION**			
			LEVEL	HIGHEST LEVEL COMPANY	X-1 YEAR	X YEAR	INCREASED BY %	PLAN OF X+1 YEAR	INCREASED BY %
	Capacity	Output (00,000 units) Variety						
	Financial Performance	Sales ($000,000,000) Profit ($000,000,000)						
	Productivity	Productivity (Units per person, year)						
		Profit per person ($10,000 per person, year) Income per person						
	Management	Quality Institutional Reform Infrastructure Management						
	Market	New Products						
		Market Star Products						
		Products Cash Cow Products						
		Dog Products						
		Target Market						
		Market Position						
	Development	Science and Technology New Projects Fields or Business Lines						
Prepared by:		Verified by:			Approved by:			

3E Card Evaluation Criteria
(Note: U.S. $1 = 8.27 Yuans)

The 3E cards feature seven criteria items with 30 check-points. Employees complete a 3E card every day, which a supervisor then reviews. Beyond the seven criteria there are additional sections on the card relating to penalties and rewards as well as inspections. Here are examples from each of the seven OEC items.

PRODUCTION PLAN
If less-than-plan production occurs because of external factors, production plan should be achieved by nonpaid overtime.

QUALITY
Daily defective product costs should be fined according to the defective product prices announced by the Quality inspection department.

TECHNOLOGY LEVEL AND PRODUCTION DISCIPLINE
Employees who fail to follow the technical requirements in production should be fined ¥20.

EQUIPMENT
Employees who violate equipment operation procedures should be fined ¥50.

MATERIAL
Employees who produce defective products should be fined an amount of up to 10% of the material price.

LABOR DISCIPLINE
Employees who are late for work should be fined ¥2; those who leave early from work should be fined the daily wage.

PRODUCTION SAFETY
Employees who operate without knowledge of safety operation rules and procedures should be fined ¥10.

OTHER AWARDS AND PENALTIES
This section will handle actions not mentioned above.

ENDORSEMENT
Additional explanations from the operators or inspectors will be recorded in this section.

INSPECTION AND REVIEW
Inspectors (team chiefs) are required to schedule inspections of the 3E card and give comments on evaluation and endorsement results. Reviewers are required to schedule reviews of the 3E card and release a review opinion. Employees' wages will be determined according to review results.

TABLE 2: DIVISIONAL MANAGEMENT ACCOUNT

_____ Division _____ Fiscal Year

		GUIDELINES		
	ADVANCED GOALS			
(1) NUM-BER	(2) GOALS	(3) TARGET VALUES	(4) EXISTING PROBLEMS	(5) ACTION PROGRAMS
(1)	(2)	(3)	(4)	(a) Through the daily clearance control procedure, we should integrate daily clearance into worker's daily life to ensure goal realization: task assignment, daily worksheet, error correction, result review, and salary compensation.
5	Management	■ Reforms of daily clearance management to achieve group's A level.	■ Lower error-correction rate of daily clearance.	
			■ Problems in on-spot management and low standards.	(b) Achieve goals of: daily plan control; scheduled work achievement inspection timetable; error correction controlled by daily clearance; 100% item controlled rate; 100% "A level" goal attainment; larger than 95% "B level" goal attainment.
				(c) Use the industrial engineering method to streamline on-site management model.
		■ Raise team management skill level■Benchmark goals to achieve the competitive advantage.		(d) Cultivate, educate, and select future higher-level managers and executive elites.
				(e) Set up a bulletin board to announce monthly job rotation and promotion results.
				(f) Prepare a compensation reform plan to solve unfairness in compensation.
				(g) Strengthen factory safety system to ensure zero occurrence rates in major accidents and less than 0.3% minor accidents.
				(h) Train and establish six to eight honor teams.
				(i) Train and establish three self-management teams and 10 exam-waiver teams.

Note: This table skips 1 to 4 and shows only No. 5 as an example.

(6) PERIOD	(7) DEPARTMENTS RESPONSIBLE				⊗ RESPONSIBLE		* ASSISTANT		X SUPPORTING			(8) STANDARD	(9) VERIFICATION MATERIALS	(10) REVIEW METHODS
	HR	FRANCE	PLANNING	MATERIAL	QUALITY	EQUIPMENT	INSPECTION	AFTER SALE SERVICE	FACTORY I	FACTORY II	FACTORY III			
(a) Aug	⊗	*	*	*	*	*	*	*	*	*	*	New Standard Q19509 A	Mode Material Exam Sheet Evaluation Result	Monthly Review Monthly Report and Review
(b) All Year	*		⊗			*						:	:	Monthly Plan Review
(c) May					⊗				*	*	*	:	:	
(d) All Year	⊗					*						New Standard	Operation Evaluation Result	Quarterly Plan Review
(e) March	⊗											:	Announce Result	Monthly Review
(f) March	⊗					*						:	Evaluation Result	:
(g) All Year	⊗				*			*	*	*	*	954401-954405	Not Exceeding Standard; Announce Result	Daily Report, Monthly Review
(h) Sept.	⊗	×	×	×	*	×	×	*	*	*	*	:	Evaluation Result	Monthly Plan Review
(i) Oct.	*	*			*	⊗	*		*	*	*	929501-929504	Standard Attainment Result	Monthly Report and Review

Prepared by: Approved by:

A department management account is the same as the divisional action program. Before the 26th day of each month, every department head submits an OEC monthly control general ledger to his or her superior for approval. It includes a list of items, target value, last month's value, expected evaluation result, last month's error-correction numbers, this month's error-correction numbers, responsible persons, work hours, and daily clearance control evaluation summary.

Every employee also completes a daily activity control clearing account called an employee management account. It consists of task items, evaluation criteria (benchmark, past-period performance, and this-period goal), values, name of the responsible employee, daily actual results, evaluation results, actual compensation, and reviewer. To track performance, each job is assigned to a specific employee along with a clear delineation of the job's supervising manager, the responsible employee, the employee's partner, and the quality-check person. For example, each piece of glass in a particular building is associated with an employee who must take care of it.

CONTROL, CHECKING, AND CLEARANCE: THE OEC DAILY CLEARING ROUTINE

The second subsystem—control, checking, and clearance—includes the OEC daily clearing routine, which involves a nine-step list of procedures:

1. Each team supervisor gives a daily briefing to workers before they start their work.
2. Production workers conduct their activities by following the seven OEC criteria to check and control: production quantity, quality, material consumption, technology level, equipment maintenance and condition, production safety and workplace condition, and labor discipline. For other workers, the criteria consist of activity items and specific targets.
3. Supervisors conduct on-site inspection tours every two hours, detect and solve problems, and complete the production site OEC form with the seven OEC criteria items.
4. At the end of the day, all workers conduct a self-check of their own work with the OEC criteria, fill out their 3E (Everyone, Everything, and Everyday) cards with seven OEC criteria items, and submit them to their supervisors. The OEC evaluation criteria include 30 items (see "3E Card Evaluation Criteria" sidebar on p. 41 for examples as well as fines if employees don't uphold the criteria related to the seven OEC areas).
5. Each supervisor examines the 3E cards, corrects errors, gives a comprehensive evaluation, and submits the evaluation results to the work area manager. Evaluation results are graded as A, B, and C. If an employee achieves an A, ¥5 are added to that employee's daily compensation; if an employee receives a C, it's minus ¥5.

THE EMPLOYEES WHO ARE ACKNOWLEDGED AS THE BEST WORKERS FOR THREE CONSECUTIVE DAYS HAVE THE HONOR OF TELLING THEIR EXPERIENCES TO FELLOW WORKERS.

6. Each work area manager checks the sample 3E cards then fills out his or her own 3E card and submits it to the factory director.

7. Each factory director reviews the 3E cards and records the results in the factory OEC account. He or she then files a daily progress report to the Deputy Division General Manager regarding problems that have been solved, problems that haven't been solved, and suggested solutions to unsolved problems.

8. The Deputy Division General Manager reviews daily progress reports and suggested solutions and provides feedback before reporting to the Division General Manager.

9. If necessary, all production and supporting department heads get together to discuss and analyze problems found through the OEC process and work together to suggest corrections, improvement, and prevention that are needed.

INCENTIVE MECHANISM

Haier's third subsystem is the incentive mechanism, and its incentive policies are openness and fairness. The company adopts a point system for production workers using the 3E card, and if an employee earns more points, he or she makes a higher wage and bonus (this way, both management and employee know the daily wage and why).

The firm also uses quality-check coupons to provide an additional incentive mechanism. Each employee has a quality-check coupon booklet with red and yellow coupons for rewards and penalties. The booklet lists all quality problems the firm has detected and provides guidelines for checking each defect. If an employee failed to self-check a quality problem that was later found by his or her team member during a cross-check or by the superior during a managerial check, the employee will lose a red coupon and receive a yellow coupon that will be counted against that day's wage and bonus.

As further motivation, each employee receives a daily grade for actual performance and progress toward achieving his or her target. Daily evaluation results are shown to workers the next day on the bulletin boards in the factory. The employees who are acknowledged as the best workers for three consecutive days have the honor of telling their experiences to fellow workers. The employees who become the best workers most frequently in one month are considered the best workers of the month. They have more opportunities to attend job training and more social benefits, while employees who become the worst workers most frequently in one month are demoted to probation workers.

Finally, the firm has an open competitive bidding system for job placement. When there's a job opening within the group, employees who have reached the qualified skill level through internal training seminars or on-the-job training can bid for that job. Management then makes the final decision and selects the best candidate based on the submitted bids.

SUSTAINABILITY

From a nearly bankrupt company to a recognized worldwide brand, Haier has come a long way. Through making employees responsible for meeting OEC criteria, Haier will continue to excel and achieve its short-term goal of becoming one of the world's top three white-goods manufacturers. In this current competitive market economy, many companies have much to learn from Haier's culture and OEC management-control system.

Thomas W. Lin, CMA, Ph.D., is a professor of accounting and the Leventhal International Faculty Fellow in the Marshall School of Business at the University of Southern California in Los Angeles. You can reach him at (213) 740-4851 or wtlin@marshall.usc.edu.

The author acknowledges the financial support provided by the IMA Foundation for Applied Research and would like to thank Haier University President Zou Xiwen for providing the tables, which were originally in Chinese.

QUESTION

5.3 What are the five characteristics of Haier's OEC management control system and enterprise culture?

Chapter 6

Cost Information for Pricing and Product Planning

Reading 6.1, *How Manufacturers Price Products*, by Eunsup Shim and Ephraim Sudit presents the results of a survey on pricing practice. The authors report data from 141 surveys across major U.S. industries. Typically, the respondents were from top management such as CFOs, controllers and vice-presidents. Survey results show that full-cost pricing was the dominant pricing strategy (69.5%) with variable costing second (17.7%) and market-based costing third (12.1%). Further, for those companies using full cost pricing, 49 percent determine prices based on a percentage of manufacturing costs with 51 percent using a percentage of all costs. Forty-seven percent of companies using variable costing report using a percent of variable manufacturing costs to determine prices while 53 percent use a percentage of all variable costs. The authors suggest that the continued use of full-costing, consistent with another survey conducted in 1983, may be the result of companies adopting ABC. ABC enables companies to trace traditional fixed costs more directly to products.

Ronald Lewis' piece, *Activity-Based Costing for Marketing* (Reading 6.2), focuses on the problem of how to account for marketing costs, and in particular, distribution costs. Since marketing costs constitute more than 50% of the total costs in many product lines, not considering them appropriately can result in inaccurate product costing and pricing. Using data from the Atlanta Company, Lewis develops an activity-based costing approach to handling marketing costs. Cost drivers for activities such as selling, advertising, warehousing, packing and shipping, and general office are developed, and costs are assigned accordingly. Analyses can then be undertaken by product, sales territory and product line.

Reading 6.3 is Kenneth Manning's article *Distribution Channel Profitability*. Many companies still do not scrutinize their sales, general and administrative costs (SG&A) to the same extent that they do their manufacturing costs. Without such detailed scrutiny, revenue and cost trade-offs related to the various distribution channels through which companies deliver products cannot be made. This article discusses three approaches to distribution channel profitability - a standard approach, an ABC approach, and a strategic cost management approach. Manning develops a four-step process to developing accurate channel and customer costs, which is applied to two companies facing different competitive issues.

In Reading 6.4, *Smart Pricing*, Moritz Fleischmann, Joseph Hall and David Pyke, discuss new insights in the way that pricing decisions are linked to a company's operations. While Internet shopping has allowed companies to make price changes quickly based on different customer segment information (dynamic pricing), unintended consequences can arise. One of these consequences is that any pricing decision can have a large effect on operations. For instance, promotions, and their associated lower costs, can cause consumers to stockpile items and then slow down their purchases of these items. Such a strategy can cause inventory management problems for the selling company. The article discusses ways in which the process of dynamic pricing and its consequences can be better managed across an entire organization.

Readings
Chapter 6

6.1 How Manufacturers Price Products
Companies continue to practice full-cost pricing, but there is a shift toward target costing.

by Eunsup Shim, CMA, and Ephraim F. Sudit*

In 1983, V. Govindarajan and R. N. Anthony (G & A) surveyed Fortune 1,000 companies, finding that most large companies price their products based on full cost rather than variable cost.[1] Full-cost pricing is based on variable costs plus allocated fixed costs.

In 1993, Eunsup Shim conducted a similar survey of pricing practices in U.S. manufacturing companies.[2] These results are compared with the 1983 survey by G&A and are used to assess the relationship between ABC implementation by U.S. manufacturers and their pricing practices. In addition, the rationale for choosing certain product pricing methods is discussed.

Why are pricing practices important? In a new manufacturing environment, managers are faced with global competition and increased productivity. Companies have become customer driven, focusing on delivering quality products at competitive prices. In many areas of manufacturing, domestic and foreign competition demand well-defined pricing strategies. Comprehensive product-cost systems should provide increased accuracy for managerial decisions concerning new products, pricing, and discontinuing and/or reengineering existing products.[3] Some evidence suggests that the distortion in reported product costs and, in turn, product pricing could be reduced by using activity-based costing (ABC).[4]

The use of costing information for pricing decisions has generated considerable debate over the years among economists, accounting researchers, and practitioners. Economists argue that, in order to maximize profits, prices should be set at the level of production where marginal cost intersects marginal revenue. In other words, pricing is based on marginal cost and marginal revenue; fixed charges for associated services are not used. The "profit maximization model" advocates the use of variable-cost pricing.

G&A drew on Herbert Simon's "satisfying" model, which states that the primary objective for companies is to seek a satisfactory return, as opposed to the "profit maximization" model. The "satisfying" model leads companies to use full-cost pricing and provides a

possible rationale for the prevalent use of this method. Practitioners cite savings in gathering cost information as well as its simplicity.

1993 PRICING PRACTICES
In the Shim survey, data were gathered across U.S. industries garnering 141 usable responses, a response rate of 23.5%. The majority of the respondents (81.5%) were in top management including controllers, vice presidents, general managers, or chief financial officers. Most of the responding companies (91%) were in the multi-products environment, averaging 75 products. The reported high product diversification is a phenomenon consistent with companies being more flexible in response to the new manufacturing environment.

The survey showed that full-cost pricing dominated pricing practices (69.5%), with slightly more than 10% (12.1%) of the respondents using a variable cost method (see Table 1). Full-cost pricing determines the selling prices based on full cost plus a certain percentage of profit. The full-cost pricing method is further broken into "percentage of manufacturing costs" and "percentage of all costs." Of the 98 full-cost pricing companies, 48 (49%) are reported to determine the prices based on percentage of manufacturing costs, and 50 (51%) used percentage of all costs in deriving product prices.

Variable-cost pricing follows similar procedures in arriving at product prices except for the use of "percentage of *variable* manufacturing costs" and "percentage of *all variable* costs."

Full-cost pricing, the predominant method, is used especially in the chemicals (80%) and electronics (72%) industries (see Table 2A). The prevalence of full-cost pricing, which requires considerable overhead cost allocation, underscores the importance of rational cost allocation. ABC tends to offer a better allocation scheme with activity analysis.

The 1993 survey reported that almost 20% of the respondents' companies use market-based (competitive) pricing. This result seems to indicate a movement to market or "target cost" pricing from cost-based pricing.

* From E. Shim and E. F. Sudit, "How Manufacturers Price Products," *Management Accounting* (February 1995): 37–39. Reprinted with permission.

TABLE 1. COMPARISON OF PRODUCT PRICING METHODS

Pricing Method		Shim (1993) Frequency	Percent	G&A (1983) Frequency	Percent
Full-Cost Pricing	Percent of Manufacturing Costs	48	34.0	209	41.0
	Percent of All Costs	50	35.5	208	41.0
	Subtotal	50	59.5	417	82.0
Variable-Cost Pricing	Percent of Variable Manufacturing Costs	8	5.7	54	11.0
	Percent of All Variable Costs	9	6.4	30	6.0
	Subtotal	17	12.1	84	17.0
Market-based Pricing (Competitive Pricing)		25	17.7	Not Surveyed	Not Surveyed
Other		1	0.7	4	1.0
Total Respondents		141	100	505	100

TABLE 2. PRODUCT PRICING METHODS BY:

A/INDUSTRY	Full-Cost Pricing	Variable-Cost Pricing	Market-Based Pricing	Total (%)
Chemicals	4	0	1	5 (3%)
Machining	17	4	6	27 (19%)
Electronics	27	4	6	37 (26%)
Transportation	2	0	1	3 (2%)
Medical	34	7	9	50 (36%)
Others	14	2	3	19 (14%)
Total (%)	98 (70%)	17 (12%)	26 (18%)	141 (100%),

B/SIZE (ANNUAL SALES) OF COMPANY				
Under $10 Million	11	0	3	14 (10%)
$11–100 Million	59	11	19	89(63%)
$101–500 Million	25	6	4	35(25%)
$501 Million-1 Billion	1	0	0	1 (0.7%)
1–5 Billion	2	0	0	2(1.3%)
Total (%)	98(70%)	17(12%)	26(18%)	141 (100%)

C/ABC IMPLEMENTATION				
Fully or Partially Implemented	26	6	6	38 (26.9%)
Plan to Implement	33	7	13	53 (37.6%)
Not Plan to Implement	39	4	7	50 (35.5%)
Total (%)	98 (70%)	17(12%)	26 (18%)	141 (100%)

Target costing is the long-run cost that a customer will bear or a market-based cost that is calculated using a sales price necessary to capture a predetermined market share.[5]

Full-cost pricing is the most popular method in companies of all sizes. Of the 14 small companies (sales under $10 million), 11 use full-cost pricing. For mid-sized companies ($11 million-$500 million in sales) there was a higher incidence of variable-cost pricing and competitive pricing (Table 2B).

The relationship between pricing method and stages of ABC implementation is highlighted in Table 2C. Companies that do not plan to implement ABC show the highest use of full-cost pricing (78%). Companies that have implemented or plan to implement ABC systems exhibit a slightly higher percentage of variable-cost pricing or market-based pricing methods (32% and 39%) than companies that do not plan to implement ABC systems (22%). The majority of companies, however, adhere to full-cost pricing.

The 1983 G&A survey showed similar results to the 1993 Shim survey, with 82% of the responding companies using full-cost pricing and 17% using variable-cost pricing. Thus, both surveys reveal the continuously prevailing use of full-cost pricing from 1983 to 1993. The consistent practice of full-cost pricing underscores the importance of proper cost allocation and product costing.

An interesting result of the 1993 survey is that 25 companies (18%) reported using market-based (competitive) pricing, which was not reported in the 1983 survey.

This result indicates an important change in arriving at prices, one that is based on competitive market conditions rather than cost structures.

RATIONALE FOR FULL COST

There are a number of plausible reasons for the continuing use of full-cost pricing. First, increased implementation of ABC systems is likely to rationalize the allocation of fixed costs and makes more seemingly fixed costs variable or semi-variable. ABC systems enhance ways of tracing fixed costs to a specific product and lead to a better allocation of these costs. ABC systems provide more accurate product cost estimates that serve as a basis of determining full-cost price. The rapid implementation of ABC systems, therefore, tends to supply a support for the prevalent use of full-cost pricing practice.

Second, full-cost pricing provides a motivation to control fixed costs. For example, allocation of fixed costs to profit centers affects the performance of those centers. Accordingly, the profit center managers, whose performance varies with the amount of allocated fixed costs, can raise questions about the amount of corporate overhead (that is, fixed costs) and, as a result, may reduce the "empire building" phenomenon.[6] The use of fully allocated fixed costs in determining price could provide an alternative risk-sharing arrangement between profit center managers and top managers.

Finally, the difficulty in estimating marginal cost and marginal revenue for various products may prevent companies from using the marginal-cost approach. With manufacturing companies producing an average of 75 products, estimating marginal cost and marginal revenue may not be feasible or economical.

The majority of companies in the new manufacturing environment continue to practice full-cost pricing. The possible reasons for this practice are: "satisfying" behavior, availability of finer product costing information with implementation of ABC systems, possibility of controlling fixed costs, and difficulty in estimating marginal cost and marginal revenue in a multiproduct environment.

THE FUTURE?

Full-cost pricing continues to be the most popular product pricing method, but there is a shift toward variable-cost pricing or market-based (competitive) pricing. The 1993 survey exhibits only a very slow trend in this direction. The fierce domestic and foreign competition in the new manufacturing environment may bolster the use of some form of competitive pricing in the future.

ENDNOTES

1. V. Govindarajan and R. N. Anthony, "How Firms Use Cost Data in Pricing Decisions," MANAGEMENT ACCOUNTING ®, July 1983, p. 30–37.
2. Eunsup Shim, "Cost Management and Activity Based Cost Allocation in a New Manufacturing Environment," Unpublished Dissertation, Rutgers University, Newark, N.J., January 1993.
3. R. Cooper and R. S. Kaplan, "How Cost Accounting Systematically Distorts Product Costs," *Accounting and Management: Field Study Perspective*, Harvard Business School Press, Boston, Mass., 1987, p. 226.
4. R. Cooper, "Implementing an Activity-Based Cost System," *Emerging Practices in Cost Management*, Warren, Gorham & Lamont, Inc., Boston, Mass., 1990, p. 69.
5. C. Berliner, and J. A. Brimson, *Cost Management for Today's Advanced Manufacturing: The CAM-I Conceptual Design*, Harvard Business School Press, Boston, Mass., 1988.
6. Anthony Dearden, and Govindarajan, *Management Control Systems*, 7th ed., Irwin, Homewood, IL., 1992, p. 184.

Eunsup Shim, CMA, CPA, Ph.D, is assistant professor of accounting at Saint Joseph's University, Philadelphia, Pa. He is a member of the Philadelphia Chapter, through which this article was submitted, and can be reached at (610) 660–1660.

Ephraim F. Sudit, Ph.D., is a professor of accounting and information systems at the Graduate School of Management, Rutgers University, Newark, N. J. He is a member of the IMA and can be reached at (201) 648–5241.

QUESTION

6.1 Based on Table 1 of Shim and Sudit's article, what are the biggest differences between the 1983 and 1993 survey? Are these differences significant? Explain.

6.2 Activity-Based Costing for Marketing

by Ronald J. Lewis*

CERTIFICATE OF MERIT, 1990–91

Manufacturing costs and traditional cost accounting systems are not the only cause of America's problems in the world-class Competitiveness arena. Marketing functions, particularly physical distribution, are a significant cost factor, yet marketing costs are being ignored in the mainstream discussions today. Also, activity-based costing (ABC) techniques and total cost management (TCM) concepts have been recommended and used by some companies for marketing activities since the late 1960s. How can they be merged with the concepts being promoted today?

THE PROBLEM'S HIDDEN CAUSE

Critics of traditional cost control systems who concentrate on production costs alone are overlooking a significant portion of the total costs of many manufactured products.

A major cause of the higher cost of these products is the cost of physical distribution activities and other marketing functions. Marketing costs make up more than 50% of the total costs in many product lines and approximately 20% of the U.S. Gross National Product.

Physical distribution is a major cost factor in the United States. It may not be a major cost factor in geographically small countries, such as Japan or Great Britain, within their own domestic markets. Nevertheless, when foreign companies establish factories in the United States, they face the same logistics problems that U.S. companies encounter.

The theoretical advantages of just-in-time (JIT) methods may not work in all real-life situations, even in Japanese transplants. In addition, the familiarity that U.S. companies have had with physical distribution problems may be an advantage for them over their foreign competitors. For example, a Japanese-American joint venture established a plant in Michigan to provide parts to a Japanese assembly plant in Ohio. In the Michigan plant, observers found that boxes of parts were stacked to the ceiling in all available floor space of the factory. When asked about JIT and other inventory reduction methods, the plant manager explained that parts were shipped from Japan by freighter to the West Coast, then by rail to Chicago, and finally by truck to Michigan. Therefore, it was more economical to ship in large quantities and store the extra supplies on the factory floor.

The joint-venture supplier in this example is majority owned by the Japanese company, which supplies another Japanese company, an automobile manufacturer, with these particular parts. Competition is not a factor because the two Japanese companies have prearranged agreements, so these physical distribution costs are considered unavoidable under the circumstances.

Although this example illustrates the fallacy of assuming that the Japanese have some magic formula for manufacturing efficiency, it also indicates that marketing costs, particularly the costs of physical distribution, are a major factor in worldwide competition and should not be ignored in discussions of performance measurements and integrated cost systems.

ABC TECHNIQUES FOR MARKETING

The objective of marketing cost analysis is to provide relevant quantitative data that will assist marketing managers in making informed decisions regarding such important areas as profitability, pricing, and adding or dropping the product lines or territories. In achieving this objective it is necessary to be able to trace costs directly to product lines or to territories where possible and to establish a rational system of allocating nontraceable costs to the cost objective. The accounting profession has not pursued this challenge!

ABC principles can be applied in attempting to trace marketing costs to product lines and territories in order to measure profitability. I'll show you how. All you have to do is follow the procedure outlined next.

1. Establish activities performed as advertising, selling, order filling, shipping, and warehousing.
2. Accumulate direct costs for each activity, and separate into variable and fixed categories.
3. Determine cost drivers for each activity. For *selling*, the cost driver is gross sales, or orders received, or number of sales calls. For the activity of *order filling*, *shipping*, and *warehousing*, the cost driver would be number, weight, or size of units shipped. For the activities of *credit* and *collection* and *general office*, the cost driver is number of customer orders or number of invoice lines.
4. Calculate unit costs for each activity. The unit cost of each activity is determined by dividing the total activity cost by the cost driver selected. Where conditions justify the practice, the unit cost can be used as the basis for budgeting and for the establishment of standards in a standard cost system.
5. Apply contribution cost analysis. The accumulation of direct costs and the allocation of indirect costs to marketing activities enables management to assign total cost responsibility to each marketing activity

* From R. J. Lewis, "Activity-Based Costing for Marketing," *Management Accounting* (November 1991): 33–36. Reprinted with permission.

although the identification of total costs does not always provide relevant information for specific decisions. Only by applying contribution analysis will the company be able to determine profit contribution by product line or by territory.

Tables 1-5 were prepared by the controller of Atlanta Company to provide information about marketing profitability. Table 1 shows selling prices, unit manufacturing costs, units sold, and other bases of variability. Table 2 shows total variable and fixed costs for each activity and develops unit rates for variable and fixed costs of each major marketing activity: selling, warehousing, packing and shipping, and general office.

Selling. The selling function is represented by the dollar value of sales. There may be justification for basing variability of selling cost on other factors, such as the number of sales calls or orders obtained, and the controller must select the basis that has the main causal effect on cost variability. Atlanta Company uses the basis of dollar value of sales.

Advertising. Advertising is a promotional activity, similar to selling, which possibly could be attributed to the cost factors. Atlanta selected units of product sold. Note that advertising may or may not have variable cost characteristics. Some companies increase their advertising when sales are down, so the cost may bear an inverse relationship with sales. Atlanta found that a portion of advertising varies with sales and that a larger portion is fixed.

Warehousing. Warehousing is the general distribution function of storage terminating. The factor of variability selected by Atlanta is weight of product sold.

Packing and Shipping. Another physical distribution function, packaging and shipping, usually has a greater proportion of variable expenses and is related to the quantity of units of product shipped. Atlanta assumes units shipped are equal to units sold.

TABLE 1. ATLANTA COMPANY PRODUCT LINE DATA YEAR 19X1

Product Line Information	A	B	C
Selling price	$10.00	$8.00	$12.00
Unit manufacturing cost	$ 8.00	$5.00	$11.00
Quantity of units sold and shipped	50,000	30,000	20,000
Average weight of units sold	2.0 lbs.	3.0 lbs.	4.0 lbs.
Number of customers' orders	100	200	200
Variable portion of manufacturing cost	60%	60%	60%

TABLE 2. ATLANTA COMPANY CALCULATION FOR PER UNIT COST RATES

TOTAL COSTS

Marketing Activity	Cost Driver	Total Volume	Cost of Marketing Activity Total	Unit Rate
Selling	Dollar value of sales	$980,000	$49,000	5.0%
Advertising	Quantity of units sold	100,000	$40,000	$.40
Warehousing	Weight of shipped	270,000 lb.	$27,000	$.10
Packing and shipping	Quantity of shipped	100,000	$20,000	$.20
General office	Number of customers' orders	500	$10,000	$20.00

VARIABLE AND FIXED COST RATES

Marketing Activity	Variable Cost	Unit Rate	Fixed Cost	Unit Rate
Selling	$29,400	3.0%	$19,600	$2.0%
Advertising	$10,000	$ .10	$30,000	$.30
Warehousing	$13,500	$ 05	$13,500	$.05
Packing and shipping	$12,000	$ .12	$ 8,000	$.08
General Office	$ 2,000	$4.00	$ 8,000	$16.00

TABLE 3. ATLANTA COMPANY SALES AND ORDERS BY TERRITORY (IN UNITS) YEAR 19XI

Transaction by Territory	Products Total	A	B	C
Products sold:				
West	60,000	26,000	20,000	14,000
South	40,000	24,000	10,000	6,000
Total	100,000	50,000	30,000	20,000
Customers' Orders:				
West	280	50	80	150
South	220	50	120	50
Total	500	100	200	200

TABLE 4. ATLANTA COMPANY PROFITABILITY STATEMENT BY TERRITORY (ALL PRODUCTS) YEAR 19X1

	Total Company	Territory West	South	Allocation Basis
Sales revenue	$980,000	$588,000	$392,000	
Less cost of soles	770,000	462,000	$308,000	
Gross margin	$210,000	$126,000	$ 84,000	
Less Expenses				
Selling	$ 49,000	$ 29,400	$ 19,600	5% of sales
Advertising	40,000	24,000	16,600	$.40/unit sold
Warehousing	27,000	16,800	10,200	10/lb. shipped
Packing and shipping	20,000	12,000	8,000	$.20/unit sold
General office	10,000	5,600	4,400	$20/order
Total expense	$146,000	$ 87,800	$ 58,200	
Operating Income (Loss)	$ 64,000	$ 38,200	$ 25,800	

TABLE 5. ATLANTA COMPANY: PROFITABILITY STATEMENT BY PRODUCT LINE (ALL TERRITORIES) YEAR 19X1

	Total Company	Product Line A	B	C	Allocation Basis
Sales revenue	$980,000	$500,000	$240,000	$240,000	
Cost of sales	770,000	400,000	150,000	220,000	
Gross margin	$210,000	$100,000	$90,000	$20,000	
Less: Expenses					
Selling	$ 49,000	$25,000	$12,000	$12,000	5% of sales
Advertising	40,000	20,000	12,000	8,000	$.40/unit sold
Warehousing	27,000	10,000	9,000	8,000	$.10/lb. shipped
Packing and shipping	20,000	10,000	6,000	4,000	$.20/unit sold
General office	10,000	2,000	4,000	4,000	$20/order
Total expense	$146,000	$67,000	$43,000	$36,000	
Operating income (Loss)	$ 64,000	$33,000	$47,000	$(16,000)	

General Office. Atlanta needs clerical accounting, credit and collection, and other activities to service the overall marketing function. Each service has its own variability, but Atlanta assumes that number of orders affects all.

Table 3 provides additional product and territory transactions data. For example, the quantity of product C sold in the West territory during the period was 14,000 units. Customers' orders for product A in the South total 50. These data form the basis for the determination of the cost calculations in subsequent tables.

The profitability analysis by territory (shown in Table 4) reveals that both territories show a profit from operations. Table 5 shows the total company profitability by product line. The profitability statement by product line provides additional information for marketing managers. Product lines A and B are profitable, whereas product line C shows an operating loss of $16,000. This statement has revealed that although the overall company shows a profit and that both territories are profitable, one product line requires further analysis. Additional tables could be presented with data by product line for each territory separately to further isolate the operating loss of product C.

As you can see, "Charging costs direct eliminates the need to allocate or assign costs. Costs that cannot be charged directly should be assigned to the product through activitybased costing."[1]

This modern advice dovetails with my illustration, which demonstrates that the techniques recommended for marketing cost analysis at least 20 years ago are conceptually equal to those now being recommended for production costs by Robert Kaplan, William Ferrara, Michael Ostrenga, and others contributing to the deluge of activity-based costing literature.[2] The only differences are that only marketing costs were involved, the state of technology was less developed, and the accounting profession did not recognize the importance of marketing costs and the methods being recommended.

WE MUST EMPHASIZE MARKETING COSTS

The main theme of management accounting journal articles in recent years has been world-class competition emphasizing the gradual slipping of U.S. manufacturers, particularly in comparison with Japanese manufacturers. Production costs have been the center of attention, while marketing costs have been ignored. We must focus on marketing costs as an important component of the total cost of a product.

The use of activity-based costing techniques for marketing functions arose during the years 1968 through

1973 when marketing executives urged members of the accounting profession to develop a better system of identifying, classifying, and allocating physical distribution costs. At that time, several articles (including one of mine[3]) isolated the activities in the major marketing functions. Cost drivers, a modern euphemism for activity bases, were identified for each activity within the marketing functions.

Techniques that resemble the recently discovered activity-based costing system and the total cost concept which is the forerunner of total cost management were discussed thoroughly and recommended for physical distribution costs at the request of the marketing managers of several hundred U.S. corporations. The accounting profession largely ignored the recommendations of the practitioners and overlooked the fact that physical distribution activities have cost characteristics similar to those of production activities. Now, 20 years later, accountants are attaching new names to these same techniques. Activity-based costing techniques have been and should continue to be applied to marketing costs to assist companies in management decision making.

ENDNOTES

1. Michael R. Ostrenga, "Activities: The Focal Point of Total Cost Management." MANAGEMENT ACCOUNTING®, February 1990, pp. 42–49.
2. Robert S. Kaplan, "The Four-Step Model of Coat Systems Design." MANAGEMENT ACCOUNTING® February 1990, pp. 22–26. Also, William L. Ferrara, "The New Cost/Management Accounting: More Questions than Answers," MANAGEMENT ACCOUNTING®, October 1990, pp. 48–52.
3. Ronald J. Lewis, "Strengthening Control of Physical Distribution Costs," *Management Services* (AICPA), January–February 1968. Also, J. L. Heskett, R. M. Ivie, and N. A. Glaskowsky, Jr., *Business Logistics Management of Physical Supply and Distribution,* The Ronald Press Company, New York, N. Y., 1964.

Ronald J. Lewis is Professor of accounting at Central Michigan University in Mt. Pleasant, Mich., and a member of the Saginaw Valley Chapter of the IMA, through which this article was submitted. He holds A.B. and A.M. degrees from Wayne State University and a Ph.D. degree from Michigan State University. Formerly he was the vice-president of academic affairs at Tri-State University, Angola, IN. He may be reached at (517) 774–3796.

QUESTION

6.2 In Lewis' article, what are the appropriate cost drivers for selling, advertising, warehousing, packing and shipping, and general office activities? Is there any flexibility in the choice of cost drivers for these categories? Explain.

6.3 Distribution Channel Profitability

ABC concepts can help companies make strategic decisions.

by Kenneth H. Manning*

Which of your distribution channels is most profitable? If you analyze them using an approach built on activity-based costing (ABC) concepts, you may find an unexpected answer.

Distribution costs are a fact of life for almost every manufacturer, distributor, and supplier. As major retailers, wholesalers, distributors, and manufacturers reconfigure their supply chains, all participants in the supply chain need to understand the revenue and cost tradeoffs associated with the various channels through which they deliver products and services.

To evaluate strategic issues within the distribution system, formulate potential responses to those issues, and estimate the impact of improvements on the overall business, you need reliable and accurate information. One approach to gaining the necessary data is constructed around activity-based costing (ABC) concepts that many companies have adopted over the last several years.[1] ABC provides a more accurate view of a company's cost structure than a standard cost approach, particularly for companies that produce a broad range of products and volumes. The benefits of ABC have been discussed in great detail in other publications and will not be presented here.[2] Building on these ABC concepts, the methodology presented here allows practitioners to determine the relative profitability of their distribution channels and customer groups. The methodology assumes that the practitioners have at least a conceptual view of an ABC approach, although a working knowledge of ABC techniques is highly recommended.

COMPARISON OF THREE APPROACHES

The typical approach to developing knowledge of channel profitability, using standard product costing, is shown in Figure 1. This approach creates two cost pools:

* From K.H. Manning, "Distribution Channel Profitability," *Management Accounting* (January 1995): 44–48. Reprinted with permission.

product costs and sales, general, and administrative (SG&A) costs. The product costs are transferred to the channels based on standard unit costs and the product mix sold through that channel. The SG&A expenses typically are allocated to the channels based on net revenue or sales volume by channel.

If the organization is aligned by channel or customer group, this approach may yield accurate profitability figures. But most often, companies are aligned by region, product line, or facility location, which makes the translation to channel or customer difficult using conventional approaches.

This approach may help answer some questions related to distribution costs, but there are numerous issues that it cannot address. In addition, it has all the drawbacks associated with traditional standard product costing, which have been shown to distort costs in many situations. Because this approach makes no attempt to adjust product costs, the analysis related to product costs can be misleading.

A more refined approach to channel profitability is to use an ABC methodology. Figure 2 illustrates the more accurate ABC approach to this problem. The ABC approach has one large advantage over the conventional approach: It costs products more accurately. Overhead costs are allocated to product lines in a more logically related fashion than under the conventional approach. The result is improved accuracy over the typical standard costing approach.

The drawback to this approach is that while we are allocating cost in a much more logical and rigorous manner, the analysis is based on one major assumption that is probably not true: that all costs are product-driven costs and therefore must be traced or allocated to products. For most companies, organizational costs are driven by more than just the products they produce.

FIGURE 1. STANDARD APPROACH TO CHANNEL PROFITABILITY

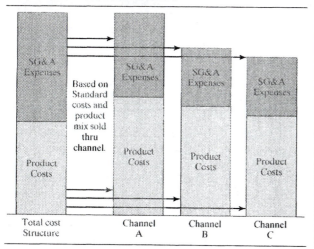

FIGURE 2. ABC APPROACH TO CHANNEL PROFITABILITY

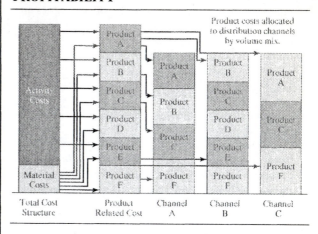

The strategic cost management approach outlined below recognizes that cost is not driven solely by the products produced but also by the customers served and the channels through which the product is offered. Removing the restriction that all costs must be related to products allows the development of a more accurate view of cost consumption. Under the traditional ABC methodology, it was not possible to detect if product costs were high due to certain customer groups or to certain channels. However, this approach gives us additional insight into the reasons for the product line cost position by creating three different types of costs: product-related costs, channel-related costs, and customer-related costs. Examining the cost structure from this perspective allows management to understand cost differences related to any one of these categories or related to interactions between these categories. (See Figure 3.)

FIGURE 3. SCM APPROACH TO CHANNEL PROFITABILITY

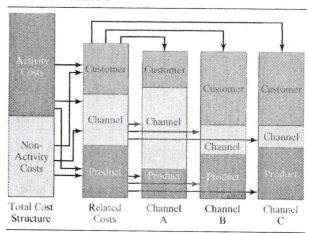

DEVELOPING ACCURATE CHANNEL AND CUSTOMER COSTS

The approach used to develop this view of costs relies on several guidelines:

- Include all costs (direct, indirect, overhead, implicit).
- Focus on relevance over precision.
- Use issues to drive analysis.

The methodology follows a four-step process, which is outlined below.

1. *Separate the organization's cost structure into activity costs and nonactivity costs.* The cost structure of the organization should be translated into activity and nonactivity components that reflect the operations of the enterprise. The number and detail of these components should be determined by the issues the study is addressing. Table 1 lists several activity and nonactivity components one would expect to see in a manufacturing company. Through the use of traditional ABC concepts, the cost associated with each of these components should be estimated. The sum of these component costs should equal the organization's total cost structure.

2. *Identify the cost behavior of all activity and nonactivity costs.* The activity and nonactivity components are organized into three categories of cost behavior: product-related, customer-related, and channel-related (see Table 1). Each cost component should be related to only one category. If a cost component cannot be related to just one category, either further decompose the activity or nonactivity definition, or, if it is judged immaterial, assign the component to the primary behavior category.

3. *Trace these costs to the individual products, channels, and customers.* Once the different cost components are classified as product-related, channel-related, or customer-related, it is necessary to identify the tracing factor that relates those costs back to the appropriate products, channels, or customers. *Tracing factors are quantifiable, repeatable measures that closely approximate the level of effort associated with an activity.* They are used to trace the activity cost to the individual component groups, e.g., product line A, product line B, channel A, and so on.

For example, the activity cost of "non-EDI order processing" was determined to be $432,500 for the one-year period. The number of order lines filled was identified as the tracing factor, as shown in Table 2.

This same procedure is performed for all cost components to develop a total cost view for the three types of cost categories. Nonactivity costs are treated in a similar manner, except direct cost linkages are easier to find for these items. In most cases it will be possible to allocate those costs directly to the product, customer, or channel that created them.

TABLE 1. COST BEHAVIOR OF ACTIVITY COSTS AND NONACTIVITY COSTS

		Product Related	Channel Related	Customer Related
Activity Costs	■	Schedule Production	■ Attend Trade Shows	■ EDI and Computer Interfaces to Customer
	■	Setup and Changeover for Machine A	■ Order/invoice Processing	■ Special Shipping and Handling Requests
	■	Test Quality Parameters	■ Sales Force	■ Collect Bad Debt
	■	Maintain Equipment	■ Telemarketing	■ Technical Support for Customer A
			■ Advertising Brand A	■ Prepare/Deliver Annual Sales Bid
			■ Arrange for Shipping	
Nonactivity Costs	■	Material Costs	■ Trade Discounts	■ Bad Debt Expense
	■	Royalties	■ Freight	■ Customer Rebates

TABLE 2. ACTIVITY COST OF NON-EDI ORDER PROCESSING

	Activity: Non-EDI Order Processing	Tracing Factor: Number of Order Lines
Channel A	$78,140	$123,045
Channel B	208,358	328,095
Channel C	146,002	229,903
Total	$432,500	$681,043

4. *Translate the product, channel, and customer cost elements into a total cost view for the business.* The final step requires that two matrices be constructed for the purpose of linking these three views. The first matrix links the product and customer view by capturing the customer purchases by product. The second matrix links the customer and channel view by capturing the customer purchases by distribution channel. These two matrices then are used to

translate the costs driven by each channel into a total cost view for product, customer, or channel.

Following this methodology will provide any necessary cost view of the organization. Obviously, it is also necessary to capture revenue information for the same products, channels, and customers for which costs were calculated.

PRODUCT VIEW VS. CHANNEL/CUSTOMER VIEW

The traditional ABC approach is probably most consistent with the way corporate planners think about business strategy and planning: by product area. The majority of businesses are formed around product lines and product groups, a fact that obviously influences the way we think about them. But alternative views certainly are becoming more important as products are served through increasingly varied channels—distributors, catalogs, megastores, direct mail, and so on. As companies develop future business plans, understanding the cost and profitability of serving different channel and customer groups will become critical to making good business decisions.

In essence, we have recast the entire company's costs and created a database of costing information around several new views: activity, nonactivity, product, channel, and customer. Attempting to perform these manipulations without the assistance of a powerful PC would be impossible, but with the introduction of the PC and numerous software applications, it is now relatively easy. The data are organized in a way that encourages analysis of number of different issues.

The best results have been obtained when this methodology was used in an issues-driven approach—the type and nature of the decision being made should drive the level of detail and direction of the analysis. The effort to arrive at good, accurate channel and customer costs is worth making only if you need to address business issues. The key issues should be identified, documented, and articulated in advance of any analysis. For instance, the sections below describe how two companies facing different competitive issues could use the approach to develop their strategic responses.

FOCUSED COMPETITOR ENTERING MARKET

A specialty chemical manufacturer supplied products to a broad range of customers in the food, consumer products, and manufacturing industries. The products were made primarily in-house although some were purchased and repackaged and then sold through a network of representatives, a direct sales force, and a telemarketing customer service center. Customers could opt for several delivery and pricing options including customer pick-up, bulk delivery, or less-than-truckload (LTL) delivery.

It recently had become known that a new competitor was planning to enter a key segment of the company's market. The management team knew that the impact would be negative but did not know to what extent. The vice president of sales & marketing particularly was concerned. He believed that the targeting segment provided a significant portion of the division's profit although the financial report indicated that it was not very profitable due to above average discounts. The head of sales and marketing decided to sponsor a study to understand the "true" profitability of the various delivery options and customer groups (or market segments).

The study team uncovered several significant findings:

- The large customers did provide a disproportionate percentage of the division's profits, despite their much lower gross margin, due primarily to less customer service, lower bad credit expenses, and reduced handling charges on large orders.
- Cost differentials within the large customer grouping depended on the use of the product. Customers in the food industry consumed more technical marketing, demanded more research support, and required a finer grade product, which slowed process run rates.
- The "true" cost difference among the different delivery options was surprising. The conventional cost approach assumed that the only difference between these options was the freight costs. The study revealed that the customer pick-up option after adjustment for freight charges actually cost less than the other delivery options due to much lower damage claim losses and reduced freight scheduling costs.
- The gross sales generated by small customers did not cover even the cost of selling and servicing these accounts. It turned out that smaller customers often had limited resources with which to solve technical problems and relied on the company's assistance in this area. Because there was no rationing mechanism or internal R&D tracking system, these costs went undetected for the most part.
- Several of the large-volume outsourced products did not provide sufficient margin to cover their full distribution costs. While they appeared profitable under the standard cost and profit reporting system, the study indicated they were unprofitable once the inbound logistics cost and purchasing cost were taken into account.

Given this information, the head of sales & marketing worked with the vice presidents of operations, R&D, and finance to develop the following set of responses:

1. Technical resources were shifted away from smaller customers and assigned to work exclusively on the

large consumer product and manufacturing accounts. The sales force then attempted to discover customer problems that could be solved by making these valuable resources available to the customers. The R&D department also created a simple time reporting system to track these "soft" costs better.

2. The customer pick-up delivery price was lowered to attract more volume through this channel. This move was intended to attract the largest-volume users of the product-consumer product and manufacturing. It also had the advantage of encouraging the competitor to take away our lowest-margin business, food processors, because these companies did not use sufficient volume to take advantage of the new price discounts.

3. The company began to look actively for other suppliers for the products they outsourced so as to improve the profitability of this operation. In addition, they decided to redesign the vendor relations group and reengineer the purchasing process with the goal of reducing the overall handling cost by 50% for purchased goods.

Using the cost and revenue information in the model management was able to estimate the impact of these changes on the overall results under several different scenarios. While the impact of the new competitor definitely would be negative, the overall effect would be mitigated substantially by these responses.

SALES FORCE RESTRUCTURING

An industrial equipment supplier had one of the oldest and most capable sales forces of all the suppliers in its field. As a result, several competitors recently had started to shift their focus to other distribution channels. While competitors moved away from dedicated sales forces, the management team chose not to pursue these alternative methods because they still considered the in-house sales force a source of real advantage in the marketplace. Due to several periods of unsatisfactory results and the continued growth of alternative distribution and sales channels, however, the company's management decided to undertake a distribution profitability study focused on understanding the strategic value of the sales force.

The primary issues management wanted to address was sales force effectiveness, so the analysis was structured to focus on this aspect of the cost structure. The detailed log of sales-force activity was tracked to customers or channels, depending on the activity. By creating a very detailed cost picture of the various channels, the company could see the relative profitability of the various channel configurations and the source of cost differentials. By building this detail, management was able to see the sales force costs consumed by different customer and product groups.

With this cost baseline, management estimated the impact of several changes to the structure. In addition, the cost differential between the company and its competitors was estimated from knowledge of how its competitors' activities and sales volumes differed across their sales forces. Combining these cost and profitability views with an understanding of the customer buying factors provided insight into several issues.

A FRAMEWORK FOR DISTRIBUTION ISSUES

After performing the analysis, management became aware of several points that had not been clear before:

■ Some high-margin product lines that were thought to be profitable were, in fact, unprofitable due to the channel-related costs.

■ Sales volume did not correlate with restated customer profitability.

■ The cost of selling product differed dramatically depending on the customer application.

■ One product line that was low margin and thought to be a loss leader was, in fact, relatively profitable.

Based on these findings, management formulated several changes in response to this new information:

■ The loss leader was priced lower to attract additional volume from existing customers.

■ Another product line was dropped because the primary customer base for it was extremely unlikely to buy any of the other products, and the revenue from these single-product customers would never justify the cost to serve them through a sales force.

■ In addition, several representatives were taken on to serve those customers who were small- to medium-volume purchasers and did not require technical expertise from the sales force. These reps were offered a margin that encouraged them to deal exclusively with this company. The cost savings from shifting the sales force more than compensated for the margin passed on to the distributors.

The sales force then was refocused on those customers who valued their technical expertise and would be likely to buy additional product lines from this supplier in the future.

By assessing the cost and profit differentials among customers and channels, this company was able to shift its sales resources to those opportunities that provided better long-term growth and profitability.

The analysis described above forms the basis for multiple types of decisions including: pricing levels, warehouse investments, cost reduction targets, make/buy decisions, new channel options, channel rationalization, and selection of target markets and key customers.

This approach is not presented as the complete solution to the distribution issues of the 1990s, but it is a very important analytical framework that should accompany most distribution strategy developments. It forms the basis for developing a solid quantitative understanding of the current distribution and customer situation. The findings and models developed in this phase can be used to evaluate current performance, estimate future impacts, and track improvements from new distribution strategies.

ENDNOTES

1. Robin Cooper and Robert S. Kaplan, "Measure Cost Right Make the Right Decision," *Harvard Business Review*, September/October 1988, pp. 96–103.

2. Philip Rhodes, "Activity-Based Costing: What Will It Do for You," *APICS*, August 1992, pp. 29–31.

Kenneth H. Manning is with Deloitte & Touche in Atlanta, Ga. He can be reached at (404) 220–1147.

QUESTIONS

6.3a Discuss the four-step process that Manning uses for developing accurate channel and customer costs.

6.3b In developing the four-step process, Manning discusses both activity and nonactivity costs. What are two examples of two nonactivity customer-related costs? Why are these labeled as "nonactivity costs?"

6.4 Smart Pricing

by Moritz Fleischmann, Joseph M. Hall & David F. Pyke*

The past decade has seen a virtual explosion of information about customers and their preferences. Many companies have the ability to gauge customers' willingness to pay for their products and can determine with some accuracy the effect of price changes on sales volumes. With Internet shopping, it is possible to effect such price changes at minimal cost for different customer segments and even for individual customers. Perhaps more enticing is the development of electronic shelf-labeling systems, which open the door to a remarkable array of possibilities for dynamic pricing in brick-and-mortar stores. The potential for increased revenue is huge.

At the same time, companies have taken major strides in understanding and managing the dynamics of the supply chain. Internally, many companies have implemented the tools and concepts of lean manufacturing. And externally, they have aggressively pursued supply chain initiatives, such as electronic procurement; vendor-managed inventory and collaborative planning; forecasting; and replenishment. The potential for cost reduction and service improvement is great.

Yet despite these potential benefits, there is a persistent dilemma. Pricing decisions have a direct, and sometimes dramatic, effect on operations and vice versa. This is vividly illustrated by the bullwhip effect, which can be initiated by price promotions (a classic 1997 paper by Lee et al. explains this effect). A more recent paper by Macé and Neslin (2000) provides new insight into consumer stockpiling in response to a promotion and deceleration (their willingness to reduce inventories in anticipation of a promotion). This insight has led many to suggest that firms should eliminate promotions in favor of "everyday low pricing" — evoking the disdain of their marketing colleagues. Also, the operations community has recently identified drivers for dynamic pricing, inspired by the widely acclaimed successes of revenue management in the airline industry (McCartney, 2000). These developments call for thorough integration of marketing and operations insights — which today still appears to be lacking. Conversations with a significant number of managers indicate that this integration is no more complete in industry than it is in academia.

Nevertheless, the linkage between pricing and operations is increasingly being scrutinized by academics and managers alike. For an extensive discussion of the literature, including technical aspects, see Rao (1993); Radjou et al. (2003); Chan et al. (in press); and Elmaghraby and Keskinocak (2003). In this article, we offer a snapshot of the work being done in this rich and evolving field, and we highlight different drivers for dynamic pricing strategies.

REVENUE MANAGEMENT

Revenue management (or yield management) — the most mature area in dynamic pricing — is concerned with pricing a perishable resource in accordance with demand from multiple customer segments so as to maximize revenue or profit. To this end, prices are adjusted dynamically as a function of inventory level and time left in the selling season. Typical applications are in the airline and hospitality industries, where there is a fixed capacity that cannot be inventoried. In such applications, the cost side of the profit equation is largely irrelevant because the incremental cost of adding another passenger or filling another room is very low.

---

* From: M. Fleischmann, J. M. Hall and D. F. Pyke, "Smart Pricing," *MIT Sloan Management Review* (Winter 2004): 9–13. Reprinted with permission.

Research in revenue management has been impressive. McGill and van Ryzin (1999) provide a review of the literature and directions for future research; Boyd and Bilegan (2003) present an updated review with a focus on e-commerce applications. Revenue management has been the driving force behind many attempts to integrate pricing and operations.

Management practice and software solutions have likewise shown remarkable progress. The airlines' successful use of revenue management is widely understood. Recently, similar concepts have been applied to manage rebates in car sales, contributing to, for example, $260 million of the $896 million first-quarter 2003 profits of Ford Motor Co. (Welch, 2003). Other examples in nontraditional industries include pricing of advertising time in the broadcast industry and capacity auctions in the natural gas pipeline industry (Secomandi et al., 2002).

RETAIL MARKDOWNS

Retailers of seasonal goods — apparel, school supplies, Christmas toys — regularly face the perplexing problem of when, and by how much, to decrease prices as the season draws to a close. The underlying trade-offs are similar to those associated with the revenue management problem. In particular, product cost is largely irrelevant; the primary focus is on maximizing revenue from leftover goods.

A seminal reference for this research area is Gallego and van Ryzin (1994), which investigates static pricing policies that are much easier to implement than "jittery" dynamic prices. The authors find that the lost revenue due to static pricing is minimal, at least for the situations they investigated.

Another reference of interest about markdowns is Smith and Achabal (1998). Their model, which was tested and implemented at three retailers, sets prices optimally in conjunction with inventory policies, taking into account the impact of reduced assortment, price and seasonal changes on sales rates. Implementation was complex because of soft input data, existing management practices and related difficulties; thus, results were mixed. In one case, for instance, a revenue increase of only 1% was reported, although this represented a $15 million increase in gross margin. More recently, markdown analyses have been extended to multiple supply chain stages (Jorgensen and Kort, 2002).

Developments in software to manage markdowns have been more recent than in the field of revenue management. Marshall (2001) reports that retailers have experienced improvements in gross margins of 5% to 20% after implementing markdown optimization software, so we expect to see a rapid expansion of these implementations.

PROMOTIONS AND DYNAMIC PRICING

Promotions are commonly used for new product introductions, but they are also frequently used with staple consumer goods such as tuna, soda and paper towels. It is this latter category that has generated most of the research. The literature suggests that price discrimination is a key driver of promotion offerings. For example, if customers differ in their brand loyalty, their access to information about current prices or their willingness to stockpile, periodic promotions may allow a firm to price discriminate profitably among these customers. However, price discrimination isn't the only motivation for price promotions; promotions that are loss leaders also can drive store traffic. Neslin (2002) is a key reference, an excellent book that provides a full understanding of the reasons for promotions as well as an extensive review of the marketing literature in this area. Several recent papers merit further comment as well.

Kannan and Kopalle (2001) focus on Internet sales and generate a number of hypotheses about how consumers will react to dynamic pricing, both on the Internet and in physical stores. This paper explicitly considers the effects of consumer learning, reference price effects and consumer price expectations — all of which are largely ignored in the operations literature. Kopalle et al. (1999) conclude that higher-share brands tend to be overpromoted, while lower-share brands are not promoted frequently enough. They project profitability increases of 7% to 31% if their insights are employed. And as already noted in the introduction, Macé and Neslin (2000) provide evidence that promotions increase near-term sales but also decrease off-promotion sales. Unfortunately, the exact dynamics remain uncertain.

One open issue is the relationship of customer consumption and promotions. Our own research (Fleischmann et al., 2003) has investigated pricing policies for a firm facing a downward-sloping demand curve and an upward-sloping, concave consumption curve. The shape of this curve reflects the belief that consumers use more product when they have more. This consumption effect, if it is sufficiently strong, may sometimes justify periodic price promotions. However, in many cases constant pricing is preferable.

While these papers are representative of the marketing literature in the sense that they focus on consumer-behavior aspects of promotion, some work is beginning to include upstream supply considerations as well. Sogomonian and Tang (1993) study the coordination of promotion and production decisions and detail the increase in profit and decrease in inventory that result. Iyer and Ye (2000) study a three-level supply chain composed of retail customers, a retailer and a manufacturer, and they develop several interesting insights into promotions. For instance, if there is great uncertainty about the sales impact of promotions, it may be more profitable for the retailer not to promote. From the perspective of integrating operations and marketing decisions, the most interesting result is that as customer inventory-holding cost decreases, stockpiling increases. This suggests that retailers will promote less frequently, and less frequent promotions mean that stockpilers will purchase more with each promotion. Retailer profits increase in this scenario, but manufacturer profits decrease if the manufacturer is not made aware of the promotion schedule. Huchzermeier et al. (2002) model a case in which customers react to promotions by stockpiling and by switching package sizes, research incorporating the behavior of "smart" customers who calculate a per-unit cost of product and thereby choose package sizes optimally. Understanding the response of these smart customers can reduce inventory costs at the store and suggests that the retailer can benefit from offering a variety of product sizes.

The status of theoretical and empirical research suggests that promotions are heavily studied, but that there remain significant gaps in our knowledge. The research also reveals that managers rely on simple rules when making pricing and promotion decisions, although there are some notable exceptions. Software application developers are beginning to provide tools that can help managers add a level of science to the art of pricing.

OPERATIONS: PRICING, LEAD TIME AND CAPACITY

Research that integrates pricing with management of lead time and production capacity can be divided into two segments. One integrates pricing concerns into the capacity-procurement decision, which reflects a long time horizon; the other focuses on a shorter time horizon, using pricing to make the best use of available capacity—akin to revenue management. The latter aims at smoothing out demand imbalances that are due to either structural seasonal patterns or short-term random fluctuations.

Three recent papers model the long-term capacity choice. So and Song (1998) study capacity expansion and pricing for a firm that uses delivery time guarantees as a competitive strategy. Along these same lines, Van Mieghem and Dada (1999) illustrate how competition, uncertainty and the timing of operational decisions influence capacity investment. Boyaci and Ray (2003) model pricing, delivery time and capacity decisions in conjunction with two substitutable products. They develop insights into the relationship between the relative cost of capacity for the two products and the price or time differentiation that the firm offers the market. For instance, firms that face increasing capacity costs should prefer a time-based strategy over a price-based strategy due to the increased demand that can result from fast delivery coupled with the price premium that can be charged for it.

Among the research that addresses dynamic pricing as a tool to improve capacity utilization, Swann (2001) investigates the joint setting of prices and production quantities when one or the other or both must be committed to at the beginning of the planning horizon. Chan et al. (2002) study the benefits of using price to influence demand levels when demand is seasonal and production is constrained so as to ensure inventory availability for periods of high demand. In a similar vein, Olsen (2003) examines optimal policies for quotation of prices and lead times dynamically as capacity "slots" become filled. Hall et al. (2003b) study the extent to which a firm can benefit from knowing the status of a production facility when making pricing decisions. In particular, they study the relationship between pricing-policy performance and the complexity of the pricing policy, measured by the amount of information required from the factory floor. The gains from using factory information can be quite high — up to a 65% increase in profit; and a fairly simple heuristic policy achieves most of these benefits. Cattani et al. (2002) study pricing decisions when a blend of make-to-order and make-to-stock production is carried out at a single facility. The analysis is designed to determine when a firm should engage in both types of production in a single facility, but there is value derived from making this decision in concert with the pricing decision.

Examples of management practice where pricing and lead time or capacity decisions are explicitly linked are few. Our conversations with managers suggest that many are pursuing more rigorous and sophisticated pricing and operations decisions, but they are doing so on parallel tracks. One exception is Tickets.com Inc., which has improved revenue per event by 45% by modifying price on the basis of supply and demand (Marshall, 2001).

OPERATIONS: PRICING AND INVENTORY

Research on inventory management dates back to at least 1913 (Harris 1913) and perhaps even to 1888 (Edgeworth 1888), so it is not surprising that the operations community has taken steps to link inventory and pricing decisions. In fact, research on the integration of pricing and inventory was pursued almost half a century ago by Whitin (1955). That paper incorporated pricing decisions into two classic inventory-ordering models: the economic order quantity model and the newsvendor model. More generally, linking prices to inventory levels may result in dynamic pricing policies.

Two primary functions of inventory are to take advantage of economies of scale in ordering or production, leading to "cycle stocks," and to protect against uncertainties in demand or replenishment times, leading to "safety stocks."

Among salient research on cycle stocks, Blattberg et al. (1981) investigate why retailers promote, presenting evidence that promotions transfer the inventory-holding cost to consumers when both parties act to minimize their own costs. Hall et al. (2003a) study dynamic pricing and inventory-ordering decisions in a setting where manufactures offer trade deals (discounts) to retailers and retailers manage a category of substitutable products rather than managing individual brands independently. They conclude that managing pricing and ordering for an entire category of products instead of on a product-by-product basis can create benefits that range from 15% to 50%.

While cycle-stock models generally assume that demand is known with certainty, safety-stock models allow for demand and sometimes lead time uncertainty. Safety-stock models may or may not incorporate the impact of order or production setup costs. In the absence of setup costs, safety-stock models generally lead to a "base stock" policy in which one replenishes inventory in each period to a constant level. In the presence of setup costs, it is generally only optimal to place an order when inventory has fallen below a certain reorder point.

In this regard, Federgruen and Heching (1999) studied a firm that must repeatedly decide how much inventory to have and what price to set in the absence of order setup costs. They term the optimal policy a "base-stock, list-price policy." When the inventory level drops below a base-stock level, the firm should charge the list price and order up to the base-stock level for that period. When inventory is above the base-stock level, the firm should order nothing and charge less than the list price, in effect a type of markdown policy. However, in the absence of extraordinary increases in inventory, a single price is employed. The work of Zhu and Thonemann (2003) extends this analysis to two products with interrelated demand. For cases where demand is stable over time, the authors find that dynamic pricing has minimal impact on profit. However, when demand is non-stationary, they find that dynamic pricing can increase profits by up to 49%.

Several papers have expanded on the work of Federgruen and Heching by incorporating ordering or production setup costs. Findings differ, depending on how they model consumer demand. Feng and Chen (2003) study a case where only two prices are allowed. They find that it is optimal to employ a high price under very low and very high inventory levels and a low price under intermediate levels. Chen and Simchi-Levi (2002a, 2002b) explore the optimality of more general pricing policies under different models of consumer demand.

Software developers have taken some significant steps to integrate pricing and inventory management. Few providers, however, offer real joint optimization of pricing with inventory or other supply chain dynamics.

CONCLUSION

There is much work yet to be done to capture a full understanding of dynamic pricing, along with a sophisticated grasp of operations and the supply chain. Marketing faculty and managers need to recognize that a unit cost is not a given number, nor is a lead time a given value. Rather, their decisions to adjust price can have a dramatic effect on the supply chain and hence on profitability. Operations faculty and managers, for their part, need to appreciate the many reasons for and benefits of dynamic pricing and be willing to explore the interactions among dynamic pricing and inventory, production planning and capacity management decisions. The good news is that managers recognize the possibilities of this integration, researchers are actively pursuing increasingly more sophisticated models and implementable approaches, and software developers are building the best insights into their existing offerings.

QUESTION

6.4 Describe the process of revenue management as it pertains to dynamic pricing.

REFERENCES

1. **Blattberg, R.C., G.D. Eppen and J. Lieberman, "A Theoretical and Empirical Evaluation of Price Deals for Consumer Nondurables,"** *Journal of Marketing* 45, no. 1 (1981): 116–129.

2. **Boyaci, T., and S. Ray, "Product Differentiation and Capacity Cost Interaction in Time and Price Sensitive Markets,"** *Manufacturing and Service Operations Management* 5, no. 1 (2003): 18–36.

3. **Boyd, E.A., and I.C. Bilegan, "Revenue Management and E-Commerce,"** *Management Science* 49, no. 10 (2003): 1363–1386.

4. **Cattani, K., E. Dahan and G. Schmidt,** *Spackling: Smoothing Make-To-Order Production of Custom Products With Make-To-Stock Production of Standard Items,* marketing working paper 384, UCLA Anderson Graduate School of Management, Oct. 1, 2002.

5. **Chan, LM.A., Z.J.M. Shen, D. Simchi-Levi and J.L. Swann, "Coordination of Pricing and Inventory Decisions: A Survey and Classification,"** in *Supply Chain Analysis in the eBusiness Era,* eds. D. Simchi-Levi, D. Wu and Z.J.M. Shen (New York: Kluwer, in press).

6. **Chan, L.M.A., D. Simchi-Levi and J. Swann,** *Dynamic Pricing Strategies for Manufacturing With Stochastic Demand and Discretionary Sales,* working paper, Georgia Institute of Technology, Atlanta, 2002.

7. **Chen, X., and D. Simchi-Levi,** *Coordinating Inventory Control and Pricing Strategies With Random Demand and Fixed Ordering Cost: The Finite Horizon Case,* working paper 157, MIT Center for eBusiness, Cambridge, Massachusetts (April 2002a).

8. **Chen, X., and D. Simchi-Levi,** *Coordinating Inventory Control and Pricing Strategies With Random Demand and Fixed Ordering Cost: The Infinite Horizon Case,* working paper, Operations Research Center, MIT, Cambridge, Massachusetts (2002b).

9. Edgeworth, F.Y., "The Mathematical Theory of Banking," *Journal of the Royal Statistical Society* 51 (March 1888): 113–127.

10. Elmaghraby, W., and P. Keskinocak, "Dynamic Pricing in the Presence of Inventory Considerations: Research Overview, Current Practices and Future Directions," *Management Science* 49, no. 10 (2003): 1287–1309.

11. Federgruen, A., and A. Heching, "Combined Pricing and Inventory Control Under Uncertainty," *Operations Research* 47, no. 3 (1999): 454–475.

12. Feng, Y., and F.Y. Chen, *Joint Pricing and Inventory Control With Setup Costs and Demand Uncertainty,* working paper, Department of Systems Engineering and Engineering Management, Chinese University of Hong Kong, Shatin, N.T., Hong Kong, Oct. 30, 2003.

13. Fleischmann, M., J.M. Hall and D.F. Pyke, *Coordinating Inventory and Pricing Decisions When Customers Stockpile* (presentation at the International Conference on Operations Research, Heidelberg, Germany, September 3–5, 2003).

14. Gallego, G., and G. van Ryzin, "Optimal Dynamic Pricing of Invertories With Stochastic Demand Over Finite Horizons," *Management Science* 40 (August 1994): 999–1020.

15. Hall, J.M., P.K. Kopalle and A. Krishna, *A Category Management Model of Retailer Dynamic Pricing and Ordering Decisions: Normative and Empirical Analysis,* working paper, Tuck School of Business, Dartmouth College, March 28, 2003a.

16. Hall, J.M., P.K. Kopalle and D.F. Pyke, *Static and Dynamic Pricing of Excess Capacity in a Make-To-Order Environment,* working paper, Tuck School of Business, Dartmouth College, 2003b.

17. Harris, F.W., "How Many Parts To Make at Once," *Factory, The Magazine of Management* 10 (1913): 135–136, 152.

18. Huchzermeier, A., A., Iyer and J. Freiheit, "The Supply Chain Impact of Smart Customers in a Promotional Environment," *Manufacturing and Service Operations Management* 4, no. 3 (2002): 228–240.

19. Iyer, A.V., and J. Ye, "Assessing the Value of Information Sharing in a Promotional Retail Environment," *Manufacturing and Service Operations Management* 2, no. 2(2000): 128–143.

20. Jorgensen, S., and P. Kort, "Optimal Pricing and Inventory Policies: Centralized and Decentralized Decision Making." *European Journal of Operations Research* 138 (May 2002): 578–600.

21. Kannan, P.K., and P.K. Kopalle, "Dynamic Pricing on the Internet: Importance and Implications for Consumer Behavior," *International Journal of Electronic Commerce* 5 (spring 2001): 63–83.

22. Kopalle, P., C.F. Mela and L. Marsh, "The Dynamic Effect of Discounting on Sales: Empirical Analysis and Normative Pricing Implications," *Marketing Science* 18, no. 3 (1999): 317–332.

23. Lee, H.L., V. Padmanabhan and S. Whang, "The Bullwhip Effect in Supply Chains," *Sloan Management Review* 38 (Spring 1997): 93–102.

24. Macé, S., and S.A. Neslin, *The Determinants of Promotion-Induced Stockpiling and Deceleration,* working paper #99-133, Tuck School of Business, Dartmouth College, 2000.

25. Marshall, J., *Digitas: Contextual Pricing and the Internet* (presentation at Tuck School of Business, Dartmouth College, November 5, 2001).

26. McCartney, S., "Computer Class: Airlines Find a Bag of High Tech Tricks To Keep Income Aloft," *Wall Street Journal,* Jan. 20, 2000, p. A1.

27. McGill, J.I., and G.J. van Ryzin, "Revenue Management: Research Overview and Prospects," *Transportation Science* 33, no. 2 (1999): 233–256.

28. Neslin, S.A., *Sales Promotion,* report no. 02-600, Marketing Science Institute, Cambridge, Massachusetts, 2002.

29. Olsen, T., *Dynamic Quotation of Prices and Lead Times* (presentation at Tuck School of Business, Dartmouth College, January 24, 2003).

30. Radjou, N., L.M. Orlov and L. Herbert, *Helping Supply Chain Cope With Demand,* TechStrategy Report, Forrester Research, Cambridge, Massachusetts, June 2003.

31. Rao, V.R., "Pricing Models in Marketing," chap. 11 in *Handbooks in Operations Research and Management Science, 5: Marketing,* eds. J. Eliashberg and G.L. Lilien (Amsterdam: North-Holland, 1993), pp. 517–552.

32. Secomandi, N., K. Abbott, T. Atan and E.A. Boyd, "From Revenue Management Concepts to Software Systems," *Interfaces* 32, no. 2 (2002): 1–11.

33. Smith, S., and D. Achabal, "Clearance Pricing and Inventory Policies for Retail Chains," *Management Science* 44 (March 1998): 285–300.

34. So, K.C., and J.-S. Song, "Price, Delivery Time Guarantees and Capacity Selection," *European Journal of Operational Research* 111 (November 1998): 28–49.

35. Sogomonian, A.G., and C.S. Tang, "A Modeling Framework for Coordinating Promotion and Production Decisions Within a Firm," *Management Science* 39 (February 1993): 191–203.

36. Swann, J.L, *Dynamic Pricing Models To Improve Supply Chain Performance* (Ph.D. diss., Northwestern University, Evanston, Illinois, 2001).

37. Van Mieghem, J.A., and M. Dada, "Price Versus Production Postponement: Capacity and Competition," *Management Science* 45 (December 1999): 1631–1649.

38. **Welch, D., "Ford Tames the Rebate Monster. Smart Pricing Has Saved the Company Millions,"** *Business Week,* May 5, 2003, p. 38.

39. **Whitin, T.M., "Inventory Control and Price Theory,"** *Management Science* 2, no. 1 (1955): 61–68.

40. **Zhu, K., and U.W. Thonemann, "Coordination of Pricing and Inventory Control Across Products,"** *Working paper,* University of Science and Technology Hong Kong and University of Münster, 2002.

Moritz Fleischmann is an assistant professor of quantitative methods, Rotterdam School of Management, Erasmus University Rotterdam; Joseph M. Hall is an assistant professor of business administration, Tuck School of Business, Dartmouth College; and David F. Pyke is professor of business administration and associate dean at the Tuck School. Contact the authors at MFleischmann@fbk. eur.nl.joseph.m.hall@dartmouth.edu and david.f.pyke@ dartmouth.edu.

Chapter 7

Management Accounting and Control Systems: Assessing Performance Over the Entire Value Chain

---

R. Cooper and W. B. Chew, *Control Tomorrow's Costs Through Today's Designs* (Reading 7.1), discusses the importance of target costing for many of today's manufacturing organizations. In short, target costing is a management process in which companies work backwards to arrive at product costs, after making a detailed assessment of what customers' requirements are for a given product. Once the level of quality and functionality are set and a target price and volume are determined, companies focus on developing manufacturing processes and materials sourcing at a target cost to achieve a target profit. This process is distinct from many traditional Western approaches in which the manufacturing cost plus a desired profit determines selling price. Using examples from Japanese firms such as Olympus Optical Company, one of the world's leaders in single-lens reflex cameras, and Komatsu, manufacturer of earth-moving products, Cooper and Chew detail the process of developing target costs at each firm. The authors also discuss how target costing can be applied in process and service industries.

Reading 7.2, *The Use of Target Costing in Developing the Mercedes-Benz M-Class*, by Tom Albright describes how Mercedes-Benz used target costing in the design and production of the M-class, a sports utility vehicle (SUV). Mercedes used cross-functional teams and included project and process engineers, marketing people, engineers and customers to help define key features that potential customers would value in an SUV. Professor Albright traces the development of the SUV through the concept, product realization and production phases. The article provides great insight into the target costing process.

Reading 7.3 by Tom Albright and Stan Davis, "*The Elements of Supply Chain Management*," provides a very good overview of what companies should consider before starting a supply chain management (SCM) program within the context of the Mercedes M-Class Sports Utility Program. The article covers numerous topics including: (a) developing and improving alliances with suppliers, (b) synchronizing flow of products, services and information across the value chain, (c) supplier involvement with JIT and TQM, (d) target costing, and (e) outsourcing. This article can also be used as a supplement to Chapter 6 on activity and process decisions.

Reading 7.4 is my article, *Implementing Management Innovations Successfully: Principles for Lasting Change*. I wrote this article based on many years of listening to managers complain about why management innovations such as TQM, ABC, reengineering, etc., continue to fail in their companies. These complaints were also borne out by articles in the business press that cited very low success rates at innovation implementation. The article defines a successful innovation implementation as on in which, "Managers and employees permanently alter the way they perform their job responsibilities to conform to the principles dictated by a particular innovation." The distinction I was trying to make was that organizations often don't do what is necessary to get managers and employees behind an innovation. I then suggest eight principles that organizations should consider as they are deciding whether to adopt an innovation.

Readings
Chapter 7

7.1 Control Tomorrow's Costs Through Today's Designs

*by Robin Cooper and W. Bruce Chew**

Over the past 15 years, company after company has learned that quality must be designed into products before they are manufactured—that it is expensive, if not misguided, to attempt to inspect in quality after the product has left the production line. Today the most competitive companies are applying the same logic to determining the price of new products. Before a company launches a product (or family of products), senior managers determine its ideal selling price, establish the feasibility of meeting that price, and then control costs to ensure that the price is met. They are using a management process known as *target costing*.

Target costing drives a product development strategy that focuses the design team on the ultimate customer and on the real opportunity in the market. Leading Japanese electronics and vehicle manufacturers have used target costing to their advantage, and companies are now introducing it in the United States, Germany, and elsewhere. Its rigorous cost-management technique helps prevent senior managers from launching low-margin products that do not generate appropriate returns to the company, but its greater value lies in its ability to bring the challenge of the marketplace back through the chain of production to product designers. Target costing ensures that development teams will bring profitable products to market not only with the right level of quality and functionality but also with appropriate prices for the targeted customer segments. It is a discipline that harmonizes the labor of disparate participants in the development effort, from designers and manufacturing engineers to market researchers and suppliers.

The logic of target costing is simple. Looking at tomorrow's marketplace, the organization maps customer segments and targets the most attractive ones. It determines what level of quality and functionality will succeed within each segment, given a predetermined target price (and volume and launch date). The organization then designs the sourcing, production, and delivery processes that will enable it to achieve its desired profits at this target. In effect, the company reasons backward from customers' needs and willingness to pay instead of following the flawed but common practice of cost-plus pricing. Target costing ensures that success with the customers will yield economic success for the company.

COST DISCIPLINE: WHY NOW?

The logic of target costing is so simple and compelling that one may wonder why it has only recently begun to receive attention. After all, at any time in the past, senior managers could have gained much from becoming involved in the process of pricing and costing a product before it was designed. Their lack of involvement gave engineers and enthusiasts, who were unlikely to see the whole picture, undue influence over the company's competitive position. When senior managers tried to drive costs out of their operations ex post facto by cutting staff, eliminating frills, outsourcing, or reengineering downstream processes, they often discovered that as much as 70% to 80% of a product's costs were effectively immutable after it left the designers' hands. As product and process technologies have become more integrated, a product's cost has become even more strongly tied to its design.

Nevertheless, although a preemptive and disciplined approach to costs has always been reasonable, it has not always been urgent, and companies do not usually undertake difficult tasks if the tasks are avoidable. These days, however, price and cost targeting are no longer avoidable, largely because of the erosion of important first-mover advantages in the new global economy. In the past, many leading companies, especially those that led by technical differentiation, found that they could take a cost-plus approach to releasing new products because they anticipated profiting from serial generations of products. They believed that being first to market was most important; that in preparing to be first, design teams needed to focus only on selecting and executing well the appropriate bundle of product attributes; and that ultimately, over several iterations of the product, the marketplace would allow the company to earn a reasonable return on total capital employed.

By that logic, when the product was first released, it might carry a comparatively high price considered affordable by only a small number of lead users, such as businesses hoping to turn a new technology to their advantage or comparatively wealthy, adventurous technologies. Lead users would pay a premium for the first-generation product and help create excitement for its new features; they would even help establish the brand. The revenues

---

* From R. Cooper and W. B. Chew, "Control Tomorrow's Costs Through Today's Designs," *Harvard Business Review* (January–February 1996): 88–97. Reprinted with permission.

from lead users would rarely cover the cost of developing the product. Hewlett-Packard Company, for example, did not expect the first releases of its laser printers to recover R&D costs. But first-mover companies have assumed that they would have time to scale up to mass production and introduce serially cheaper versions of products for increasingly broader segments of customers. The mass market would be the source of most profits—as indeed it was for consumer products such as the 35-millimeter camera and the fax, and for components such as ABS brakes and digital TV controls.

Today that strategic assumption would be disastrous for all but the most advanced products, those with highly proprietary technologies. Global markets no longer allow a company time to introduce a product and then scale up. Now imitators—usually lean enterprises—can bring "me too" products to market so rapidly that first-mover companies have no time to inculcate brand loyalty, let alone recover their development costs. Lean competitors, with faster reflexes than old mass-production companies, work on shorter product-development and life cycles, and they manufacture almost anywhere—Korea, Mexico, Israel.

The growing number and increasing ubiquity of lean competitors means that copycat versions of most new products will be available within months, not years. So if market leaders can't recover costs as they used to, they have no choice but to manage costs from the design phase forward and to launch products at prices that will attract broad segments of customers and forestall imitation. How long they can hold on to their market, then, will often depend on how quickly they can offer greater functionality without raising price.

For companies to gain and hold market leadership today, they have to design the cost out of their products when they set initial levels of quality and functionality and they have to calibrate product performance to an identified price niche. In other words, senior managers need to approach new product development controlling for tomorrow's costs, not just today's. And tomorrow comes more quickly than it used to.

OLYMPUS: FROM COST TARGETS TO TARGET COSTING

In Japan, competition among lean companies has become so intense that aggressive cost management is critical to survival in sonic sectors. It is thus no accident that leading organizations such as Olympus Optical Company and Komatsu developed and adapted target costing early on.

Olympus was a leader in single-lens reflex (SLR) cameras, which had no technological competitor for a generation. But by 1987, "compact" cameras built around a miniaturized electronic shutter had absorbed so many advanced electronic controls—features such as automatic exposure and zoom—that consumers began to view them as a serious alternative to the SLR. Olympus had introduced a compact of its own as early as 1978, but not as a main focus of its product portfolio. In the mid-1980s, Olympus began losing money, and by 1987 its losses were substantial.

Senior managers saw severe problems. Cameras incorporating the new electronic technologies suffered from poor quality and there were no individual product "hits." The managers concluded that the planning and development of product families needed improvement. Externally, Olympus suffered from the sudden shift from SLR cameras to competitors' compact cameras and from a steady appreciation of the yen.

The company reacted first with an effort to regain lost share by introducing a number of new products—for example, SLRs with advanced electronics and compacts with an advanced zoom. A second initiative was aimed at improving quality, which historically had been high at Olympus and which continued to be crucial to its ability to lower the total costs associated with its products.

But most important to Olympus was the third initiative: reconciling production costs to a volatile market. Managers believed that the company's ability to manufacture cameras at a cost that would meet the increasingly stringent expectations of its customers would be central to the success of any new product. Moreover, the company's product development process would have to meet challenging price and profit targets within 18 months of their being set—before the competitive environment could shift again.

This was not the first time that Olympus managers had set cost targets for new products, but earlier targets had been more or less hypothetical. Senior managers had created no imperative to meet them, and missed targets did not prevent products from being launched. Essentially, designers did their best on functionality, manufacturing engineers pursued efficiency, and marketing sold what was produced. All that changed in 1987.

First, Olympus tried to establish a clearer picture of what features future customers would value in new product families. It produced a corporate plan that identified the future mix of businesses by major product line, the desired levels of profitability, and the contribution of each product to the cultivation of the brand, and it performed a technology review to learn how current and future technologies would affect the camera business. The technology review included an audit of Olympus's proprietary technologies that could be turned to the company's advantage. Its market mapping included an analysis of the general business environment to determine how macro-economic factors, such as changing exchange rates and the further segmentation of income groups, were likely to affect consumer demand. Finally, the marketing research included a survey of information collected from such sources as Olympus questionnaires, group interviews, interviews at fashion centers, and interviews with photographers as well as a competitive analysis that examined areas such as competitors' capabilities, likely price points, and filed patents.

With a clearer sense of what the camera market would bear and what Olympus's profitability goals required, the company identified the price points at which new compact cameras would sell. The U.S. market price for basic compact-camera models in 1991 was about $100. With that price as a baseline, Olympus analyzed consumer trends, competitors' performance, and forward-looking technology to establish what relationship it could anticipate between distinctive camera features, such as magnification capability or smaller size, and higher price points. From each price point, Olympus subtracted the appropriate margins for dealers and its U.S. subsidiary and also subtracted import costs, such as freight and duties, to arrive at the price that would be paid to the factory for any new model. Then, by subtracting its own margin requirement, Olympus finally arrived at a preliminary target cost for each new product.

Now what it needed was a disciplined process for developing products that could be made at those costs. The responsibility for ensuring that the company could produce cameras with the features customers wanted and at costs within the targeted limits fell to a product-development management team at Tatsuno, the site of Olympus's primary manufacturing operations. Only when designers and manufacturing engineers could demonstrate that estimated production costs did not exceed target costs would a camera be submitted for release to production.

OLYMPUS MOVES TO CLOSE THE GAPS

This process may sound straightforward, but it was not: Only about 20% of proposed new models cleared Olympus's hurdle on the first pass. However, the 80% that missed were not abandoned. As at many companies, it was not uncommon at Olympus for product managers to design "nice-to-have," but not "need-to-have" features into their products. The product-development management team's job was to ask whether the value those features added really outweighed their costs. Correspondingly, they would ask whether an enhanced product could justifiably be moved to the next higher price point so that its estimated costs would generate acceptable returns.

Soon enough, those reviews ended. If target costs could not be met or price points could not be changed, the team returned the product to research and development for redesign.

In the context of this review, Olympus managers used a life-cycle analysis to reckon the costs of important new technologies incorporated in new product designs. That is, they assessed the value of a technology's contribution to features that could be expected to serve a variety of models over the life cycle of a whole product family; they did not attribute the technology's costs only to the first models introduced. Further, they separated the whole cost of a new technology into its two components: the costs of research and development and the costs of production.

The Olympus product-development team determined that in allocating research and development costs, product designers should consider how long a camera family is likely to be on the market (on the order of three years) or how long a specific feature is likely to find application in other camera families. As for production costs, Olympus managers learned that even after a product family comes to market, the costs associated with new technology often decline quickly and dramatically with the adoption of manufacturing programs that actually increase product quality—for instance, by reducing the number of parts in a subassembly, eliminating labor-intensive mechanical adjustments, or moving from metal or glass to plastic. The number of parts in the shutter unit of one entire class of compact cameras, for example, fell from 105 to 56, a reduction that led to a 58% decrease in production costs for this widely used component. By 1990, Olympus managers had discovered that the company could generally reduce its production costs by approximately 35% across the production lifetime of its new products. The product-development management team incorporated this figure into its target costing of future products.

On the whole, life-cycle analysis helped many potentially profitable products clear the hurdle. The practice may sound vaguely like the old strategy of distributing costs over successive generations of buyers, from lead users to mass markets, but it is different. There is no thought here of introducing the product family at high prices that then fall as volume increases. Cost, not price, is expected to fall.

Cost reductions of this magnitude don't happen without strenuous effort. For existing products and processes, Olympus monitored and managed fixed costs, purchased-parts costs, routine production costs, the costs of defective production, capacity utilization targets, and overhead expenses. And Olympus used its falling production costs in a number of ways. At times, it raised margins; at other times, it selectively dropped price points. On the whole, however, the company used cost savings to improve its products over time. The one thing it did not do was take a short-term profit, which, in the unforgiving environment of lean competition, would have been the most dangerous option. A company that just cashes in its market advantage invites imitation and invests nothing in sustaining its technical differentiation.

KOMATSU'S SUPPLIERS BRING COSTS DOWN

As the Olympus experience illustrates, target costing issues a clear-cut but daunting challenge to product designers. They cannot call a design a success unless they meet the functionality needs of the customer, the price demands of the distribution channel, the manufacturability requirements of the plant, and the financial projections of the corporation.

Komatsu's experience illustrates another way to use target costing—in this case to pressure suppliers to drive their costs down. Komatsu's earth-moving products contain many more components than do Olympus's cameras, and the company relies more heavily on outside suppliers for complete subsystems: hydraulic devices, electrical subassemblies, and the like. In 1993, for example, Komatsu manufactured roughly 30% of the content in its heavy equipment products, designed and subcontracted 50%, and purchased the remaining 20% from outside suppliers.

Moreover, the number of choices Komatsu must make regarding components makes it difficult to control development costs. Which features will the F company offer on which models? Which teams need additional support? Where should the company be refining designs and where should it be rethinking entire design approaches? Komatsu must involve suppliers in product design early in order to make informed decisions in those and other important matters.

Throughout the entire product-development process, Komatsu poses a challenge to its suppliers: to maintain the performance specifications of components and deliver at prices consistent with Komatsu's overall target costs. Komatsu's target costing program provides the parameters that guide its negotiations with suppliers and subassembly makers to ensure a profitable product launch. By linking performance needs and the company's margin requirements back to each major subassembly, Komatsu's design team can track the performance of whole vehicle and keep an eye on the integrated goal: a product launched at a price the end user will find attractive, not simply a subassembly that satisfies product designers.

To develop system and component targets for its suppliers, Komatsu relies on data on historical performance and cost that it has recorded in function and cost tables. Function tables, containing information about the physical characteristics of each component, help designers determine the company's best-performing components, Cost tables, containing information about the costs of components, help designers identify the low-cost components. By, in effect, overlaying one table on the other, Komatsu engineers identify the target cost of the best component for a given project. This target cost becomes the suppliers' target price.

In developing the target cost of an excavator's cooling system, for instance, Komatsu's engineers determined that the most important performance factor was the surface area of the system's radiator, They consulted function tables to calculate he minimum radiator surface area required. They consulted cost tables to calculate the most cost-effective design. Then they calculated the target cost of their radiator to reflect both minimums: least surface area and minimum cost per unit of area. In demanding that the radiator in the excavator's cooling system be both the most efficient at cooling and the most cost-effective, Komatsu forced its suppliers to push the frontiers of their own technology to achieve more efficient designs.

It is important to remember that subsystem target costs must fit within an overall target cost, which has been derived from a projected market price. But if a subsystem's cost exceeds its projected share of the product's target cost, Komatsu does not automatically reject the design or reduce the cost targets for other components. Like Olympus, Komatsu focuses not on some mechanistic algorithm but on the complex relationship between cost and price and the effects of both on value. Komatsu asks whether particular functions need to be continued. It provides engineering support to suppliers that cannot meet targets. It seeks unexploited opportunities to reduce costs even further among components that have already met their targets. Komatsu managers do not measure success one department at a time. They know that the marketplace does not reward an outstanding component, only an outstanding integrated design.

SMOOTHING OUT THE TARGET-COSTING PROCESS

Clearly, target costing involves more than listing dollar targets and projected margins. It is a highly structured product-development discipline, adapted to such specific elements of a company's strategic positioning as industry pricing dynamics, product-complexity and life-cycle analyses, and supplier relations. It requires a company to make a series of decisions that include defining the product that customers want, ascertaining the economics required for profitability, allocating targets to components, and identifying the gap between target costs and initial projections of manufacturing costs. (See the diagram "The Target-Costing Process.")

On the other hand, as the experiences of Olympus and Komatsu suggest, target costing is not an exact science. It depends on credible data and on people who have the courage to make difficult judgments. Target costing is an iterative process that cannot be decoupled from the ordinary push and pull of the design process. The targets evolve as teams seek to balance functionality, price, volumes, capital investment, and costs. Also, because target costing is integrative, responsibility for achieving targets must be shared across functions. Finally, if they are to use target costing, companies must treat their suppliers as partners both during the design process and when they are setting cost targets.

Our description may make target costing sound like a smooth ride, but troublesome roadblocks can show up at different stages.

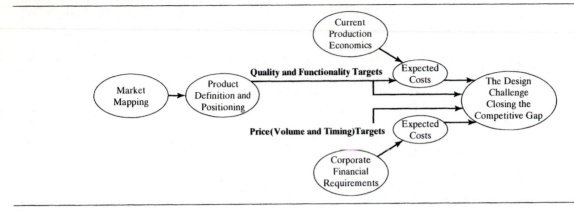

Defining the Product, Targeting the Marketplace. The choices that drive the entire target-costing process are the customer's. What prices will customers accept? What functionality will they insist on? What will competitors offer them? Because the ultimate goal of target costing is to maximize a product's total profitability, not minimize its cost, companies must do their best to understand how their customers' preferences and their competitors' products will evolve over time. That requires a thorough understanding of the customers' behavior in each market segment.

When the Japanese targeted the luxury car market, for example, they already knew one critical feature of luxury cars: They had to be quiet. For years, manufacturers had tried to lower sound levels in luxury cars and found the task inherently difficult. Sound level not only traded off against acceleration—high-revving engines tended to be loud—but was also an integrative challenge, because sound came from many other design components, including the drive train, tires, and door seals. Japanese researchers discovered, however, that frequency was as important to customers as decibel level; that is, the nature of the sound was as important as its loudness. This discovery pointed to a different design challenge: Instead of minimizing, sound, designers could try to "tune" the car in a pleasing fashion—an approach with enormous ramifications for the way companies set their target costs.

The relationship between volume and frequency points to the challenge facing anyone engaged in product positioning. Any approach that asks customers, "Do you like this offering better than that one?" and stops there will not yield much insight. Marketers need an approach that will reveal deeper patterns of customer preference. Fortunately, researchers can use sophisticated surveying techniques such as conjoint analysis to reveal how potential customers cluster around multiple product features and functionalities. These preferences must then be expressed as innovative design options—what we might think of as quality and functionality targets. It is at this point that companies might use such interfunctional design techniques as the House of Quality, which maps the relationship between customers' desired features and specific engineering characteristics.

It is not enough to focus on the customer; competitors are a parallel concern. Most companies define competitors as "companies that make things similar to what we make," which is the producers' view of competition. In target costing, the Japanese companies we have studied tend to define competitors from the customers' perspective: "I am about to make a purchase, so what are my options?" Olympus, for example, benchmarked itself not only against camera manufacturers but also against the makers of CD players and Walkman-type products. The company understood that it was competing for discretionary dollars against makers of all kinds of consumer gadgets, not just against camera makers.

Computing Overall Target Costs. Companies derive overall targets in a number of different ways but the purpose is always the same: to think rigorously about the company's future profitability. In fact, some Japanese companies classify target costing as a profit-management tool rather than as a cost-control tool. In any case, the task is to compute the costs that must not be exceeded if acceptable margins from specific products at specific price points are to be guaranteed.

For most companies, this order of logic represents a radical shift in thinking. Traditionally, companies perform the financial analysis associated with product development only after much of the development work has been done, and then only to determine whether to continue investment. In contrast, a financial analysis done early in the design process can accomplish much more. In target costing, it can tell design teams and general managers a great deal about what is required to make the product a success. The nature of the analysis may be the same, but shifts in timing and focus make a huge difference.

One U.S. vehicle maker we have worked with performed a financial analysis to estimate a likely return on investment for a redesigned product launched under a single set of hypothetical conditions. The purpose of the analysis was to make senior managers more comfortable with their decision to go ahead. So although the analysis

126

aided the approval process, it provided little guidance to the design team. It displayed no sensitivity to the fact that conditions such as launch date, cost, and volume are variable and that small changes matter. Our analysis of the company's data showed that to miss cost targets would have been catastrophic: A 5% error would have eliminated any return on the company's $200 million investment.

Allocating Target Costs, Identifying the Gap. Once a target cost has been calculated for a new product, the design team has to divide it up among the product's various functions. How much can the team spend on one function as against all the others? The team must first calculate the gap between the target cost and what it estimates it would cost to build the product with today's processes, suppliers, productivity levels, and materials. The difference is a good approximation of the excess cost that must be wrung out of the new product.

It usually makes no sense to apply cost-reduction requirements uniformly across all the components and subsystems of the contemplated product. Rather, the design team can consult customer-value surveys, historical trends, and other data to guide it in determining how much cost it can remove from each component or subassembly. The team will allocate more costs to critical features (allowing for increased engine cost in a car that is intended to have a peppier ride, for example). But every extra dollar it allocates to improving one product feature must come from another function's allocation, because the target cost remains fixed.

Isuzu Motors' target-costing system, like others, aims to keep prices constant while adding as much functionality as possible to each new generation of vehicles. The system therefore attaches great importance to determining what features and level of performance the customer will want most, and it uses those preferences as the basis for allocating costs to major functions and group components. Market researchers ask customers to estimate how much they would pay for a given function. Then they develop ratios of preference by asking customers to estimate the relative importance of each function on a 100-point scale.

Isuzu uses this information to spread a product's target cost among the major specified function improvements. If the target cost for a component is too low to allow a sufficiently attractive or safe version to be produced, the component's target cost is increased and the target cost of other components is decreased. Thus, Isuzu continually uses its best sense of customer value to drive its design team's cost allocation decisions.

Obeying the Cardinal Rule. All design-team members, whatever their function specialty, must regard the overall final cost target as an unalterable commitment; target commitments outrank design commitments. The idea is that aggressive targets focus the efforts of the design team on creative solutions and press value engineering to its limits.

In other words, to say that target costing is an iterative process is not to say that target costs, once set, are then subject to ongoing debate. They are not. Targets must fall under the protection of what we call the *cardinal rule:* If you cannot meet the targets, you cannot launch the product. That being the case, the process of product definition and target generation continues, but not in the factory.

Some companies have a layered set of targets. The first pass is the simplest, and failure here leads to a more sophisticated life-cycle analysis. But this approach must not become a game with ever lower hurdles, each test becoming less rigorous than the one before. As one manager puts it, "In the past, if a specific project failed the test for funding, we just kept changing the assumptions for the project or revising the test until the project passed. Target costing will not tolerate that."

The cardinal rule applies to the product as a whole. When targets are assigned to individual subassembly teams, some teams will beat their targets, some will meet them, and some will fall short. But success is not determined component by component; it is achieved—or not— by the final product. When components turn out to be more expensive than anticipated, that cost must be offset somewhere else in the design. This requirement demands a degree of cooperation and team spirit that will necessitate change for many organizations.

TARGET COSTING AND THE ORGANIZATION

Any system that cuts across organizational boundaries and communicates so many vital economic and market objectives is bound to have a profound impact on how the organization does business. One of the main benefits of target costing is that it forces companies to delineate their product-development goals very precisely and in a single vernacular.

In many companies, clarity of communication may be sacrificed to a general commitment to decentralization. At one large U.S. industrial company we have worked with, for example, nearly every functional department was using a unit of analysis that it had developed to answer a question of importance to itself only and that varied subtly from every other functional department's unit of analysis. Competitors' specifications were collected by product, existing costs were computed by part, customers' needs were defined in terms of product attribute, manufacturing constraints were determined by installation point, and the capabilities of the supplier were measured by module.

All those measures were related, but none addressed overall cost targets. There was no overall context within which to work. As a result, a product designer assigned to a particular subsystem could not get a clear answer to the question: "How much do customers value this subsystem?" or "What does this subsystem cost?"

Target costing requires that such problems be addressed directly. It forces companies to be specific about what customers want and what prices they are prepared to pay. Finally, target costing creates opportunities to demonstrate a commitment to customers. If targets cannot be met, the company cannot simply raise the price and launch the product. Such discipline may be painful to the people who work on a project, but it sends an important message to the organization as a whole: that customers come first and that if the company doesn't create value for them, a competitor will.

MAKING IT WORK

For target costing to succeed, targets must not only be valid, people must also see them as valid. They cannot be the outcome of a "political" process. The market analysis that yields the target prices, the financial analysis that generates the target costs, and the disaggregation procedures that allocate costs among components and subassemblies—all must be trusted. The target-costing process must, therefore, be highly transparent.

Moreover, cost-reduction objectives must be achievable most of the time. Setting the bar too high can be as damaging as having no bar at all; in fact, the Japanese set a series of what they call *tip-toe objectives*, that is, objectives that may be reached by "standing on tiptoes"—a stretch that strains the organization but does not defeat it. Also, the requirements for product functionality must be clearly and publicly articulated so that nobody tries to achieve the target cost by reducing product functionality below acceptable levels. It is no good to reduce costs by shortchanging customers. When target costing works well, quantifiable hurdles are established in a transparent process, and senior managers commit themselves to what the numbers show. Engineers receive goals that are clear and achievable, and everyone adheres to the cardinal rule. A company that meets those requirements is not guaranteed a victory in the markets it enters. It does earn the right to compete.

The authors gratefully acknowledge the assistance of Bernard Avishai in developing and writing this article.

Robin Cooper is a professor at the Claremont Graduate School's Peter F. Drucker Graduate Management Center in Claremont, California, and author of When Lean Enterprises Collide: Competing Through Confrontation *(Harvard Business School Press, 1995), which draws on Cooper's five-year study of the management systems of 20 Japanese companies. W. Bruce Chew is a senior consultant at Monitor Company, a global consulting firm in Cambridge, Massachusetts. He is a former associate professor of technology and operations management at the Harvard Business School in Boston, Massachusetts.*

TARGETING COSTS IN PROCESS AND SERVICE INDUSTRIES

Target costing has made its mark in industries in which products require a good deal of production assembly—cars, cameras, and bulldozers, for example. However, the discipline target costing offers has uses outside the assembly environment.

In processing companies, where the characteristics of the process—time, temperature, and pressure—determine the performance of the product, the focus of target costing shifts from the product to the process. A steel company would tend to focus on the costs associated with routings and processing time; a paper mill, on those associated with speed and breakage. The key issues—understanding market needs, ensuring satisfactory financial performance at a given price, and not exceeding the target cost—remain.

Similarly, target costing can be applied to services, for which the focus is the service delivery system. As in process—intensive manufacturing, process is inextricable from product. Think of the issues that are important to the delivery of health care and fast-food functions. Where services and process-intensive manufacturing diverge is in their flexibility. It is enormously expensive to convert a paper machine so that it can produce a grade or weight that was not considered in its initial design. Service delivery systems, however, are a different matter. In people-intensive, customer-responsive service-delivery systems, it is not only possible to add new services, it can be hard not to. Menus are easy to extend. Room services can easily be added. Consulting firms or law firms can always enter a new area of practice. Where is the discipline that ensures that these extensions are profitable?

Because a single service-delivery system may be used to deliver a wide range of services, determining the profitability of individual services becomes an exercise in the arbitrary allocation of costs. In services, particularly those in which waiting time is critical, it is the systemic effects of individual new service—for instance, the extent to which they make the process more complex—that determine whether their revenues and value to customers offset their costs. Target costing can still facilitate a discussion of the appropriateness of a new service, but only if it focuses on the systemic impact of the service extension and questions whether this impact aligns with company strategy and profitability goals. In service industries as in other industries, target costing can help organizations resist the urge to create new market offerings simply because they have the ability.

QUESTIONS

7.1a Describe the procedure (as characterized by Cooper and Chew) that Isuzu Motors goes through to allocate its target cost among major functional improvements to its vehicles.

7.1b What are "tip-toe" objectives as discussed in the Cooper and Chew article, and what is their role in target costing?

7.2 The Use of Target Costing in Developing the Mercedes-Benz M-Class

by Tom Albright*

EXECUTIVE SUMMARY

- Target costing techniques are important tools for controlling costs in the early stages of product development.
- This article describes how Mercedes-Benz used target costing in the design and production of the M-class, a new sports utility vehicle.
- Mercedes' marketing research showed that customers in this market segment hold established expectations about product characteristics and price levels.
- This marketing information was used to design a vehicle with the characteristics that customers wanted, at a selling price that customers would pay, and that would produce an acceptable level of profitability for investors.

Target costing systems have three major characteristics (Cooper, 1995):

- Targets for price, quality, and function are set in advance.
- Major costs are identified in the design phase.
- The approach is multifunctional.

To develop the M-class, Mercedes used multifunctional teams that included product and process engineers, marketing professionals, and suppliers. The company held focus groups to help define features that potential customers expected to see in a sports utility vehicle from Mercedes.

Target costing was a logical cost management technique for Mercedes to use because the company was designing a completely new vehicle and concurrently constructing a new production facility. As a result, Mercedes could define a significant portion of the production costs that would be incurred before the costs were actually committed.

SUCCESS AT TARGET COSTING

Successful implementation of target costing principles requires managing many interrelated components, including the following (Ansari and Bell, 1997):

- Price-led costing
- Customer orientation
- Focus on product and process design
- Cross-functional teams
- Life-cycle cost reduction
- Value chain involvement

Price-led costing. In many industries, pricing has traditionally been a function of cost. Markups, or profit margins, are simply added to the estimated cost of a product to set an initial market price. If customers reject a price determined in this manner, producers have little recourse other than to reduce their margin, though they can also attempt to trim production costs.

Target costing practices treat selling prices and margins as uncontrollable variables, because the markets determine selling prices, and companies must earn adequate margins to remain in business over the long term. Thus, cost is the only variable that can be influenced by management.

Customer orientation. Delivering products customers want at a price they are willing to pay is a fundamental premise "of target" costing. Lean enterprises survive by gaining a series of short-term advantages over their competitors in one of three customer-oriented variables (the *survival triplet*) (Cooper, 1995):

- Price
- Quality
- Functionality

Ultimately consumers determine minimum acceptable standards for quality and functionality and they define a maximum acceptable market price.

Short-term competitive advantage can be gained by managing the elements of the survival triplet more effectively than does the competition. For example, competitive advantage can be gained if a company can deliver comparable quality and functionality at a price significantly below that of its competitors. Similarly, a company can also gain a competitive advantage by providing greater functionality, higher quality, or both at comparable prices.

Focus on product and process design. Many production costs derive from decisions made during the design phase. Consequently, cost-reduction efforts should focus on phases before production begins. Mercedes, for example, made decisions early in the product-development process to reduce the level of value-added (or conversion) activities and costs within its planned facility.

Traditionally, purchased components have made up from 55% to 60% of unit production costs at Mercedes,

---

* From: T. Albright, "The Use of Target Costing in Developing the Mercedes Benz M-Class," *International Journal of Strategic Cost Management* (Autumn 1998): 13–23. Reprinted with permission.

which means that value-added percentages have ranged from 40% to 45%. During the product- and process-design phase for the M-class, Mercedes made the strategic decision to rely heavily on systems suppliers. As a result, the value-added percentage in the new plant where the M-class is made is only 20% to 25% of manufacturing cost.

Cross-functional teams. Target costing begins with customer needs. It should end with a product that meets or exceeds customer expectations. For this to happen, however, a wide variety of professional expertise is required. At Mercedes the cross-functional design team included cost planners, design engineers, systems suppliers, and marketing professionals had to coordinate their work to enhance quality and control costs.

Life-cycle cost reduction. Target costing also encourages designers to consider costs that extend beyond the manufacturing stage. Because target costing principles are customer-oriented, design decisions should seek to minimize both manufacturing costs and the ownership costs that customers will incur.

For example, although the Mercedes E300 diesel has a relatively high sticker price, it is the choice of many European cab companies because its maintenance costs are low, and its life commonly exceeds 300,000 miles. Lower operating costs during the vehicle's useful life and higher resale values are examples of life cycle cost-reduction strategies affected by engineering design choices.

Value chain involvement. Target costing principles stress the importance of managing costs throughout the value chain. Involving "upstream" suppliers early in development is crucial. Involving suppliers early during the design phase helped Mercedes improve quality and reduce costs. "Downstream" input—the involvement, for example, of the marketing and customer service departments—is also necessary to achieve the strategic benefits of target costing.

BACKGROUND OF THE MERCEDES M-CLASS PROJECT

To explain how Mercedes used target costing techniques in developing the M class, the following sections discuss each of the major target costing characteristics mentioned previously. Also discussed are innovations Mercedes developed, which include various indexes that explicitly link engineering and financial concepts.

Background. In the early 1990s, Mercedes struggled with problems in product development, cost efficiency, material purchasing, and adapting to changing markets. By 1993 Mercedes had experienced its worst sales slump in decades, and it lost money for the first time in its history.

Since that time, Mercedes has streamlined its core business, reduced parts and system complexity, and established simultaneous engineering programs with suppliers.

New products. In a search for additional market share, new segments, and new niches, Mercedes started developing a range of new products. The new C-class debuted in 1993, the E-class in 1995, the new sportster SLK in 1996, and both the A-class and the M-class All Activity Vehicle in 1997. Perhaps the largest and most radical of all the new projects was the M-class.

In April 1993, Mercedes announced it would build its first passenger vehicle manufacturing facility in the United States. The decision emphasized the company's globalization strategy and desire to move closer to customers and markets. After an intensive, six-month effort to evaluate locations suitable for a new plant costing $300 million, Mercedes chose Tuscaloosa County, Alabama. Annual production at the plant is now about 65,000 vehicles, with North American and export volumes approximately equal.

The M-class project can justifiably be called a radical, high-stake experiment (Woodruff and Miller, 1995). Mercedes had to build a new factory in a new country and also develop a new product for a new market segment. While Japanese manufacturing plants built outside Japan typically copy Japanese factories and models (at least at first), Mercedes simultaneously had to debug a new product, a new manufacturing process, and a new work force. During the early stages of product and rocess development, the popular press described the Mercedes venture as a prescription for disaster because of the many variables and unknowns involved.

THE M-CLASS PROJECT PHASES

The M-class moved from concept to production relatively quickly. The *concept phase* began in 1992, which led to a feasibility study that the board of directors approved. The project *realization phase* began in 1993. Finally, *production* began in 1997. Key elements of these various phases are described next.

Concept phase (1992–1993). The cross-functional team at Mercedes compared the company's existing product line with various market segments in order to find opportunities to introduce new types of vehicles. The analysis revealed opportunities in the rapidly expanding market for sports utility vehicles, dominated by Jeep, Ford, and GM.

The team conducted market research to estimate potential sales opportunities worldwide for a high-end sports utility vehicle having the characteristics of a Mercedes-Benz. A rough cost estimate was developed that included materials, labor, overhead, and one-time development and project costs. Then cash flows were projected and analyzed over a 10-year period. Net present value (NPV) analysis was used to acquire approval of the project from the board of directors. Because of the capital-intensive nature of the automobile manufacturing industry, estimates of production volume are critical factors in the NPV calculation.

Risks and opportunities. The sensitivity of the NPV calculation was analyzed by simulating various "what-if" scenarios involving different risks and opportunities. The risk factors that were tested included fluctuations in monetary exchange rate, different sales levels due to consumer substitution of M-class vehicles for other Mercedes products, and product and manufacturing costs that differed from projections.

Based on the economic feasibility study of the concept phase, the board approved the project. The search for manufacturing locations included sites in Germany, other European countries, and the United States. Partly because of Mercedes globalization strategy, the decisive factor in placing the plant in the United States was the desire to be close to the biggest market for sports utility vehicles.

Project realization phase (1993–1996). The target costing process requires broad, cross-functional activities to acquire market information necessary to develop a new vehicle. Mercedes used customer focus groups to obtain this information. The company held regular customer clinics to explain the new vehicle concept and to view the prototype. These clinics elicited important information about how the proposed vehicle would be received by potential customers and the press. Customers were asked to rank the importance of various characteristics including safety, comfort, economy, and styling. Engineers organized in function groups designed systems to deliver these essential characteristics.

Furthermore, Mercedes would not lower its internal standards for components, even if initial customer expectations were lower than the Mercedes standard. For example, many automotive experts believe the handling of Mercedes products results from manufacturing a world-class chassis. Thus, each new class within the Mercedes line must meet strict standards for handling, even though these standards may actually exceed customer expectations for some classes.

Mercedes did not use target costing to produce the lowest-priced vehicle in an automotive class. Rather, the company's strategic objective was to deliver products that were slightly more expensive than competitive models but with a greater perceived value on the part of the customer.

Goal-oriented approach. Another difference between Mercedes' and other companies' use of target costing lies in the goal-oriented approach to achieving target cost. Cooper cites examples of Japanese companies that strive in a single-minded effort to achieve a static target cost. In contrast, the M-class (and M-class target cost) remained alive throughout the product realization phase because of changing dynamics.

Mercedes found it beneficial to place the design and testing team members in close physical proximity to other functions within the project to promote fast communication and decision making. In this way the company was able to respond quickly to changing conditions. For example, while the vehicle was under development, the market moved toward the luxury end of the spectrum. Crash test results were also incorporated into the evolving M-class design. In addition, Mercedes developed new technical features such as side airbags. (The decision to include this new feature on all Mercedes lines was made at the corporate level because experience has shown that customers' reactions to a vehicle class can affect the entire brand.)

As demonstrated above, Mercedes recognized the importance of flexibility in setting and achieving target costs.

Production phase 1997–present. The M-class project was monitored by annual updates of the net present value (NPV) analysis. In addition, a three-year plan (including income statements) was prepared annually and reported to the headquarters in Germany. Monthly departmental meetings were held to discuss actual cost performance compared with standards developed during the cost estimation process. Thus, the accounting system served as a control mechanism to ensure actual production costs conformed to target (or standard) costs.

TARGET COSTING AND THE M-CLASS

The target costing process was led by cost planners who were engineers, not accountants. Because the cost planners were engineers with manufacturing and design experience, they could make reasonable estimates of costs that suppliers would incur in providing various systems. Also, Mercedes already owned much of the tooling, such as dies to form sheet metal, used by suppliers to produce components. Tooling costs are a substantial part of the one-time costs in the project phase.

Mercedes divided the vehicle into function groups that included doors, sidewall and roof, electrical system, bumpers, powertrain, seats, heating system, cockpit, and front end. As shown in Exhibit 1, the process of achieving target cost for the M-class began with an estimate of the existing cost for each function group. Next, components of each function group were identified with their associated costs. Team members set cost reduction targets by comparing the estimated existing cost with the target cost for each function group. Finally, cost reduction targets were established for each component. As part of the competitive benchmarking process, Mercedes purchased and disassembled competitors' vehicles to help understand costs and manufacturing processes within the competitor's manufacturing plant.

A modular construction process that relied on high-value-added systems suppliers was used to produce the M-class. Advantages of this process include higher quality, shorter development time, and greater cost efficiency. First-tier suppliers provide entire systems rather than individual parts or components. For example, the entire cockpit was purchased as a unit from an external vendor.

Function Group: Chassis
Component 1
Component 2   **Influence Factors**
Component 3   Materials
Component 4   Labor
Component 5   Overhead   **Function Group: Chassis**
Component 6   Component 1
                     Tooling,   Component 2
                     Development,   Component 3
                     Marketing, and Sales costs; Component 4
                     Startup and   Component 5
                     Project Costs   Component 6

Systems suppliers were part of the development process from the beginning of the project. Approximately 70 suppliers worked with teams from finance and controlling, engineering, purchasing, marketing, sales, logistics, and quality control to ensure the delivery of systems that meet expectations. Mercedes expected suppliers to meet established cost targets. To enhance function group effectiveness, suppliers were brought into the discussion at an early stage in the process.

Index development to support target costing. During the concept development phase, Mercedes team members used various indexes to help determine critical performance, design, and cost relationships for the M-class. The purpose of the indexes is to ensure that resources are applied in the most effective manner. An importance index is created by to conceptually linking the contribution of each major function group to an attribute desired by a customer. In the final stage of analysis, the value of each function group is compared with its cost. Thus, engineers can assess cost/benefit relationships during the design phase.

Exhibits 2–6 illustrate the calculations used to quantify various aspects of the target costing process. (All numbers have been altered for proprietary reasons; however, the tables illustrate the actual process used in the development of the M-class.) To construct the indexes, various forms of information were gathered from customers, suppliers, and the M-class design team. Though the actual number of categories used by Mercedes was much greater, Exhibit 2 illustrates the calculations used to quantify customer responses to the M-class concept. For example, values shown in the importance column of Exhibit 2 resulted from asking a sample of potential customers, whether they consider each category important when contemplating the purchase of a new Mercedes product. Individuals could respond affirmatively to all categories that applied.

Target costs for functions. To gain a better understanding of the various sources of costs, function groups were identified together with their target cost estimates. Exhibit 3 shows the function groups, the target cost for each, and what percentage of the total cost each represents. The target cost percentage is used in the calculation of a target cost index.

Exhibit 4 summarizes how each function group contributes to the consumer requirements identified in Exhibit 2. The rows explain the relative importance of each function group to satisfying each category defined by customers. An interesting aspect of this table is that it makes explicit the link between consumer preferences and engineering components. For example, a large proportion of potential customers identified safety as the most important characteristic of the M-class; some function groups contributed more to safety than others. Mercedes engineers determined that chassis quality was an important element of safety (60% of the total function group contribution in this example).

Exhibit 5 combines the category weighting percentages from Exhibit 2 with the function group contribution from Exhibit 4. The key point is to understand which function groups contribute the most (least) to important (less important) consumer categories. The result is an importance index that measures the relative importance of each function group across all categories. For example, potential customers weighted the categories of safety, comfort, economy, and styling as .47, .32, .05, and .16, respectively. The rows in Exhibit 5 represent the contribution of each function group to the various categories. The importance index for the chassis is calculated by multiplying each row value by its corresponding category value and summing the results: $(.47 \times .60) + (.32 \times .20) + (.05 \times .05) + (.16 \times .05) = .36$.

EXHIBIT 2. RELATIVE IMPORTANCE RANKING BY CATEGORY

Category	Importance	Relative Percentage
Safety	45	47
Comfort	30	32
Economy	5	5
Styling	15	16
Total	95	100

As shown in Exhibit 6, the target cost index is calculated by dividing the importance index by the target cost percentage by function group. Managers at Mercedes used indexes such as these during the concept design phase to understand the relationship of the *importance* of a function group to the *target cost* of a function group. Indexes less than one may indicate a cost in excess of the perceived value of the function group. Choices made during the project realization phase were largely irreversible during the production phase because approximately 80% of the production cost of the M-class represented materials and systems provided by external suppliers. Thus, opportunities for cost reduction, known as value engineering, are best identified and managed during the early stages of product development.

VALUE ENGINEERING

Having established a target cost index, value engineering techniques may be applied to align target cost and perceived value. As defined by Cooper (1995), value engineering is the systematic, interdisciplinary examination of factors affecting cost to devise a means of achieving cost, quality, and functionality at the target cost.

Many value-engineering techniques are available. For example, purchasing, disassembling, and analyzing competitors' products provide insights into manufacturing processes and costs. This technique often is used as part of a competitive benchmarking program. Redesigning production processes and key components involves the cross-functional analysis of each component within a function group. Cooper describes how camera manufacturers may substitute a plastic lens to reduce costs when designing a new product. Supplier involvement early in the design phase can create opportunities for cost reduction, such as recycling reusable materials or adjusting tolerances where feasible.

EXHIBIT 3. TARGET COST AND PERCENTAGE BY FUNCTION GROUP

Function Group	Target Cost	Percentage of Total
Chassis	$x,xxx	25
Transmission	$x,xxx	20
Air conditioner	$x,xxx	8
Electrical system	$x,xxx	15
Other function groups	$x,xxx	32
Total	$xx,xxx	100

EXHIBIT 4. FUNCTION GROUP CONTRIBUTION TO CUSTOMER REQUIREMENTS

Category–Function Group	Safety	Comfort	Economy	Styling
Chassis	60%	20%	5%	5%
Transmission	20	30	30	
Air conditioner		20		5
Electrical system	5	5	25	
Other systems	15	25	40	90
Total	100%	100%	100%	100%

EXHIBIT 5. IMPORTANCE OF VARIOUS FUNCTION GROUPS

Category–Function Group	Safety .47	Comfort .32	Economy .05	Styling .16	Importance Index
Chassis	.60	.20	.05	.05	.36
Transmission	.20	.30	.30		.21
Air conditioner		.20		.05	.07
Electrical systems	.05	.05	.25		.05
Other systems	.15	.25	.40	.90	.31
Total	1.00	1.00	1.00	1.00	

EXHIBIT 6. TARGET COST INDEX

Index–Function Group	(A) Importance Index	(B) % of Target Cost	(C)A/B Target Cost Index
Chassis	.36	.25	1.44
Transmission	.21	.20	1.05
Air conditioner	.07	.08	.87
Electrical system	.05	.15	.33
Other systems	.31	.32	.97
Total		1.00	

SUMMARY

The Mercedes organization produced an entirely new vehicle from concept to production in four years, on time, and within budget. Mercedes launched the M-class in September 1997 in the United States market; the export market launch occurred in March 1998. The production facility originally constructed to produce 65,000 M-class vehicles annually is currently being expanded to permit annual production of 80,000 vehicles.

The M-class project used a streamlined management structure in order to facilitate efficient and rapid development. Target costing proved to be a key management element in the success of this venture.

REFERENCES

Albright, T. L. *Cases in Strategic Cost Management: Mercedes-Benz AAV.* (1998). The Institute of Management Accountants–REAP Program.

Ansari, S. and Bell, J. *Target Costing, The Next Frontier in Strategic Cost Management.* Chicago: Irwin, 1995.

Cooper, R. *When Lean Enterprises Collide.* Boston: Harvard Business School Press, 1995. Woodruff & Miller. 1995.

Tom Albright is J. Reese Phifer Faculty Fellow at the Culverhouse School of Accountancy at The University of Alabama. The author thanks Ola Kallenius, Jonathan DeHart, Jason Hoff, Henrik Jönsson, Josef Pfau, and Günther Thuss of Mercedes-Benz for their generous contributions to this article.

QUESTIONS

7.2a   What are the six critical components of a target costing system?

7.2b   Was the M-class project a risky one for Mercedes Benz? Explain.

7.3 The Elements of Supply Chain Management

*by Tom Albright and Stan Davis**

EXECUTIVE SUMMARY

- *Supply chain management* (SCM) has received increasing attention as companies seek to gain and maintain a competitive advantage in the market.

- This article discusses points that companies beginning a SCM program should consider. Although it provides many illustrations, the article concentrates on the supply-chain practices followed by Mercedes U.S. International in developing the new M-class sports utility vehicle.

- SCM encompasses not only planning and controlling the flow of materials from suppliers to end users *(logistics-based SCM)* but also the philosophy adopted by a company toward supplier relationships *(strategic SCM).*

- SCM seeks to unify skills and resources of business functions found both within an enterprise and outside. The thrust is to develop relationships and to synchronize the flow of products, services, and information.

- Supply-chain considerations are an integral part of an organization's value chain and essential to many business initiatives, including just-in-time (JIT) manufacturing, total quality management (TQM), electronic data interchange (EDI), outsourcing, and target costing.

Supply chain logistics is a primary activity in an organization's value chain. To engage in strategic cost management, managers must identify and assess primary and secondary activities and the processes necessary for the organization to compete. These activities and processes are referred to as an organization's *value chain.*

A company's value chain includes primary activities that create value for customers both *inside and outside* the firm (Thompson and Strickland 1996). Understanding the costs associated with each activity of the value chain provides an understanding of the organization's cost structure, which allows a firm to set cost or niche strategies. Typically, a value chain includes six primary activities (Thompson and Strickland, 1996):

1.   Purchased supplies and inbound logistics;
2.   Operations;
3.   Outbound logistics;
4.   Sales and marketing;
5.   Service; and
6.   Profit margin.

Supply chain management is integrally involved in the first three links in the chain and is becoming integrated into a firm's strategy. In developing a strategic plan, a company should carefully analyze potential relationships with suppliers. Because successful SCM is a key element in other management techniques, such as JIT, TQM, EDI, target costing, and outsourcing, assessing the power relationship is important. Given the

* From: T. Albright and S. Davis, "The Elements of Supply Chain Management," *International Journal of Strategic Cost Management* (Autumn 1999): 49–65. Reprinted with permission.

demands that these programs place on suppliers, proper relationships with key suppliers are essential.

ALLIANCES WITH SUPPLIERS

Successful SCM practices begin with the selection of key suppliers, then developing trusting, mutually beneficial relationships that last over long periods. Alliances with suppliers are usually necessary only for vendors that supply integral, strategically important components to the manufacturing process.

The objective of aligning closely with suppliers is not to acquire the lowest possible price but, rather, to secure acceptable prices in return for superior service and reliability. Another benefit of developing strong alliances with suppliers of key components is the assistance suppliers can offer in designing new components and production processes.

But developing strong alliances is often difficult because of mistrust on both sides of the purchase arrangement. The supplier-purchaser relationship has long been an arm's-length transaction, with both sides seeking as much short-term gain as possible. Thus, developing long-lasting ties and sharing sensitive information is often difficult. Seeking to develop alliances built on trust and mutually beneficial outcomes requires a change in mind-set at many companies.

IMPROVING RELATIONSHIPS WITH SUPPLIERS OF STRATEGIC PARTS

The following four practices help foster improved relations with suppliers of strategic parts (Landry 1998):

1. *Power balancing.* In buyer-supplier relationships in which a buyer represents a large proportion of a supplier's business, the buyer may be in a position to demand price (or other) concessions. Such an uneven power distribution is not conducive to building a healthy strategic alliance. Equal dependence between partners occurs when the proportion of a supplier's total output that is sold to a customer roughly equals the proportion of total purchases acquired by a customer from that supplier. For example, if a supplier sells about 25% of its total output to a strategic partner, then a power balance is achieved if the buyer's proportion of total purchases is 25% for that supplier. Maintaining relative dependence between suppliers and buyers increases the likelihood that both parties will have a vested interest in the success of the other partner as the degree of relative dependence increases.

2. *Codependency.* Apart from balancing power in a supplier-buyer relationship, developing a code-pendency in the relationship can benefit the alliance. When a supplier commits substantial specialized resources to meeting the demands of a purchaser and the purchaser chooses to single-source with that supplier, both parties have a vested interest in the success of the purchaser. This relationship reduces maneuvering for short-term gains by suppliers and strengthens the desire for mutually beneficial outcomes for both parties.

3. *Target costing.* Instead of seeking the lowest bid, establishing target costs for components, then rewarding suppliers when those targets are reached encourages joint problem solving.

4. *Personal ties.* Developing trust between suppliers and purchasers usually begins at the individual level. Establishing joint teams consisting of employees from both the purchaser and the supplier helps foster good working relationships. Trust increases as each side begins to feel more comfortable with members from the other organization.

Many organizations often single-source numerous strategic components yet fail to establish the trust and partnership ties that can provide additional benefits for both parties. As the following example illustrates, treating suppliers as partners in strategic alliances provides long-term benefits other than obtaining low costs on supplied components.

THE MERCEDES M-CLASS SPORTS UTILITY VEHICLE

During the recession that began in the early 1990s, Mercedes-Benz struggled with product development, cost efficiency, material purchasing, and problems in adapting to changing markets. In 1993, these problems caused the worst sales slump in decades, and Mercedes lost money for the first time in its history.

In a search for additional market share, new segments, and new niches, Mercedes started developing a range of new products. Perhaps the largest and most radical of these new projects was the M-class, a sports utility vehicle that moved from concept to production in a relatively short time.

To design vehicle and production systems, Mercedes-Benz US. International used *function groups* that included representatives from every area of the company (marketing, development, engineering, purchasing, production, and controlling). The role of these function groups was to develop specifications and cost projections. Note also that a modular construction process was used to produce the M-class. First-tier suppliers provided modular systems (rather than individual parts or components) for production of about 65,000 vehicles annually.

Mercedes included suppliers early in the design stage of the vehicle. By including suppliers as members of the function groups, Mercedes was able to take advantage of their expertise and advice on matters such as supplier capability, cost, and quality. The synergy generated by these cross-function groups also allowed the groups to solve larger design issues, such as how to more efficiently and economically switch from manufacturing left-side-drive vehicles to right-side-drive vehicles. Significant time savings were recognized because of the design improvements implemented by the function groups. Because supplier personnel were at the Mercedes plant on a full-time basis during the launch, other issues (such as quality problems or slight modifications to the product) could be addressed in a more timely fashion.

SUPPLIER INVOLVEMENT IN JIT AND TQM
Initiating cost savings and quality programs requires a commitment not only from an organization itself, but also from parties outside the organization, such as transporters and suppliers of goods. Management initiatives such as JIT, TQM, target costing, and outsourcing require significant cooperation between suppliers and purchasers.

The JIT philosophy advocates *waste elimination*, including wasted materials resulting from a manufacturing process and wasted time in delivery and movement of goods. Additional sources of waste include machine setups, rework, warehouse space required by large inventories, and capital required to carry large inventory levels (which can mask production problems).

The success of JIT and TQM depends on developing innovative *performance measures* for suppliers. These measures include quality, response time, and number of delivery points. The ability to sustain a long-term relationship enables purchasers to work with suppliers over time to achieve acceptable performance on such measures. Buyers that frequently change suppliers end up buying from companies that are at the beginning of the learning curve. Thus, many benefits of a long-term relationship are foregone.

In addition to quality issues, lower inventory levels require suppliers to provide more shipments in smaller quantities. Suppliers must be able to respond quickly to orders and ship in lot sizes desired by the purchaser. In some cases, manufacturers may also require delivery of goods *to the point of production*, thus reducing the need for inventory and also reducing the expense and time of moving materials from a receiving dock to a holding area, then to the point of production.

These demands have caused a different type of relationship to develop between purchasers and suppliers. Many purchasers and suppliers are forging relationships based on long-term commitments, thus saving negotiation, inspection, and other costs associated with contracting with many suppliers. Properly orchestrated, a close relationship between suppliers and purchasers can be a win-win situation when organizations initiate programs such as JIT and TQM. Buyers receive high-quality goods delivered on schedule, and suppliers gain long-term commitments that enable them to plan for future orders with the understanding that buyers will continue to assist them in improving quality and service. These quality and service improvements can then be transferred to other customers the supplier may service.

MERCEDES AND IN-SEQUENCE DELIVERY
Mercedes designed its manufacturing facility consistent with the JIT philosophy, so there is little warehouse space at the factory where the M-class is made. Instead, Mercedes relies on *in-sequence delivery*, a system whereby preconstructed modules arrive in a prescribed sequence and are placed on the manufacturing line.

For example, from the moment a new vehicle order is initiated, manufacturers of the cockpit module have 169 minutes to manufacture (to specifications) and deliver the module to the proper place in the manufacturing line at the Mercedes plant. Mercedes and its suppliers stay in constant contact through EDI facilities that transmit order specifications and other information between the plant and first-tier suppliers.

Exhibit 1 illustrates Mercedes' in-sequence delivery system. When an order is initiated, suppliers are notified through an EDI transmission of the specifications for the new vehicle. Suppliers are then expected to deliver their products in a predetermined order as each module is needed in the manufacturing process. This system moves one step beyond the simple JIT philosophy by requiring various suppliers to synchronize their efforts so that production can occur uninterrupted.

TARGET COSTING
Because most costs are designed into a product, target costing must begin at the design stage of product development. It is at this stage that supplier selection becomes most critical. The indexes developed by Mercedes allowed the company and its suppliers to work closely to align the cost of a function group with its perceived value, as defined by customers. (All numbers provided here have been altered for proprietary reasons; however, the tables illustrate the actual process used in the development of the M-class.)

MERCEDES AND TARGET COSTING
During the concept development phase for the M-class, Mercedes team members used various indexes to help determine critical performance, design, and cost relationships. To construct the indexes, various forms of information were gathered from customers, suppliers, and members of the design team.

Although the actual number of categories used by Mercedes was much higher, Exhibit 2 illustrates the calculations used to quantify customer responses to the M-class concept. For example, values shown in the *importance column* resulted from asking a sample of potential customers whether they consider each category extremely important when considering the purchase of a new Mercedes product. Customers could respond affirmatively to all categories that applied.

EXHIBIT 1. IN-SEQUENCE DELIVERY

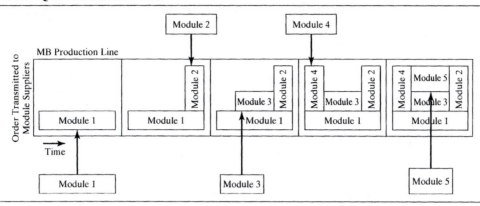

EXHIBIT 2. RELATIVE IMPORTANCE RANKING BY CATEGORY

Category	Importance	Relative Percentage
Safety	32	41%
Comfort	25	32
Economy	15	18
Styling	7	9
Total	79	100%

WORK OF THE FUNCTION GROUPS

To gain a better understanding of various sources of costs, function groups were identified together with target cost estimates. As shown in Exhibit 3, the relative target cost percentage of each function group was computed.

Exhibit 4 summarizes how each function group contributed to the consumer requirements identified in Exhibit 2. For example, potential customers identified safety as an important characteristic of the M-class; some function groups contributed more to the safety category than did others. Mercedes engineers determined that chassis quality was an important element of safety (50% of the total function group contribution).

Exhibit 5 combines the category weighting percentages from Exhibit 2 with the function group contribution from Exhibit 4. The result is an importance index that measures the relative importance of each function group across all categories. For example, potential customers weighted the categories of safety, comfort, economy, and styling as .41, 32, .18, and .09, respectively. The rows in Exhibit 5 represent the contribution of each function group to the various categories. The importance index for the function group is calculated by multiplying each row value by its corresponding category value, then summing the results. For example, the chassis importance index of .33 is computed as follows: $(.50 \times .41) + (.30 \times .32) + (.10 \times .18) + (.10 \times .09) = .33$).

As shown in Exhibit 6, the target cost index is calculated by dividing the importance index by the target cost percentage by function group. Managers at Mercedes used indexes such as these during the concept design phase to understand the relationship of the *importance* of a function group to the *target cost* of a function group. Indexes less than one may indicate a cost in excess of the perceived value of the function group. Thus, opportunities for cost reduction—consistent with customer demands— may be identified and managed during the early stages of product development.

OUTSOURCING

A popular trend among manufacturing organizations is to minimize on-site value-added activities by outsourcing significant portions of the assembly processes. Original equipment manufacturers (OEMs) have increasingly begun to outsource their production processes to contract manufacturers in an effort to reduce costs.

OEMs now outsource some of the manufacturing processes that they formerly considered core competencies. OEMs are focusing their efforts on design and innovation issues. It has been estimated that contract manufacturers will achieve a cumulative annual growth rate of 25% between 1996 and 2001. EDI and partnering with suppliers are essential for OEMs that seek to reduce costs by using contract manufacturers (Roberts 1998).

Outsourcing Manufacturing Assembly Processes at Mercedes. Many manufacturers contract with suppliers for parts, then manage assembly in-house, but Mercedes took a different strategy by outsourcing assemblies of the M-class to suppliers. Engineers divided the M-class into systems that were combined to form a completed vehicle. As many as 18 modules to be delivered in sequence have been outsourced to suppliers, which purchase the sub-components and assemble the module for Mercedes.

By assembling the modules off-site, Mercedes has reduced plant and warehouse space requirements. In addition, the number of suppliers used has been drastically reduced by this outsourcing of systems. For example, the cockpit requires more than 150 parts from about 35 vendors. By outsourcing the cockpit to one vendor, Mercedes has reduced its involvement from potentially 35 vendors to only one.

EXHIBIT 3. TARGET COST AND PERCENTAGE BY FUNCTIONAL GROUP

Function Group	Target Cost	Percentage of Total
Chassis	$x,xxx	20%
Transmission	$x,xxx	25
Air conditioner	$x,xxx	5
Electrical system	$x,xxx	7
Other function groups	$x,xxx	43
Total	$xx,xxx	100%

EXHIBIT 4. FUNCTION GROUP CONTRIBUTION TO CUSTOMER REQUIREMENTS

	Category			
Function group	Safety	Comfort	Economy	Styling
Chassis	50%	30%	10%	10%
Transmission	20	20	30	
Air conditioner		20		5
Electrical system	5		20	
Other systems	25	30	40	85
Total	100%	100%	100%	100%

EXHIBIT 5. IMPORTANCE INDEX OF VARIOUS FUNCTIONAL GROUPS

	Category				
Function group	Safety .41	Comfort .32	Economy .18	Styling .09	Importance Index
Chassis	.50	.30	.10	.10	.33
Transmission	.20	.20	.30		.20
Air conditioner		.20		.05	.07
Electrical system	.05		.20		.06
Other systems	.25	.30	.40	.85	.35
Total	1.00	1.00	1.00	1.00	

EXHIBIT 6. IMPORTANCE INDEX OF VARIOUS FUNCTIONAL GROUPS

	(A) Importance Index	Index (B) % of Target Cost Index	(c) A/B Target Cost
Function group			
Chassis	.33	.20	1.65
Transmission	.20	.25	.80
Air conditioner	.07	.05	1.40
Electrical system	.06	.07	.86
Other systems	.35	.43	.81
Total		1.00	

First- and Second-Tier Suppliers. Note that Mercedes has developed a two-tier supplier network. First-tier suppliers provide finished modules to Mercedes. Second-tier suppliers are the vendors from which first-tier suppliers purchase parts. At the beginning of the production process, Mercedes maintained strict control over both first-tier and second-tier suppliers with respect to cost and quality issues. As the level of comfort and trust grew between Mercedes and first-tier suppliers, Mercedes gave first-tier suppliers more freedom to make their own arrangements with second-tier suppliers. Exhibit 7 illustrates Mercedes' two-tier relationship with suppliers.

The benefits to Mercedes are numerous. By outsourcing more than 80% of vehicle components to a limited number of first-tier suppliers, Mercedes reduces the overhead associated with purchasing activities and also saves on labor and employee-related costs. Further, by having established strong alliances with first-tier suppliers, Mercedes enjoys a higher level of service from suppliers and benefits from the expertise developed by suppliers as they seek ways to improve current operations. Finally, because much of the product is manufactured off-site, suppliers of major modules are encouraged to work together to continuously improve not only their own module but the integrated product as well.

DEVELOPING SUPPLIER RELATIONSHIPS
Developing strategic alliances with suppliers can be very rewarding. Although each organization's experience with building supplier relationships is unique, three suggestions can make a venture more likely to succeed.

Commit to Partnering Before Seeking Partners. Because developing strategic alliances with suppliers will change many practices, top management must be committed to establishing these relationships and accepting the changes that they will bring. Some of these changes include:

- Accepting a smaller vendor base from which to purchase supplies;
- Including suppliers in the early stages of design and development of new products; and
- Developing the ability to share information with vendors that will make their jobs easier.

An organization's commitment also may include agreeing to train a supplier's employees in various areas of importance (e.g., the organization's production practices), developing joint objectives with suppliers (e.g., joint profit levels), and striving to be a better customer.

Before seeking strategic partners, however, organizations need to accept the fact that the best supplier may not necessarily be the cheapest provider of goods and services. Higher-quality products and smaller, more frequent deliveries (as required by TQM and JIT) are more costly, and suppliers should not be expected to bear the entire burden of increased costs. Such an arrangement would not foster the trust between suppliers and buyers that is necessary in a long-term, mutually beneficial partnership (Duncan and Breen, 1988; Adair-Heeley, 1988; Hay, 1990b; Kepp, 1994; Tait, 1998).

EXHIBIT 7. MERCEDES TWO-TIER SUPPLIER NETWORK

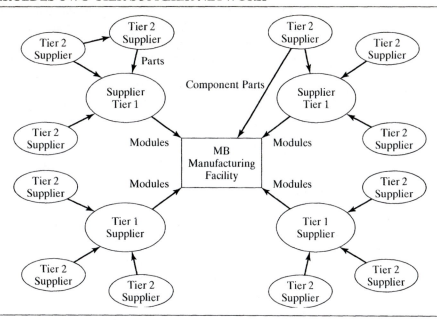

Select Appropriate Suppliers for Alliances. The first thing to remember when selecting suppliers is that the best supplier may not be among the current set of companies that provides goods to your organization. It may be necessary to sever business relations with some current vendors (even if they have been suppliers for a long time) if they are unwilling or unable to commit to a partnering relationship.

Make sure that a supplier can provide the level of service and quality your business will require. Some vendors, eager to earn business, may "promise the world" but lack the capacity, manpower, or infrastructure required to deliver on their end of the bargain.

Another important point to consider is the supplier's commitment to entering into a partnership arrangement. Because a strategic alliance requires two-way commitment, suppliers should be willing to accept their responsibilities in the partnership, such as the requirements imposed on suppliers under such initiatives as TQM or JIT, or a commitment to continuous improvement. Finally, inquire about the performance of suppliers with a few of their other customers to ensure that their dependability, quality, and service are acceptable (Hay, 1990a; Anonymous, 1994).

Be Prepared to Sell the Relationship. Ask the question, "Why would a supplier want to align itself with this organization?" A cursory glance at the requirements imposed by TQM or JIT programs may leave a vendor asking, "What's in it for me?"—a valid question. A supplier's willingness to enter into such a relationship depends in part on its ability to meet the increased requirements.

Key selling points include the fact that, because fewer vendors will be supplying like goods, the result should be an increased volume for supplier partners.

Other rewards for suppliers include the assurance of business, technical, production, and training assistance; financial help (if necessary) to acquire facilities needed to meet the customer's needs; and the ability to take advantage of any production or technological gains that result from doing business with other customers. Unless the arrangement is mutually beneficial, the prospects that suppliers will enter into helpful strategic alliances are greatly reduced (Duncan and Breen, 1988; Morgan, 1993a, 1993b).

LOGISTICS-BASED SUPPLY CHAIN MANAGEMENT

Logistics-based supply chain management (LSCM) has long held a prominent place within operations management as an area for cost savings. Traditionally, LSCM has involved management of material flow from supplier to manufacturer (inbound logistics) or from manufacturer to customer (outbound logistics). This approach, however, was restricted because it ignored material flow *within* an organization. Recent approaches have encompassed total materials flow: from the supplier of materials, through the manufacturing organization, to purchasers of finished goods.

Specifically, LSCM activities include (Copacino, 1997):

- Sourcing and purchasing;
- Conversion (manufacturing), including capacity planning and operations management;
- Production scheduling and materials planning;
- Distribution planning and warehouse operations:
- Inventory management (including inbound and outbound transportation); and

- The linkage with customer service, sales, promotion, and marketing activities.

LSCM can provide value-added activities in many areas including transportation, inventory, and information (Ross, 1998). Each is discussed in more detail here.

Transportation. The primary goal of transportation is to have goods delivered on time, undamaged, and cost-effectively. Deregulation of the transportation industry has made contracting for the delivery of inbound and outbound freight more beneficial. Although a common practice is to contract with the lowest bidder for transportation services, many shippers are beginning to demand not only low prices but also a higher level of service. Given the increased importance of JIT deliveries and maintaining low inventories, managers often incorporate the cost of missed delivery schedules into the cost of transportation.

Two philosophies exist toward selecting carriers:

- Repeatedly soliciting bids for individual transportation engagements; and
- Developing a relationship with certain carriers to encourage higher quality performance.

By sharing shipment responsibilities, sellers and buyers can include carriers in negotiations and reach agreements on such issues as:

- Traffic volume;
- Frequency and quality of service;
- Rates; and
- The carrier's liability for loss, delay, or damage.

Agreements that include all three parties—buyer, supplier, and transporter—will likely be more beneficial to all parties. The buyer gets to specify its issues of importance (e.g., on-time delivery vs. cost; damaged goods vs. on-time delivery), whereas the seller gets to specify its own issues of importance. The transporter gains a better understanding of what the buyer expects, what the seller expects, and what services are most important to customers-including what services the customers are willing to pay for (Carter and Ferrin, 1995).

Inventory. LSCM can also aid in controlling inventory levels and ensuring that goods are delivered in good order to other manufacturing units or to buyers outside the organization. Marketing, manufacturing, and purchasing personnel should all participate in forecasting material needs to achieve an effective purchasing and delivery plan.

Traditional solutions for inventory management include mathematical formulas such as the *economic order quantity* (EOQ) formula and *materials requirement planning* (MRP) techniques, which are used to optimize production schedules. Many computerized programs exist to aid manufacturers and wholesalers in maintaining an effective inventory management system (software packages used for SCM are discussed later in this article).

In managing inventory levels, it is essential for businesses to know with as much certainty as possible the lead time for delivery of supplies and for the production of goods. Without understanding the time required between recognizing the need for a good and its production, maintaining an optimal inventory balance is difficult. Unknown lead times increase the chance of over- or understocked inventory, both of which are costly to a business (Ross, 1998; Copacino, 1997).

LSCM at Hewlett-Packard. At Hewlett-Packard (HP), benchmarking is used to aid LSCM planning. Inventory is an insurance against uncertainty HP attacks this uncertainty at three sources: suppliers, manufacturing, and customers. Although not all sources of uncertainty can be eliminated, tracking certain measures enables manufacturing organizations to reduce their exposure to uncertainty. At HP, benchmark indicators include the following:

1. *Suppliers.* HP tracks on-time performance, average days or hours late, and the degree of inconsistency (the standard deviation of late measures). Tracking these measures helps HP know how much extra stock to keep on hand per supplier while minimizing the probability of stockouts.
2. *Manufacturing.* Downtime (for the process, not just a machine), repair time, and variation in repair time are key performance indicators. HP uses a probability distribution of performance and focuses on the reliability of the process.
3. *Customers.* Greater levels of order variation require greater levels of safety stock. HP tracks average demand and the variability of demand by customer (Davis, 1993).

Vendor-Managed Inventory. To control costs and improve the supply chain, leading companies use vendor managed inventory (VMI). By yielding (or at least sharing) the responsibility of managing inventories with suppliers, buyers reduce inventory carrying costs and receive improved service from suppliers (Tyndall et al., 1998). Suppliers benefit by gaining better insight into buyers' requirements and processes, and also from the increased information flow concerning future demands. By entering into a VMI agreement with a supplier, one wholesaler reduced delivery and administrative charges and also average inventory (from 10 days to 6 days) while keeping service levels constant. The company also reduced the time from order to delivery from 48 hours to 10 hours. Finally, the company gained a competitive advantage by sharing some of the associated cost savings with customers (Holstrom, 1998).

Organizing suppliers into a consortium can enable manufacturers to control inventory costs. Coordinating the activities of first and second tier suppliers can yield lower transaction costs by sharing operating insights and best practices. The increased cooperation among consortium members facilitates the sharing of information learned about third-tier suppliers and thus helps identify substandard suppliers. FedEx, among other organizations, has begun offering management services explicitly to help other companies set up consortium buying arrangements. Toyota has also developed supplier associations that foster communication and cooperation across major suppliers. The associations do the following (Stuart et al., 1998; Tyndall et al., 1998):

- Standardize quality control;
- Facilitate supplier interaction; and
- Provide forums that build trust.

Information Technology. With shorter turnaround times and smaller orders becoming the norm, the ability to withdraw information from a logistics management system is crucial. Many buyers and suppliers set up EDI facilities that provide an unfettered information flow to ensure that orders and inventory levels are constantly monitored and maintained.

Characteristics of an LSCM system include:

- Rapid and accurate transaction processing;
- Real-time technologies integrated with other functions in the organization; and
- Advanced decision-support capabilities.

These systems also should include modeling, transportation, routing, and scheduling capabilities that are linked to suppliers and purchasers (Copacino, 1997).

By choosing to link with suppliers through some form of EDI, companies can share long-term and short-term forecast demands to aid upstream suppliers in their scheduling requirements. One Volvo plant uses EDI hookups with a supplier to share forecasts of goods three to four days in the future. The EDI system then creates sales orders and initiates purchase orders so that the forecast can be met. Further, EDI links are planned for suppliers of Volvo's suppliers (second-tier suppliers) to further expedite the transfer of information and maintain proper materials flow among suppliers and Volvo (Anonymous, 1998a).

Other organizations use the Internet to share information with key suppliers. Using secure websites, manufacturers such as Boeing, Dell, and Thompson Consumer Electronics have designed ways to improve communications with suppliers and customers. Boeing allows customers to browse its catalog and order spare parts from an Internet site, which processes about 4,000 transactions per day. This has reduced order-processing costs by 25% and also shortened delivery time.

Thompson Consumer Electronics receives customer demand forecasts on its secured Internet site. This information is entered into Thompson's SCM software for scheduling and production requirements (Thompson uses SCM software manufactured by i2 Technologies). Further, Thompson posts its demand forecasts on line, thereby allowing suppliers to know when components are needed. As a result, Thompson has shortened lead times from three or four weeks to as little as one week in many cases.

Dell has taken information-sharing one step further. By customizing about 30 web pages for top suppliers, Dell allows the suppliers to view its customers' demands so that the suppliers can better plan for future demands. Dell also has linked websites to bulletin boards where suppliers can post messages and share information. Manufacturers on the leading edge of SCM continually seek ways to increase information flow between suppliers and its customers (Stein and Sweat, 1998).

SCM SOFTWARE

SCM software integrates external communications (i.e., communications with suppliers and purchasers through either the Internet or EDI) and internal communications. SCM software includes (but is not limited to) products from:

- Manugistics, Inc.
- American Software, Inc.
- i2 Technologies, Inc.
- Numertrix Ltd.
- Red Pepper Software Co.

Using the PC-based Manugistics Routing and Scheduling Version 10 (MRS 10), Domino's Pizza updates and optimizes its routing schedules for delivery to production sites on a daily basis. Domino's previous system allowed updates only on a semiannual basis. Given dramatic changes in demand, Domino's hopes to save $1 million during its first year by optimizing its trucking routes on a daily basis.

By linking with suppliers and purchasing an integrated SCM software package, Molson Breweries not only notifies suppliers in various manufacturing locations of upcoming demand but also gains valuable information about margins for particular production sites. Production scheduling and transportation now is handled more efficiently based on profit margins of products, demand in given areas, and supplier capabilities at a given time.

3-Com Corp., a network equipment supplier, relied on linked Excel spreadsheets to keep production lines near target utilizations. As volume grew, planning and scheduling became more difficult. Therefore, 3-Com started using Red Pepper's Response Agent to aid in its SCM efforts. Now schedules that balance material and capacity constraints are generated and what-if scenarios can be run in a matter of hours; previously, what-if scenarios took days to run (Mayer, 1996).

By using Internet technology, EDI, and SCM software, suppliers know what a customer needs before the customer asks (or, possibly, before the customer even realizes that it needs anything). Thus, technology has made the concept of a "seamless" supply chain a reality. Developing creative links with suppliers and customers appears to be a rich opportunity for innovative manufacturers to enjoy a competitive advantage over competitors that are unwilling or unable to invest the time and resources into improving their supply chains.

FUTURE TRENDS IN LSCM
Trends in LSCM include the following:

- A greater emphasis on establishing a balance between cost and service in the logistics function;
- Increasing third-party services for LSCM activities;
- Increasing emphasis on channel integration, and
- Expanding roles for EDI relationships between suppliers and purchasers.

The transportation and warehousing industry is slowly transforming itself into a full-service logistics manager for manufacturing organizations that outsource logistics functions. Successful third-party providers of logistics services will tailor their services to specific industries and manufacturers to develop an expertise and relationship not offered by ordinary transportation providers. Included in these services are EDI hookups linking suppliers and purchasers to further facilitate transactions among organizations (Copacino, 1997). Competition among third-party transportation providers (transporters of goods other than the supplier or the purchaser of the goods) is increasing. Thus, customers can not only demand lower prices but also expect more extensive services, furthering the benefits to businesses deciding to outsource logistics functions (Mireles, 1998).

Channel integration is the management of inventory, warehousing, and transportation across corporate boundaries (Copacino, 1997). Strategic supply chain management and logistical supply chain management techniques discussed in this article enable managers to reduce interorganizational barriers. Segmenting product offerings into channels allows manufacturers to better determine profitable and unprofitable product lines, differentiate between the levels of service required by these channels, and possibly eliminate unneeded layers within some channels.

Another major trend in LSCM is an increased dependence on EDI. Organizations are just beginning to realize the vast array of benefits available from EDI and advanced information systems capabilities. Unfortunately, a recent survey conducted by KPMG as part of a

Global Supply Chain Benchmark Study reports that many organizations are not taking advantages of recent information technology advances. The report indicates that organizations are making more use of SCM software for internal purposes, but that the exchange of information between organizations is still far behind where it could be with the capabilities of today's information technology (Anonymous, 1998b).

ENDNOTES
C. B. Adair-Heeley, "JIT Purchasing: Seven Steps for Successful Implementation," *Production and Inventory Management Review and APICS* 8 (1988): 22–23.

Anonymous, "Service Is the Difference When Choosing a Copier Supplier," *Managing Office Technology* 39 (1994): 79–80.

Anonymous, "Make Supply Chain Technology Work for You," *Works Management* (July 1998a): 37–41.

Anonymous, "Key Trends and Analysis," *Stores* (April 1988b): S9–S20.

J. R. Carter and B. G. Ferrin, "The Impact of Transportation Costs on Supply Chain Management," *Journal of Business Logistics* 16 (1996): 207.

W. C. Copacino, *Supply Chain Management: The Basics and Beyond.* (Boca Raton, FL: St. Lucie Press, 1997).

T. Davis, "Effective Supply Chain Management," *Sloan Management Review* (Summer 1993): 35–46.

W. L. Duncan and S. Breen, "Making JIT Attractive to Suppliers," *Manufacturing Systems* 6 (1988): 54–55.

E. J. Hay, "Implementing JIT Purchasing: Phase III-Selection," *Production and Inventory Management Review and APICS News* 10 (1990a): 28–29.

E. J. Hay, "Implementing JIT Purchasing: Phase IV-Relationship Building," *Production and Inventory Management Review and APICS News* 10 (1990b): 38–40.

J. Holmstrom, "Implementing Vendor-Managed Inventory the Efficient Way: A Case Study of Partnership in the Supply Chain," *Production and Inventory Management Journal* (3rd Quarter 1998): 1–5.

M. Kepp. "Relationship-Building," *Business Latin America* 29 (1994): 6–7.

J. T. Landry, "Supply Chain Management," *Harvard Business Review* (November 1998): 24–25.

J. H. Mayer, "Supply-Chain Tools Cut Inventory Fat," *Applications Software Magazine* (May 1996): 77–80.

R. C. Mireles, "Supply Chain Management Trends," *Transportation and Distribution* (July 1998): 75.

J. Morgan, "Building a World Class Supply Base from Scratch," *Purchasing* (August 19, 1993a): 56–61.

J. Morgan, "Supplier Programs Take Time to Become World Class," *Purchasing* (August 19, 1993b): 61–63.

B. Roberts, "Ties that Bind," *Electronic Business* (August 1998): 62–68.

D. F. Ross, *Competing Through Supply Chain Management: Creating Market Winning Strategies Through Supply Chain Partnerships.* (New York: Chapman & Hall, 1998.)

T. Stein and J. Sweat, "Killer Supply Chain," *Information Week* 708 (1998): 36–41.

I. Stuart, R. Deckert, D. McCutcheon, and R. Kunst, "Case Study: A Leveraged Learning Network," *Sloan Management Review* 39 (1998): 81–93.

D. Tait, "Make Strong Relationships a Priority," *Canadian Manager* 23 (1998): 21–28.

A. A. Thompson and A. J. Strickland, III. *Strategic Management Concepts and Cases* (9th ed.). (Chicago: Irwin, 1996.)

G. Tyndall, C. Gopal, W. Partsch, and J. Kamauff, "Ten Strategies to Enhance Supplier Management," *National Productivity Review* (Summer 1998): 31–44.

Tom Albright is the J. Reese Phifer Faculty Fellow and Stan Davis is a doctoral student, both at the Culverhouse School of Accountancy at the University of Alabama in Tuscaloosa. Alabama. The authors thank Ola Kallenius and Bob Birch of Mercedes for their generous contributions.

QUESTIONS

7.3a What are the four practices that help organizations foster improved relations with suppliers of strategic parts? Explain.

7.3b What is the latest improvement in logistics-based supply chain management (LSCM)? What are its key elements?

7.4 Implementing Management Innovations Successfully: Principles for Lasting Change

by S. Mark Young*

Over the past decade, the pace with which organizations worldwide have been experimenting with innovations to remain competitive has increased frenetically. Activity-based cost management (ABCM), Total Quality Management (TQM), and business process reengineering (BPR) have been attempted by many organizations separately, and in some cases, simultaneously. The financial and human resources that have been poured into these innovation attempts are truly staggering, but unfortunately, many innovations have failed.

The purpose of this article is to offer some principles for successful implementation that often are not explicitly incorporated, or are underemphasized in many approaches to implementation.

Successful implementation occurs when, "Managers and employees permanently alter the way they perform their job responsibilities to conform to the principles dictated by a particular innovation."

Principle 1: The Importance of organizational culture.
Some organizational cultures embrace change while others retreat from change. Knowing what kind of culture exists is an extremely important factor to understand.

Principle 2: Only adopt those innovations consistent with current corporate, divisional, and plant strategies.
The assumption underlying this principle is that employees will be more willing to adopt an innovation if it is consistent with the organization's strategy to which they have already committed.

Principle 3: Don't attempt an innovation if an organization is simultaneously engaging in downsizing.
Employees have great difficulty committing to change when they see that their organization is not committing to them. Have a strong feeling of job security allows employees to accept change more easily.

Principle 4; Spend as much time and resources on managing the human side of change as the technical side.
Managing the technical side of an innovation is often not the most significant problem for organizations. Successful change involves placing a great deal of effectively managing people so that they may embrace change.

Principle 5: Educate and train employees at all levels of the organization regarding the purpose and benefits of the innovation.
Educating employees only at the managerial level as to why change is occurring is an enormous mistake. Because most innovation success rests on improvements in variables related to quality, cost and time, employees at the point of production and service need to be included in any training and education programs. Only then can the entire organization embrace change.

---

* This article has been summarized from the original article by S. Mark Young, "Implementing Management Innovations Successfully: Principles for Lasting Change," in the *Journal of Cost Management* (September/October 1997): 16–20.

Principle 6: Use medium- and long-term performance measures to gauge innovation success.

Many organizations simply rely on short term (often financial) performance measures such to gauge success. The key to assessing real change is to use measures that will answer questions such as, "Is the innovation leading to the intended consequences?" and "Are employees thinking differently about problems and are they making better decisions?" Answers to these questions may require more qualitative measures such as attitudinal surveys and direct observation of behavior. Such measures serve as medium term assessments of true behavioral change. The organization should also rely on long-term (3 to 5 year) measures as it takes several years for true change to occur.

Principle 7: Generate useful and understandable reports to illustrate the effects of change programs.

Managers are typically inundated with a lot of information and many reports that don't provide them with the answers they need. Reports related to change programs must be easily understandable and useful. They should detail measures that a manager can look at to determine if change is occurring.

Principle 8: Make explicit agreements regarding when and if existing information systems should be turned off once a new system is in place.

Determining when to switch off an old system and turn on the new one is of immense importance. Once a system like ABC has been implemented the old direct labor based system must be turned off quickly. If this does not happen then managers will be constantly looking at both the old and new systems. The numbers generated from both may cause confusion and reliance on the old system may not allow managers to make the transition to the new system.

QUESTION

7.4a Principle 4 says, "Spend as much time and resources on managing the human side of change as the technical side." Why is this so important?

7.4b Why does Young advocate, in Principle 6 that organizations should use both medium- and long-term measures to gauge innovation success?

Chapter 8

Motivating Behavior in Management Accounting and Control Systems

---

Kenneth Merchant's classic article, *The Control Function of Management*" (Reading 8.1), presents a framework for determining the appropriate use of management controls. Merchant discusses specific action controls, those designed to make sure that individuals take the most appropriate actions; controls over results, those related to meeting targets such as budgets; and personnel controls, those based on hiring people who will do what is best for the organization. Using this framework, Merchant discusses a number of topics including how to choose among the various forms of control and the kinds of financial and behavioral costs that are incurred in using each form of control.

Alfie Kohn's *Why Incentive Plans Cannot Work* (Reading 8.2), argues strongly that incentive plans that link rewards to measured performance are fundamentally flawed. Citing research evidence, Kohn believes that employees who expect to receive a reward for their efforts do not perform as well as those who do not expect rewards. What is lacking with current pay-for-performance systems is that they do not foster a work environment in which employees can experience intrinsic rewards. Ultimately, the preoccupation with extrinsic rewards does not lead to organizational commitment, discourages risk taking, and reduces creativity and innovation. Ever controversial, Kohn closes with the following, "Managers who insist that the job won't get done right without rewards have failed to offer a convincing argument for behavioral manipulation. Promising a reward to someone who appears unmotivated is a bit like offering salt water to someone who is thirsty. Bribes in the workplace simply won't work."

Reading 8.3 is an article by Jeffrey Pfeffer, *Six Dangerous Myths About Pay*. This provocative article addresses key questions regarding employee compensation: (1) how much should employees be paid?, (2) how much emphasis should be on financial compensation as part of a total reward system?, (3) how much emphasis should be placed on attempting to hold down the rate of pay?, and (4) whether to implement a reward system that recognizes and rewards employees based on individual performance. To tackle these questions Pfeffer discusses six "dangerous" myths about compensation and then uses a wide variety of examples to dispel them.

David Gebler's "Creating an Ethical Culture," (Reading 8.4), was published shortly before Kenneth Lay and Jeffrey Skilling were convicted of fraud and conspiracy (Lay subsequently died of a heart attack while awaiting sentencing in July 2006). The article is very timely as major fraud by very senior company officials has clearly been on the rise over the past decade. Gebler states that despite an increase in the number of ethics programs in companies, reduced levels of misconduct have not occurred. Companies need to build the right organizational culture first rather than superimposing an ethics program a culture that cannot respond.

In Reading 8.5, *Pay Without Performance: An Overview of the Issues*, Lucian Bebchuk and Jess Fried, provide a critique of current executive compensation plans and existing corporate governance systems that perpetuate them. Central to their discussion is that so-called "arm's length" contracting between executives and boards of directors has been compromised due to conflicts of interests with incentives. The authors point out that an organization's governance system can provide differential latitude for top executives to influence their own boards. They suggest a number of ways in which much more transparency about compensation arrangements can be made.

Readings
Chapter 8

8.1 The Control Function of Management

by Kenneth A. Merchant, Harvard University*

After strategies are set and plans are made, management's primary task is to take steps to ensure that these plans are carried out, or, if conditions warrant, that the plans are modified. This is the critical control function of management. And since management involves directing the activities of others, a major part of the control function is making sure other people do what should be done.

The management literature is filled with advice on how to achieve better control. This advice usually includes a description of some type of measurement and feedback process:

> The basic control process, wherever it is found and whatever it controls, involves three steps: (1) establishing standards, (2) measuring performance against these standards, and (3) correcting deviations from standards and plans.[1]
>
> A good management control system stimulates action by spotting the significant variations from the original plan and highlighting them for the people who can set things right.[2]
>
> Controls need to focus on results[3]

This focus on measurement and feedback, however, can be seriously misleading. In many circumstances, a control system built around measurement and feedback is not feasible. And even when feasibility is not a limitation, use of a feedback-oriented control system is often an inferior solution. Yet, good controls can be established and maintained using other techniques.

What is needed is a broader perspective on control as a management function: this article addresses such a perspective. The first part summarizes the general control problem by discussing the underlying reasons for implementing controls and by describing what can realistically be achieved. In the second part, the various types of controls available are identified. The last part discusses why the appropriate choice of controls is and should be different in different settings.

WHY ARE CONTROLS NEEDED?
If all personnel always did what was best for the organization, control—and even management—would not be needed. But, obviously individuals are sometimes unable or unwilling to act in the organization's best interest, and a set of controls must be implemented to guard against undesirable behavior and to encourage desirable actions.

One important class of problems against which control systems guard may be called *personal limitations*. People do not always understand what is expected of them nor how they can best perform their jobs, as they may lack some requisite ability, training, or information. In addition, human beings have a number of innate perceptual and cognitive biases, such as an inability to process new information optimally or to make consistent decisions, and these biases can reduce organizational effectiveness.[4] Some of these personal limitations are correctable or avoidable, but for others, controls are required to guard against their deleterious effects.

Even if employees are properly equipped to perform a job well, some choose not to do so, because individual goals and organizational goals may not coincide perfectly. In other words, there is a *lack of goal congruence*. Steps must often be taken either to increase goal congruence or to prevent employees from acting in their own interest where goal incongruence exists.

If nothing is done to protect the organization against the possible occurrence of undesirable behavior or the omission of desirable behavior caused by these personal limitations and motivational problems, severe repercussions may result. At a minimum, inadequate control can result in lower performance or higher risk of poor performance. At the extreme, if performance is not controlled on one or more critical performance dimensions, the outcome could be organizational failure.

WHAT IS GOOD CONTROL?
Perfect control, meaning complete assurance that actual accomplishment will proceed according to plan, is never possible because of the likely occurrence of unforeseen events. However, good control should mean that an informed person could be reasonably confident that no major unpleasant surprises will occur. A high probability of forthcoming poor performance, despite a reasonable operating plan, sometimes is given the label "out of control."

Some important characteristics of this desirable state of good control should be highlighted. First, control is future-oriented: the goal is to have no unpleasant surprises in the future. The past is not relevant except as a

* From: K. Merchant, "The Control Function of Management, *Sloan Management Review* (Summer 1982): 43–55. Reprinted with permission.

guide to the future. Second, control is multidimensional, and good control cannot be established over an activity with multiple objectives unless performance on all significant dimensions has been considered. Thus, for example, control of a production department cannot be considered good unless all the major performance dimensions, including quality, efficiency, and asset management, are well controlled. Third, the assessment of whether good performance assurance has been achieved is difficult and subjective. An informed expert might judge that the control system in place is adequate because no major bad surprises are likely, but this judgment is subject to error because adequacy must be measured against a future that can be very difficult to assess. Fourth, better control is not always economically desirable. Like any other economic good, the control tools are costly and should be implemented only if the expected benefits exceed the costs.

HOW CAN GOOD CONTROL BE ACHIEVED?
Good control can be achieved by avoiding some behavioral problems and/or by implementing one or more types of control to protect against the remaining problems. The following sections discuss the major control options.

Control-Problem Avoidance. In most situations, managers can avoid some control problems by allowing no opportunities for improper behavior. One possibility is automation. Computers and other means of automation reduce the organization's exposure to control problems because they can be set to perform appropriately (that is, as the organization desires), and they will perform more consistently than do human beings. Consequently, control is improved.

Another avoidance possibility *is centralization,* such as that which takes place with very critical decisions at most organization levels. If a manager makes all the decisions in certain areas, those areas cease to be control problems in a managerial sense because no other persons are involved.

A third avoidance possibility is *risk-sharing* with an outside body, such as an insurance company. Many companies bond employees in sensitive positions, and in so doing, they reduce the probability that the employees' behavior will cause significant harm to the firm.

Finally, some control problems can and should be avoided by *elimination* of a business or an operation entirely. Managers without the means to control certain activities, perhaps because they do not understand the processes well, can eliminate the associated control problems by turning over their potential profits and the associated risk to a third party, for example, by subcontracting or divesting.

If management cannot, or chooses not to, avoid the control problems caused by relying on other individuals, they must address the problems by implementing one or more control tactics. The large number of tactics that are available to help achieve good control can be classified usefully into three main categories, according to the *object* of control; that is, whether control is exercised over *specific actions, results,* or *personnel.* Table 1 shows many common controls classified according to their control object; these controls are described in the following sections.

Control of Specific Actions. One type of control, specific-action control, attempts to ensure that individuals perform (or do not perform) certain actions that are known to be desirable (or undesirable). Management can limit the incidence of some types of obviously undesirable activity by using *behavioral constraints* that render the occurrence impossible, or at least unlikely. These constraints include physical devices, such as locks and key personnel identification systems, and administrative constraints, such as segregation of duties, which make it very difficult for one person to carry out an improper act.

TABLE 1. A CONTROL TOOL CLASSIFICATION FRAMEWORK

Object of Control Specific Actions	Results	Personnel
Behavioral Constraint:	Results Accountability:	Upgrade Capabilities:
—Physical (e.g., locks, security guards)	—Standards	—Selection
	—Budgets	—Training
—Administrative (e.g., separation of duties)	—Management by Objective (MBO)	—Assignment
		Improve Communication:
Action Accountability:		—Clarify Expectations
—Work Rules		—Provide Information for Coordination
—Policies and Procedures		
—Codes of Conduct		Encourage Peer Control:
		—Work Groups
Preaction Review:		—Shared Goals
—Direct Supervision		
—Approval Limits		
—Budget Reviews		

A second type of specific-action control is *action accountability*—a type of feedback control system by which employees are held accountable for their actions. The implementation of action-accountability control systems requires: (1) defining the limits of acceptable behavior, as is done in procedures manuals; (2) tracking the behaviors that employees are actually engaged in; and (3) rewarding or punishing deviations from the defined limits. Although action-accountability systems involve the tracking and reporting of actual behaviors, their objective is to motivate employees to behave appropriately in the future. These systems are effective only if employees understand what is required of them, and they feel that their individual actions will be noticed and rewarded or punished in some significant way.

A third type of specific-action control is *preaction review*. This involves observing the work of others before the activity is complete, for example, through direct supervision, formal planning reviews, and approvals on proposals for expenditures. Reviews can provide effective control in several ways by: correcting potentially harmful behavior before the full damaging effects are felt; or influencing behavior just by the threat of an impending review, such as causing extra care in the preparation of an expenditure proposal. One advantage of reviews is that they can be used even when it is not possible to define exactly what is expected prior to the review.

Control of Results. Control can also be accomplished by focusing on results: this type of control comes in only one basic form, results accountability, which involves holding employees responsible for certain results. Use of results-accountability control systems requires: (1) defining the dimensions along which results are desired, such as efficiency, quality, and service; (2) measuring performance on these dimensions; and (3) providing rewards (punishments) to encourage (discourage) behavior that will lead (not lead) to those results. As with action-accountability systems, results-accountability systems are future-oriented; they attempt to motivate people to behave appropriately. But they are effective only if employees feel that their individual efforts will be noticed and rewarded in some significant way.

Control of Personnel. A third type of control can be called *personnel control* because it emphasizes a reliance on the personnel involved to do what is best for the organization, and it provides assistance for them as necessary. Personnel controls can be very effective by themselves in some situations, such as in a small family business or in a professional partnership, because the underlying causes of the needs for controls (personal limitations and lack of goal congruence) are minimal. However, even when control problems are present, they can be reduced to some extent by: (1) upgrading the capabilities of personnel in key positions, such as tightening hiring policies, implementing training programs, or

improving job assignments; (2) improving communications to help individuals know and understand their roles better and how they can best coordinate their efforts with those of other groups in the organization; and (3) encouraging peer (or subordinate) control by establishing cohesive work groups with shared goals.

FEASIBILITY CONSTRAINTS ON THE CHOICE OF CONTROLS

The design of a control system often depends partly on the feasibility of the various types of controls: not all of these tools can be used in every situation. Personnel controls are the most adaptable to a broad range of situations.

To some extent, all organizations rely on their employees to guide and motivate themselves, and this self-control can be increased with some care in hiring, screening, and training. Even in a prison, where administrators are faced with a sharp lack of goal congruence and where few control options are available other than physical constraints, inmates are screened so that dangerous ones are not assigned to high-risk positions, such as in a machine shop.

Most situations, however, require reinforcing personnel controls by placing controls over specific actions, results, or a combination of the two. This is where feasibility becomes a limiting factor.

For control over specific actions, management must have some knowledge of which actions are desirable. While it may be easy to define precisely the required behavior on a production line, the definition of preferred behavior for a research engineer cannot be as precise. Being able to keep track of specific actions is also necessary to enforce actions accountability; however, this is usually not a limiting factor, except in rare situations such as a remote outpost, because actions can be observed directly or assessed indirectly through action reports, such as hours worked, sales calls made, or procedural violations.

For control over results, the most serious constraint is the ability to measure the desired results effectively. (Management usually knows what results are desirable.) Ideally, measurements should: (1) assess the *correct* performance areas—the ones for which results are truly desired; (2) be *precise*—not determined by only crude estimations; (3) be *timely* and (4) be *objective*—not subject to manipulation. While perfect measures are rarely available, reasonable surrogates can often be found or developed. For example, "complaints received" might be a good (negative) indicator of the performance of hotel staff personnel along the customer-service dimension. Significant difficulty in achieving any of these four measurement qualities, however, can lead to failure of a results-oriented control system.

Figure 1 shows how the two factors most limiting control feasibility knowledge of desirable actions and the ability to measure results on the important performance dimensions—can influence the choice of controls used.[5] The most difficult control situation, shown in box 4 of Figure 1, is one in which the desirable actions are not known and the important result areas cannot be measured well. Only personnel controls (or problem avoidance) are available options. In a research laboratory, for example, success might be difficult to assess for years, yet prescription of specific actions could be counterproductive. Fortunately, in this specific setting, control is not a serious problem because research scientists tend to be professional—well trained and responsible to the standards of their profession. They tend to control themselves, and consequently, control of research laboratories tend to be dominated by controls over personnel.

In box 3 of Figure 1, where knowledge of desirable specific actions is poor but good results measurements are available, control is best accomplished by controlling results. Movie production is a good example. It is probably impossible to dictate what a movie director should do or even to observe his or her behavior and predict whether the finished product will be good. It is, however, a relatively easy task to measure the economic performance of the movie and the artistic merit, if that is a concern. In this situation, the best control system would seem to be a results accountability system that defines to the director the results expected, holds him or her responsible for achieving them, and provides some reinforcement in the form of compensation and/or recognition.

For similar reasons, results controls tend to be dominant at most upper-management levels. It is usually not possible to prescribe and keep track of the specific actions each manager should be performing, but it is relatively easy to define the results desired, in terms similar to those desired by shareholders.

Specific-action controls should dominate where there is knowledge about which actions are desirable but where results measurement is impossible or difficult, as indicated in box 2 of Figure 1. Consider, for example, control over a real-estate development business where large capital investment decisions are made frequently. Results of these decisions are difficult to measure in a timely, accurate fashion because of their long-term nature; they tend to be inseparable from the results of other actions and are confounded by changes in the environment. However, the techniques of investment analysis are well developed (e.g., net present value analysis with tests of the sensitivity of assumptions), and control may be accomplished by formally reviewing the techniques used and the assumptions made.

FIGURE 1. KEY CONTROL OBJECT FEASIBILITY DETERMINANTS

		Ability to Measure Results on Important Performance Dimensions	
		High	Low
Knowledge of Which Specific Actions are Desirable	Excellent	1. Specific-Action and/or Results Control	2. Specific-Action Control (e.g., real-estate venture)
	Poor	3. Results Control (e.g., movie director)	4. Personal control (e.g., research laboratory)

HOW TO CHOOSE AMONG THE FEASIBLE OPTIONS

Often managers cannot rely completely on the people involved in a given area and cannot employ one or more of the avoidance strategies mentioned earlier. When this is the case, the best situation is one in which either specification or results controls, or both, can be chosen, as is shown in box 1 of Figure 1. In general, the choice of one or more tools should involve consideration of: (1) the total need for control; (2) the amount of control that can be designed into each of the control devices; and (3) the costs of each, both in terms of money spent and unintended behavioral effects, if any. These decision parameters will be described more fully.

Need for Controls. The need for controls over any particular behavior or operation within an organization depends very simply on the impact of that area on overall organizational performance. Thus, more control should be exercised over a strategically important behavior rather than over a minor one, regardless of how easy it is to control each. For example, controlling the new-product-development activity is far more important in many companies than making sure that the production of existing products is accomplished as efficiently as possible. Consequently, more resources should be devoted to controlling the new-product activity, even though it is a far more difficult area to control.

Amount of Control Provided by Feasible Options. The amount of control provided by each of the control tools depends both on their design and on how well they fit the situation in which they are used. Personnel controls should usually provide some degree of control. But although they may be totally effective in some situations, such as in a small business, they provide little or no warning of failure. They can break down very quickly if demands, opportunities, or needs change.

Specific-action and results controls can provide widely varying amounts of control. In general, reasonably certain (or tight) control requires: (1) detailed specification of what is expected of *each individual;* (2) prevention of undesired actions, or effective and frequent monitoring of actions or results; and (3) administration of penalties or rewards that are significant to the individuals involved.

For example, with specific-action-accountability systems, the amount of control can be affected by changing one or more of the elements of the system. First, tighter control can be effected by making the definitions of acceptability more specific. This might take the form of work rules (e.g., no smoking) or specific policies (e.g., a purchasing policy to secure three competing bids before releasing the purchase order), as opposed to general guidelines or vague codes of conduct (e.g., act professionally). Second, control can be made tighter by improving the effectiveness of the action-tracking system. Personnel who are certain that their actions will be noticed relatively quickly will be affected more strongly by an action-accountability system than will those who feel that the chance of their being observed is small. Thus, constant direct supervision should provide tighter control than would an audit sampling of a small number of action reports some time later. Third, control can be made tighter by making the rewards or punishments more significant to the individuals involved. In general, this impact should vary directly with the size of the reward (or the severity of the punishment), although different individuals may react differently to identical rewards or punishments.

Results-accountability systems can be varied along similar lines. Expected performance can be defined broadly, for instance, with a goal for annual net income. Alternatively, expected performance can be defined in more detailed form by prescribing goals for specific result areas (for example, sales growth, efficiency, quality) and by using line items with short time horizons (e.g., month or quarter). Control is tighter when the performance dimensions for which desired results are defined explicitly and, of course, correctly: this type of control is particularly effective if well-established results standards are available, perhaps in the form of output from an engineering study, industry survey, or historical analysis. Results-accountability control can also be tightened by improving the measurement of results. This can be accomplished by making the measures more precise, more timely, and/or less subject to manipulation.

In addition, reviews can be used to provide either tight or loose assurance. Tight assurance is more likely if the reviews are detailed, comprehensive, and frequent.

Of course, managers do not have to rely exclusively on a single type of control in a control system. Use of more than one type of control—in effect, overlapping controls—will often provide reinforcement. For example, most organizations rely on selecting good people, establishing some set procedures, implementing some accountability for results, and reviewing some key decisions before they are made.

Costs: Outlay and Behavioral. The cost of a control depends on two factors: the incremental dollar cost of the tool and the cost of any unintended behavioral effects. The actual dollar cost of a control might be considerably less than it first appears because some devices that provide control may already be in place for other reasons. For example, a budgeting process for a small firm does not have to justify its cost on the basis of control reasons alone. Creditors probably already require pro forma financial statements, so the incremental cost might involve only additional detail (e.g., down to the operations level) and involvement of a greater number of participants.

The costs of any unintended negative effects must also be considered, and these can be very significant. It is beyond the scope of this article to provide an exhaustive enumeration of the many negative side effects possible. Indeed, they come in many different forms, but it is nevertheless useful to mention a few examples.

A common problem with specific-action controls is that they cause operating delays. These can be relatively minor, such as delays caused by limiting access to a stockroom, but they can also be major. For example, after the executives of Harley-Davidson Motor Company bought the firm from AMF, Inc., they were able to implement a rebate program in ten days, rather than the six to eight weeks it would have taken with all the reviews required in the multilayered AMF organization.[6] Obviously, where timely action is important, delays caused by control processes can be very harmful.

Another problem with specific-action controls is that they can cause rigid, bureaucratic behavior. Individuals who become accustomed to following a set routine are not as apt to sense a changing environment, nor are they likely to search for better ways of doing the tasks at hand in a stable environment.

Results controls can create severe, unintended negative effects when all the measurement criteria are not met satisfactorily. Perhaps the most serious common problem is a failure to define the results areas correctly. This causes goal "displacement," a situation where individuals are encouraged to generate the wrong results—in response to the goals defined in the control system—rather than those results truly needed by the organization. For example, a department store introduced an incentive compensation plan to pay employees on the basis of sales volume. The immediate impact was indeed an increase in sales volume, but the increase was accomplished in ways that were inconsistent with long-term organizational goals. The employees competed among themselves for customers and neglected important but unmeasured and unrewarded activities such as stocking, and merchandising.[7] Another common example of goal displacement is caused by the practice of rewarding managers on the oft criticized return-on investment criterion.[8]

Data distortion is another dangerous potential side effect of results controls. If the measurement methods are not objective, then the employees whose performances are being measured might falsify the data or change the measurement methods, and, in so doing, undermine the whole organization's information system.

Many of the ramifications of these unintended effects of control systems are not well understood, and their costs are very difficult to quantify. However, consideration of these effects is an important control-system design factor: they cannot be ignored.

WHERE DOES FEEDBACK FIT IN?

Because feedback does not appear prominently in the preceding discussion, it is useful for clarification purposes to consider where feedback fits in. Control is necessarily future-oriented, as past performance cannot be changed, but analysis of results and feedback of variances can often provide a particularly strong addition to a control system. A prerequisite, of course, is the ability to measure results, so feedback can only be useful in the situations presented in boxes 1 and 3 of Figure 1.

There are three reasons why feedback of past results is an important part of many control systems. First, feedback is necessary as reinforcement for a results-accountability system. Even if the feedback is not used to make input adjustments, it signals that results are being monitored. This can heighten employee awareness of what is expected of them and should help stimulate better performance.

Second, in repetitive situations, measurement of results can provide indications of failure in time to make useful interventions. This is shown in the simple feedback control model presented in Figure 2. When the results achieved are not satisfactory, the inputs, which include the specific actions and types of persons involved, can be changed to provide different results. Obviously, these input adjustments are more likely to improve results when there is a good understanding of how inputs relate to results; otherwise, the interventions are essentially experiments.

Third, analysis of how the results vary with different combinations of inputs might improve understanding of how the inputs relate to results. This process is depicted in loop A of Figure 3, a slightly more complicated feedback control model. As this input results understanding improves, it provides the opportunity to shift the control system from a results-oriented to a specific-action-oriented focus. If managers discover that certain specific actions produce consistently superior results, then it might be beneficial to inform employees of the specific actions that are expected of them, for example, by publishing

these desired actions in a procedures manual. The greater the knowledge about how actions bring about results, the greater the possibilities of using a tight, specific-action-oriented control system.

Note that these latter two reasons for analyzing feedback—for making interventions and for learning—are only useful in situations that at least partially repeat themselves. If a situation is truly a one-time occurrence, such as a major divestiture or a unique capital investment, management has little use for feedback information. In these cases, by the time the results are available, it is too late to intervene, and a greater understanding of how results are related to inputs is not immediately useful.

FIGURE 2. A SIMPLE FEEDBACK CONTROL MODEL

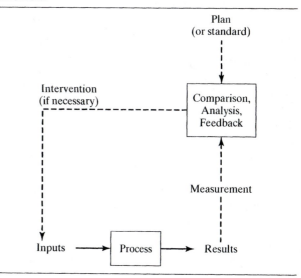

FIGURE 3. A FEEDBACK CONTROL MODEL WITH LEARNING

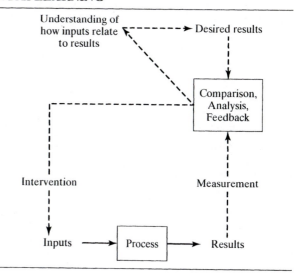

There are other circumstances where feedback need not, and perhaps should not, be a part of a good control system. In many cases, although feedback control systems are not really feasible, they are used anyway. This occurs because of the consistent tendency "to concentrate an matters that are concrete and quantifiable, rather than intangible concepts," which may be equally or more important.[9] Invariably, this will lead to dysfunctional effects, as will all other failures to satisfy the measurement criteria or to define results appropriately.

Cost considerations also commonly lead to decisions not to include feedback in a control system. The design, implementation, and maintenance of results-tracking information systems can often be very expensive. Thus, it is not feasible to have feedback as part of every control system, nor is it necessarily desirable even when feasibility constraints are not present.

THE DESIGN PROCESS

As discussed at the beginning of this article, management control is a problem of human behavior. The challenge is to have each individual acting properly as often as possible. Thus, it seems logical to start the control-system design process by considering the personnel component of the organization by itself. In some situations, well-trained, highly motivated personnel can be expected, with a high degree of certainty, to perform their jobs satisfactorily without any additional control steps being taken. A confident reliance on personnel controls is a very desirable situation because additional controls cost money and may have undesirable side effects.

If, however, management determines that personnel controls should be supplemented, the first step should be to examine the feasibility of the various control options. To do this, management must assess two factors: how much is known about which specific actions are desirable, and how well measurement can be accomplished in the important performance areas. This feasibility test might immediately determine whether the controls that can be added should be oriented toward specific actions or results. Control can be made tighter by strengthening the controls in place, along the lines discussed earlier, or by implementing overlapping controls, such as controls over results and specific actions.

In most cases, management has same, but less than complete, knowledge of which specific actions are desirable and some, but not perfect, ability to measure the important result areas. This situation usually calls for implementation of both specific-action and results controls, with feedback loops to improve understanding of the relevant processes.

AN EXAMPLE: CONTROL OF A SALES FORCE

The above observations about control can be illustrated by describing how control of a sales force might work. Generally, personnel controls are some part of every sales force control system. Consider, for example, this statement by a sales and marketing consultant:

I think I can tell a good salesman just by being around him. If the guy is experienced, confident, well prepared, speaks well, maintains control of situations, and seems to have his time planned, I assume I have a good salesman.

If a sales manager feels confident about all of the salespeople employed, he or she might wish to allow personnel controls to dominate the control system. This is likely, for example, in a small business with a sales force comprised solely of relatives and close friends. But most sales managers are not willing to rely exclusively on hiring and training good people.

What controls should be added? The answer, of course, depends on the type of sales involved. In a single-product, high-volume operation, the volume of sales generated is probably a good simple factor on which to base a results-oriented control system. It provides a reasonable, although not perfect, surrogate for long-range profitability, and the measurements are very inexpensive because the data are already gathered as a necessary input to the financial reporting system. The results-accountability system can then be completed by providing reinforcement in the form of sales commissions. This simple solution will also work where multiple products with varying profitability are involved, if the commission schedules are varied so that rewards are assigned in proportion to the profitability of the sales generated.

Consider, however, a situation where salespeople sell large-scale construction equipment and where sales come in very large but infrequent chunks. A commission-type, results-accountability system is still feasible. Measurement of results is not difficult and can be accurate to the penny. The amount of control provided, however, is not high because the measurements fail on the timeliness dimension. Because sales are infrequent, zero sales are not an unusual situation in any given month. Therefore, a salesperson could be drawing advances on hypothetical future commissions for many months without performing any of the desired promotional activities.

Two solutions are possible. One is to augment the commission system with some specific-action controls, such as activity reports. Some activities are probably known to be desirable, such as the number of hours worked and the quantity of calls made. If the product mix and market environment are fairly stable, then requiring and monitoring activity reports is not as costly as it might seem, because it could provide an important side benefit—an activity-oriented data base. The patterns in this data base can be analyzed and compared with results over time to add to knowledge about which activities yield the best results.

An alternate solution is to improve the results-accountability system. It might be possible to define some factors that are strong predictors of sales success, such as customer satisfaction with the salesperson or customer familiarity with the company's products. Measurement of these intangibles, of course, would have to be done by surveying customers. Even though these measures do not directly assess the desired result area (long-range profitability), and measurement is imprecise, they could provide a better focus for a results-oriented control system than a sales-generated measure because of the improvement in timeliness. Over time, it is likely that the choice of measures and measurement methodologies could be improved. The advantage of this results-oriented solution over an action-oriented system is that it is more flexible and less constraining to the salespeople; they can continue to use styles best suited to their personalities.

CONCLUSIONS

This article has taken a new look at the most basic organizational control problem—how to get employees to live up to the plans that have been established. In the course of discussion, the following major points were made:

1. Management control is a behavioral problem. The various control tools are only effective to the extent that they influence behavior in desirable directions.
2. Good control can often be achieved in several different ways. In some circumstances, the control problems can be avoided, for example, by centralizing or automating certain decisions. If problems cannot be avoided, one or more types of controls are usually desirable or necessary. The options can be classified according to the object of control, labeled in this article as specific actions, results, and personnel.
3. Not all types of controls are feasible in all situations. Figure 4 presents the questions to ask when assessing the feasibility of control types. If none of the controls is feasible, the probability of undesirable results occurring is high.
4. Control can be strengthened either by employing a tighter version of a single type of control or by implementing more than one type of control. However, tighter control is not always desirable because of additional system costs and the potential of undesirable side effects, such as destruction of morale, reduction of initiative, or displacement of employee focus toward measurable result areas only.

FIGURE 4. QUESTIONS TO DETERMINE FEASIBILITY OF CONTROL TYPES

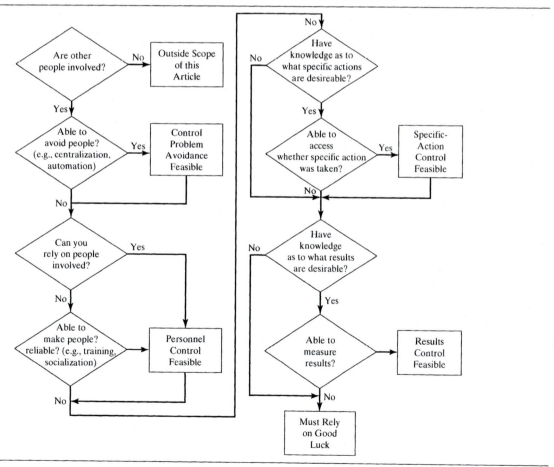

Some of the qualities, benefits, and costs of each of the major control types are listed in Table 2.

5. The basic management control problems and alternatives are the same in all functional areas and at all levels in the organization, from the lowest supervisory levels to the very top levels of management. The best solutions, however, vary between situations.

An understanding of control can be an important input into many management decisions. For example, control problems should be considered in making some types of investments. An investment in an operation in which control is very difficult—such as a highly specialized and technical area where control must depend heavily on personnel controls—is, by definition, risky. Thus, investments in such areas should promise high returns to compensate for this risk.

Similarly, control considerations should affect the design of the other parts of the management system. Consider, for example, the organizational structure. If independent areas of *responsibility* cannot be carved out as part of the organizational structure, results-accountability control systems will not work well because employees will not feel that their individual actions have a noticeable effect on results. (It should be noted that many of the prescriptions calling for "responsibility accounting" only provide the illusion of results independence because of the many allocations of the costs and/or benefits of shared resources.) If independent areas of *authority* are not established, specific-action-accountability control systems cannot work. This principle underlies the internal control principle of "separation of duties." In addition, if tighter reviews of specific actions are necessary for adequate performance assurance, it is likely that the supervisory spans of control will have to be reduced. Similar observations can be made about other management functions, but they are beyond the scope of this article.

This article has attempted to provide a new look at this basic, but often overlooked, management problem. The control area is decidedly complex, and there is much that is not known about how controls work and how employees respond to different types of controls. For example, it would be worthwhile to know more about how controls can be designed to maximize the amount of control provided while minimizing the cost in the form of employee feelings of lost autonomy. However, an increased awareness of the control problem, of what can be accomplished and of the options available should provide a new perspective that will suggest ways to improve control systems and overall organizational performance.

The author wishes to acknowledge Robert N. Anthony, Peter Brownell, and Martha S. Hayes for their helpful comments.

The control function of management can be a critical determinant of organizational success. Most authors discuss control only through feedback and adjustment processes. This article takes a broader perspective on control and discusses the following questions: What is good control? Why are controls needed? How can good control be achieved? If multiple control strategies are feasible, how should the choice among them be made? Ed.

ENDNOTES

1. See H. Koontz, C. O'Donnell, and H. Weihrich. *Management*, 7th ed. (New York: McGraw-Hill, 1980), p. 722.
2. See W. D. Brinckloe and M. T. Coughlin, *Managing Organizations* (Encino, CA: Glencoe Press, 1977), p. 298.
3. See P. F. Drucker, *Management: Tasks, Responsibilities, Practices* (New York: Harper & Row, 1974), p. 497.
4. A recent summary of many of the findings in this area (illustrating such cognitive limitations as conservative revision of prior subjective probabilities when new information is provided, and the use of simplifying decision-making heuristics when faced with complex problems) is provided by W. F. Wright, "Cognitive Information Processing Biases: Implications for Producers and Users of Financial Information," *Decision Sciences* (April 1980): 284–298.

TABLE 2. QUALITIES OF CONTROL TOOLS

Object of Control:		SPECIFIC ACTIONS		RESULTS	PERSONNEL
	Constraint	Accountability	Review	Accountability	
Amount of Control Provided (tight or loose)	Tight	Tight if Specific; Loose if Vague	Tight if Detailed And Frequent	Tight if Expectations Are Specific And Detailed	Loose
Out-of-Pocket-Cost (relative)	Low	Low	High	High	Varies
Possible Unintended Effects (examples)	Slight Operating Delays	Rigid Bureaucratic Behavior	Operating Delays	Goal Displacement Data Distortion	

5. A similar scheme is presented in W. G. Ouchi, "A Conceptual Framework for the Design of Organizational Control Mechanisms," *Management Science* (September 1979): 833–848.

6. See H. Klein, "At Harley-Davidson, Life without AMF Is Upbeat but Full of Financial Problems," *Wall Street Journal*, 13 April 1982, p. 37.

7. See N. Babchuk and W. J. Goode, "Work Incentives in a Self-Determined Group," *American Sociological Review* (1951): 679–687.

8. For a summary of criticisms of return-on-investment (ROI) measures of performance, see J. Dearden, "The Case against ROI Control," *Harvard Business Review*, May–June 1969, pp. 124–135.

9. See D. Mitchell, *Control without Bureaucracy* (London: McGraw-Hill Book Company Limited, 1979), p. 6.

Kenneth A. Merchant is Assistant Professor of Business Administration at Harvard University. Dr. Merchant holds the B.A. degree from Union College, the M.B.A. degree from Colombia University, and the Ph.D. degree from the University of California, Berkeley. His main interests lie in the areas of accounting, information systems, and planning and control. Dr. Merchant has published articles for such journals as The Accounting Review and Accounting, Organizations, and Society.

QUESTION

8.1 Merchant discusses specific action, results, and personnel controls. Provide three examples of each. Can organizations focus on just one major type of control method (e.g. action controls)?

8.2 Why Incentive Plans Cannot Work
When reward systems fail, don't blame the program— look at the premise behind it.

*by Alfie Kohn**

It is difficult to overstate the extent to which most managers and the people who advise them believe in the redemptive power of rewards. Certainly, the vast majority of U.S. corporations use some sort of program intended to motivate employees by tying compensation to one index of performance or another. But more striking is the rarely examined belief that people will do a better job if they have been promised some sort of incentive. This assumption and the practices associated with it are pervasive, but a growing collection of evidence supports an opposing view. According to numerous studies in laboratories, workplaces, classrooms, and other settings, rewards typically undermine the very processes they are intended to enhance. The findings suggest that the failure of any given incentive program is due less to a glitch in that program than to the inadequacy of the psychological assumptions that ground all such plans.

TEMPORARY COMPLIANCE

Behaviorist theory, derived from work with laboratory animals, is indirectly responsible for such programs as piecework pay for factory workers, stock options for top executives, special privileges accorded to employees of the Month, and commissions for salespeople. Indeed, the livelihood of innumerable consultants has long been based on devising fresh formulas for computing bonuses to wave in front of employees. Money, vacations, banquets, plaques—the list of variations on a single, simple behaviorist model of motivation is limitless. And today even many people who are regarded as forward thinking—those promote teamwork, participative management, continuous improvement, and the like—urge the use of rewards to institute and maintain these very reforms. What we use bribes to accomplish may have changed, but the reliance on bribes, on behaviorist doctrine, has not.

Moreover, the few articles that appear to criticize incentive plans are invariably limited to details of implementation. Only fine-tune the calculations and delivery of the incentive—or perhaps hire the author as a consultant—and the problem will be solved, we are told. As Herbert H. Meyer, professor emeritus in the psychology department the College of Social and Behavioral Sciences at the University of South Florida, has written, "Anyone reading literature on this subject published 20 years ago would find that the articles look almost identical to those published today." That assessment, which could have been written this morning, was actually offered in 1975. In nearly forty years, the thinking hasn't changed.

Do rewards work? The answer depends on what we mean by "work." Research suggests that, by and large, rewards succeed at securing one thing only: temporary compliance. When it comes to producing lasting change in attitudes and behavior, however, rewards, like punishment, are strikingly ineffective. Once the rewards run out, people revert to their old behaviors. Studies show that offering incentives for losing weight, quitting smoking, using seat belts, or (in the case of children) acting generously is not only less effective than other strategies but often proves worse than doing nothing at all. Incentives, a version of what psychologists call extrinsic motivators, do not alter the attitudes that underlie our behaviors. They do not create an enduring *commitment* to any value or action. Rather incentives merely—and temporarily—change what we do.

As for productivity, at least two dozen studies over the last three decades have conclusively shown that people who expect to receive a reward for completing a task or for doing that task successfully simply do not perform as well as those who expect no reward at all. These studies examined rewards for children and adults, males and females, and included tasks ranging from memorizing facts to creative problem-solving to designing collages. In general, the more cognitive sophistication and open-ended thinking that was required, the worse people performed when working for a reward. Interestingly enough, the researchers themselves were often taken by surprise. They assumed that rewards would produce better work but discovered otherwise.

The question for managers is whether incentive plans can work when extrinsic motivators more generally do not. Unfortunately, as author C. Douglas Jenkins, Jr., has noted, most organizational studies to date—like the articles published—have tended "to focus on the effects of *variations* in incentive conditions, and not on whether performance-based pay per se raises performance levels."

A number of studies, however, have examined whether or not pay, especially at the executive level, is related to corporate profitability and other measures of organizational performance. Often they have found slight or even *negative* correlations between pay and performance. Typically, the absence of such a relationship is interpreted as evidence of links between compensation and something other than how well people do their jobs. But most of these data could support a different conclusion, one that reverses the causal arrow. Perhaps what these studies reveal is that higher pay does not, produce better performance. In other words, the very idea of trying to reward quality may be a fool's errand.

Consider the findings of Jude T. Rich and John A. Larson, formerly of McKinsey & Company. In 1982, using interviews and proxy statements, they examined compensation programs at 90 major U.S. companies to determine whether return to shareholders was better for corporations that had incentive plans for top executives than it was for those companies that had no such plans. They were unable to find any difference.

Four years later, Jenkins tracked down 28 previously published studies that measured the impact of financial incentives on performance. (Some were conducted in the laboratory and some in the field.) His analysis, "Financial Incentives," published in 1986, revealed that 16, or 57%, of the studies found a positive effect on performance. However, all of the performance measures were quantitative in nature: a good job consisted of producing more of something or doing it faster. Only five of the studies looked at the quality of performance. And none of those five showed any benefits from incentives.

Another analysis took advantage of an unusual situation that affected a group of welders at a Midwestern manufacturing company. At the request of the union, an incentive system that had been in effect for some years was abruptly eliminated. Now, if a financial incentive supplies motivation, its absence should drive down production. And that is exactly what happened, at first. Fortunately, Harold F. Rothe, former personnel manager and corporate staff assistant at the Beloit Corporation, tracked production over a period of months, providing the sort of long-term data rarely collected in this field. After the initial slump, Rothe found that in the absence of incentives the welders' production quickly began to rise and eventually reached a level as high or higher than it had been before.

One of the largest reviews of how intervention programs affect worker productivity, a meta-analysis of some 330 comparisons from 98 studies, was conducted in the mid-1980s by Richard A. Guzzo, associate professor of psychology at the University of Maryland, College Park, and his colleagues at New York University. The raw numbers seemed to suggest a positive relationship between financial incentives and productivity, but because of the huge variations from one study to another, statistical tests indicated that there was no significant effect overall. What's more, financial incentives were virtually unrelated to the number of workers who were absent or who quit their jobs over a period of time. By contrast, training and goal-setting programs had a far greater impact on productivity than did pay-for-performance plans.

WHY REWARDS FAIL

Why do most executives continue to rely on incentive programs? Perhaps it's because few people take the time to examine the connection between incentive programs and problems with workplace productivity and morale. Rewards buy temporary compliance, so it looks like the problems are solved. It's harder to spot the harm they cause over the long term. Moreover, it does not occur to most of us to suspect rewards, given that our own teachers, parents, and managers probably used them. "Do this and you'll get that" is part of the fabric of American life. Finally, by clinging to the belief that motivational problems are due to the particular incentive system in effect at the moment, rather than to the psychological theory behind all incentives, we can remain optimistic that a relatively minor adjustment will repair the damage.

Over the long haul, however, the potential cost to any organization of trying to fine-tune reward-driven compensation systems may be considerable. The fundamental flaws of behaviorism itself doom the prospects of affecting long-term behavior change or performance improvement through the use of rewards. Consider the following six-point framework that examines the true costs of an incentive program.

1. **"Pay is not a motivator."** W. Edward Deming's declaration may seem surprising, even absurd. Of course, money buys the things people want and need. Moreover, the less people are paid, the more concerned they are likely to be about financial matters. Indeed, several studies over the last few decades have found that when people are asked to guess what matters to their coworkers—or, in the case of managers, to their subordinates—they assume money heads the list. But put the question directly—"what do you care about?"—and pay typically ranks only fifth or sixth.

   Even if people were principally concerned with their salaries, this does not prove that money is motivating. There is no firm basis for the assumption that paying people more will encourage them to do better work or even, in the long run, more work. As Frederick Herzberg, Distinguished Professor of Management at the University of Utah's Graduate School of Management, has argued, just because too little money can irritate and demotivate does not mean that more and more money will bring about increased satisfaction, much less increased motivation. It is plausible to assume that if someone's take-home pay was cut in half, his or her morale would suffer enough to undermine performance. But it doesn't necessarily follow that doubling that person's pay would result in better work.

2. **Rewards punish.** Many managers understand that coercion and fear destroy motivation and create defiance, defensiveness, and rage. They realize that punitive management is a contradiction in terms. As Herzberg wrote in HBR some 25 years ago ("One More Time: How Do You Motivate Employees?" January–February 1968), a "KITA"—which, he coyly explains, stands for "kick in the pants"—may produce movement but never motivation.

   What most executives fail to recognize is the Herzberg's observation is equally true of rewards. Punishment and rewards are two sides of the same coin. Rewards have a punitive effect because they, like out right punishment, are manipulative. "Do this and you'll get that" is not really very different from "Do this or here's what will happen to you." In the case of incentives, the reward itself may be highly desired; but by making that bonus contingent on certain behaviors, managers manipulate their subordinates, and that experience of being controlled is likely to assume a punitive quality over time.

   Further, not receiving a reward one had expected to receive is also indistinguishable from being punished. Whether the incentive is withheld or withdrawn deliberately, or simply not received by someone who had hoped to get it, the effect is identical. And the more desirable the reward, the more demoralizing it is to miss out.

   The new school, which exhorts us to catch people doing something right and reward them for it, is not very different from the old school, which advised us to catch people doing something wrong and threaten to punish them if they ever do it again. What is essentially taking place in both approaches is that a lot of people are getting caught. Managers are creating a workplace in which people feel controlled, not an environment conducive to exploration, learning, and progress.

3. **Rewards rupture relationships.** Relationships among employees are often casualties of the scramble for rewards. As leaders of the Total Quality Management movement have emphasized, incentive programs, and the performance appraisal systems that accompany them, reduce the possibilities for cooperation. Peter R. Scholtes, senior management consultant at Joiner Associates Inc., put it starkly, "Everyone is pressuring the system for individual gain. No one is improving the system for collective gain. The system will inevitably crash." Without teamwork, in other words, there can be no quality.

   The surest way to destroy cooperation and, therefore, organizational excellence, is to force people to compete for rewards or recognition or to rank them against each other. For each person who wins, there are many others who carry with them the feeling of having lost. And the more these awards are publicized through the use of memos, newsletters, and awards banquets, the more detrimental their impact can be. Furthermore, when employees compete for a limited number of incentives, they will most likely begin to see each other as obstacles to their own success. But the same result can occur with any use of rewards; introducing competition just makes a bad thing worse.

   Relationships between supervisors and subordinates can also collapse under the weight of incentives. Of course, the supervisor who punishes is about as welcome to employees as a glimpse of a police car in their rearview mirrors. But even the supervisor who rewards can produce some damaging reactions. For instance, employees *may be* tempted to conceal any problems they might be having and present themselves as infinitely competent to the manager in control of the money. Rather than ask for help—a *prerequisite* for optimal performance—they might opt instead for flattery, attempting to convince the manager that they have everything under control. Very few things threaten an organization as much as a hoard of incentive-driven individuals trying to curry favor with the incentive dispenser.

4. **Rewards ignore reasons.** In order to solve problems in the workplace, managers must understand what caused them. Are employees inadequately prepared for the demands of their jobs? Is long-term growth being sacrificed to maximize short-term return? Are workers unable to collaborate effectively? Is the rigidly hierarchical that employees are intimidated about making recommendations and feel powerless and burned out? Each of these situations calls for a different response. But relying on incentives to boost productivity does nothing to address possible underlying problems and bring about meaningful change.

Moreover, managers often use incentive systems as a substitute for giving workers what they need to do a good job. Treating workers well—providing useful feedback, social support, and the room for self-determination—is the essence of good management. On the other hand, dangling, a bonus in front of employees and waiting for the results requires much less effort. Indeed, some evidence suggests that productive managerial strategies are less likely to be used in organizations that lean on pay-for-performance plans. In his study of welders' performance, Rothe noted that supervisors tended to "demonstrate relatively less leadership" when incentives were in place. Likewise, author Carla O'Dell reports in *People, Performance, and Pay* that a survey of 1,600 organizations by the American Productivity Center discovered little in the way of active employee involvement in organizations that used small-group incentive plans. As Jone L. Pearce, associate professor at the Graduate School of Management, University of California at Irvine, wrote in "Why Merit Pay Doesn't Work: Implications from Organization Theory," pay for performance actually "impedes the ability of managers to manage."

5. **Rewards discourage risk-taking.** "People will do precisely what they are asked to do if the reward is significant," enthused Monroe J. Haegele, a proponent of pay-for-performance programs, in "The New Performance Measures." And here is the root of the problem. Whenever people are encouraged to think about what they will get for engaging in a task, they become less inclined to take risks or explore possibilities, to play hunches or to consider incidental stimuli. In a word, the number one casualty of rewards is creativity.

Excellence pulls in one direction; rewards pull in another. Tell people that their income will depend on their productivity or performance rating, and they will focus on the numbers. Sometimes they will manipulate the schedule for completing tasks or even engage in patently unethical and illegal behavior. As Thane S. Pittman, professor and chair of the psychology department at Gettysburg College, and his colleagues point out, when we are motivated by incentives, "features such as predictability and simplicity are desirable, since the primary focus associated with this orientation is to get through the task expediently in order to reach the desired goal." The late Cornell University professor, John Condry, was more succinct: rewards, he said, are the "enemies of exploration."

Consider the findings of organizational psychologist Edwin A. Locke. When Locke paid subjects on a piece-rate basis for their work, he noticed that they tended to choose easier tasks as the payment for success increased. A number of other studies have also found that people working for a reward generally try to minimize challenge. It isn't that human beings are naturally lazy or that it is unwise to give employees a voice in determining the standards to be used. Rather, people tend to lower their sights when they are encouraged to think about what they are going to get for their efforts. "Do this and you'll get that," in other words, focuses attention on the "that" instead of the "this." Emphasizing large bonuses is the last strategy we should use if we care about innovation. Do rewards motivate people? Absolutely. They motivate people to get rewards.

6. **Rewards undermine interest.** If our goal is excellence, no artificial incentive can ever match the power of intrinsic motivation. People who do exceptional work may be glad to be paid and even more glad to be well paid, but they do not work to collect a paycheck. They work because they love what they do.

Few will be shocked by the news that extrinsic motivators are a poor substitute for genuine interest in one's job. What is far more surprising is that rewards, like punishment, may actually undetermined the intrinsic motivation that results in optimal performance. The more a manager stresses what an employee can earn for good work, the less interested that employee will be in the work itself.

The first studies to establish the effect of rewards on intrinsic motivation were conducted in the early 1970s by Edward Deci, professor and chairman of the psychology department at the University of Rochester. By now, scores of experiments across the country have replicated the finding. As Deci and his colleague Richard Ryan, senior vice president of investment and training manager at Robert W. Baird and Co., Inc., wrote in their 1985 book, *Intrinsic Motivation and Self-Determination in Human Behavior*, "the research has consistently shown that any contingent payment system tends to undermine intrinsic motivation." The basic effect is the same for a variety of rewards and tasks, although extrinsic motivators are particularly destructive when tied to interesting or complicated tasks.

Deci and Ryan argue that receiving a reward for a particular behavior sends a certain message about what we have done and controls, or attempts to control, our future behavior. The more we experience being controlled, the more we will tend to lose interest in what we are doing. If we go to work thinking about the possibility of getting a bonus, we come to feel that our work is not self-directed. Rather, it is the reward that drives our behavior.

Other theorists favor a more simple explanation for the negative effect rewards have on intrinsic motivation: anything presented as a prerequisite for something else—that is, as a means toward another end—comes to be seen as less desirable. The recipient of the reward assumes, "If they have to bribe me to do it, it must be something I wouldn't want to do." In fact, a series of studies, published in 1992 by psychology professor Jonathan L. Freedman and his colleagues at the University of Toronto, confirmed that the larger the incentive we are offered, the more negatively we will view the activity for which the bonus was received. (The activities themselves don't seem to matter; in this study, they ranged from participating in a medical experiment to eating unfamiliar food.) Whatever the reason for the effect, however, any incentive or pay-for performance system tends to make people less enthusiastic about their work and therefore less likely to approach it with a commitment to excellence.

DANGEROUS ASSUMPTIONS
Outside of psychology departments, few people distinguish between intrinsic and extrinsic motivation. Those who do assume that the two concepts can simply be added together for best effect. Motivation comes in two flavors, the logic goes, and both together must be better than either alone. But studies show that the real world works differently.

Some managers insist that the only problem with incentive programs is that they don't reward the right things. But these managers fail to understand the psychological factors involved and, consequently, the risks of sticking with the status quo.

Contrary to conventional wisdom, the use of rewards is not a response to the extrinsic orientation exhibited by many workers. Rather, incentives help create this focus on financial considerations. When an organization uses a Skinnerian management or compensation system, people are likely to become less interested in their work, requiring extrinsic incentives before expending effort. Then supervisors shake their heads and say, "You see? If you don't offer them a reward, they won't do anything." It is

a classic self-fulfilling prophecy. Swarthmore College psychology professor Barry Schwartz has conceded that behavior theory may seem to provide us with a useful way of describing what goes on in U.S. workplaces. However, "It does this not because work is a natural exemplification of behavior theory principles but because behavior theory principles … had a significant hand in transforming work into an exemplification of behavior theory principles."

Managers who insist that the job won't get done right without rewards have failed to offer a convincing argument for behavioral manipulation. Promising a reward to someone who appears unmotivated is a bit like offering salt water to someone who is thirsty. Bribes in the workplace simply can't work.

Alfie Kohn is the author of four books, including No Contest: The Case Against Competition *and the newly published* Punished by Rewards: The Trouble with Gold Stars, Incentive Plans, A's, Praise, and Other Bribes, *from which this article is adapted. Kohn lectures widely at universities, conferences, and corporations on education and management.*

ON INCENTIVES
"The Pay-for-Performance Dilemma"
by Herbert H. Meyer, *Organizational Dynamics*, Winter 1975.

"Financial Incentives"
by G. Douglas Jenkins, Jr. in *Generalizing from Laboratory to Field Settings* edited by Edwin A. Locke Lexington, MA: Lexington Books, 1986,

"Why Some Long-Term Incentives Fail"
by Jude T. Rich and John A. Larson in *Incentives, Cooperation, and Risk Sharing* edited by Haig R. Nalbantian, Totowa, NJ: Rowman & Littlefield, 1987.

"Output Rates Among Welders: Productivity and Consistency Following Removal of a Financial Incentive System"
by Harold E. Rothe, *Journal of Applied Psychology*, December 1970.

"The Effects of Psychologically Based Intervention Programs on Worker Productivity: A Meta-Analysis"
by Richard A. Guzzo, Richard D. Jette, and Raymond A. Katzell, *Personnel Psychology*, Summer 1985.

"One More Time: How Do You Motivate Employees?"
by Frederick Herzberg, *Harvard Business Review*, January–February 1968.

"An Elaboration on Deming's Teachings on Performance Appraisal"
by Peter R. Scholtes in *Performance Appraisal: Perspectives on a Quality Management Approach* edited by Gary

N. McLean, et al., Alexandria, VA: University of Minnesota Training and Development Research Center and American Society for Training and Development, 1990.

People, Performance, and Pay
by Carla O'Dell, Houston: American Productivity Center, 1987.

"Why Merit Pay Doesn't Work: Implications from Organization Theory"
by Jone L. Pearce in *New Perspectives on Compensation* edited by David B. Balkan and Luis R. Gomez-Mejia, Englewood Cliffs, NJ: Prentice-Hall, 1987.

"The New Performance Measures"
by Monroe J. Haegele in *The Compensation Handbook*, Third Edition edited by Milton L. Rock and Lance A. Berger, New York: McGraw-Hill, 1991.

"Intrinsic and Extrinsic Motivational Orientations: Reward Induced Changes in Preference for Complexity"
by Thane S. Pittman, Jolee Emery, and Ann K. Boggiano, *Journal of Personality and Social Psychology*, March 1982.

"Enemies of Exploration: Self-Initiated Versus Other-initiated Learning"
by John Condry, *Journal of Personality and Social Psychology*, July 1977.

"Toward a Theory of Task Motivation and Incentives"
by Edwin A. Locke, *Organizational Behavior and Human Performance*, Volume 3, 1968.

Intrinsic Motivation and Self-Determination in Human Behavior
by Edward L. Deci and Richard M. Ryan, New York: Plenum Press, 1985.

"Inferred Values and the Reverse-Incentive Effect in Induced Compliance"
by Jonathan L. Freedman, John A. Cunningham, and Kirsten Krismer, *Journal of Personality and Social Psychology*, March 1992.

The Battle for Human Nature: Science, Morality and Modern Life
by Barry Schwartz, New York: W. W. Norton and Company, 1986.

RECOMMENDED READING

"A Model of Creativity and Innovation in Organizations"
by Teresa M. Amabile in *Research in Organizational Behavior*, Volume 10 edited by Barry M. Staw and L. L. Cummings, Greenwich, CT: JAI Press, Inc., 1988.

Out of the Crisis
by W. Edwards Darning, Cambridge, MA: MIT Center for Advanced Engineering Study, 1986.

"Merit Pay, Performance Targeting, and Productivity"
by Alfie Halachmi and Marc Holzer, *Review of Public Personnel Administration*, Spring 1987.

No Contest: The Case Against Competition
Revised Edition by Alfie Kohn, Boston: Houghton Mifflin, 1992.

Punished by Rewards: The Trouble with Gold Stars, Incentive Plans, A's, Praise, and Other Bribes
by Alfie Kohn, Boston: Houghton Mifflin, 1993.

The Market Experience
by Robert B. Lane, Cambridge, England: Cambridge University Press, 1991.

The Hidden Costs of Reward: New Perspectives on the Psychology of Human Motivation
edited by Mark R. Lepper and David Greene, Hillsdale, NJ: L. Erlbaum Associates, 1978.

The Great Jackass Fallacy
by Harry Levinson, Cambridge, MA: Harvard University Press, 1973.

The Human Side of Enterprise
by Douglas McGregor, New York: McGraw-Hill, 1960.

Wealth Addiction
by Philip Slater, New York: Dutton, 1980.

Money and Motivation: An Analysis of Incentives in Industry
by William Foote Whyte and Melville Dalton, et al. New York: Harper, 1955.

QUESTION

8.2   What are the six reasons that incentive programs fail, according to Alfie Kohn? Explain.

8.3 Six Dangerous Myths About Pay

*Many managers have bought into expensive fictions
about compensation. Have you?*

by Jeffrey Pfeffer*

Consider two groups of steel minimills. One group pays an average hourly wage of $18.07. The second pays an average of $21.52 an hour. Assuming that other direct-employment costs, such as benefits, are the same for the two groups, which group has the higher labor costs?

An airline is seeking to compete in the low-cost, low-frills segment of the U.S. market where, for obvious reasons, labor productivity and efficiency are crucial for competitive success. The company pays virtually no one on the basis of individual merit or performance. Does it stand a chance of success?

A company that operates in an intensely competitive segment of the software industry does not pay its sales force on commission. Nor does it pay individual bonuses or offer stock options or phantom stock, common incentives in an industry heavily dependent on attracting and retaining scarce programming talent. Would you invest in this company?

Every day, organizational leaders confront decisions about pay. Should they adjust the company's compensation system to encourage some set of behaviors? Should they retain consultants to help them implement a performance-based pay system? How large a raise should they authorize?

In general terms, these kinds of questions come down to four decisions about compensation:

- how much to pay employees;
- how much emphasis to place on financial compensation as a part of the total reward system;
- how much emphasis to place on attempting to hold down the rate of pay; and
- whether to implement a system of individual incentives to reward differences in performance and productivity and, if so, how much emphasis to place on these incentives.

For leaders, there can be no delegation of these matters. Everyone knows decisions about pay are important. For one thing, they help establish a company's culture by rewarding the business activities, behaviors, and values that senior managers hold dear. Senior management at Quantum, the disk drive manufacturer in Milpitas, California, for example, demonstrates its commitment to teamwork by placing all employees, from the CEO to hourly workers, on the same bonus plan, tracking everyone by the same measure—in this case, return on total capital.

Compensation is also a concept and practice very much in flux. Compensation is becoming more variable as companies base a greater proportion of it on stock options and bonuses and a smaller proportion on base salary, not only for executives but also for people further down the hierarchy. As managers make, organization-defining decisions about pay systems, they do so in a shifting landscape while being bombarded with advice about the best routes to stable ground.

Unfortunately, much of that advice is wrong. Indeed, much of the conventional wisdom and public discussion about pay today is misleading, incorrect, or sometimes both at the same time. The result is that businesspeople end up adopting wrongheaded notions about how to pay people and why. They believe in six dangerous myths about pay—fictions about compensation that have somehow come to be seen as the truth.

Do you think you have managed to avoid these myths? Let's see how you answered the three questions that open this article. If you said the second set of steel minimills had higher labor costs, you fell into the common trap of confusing labor *rates* with labor *costs*. That is Myth #1: that labor rates and labor costs are the same thing. But how different they really are. The second set of minimills paid its workers at a rate of $3.45 an hour more than the first. But according to data collected by Fairfield University Professor Jeffrey Arthur, its labor costs were much lower because the productivity of the mills was higher. The second set of mills actually required 34% fewer labor hours to produce a ton of steel than the first set and also generated 63% less scrap. The second set of mills could have raised workers' pay rate by 19% and still had lower labor costs.

Connected to the first myth are three more myths that draw on the same logic. When managers believe that labor costs and labor rates are the same thing, they also tend to believe that they can cut labor costs by cutting labor rates. That's Myth #2. Again, this leaves out the important matter of productivity. I may replace my $2,000-a-week engineers with ones that earn $500 a week, but my costs may skyrocket because the new, lower-paid employees are inexperienced, slow, and less capable. In that case, I would have increased my costs by cutting my rates.

* From: J. Pfeffer, "Six Dangerous Myths About Pay," *Harvard Business Review* (May–June, 1998): 109–119. Copyright © 1998 by the President and Fellows of Harvard College; all rights reserved. Reprinted with permission.

Managers who mix up labor rates and labor costs also tend to accept Myth #3: that labor costs are a significant portion of total costs. Sometimes, that's true. It is, for example, at accounting and consulting firms. But the ratio of labor costs to total costs varies widely in different industries and companies. And even where it is true, it's not as important as many managers believe. Those who swallow Myth #4—that low labor costs are a potent competitive strategy—may neglect other, more effective ways of competing, such as through quality, service, delivery, and innovation. In reality, low labor costs are a slippery way to compete and perhaps the least sustainable competitive advantage there is.

Those of you who believed that the airline trying to compete in the low-cost, low-frills segment of the U.S. market would not succeed without using individual incentives succumbed to Myth #5: that the most effective way to motivate people to work productively is through individual incentive compensation. But Southwest Airlines has never used such a system, and it is the cost *and* productivity leader in its industry. Southwest is not alone, but still it takes smart, informed managers to buck the trend of offering individual rewards.

Would you have invested in the computer software company that didn't offer its people bonuses, stock options, or other financial incentives that could make them millionaires? You should have because it has succeeded mightily, growing over the past 21 years at a compound annual rate of more than 25%. The company is the SAS Institute of Cary, North Carolina. Today it is the largest privately held company in the software industry, with 1997 revenues of some $750 million.

Rather than emphasize pay, SAS has achieved an unbelievably low turnover rate below 4%—in an industry where the norm is closer to 20%—by offering intellectually engaging work; a family-friendly environment that features exceptional benefits, and the opportunity to work with fun, interesting people using state-of-the-art equipment.

In short, SAS has escaped Myth #6: that people work primarily for money. SAS, operating under the opposite assumption, demonstrates otherwise. In the last three years, the company has lost *none* of its 20 North American district sales managers. How many software companies do you know could make that statement, even about the last three months?

Every day, I see managers harming their organizations by believing in these myths about pay. What I want to do in these following pages is explore some factors that help account for why the myths are so pervasive, present some evidence to disprove their underlying assumptions, and suggest how leaders might think more productively and usefully about the important issue of pay practices in their organizations.

WHY THE MYTHS EXIST

On October 10, 1997, the *Wall Street Journal* published an article expressing surprise that a "contrarian Motorola" had chosen to build a plant in Germany to make cellular phones despite the notoriously high "cost" of German labor. The *Journal* is not alone in framing business decisions about pay in this way. The *Economist* has also written articles about high German labor "costs," citing as evidence labor rates (including fringe benefits) of more than $30 per hour.

The semantic confusion of labor rates with labor costs, endemic in business journalism and everyday discussion, leads managers to see the two as equivalent. And when the two seem equivalent, the associated myths about labor costs seem to make sense, too. But, of course, labor rates and labor costs simply aren't the same thing. A labor rate is total salary divided by time worked. But labor costs take productivity into account. That's how the second set of minimills managed to have lower labor costs than the mills with the lower wages. They made more steel, and they made it faster and better.

Another reason why the confusion over costs and rates persists is that labor rates are a convenient target for managers who want to make an impact. Labor rates are highly visible, and it's easy to compare the rates you pay with those paid by your competitors or with those paid in other parts of the world. In addition, labor rates often appear to be a company's most malleable financial variable. It seems a lot quicker and easier to cut wages than to control costs in other ways, like reconfiguring manufacturing processes, changing corporate culture, or altering product design. Because labor costs appear to be the lever closest at hand, managers mistakenly assume it is the one that has the most leverage.

For the myths that individual incentive pay drives creativity and productivity, and that people are primarily motivated by money, we have economic theory to blame. More specifically, we can blame the economic model of human behavior widely taught in business schools and held to be true in the popular press. This model presumes that behavior is rational—driven by the best information available at the time and designed to maximize the individual's self-interest. According to this model, people take jobs and decide how much effort to expend in those jobs based on their expected financial return. If pay is not contingent on performance, the theory goes, individuals will not devote sufficient attention and energy to their jobs.

Additional problems arise from such popular economic concepts as agency theory (which contends that there are differences in preference and perspective between owners and those who work for them) and transaction-cost economies (which tries to identify which transactions are best organized by markets and which by hierarchies). Embedded in both concepts is the idea that individuals not only pursue self-interest but do so on occasion with guile and opportunism. Thus agency theory suggests that employees have different objectives than their employers and, moreover, have opportunities to misrepresent information and divert resources to their personal use. Transaction-cost theory suggests that people will make false or empty threats and promises to get better deals from one another.

All of these economic models portray work as hard and aversive—implying that the only way people can be induced to work is through some combination of rewards and sanctions. As professor James N. Baron of Stanford Business School has written, "The image of workers in these models is somewhat akin to Newton's first law of motion: employees remain in a state of rest unless compelled to change that state by a stronger force impressed upon them—namely, and optimal labor contract."

Similarly, the language of economics is filled with terms such as *shirking* and *free riding*. Language is powerful, and as Robert Frank, himself an economist, has noted, theories of human behavior become self-fulfilling. We act on the basis of these theories, and through our own actions produce in others the behavior we expect. If we believe people will work hard only if specifically rewarded for doing so, we will provide contingent rewards and thereby condition people to work only when they are rewarded. If we expect people to be untrustworthy, we will closely monitor and control them and by doing so will signal that they can't be trusted—an expectation that they will most likely confirm for us.

So self-reinforcing are these ideas that you almost have to avoid mainstream business to get away from them. Perhaps that's why several companies known to be strongly committed to managing through trust, mutual respect, and true decentralization—such as AES Corporation, Lincoln Electric, the Men's Wearhouse, the SAS Institute, ServiceMaster, Southwest Airlines, and Whole Foods Market—tend to avoid recruiting at conventional business schools.

There's one last factor that helps perpetuate all these myths: the compensation-consulting industry. Unfortunately, that industry has a number of perverse incentives to keep these myths alive.

First, although some of these consulting firms have recently broadened their practices, compensation remains their bread and butter. Suggesting that an organization's performance can be improved in some way other than by tinkering with the pay system may be empirically correct but is probably too selfless a behavior to expect from these firms.

TRUTH AND CONSEQUENCES: THE SIX DANGEROUS MYTHS ABOUT COMPENSATION

Myth	Reality
1. Labor rates and labor costs are the same thing.	1. They are not, and confusing them leads to a host of managerial missteps. For the record, labor rates are straight wages divided by time—a Wal-Mart cashier earns $5.15 an hour, a Wall Street attorney $2,000 a day. Labor costs are a calculation of how much a company pays its people and how much they produce. Thus German factory workers may be paid at a rate of $30 an hour and Indonesians $3, but the workers' relative costs will reflect how many widgets are produced in the same period of time.
2. You can lower your labor costs by cutting labor rates.	2. When managers buy into the myth that labor rates and labor costs are the same thing, they usually fall for this myth as well. Once again, then, labor costs are a function of labor rates and productivity. To lower labor costs, you need to address *both*. Indeed, sometimes lowering labor rates increases labor costs.
3. Labor costs constitute a significant proportion of total costs.	3. This is true—but only sometimes. Labor costs as a proportion of total costs vary widely by industry and company. Yet many executives assume labor costs are the biggest expense on their income statement. In fact, labor costs are only the most immediately malleable expense.
4. Low labor costs are a potent and sustainable competitive weapon.	4. In fact, labor costs are perhaps the most slippery and least sustainable way to compete. Better to achieve competitive advantage through quality; through customer service; through product, process, or service innovation; or through technology leadership. It is much more difficult to imitate these sources of competitive advantage than to merely cut costs.
5. Individual incentive pay improves performance.	5. Individual incentive pay, in reality, undermines performance—of both the individual and the organization. Many studies strongly suggest that this form of reward undermines teamwork, encourages a short-term focus, and leads people to believe that pay is not related to performance at all but to having the "right" relationships and an ingratiating personality.
6. People work for money.	6. People do work for money—but they work even more for meaning in their lives. In fact, they work to have fun. Companies that ignore this fact are essentially bribing their employees and will pay the price in a lack of loyalty and commitment.

Second, if it's simpler for managers to tinker with the compensation system than to change an organization's culture, the way work is organized, and the level of trust and respect the system displays, it's even easier for consultants. Thus both the compensation consultants and their clients are tempted by the apparent speed and ease with which reward-system solutions can be implemented.

Third, to the extent that changes in pay systems bring their own new predicaments, the consultants will continue to have work solving the problems that the tinkering has caused in the first place.

FROM MYTH TO REALITY: A LOOK AT THE EVIDENCE

The media are filled with accounts of companies attempting to reduce their labor costs by laying off people, moving production to places where labor rates are lower, freezing wages, or some combination of the above. In the early 1990s, for instance, Ford decided not to award merit raises to its white-collar workers as part of a new cost-cutting program. And in 1997, General Motors endured a series of highly publicized strikes over the issue of out-sourcing. GM wanted to move more of its work to nonunion, presumably lower-wage, suppliers to reduce its labor costs and become more profitable.

Ford's and GM's decisions were driven by the myths that labor rates and labor costs are the same thing, and that labor costs constitute a significant portion of total costs. Yet hard evidence to support those contentions is slim. New United Motor Manufacturing, the joint venture between Toyota and General Motors based in Fremont, California, paid the highest wage in the automobile industry when it began operations in the mid-1980s, and it also offered a guarantee of secure employment. With productivity some 50% higher than at comparable GM plants, the venture could afford to pay 10% more and still come out ahead.

Yet General Motors apparently did not learn the lesson that what matters is not pay rate but productivity. In May 1996, as GM was preparing to confront the union over the issue of outsourcing the "Harbour Report," the automobile industry's bible of comparative efficiency, published some interesting data suggesting that General Motors' problems had little to do with labor rates. As reported in the *Wall Street Journal* at the time, the report showed that it took General Motors some 46 hours to assemble a car, while it took Ford just 37.92 hours, Toyota 29.44, and Nissan only 27.36. As a way of attacking cost problems, officials at General Motors should have asked why they needed 21 more hours than Ford to accomplish the same thing or why GM was some 68% less efficient than Nissan.

For more evidence of how reality really looks, consider the machine tool industry. Many of its senior managers have been particularly concerned with low-cost foreign competition, believing that the cost advantage has come from the lower labor rates available offshore. But for machine tool companies that stop fixating on labor rates and focus instead on their overall management system and manufacturing processes, there are great potential returns. Cincinnati Milacron, a company that had virtually surrendered the market for low-end machine tools to Asian competitors by the mid-1980s, overhauled its assembly process, abolished its stockroom, and reduced job categories from seven to one. Without any capital investment, those changes in the production *process* reduced labor hours by 50%, and the company's productivity is now higher than its competitors' in Taiwan.

Even U.S. apparel manufacturers lend support to the argument that labor costs are not the be-all and end-all of profitability. Companies in this industry are generally obsessed with finding places where hourly wages are low. But the cost of direct labor needed to manufacture a pair of jeans is actually only about 15% of total costs, and even the direct labor involved in producing a man's suit is only about $12.50.[1]

Compelling evidence also exists to dispute the myth that competing on labor costs will create any sustainable advantage. Let's start close to home. One day, I arrived at a large discount store with a shopping list. Having the good fortune to actually find a sales associate, I asked him where I could locate the first item on my list. "I don't know," he replied. He gave a similar reply when queried about the second item. A glance at the long list I was holding brought the confession that because of high employee turnover, the young man had been in the store only a few hours himself. What is that employee worth to the store? Not only can't he sell the merchandise, he can't even find it! Needless to say, I wasn't able to purchase everything on my list because I got tired of looking and gave up. And I haven't returned since. Companies that compete on cost alone eventually bump into consumers like me. It's no accident that Wal-Mart combines its low-price strategy with friendly staff members greeting people at the door and works assiduously to keep turnover low.

Another example of a company that understands the limits of competing solely on labor costs is the Men's Wearhouse, the enormously successful off-price retailer of tailored men's clothing. The company operates in a fiercely competitive industry in which growth is possible primarily by taking sales from competitors, and price wars are intense. Still, less than 15% of the company's staff is part-time, wages are higher than the industry average, and the company engages in extensive training. All these policies defy conventional wisdom for the retailing industry. But the issue isn't what the Men's Wearhouse's employees cost, it's what they can do: sell very effectively because of their product knowledge and sales skills. Moreover, by keeping inventory losses and employee turnover low, the company saves money on shrinkage and hiring. Companies that miss this point—that costs, particularly labor costs, aren't everything—often overlook ways of succeeding that competitors can't readily copy.

Evidence also exists that challenges the myth about the effectiveness of individual incentives. Thus evidence, however, has done little to stem the tide of individual merit pay. A survey of the pay practices of the *Fortune* 1,000 reported that between 1987 and 1993, the proportion of companies using individual incentives for at least 20% of their workforce increased from 38% to 50% while the proportion of companies using profit sharing—a more collective reward—decreased from 45% to 43%. Between 1981 and 1990, the proportion of retail salespeople that were paid solely on straight salary, with no commission, declined from 21% to 7%. And this trend toward individual incentive compensation is not confined to the United States. A study of pay practices at plants in the United Kingdom reported that the proportion using some form of merit pay had increased every year since 1986 such that by 1990 it had reached 50%.[2]

Despite the evident popularity of this practice, the problems with individual merit pay are numerous and well documented. It has been shown to undermine teamwork, encourage employees to focus on the short term, and lead people to link compensation to political skills and ingratiating personalities rather than to performance. Indeed, those are among the reasons why W. Edwards Deming and other quality experts have argued strongly against using such schemes.

Consider the results of several studies. One carefully designed study of a performance-contingent pay plan at 20 Social Security Administration offices found that merit pay had no effect on office performance. Even though the merit pay plan was contingent on a number of objective indicators, such as the time taken to settle claims and the accuracy of claims processing, employees exhibited no difference in performance after the merit pay plan was introduced as part of a reform of civil service pay practices. Contrast that study with another that examined the elimination of a piecework system and its replacement by a more group-oriented compensation system at a manufacturer of exhaust system components. There, grievances decreased, product quality increased almost tenfold, and perceptions of teamwork and concern for performance all improved.[3]

Surveys conducted by various consulting companies that specialize in management and compensation also reveal the problems and dissatisfaction with individual merit pay. For instance, a study by the consulting form William M. Mercer reported that 73% of the responding companies had made major changes to their performance-management plans in the preceding two years, as they experimented with different ways to tie pay to individual performance. But 47% reported that their employees found the systems neither fair nor sensible,

and 51% of the employees said that the performance-management system provided little value to the company. No wonder Mercer concluded that most individual merit or performance-based pay plans share two attributes: they absorb vast amounts of management time and resources, and they make everybody unhappy.

One concern about paying on a more group-oriented basis is the so-called free-rider problem, the worry that people will not work hard because they know that if rewards are based on collective performance and their colleagues make the effort, they will share in those rewards regardless of the level of their individual efforts. But there are two reasons why organizations should not be reluctant to design such collective pay systems.

First, much to the surprise of people who have spent too much time reading economics, empirical evidence from numerous studies indicates that time extent of free riding is quite modest. For instance, one comprehensive review reported that "under the conditions described by the theory as leading to free riding, people often cooperate instead."[4]

Second, individuals do not make decisions about how much effort to expend in a social vacuum; they are influenced by peer pressure and the social relations they have with their workmates. This social influence is potent, and although it may be somewhat stronger in smaller groups, it can be a force mitigating against free riding even in large organizations. As one might expect, then, there is evidence that organizations paying on a more collective basis, such as through profit sharing or gain sharing, outperform those that don't.

Sometimes, individual pay schemes go so far as to affect customers. Sears was forced to eliminate a commission system at its automobile repair stores in California when officials found widespread evidence of consumer fraud. Employees, anxious to meet quotas and earn commissions on repair sales, were selling unneeded services to unsuspecting customers. Similarly, in 1992, the *Wall Street Journal* reported that Highland Superstores, an electronics and appliance retailer, eliminated commissions because they had encouraged such aggressive behavior on the part of salespeople that customers were alienated.

Enchantment with individual merit pay reflects not only the belief that people won't work effectively if they are not rewarded for their individual efforts but also the related view that the road to solving organizational problems is largely paved with adjustments to pay and measurement practices. Consider again the data from the Mercer survey; nearly three-quarters of all the companies surveyed had made *major* changes to their pay plans in just the past two years. That's tinkering on a grand scale. Or take the case of Air Products and Chemicals of Allentown, Pennsylvania. When on October 23, 1996, the company reported mediocre sales and profits, the stock price declined from the low $60s to the high $50s. Eight days later, the company announced a new set of management-compensation and stock-ownership initiatives designed to reassure Wall Street that management cared about its shareholders and was demonstrating that concern by changing compensation arrangements. The results were dramatic. On the day of the announcement, the stock price went up 1 1/4 points, and the next day it rose an additional 4 3/4 points. By November 29, Air Products' stock had gone up more than 15%. According to Value Line, this rise was an enthusiastic reaction by investors to the new compensation system. No wonder managers are so tempted to tamper with pay practices!

But as Bill Strusz, director of corporate industrial relations at Xerox in Rochester, New York, has said, if managers seeking to improve performance or solve organizational problems use compensation as the only lever, they will get two results: nothing will happen, and they will spend a lot of money. That's because people want more out of their jobs than just money. Numerous surveys—even of second-year M.B.A. students, who frequently graduate with large amounts of debt—indicate that money is far from the most important factor in choosing a job or remaining in one.

Why has the SAS Institute had such low turnover in the software industry despite its tight labor market? When asked this question, employees said they were motivated by SAS's unique perks—plentiful opportunities to work with the latest and most up-to-date equipment and the ease with which they could move back and forth between being a manager and being an individual contributor. They also cited how much variety there was in the projects they worked on, how intelligent and nice the people they worked with were, and how much the organization cared for and appreciated them. Of course, SAS pays competitive salaries, but in an industry in which people have the opportunity to become millionaires through stock options by moving to a competitor, the key to retention is SAS's culture, not its monetary rewards.

People seek, in a phrase, an enjoyable work environment. That's what AES, the Men's Wearhouse, SAS, and Southwest have in common. One of the core values at each company is *fun*. When a colleague and I wrote a business school case on Southwest, we asked some of the employees, a number of whom had been offered much more money to work elsewhere, why they stayed. The answer we heard repeatedly was that they knew what the other environments were like, and they would rather be at a place, as one employee put it, where *work* is not a four-letter word. This doesn't mean work has to be easy. As an AES employee noted, fun means working in a place where people can use their gifts and skills and can work with others in an atmosphere of mutual respect.

There is a great body of literature on the effect of large external rewards on individuals' intrinsic motivation. The literature argues that extrinsic rewards diminish intrinsic motivation and, moreover, that large extrinsic rewards can actually decrease performance in tasks that require creativity and innovation. I would not necessarily go so far as to say that external rewards backfire, but they certainly create their own problems. First, people receiving such rewards can reduce their own motivation through a trick of self-perception, figuring, "I must not like the job if I have to be paid so much to do it" or "I make so much, I must be doing it for the money." Second, they undermine their own loyalty or performance by reacting against a sense of being controlled, thinking something like, "I will show the company that I can't be controlled just through money."

But most important, to my mind, is the logic in the idea that any organization believing it can solve its attraction, retention, and motivation problems solely by its compensation system is probably not spending as much time and effort as it should on the work environment—on defining its jobs, on creating its culture, and on making work fun and meaningful. It is a question of time and attention, of scare managerial resources. The time and attention spent managing the reward system are not available to devote to other aspects of the work environment that in the end may be much more critical to success.

SOME ADVICE ABOUT PAY

Since I have traipsed you through a discussion of what's wrong with the way most companies approach compensation, let me now offer some advice about how to get it right.

The first, and perhaps most obvious, suggestion is that managers would do well to keep the difference between labor rates and labor costs straight. In doing so, remember that only labor costs—and not labor rates—are the basis for competition, and that labor costs may not be a major component of total costs. In any event, managers should remember that the issue is not just what you pay people, but also what they produce.

To combat the myth about the effectiveness of individual performance pay, managers should see what happens when they include a large dose of collective rewards in their employees' compensation package. The more aggregated the unit used to measure the performance, the more reliably performance can be assessed. One can tell pretty accurately how well an organization, or even a subunit, has done with respect to sales, profits, quality, productivity, and the like. Trying to parcel out who, specifically, was responsible for exactly how much of that productivity, quality, or sales is frequently much more difficult or even impossible. As Herbert Simon, the Nobel-prize-winning economist, has recognized, people in organizations are interdependent, and therefore organizational results are the consequence of collective behavior and performance. If you could reliably and easily measure and reward individual contributions, you probably would not need an organization at all as everyone would enter markets solely as individuals.

In the typical individual-based merit pay system, the boss works with a raise budget that's some percentage of the total salary budget for the unit. It's inherently a zero-sum process: the more I get in my raise, the less is left for my colleagues. So the worse my workmates perform, the happier I am because I know I will look better by comparison. A similar dynamic can occur across organizational units in which competition for a fixed bonus pool discourages people from sharing best practices and learning from employees in other parts of the organization. In November 1995, for example, *Fortune* magazine reported that at Lantech, a manufacturer of packaging machinery in Louisville, Kentucky, individual incentives caused such intense rivalry that the chairman of the company, Pat Lancaster, said, "I was spending 95% of my time on conflict resolution instead of on how to serve our customers."

Managers can fight the myth that people are primarily motivated by money by de-emphasizing pay and not portraying it as the main thing you get from working at a particular company. How? Consider the example of Tandem Computer, which in the years before it was acquired by Compaq, would not even tell you your salary before expecting you to accept a job. If you asked, you would be told that Tandem paid good, competitive salaries. The company had a simple philosophy—if you came for money, you would leave for money, and Tandem wanted employees who were there because they liked the work, the culture, and the people, not something—money—that every company could offer. Emphasizing pay as the primary reward encourages people to come and to stay for the wrong reasons. AES a global independent power producer in Arlington, Virginia, has a relatively short vesting period for retirement-plan contributions and tries not to pay the highest salaries for jobs in its local labor market. By so doing, it seeks to ensure that people are not locked into working at a place where they don't want to be simply for the money.

Managers must also recognize that pay has substantive and symbolic components. In signaling what and who in the organization is valued, pay both reflects and helps determine the organization's culture. Therefore, managers must make sure that the messages sent by pay practices are intended. Talking about teamwork and co-operation and then not having a group-based component to the pay system matters because paying solely on an individual basis signals what the organization believes is actually important—individual behavior and performance. Talking about the importance of *all* people in the organization and then paying some disproportionately more than others believes that message. One need not go to the extreme of Whole Foods Market, which pays no one more than eight times the average company salary (the result being close to $1 billion in sales at a company where the CEO makes less than $200,000 a year). But paying large executive bonuses while laying off people and asking for wage freezes, as General motors did in the 1980s, may not send the right message, either. When Southwest Airlines asked its pilots for a five-year wage freeze, CEO Herb Kelleher voluntarily asked the compensation committee to freeze his salary for at least four years as well. The message of shared, common fate is powerful in an organization truly seeking to build a culture of teamwork.

Making pay practices public also sends a powerful symbolic message. Some organizations reveal pay distributions by position or level. A few organizations, such as Whole Foods Market, actually make data on individual pay available to all members who are interested. Other organizations try to maintain a high level of secrecy about pay. What messages do those organizations send? Keeping salaries secret suggests that the organization has something to hide or that it doesn't trust its people with the information. Moreover, keeping things secret just encourages people to uncover the secrets—if something is worth hiding, it must be important and interesting enough to expend effort discovering. Pay systems that are more open and transparent send a positive message about the equity of the system and the trust that the company places in its people.

Managers should also consider using other methods besides pay to signal company values and focus behavior. The head of North American sales and operations for the SAS Institute has a useful perspective on this issue. He didn't think he was smart enough to design an incentive system that couldn't be gamed. Instead of using the pay system to signal what was important, he and other SAS managers simply told people what was important for the company and why. That resulted in much more nuanced and rapid changes in behavior because the company didn't have to change the compensation system every time business priorities altered a little. What a novel idea—actually talking to people about what is important and why, rather than trying to send some subtle signals through the compensation system!

Perhaps most important, leaders must come to see pay for what it is: just one element in a set of management practices that can either build or reduce commitment, teamwork, and performance. Thus my final piece of advice about pay is to make sure that pay practices are congruent with other management practices and reinforce rather than oppose their effects.

BREAKING WITH CONVENTION TO BREAK THE MYTHS

Many organizations devote enormous amounts of time and energy to their pay systems, but people, from senior managers to hourly workers, remain unhappy with them. Organizations are trapped in unproductive ways of approaching pay, which they find difficult to escape. The reason, I would suggest, is that people are afraid to challenge the myths about compensation. It's easier and less controversial to see what everyone else is doing and then to do the same. In fact, when I talk to executives at companies about installing pay systems that actually work, I usually hear, "But that's different from what most other companies are saying and doing."

It must certainly be the case that a company cannot earn "abnormal" returns by following the crowd. That's true about marketplace strategies, and it's true about compensation. Companies that are truly exceptional are not trapped by convention but instead see and pursue a better business model.

Companies that have successfully transcended the myths about pay know that pay cannot substitute for a working environment high on trust, fun, and meaningful work. They also know that it is more important to worry about what people do than what they cost, and that zero-sum pay plans can set off internal competition that makes learning from others, teamwork, and cross-functional cooperation a dream rather than the way the place works on an everyday basis.

There is an interesting paradox in achieving high organizational performance through innovative pay practices—if it were easy to do, it wouldn't provide as much competitive leverage as it actually does. So while I can review the logic and evidence and offer some alternative ways of thinking about pay, it is the job of leaders to exercise both the judgment and the courage necessary to break with common practice. Those who do will develop organizations in which pay practices actually contribute rather than detract from building high-performance management systems. Those who are stuck in the past are probably doomed to endless tinkering with pay; at the end of the day, they won't have accomplished much, but they will have expended a lot of time and money doing it.

ENDNOTES

1. John T. Dunlop and David Weil, "Diffusion and Performance of Modular Production in the U.S. Apparel Industry," *Industrial Relations*, July 1996, p. 337.

2. For the survey of the pay practices of *Fortune* 1,000 companies, see Gerald E. Ledford, Jr., Edward E. Lawler III, and Susan A. Mohrman, "Reward Innovations in *Fortune* 1,000 Companies," *Compensation and Benefits Review*, April 1995, p. 76; for the salary and commission data, see Gregory A. Patterson, "Distressed Shoppers, Disaffected Workers Prompt Stores to Alter Sales Commissions," the *Wall Street Journal*, July 1, 1992, p. B1; for the study of U.K. pay practices, see Stephen Wood, "High Commitment Management and Payment Systems," *Journal of Management Studies*, January 1996, p. 53.

3. For the Social Security Administration study, see Jone L. Pearce, William B. Stevenson, and James L. Perry, "Managerial Compensation Based on Organizational Performance: A Time Series Analysis of the Effects of Merit Pay," *Academy of Management Journal*, June 1985, p. 261; for the study of group-oriented compensation, see Larry Hatcher and Timothy L. Ross, "From Individual Incentives to an Organization-Wide Gainsharing Plan: Effects on Teamwork and Product Quality," *Journal of Organizational Behavior*, May 1991, p. 169.

4. Gerald Marwell, "Altruism and the Problem of Collective Action," in V.J. Derlega and J. Grzelak, eds., *Cooperation and Helping Behavior: Theories and Research* (New York: Academic Press, 1982), p. 208.

Jeffrey Pfeffer is the Thomas D. Dee Professor of Organizational Behavior at the Stanford Graduate School of Business in Stanford, California. He is the author of The Human Equation: Building Profits by Putting People First *(Harvard Business School Press, 1998).*

QUESTION

8.3   Describe the six myths about compensation and their realities.

8.4 Creating an Ethical Culture
Values-based ethics programs can help employees judge right from wrong.

*by DAVID GEBLER**

WHILE THE FATE of former Enron leaders Kenneth Lay and Jeffrey Skilling is being determined in what has been labeled the "Trial of the Century," former WorldCom managers are in jail for pulling off one of the largest frauds in history.

Yes, criminal activity definitely took place in these companies and in dozens more that have been in the news in recent years, but what's really important is to take stock of the nature of many of the perpetrators.

Some quotes from former WorldCom executives paint a different picture of corporate criminals than we came to know in other eras:

"I'm sorry for the hurt that has been caused by my cowardly behavior." —*Scott Sullivan, CFO*

"Faced with a decision that required strong moral courage, I took the easy way out.... There are no words to describe my shame."
—*Buford Yates, director of general accounting*

"At the time I consider the single most critical character-defining moment of my life, I failed. It's something I'll take with me the rest of my life."
—*David Myers, controller*

These are the statements of good people gone bad. But probably most disturbing was the conviction of Betty Vinson, the senior manager in the accounting department who booked billions of dollars in false expenses. At her sentencing, U.S. District Judge Barbara Jones noted that Vinson was among the lowest-ranking members of the conspiracy that led to the $11 billion fraud that sank the telecommunications company in 2002. Still, she said, "Had Ms. Vinson refused to do what she was asked, it's possible this conspiracy might have been nipped in the bud."

Judge Jones added that although Ms. Vinson "was among the least culpable members of the conspiracy" and acted under extreme pressure, "that does not excuse what she did."

Vinson said she improperly covered up expenses by drawing down reserve accounts—some completely unrelated to the expenses—and by moving expenses off income statements and listing them as assets on the balance sheet.

Also the company's former director of corporate reporting, Vinson testified at Bernie Ebbers's trial that, in choosing which accounts to alter, "I just really pulled some out of the air. I used some spreadsheets." She said she repeatedly brought her concerns to colleagues and supervisors, once describing the entries to a coworker as "just crazy." In spring 2002, she noted, she told one boss she would no longer make the entries. "I said that I thought the entries were just being made to make the income statement look like Scott wanted it to look."

Standing before the judge at her sentencing, Vinson said: "I never expected to be here, and I certainly won't do anything like this again." She was sentenced to five months in prison and five months of house arrest.

PRESSURE REIGNS
While the judge correctly said that her lack of culpability didn't excuse her actions, we must carefully note that Betty Vinson, as well as many of her codefendants, didn't start out as criminals seeking to defraud the organization. Under typical antifraud screening tools, she and others like her wouldn't have raised any red flags as being potential committers of corporate fraud.

Scott Sullivan was a powerful leader with a well-known reputation for integrity. If any of us were in Betty Vinson's shoes, could we say with 100% confidence that we would say "no" to the CFO if he asked us to do something and promised that he would take full responsibility for any fallout from the actions we were going to take?

Today's white-collar criminals are more likely to be those among us who are unable to withstand the blistering pressures placed on managers to meet higher and tougher goals. In this environment, companies looking to protect themselves from corporate fraud must take a hard look at their own culture. Does it promote ethical behavior, or does it emphasize something else?

In most companies, "ethics" programs are really no more than compliance programs with a veneer of "do the right thing" messaging to create an apparent link to the company's values. To be effective, they have to go deeper than outlining steps to take to report misconduct. organizations must understand what causes misconduct in the first place.

We can't forget that Enron had a Code of Ethics. And it wasn't as if WorldCom lacked extensive internal controls. But both had cultures where engaging in

---

* From: D. Gebler, "Creating an Ethical Culture," *Strategic Finance* (May 2006): 29–34. Reprinted with permission.

unethical conduct was tacitly condoned, if not encouraged.

BUILDING THE RIGHT CULTURE

Now the focus has shifted toward looking at what is going on inside organizations that's either keeping people from doing the right thing or, just as importantly, keeping people from doing something about misconduct they observe. If an organization wants to reduce the risk of unethical conduct, it must focus more effort on building the right culture than on building a compliance infrastructure.

The Ethics Resource Center's 2005 National Business Ethics Survey (NBES) clearly confirms this trend toward recognizing the role of corporate culture. Based on interviews with more than 3,000 employees and managers in the U.S., the survey disclosed that, despite the increase in the number of ethics and compliance program elements being implemented, desired outcomes, such as reduced levels of observed misconduct, haven't changed since 1994. Even more striking is the revelation that, although formal ethics and compliance programs have some impact, organizational culture has the greatest influence in determining program outcomes.

The Securities & Exchange Commission (SEC) and the Department of Justice have also been watching these trends. Stephen Cutler, the recently retired SEC director of the Division of Enforcement, was matter of fact about the importance of looking at culture when it came to decisions of whether or not to bring an action. "We're trying to induce companies to address matters of tone and culture.... What we're asking of that CEO, CFO, or General Counsel goes beyond what a perp walk or an enforcement action against another company executive might impel her to do. We're hoping that if she sees that a failure of corporate culture can result in a fine that significantly exceeds the proverbial 'cost of doing business,' and reflects a failure on her watch—and a failure on terms that everyone can understand: the company's bottom line—she may have a little more incentive to pay attention to the environment in which her company's employees do their jobs."

MEASURING SUCCESS

Only lagging companies still measure the success of their ethics and compliance programs just by tallying the percentage of employees who have certified that they read the Code of Conduct and attended ethics and compliance training. The true indicator of success is whether the company has made significant progress in achieving key program outcomes. The National Business Ethics Survey listed four key outcomes that help determine the success of a program:

- Reduced misconduct observed by employees,
- Reduced pressure to engage in unethical conduct,
- Increased willingness of employees to report misconduct, and
- Greater satisfaction with organizational response to reports of misconduct.

What's going to move these outcomes in the right direction? Establishing the right culture.

Most compliance programs are generated from "corporate" and disseminated down through the organization. As such, measurement of the success of the program is often based on criteria important to the corporate office: how many employees certified the Code of Conduct, how many employees went through the training, or how many calls the hotline received.

Figure 1: SEVEN LEVELS OF AN ETHICAL ORGANIZATION

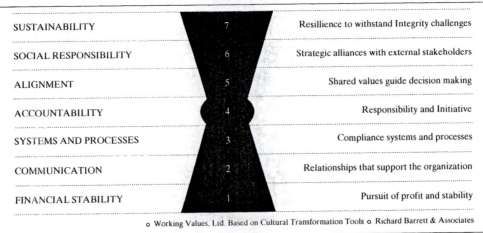

SUSTAINABILITY	7	Resilience to withstand Integrity challenges
SOCIAL RESPONSIBILITY	6	Strategic alliances with external stakeholders
ALIGNMENT	5	Shared values guide decision making
ACCOUNTABILITY	4	Responsibility and Initiative
SYSTEMS AND PROCESSES	3	Compliance systems and processes
COMMUNICATION	2	Relationships that support the organization
FINANCIAL STABILITY	1	Pursuit of profit and stability

o Working Values, Ltd. Based on Cultural Transformation Tools o Richard Barrett & Associates

Culture is different—and is measured differently. An organization's culture isn't something that's created by senior leadership and then rolled out. A culture is an objective picture of the organization, for better or worse. It's the sum total of all the collective values and behaviors of all employees, managers, and leaders. By definition, it can only be measured by criteria that reflect the individual values of all employees, so understanding cultural vulnerabilities that can lead to ethics issues requires knowledge of what motivates employees in the organization. Leadership must know how the myriad human behaviors and interactions fit together like puzzle pieces to create a whole picture. An organization moves toward an ethical culture only if it understands the full range of values and behaviors needed to meet its ethical goals. The "full-spectrum" organization is one that creates a positive sense of engagement and purpose that drives ethical behavior.

Why is understanding the culture so important in determining the success of a compliance program? Here's an example: Most organizations have a policy that prohibits retaliation against those who bring forward concerns or claims. But creating a culture where employees feel safe enough to admit mistakes and to raise uncomfortable issues requires more than a policy and "Code training." To truly develop an ethical culture, the organization must be aware of how its managers deal with these issues up and down the line and how the values they demonstrate impact desired behaviors. The organization must understand the pressures its people are under and how they react to those pressures. And it must know how its managers communicate and whether employees have a sense of accountability and purpose.

CATEGORIZING VALUES

Determining whether an organization has the capabilities to put such a culture in place requires careful examination. Do employees and managers demonstrate values such as respect? Do employees feel accountable for their actions and feel that they have a stake in the success of the organization?

How does an organization make such a determination? One approach is to categorize different types of values in a way that lends itself to determining specific strengths and weaknesses that can be assessed and then corrected or enhanced.

The Culture Risk Assessment model presented in Figure 1 has been adapted from the Cultural Transformation Tools® developed by Richard Barrett & Associates. Such tools provide a comprehensive framework for measuring cultures by mapping values. More than 1,000 organizations in 24 countries have used this technique in the past six years. In fact, the international management consulting firm McKinsey & Co. has adopted it as its method of choice for mapping corporate cultures and measuring progress toward achieving culture change.

The model is based on the principle, substantiated through practice, that all values can be assigned to one of seven categories:

Levels 1, 2, and 3—The Organization's Basic Needs
Does the organization support values that enable it to run smoothly and effectively? From an ethics perspective, is the environment one in which employees feel physically and emotionally safe to report unethical behavior and to do the right thing?

Level 1—Financial Stability. Every organization needs to make financial stability a primary concern. Companies that are consumed with just surviving struggle to focus enough attention on how they conduct themselves. This may, in fact, create a negative cycle that makes survival much more difficult. Managers may exercise excessive control, so employees may be working in an environment of fear.

In these circumstances, unethical or even illegal conduct can be rationalized. When asked to conform to regulations, organizations do the minimum with an attitude of begruding compliance.

Organizations with challenges at this level need to be confident that managers know and stand within clear ethical boundaries.

Level 2—Communication. Without good relationships with employees, customers, and suppliers, integrity is compromised. The critical issue at this level is to create a sense of loyalty and belonging among employees and a sense of caring and connection between the organization and its customers.

The most critical link in the chain is between employees and their direct supervisors. If direct supervisors can't effectively reinforce messages coming from senior leadership, those messages might be diluted and confused by the time they reach line employees. When faced with conflicting messages, employees will usually choose to follow the lead of their direct supervisor over the words of the CEO that have been conveyed through an impersonal communication channel. Disconnects in how local managers "manage" these messages often mean that employees can face tremendous pressure in following the lead established by leadership.

Fears about belonging and lack of respect lead to fragmentation, dissension, and disloyalty. When leaders meet behind closed doors or fail to communicate openly, employees suspect the worst. Cliques form, and gossip becomes rife. When leaders are more focused on their own success, rather than the success of the organization, they begin to compete with each other.

Level 3—Systems and Processes. At this level, the organization is focused on becoming the best it can be through the adoption of best practices and a focus on quality, productivity, and efficiency.

Level 3 organizations have succeeded in implementing strong internal controls and have enacted clear standards of conduct. Those that succeed at this level are the ones that see internal controls as an opportunity to create better, more efficient processes. But even those that have successfully deployed business processes and practices need to be alert to potentially limiting aspects of being too focused on processes. All organizations need to be alert to resorting to a "check-the-box" attitude that assumes compliance comes naturally from just implementing standards and procedures. Being efficient all too often leads to bureaucracy and inconsistent application of the rules. When this goes badly, employees lose respect for the system and resort to self-help to get things done. This can lead to shortcuts and, in the worst case, engaging in unethical conduct under the guise of doing what it takes to succeed.

Level 4—Accountability
The focus of the fourth level is on creating an environment in which employees and managers begin to take responsibility for their own actions. They want to be held accountable, not micromanaged and supervised every moment of every day. For an ethics and compliance program to be successful, all employees must feel that they have a personal responsibility for the integrity of the organization. Everyone must feel that his or her voice is being heard. This requires managers and leaders to admit that they don't have all the answers and invite employee participation.

Levels 5, 6, and 7—Common Good
Does the organization support values that create a collective sense of belonging where employees feel that they have a stake in the success of the ethics program?

Level 5—Alignment. The critical issue at this level is developing a shared vision of the future and a shared set of values. The shared vision clarifies the intentions of the organization and gives employees a unifying purpose and direction. The shared values provide guidance for making decisions.

The organization develops the ability to align decision making around a set of shared values. The values and behaviors must be reflected in all of the organization's processes and systems, with appropriate consequences for those who aren't willing to walk the talk. A precondition for success at this level is building a climate of trust.

Level 6—Social Responsibility. At this level, the organization is able to use its relationships with stakeholders to sustain itself through crises and change. Employees and customers see that the organization is making a difference in the world through its products and services, its involvement in the local community, or its willingness to fight for causes that improve humanity.

They must feel that the company cares about them and their future. Companies operating at this level go the extra mile to make sure they are being responsible citizens. They support and encourage employees' activities in the community by providing time off for volunteer work and/or making a financial contribution to the charities that employees are involved in.

Level 7—Sustainability. To be successful at Level 7, organizations must embrace the highest ethical standards in all their interactions with employees, suppliers, customers, shareholders, and the community. They must always consider the long-term impact of their decisions and actions.

Employee values are distributed across all seven levels. Through surveys, organizations learn which values employees bring to the workplace and which values are missing. Organizations don't operate from any one level of values: They tend to be clustered around three or four levels. Most are focused on the first three: profit and growth (Level 1), customer satisfaction (Level 2), and productivity, efficiency, and quality (Level 3). The most successful organizations operate across the full spectrum with particular focus in the upper levels of consciousness—the common good—accountability, leading to learning and innovation (Level 4), alignment (Level 5), sustainability (Level 6), and social responsibility (Level 7).

Some organizations have fully developed values around Levels 1, 2, and 3 but are lacking in Levels 5, 6, and 7. They may have a complete infrastructure of controls and procedures but may lack the accountability and commitment of employees and leaders to go further than what is required.

Similarly, some organizations have fully developed values around Levels 5, 6, and 7 but are deficient in Levels 1, 2, and 3. These organizations may have visionary leaders and externally focused social responsibility programs, but they may be lacking in core systems that will ensure that the higher-level commitments are embedded into day-to-day processes.

Once an organization understands its values' strengths and weaknesses, it can take specific steps to correct deficient behavior.

STARTING THE PROCESS
Could a deeper understanding of values have saved WorldCom? We will never know, but if the culture had encouraged open communication and fostered trust, people like Betty Vinson might have been more willing to confront orders that they knew were wrong. Moreover, if the culture had embodied values that encouraged transparency, mid-level managers wouldn't have been asked to engage in such activity in the first place.

The significance of culture issues such as these is also being reflected in major employee surveys that highlight what causes unethical behavior. According to the

NBES, "Where top management displays certain ethics-related actions, employees are 50 percentage points less likely to observe misconduct." No other factor in any ethics survey can demonstrate such a drastic influence.

So how do compliance leaders move their organizations to these new directions?

1. **The criteria for success of an ethics program must be outcomes based.** Merely checking off program elements isn't enough to change behavior.

2. **Each organization must identify the key Indicators of its culture.** Only by assessing its own ethical culture can a company know what behaviors are the most influential in effecting change.

3. **The organization must gauge how all levels of employees perceive adherence to values by others within the company.** One of the surprising findings of the NBES was that managers, especially senior managers, were out of touch with how nonmanagement employees perceived their adherence to ethical behaviors. Nonmanagers are 27 percentage points less likely than senior managers to indicate that executives engage in all of the ethics-related actions outlined in the survey.

4. **Formal programs are guides to shape the culture, not vice versa.** People who are inclined to follow the rules appreciate the rules as a guide to behavior. Formal program elements need to reflect the culture in which they are deployed if they are going to be most effective in driving the company to the desired outcomes.

Culture may be new on the radar screen, but it isn't outside the scope or skills of forward-thinking finance managers and compliance professionals. Culture can be measured, and finance managers can play a leadership role in developing systematic approaches to move companies in the right direction.

David Gebler, J.D., is president of Working Values, Ltd., a business ethics training and consulting firm specializing in developing behavior-based change to support compliance objectives. You can reach him at dgebler@workingvalues.com.

QUESTIONS

8.4a   What are the four key outcomes that determine the success of an ethics program?

8.4b   What are the seven level of an ethical organization? Does an organization need all seven levels?

8.5 Pay without Performance: Overview of the issues

by Lucian A. Bebchuk and Jesse M. Fried*

EXECUTIVE OVERVIEW

In a recent book, *Pay without Performance: The Unfulfilled Promise of Executive Compensation*, Bebchuk and Fried critique existing executive pay arrangements and the corporate governance processes that produce them. They also put forward proposals for improving both executive pay and corporate governance. This paper provides an overview of the main elements of their critique and proposals. The authors show that, under current legal arrangements, boards cannot be expected to contract at arm's length with the executives whose pay they set. They discuss how managers' influence can explain many features of the executive compensation landscape, including ones that researchers subscribing to the arm's-length contracting view have long considered as puzzling. The authors also explain how managerial influence can lead to inefficient arrangements that generate weak or even perverse incentives, as well as to arrangements that make the amount and performance-insensitivity of pay less transparent. Finally, they outline proposals for improving the transparency of executive pay, the connection between pay and performance, and the accountability of corporate boards.

> *In judging whether Corporate America is serious about reforming itself, CEO pay remains the acid test. To date, the results aren't encouraging.*
> —Warren Buffett, letter to shareholders of Berkshire Hathaway, Inc., February 2004

In *Pay without Performance* and several prior and accompanying papers,[1] we seek to provide a full account of how managerial power and influence have shaped the executive compensation landscape. The dominant paradigm for financial economists' study of executive compensation has assumed that pay arrangements are the product of *arm's-length contracting*—contracting between executives attempting to get the best possible deal for themselves and boards seeking to get the best possible deal for shareholders. This assumption also has been the basis for the corporate law rules governing the

---

* From: L. A. Bebchuk and J. M. Fried, "Pay Without Performance Overview of the Issues," *Academy of Management Perspectives* (February 2006): 5–23. Reprinted with permission.

subject. We aim to show, however, that the pay-setting process in publicly traded companies has strayed far from the arm's-length model.

Our analysis indicates that managerial power has played a key role in shaping managers' pay arrangements. The pervasive role of managerial power can explain much of the contemporary landscape of executive compensation. Indeed, it can explain practices and patterns that have long puzzled financial economists studying executive compensation. Furthermore, managerial influence over the design of pay arrangements has produced considerable distortions and costs to investors and the economy. It has distorted pay arrangements, diluted managers' incentives to enhance firm value, and even provided perverse incentives to take actions that reduce long-term firm value.

Executive compensation has long been a topic of heated debate. The rise in executive pay has been the subject of much public criticism, which further intensified following the corporate governance scandals that began erupting in late 2001. This wave of corporate scandals shook confidence in the performance of public company boards and drew attention to potential flaws in their executive compensation practices. As a result, there is now recognition that many boards have employed compensation arrangements that do not serve shareholders' interests. But there is still substantial disagreement about the scope and source of such problems and, not surprisingly, about how to address them.

Many take the view that concerns about executive compensation have been exaggerated. There are some who maintain that flawed compensation arrangements have been limited to a relatively small number of firms, and that most boards have carried out effectively their role of setting executive pay. Others concede that flaws in compensation arrangements have been widespread, but maintain that these flaws have resulted from honest mistakes and misperceptions on the part of boards seeking to serve shareholders. According to this view, now that the problems have been recognized, corporate boards can be expected to fix them on their own. Still others argue that, even though regulatory intervention was necessary, recent reforms that strengthen director independence will fully address past problems. Accordingly, at least going forward, one can expect boards to set pay policies in shareholders' interest.

Our work seeks to persuade readers that such complacency is hardly warranted. To begin, flawed compensation arrangements have not been limited to a small number of "bad apples:" they have been widespread, persistent, and systemic. Furthermore, the problems have not resulted from temporary mistakes or lapses of judgment that boards can be expected to correct on their own; rather, they have stemmed from structural defects in the underlying governance structures that enable executives to exert considerable influence over their boards. The absence of effective arm's-length dealing under today's system of corporate governance has been the primary source of problematic compensation arrangements. Finally, while recent reforms that seek to increase board independence will likely improve matters, they will not be sufficient to make boards adequately accountable; much more needs to be done.

Another, broader aim of our work has been to contribute to a better understanding of some of the basic problems afflicting the corporate governance system. The study of executive compensation opens a window through which we can examine our current reliance on boards to act as guardians of shareholders' interests. Our corporate governance system gives boards substantial power and counts on them to monitor and supervise the company's managers. As long as corporate directors are believed to carry out their tasks for the benefit of shareholders, current governance arrangements—which insulate boards from intervention by shareholders—appear acceptable. Our analysis of the executive pay landscape casts doubt on the validity of this belief and the wisdom of insulating boards from shareholders.

A full understanding of the flaws in current compensation arrangements, and in the governance processes generating them, is necessary for addressing these problems. After providing a full account of the existing problems, our work also puts forward a set of proposals for improving both executive pay and corporate governance. We provide detailed suggestions for making pay, and its relationship to performance, more transparent. Such transparency will provide a better check on managers' power to influence their own pay. It will also eliminate existing incentives to choose compensation arrangements that are less efficient but more effective in camouflaging the amount of pay or its insensitivity to performance.

Furthermore, our analysis of the myriad ways in which pay is decoupled from performance and weakens or distorts incentives provides a basis for recommending how firms could better tie pay to performance and provide incentives more cost-effectively. Finally, we put forward reforms that make directors not only more independent of insiders but also more dependent on shareholders, thus improving board accountability to shareholders. Such reforms may well offer the most promising route for improving executive compensation and corporate governance more generally.

This paper draws on their earlier work on executive compensation, especially the authors' recent book, *Pay without Performance: The Unfulfilled Promise of Executive compensation* (Harvard University Press, 2004). The paper is a revision of a paper prepared for a *Journal of Corporation law* symposium on this book. For financial support, they would like to thank the Guggenheim, Lens, and Nathan Cummins Foundations and the John M. Olin center for Law, Economics, and Business (Bebchuk); and the Boalt Hall Fund and the U.C. Berkeley Committee on Research (Fried).

In this paper, we outline some of the main elements of our critique of contemporary executive compensation and corporate governance arrangements, as well as of our proposals and suggested reforms. We start by describing the limitations of the official arm's-length model of executive compensation. We then turn to the managerial power perspective, and discuss how managerial influence can explain many features of the compensation landscape, as well as the flaws and problems with existing pay arrangements, including their weak relationship to managers' own performance and their inadequate disclosure. We conclude with a discussion of our proposals for making pay more transparent, improving the design of pay arrangements, and increasing board accountability.

Before proceeding, we wish to emphasize that our strong critique of existing pay arrangements and pay-setting processes should not be understood as a claim that directors and executives are less ethical or have acted with less decency than one would expect from others if they were placed in the same circumstances. Our problem is with the system of arrangements and incentives within which directors and executives operate, not with the moral virtue or caliber of directors and executives.

As currently structured, the system unavoidably creates incentives and psychological and social forces that distort pay choices. They can be expected to lead anybody (who is not a saint) to support, at least as long as they remain within prevailing practices and conventions, that favor themselves, their colleagues, or people who can in turn favor them. If we were to maintain the basic structure of our corporate governance system and merely replace directors and executives with an entirely different group of people, their replacements would be exposed to the very same incentives and forces and, by and large, we would not expect them to act differently. To address the problems, we need to change the basic arrangements that produce these distortions.

THE STAKES

What is at stake in the debate over executive pay? Some might question whether executive compensation has a significant economic impact on shareholders and the economy. The problems with executive compensation, it might be argued, do not much affect shareholders' bottom line and are mainly symbolic.

However, the question of whether and to what extent pay arrangements are flawed is an important one for shareholders and policymakers— even if symbolism were unimportant. The existing flaws in compensation arrangements impose substantial costs on shareholders. To begin, there is the excess pay that managers receive as a result of their power: that is, the difference between what managers' influence enables them to obtain and what they would get under arm's-length contracting. As

a recent study by Yaniv Grinstein and one of us documents in detail,[2] the amounts involved are hardly pocket change for shareholders.

The study finds that, during the period of 1993-2003, the aggregate compensation paid by public firms to their top-five executives totaled about $350 billion (in 2002 dollars). This aggregate top-five compensation accounted for 6.6 percent of the aggregate earnings (net income) of these firms during the period under consideration. The aggregate compensation paid by public firms to their top-five executives was 9.8 percent of the aggregate earnings of these firms during 2001-2003, up from 5 percent during 1993-1995. Note that this study relies on a standard executive compensation dataset that (like other such datasets) does not include various forms of compensation not reported in publicly filed summary compensation tables, such as the retirement benefits and packages that comprise a significant component of executives' total career compensation.

If such compensation could be cut without weakening managerial incentives, the gain to investors would not be merely symbolic. Rather, it would have real practical significance. Further-more, and perhaps even more importantly, managers' influence over compensation arrangements dilutes and distorts managerial incentives. In our view, the reduction in shareholder value caused by these inefficiencies—rather than that caused by excessive managerial pay—could well be the biggest cost arising from managerial influence over compensation.

Existing pay arrangements have been producing two types of incentive problems. First, compensation arrangements have been providing weaker incentives to reduce managerial slack and to increase shareholder value than would be the case under arm's-length contracting. Both the non-equity and equity components of managerial compensation have been more severely decoupled from managers' contribution to company performance than superficial appearances might suggest. Making pay more sensitive to performance may well benefit shareholders substantially.

Second, prevailing practices not only fail to provide cost-effective incentives to reduce slack but also create perverse incentives. For example, managers' broad freedom to unload company options and stock can lead managers to act in ways that reduce shareholder value. Executives who expect to unload shares have incentives to misreport results, suppress bad news, and choose projects and strategies that are less transparent to the market. The efficiency costs of such distortions might exceed, possibly by a large margin, whatever liquidity or risk-bearing benefits executives obtain from being able to unload their options and shares at will. Similarly, because existing pay practices often reward managers for increasing firm size, they provide executives with incentives to pursue expansion via acquisitions or otherwise, even when that strategy is not value-maximizing.

THE ARM'S-LENGTH CONTRACTING VIEW

According to the "official" view of executive compensation, corporate boards setting pay arrangements are guided solely by shareholder interests and operate at arm's length from the executives whose pay they set. The premise that boards contract at arm's length with executives has long been and remains a central tenet in the corporate world and in most research on executive compensation by financial economists.

In the corporate world, the official view serves as the practical basis for legal rules and public policy. It is used to justify directors' compensation decisions to shareholders, policymakers, and courts. These decisions are portrayed as being made largely with shareholders' interests at heart and therefore deserving of deference.

The premise of arm's-length contracting has also been shared by most of the research on executive compensation. Managers' influence over directors has been recognized by those writing on the subject from legal, organizational, and sociological perspectives, as well as by media coverage of executive pay. But most of the research on executive pay (especially empirical research) has been done by financial economists, and the premise of arm's-length contracting has guided most of their work. Some financial economists, whose studies we discuss in our book in detail, have reported findings they viewed as inconsistent with the arm's-length model.[3] However, the majority of work in the field has assumed arm's-length contracting between boards and executives.

In the paradigm that has dominated financial economics, boards, operating at arm's length from executives, seek to serve shareholder interests by adopting compensation schemes designed to provide managers with efficient incentives to maximize shareholder value. In this paradigm, managers' pay arrangements are viewed as a (partial) remedy to the agency problem, reducing potential costs from self-serving decisions by managers. Like other rational and informed parties who contract at arm's length, boards and managers are assumed to have powerful incentives to avoid inefficient provisions that shrink the pie produced by their contractual arrangements. The arm's-length contracting view has thus led researchers to assume that executive compensation arrangements will tend to increase value, which is why we have used the terms "efficient contracting" or "optimal contracting" to label this approach in some of our earlier work.[4]

Financial economists, both theorists and empiricists, have largely worked within the arm's-length model in attempting to explain common compensation arrangements as well as variation in compensation practices among firms.[5] In fact, upon discovering practices that appear inconsistent with the cost-effective provision of incentives, financial economists have often labored to come up with clever explanations for how such practices might be consistent with arm's-length contracting after all. Practices for which no explanation has been found have been considered "anomalies" or "puzzles" that will ultimately either be explained within the paradigm or disappear.

In our book, we identified many compensation practices that are difficult to understand under the arm's-length contracting view but can be readily explained by managerial influence over the paysetting process. Some of our critics suggested reasons why some of these practices could still be consistent with arm's-length contracting and argued that we have therefore not succeeded in ruling out completely the possiblity of arm's-length dealing. For example, in response to our showing that pay is significantly decoupled from performance, critics argued that it might be desirable to provide managers with large amounts of non-performance pay.[6] This type of response reflects an implicit presumption in favor of arm's-length contracting. The burden of proof rests on those skeptical of arm's-length contracting, and arm's-length contracting should be assumed true until the skeptics prove otherwise.

The presumption of arm's-length contracting, however, does not seem warranted. As we discuss below, an examination of the pay-setting process suggests that managerial influence plays a key role. Thus, given the *a priori* plausibility of managerial influence, one might place the burden of proof on those arguing that the executive pay arrangements produced by existing processes are not significantly shaped by such influence. In any event, that sophisticated financial economists continue to implicitly or explicitly use arm's-length contracting as their baseline presumption indicates the dominance and power of this long-held view.

LIMITS OF THE ARM'S-LENGTH VIEW

The official arm's-length story is neat, tractable, and reassuring. However, this model fails to account for the realities of executive compensation.

The arm's-length contracting view recognizes that managers are subject to an agency problem and do not automatically seek to maximize shareholder value. The potential divergence between managers' and shareholders' interests makes it important to provide managers with adequate incentives. Under the arm's-length contracting view, the board, working in shareholders' interest, attempts to cost-effectively provide such incentives through managers' compensation packages. However, just as there is no reason to presume that managers automatically seek to maximize shareholder value, there is no reason to expect *a priori* that directors will either. Indeed, an analysis of directors' incentives and circumstances suggests that directors' behavior is also subject to an agency problem.

Directors have had and continue to have various economic incentives to support, or at least go along with, arrangements favorable to the company's top executives.

Social and psychological factors—collegiality, team spirit, a natural desire to avoid conflict within the board, friendship and loyalty, and cognitive dissonance—exert additional pressure in that direction. Although many directors own shares in their firms, their financial incentives to avoid arrangements favorable to executives have been too weak to induce them to take the personally costly, or at the very least unpleasant, route of resisting compensation arrangements sought by executives. In addition, limitations on time and resources have made it difficult for even well-intentioned directors to do their pay-setting job properly. Finally, the market constraints within which directors operate are far from tight and do not prevent deviations from arm's-length contracting outcomes in favor of executives. Below we briefly discuss each of these factors.

INCENTIVES TO BE RE-ELECTED

Most directors might wish to be re-appointed to the board. Besides an attractive salary, a directorship provides prestige and valuable business and social connections. The financial and nonfinancial benefits of holding a board seat give directors an interest in keeping their positions.

In a world where shareholders selected individual directors, board members seeking re-appointment might have an incentive to develop reputations as shareholder-serving. Typically, however, the director slate proposed by management is the only one offered. The key to a board position is thus being placed on the company's slate. And because the CEO has had significant influence over the nomination process, displeasing the CEO has been likely to hurt one's chances of being put on the company slate. Directors thus have had an incentive to "go along" with the CEO's pay arrangement, a matter dear to the CEO's heart, at least as long as the compensation package remains within the range of what can be plausibly defended and justified. In addition, developing a reputation as a director who blocks compensation arrangements sought by executives could hurt rather than help a director's chances of being invited to join other companies' boards.

The new stock exchange listing requirements, which attempt to give independent directors a greater role in director nominations, weaken but do not eliminate executives' influence over director nominations. The CEO's wishes can be expected to continue to influence the decisions of the nominating committee; after all, the directors appointed to the board are expected to work closely with the CEO. As a practical matter, director candidates opposed by the CEO are not expected to be offered board nomination and would likely turn it down even if they were to receive such an offer.[7]

Even if the CEO had no influence over nominations, fighting with the CEO over the amount or performance sensitivity of her compensation might be viewed unfavorably by independent directors on the nominating committee. These directors might prefer to keep off the board an individual whose poor relationship with the CEO undermines board collegiality. They might also wish to avoid the friction and unpleasantness likely to accompany disputes over the CEO's pay. Finally, the independent directors also might side with the CEO for other reasons to be discussed below.

CEOS' POWER TO BENEFIT DIRECTORS

There are a variety of ways in which CEOs can benefit individual directors or board members as a group. For example, CEOs have influence over director compensation, in which directors have a natural interest. As the company leader, usually as a board member, and often as board chairman, the CEO can choose to either discourage or encourage director pay increases. Independent directors who are generous toward the CEO might reasonably expect the CEO to use her bully pulpit to support higher director compensation. At a minimum, generous treatment of the CEO contributes to an atmosphere that is conducive to generous treatment of directors. Indeed, a study finds that companies with higher CEO compensation have higher director compensation as well—and that this relationship is caused by cooperation between directors and the CEO rather than by company performance.[8]

In the past, CEOs have often used their power over corporate resources to reward cooperative directors. The new stock exchange listing standards now place some limits on CEOs' ability to reward independent directors, but they do leave CEOs with substantial power in this area. For example, these requirements do not prohibit additional compensation to an independent director. Rather, they only limit such compensation to $100,000 annually, and do not restrict payments to immediate family members who are non-executive employees.

Similarly, the requirements limit but do not prohibit business dealings between a company and an independent director's firm, and they place absolutely no limit on the firm's dealing with the director's firm before or after the director qualifies for independent director status. And the standards permit unlimited contributions to charitable organizations that independent directors run, are affiliated with, or simply favor. In sum, executives' control over corporate resources continues to enable them to provide many directors with rewards exceeding the small direct personal cost to most directors of approving pay arrangements that deviate from those expected under arm's-length contracting.

FRIENDSHIP AND LOYALTY

Many independent directors have some prior social connection to, or are even friends with, a company's CEO or other senior executives. Even directors who did not know the CEO before their appointment may well have begun their service with a sense of obligation and loyalty to the

CEO. The CEO often will have been involved in bringing the director onto the board—even if only by not blocking the director's nomination. With such a background, directors often start serving with a reservoir of good will toward the CEO, which will contribute to a tendency to favor the CEO in setting her pay. This kind of reciprocity is expected and observed in many social and professional contexts. Not surprisingly, studies find that compensation committees whose chairs have been appointed after the CEO takes office have tended to award higher CEO compensation.[9]

COLLEGIALITY AND AUTHORITY

In addition to friendship and loyalty considerations, there are other social and psychological forces that make it difficult for directors to resist executive-serving compensation arrangements. The CEO is the directors' colleague, and directors are expected in most circumstances to treat their fellow directors collegially. The CEO is also the firm's leader, the person whose decisions and visions have the most influence on the firm's future direction. In most circumstances, directors treat the CEO with respect and substantial deference. Switching hats to contract at arm's length with one's colleague and leader is naturally difficult.

COGNITIVE DISSONANCE AND SOLIDARITY

Many members of compensation committees are current and former executives of other companies. Individuals are known to develop views consistent with their self-interest. Executives and former executives are likely to have formed beliefs that support the type of pay arrangements from which they have benefited. An executive who has benefited from a conventional option plan, for example, is more likely to resist the view that such plans provide executives with excessive windfalls.

Further reinforcing such cognitive dissonance, an executive who serves as a director in another firm might identify and feel some solidarity or sympathy with that firm's executives; she naturally would be inclined to treat these executives the same way she would like to be treated by her own board of directors. Not surprisingly, there is evidence that CEO pay is correlated with the pay levels of the outside directors serving on the compensation committee.[10]

THE SMALL COSTS OF FAVORING EXECUTIVES

Directors typically own only a small fraction of the firm's shares. As a result, the direct personal cost to board members of approving compensation arrangements that are too favorable to executives—the reduction in the value of their shareholdings—is small. This cost is therefore unlikely to outweigh the economic incentives and social and psychological factors that induce directors to go along with pay schemes that favor executives.

RATCHETING

It is now widely recognized that the rise in executive compensation has in part been driven by many boards seeking to pay their CEO more than the industry average; this has led to an ever-increasing average and a continuous escalation of executive pay.[11] A review of reports of compensation committees in large companies indicates that a large majority of them used peer groups in determining pay and set compensation at or above the fiftieth percentile of the peer group.[12] Such ratcheting is consistent with a picture of boards that do not seek to get the best deal for their shareholders but rather are happy to go along with whatever can be justified as consistent with prevailing practices.

LIMITS OF MARKET FORCES

Some writers have argued that even if directors are subject to considerable influence from corporate executives, market forces can be relied on to force boards and executives to adopt the compensation arrangements that arm's-length contracting would produce. Our analysis, however, finds that market forces are neither sufficiently finely tuned nor sufficiently powerful to compel such outcomes. The markets for capital, corporate control, and managerial labor do impose *some* constraints on executive compensation. These constraints are hardly stringent, however, and they permit substantial deviations from arm's-length contracting.

Consider, for example, the market for corporate control—the threat of a takeover. Firms frequently have substantial defenses against takeovers. For example, a majority of companies have a staggered board, which prevents a hostile acquirer from gaining control before two annual elections are held, and often enables incumbent managers to block hostile bids that are attractive to shareholders. To overcome incumbent opposition, a hostile bidder must be prepared to pay a substantial premium.[13] The disciplinary force of the market for corporate control is further weakened by the prevalence of golden parachute provisions, as well as by payoffs made by acquirers to target managers to facilitate the acquisition. The market for corporate control thus exerts little disciplining force on managers and boards, leaving them considerable slack and ability to negotiate manager-favoring pay arrangements.

NEW CEOs

Some critics of our work assumed that our analysis of departures from arm's-length contracting did not apply to cases in which boards negotiate pay with a CEO candidate from outside the firm.[14] However, while such negotiations might be closer to the arm's-length model than negotiations with an incumbent CEO, they still fall quite short of this benchmark.

Among other things, directors negotiating with an outside CEO candidate know that, after the candidate becomes CEO, she will have influence over their re-nomination to the board and over their compensation and perks. The directors will also wish to have good personal and working relationships with the individual who is expected to become the firm's leader and a fellow board member. And while agreeing to a pay package that favors the outside CEO hire imposes little financial cost on directors, a breakdown in the negotiations, which might embarrass the directors and force them to re-open the CEO selection process, would be personally costly to them. Finally, directors' limited time forces them to rely on information shaped and presented by the company's human resources staff and compensation consultants, all of whom have incentives to please the incoming CEO.

FIRING OF EXECUTIVES

Some critics of our work have suggested that the increased willingness of directors to fire CEOs over the past decade, especially in recent years, provides evidence that boards do in fact deal with CEOs at arm's length.[15] Although the incidence of firing has gone up over time, firings are still limited to unusual situations in which the CEO is accused of legal or ethical violations (e.g., Fannie Mae, AIG, Boeing, Marsh) or is viewed by revolting shareholders as having a terrible record of performance (Morgan Stanley, HP). Without strong outside pressure to fire the CEO, mere mediocrity is far from enough to get a CEO pushed out. Furthermore, in the rare cases in which boards fire executives, boards often provide the departing executives with benefits beyond those required by the contract to sweeten the CEO's departure and alleviate the directors' guilt and discomfort. All in all, boards' record of dealing with failed executives does not support the view that boards treat CEOs at arm's length.

In sum, a realistic picture of the incentives and circumstances of board members reveals myriad incentives and tendencies that lead directors to behave very differently than boards contracting at arm's-length with their executives over pay. Recent reforms, such as the new stock exchange listing requirements, may weaken some of these factors but will not eliminate them. Without additional reforms, the pay-setting process will continue to deviate substantially from arm's-length contracting.

POWER AND PAY

The same factors that limit the usefulness of the arm's-length model in explaining executive compensation suggest that executives have had substantial influence over their own pay. Compensation arrangements have often deviated from arm's-length contracting because directors have been influenced by management, sympathetic to executives, insufficiently motivated to insist on shareholder-serving compensation, or simply ineffectual. Executives' influence over directors has enabled them to obtain "rents"—benefits greater than those obtainable under true arm's-length contracting.

In our work, we find that the role of managerial power can explain many practices and aspects of the executive compensation landscape. It is worth emphasizing that our conclusion is not based on the amount of compensation received by executives. In our view, high absolute levels of pay do not by themselves imply that compensation arrangements deviate from arm's-length contracting. Our finding that such deviations have been common is based primarily on an analysis of the processes by which pay is set, as well as on an examination of the inefficient, distorted, and non-transparent structure of pay arrangements. For us, the "smoking gun" of managerial influence over pay is not high levels of pay, but rather such things as the correlation between power and pay, the systematic use of compensation practices that obscure the amount and performance insensitivity of pay, and the showering of gratuitous benefits on departing executives.

POWER-PAY RELATIONSHIPS

Although top executives generally have some degree of influence over their boards, the extent of their influence depends on various features of the firm's governance structure. The managerial power approach predicts that executives who have more power vis-à-vis their boards should receive higher pay—or pay that is less sensitive to performance—than their less powerful counterparts. A substantial body of evidence does indeed indicate that pay has been higher, and less sensitive to performance, when executives have more power.

To begin, there is evidence that executive compensation is higher *when the board is relatively weak or ineffectual* vis-à-vis the CEO. In particular, CEO compensation is higher when the board is large, which makes it more difficult for directors to organize in opposition to the CEO; when more of the outside directors have been appointed by the CEO, which could cause them to feel gratitude or obligation to the CEO; and when outside directors serve on three or more boards, and thus are more likely to be distracted.[16] Also, CEO pay is 20 to 40 percent higher if the CEO is the chairman of the board, and it is negatively correlated with the stock ownership of compensation committee members.[17]

Second, studies find a connection between executive pay and the *presence of a large outside shareholder*. Such presence is likely to result in closer monitoring and thus can be expected to reduce managers' influence over their compensation. One study finds a negative correlation between the equity ownership of the largest shareholder and the amount of CEO compensation; doubling the percentage ownership of the outside shareholder reduces non-salary compensation by 12 to 14 percent.[18] Another study finds that CEOs in firms that lack a 5 percent (or larger) external shareholder tend to receive more "luck-based" pay—that is, pay associated with profit increases that are entirely generated by external factors (e.g., changes in oil prices and exchange rates) rather than by managers' own efforts.[19] This study also finds that, in firms lacking large external shareholders, the cash compensation of CEOs is reduced less when their option-based compensation is increased.

Third, there is evidence linking executive pay to the *concentration of institutional shareholders*, which are more likely to engage in monitoring and scrutiny of the CEO and the board. One study finds that more concentrated institutional ownership leads to lower executive compensation as well as to more performance-sensitive compensation.[20] Another study finds that the effect of institutional shareholders on CEO pay depends on the types of relationships they have with the firm.[21] CEO pay is negatively correlated with the presence of institutions that have other business relationship with the firm and thus concerned only with the firm's share value ("pressure-resistant" institutions); however, CEO pay is positively correlated with the presence of firms with business relationships with the firm (e.g., managing a pension fund) and thus vulnerable to management pressure ("pressure-sensitive" institutions).

Finally, studies find a connection between pay and *anti-takeover provisions* that make CEOs and their boards less vulnerable to a hostile takeover. One study finds that CEOs of firms adopting anti-takeover provisions enjoy above-market compensation before adoption of the anti-takeover provisions and that adoption of these provisions increases their excess compensation significantly.[22] This pattern is not readily explainable by arm's-length contracting; indeed, if managers' jobs are more secure, shareholders should be able to pay risk-averse managers less. Another study finds that CEOs of firms that became protected by state anti-takeover legislation enacted during the period of 1984–1991 reduced their holdings of shares by an average of 15 percent, apparently because the shares were not as necessary for maintaining control.[23] Arm's-length contracting might predict that a CEO protected by anti-takeover legislation would be required to buy more shares to restore her incentive to increase shareholder value.

LIMITS TO MANAGERIAL INFLUENCE
There are, of course, limits to the arrangements that directors will approve and executives will seek. Although market forces are not sufficiently powerful to compel arm's-length outcomes, they do impose *some* constraints on executive compensation. If a board were to approve a pay arrangement viewed as egregious, for example, shareholders would be less willing to support incumbents in a hostile takeover or proxy fight. In addition, directors and executives adopting such an arrangement might bear social costs. The constraints imposed by markets and by social forces are far from tight, however, and they permit substantial deviations from arm's-length outcomes. The adoption of arrangements favoring executives is unlikely to impose substantial economic or social costs if the arrangements are not patently abusive or indefensible.

One important building block of the managerial power approach is that of "outrage" costs. When a board approves a compensation arrangement favorable to managers, the extent to which directors and executives bear economic and social costs will depend on how the arrangement is perceived by outsiders whose views matter to the directors and executives. Outrage might also lead to shareholder pressure on managers and directors, as well as possibly embarrass directors and managers or harm their reputations. The more outrage a compensation arrangement is expected to generate, the more reluctant directors will be to approve it and the more hesitant managers will be to propose it in the first place.

There is evidence that the design of compensation arrangements is indeed influenced by how outsiders perceive them. One study finds that, during the 1990s, CEOs who were the target of shareholder resolutions criticizing executive pay had their annual (industry-adjusted) compensation reduced over the following two years.[24]

CAMOUFLAGE AND STEALTH COMPENSATION
The critical role of outsiders' perception of executives' compensation and the significance of outrage costs explain the importance of yet another component of the managerial power approach: "camouflage." The desire to minimize outrage gives designers of compensation arrangements a strong incentive to try to legitimize, justify, or obscure—or, more generally, to camouflage—the amount and performance-insensitivity of executive compensation.

After the board's compensation committee approves the compensation package, firms use compensation consultants and their reports to justify the compensation to shareholders. Wade, Porac, and Pollack find that companies that pay their CEOs larger base salaries, and firms with more concentrated and active outside ownership, are more likely to cite the use of surveys and consultants in justifying executive pay in their proxy reports to shareholders.[25] This study also finds that, when accounting returns are high, firms emphasize these accounting returns and downplay market returns.

For our purposes, attempts to justify compensation arrangements are less important than how managers' interest in camouflage affects the choice of arrangements in the first place. The latter is quite important because the desire to camouflage might lead to the adoption of compensation structures that are less efficient for incentive generation (and thus hurt managerial incentives and firm performance) but offer camouflage benefits. In our work we present evidence that compensation arrangements have often been chosen and designed with an eye to camouflaging the amount of pay and the extent to which it is decoupled from performance. Overall, the camouflage motive turns out to be quite useful in explaining many otherwise puzzling features of the executive compensation landscape.

Among the arrangements that camouflage the amount and the performance-insensitivity of compensation are executive pension plans, deferred compensation arrangements, and post-retirement perks. Most of the pension and deferred compensation benefits given to executives are not eligible for the large tax subsidy granted to the standard retirement arrangements provided to other employees. In the case of executives, such arrangements merely shift tax liability from the executive to the firm. The efficiency grounds for providing compensation through in-kind retirement perks are also far from clear. All of these arrangements, however, make pay less salient.

Among other things, under existing disclosure rules, firms do not have to place a dollar value on—and include in the firm's publicly filed summary compensation tables—amounts provided to executives after they retire. Although the existence of executives' retirement arrangements must be noted in certain places in the firm's public filings, this disclosure is less salient because outsiders focus on the dollar amounts reported in the compensation tables. Indeed, the standard compensation datasets generally used by media reporters and researchers do not include information about executives' retirement benefits.

In a recent empirical study, Robert Jackson and one of us use the information provided in proxy statements to estimate the value of the executive pension plans of S&P 500 CEOs.[26] About two-thirds of CEOs have such plans, and the study provides estimates of the value of these plans for all the CEOs who recently left their firms or are close to retirement age. For the median CEO in the study's sample, the actuarial value of the CEO's pension was $15 million, which comprised about one-third of the total compensation (both equity-based and non-equity) they had received during their service as CEOs. When pension value is included in calculating executive pay, compensation is much less linked to performance than commonly perceived. Such inclusion increases the fraction that is salary-like (basic salary during the CEO's service and pension afterwards) from 16 percent to 39 percent. The study documents that the current omission of retirement benefits from standard compensation datasets has distorted investors' picture of pay arrangements. In particular, this omission has led to: (i) significant under-estimations of the total magnitude of pay; (ii) considerable distortions in comparisons among executive pay packages; and (iii) substantial over-estimations of the extent to which executive pay is linked to performance.

While firms do not make the value of executive pensions transparent, they do disclose the information that enables one to estimate the value of these pensions. In contrast, the information provided about deferred compensation arrangements does not allow even the most diligent outsider to estimate with any precision the value conferred on executives through these arrangements. Thus, this form of compensation is especially effective in camouflaging potentially large amounts of non-performance pay. How large these amounts are for any given executive is not something that we can currently estimate.

GRATUITOUS GOODBYE PAYMENTS

In many cases, boards give departing CEOs payments and benefits that are gratuitous—that are not required under the terms of a CEO's compensation contract. Such gratuitous "goodbye payments" are common even when CEOs perform so poorly that their boards feel compelled to replace them. For example, when Mattel CEO Jill Barad resigned under fire, the board forgave a $4.2 million loan, gave her an additional $3.3 million in cash to cover the taxes for forgiveness of another loan, and allowed her unvested options to vest prematurely. These gratuitous benefits were offered in addition to the considerable benefits that she received under her employment agreement, which included a termination payment of $26.4 million and a stream of retirement benefits exceeding $700,000 per year.

It is not easy to reconcile such gratuitous payments with the arm's-length contracting model. The board has the authority to fire the CEO and pay the CEO her contractual severance benefits. Thus, there is no need to "bribe" a poorly performing CEO to step down. In addition, the signal sent by the golden goodbye payment will, if anything, only weaken the incentive of the next CEO to perform.

The making of such gratuitous payments, however, is quite consistent with the existence of managerial influence over the board. Because of their relationship with the CEO, some directors might be unwilling to replace the existing CEO unless she is very generously treated. Other directors might be willing to replace the CEO but prefer to accompany the move with a goodbye payment, either to reduce the personal discomfort they feel in forcing out the CEO, or to make the difficult separation process more pleasant and less contentious. In all of these cases, directors' willingness to make gratuitous payments to the (poorly performing) CEO results from the CEO's relationship with the directors.

It is important to note that, taking managerial power *as given*, providing gratuitous payments to fired CEOs might be beneficial to shareholders in some instances. If many directors are loyal to the CEO, such payments might be necessary to assemble a board majority in favor of replacing him. In such a case, the practice would help shareholders when the CEO's departure is more beneficial to shareholders than the cost of the goodbye payment. For our purposes, however, what is important is that these gratuitous payments—whether they are beneficial to shareholders or not—reflect the existence and significance of managerial influence.

THE DECOUPLING OF PAY FROM PERFORMANCE

Those applauding the rise in executive compensation have emphasized the benefits of strengthening managers' incentives to increase shareholder value. Indeed, in the beginning of the 1990s, prominent financial economists such as Michael Jensen and Kevin Murphy urged shareholders to be more accepting of large pay packages that would provide high-powered incentives.[27] Shareholders, it was argued, should care much more about providing managers with sufficiently strong incentives than about the amounts spent on executive pay.

Indeed, throughout the past 15 years, investors have often accepted increases in executive pay as the price for improving managers' incentives. Higher compensation has been presented as essential for improving managers' incentives and therefore worth the additional cost. Pay, however, is hardly as tied to managers' own performance as investors commonly assume. Shareholders have not received as much bang for their buck as possible. Firms could have generated the same increase in incentives at a much lower cost, or they could have used the amount spent to obtain more powerful incentives. Executive pay is much less sensitive to performance than has commonly been recognized.

NON-EQUITY COMPENSATION

Although the equity-based fraction of managers' compensation has increased considerably during the past decade and has therefore received the most attention, non-equity compensation continues to be substantial. In 2003, non-equity compensation comprised on average about half the total compensation (as reported in the standard ExecuComp dataset) of CEOs, as well as of other top-five executives, in S&P 1500 companies not classified as new economy firms.[28]

Although significant non-equity compensation comes in the form of base salary and sign-up "golden hello" payments that do not purport to be performance-related, much non-equity compensation comes in the form of bonus compensation which purports to be performance-based. Nonetheless, empirical studies have failed to find any significant correlation between non-equity compensation and managers' own performance during the 1990s.[29]

A close examination of firms' practices suggests why non-equity compensation is not tightly connected to managers' own performance. To begin, many firms use subjective criteria for at least some of their bonus pay-merits. While subjective criteria could play a useful role in the hands of boards guided solely by shareholder interests, boards favoring managers can use discretionary criteria to ensure that managers are well paid even when, because of poor performance, bonuses based on objective criteria are low.

Furthermore, when firms do use objective criteria, these criteria and their implementation do not seem to be designed to reward managers for their own performance. Firms commonly do not base bonuses on how the firm's operating performance or earnings increased relative to peer firms. Instead, some firms base bonuses on how earnings or other financial variables compared to prior year figures. However, bonuses that are paid whenever there is improvement over prior year outcomes will often reward managers whose results fluctuate from year to year around a level reflecting poor performance.

Other firms base bonuses on how financial performance fared relative to a threshold specified by the board. In such cases, how well an executive fares depends not only on how well the executive performs but also on how low the goal is set. By setting goals low enough, directors can ensure executives receive rich bonuses. And when the firms fail to meet the established targets, they can reset the target (as happened at Coca-Cola in 2001 and AT&T Wireless in 2002) or compensate the executives by setting especially low figures going forward. Importantly, boards rarely attempt to filter out improvements in financial performance reflecting industry-wide changes that have nothing to do with the managers' own performance.

Many boards award bonuses to managers for buying other firms. In about 40 percent of large acquisitions, the CEO of the acquiring firm receives a multi-million dollar bonus for completing the deal.[30] But making acquisitions appears hardly something for which managers should receive a special reward beyond whatever positive effects the acquisition might have on the value of the managers' options and shares and earning-based bonuses. Executives do not lack incentives to make acquisitions. If anything, investors' concern is that executives may engage in empire-building and make too many acquisitions. Thus, although the making of a large acquisition might provide a convenient excuse for a large bonus, acquisition bonuses are not called for by incentive considerations.

WINDFALLS IN EQUITY-BASED COMPENSATION

In light of the historically weak link between non-equity compensation and managerial performance, shareholders and regulators wishing to make pay more sensitive to performance have increasingly looked to, and encouraged, equitybased compensation—that is, compensation based on the value of the company's stock. Most equity-based compensation has taken the form of stock options—options to buy a certain number of company shares for a specified price (the "exercise" or "strike" price). We strongly support equity-based compensation, which in principle can provide managers with desirable incentives. Unfortunately, however, the conventional design of options enables executives to reap substantial rewards even when their performance was merely passable or even poor.

Rewards for Market-Wide and Industry-Wide Movements: Conventional stock options enable executives to gain from any increase in the nominal stock price above the grant-date market price. Thus, executives can gain even when their performance is unimpressive or mediocre relative to their peers, as long as the firm's stock price rises largely due to market-wide and industry-wide movements. In fact, much of the variation in executives' payoffs from options comes from such fluctuations rather than from firm-specific movements that might be due to the manager's own performance.

Although there is a whole range of ways in which such windfalls could be filtered out, a large majority of firms have failed to adopt equity-based plans that filter out such windfalls. Unfortunately, most of the boards now changing their equity-based compensation plans in response to outside pressure are still choosing to avoid plans that would effectively eliminate such windfalls. Rather, they are moving to plans such as those based on restricted stock that fail to eliminate, and sometimes even increase, these windfalls.

Rewards for Short-Term Spikes: Option plans have been designed, and largely continue to be designed, in ways that enable executives to make considerable gains from temporary spikes in the firm's stock price, even when long-term stock performance is poor. Firms have given executives broad freedom to unwind equity incentives, a practice that has been beneficial to executives but costly to shareholders. In addition to giving executives freedom to exercise their options as soon as they vest and sell the underlying stock, firms have given executives substantial control over the timing of sales, enabling executives to benefit from their inside information. Indeed, many firms have not only failed to limit the unloading of options but have also adopted reload plans that encourage executives to lock in short-term spikes in stock prices.

The features of option plans that reward managers for short-term spikes not only provide managers rewards that might not reflect their long-term performance but also provide perverse incentives to manipulate earnings. There is, in fact, significant evidence linking executives' freedom to unload options with earnings manipulation and financial misreporting.[31]

COMPENSATION AT AND AFTER DEPARTURE
As already noted, a substantial portion of executives' compensation is not reported with a dollar figure in firms' public disclosures and consequently not included in standard executive compensation datasets. This "stealth compensation" includes executive pensions, deferred compensation arrangements, and post-retirement consulting contracts and perks. These less-noticed forms of compensation have tended to be insensitive to managerial performance, thus further contributing to the decoupling of pay from performance.

Take, for example, Franklin Raines, who was forced to retire as Fannie Mae's CEO in late 2004. Upon departure, Fannie owed him (and his surviving spouse after his death) an annual pension of approximately $1.4 million, an amount specified without any connection to the firm's performance under Raines. In a case study of his compensation, we estimated the value of this non-performance element of Raines's pay at about $25 million.[32]

Further decoupling pay from performance are severance payments given to departing executives. Executives who are pushed out by their boards due to extremely poor performance are typically paid a severance equal to their compensation over a multi-year period, often two or three years' worth. These payments are not reduced even when the firm's performance has been objectively dismal. Furthermore, standard severance provisions do not reduce the severance payment even if the executive quickly finds other employment.

Interestingly, although non-executive employees are generally more likely to be terminated, they rarely receive such generous financial protection. If anything, executives' wealth and generous retirement benefits are likely to make them more capable of bearing the risk of termination. More importantly, if executives' large compensation is justified by the importance of providing them with incentives, one should expect executives' compensation to be more sensitive to performance and provide less protection in the event of dismal failure. The existing severance practices that firms use for their executives not only fail to contribute to the link between pay and performance but also affirmatively operate to weaken it. They weaken the payoff difference between good and poor performance, a difference that shareholders spend much to create.

IMPROVING TRANSPARENCY
We now turn to the implications of our analysis—to our proposals for improving pay arrangements and the governance processes generating them. We start with reforms that we view as no-brainers, ones for which we see no reasonable basis for opposition. Specifically, firms should be required to make the amount and structure of pay more transparent.

Financial economists have paid insufficient attention to transparency because they often focus on whether information is disclosed and, therefore, whether the information can become incorporated into market pricing. It is widely believed that information can be reflected in stock prices as long as it is known and fully understood by even a limited number of market professionals.

In the case of executive compensation, there is already significant disclosure. As we have discussed, SEC regulations require detailed disclosure of the compensation of a company's CEO and of the four other most highly compensated executives. In our view, however, it is important to recognize the difference between disclosure and transparency, and it is transparency that should receive the most attention.

The primary goal of requiring the disclosure of executive compensation is not to enable accurate pricing of the firm's securities. Rather, this disclosure is primarily intended to provide some check on arrangements that are too favorable to executives. This goal is not well served by disseminating information in a way that makes the information understandable to a small number of market professionals but opaque to others.

Public officials, governance reformers, and investors should work to ensure that compensation arrangements are and remain transparent. Transparency would provide shareholders with a more accurate picture of total pay and its relationship with performance and thereby provide some check on departures from arrangements that serve shareholder interests. Furthermore, transparency would eliminate the distortions that currently arise when pay designers choose particular forms of compensation for their camouflage value rather than for their efficiency. Finally, transparency would impose little cost on firms because it would simply require them to disclose clearly information they have or can obtain at negligible cost.

Although we support improved mandatory disclosure requirements, nothing prevents companies in the meantime from voluntarily making pay more transparent. Investors should demand more openness, and companies should not continue to follow a "lawyerly" approach of not disclosing more than required. The following measures could substantially increase the transparency of pay arrangements.

(As this paper went to print, the SEC began a formal consideration of expanded disclosure requirements. The proposals put forward by the SEC staff include the first measure discussed below, and we hope that the other measures below will also be included during the process of the SEC's consideration of the subject.)

1. Placing a Monetary Value on All Forms of Compensation

Companies should be required to place a dollar value on all forms of compensation and to include these amounts in the summary compensation tables contained in company SEC filings. Firms have been able to provide executives with substantial "stealth compensation" by using pensions, deferred compensation, and post-retirement perks and consulting contracts. Although some details of these arrangements have appeared elsewhere in companies' SEC filings, firms have not been required to place a dollar value on these benefits and to include this value in the summary tables, which receive the most attention from investors and the media. These benefits have not even been included in the standard database used by financial economists to study executive compensation.

In our view, companies should be required to place a monetary value on each benefit provided or promised to an executive, and to include this value in the summary compensation table the year in which the executive becomes entitled to it. Thus, for example, the compensation tables should include the amount by which the expected value of an executive's promised pension payments increases during the year. In addition, it might be desirable to require companies to place a monetary value on any tax benefit that accrues to the executive at the company's expense (for example, under deferred compensation arrangements)—and to report this value.

2. Disclosing All Non-Deductible Compensation

Efficient arrangements should take into account their effect on the combined tax bill of the company and the executive. The tax code permits companies to deduct certain payments to executives but not others. Companies routinely include in their disclosure boilerplate language putting shareholders on notice that some of the arrangements may result in the firm being unable to take a deduction for the compensation paid to executives. But firms now do not provide details about what particular amounts end up not being deductible. Firms should provide full details about the components of pay that are not deductible, place a monetary value on the costs of this non-deductibility to the firm, and disclose this dollar cost to investors.

3. Disclosing the Relationship Between Pay and Performance

Companies should make transparent to their shareholders how much of managers' profits from equity and non-equity compensation is due to general market and industry movements. This could be done by requiring firms to calculate and report the gains made by managers from the exercise of options (or the vesting of restricted shares, in the case of restricted share grants) and to report what fraction, if any, was due to the company's superior performance over its industry peers. Such disclosure would make much more transparent the extent to which the company's equity-based plans reward the managers' own performance.

4. Disclosure of Option and Share Unloading

Companies should be required to make transparent to shareholders on a regular basis the extent to which their top five executives have unloaded any equity instruments received as part of their compensation. Although a diligent and dedicated researcher can obtain this information by sifting through stacks of executive trading reports filed with the SEC, requiring the firm to compile and report such information would highlight for all investors the extent to which managers have used their freedom to unwind incentives.

IMPROVING PAY ARRANGEMENTS

Well-designed executive compensation can provide executives with cost-effective incentives to generate shareholder value. We have argued, however, that the promise of such arrangements has not yet been realized. Below we note various changes that firms should consider, and investors should urge them to adopt, in order to strengthen the link between pay and performance and improve executives' incentives.

1. Reducing Windfalls in Equity-Based Compensation

Investors should encourage firms to adopt equity compensation plans that filter out at least some of the gains in the stock price that are due to general market or industry movements. With such filtering, the same amount of incentives can be provided at a lower cost, or stronger incentives can be provided at the same cost. This can be done not only through indexing of the exercise price but also in other ways. For example, by linking the exercise price of options to the stock price of the worst-performing firms in the industry, market-wide movement can be filtered out without imposing excessive risk on executives. It is important to note that moving to restricted stock is not a good way to address the windfalls problem; in fact, restricted-stock grants provide an even larger windfall than conventional options do.

2. Reducing Windfalls in Bonus Plans

For similar reasons, companies should design bonus plans that filter out improvements in financial performance due to economy- or industry-wide movements. Even assuming that it is desirable to focus on accounting performance rather than stock price performance, as bonus plans seek to do, rewarding executives for improvements shared by all firms in the industry is not a cost-effective way to provide incentives. Thus, bonus plans should not be based on absolute increases in earnings, sales, revenues, and so forth, but rather on such increases relative to peer companies.

3. Limiting the Unwinding of Equity Incentives

Investors also should seek to limit executives' broad freedom to unwind the equity-based incentives provided by their compensation plans. It may well be desirable to separate the vesting of options and managers' ability to unwind them. By requiring that executives hold vested options (or the shares resulting from the exercise of such options) for a given period after vesting, firms would ensure that options that already belong to the executive will remain in his or her hands for some time, continuing to provide incentives to increase shareholder value. Furthermore, such restrictions would eliminate the significant distortions that can result from rewarding executives for short-term spikes in the stock price even when long-term stock returns are flat. To prevent circumvention, such restrictions should be backed by contractual prohibitions on executives' hedging or using any other scheme that effectively eliminates some of their exposure to declines in the firm's stock price.

In addition, it might be desirable, as one of us proposed some time ago, to require executives to disclose in *advance* their intention to sell shares, providing detailed information about the intended trade, including the number of shares to be sold.[33] Providing executives with opportunities to sell their shares when their inside information indicates the stock price is about to decline can dilute and distort their incentives.

4. Tying Bonuses to Long-Term Performance

Even assuming it were desirable to reward managers for improvements in accounting performance, such rewards should not be given for short-term fluctuations but rather only for improvements over a considerable period of time. Rewarding executives for short-term improvements is not an effective way to provide beneficial incentives and indeed might create incentives to manipulate short-term accounting results.

Similarly, compensation contracts should generally include claw-back provisions that require managers to return payments based on accounting figures that are subsequently restated. Such return of payments is warranted, regardless of whether the executive was in any way responsible for the misreporting. When the board believes it is desirable to tie executive payoffs to a formula involving a metric whose value turns out to have been inflated, correctly applying the formula requires reversing payments that were based on an erroneous value. The principle should be: "What wasn't earned must be returned."

5. Be Wary of Paying for Expansion

Because running a larger firm increases managers' power, prestige, and perquisites, executives might have an excessive incentive to expand the company. Executive compensation arrangements should seek to counter rather than reinforce this incentive. Thus, the common practice of paying executives bonuses for making acquisitions and otherwise rewarding managers for firm expansion can create perverse incentives. While the increased difficulty of running a larger firm might make it necessary to pay executives of bigger firms additional compensation, boards should keep in mind that such practices provide executives with *ex ante* incentives to expand (say, by making acquisitions) even when expansion is not value-maximizing.

6. Dividend-Neutrality

Under current option plans, terms are not updated to reflect the payment of dividends, and as a result executives' payoffs are reduced when they decide to pay a dividend. Indeed, there is evidence that executives whose pay has a large option component tend to issue lower dividends. Instead, they resort to share repurchases, which have a less adverse effect on the value of managers' options but may not always be the most efficient form of payout.[34] To reduce distortions in managers' payout decisions, all equity-based compensation should be designed in such a way that it is dividend-neutral; that is, it neither encourages nor discourages the payment of dividends. In particular, in the case of option plans, the exercise price of options should be adjusted in any case where a dividend is paid.

7. Rethinking Executive Pensions

There are reasons to doubt the efficiency of the widespread practice of using Supplemental Executive Retirement Plans (SERPs) to provide executives with a major component of their career compensation. Unlike pension plans used for non-executive employees, SERPs do not enjoy a tax subsidy. And given that firms have been generally moving away from defined benefit plans to defined contribution plans for non-executive employees, it is far from clear that providing executives with defined benefit plans is required by risk-bearing considerations. While defined benefit plans shift the risk of investment performance from the employee to the firm, executives do not seem to be less able to bear such risk than other employees.

While the efficiency benefits of SERPs are far from clear, SERPs provide executives with pay that is largely decoupled from performance and thus weakens the overall link between total pay and performance. Firms thus would do well to reconsider their heavy reliance on SERPs.

8. Avoiding Soft-Landing Arrangements

Soft-landing arrangements, which provide managers with a generous exit package when they are pushed out due to failure, dilute executives' incentives. While firms spend large amounts on producing a payoff gap between performing well and performing poorly, the money spent on soft-landing arrangements works in the opposite direction, narrowing the payoff gap between good and poor performance.

At present, executives are commonly promised generous severance arrangements in the event of termination, unless the termination is triggered by an extremely narrow set of circumstances (such as criminal indictment or "malfeasance"). Even if firms stick to the existing broad definition of termination without cause, the payoff in such a termination should depend in part on the firm's performance relative to its peers during the executive's service. An executive who is terminated against the background of extremely poor stock performance should get less than an executive who is terminated when the company's performance is reasonable. Furthermore, firms should consider provisions that make the termination payoff depend on the reasons for the executive's termination.

IMPROVING BOARD ACCOUNTABILITY

Past and current flaws in executive pay arrangements, we argue, have resulted from underlying problems within the corporate governance system: specifically, directors' lack of sufficient incentive to focus solely on shareholder interests when setting pay. If directors could be relied on to focus on shareholder interests, the pay-setting process, and board oversight of executives more generally, would be greatly improved. The most promising route to improving pay arrangements is thus to make boards more accountable to shareholders and more focused on shareholder interests.

Increasing accountability to shareholders would transform the arm's-length contracting model into a reality and lead to improved pay-setting processes. Accountability would thus lead to better-designed compensation arrangements as well as improved board performance more generally.

Recent reforms require most companies listed on the major stock exchanges (the New York Stock Exchange, NASDAQ, and the American Stock Exchange) to have a majority of independent directors—directors who are not otherwise employed by the firm or in a business relationship with it. These companies must also staff compensation and nominating committees entirely with independent directors. These reforms are likely to reduce managers' power over the board and improve directors' incentives somewhat. But they fall far short of what is necessary.

Our analysis shows that the new listing requirements weaken executives' influence over directors but do not eliminate it. More importantly, there are limits to what independence can do by itself. Independence does not ensure that directors have incentives to focus on shareholder interests or that directors will be well-selected. In addition to becoming more independent of insiders, directors also must become more dependent on shareholders. To this end, we should eliminate the arrangements that currently entrench directors and insulate them from shareholders.

To begin, shareholders' power to replace directors should be turned from myth into reality. Even in the wake of poor performance and shareholder dissatisfaction, directors now face very little risk of being ousted. Shareholders' ability to replace directors is extremely limited. A recent study by one of us provides evidence that, outside the hostile takeover context, the incidence of electoral challenges to directors has been practically negligible in the past decade.[35] This state of affairs should not continue.

To improve the performance of corporate boards, impediments to director removal should be reduced.[36] To begin, shareholders should be given the power to place director candidates on the corporate ballot. Secondly, proxy contest challengers that attract sufficient support should receive reimbursement for their expenses.

Furthermore, it would be desirable to eliminate staggered boards, which most public companies now have, and have all directors stand for annual election. Staggered

186

boards provide a powerful protection from removal in either a proxy fight or a hostile takeover. A recent empirical study by Alma Cohen and one of us finds that staggered boards bring about an economically significant reduction in firm value.[37]

In addition to making shareholder power to remove directors viable, boards should not have veto power—which current corporate law grants them—over changing governance arrangements in the company's charter. Shareholders should have the power, which they now lack, to initiate and adopt changes in the corporate charter.

Under current rules, shareholders can pass only non-binding resolutions, and a recent empirical study by one of us documents that boards commonly elect not to follow resolutions that receive majority support from shareholders, even if such resolutions pass two or three times.[38]

Allowing shareholders to amend the corporate charter would improve over time the entire range of corporate governance arrangements without outside regulatory intervention. If there is concern that shareholders are influenced by short-term considerations, shareholder-initiated changes could require approval by majority vote in two successive annual shareholder meetings. But we should not continue denying shareholders the power to change the corporate charter, no matter how widespread and long-lasting shareholder support for such a change is. Allowing shareholders to set governance arrangements would contribute to making boards more accountable to shareholders.

To fully address the existing problems in executive compensation and corporate governance, structural reforms in the allocation of power between boards and shareholders are necessary. Given political realities and the power of vested interests, such reforms would not be easy to pass. But the corporate governance flaws that we have discussed—which we have seen to be pervasive, systemic, and costly—call for such reforms.

ENDNOTES

1. Bebchuk, L.A. & Fried, J.M. 2004. *Pay without performance: The unfulfilled promise of executive compensation*. Cambridge: Harvard University Press. Accompanying articles include: Bebchuk, L.A.. & Fried, J.M. 2004. Stealth compensation via retirement benefits. *Berkeley Business Law Journal* 2: 291–325. Bebchuk, L.A. & Fried, J.M. forthcoming. Executive compensation at Fannie Mae: A case study of perverse incentives, non-performance pay, and camouflage. *Journal of Corporation Law*; Bebchuk, L.A. & Grinstein, Y. The growth of executive pay. 2005. *Oxford Review of Economic Policy* 21: 283–303. Earlier work by us on which the book draws includes Bebchuk, L.A., Fried, J.M., & Walker, D.I. 2002. Managerial power and rent extraction in the design of executive compensation. *University of Chicago Law Review* 69: 751–846; Bebchuk, L.A. & Fried, J.M. 2003. Executive compensation as an agency problem. *Journal of Economic Perspectives* 17:71–92.

2. Bebchuk & Grinstein, supra note 1.

3. See, e.g., Blanchard, O.J., Lopez-de-Silanes, F., & Shleifer, A. 1994. What do firms do with cash windfalls? *Journal of Financial Economics* 36: 337–360; Yermack, D. 1997. Good timing: CEO stock option awards and company news announcements. *Journal of Finance* 52: 449–476; Bertrand, M. & Mullainathan, S. 2001. Are CEOs rewarded for luck? The ones without principals are," *Quarterly Journal of Economics* 116: 901–932.

4. See Bebchuk, Fried, & Walker, supra note 1; Bebchuk and Fried, Executive Compensation as an Agency Problem, supra note 1.

5. For surveys from this perspective in the finance and economics literature, see, for example, Abowd, J.M. & Kaplan, D.S. 1999. Executive compensation: Six questions that need answering. *Journal of Economic Perspectives* 13: 145–168; Core, J.E., Guay, W., & Larcker, D.F. 2003. Executive equity compensation and incentives: A survey. *Economic Policy Review* 9: 27–50.

6. See, e.g., Core, J.E., Guay, W.R. & Thomas, R.S. 2005. Is U.S. CEO compensation inefficient? *Michigan Law Review* 103: 1142–1185.

7. Nasaw, D. 2003. Opening the board: The fight is on to determine who will guide the selection of directors in the future, *Wall Street Journal*, October 27, 2003, R8.

8. Brick, I.E., Palmon, O. & Wald, J.K. forthcoming. CEO Compensation, director compensation, and firm performance: Evidence of cronyism. *Journal of Corporate Finance*.

9. Main, B.G.M., O'Reilly III, C.A., & Wade, J. 1995. The CEO, the board of directors, and executive compensation: Economic and psychological perspectives. *Industrial and Corporate Change* 11: 292–332.

10. Main, O'Reilly III, & Wade, supra note 9.

11. Murphy, K.J. 1999. Executive compensation, in *Handbook of Labor Economics*, Ashenfelter, O. & Card, D. (Eds.). New York: Elsevier.

12. Bizjak, J.M., Lemmon, M.L., & Naveen, L. 2003. Has the use of peer groups contributed to higher levels of executive compensation? Working paper.

13. Bebchuk,' L.A., John Coates IV, J., & Subramanian, G. 2002. The powerful antitakeover force of staggered boards: Theory, evidence, and policy. *Stanford Law Review* 54: 887–951.

14. Murphy, K.J. 2002. Explaining executive compensation: Managerial power vs. the perceived cost of stock options. *University of Chicago Law Review* 69: 847–869.

15. See, e.g., Jenkins, H.W. 2002. Outrageous CEO pay revisited, *Wall Street Journal*, October 2, 2002, A17.
16. Core, J., Holthausen, R., & Larcker, D. 1999. Corporate governance, chief executive compensation, and firm performance. *Journal of Financial Economics* 51: 371–406.
17. Core, Holthausen, & Larcker, supra note 16; Cyert, R., Sok-Hyon Kang, S. & Kumar, P. 2002. Corporate governance, takeovers, and top-management compensation: Theory and evidence. *Management Science* 48: 453–469.
18. Cyert, Kang, & Kumar, supra note 17.
19. Bertrand, M. & Mullainathan, S. 2000. Agents with and without principals. *American Economic Review* 90: 203–208.
20. Hartzell, J.C. & Starks, L.T. 2003. Institutional investors and executive compensation. *Journal of Finance* 58: 2351–2374.
21. Parthiban, D., Kochar, R., & Levitas, R. 1998. The effect of institutional investors on the level and mix of CEO compensation. *Academy of Management Journal* 41: 200–208.
22. Borokhovich, K.A., Brunarski, K.R., & Parrino, R. 1997. CEO contracting and anti-takeover amendments. *Journal of Finance* 52: 1503–1513.
23. Cheng, S., Nagar, V., & Rajan, M.V. 2005. Identifying control motives in managerial ownership: Evidence from antitakeover legislation. *Review of Financial Studies* 8: 637–672.
24. Thomas, R.S. & Martin, K.J. 1999. The effect of shareholder proposals on executive compensation. *University of Cincinnati Law Review* 67: 1021–1065.
25. Wade, J.B., Porac, J.F., & Pollock, T.G. 1997. Worth, words, and the justification of executive pay. *Journal of Organizational Behavior* 18: 641–664.
26. Bebchuk, L.A. & Jackson, Jr., R. 2005. Executive pensions. Forthcoming. *Journal of Corporation Law.*
27. Jensen, M.C. & Murphy, K.J. 1990. Performance pay and top-management incentives. *Journal of Political Economy* 98: 225–264; Jensen, M.C. & Murphy, K.J. 1990. CEO incentives: It's not how much you pay, but how. *Harvard Business Review* 68: 138–153.
28. Bebchuk & Grinstein, supra note 1.
29. See Murphy, supra note 11.
30. Grinstein, Y. & Hribar, P. 2004. CEO compensation and incentives: Evidence from M&A bonuses. *Journal of Financial Economics* 71: 119–143.
31. Bergstresser, D. & Philippon, T. forthcoming. CEO incentives and earnings management: Evidence from the 1990s. *Journal of Financial Economics*; Summers, S.L. & Sweeney, J.T. 1998. Fraudulently misstated financial statements and insider trading: An empirical analysis. *Accounting Review* 73: 131–146.
32. Bebchuk & Fried, supra note 1.
33. See Fried, J.M. 1998. Reducing the profitability of corporate insider trading through pretrading disclosure. *Southern California Law Review* 71: 303–392.
34. See Fried, J.M. forthcoming. Informed trading and false signaling with open market repurchases. *California Law Review.*
35. Bebchuk, L.A. 2003. The case for shareholder access to the ballot. *The Business Lawyer* 59: 43–66.
36. For a fuller analysis of the ways in which shareholder power to remove directors could be made viable, see Bebchuk, L.A. 2005. The myth of the shareholder franchise. Working paper.
37. Bebchuk, L.A. & Cohen, A. 2005. The costs of entrenched boards. *Journal of Financial Economics* 78:409–433.
38. Bebchuk, L.A. 2005. The case for increasing shareholder power. *Harvard Law Review* 18: 833–914.

Lucian A. Bebchuk *is Wiliam J. Friedman and Alicia Townsend Friedman Professor of Law, Economics Finance and Director of the Program on Corporate Governance, Harvard Law School.*

Jesse M. Fried *is Professor of Law and Co-Director of the Berkeley Center for Law, Business and the Economy at the School of Law, University of California, Berkeley.*

QUESTION

8.5 What are the eight measures that could increase the transparency of executive compensation arrangements?

Chapter 9

The Balanced Scorecard

Robert Kaplan and David Norton's article, *Using the Balanced Scorecard as a Strategic Management System* (Reading 9.1), extends the authors earlier development of the balanced scorecard as described in the text. In this article, four new processes designed to link more effectively long-term strategic objectives with short-term actions are presented. The four processes are: (1) translating the vision, which aids managers in building consensus around the organization's vision and strategy, (2) communicating and linking, which helps managers communicate their strategy throughout the organization and to link it to department and individual objectives; (3) business planning, which allows companies to integrate business and financial plans; and (4) feedback and learning -which provides managers with information about how well their departments and employees have done in meeting their budgeted financial goals. The article presents examples within each category of recent company experiences in applying these processes.

Readings 9.2 and 9.3, Kaplan and Norton's *Transforming the Balanced Scorecard from Performance Measurement to Strategic Management*, Parts I and II, respectively, extend the authors' work on the balanced scorecard into the area of organizational strategy. Reading 9.2 (Part I), develops the idea of strategy maps and balanced scorecards to develop performance objective and measures linked to strategy. The key relationships are shown in Figure 2, which is a comprehensive illustration of how factors in the Learning and Growth Perspective affect processes within the Internal Perspective. In turn, these processes influence key variables in the Customer Perspective. Factors from both the Internal and Customer Perspectives affect Revenue Growth and Productivity Strategies in the Financial Perspective that ultimately improves Shareholder Value.

The implementation of the BSC at Pitney Bowes, Inc. (PBI) is the topic of Reading 9.4 (*Pitney Bowes Calls for New Metrics*), by M. Green, J. Garrity, A. Gumbus, and B. Lyons. PBI, headquartered in Stamford, CT, is a $4 billion provider of integrated mail and document solutions. The BSC allowed PBI to better integrate their performance management system so that the metrics they used were more relevant and more understandable for employees in the business. Ultimately, the BSC changed the focus on monthly financial meetings to focus on five things that PBI is doing well and three things that need to be improved, and has led to other implementations relating to capital budgeting.

In Reading 9.5, *Measuring the Strategic Readiness of Intangible Assets*, Robert Kaplan and David Norton, focus on one of the most vexing aspects of successfully implementing the balanced scorecard – aligning intangible assets in the learning and growth perspective. More specifically, the article discusses the three key categories of intangible assets and their readiness to be deployed. The three categories are: (1) human capital, (2) information capital, and (3) organization capital. Because intangible assets are considered "softer" or more subjective than financial measures, managers often ignore them or don't know how to manager them. This article provides a compelling argument as to the importance of managing intangible assets for the benefit successfully implementing the balanced scorecard and the organization as a whole.

9.1 Using the Balanced Scorecard as a Strategic Management System
Building a scorecard can help managers link today's actions with tomorrow's goals.

by Robert S. Kaplan and David P. Norton*

As companies around the world transform themselves for competition that is based on information, their ability to exploit intangible assets has become far more decisive than their ability to invest in and manage physical assets. Several years ago, in recognition of this change, we introduced a concept we called the *balanced scorecard.* The balanced scorecard supplemented traditional financial measures with criteria that measured performance from three additional perspectives—those of customers, internal business processes, and teaming and growth. (See the chart "Translating Vision and Strategy: Four Perspectives.") It therefore enabled companies to track financial results while simultaneously monitoring progress in building the capabilities and acquiring the intangible assets they would need for future growth. The scorecard wasn't a replacement for financial measures; it was their complement.

Recently, we have seen some companies move beyond our early vision for the scorecard to discover its value as the cornerstone of a new strategic management system. Used this way, the scorecard addresses a serious deficiency in traditional management systems: their inability to link a company's long-term strategy with its short-term actions.

Most companies' operational and management control systems are built around financial measures and targets, which bear little relation to the company's progress in achieving long-term strategic objectives. Thus the emphasis most companies place on short-term financial measures leaves a gap between the development of a strategy and its implementation.

Managers using the balanced scorecard do not have to rely on short-term financial measures as the sole indicators of the company's performance. The scorecard lets them introduce four new management processes that, separately and in combination, contribute to linking long-term strategic objectives with short-term actions. (See the chart "Managing Strategy: Four Processes.")

TRANSLATING VISION AND STRATEGY—FOUR PERSPECTIVES

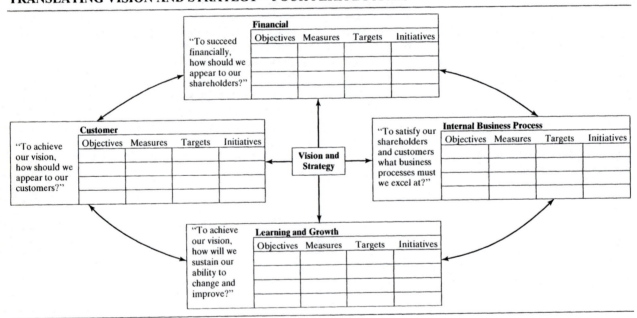

* From: R. S. Kaplan and D. P. Norton, "Using the Balanced Scorecard as a Strategic Management System," *Harvard Business Review* (January–February 1996): 75–85. Copyright © 1996 by the President and Fellows of Harvard College; all rights reserved.

MANAGING STRATEGY: FOUR PROCESSES

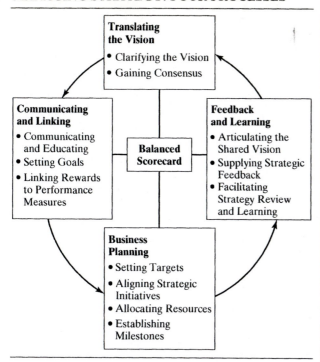

Translating the Vision
- Clarifying the Vision
- Gaining Consensus

Communicating and Linking
- Communicating and Educating
- Setting Goals
- Linking Rewards to Performance Measures

Balanced Scorecard

Feedback and Learning
- Articulating the Shared Vision
- Supplying Strategic Feedback
- Facilitating Strategy Review and Learning

Business Planning
- Setting Targets
- Aligning Strategic Initiatives
- Allocating Resources
- Establishing Milestones

The first new process—*translating the vision*—helps managers build a consensus around the organization's vision and strategy. Despite the best intentions of those at the top, lofty statements about becoming "best in class," "the number one supplier," or an "empowered organization" don't translate easily into operational terms that provide useful guides to action at the local level. For people to act on the words in vision and strategy statements, those statements must be expressed as an integrated set of objectives and measures, agreed upon by all senior executives, that describe the long-term drivers of success.

The second process—*communicating and linking*—lets managers communicate their strategy up and down the organization and link it to departmental and individual objectives. Traditionally, departments are evaluated by their financial performance, and individual incentives are tied to short-term financial goals. The scorecard gives managers a way of ensuring that all levels of the organization understand the long-term strategy and that both departmental and individual objectives are aligned with it.

The third process—*business planning*—enables companies to integrate their business and financial plans. Almost all organizations today are implementing a variety of change programs, each with its own champions, gurus, and consultants, and each competing for senior executives' time, energy, and resources. Managers find it difficult to integrate those diverse initiatives to achieve their strategic goals—a situation that leads to frequent disappointments with the programs' results. But when

managers use the ambitious goals set for balanced scorecard measures as the basis for allocating resources and setting priorities, they can undertake and coordinate only those initiatives that move them toward their long-term strategic objectives.

The fourth process—*feedback and learning*—gives companies the capacity for what we call strategic learning. Existing feedback and review processes focus on whether the company, its departments, or its individual employees have met their budgeted financial goals. With the balanced scorecard at the center of its management systems, a company can monitor short-term results from the three additional perspectives—customers, internal business processes, and learning and growth—and evaluate strategy in the light of recent performance. The scorecard thus enables companies to modify strategies to reflect real-time learning.

None of the more than 100 organizations that we have studied or with which we have worked implemented their first balanced scorecard with the intention of developing a new strategic management system. But in each one, the senior executives discovered that the scorecard supplied a framework and thus a focus for many critical management processes: departmental and individual goal setting, business planning, capital allocations, strategic initiatives, and feedback and learning. Previously, those processes were uncoordinated and often directed at short-term operational goals. By building the scorecard, the senior executives started a process of change that has gone well beyond the original idea of simply broadening the company's performance measures.

For example, one insurance company—let's call it National Insurance—developed its first balanced scorecard to create a new vision for itself as an underwriting specialist. But once National started to use it, the scorecard allowed the CEO and the senior management team not only to introduce a new strategy for the organization but also to overhaul the company's management system. The CEO subsequently told employees in a letter addressed to the whole organization that National would thenceforth use the balanced scorecard and the philosophy that it represented to manage the business.

National built its new strategic management system step-by-step over 30 months, with each step representing an incremental improvement. (See the chart "How One Company Built a Strategic Management System.") The iterative sequence of actions enabled the company to reconsider each of the four new management processes two or three times before the system stabilized and became an established part of National's overall management system. Thus the CEO was able to transform the company so that everyone could focus on achieving long-term strategic objectives—something that no purely financial framework could do.

2A *Communicate to Middle Managers*: The top three layers of management (100 people) are brought together to learn about and discuss the new strategy. The balanced scorecard is the communication vehicle. (*months 4–5*)

2B *Develop Business Unit Scorecards*: Using the corporate scorecard as a template, each business unit translates its strategy into its own scorecard. (*months 6–9*)

5 *Refine the Vision*: The review of business unit scorecards identifies several cross-business issues not initially included in the corporate strategy. The corporate scorecard is updated. (*month 12*)

7 *Update Long-Range Plan and Budget:* Five-year goals are established for each measure. The investments required to meet those goals are identified and funded. The first year of the five-year plan becomes the annual budget. (*months 15–17*)

9 *Conduct Annual Strategy Review*: At the start of the third year, the initial strategy has been achieved and the corporate strategy requires updating. The executive committee lists ten strategic issues. Each business unit is asked to develop a position on each issue as a prelude to updating its strategy and scorecard. (*months 25–26*)

Time Frame *(in months)*

0	1	2	3	4	5	6	7	8	9	10	11	12	13	14	15	16	17	18	19	20	21	22	23	24	25	26

Actions:

1 *Clarify the Vision*: Ten members of a newly formed executive team work together for three months. A balanced scorecard is developed to translate a generic vision into a strategy that is understood and can be communicated. The process helps build consensus and commitment to the strategy.

3A *Eliminate Nonstrategic Investments*: The corporate scorecard, by clarifying strategic priorities, identifies many active programs that are not contributing to the strategy. (*month 6*) **3B** *Launch Corporate Change Programs*: The corporate scorecard identifies the need for cross-business change programs. They are launched while the business units prepare their scorecards. (*month 6*)

4 *Review Business Unit Scorecards*: The CEO and the executive team review the individual business units' scorecards. The review permits the CEO to participate knowledgeably in shaping business unit strategy. (*months 9–11*)

6A *Communicate the Balance Scorecard to the Entire Company*: At the end of one year, when the management teams are comfortable with the strategic approach, the scorecard is disseminated to the entire organization. (*month 12–ongoing*) **6B** *Establish Individual Performance Objectives*: The top three layers of management link their individual objectives and incentive compensation to their scorecards. (*months 13–14*)

8 *Conduct Monthly and Quarterly Reviews*: After corporate approval of the business unit scorecards, a monthly review process, supplemented by quarterly reviews that focus more heavily on strategic issues, begins. (*month 18–ongoing*)

10 *Link Everyone's Performance to the Balanced Scorecard*: All employees are asked to link their individual objectives to the balanced scorecard. The entire organization's incentive compensation is linked to the scorecard. (*months 25–26*)

Note: Steps 7, 8, 9, and 10 are performed on a regular schedule. The balanced scorecard is now a routine part of the management process.

TRANSLATING THE VISION

The CEO of an engineering construction company, after working with his senior management team for several months to develop a mission statement, got a phone call from a project manager in the field. "I want you to know," the distraught manager said, "that I believe in the mission statement. I want to act in accordance with the mission statement. I'm here with my customer. What am I supposed to do?"

The mission statement, like those of many other organizations, had declared an intention to "use high-quality employees to provide services that surpass customers' needs." But the project manager in the field with his employees and his customer did not know how to translate those words into the appropriate actions. The phone call convinced the CEO that a large gap existed between the mission statement and employees' knowledge of how their day-to-day actions could contribute to realizing the company's vision.

Metro Bank (not its real name), the result of a merger of two competitors, encountered a similar gap while building its balanced scorecard. The senior executive group thought it had reached agreement on the new organization's overall strategy: "to provide superior service to targeted customers." Research had revealed five basic market segments among existing and potential customers, each with different needs. While formulating the measures for the customer-perspective portion of their balanced scorecard, however, it became apparent that although the 25 senior executives agreed on the words of the strategy, each one had a different definition of *superior service* and a different image of the *targeted customers*.

The exercise of developing operational measures for the four perspectives on the bank's scorecard forced the 25 executives to clarify the meaning of the strategy statement. Ultimately, they agreed to stimulate revenue growth through new products and services and also agreed on the three most desirable customer segments. They developed scorecard measures for the specific products and services that should be delivered to customers in the targeted segments as well as for the relationship the bank should build with customers in each segment. The scorecard also highlighted gaps in employees' skills and in information systems that the bank would have to close in order to deliver the selected value propositions to the targeted customers. Thus, creating a balanced scorecard forced the bank's senior managers to arrive at a consensus and then to translate their vision into terms that had meaning to the people who would realize the vision.

COMMUNICATING AND LINKING

"The top ten people in the business now understand the strategy better than ever before. It's too bad," a senior executive of a major oil company complained, "that we can't put this in a bottle so that everyone could share it." With the balanced scorecard, he can.

One company we have worked with deliberately involved three layers of management in the creation of its balanced scorecard. The senior executive group formulated the financial and customer objectives. It then mobilized the talent and information in the next two levels of managers by having them formulate the internal-business-process and learning-and-growth objectives that would drive the achievement of the financial and customer goals. For example, knowing the importance of satisfying customers' expectations of on-time delivery, the broader group identified several internal business processes—such as order processing, scheduling, and fulfillment in which the company had to excel. To do so, the company would have to retrain front line employees and improve the information systems available to them. The group developed performance measures for those critical processes and for staff and systems capabilities.

Broad participation in creating a scorecard takes longer, but it offers several advantages: Information from a larger number of managers is incorporated into the internal objectives; the managers gain a better understanding of the company's long-term strategic goals; and such broad participation builds a stronger commitment to achieving those goals. But getting managers to buy into the scorecard is only a first step in linking individual actions to corporate goals.

The balanced scorecard signals to everyone what the organization is trying to achieve for shareholders and customers alike. But to align employees' individual performances with the overall strategy, scorecard users generally engage in three activities: communicating and educating, setting goals, and linking rewards to performance measures.

Communicating and Educating. Implementing a strategy begins with educating those who have to execute it. Whereas some organizations opt to hold their strategy close to the vest, most believe that they should disseminate it from top to bottom. A broad-based communication program shares with all employees the strategy and the critical objectives they have to meet if the strategy is to succeed.

Onetime events such as the distribution of brochures or newsletters and the holding of "town meetings" might kick off the program. Some organizations post bulletin boards that illustrate and explain the balanced scorecard measures, then update them with monthly results. Others use group-ware and electronic bulletin boards to distribute the scorecard to the desktops of all employees and to encourage dialogue about the measures. The same media allow employees to make suggestions for achieving or exceeding the targets.

... AROUND THE BALANCED SCORECARD

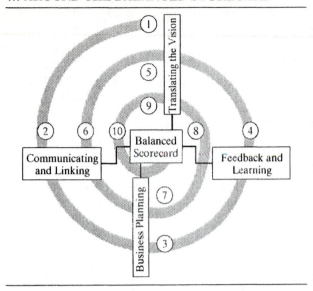

The balanced scorecard, as the embodiment of business unit strategy, should also be communicated upward in the organization—to corporate headquarters and to the corporate board of directors. With the scorecard, business units can quantify and communicate their long-term strategies to senior executives using a comprehensive set of linked financial and nonfinancial measures. Such communication informs the executives and the board in specific terms that long-term strategies designed for competitive success are in place. The measures also provide the basis for feedback and accountability. Meeting short-term financial targets should not constitute satisfactory performance when other measures indicate that the long-term strategy is either not working or not being implemented well.

Should the balanced scorecard be communicated beyond the boardroom to external shareholders? We believe that as senior executives gain confidence in the ability of the scorecard measures to monitor strategic performance and predict future financial performance, they will find ways to inform outside investors about those measures without disclosing competitively sensitive information.

Skandia, an insurance and financial services company based in Sweden, issues a supplement to its annual report called "The Business Navigator"—an instrument to help us navigate into the future and thereby stimulate renewal and development. The supplement describes Skandia's strategy and the strategic measures the company uses to communicate and evaluate the strategy. It also provides a report on the company's performance along those measures during the year. The measures are customized for each operating unit and include, for example, market share, customer satisfaction and retention, employee competence, employee empowerment, and technology deployment.

Communicating the balanced scorecard promotes commitment and accountability to the business's long-term strategy. As one executive at Metro Bank declared, "The balanced scorecard is both motivating and obligating."

Setting Goals. Mere awareness of corporate goals, however, is not enough to change many people's behavior. Somehow, the organization's high-level strategic objectives and measures must be translated into objectives and measures for operating units and individuals.

The exploration group of a large oil company developed a technique to enable and encourage individuals to set goals for themselves that were consistent with the organization's. It created a small, fold-up personal scorecard that people could carry in their shirt pockets or wallets. (See the exhibit "The Personal Scorecard.") The scorecard contains three levels of information. The first describes corporate objectives, measures, and targets. The second leaves room for translating corporate targets into targets for each business unit. For the third level, the company asks both individuals and teams to articulate which of their own objectives would be consistent with the business unit and corporate objectives, as well as what initiatives they would take to achieve their objectives. It also asks them to define up to five performance measures for their objectives and to set targets for each measure. The personal scorecard helps to communicate corporate and business unit objectives to the people and teams performing the work, enabling them to translate the objectives into meaningful tasks and targets for themselves. It also lets them keep that information close at hand—in their pockets.

Linking Rewards to Performance Measures. Should compensation systems be linked to balanced scorecard measures? Some companies, believing that tying financial compensation to performance is a powerful lever, have moved quickly to establish such a linkage. For example, an oil company that we'll call Pioneer Petroleum uses its scorecard as the sole basis for computing incentive compensation. The company ties 60% of its executives' bonuses to their achievement of ambitious targets for a weighted average of four financial indicators: return on capital, profitability, cash flow, and operating cost. It bases the remaining 40% on indicators of customer satisfaction, dealer satisfaction, employee satisfaction, and environmental responsibility (such as a percentage change in the level of emissions to water and air). Pioneer's CEO says that linking compensation to the scorecard has helped to align the company with its strategy. "I know of no competitor," he says, "who has this degree of alignment. It is producing results for us."

THE PERSONAL SCORECARD

Corporate Objectives
- ☐ Double our corporate value in seven years.
- ☐ Increase our earnings by an average of 20% per year.
- ☐ Achieve an internal rate of return 2% above the cost of capital.
- ☐ Increase both production and reserves by 20% in the next decade.

Corporate Targets					Scorecard Measures	Business Unit Targets					Team/Individual Objectives and Initiatives
1995	1996	1997	1998	1999		1995	1996	1997	1998	1999	1.
Financial											
100	120	160	180	250	Earnings (in millions of dollars)						
100	450	200	210	225	Net cash flow						
100	85	80	75	70	Overhead and operating expenses						2.
Operating											
100	75	73	70	64	Earnings (in millions of dollars)						
100	97	93	90	82	Net cash flow						
100	105	108	108	110	Overhead and operating expenses						3.
Team/Individual Measures						**Targets**					
1.											
2.											
3.											4.
4.											
5.											
Name:											5.
Location:											

As attractive and as powerful as such linkage is, it nonetheless carries risks. For instance, does the company have the right measures on the scorecard? Does it have valid and reliable data for the selected measures? Could unintended or unexpected consequences arise from the way the targets for the measures are achieved? Those are questions that companies should ask.

Furthermore, companies traditionally handle multiple objectives in a compensation formula by assigning weights to each objective and calculating incentive compensation by the extent to which each weighted objective was achieved. This practice permits substantial incentive compensation to be paid if the business unit overachieves on a few objectives even if it falls far short on others. A better approach would be to establish minimum threshold levels for a critical subset of the strategic measures. Individuals would earn no incentive compensation if performance in a given period fell short of any threshold. This requirement should motivate people to achieve a more balanced performance across short-and long-term objectives.

Some organizations, however, have reduced their emphasis on short-term, formula-based incentive systems as a result of introducing the balanced scorecard. They have discovered that dialogue among executives and managers about the scorecard—both the formulation of the measures and objectives and the explanation of actual versus targeted results—provides a better opportunity to observe managers' performance and abilities. Increased knowledge of their managers' abilities makes it easier for executives to set incentive rewards subjectively and to defend those subjective evaluations—a process that is less susceptible to the game playing and distortions associated with explicit, formula based rules.

One company we have studied takes an intermediate position. It bases bonuses for business unit managers on two equally weighted criteria: their achievement of a financial objective—economic value added—over a three-year period and a subjective assessment of their performance on measures drawn from the customer, internal-business-process, and learning-and-growth perspectives of the balanced scorecard.

That the balanced scorecard has a role to play in the determination of incentive compensation is not in doubt. Precisely what that role should be will become clearer as more companies experiment with linking rewards to scorecard measures.

BUSINESS PLANNING

"Where the rubber meets the sky": That's how one senior executive describes his company's long-range-planning process. He might have said the same of many other companies because their financially based management systems fail to link change programs and resource allocation to long-term strategic priorities.

The problem is that most organizations have separate procedures and organizational units for strategic planning and for resource allocation and budgeting. To formulate their strategic plans, senior executives go off-site annually and engage for several days in active discussions facilitated by senior planning and development managers or external consultants. The outcome of this exercise is a strategic plan articulating where the company expects (or hopes or prays) to be in three, five, and ten years. Typically, such plans then sit on executives' bookshelves for the next 12 months.

Meanwhile, a separate resource-allocation and budgeting process run by the finance staff sets financial targets for revenues, expenses, profits, and investments for the next fiscal year. The budget it produces consists almost entirely of financial numbers that generally bear little relation to the targets in the strategic plan.

Which document do corporate managers discuss in their monthly and quarterly meetings during the following year? Usually only the budget, because the periodic reviews focus on a comparison of actual and budgeted results for every line item. When is the strategic plan next discussed? Probably during the next annual off-site meeting, when the senior managers draw up a new set of three-, five-, and ten-year plans.

The very exercise of creating a balanced scorecard forces companies to integrate their strategic planning and budgeting processes and therefore helps to ensure that their budgets support their strategies. Scorecard users select measures of progress from all four scorecard perspectives and set targets for each of them. Then they determine which actions will drive them toward their targets, identify the measures they will apply to those drivers from the four perspectives, and establish the short-term milestones that will mark their progress along the strategic paths they have selected. Building a scorecard thus enables a company to link its financial budgets with its strategic goals.

For example, one division of the Style Company (not its real name) committed to achieving a seemingly impossible goal articulated by the CEO: to double revenues in five years. The forecasts built into the organization's existing strategic plan fell $1 billion short of this objective. The division's managers, after considering various scenarios, agreed to specific increases in five different performance drivers: the number of new stores opened, the number of new customers attracted into new and existing stores, the percentage of shoppers in each store converted into actual purchasers, the portion of existing customers retained, and average sales per customer.

By helping to define the key drivers of revenue growth and by committing to targets for each of them, the division's managers eventually grew comfortable with the CEO's ambitious goal.

The process of building a balanced scorecard—clarifying the strategic objectives and then identifying the few critical drivers—also creates a framework for managing an organization's various change programs. These initiatives—reengineering, employee empowerment, time-based management, and total quality management, among others—promise to deliver results but also compete with one another for scarce resources, including the scarcest resource of all: senior managers' time and attention.

Shortly after the merger that created it, Metro Bank, for example, launched more than 70 different initiatives. The initiatives were intended to produce a more competitive and successful institution, but they were inadequately integrated into the overall strategy. After building their balanced scorecard, Metro Bank's managers dropped many of those programs—such as a marketing effort directed at individuals with very high net worth—and consolidated others into initiatives that were better aligned with the company's strategic objectives. For example, the managers replaced a program aimed at enhancing existing low-level selling skills with a major initiative aimed at retraining salespersons to become trusted financial advisers, capable of selling a broad range of newly introduced products to the three selected customer segments. The bank made both changes because the scorecard enabled it to gain a better understanding of the programs required to achieve its strategic objectives.

Once the strategy is defined and the drivers are identified, the scorecard influences managers to concentrate on improving or reengineering those processes most critical to the organization's strategic success. That is how the scorecard most clearly links and aligns action with strategy.

The final step in linking strategy to actions is to establish specific short-term targets, or milestones, for the balanced scorecard measures. Milestones are tangible expressions of managers' beliefs about when and to what degree their current programs will affect those measures.

In establishing milestones, managers are expanding the traditional budgeting process to incorporate strategic as well as financial goals. Detailed financial planning remains important, but financial goals taken by themselves ignore the three other balanced scorecard perspectives. In an integrated planning and budgeting process, executives continue to budget for short-term financial performance, but they also introduce short-term targets for measures in the customer, internal-business process, and learning-and-growth perspectives. With those milestones established, managers can continually test both the theory underlying the strategy and the strategy's implementation.

At the end of the business planning process, managers should have set targets for the long-term objectives they would like to achieve in all four scorecard perspectives; they should have identified the strategic initiatives required and allocated the necessary resources to those initiatives; and they should have established milestones for the measures that mark progress toward achieving their strategic goals.

FEEDBACK AND LEARNING

"With the balanced scorecard," a CEO of an engineering company told us, "I can continually test my strategy. It's like performing real-time research." That is exactly the capability that the scorecard should give senior managers: the ability to know at any point in its implementation whether the strategy they have formulated is, in fact, working, and if not, why.

The first three management processes—translating the vision, communicating and linking, and business planning—are vital for implementing strategy, but they are not sufficient in an unpredictable world. Together they form an important single-loop-learning process—single-loop in the sense that the objective remains constant, and any departure from the planned trajectory is seen as a defect to be remedied. This single-loop process does not require or even facilitate reexamination of either the strategy or the techniques used to implement it in light of current conditions.

Most companies today operate in a turbulent environment with complex strategies that, though valid when they were launched, may lose their validity as business conditions change. In this kind of environment, where new threats and opportunities arise constantly, companies must become capable of what Chris Argyris calls *double-loop learning*—learning that produces a change in people's assumptions and theories about cause-and-effect relationships. (See "Teaching Smart People How to Learn," HBR May–June 1991.)

Budget reviews and other financially-based management tools cannot engage senior executives in double-loop learning—first, because these tools address

performance from only one perspective, and second, because they don't involve strategic learning. Strategic learning consists of gathering feedback, testing the hypotheses on which strategy was based, and making the necessary adjustments.

The balanced scorecard supplies three elements that are essential to strategic learning. First, it articulates the company's shared vision, defining in clear and operational terms the results that the company, as a team, is trying to achieve. The scorecard communicates a holistic model that links individual efforts and accomplishments to business unit objectives.

Second, the scorecard supplies the essential strategic feedback system. A business strategy can be viewed as a set of hypotheses about cause-and-effect relationships. A strategic feedback system should be able to test, validate, and modify the hypotheses embedded in a business unit's strategy. By establishing short-term goals, or milestones, within the business planning process, executives are forecasting the relationship between changes in performance drivers and the associated changes in one or more specified goals. For example, executives at Metro Bank estimated the amount of time it would take for improvements in training and in the availability of information systems before employees could sell multiple financial products effectively to existing and new customers. They also estimated how great the effect of that selling capability would be.

Another organization attempted to validate its hypothesized cause-and-effect relationships in the balanced scorecard by measuring the strength of the linkages among measures in the different perspectives. (See the chart "How One Company Linked Measures from the Four Perspectives.") The company found significant correlations between employees' morale, a measure in the learning-and-growth perspective, and customer satisfaction, an important customer perspective measure. Customer satisfaction, in turn, was correlated with faster payment of invoices—a relationship that led to a substantial reduction in accounts receivable and hence a higher return on capital employed. The company also found correlations between employees' morale and the number of suggestions made by employees (two learning-and-growth measures) as well as between an increased number of suggestions and lower rework (an internal-business-process measure). Evidence of such strong correlations help to confirm the organization's business strategy. If, however, the expected correlations are not found over time, it should be an indication to executives that the theory underlying the unit's strategy may not be working as they had anticipated.

Especially in large organizations, accumulating sufficient data to document significant correlations and causation among balanced scorecard measures can take a long time—months or years. Over the short term, managers' assessment of strategic impact may have to rest on subjective and qualitative judgments. Eventually, however, as more evidence accumulates, organizations may be able to provide more objectively grounded estimates of cause-and-effect relationships. But just getting managers to think systematically about the assumptions underlying their strategy is an improvement over the current practice of making decisions based on short-term operational results.

Third, the scorecard facilitates the strategy review that is essential to strategic learning. Traditionally, companies use the monthly or quarterly meetings between corporate and division executives to analyze the most recent period's financial results. Discussions focus on past performance and on explanations of why financial objectives were not achieved. The balanced scorecard, with its specification of the causal relationships between performance drivers and objectives, allows corporate and business unit executives to use their periodic review sessions to evaluate the validity of the unit's strategy and the quality of its execution. If the unit's employees and managers have delivered on the performance drivers (retraining of employees, availability of information systems, and new financial products and services, for instance), then their failure to achieve the expected outcomes (higher sales to targeted customers, for example) signals that the theory underlying the strategy may not be valid. The disappointing sales figures are an early warning.

ONE COMPANY LINKED MEASURES FROM THE FOUR PERSPECTIVES

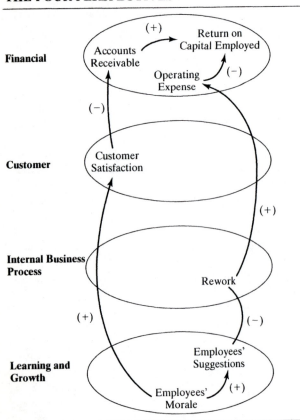

Managers should take such disconfirming evidence seriously and reconsider their shared conclusions about market conditions, customer value propositions, competitors' behavior, and internal capabilities. The result of such a review may be a decision to reaffirm their belief in the current strategy but to adjust the quantitative relationship among the strategic measures on the balanced scorecard. But they also might conclude that the unit needs a different strategy (an example of double-loop learning) in light of new knowledge about market conditions and internal capabilities. In any case, the scorecard will have stimulated key executives to learn about the viability of their strategy. This capacity for enabling organizational learning at the executive level—strategic learning—is what distinguishes the balanced scorecard, making it invaluable for those who wish to create a strategic management system.

TOWARD A NEW STRATEGIC MANAGEMENT SYSTEM

Many companies adopted early balanced scorecard concepts to improve their performance measurement systems. They achieved tangible but narrow results. Adopting those concepts provided clarification, consensus, and focus on the desired improvements in performance. More recently, we have seen companies expand their use of the balanced scorecard, employing it as the foundation of an integrated and iterative strategic management system. Companies are using the scorecard to

- clarify and update strategy,
- communicate strategy throughout the company,
- align unit and individual goals with the strategy,
- link strategic objectives to long-term targets and annual budgets,
- identify and align strategic initiatives, and
- conduct periodic performance reviews to learn about and improve strategy.

The balanced scorecard enables a company to align its management processes and focuses the entire organization on implementing long-term strategy. At National Insurance, the scorecard provided the CEO and his managers with a central framework around which they could redesign each piece of the company's management system. And because of the cause-and-effect linkages inherent in the scorecard framework, changes in one component of the system reinforced earlier changes made elsewhere. Therefore, every change made over the 30-month period added to the momentum that kept the organization moving forward in the agreed-upon direction.

Without a balanced scorecard, most organizations are unable to achieve a similar consistency of vision and action as they attempt to change direction and introduce new strategies and processes. The balanced scorecard provides a framework for managing the implementation of strategy while also allowing the strategy itself to evolve in response to changes in the company's competitive, market, and technological environments.

Robert S. Kaplan is the Arthur Lowes Dickenson Professor of Accounting at the Harvard Business School in Boston, Massachusetts. David P. Norton is the founder and president of Renaissance Solutions, a consulting firm in Lincoln, Massachusetts. They are the authors of "The Balanced Scorecard—Measures That Drive Performance"

(HBR January–February 1992) and "Putting the Balanced Scorecard to Work" (HBR September–October 1993). Kaplan and Norton have also written a book on the balanced scorecard to be published in September 1996 by the Harvard Business School Press.

QUESTION

9.1   According to Kaplan and Norton, one organization's members created a personal scorecard. What are the elements of this personal scorecard? Is this an effective tool for managers?

9.2 Transforming the Balanced Scorecard from Performance Measurement to Strategic Management: Part I

by Robert S. Kaplan and David P. Norton*

Several years ago we introduced the Balanced Scorecard (Kaplan and Norton 1992). We began with the premise that an exclusive reliance on financial measures in a management system is insufficient. Financial measures are lag indicators that report on the outcomes from past actions. Exclusive reliance on financial indicators could promote behavior that sacrifices long-term value creation for short-term performance (Porter 1992; AICPA 1994). The Balanced Scorecard approach retains measures of financial performance—the lagging outcome indicators—but supplements these with measures on the drivers, the lead indicators, of future financial performance.

THE BALANCED SCORECARD EMERGES

The limitations of managing solely with financial measures, however, have been known for decades.[1] What is different now? Why has the Balanced Scorecard concept been so widely adopted by manufacturing and service companies, nonprofit organizations, and government entities around the world since its introduction in 1992?

First, previous systems that incorporated nonfinancial measurements used *ad hoc* collections of such measures, more like checklists of measures for managers to keep track of and improve than a comprehensive system of linked measurements. The Balanced Scorecard emphasizes the linkage of measurement to strategy (Kaplan and Norton 1993) and the cause-and-effect linkages that describe the hypotheses of the strategy (Kaplan and Norton 1996b). The tighter connection between the measurement system and strategy elevates the role for nonfinancial measures from an operational checklist to a comprehensive system for strategy implementation (Kaplan and Norton 1996a).

Second, the Balanced Scorecard reflects the changing nature of technology and competitive advantage in the latter decades of the 20th century. In the industrial-age competition of the 19th and much of the 20th centuries, companies achieved competitive advantage from their investment in and management of tangible assets such as inventory, property, plant, and equipment (Chandler 1990). In an economy dominated by tangible assets, financial measurements were adequate to record investments on companies' balance sheets. Income statements could also capture the expenses associated with the use of these tangible assets to produce revenues and profits. But by the end of the 20th century, intangible assets became the major source for competitive advantage. In 1982, tangible book values represented 62% of industrial organizations' market values; ten years later, the ratio had plummeted to 38% (Blair 1995). By the end of the 20th century, the book value of tangible assets accounted for less than 20% of companies' market values (Webber 2000, quoting research by Baruch Lev).

Clearly, strategies for creating value shifted from managing tangible assets to knowledge-based strategies that create and deploy an organization's intangible assets. These include customer relationships, innovative products and services, high-quality and responsive operating processes, skills and knowledge of the workforce, the information technology that supports the work force and links the firm to its customers and suppliers, and the organizational climate that encourages innovation, problem-solving, and improvement. But companies were unable to adequately measure their intangible assets (Johnson and Kaplan 1987, 201–202). Anecdotal data from management publications indicated that many companies could not implement their new strategies in this

* From: R. S. Kaplan and D. P. Norton, "Transforming the Balanced Scorecard from Performance Measurement to Strategic Management: Part I," *Accounting Horizons* (March 2001), 15(1): 87–104.

environment (Kiechel 1982; Charan and Colvin 1999). They could not manage what they could not describe or measure.

INTANGIBLE ASSETS: VALUATION VS. VALUE CREATION

Some call for accountants to make an organization's intangible assets more visible to managers and investors by placing them on a company's balance sheet. But several factors prevent valid valuation of intangible assets on balance sheets.

First, the value from intangible assets is indirect. Assets such as knowledge and technology seldom have a direct impact on revenue and profit. Improvements in intangible assets affect financial outcomes through chains of cause-and-effect relationships involving two or three intermediate stages (Huselid 1995; Becker and Huselid 1998). For example, consider the linkages in the service management profit chain (Heskett et al. 1994):

- investments in employee training lead to improvements in service quality
- better service quality leads to higher customer satisfaction
- higher customer satisfaction leads to increased customer loyalty
- increased customer loyalty generates increased revenues and margins

Financial outcomes are separated casually and temporally from improving employees' capabilities. The complex linkages make it difficult, if not impossible, to place a financial value on an asset such as work force capabilities or employee morale, much less to measure period-to-period changes in that financial value.

Second, the value from intangible assets depends on organizational context and strategy. This value cannot be separated from the organizational processes that transform intangibles into customer and financial outcomes. The balance sheet is a linear, additive model. It records each class of asset separately and calculates the total by adding up each asset's recorded value. The value created from investing in individual intangible assets, however, is neither linear nor additive.

Senior investment bankers in a firm such as Goldman Sachs are immensely valuable because of their knowledge about complex financial products and their capabilities for managing relationships and developing trust with sophisticated customers. People with the same knowledge, experience, and capabilities, however, are nearly worthless to a financial services company such as etrade.com that emphasizes operational efficiency, low cost, and technology-based trading. The value of an intangible asset depends critically on the context—the organization, the strategy, and other complementary assets—in which the intangible asset is deployed.

Intangible assets seldom have value by themselves.[2] Generally, they must be bundled with other intangible and tangible assets to create value. For example, a new growth-oriented sales strategy could require new knowledge about customers, new training for sales employees, new data-bases, new information systems, a new organization structure, and a new incentive compensation program. Investing in just one of these capabilities, or in all of them but one, could cause the new sales strategy to fail. The value does not reside in any individual intangible asset. It arises from creating the entire set of assets along with a strategy that links them together. The value-creation process is multiplicative, not additive.

THE BALANCED SCORECARD SUPPLEMENTS CONVENTIONAL FINANCIAL REPORTING

Companies' balance sheets report separately on tangible assets, such as raw material, land, and equipment, based on their historic cost—the traditional financial accounting method. This was adequate for industrial-age companies, which succeeded by combining and transforming their tangible resources into products whose value exceeded their acquisition and production costs. Financial accounting conventions relating to depreciation and cost of goods sold enabled an income statement to measure how much value was created beyond the costs incurred to acquire and transform tangible assets into finished products and services.

Some argue that companies should follow the same cost-based convention for their intangible assets—capitalize and subsequently amortize the expenditures on training employees, conducting research and development, purchasing and developing databases, and advertising that creates brand awareness. But such costs are poor approximations of the realizable value created by investing in these intangible assets. Intangible assets can create value for organizations, but that does not imply that they have separable market values. Many internal and linked organizational processes, such as design, delivery, and service, are required to transform the potential value of intangible assets into products and services that have tangible value.

We introduced the Balanced Scorecard to provide a new framework for describing value-creating strategies that link intangible and tangible assets. The scorecard does not attempt to "value" an organization's intangible assets, but it does measure these assets in units other than currency. The Balanced Scorecard describes how intangible assets get mobilized and combined with intangible and tangible assets to create differentiating customer-value propositions and superior financial outcomes.

STRATEGY MAPS

Since introducing the Balanced Scorecard in 1992, we have helped over 200 executive teams design their scorecard programs. Initially we started with a clean sheet of paper, asking, "what is the strategy," and allowed the strategy and the Balanced Scorecard to emerge from interviews and discussions with the senior executives. The scorecard provided a framework for organizing strategic objectives into the four perspectives displayed in Figure 1):

1. *Financial*—the strategy for growth, profitability, and risk viewed from the perspective of the shareholder.
2. *Customer*—the strategy for creating value and differentiation from the perspective of the customer.
3. *Internal Business Processes*—the strategic priorities for various business processes that create customer and shareholder satisfaction.
4. *Learning and Growth*—the priorities to create a climate that supports organizational change, innovation, and growth.

From this initial base of experience, we subsequently developed a general framework for describing and implementing strategy that we believe can be as useful as the traditional framework of income statement, balance sheet, and statement of cash flows for financial planning and reporting. The new framework, which we call a "Strategy Map," is a logical and comprehensive architecture for describing strategy, as illustrated in Figure 2. A strategy map specifies the critical elements and their linkages for an organization's strategy.

- Objectives for growth and productivity to enhance shareholder value.
- Market and account share, acquisition, and retention of targeted customers where profitable growth will occur.
- Value propositions that would lead customers to do more higher-margin business with the company.
- Innovation and excellence in products, services, and processes that deliver the value proposition to targeted customer segments, promote operational improvements, and meet community expectations and regulatory requirements.
- Investments required in people and systems to generate and sustain growth.

FIGURE 1. THE BALANCED SCORECARD DEFINES A STRATEGY'S CAUSE-AND-EFFECT RELATIONSHIPS

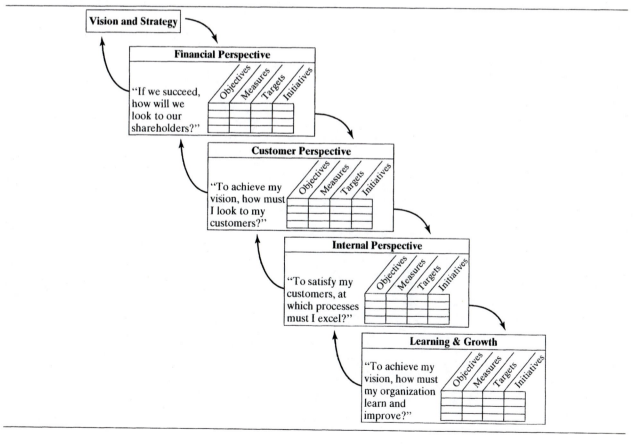

By translating their strategy into the logical architecture of a strategy map and Balanced Scorecard, organizations create a common and understandable point of reference for all organizational units and employees.

Organizations build strategy maps from the top down, starting with the destination and then charting the routes that lead there. Corporate executives first review their mission statement, why their company exists, and core values, what their company believes in. From that information, they develop their strategic vision, what their company wants to become. This vision creates a clear picture of the company's overall goal, which could be to become a top-quartile performer. The strategy identifies the path intended to reach that destination.

Financial Perspective. The typical destination for profit-seeking enterprises is a significant increase in shareholder value (we will discuss the modifications for nonprofit and government organizations later in the paper). Companies increase economic value through two basic approaches—*revenue growth* and *productivity*.[3] A revenue growth strategy generally has two components: build the franchise with revenue from new markets, new products, and new customers; and increase sales to existing customers by deepening relationships with them, including cross-selling multiple products and services,

and offering complete solutions. A productivity strategy also generally has two components: improve the cost structure by lowering direct and indirect expenses; and utilize assets more efficiently by reducing the working and fixed capital needed to support a given level of business.

Customer Perspective. The core of any business strategy is the *customer-value proposition*, which describes the unique mix of product, price, service, relationship, and image that a company offers. It defines how the organization differentiates itself from competitors to attract, retain, and deepen relationships with targeted customers. The value proposition is crucial because it helps an organization connect its internal processes to improved outcomes with its customers.

Companies differentiate their value proposition by selecting among *operational excellence* (for example, McDonalds and Dell Computer), *customer intimacy* (Home Depot and IBM in the 1960s and 1970s), and *product leadership* (Intel and Sony) (Treacy and Wiersema 1997, 31–45). Sustainable strategies are based on excelling at one of the three while maintaining threshold standards with the other two. After identifying its value proposition, a company knows which classes and types of customers to target.

FIGURE 2. THE BALANCED SCORECARD STRATEGY MAP

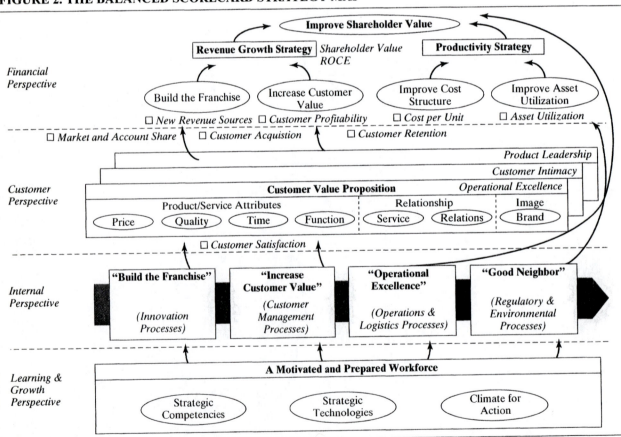

Specifically, companies that pursue a strategy of operational excellence need to excel at competitive pricing, product quality, product selection, lead time, and on-time delivery. For customer intimacy, an organization must stress the quality of its relationships with customers, including exceptional service, and the completeness and suitability of the solutions it offers individual customers. Companies that pursue a product-leadership strategy must concentrate on the functionality, features, and performance of their products and services.

The customer perspective also identifies the intended outcomes from delivering a differentiated value proposition. These would include market share in targeted customer segments, account share with targeted customers, acquisition and retention of customers in the targeted segments, and customer profitability.[4]

Internal Process Perspective. Once an organization has a clear picture of its customer and financial perspectives, it can determine the means by which it will achieve the differentiated value proposition for customers and the productivity improvements for the financial objectives. The internal business perspective captures these critical organizational activities, which fall into four high-level processes:

1. *Build the franchise* by spurring innovation to develop new products and services and to penetrate new markets and customer segments.
2. *Increase customer value* by expanding and deepening relationships with existing customers.
3. *Achieve operational excellence* by improving supply-chain management, internal processes, asset utilization, resource-capacity management, and other processes.
4. *Become a good corporate citizen* by establishing effective relationships with external stakeholders.

Many companies that espouse a strategy calling for innovation or for developing value-adding customer relationships mistakenly choose to measure their internal business process by focusing only on the cost and quality of their operations. These companies have a complete disconnect between their strategy and how they measure it. Not surprisingly, organizations encounter great difficulty implementing growth strategies when their primary internal measurements emphasize process improvements, not innovation or enhanced customer relationships.

The financial benefits from improvements to the different business processes typically occur in stages. Cost savings from increases in *operational efficiencies* and process improvements deliver short-term benefits. Revenue growth from enhancing *customer relationships* accrues in the intermediate term. Increased *innovation* generally produces long-term revenues and margin improvements. Thus, a complete strategy should generate returns from all three high-level internal processes.

Learning and Growth Perspective. The final region of a strategy map is the learning and growth perspective, which is the foundation of any strategy. In the learning and growth perspective, managers define the employee capabilities and skills, technology, and corporate climate needed to support a strategy. These objectives enable a company to align its human resources and information technology with the strategic requirements from its critical internal business processes, differentiated value proposition, and customer relationships. After addressing the learning and growth perspective, companies have a complete strategy map with linkages across the four major perspectives.

Strategy maps, beyond providing a common framework for describing and building strategies, also are powerful diagnostic tools, capable of detecting flaws in organizations' Balanced Scorecards. For example, Figure 3 shows the strategy map for the Revenue Growth theme of Mobil North America Marketing & Refining. When senior management compared the scorecards being used by its business units to this template, it found one unit with no objective or measure for dealers, an omission immediately obvious from looking at its strategy map. Had this unit discovered how to bypass dealers and sell gasoline directly to end-use consumers? Were dealer relationships no longer strategic for this unit? The business unit shown in the lower right corner of Figure 3 did not mention quality on its scorecard. Again, had this unit already achieved six sigma quality levels so quality was no longer a strategic priority? Mobil's executive team used its divisional strategy map to identify and remedy gaps in the strategies being implemented at lower levels of the organization.

STAKEHOLDER AND KEY PERFORMANCE INDICATOR SCORECARDS

Many organizations claim to have a Balanced Scorecard because they use a mixture of financial and nonfinancial measures. Such measurement systems are certainly more "balanced" than ones that use financial measures alone. Yet, the assumptions and philosophies underlying these scorecards are quite different from those underlying the strategy scorecards and maps are described above. We observe two other scorecard types frequently used in practice: the *stakeholder scorecard* and the *key performance indicator scorecard*.

FIGURE 3. MOBIL USES REVERSE ENGINEERING OF A STRATEGY MAP AS A STRATEGY DIAGNOSTIC

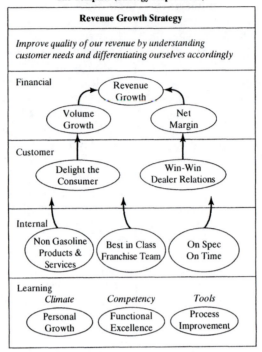

The Template (Strategy Map: Partial)

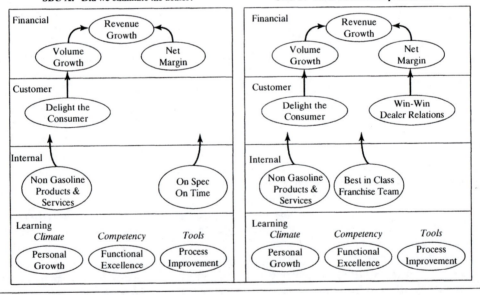

SBU A: "Did we eliminate the dealer?"   SBU B: "Have we achieved perfection?"

Stakeholder Scorecards. The *stakeholder scorecard* identifies the major constituents of the organization—shareholders, customers, and employees—and frequently other constituents such as suppliers and the community. The scorecard defines the organization's goals for these different constituents, or stakeholders, and develops an appropriate scorecard of measures and targets for them (Atkinson and Waterhouse 1997). For example, Sears built its initial scorecard around three themes:

- "a compelling place to shop"
- "a compelling place to work"
- "a compelling place to invest"

Citicorp used a similar structure for its initial scorecard—"a good place to work, to bank, and to invest."

AT&T developed an elaborate internal measurement system based on financial value-added, customer value-added, and people value-added.

All these companies built their measurements around their three dominant constituents—customers, shareholders, and employees—emphasizing satisfaction measures for customers and employees to ensure that these constituents felt well served by the company. In this sense, they were apparently *balanced*. Comparing these scorecards to the strategy map template in Figure 2 we can easily detect what is missing from such scorecards: no objectives or measures for *how* these balanced goals are to be achieved. A vision describes a desired outcome; a strategy, however, must describe *how* the outcome will be achieved, how employees, customers, and shareholders will be satisfied. Thus, a stakeholder scorecard is not adequate to describe the strategy of an organization and, therefore, is not an adequate foundation on which to build a management system.

Missing from the stakeholder card are the drivers to achieve the goals. Such drivers include an explicit value proposition such as innovation that generates new products and services or enhanced customer management processes, the deployment of technology, and the specific skills and competencies of employees required to implement the strategy. In a well-constructed *strategy scorecard*, the value proposition in the customer perspective, all the processes in the internal perspective, and the learning and growth perspective components of the scorecard define the "how" that is as fundamental to strategy as the outcomes that the strategy is expected to achieve.

Stakeholder scorecards are often a first step on the road to a strategy scorecard. But as organizations begin to work with stakeholder cards, they inevitably confront the question of "how." This leads to the next level of strategic thinking and scorecard design. Both Sears and Citicorp quickly moved beyond their stakeholder scorecards, developing an insightful set of internal process objectives to complete the description of their strategy and, ultimately, achieving a strategy Balanced Scorecard. The stakeholder scorecard can also be useful in organizations that do not have internal synergies across business units. Since each business has a different set of internal drivers, this "corporate" scorecard need only focus on the desired outcomes for the corporation's constituencies, including the communities and suppliers. Each business unit then defines how it will achieve those goals with its business unit strategy scorecard and strategy map.

Key Performance Indicator Scorecards. Key Performance Indicator (KPI) scorecards are also common. The total quality management approach and variants such as the Malcolm Baldrige and European Foundation for Quality Management (EFQM) awards generate many measures to monitor internal processes. When migrating to a "Balanced Scorecard," organizations often build on the base already established by classifying their existing measurements into the four BSC categories. KPI scorecards also emerge when the organization's information technology group, which likes to put the company database at the heart of any change program, triggers the scorecard design. Consulting organizations that sell and install large systems, especially so-called executive information systems, also offer KPI scorecards.

As a simple example of a KPI scorecard, a financial service organization articulated the 4Ps for its "balanced scorecard:"

1. Profits
2. Portfolio (size of loan volume)
3. Process (percent processes ISO certified)
4. People (meeting diversity goals in hiring)

Although this scorecard is more balanced than one using financial measures alone, comparing the 4P measures to a strategy map like that in Figure 2 reveals the major gaps in the measurement set. The company has no customer measures and only a single internal-process measure, which focuses on an initiative not an outcome. This KPI scorecard has no role for information technology (strange for a financial service organization), no linkages from the internal measure (ISO process certification) to a customer-value proposition or to a customer outcome, and no linkage from the learning and growth measure (diverse work force) to improving an internal process, a customer outcome, or a financial outcome.

KPI scorecards are most helpful for departments and teams when a strategic program already exists at a higher level. In this way, the diverse indicators enable individuals and teams to define what they must do well to contribute to higher-level goals. Unless, however, the link to strategy is clearly established, the KPI scorecard will lead to local but not global or strategic improvements.

Balanced Scorecards should not just be collections of financial and nonfinancial measures, organized into three to five perspectives. The best Balanced Scorecards reflect the strategy of the organization. A good test is whether you can understand the strategy by looking only at the scorecard and its strategy map. Many organizations fail this test, especially those that create stakeholder scorecards or key performance indicator scorecards.

Strategy scorecards along with their graphical representations on strategy maps provide a logical and comprehensive way to describe strategy. They communicate clearly the organization's desired outcomes and its hypotheses about how these outcomes can be achieved. For example, *if* we improve on-time delivery, *then* customer satisfaction will improve; *if* customer satisfaction improves, *then* customers will purchase more. The scorecards enable all organizational units and employees to understand the strategy and identify how they can contribute by becoming aligned to the strategy.

APPLYING THE BSC TO NONPROFITS AND GOVERNMENT ORGANIZATIONS

During the past five years, the Balanced Scorecard has also been applied by nonprofit and government organizations (NPGOs). One of the barriers to applying the scorecard to these sectors is the considerable difficulty NPGOs have in clearly defining their strategy. We reviewed "strategy" documents of more than 50 pages. Most of the documents, once the mission and vision are articulated, consist of lists of programs and initiatives, not the outcomes the organization is trying to achieve. These organizations must understand Porter's (1996, p. 77) admonition that strategy is not only what the organization intends to do, but also what it decides *not* to do, a message that is particularly relevant for the NPGOs.

Most of the initial scorecards of NPGOs feature an operational excellence strategy. The organizations take their current mission as a given and try to do their work more efficiently—at lower cost, with fewer defects, and faster. Often the project builds off of a recently introduced quality initiative that emphasizes process improvements. It is unusual to find nonprofit organizations focusing on a strategy that can be thought of as product leadership or customer intimacy. As a consequence, their scorecards tend to be closer to the KPI scorecards than true strategy scorecards.

The City of Charlotte, North Carolina, however, followed a customer-based strategy by selecting an interrelated set of strategic themes to create distinct value for its citizens (Kaplan 1998). United Way of Southeastern New England also articulated a customer (donor) intimacy strategy (Kaplan and Kaplan 1996). Other nonprofits—the May Institute and New Profit Inc.—selected a clear product-leadership position (Kaplan and Elias 1999). The May Institute uses partnerships with universities and researchers to deliver the best behavioral and rehabilitation care delivery. New Profit Inc. introduces a new selection, monitoring, and governing process unique among nonprofit organizations. Montefiore Hospital uses a combination of product leadership in its centers of excellence, and excellent customer relationships—through its new patient-oriented care centers—to build market share in its local area (Kaplan 2001). These examples demonstrate that NPGOs can be strategic and build competitive advantage in ways other than pure operational excellence. But it takes vision and leadership to move from continuous improvement processes to thinking strategically about which processes and activities are most important for fulfilling the organization's mission.

Modifying the Architecture of the Balanced Scorecard. Most NPGOs had difficulty with the original architecture of the Balanced Scorecard that placed the financial perspective at the top of the hierarchy. Given that achieving financial success is not the primary objective for most of these organizations, many rearrange the scorecard to place customers or constituents at the top of the hierarchy.

In a private-sector transaction, the customer plays two distinct roles—paying for the service and receiving the service—that are so complementary that most people don't even think about them separately. But in a nonprofit organization, donors provide the financial resources—they pay for the service—while another group, the constituents, receives the service. Who is the customer—the one paying or the one receiving? Rather than have to make such a Solomonic decision, organizations place both the donor perspective and the recipient perspective, in parallel, at the top of their Balanced Scorecards. They develop objectives for both donors and recipients, and then identify the internal processes that deliver desired value propositions for both groups of "customers."

In fact, nonprofit and government agencies should consider placing an over-arching objective at the top of their scorecard that represents their long-term objective such as a reduction in poverty or illiteracy, or improvements in the environment. Then the objectives within the scorecard can be oriented toward improving such a high-level objective. High-level financial measures provide private sector companies with an accountability measure to their owners, the shareholders. For a nonprofit or government agency, however, the financial measures are not the relevant indicators of whether the agency is delivering on its mission. The agency's mission should be featured and measured at the highest level of its scorecard. Placing an over-arching objective on the BSC for a nonprofit or government agency communicates clearly the long-term mission of the organization as portrayed in Figure 4.

Even the financial and customer objectives, however, may need to be re-examined for governmental organizations. Take the case of regulatory and enforcement agencies that monitor and punish violations of environmental, safety, and health regulations. These agencies, which detect transgressions, and fine or arrest those who violate the laws and regulations, cannot look to their "immediate customers" for satisfaction and loyalty measures. Clearly not; the true "customers" for such organizations are the citizens at large who benefit from effective but not harsh or idiosyncratic enforcement of laws and regulations. Figure 5 shows a modified framework in which a government agency has three high-level perspectives:

1. *Cost Incurred*: This perspective emphasizes the importance of operational efficiency. The measured cost should include both the expenses of the agency

and the social cost it imposes on citizens and other organizations through its operations. For example, an environmental agency imposes remediation costs on private-sector organizations. These are part of the costs of having the agency carry out its mission. The agency should minimize the direct and social costs required to achieve the benefits called for by its mission.

2. *Value Created*: This perspective identifies the benefits being created by the agency to citizens and is the most problematic and difficult to measure. It is usually difficult to financially quantify the benefits from improved education, reduced pollution, better health, less congestion, and safer neighborhoods. But the balanced scorecard still enables organizations to identify the outputs, if not the outcomes, from its activities, and to measure these outputs. Surrogates for value created could include percentage of students acquiring specific skills and knowledge; density of pollutants in water, air, or land; improved morbidity and mortality in targeted populations; crime rates and perception of public safety; and transportation times. In general, public-sector organizations may find they use more output than outcome measures. The citizens and their representatives—elected officials and legislators—will eventually make the judgments about the benefits from these outputs vs. their costs.

3. *Legitimizing Support*: An important "customer" for any government agency will be its "donor," the organization—typically the legislature—that provides the funding for the agency. In order to assure continued funding for its activities, the agency must strive to meet the objectives of its funding source—the legislature and, ultimately, citizens and taxpayers.

After defining these three high-level perspectives, a public-sector agency can identify its objectives for internal processes, learning, and growth that enable objectives in the three high-level perspectives to be achieved.

BEYOND MEASUREMENT TO MANAGEMENT

Originally, we thought the Balanced Scorecard was about performance measurement (Kaplan and Norton 1992). Once organizations developed their basic system for measuring strategy, however, we quickly learned that *measurement* has consequences far beyond reporting on the past. Measurement creates focus for the future. The measures chosen by managers communicate important messages to all organizational units and employees. To take full advantage of this power, companies soon integrated their new measures into a *management system*. Thus the Balanced Scorecard concept evolved from a performance measurement system to become the organizing framework, the operating system, for a new

strategic management system (Kaplan and Norton 1996c, Part II). The academic literature, rooted in the original performance measurement aspects of the scorecard, focuses on the BSC as a measurement system (Ittner et al. 1997; Ittner and Larcker 1998; Banker et al. 2000; Lipe and Salterio 2000) but has yet to examine its role as a management system.

Using this new strategic management system, we observed several organizations achieving performance breakthroughs within two to three years of implementation (Kaplan and Norton 2001a, 4–6, 17–22). The magnitude of the results achieved by the early adopters reveals the power of the Balanced Scorecard management system to focus the entire organization on strategy. The speed with which the new strategies deliver results indicates that the companies' successes are not due to a major new product or service launch, major new capital investments, or even the development of new intangible or "intellectual" assets. The companies, of course, develop new products and services, and invest in both hard, tangible assets, as well as softer, intangible assets. But they cannot benefit much in two years from such investments. To achieve their break-through performance, the companies capitalize on capabilities and assets—both tangible and intangible—that already exist within their organizations.[5] The companies' new strategies and the Balanced Scorecard unleash the capabilities and assets previously hidden (or frozen) within the old organization. In effect, the Balanced Scorecard provides the "recipe" that enables ingredients already existing in the organization to be combined for long-term value creation.

FIGURE 4. ADAPTING THE BALANCED SCORECARD FRAMEWORK TO NONPROFIT ORGANIZATIONS

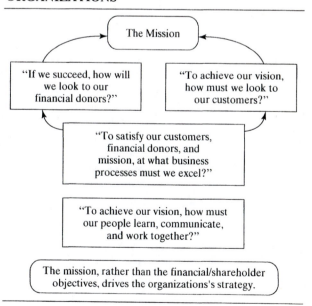

The Mission

"If we succeed, how will we look to our financial donors?"

"To achieve our vision, how must we look to our customers?"

"To satisfy our customers, financial donors, and mission, at what business processes must we excel?"

"To achieve our vision, how must our people learn, communicate, and work together?"

The mission, rather than the financial/shareholder objectives, drives the organizations's strategy.

FIGURE 5. THE FINANCIAL/CUSTOMER OBJECTIVES FOR PUBLIC SECTOR AGENCIES MAY REQUIRE THREE DIFFERENT PERSPECTIVES*

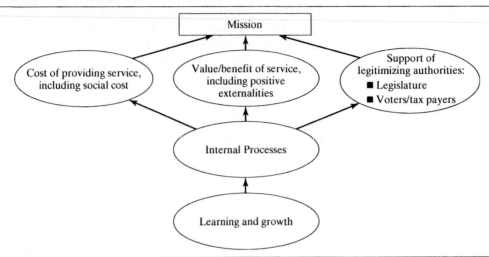

* Professor Dutch Leonard, Kennedy School of Government, Harvard University, collaborated to develop this diagram.

Part II of our commentary on the Balanced Scorecard (Kaplan and Norton 2001b) will describe how organizations use Balanced Scorecards and strategy maps to accomplish comprehensive and integrated transformations. These organizations redefine their relationships with customers, reengineer fundamental business processes, reskill the work force, and deploy new technology infrastructures. A new culture emerges, centered not on traditional functional silos, but on the team effort required to implement the strategy. By clearly defining the strategy, communicating it consistently, and linking it to the drivers of change, a performance-based culture emerges to link everyone and every unit to the unique features of the strategy. The simple act of describing strategy via strategy maps and scorecards makes a major contribution to the success of the transformation program.

ENDNOTES

American Institute of Certified Public Accountants (AICPA), Special Committee on Financial Reporting, 1994. *Improving Business Reporting—A Customer Focus: Meeting the Information Needs of Investors and Creditors*. New York, NY: AICPA.

Atkinson, A. A., and J. H. Waterhouse. 1997. A stakeholder approach to strategic performance measurement. *Sloan Management Review* (Spring).

Banker, R., G. Potter, and D. Srinivasan. 2000. An empirical investigation of an incentive plan that includes nonfinancial performance measures. *The Accounting Review* (January): 65–92.

Becker, B., and M. Huselid. 1998. High performance work systems and firm performance: A synthesis of research and managerial implications. In *Research in Personnel and Human Resources Management*, 53–101. Greenwich, CT: JAI Press.

Blair, B. B. 1995. *Ownership and Control: Rethinking Corporate Governance for the Twenty-First Century*. Washington, D.C.: Brookings Institution.

Chandler, A. D. 1990. *Scale and Scope: The Dynamics of Industrial Capitalism*. Cambridge, MA: Harvard University Press.

Charan, R., and G. Colvin. 1999. Why CEOs fail. *Fortune* (June 21).

Epstein, M., and J. F. Manzoni. 1998. Implementing corporate strategy: From Tableaux de Bord to Balanced Scorecards. *European Management Journal* (April).

Greenwood, R. G. 1974. *Managerial Decentralization: A Study of the General Electric Philosophy*. Lexington, MA: D. C. Heath.

Heskett, J., T. Jones, G. Loveman, E. Sasser, and L. Schlesinger. 1994. Putting the service profit chain to work. *Harvard Business Review* (March–April): 164–174.

Huselid, M. A. 1995. The impact of human resource management practices on turnover, productivity, and corporate financial performance. *Academy of Management Journal*: 635–672.

Ittner, C., D. Larcker, and M. Meyer. 1997. Performance, compensation, and the Balanced Scorecard. Working paper, University of Pennsylvania.

———, D. Larcker, and M. Rajan. 1997. The choice of performance measures in annual bonus contracts. *The Accounting Review* (April): 231–255.

———, and D. Larcker. 1998. Innovations in performance measurement: Trends and research implications. *Journal of Management Accounting Research*: 205–238.

Johnson, H. T., and R. S. Kaplan. 1987. *Relevance Lost: The Rise and Fall of Management Accounting*, Boston, MA: Harvard Business School Press.

Kaplan, R. S., and D. P. Norton. 1992. The Balanced Scorecard: Measures that drive performance. *Harvard Business Review* (January–February): 71–79.

———, and ———, 1993. Putting the Balanced Scorecard to work. *Harvard Business Review* (September–October): 134–147.

———, and E. L. Kaplan. 1996. United Way of Southeastern New England. Harvard Business School Case 197–036. Boston, MA.

———, and D. P. Norton. 1996a. Using the Balanced Scorecard as a strategic management system. *Harvard Business Review* (January–February): 75–85.

———, and ———. 1996b. Linking the Balanced Scorecard to strategy. *California Management Review* (Fall): 53–79.

———, and ———. 1996c. *The Balanced Scorecard: Translating Strategy Into Action.* Boston, MA: Harvard Business School Publishing.

———. 1998. City of Charlotte (A). Harvard Business School Case 199–036. Boston, MA.

———, and R. Cooper. 1998. *Cost and Effect: Using Integrated Cost Systems to Drive Profitability and Performance.* Boston, MA: Harvard Business School Press.

———, and J. Elias. 1999. New Profit, Inc.: Governing the nonprofit enterprise. Harvard Business School Case 100–052. Boston, MA.

———. 2001. Montefiore Medical Center. Harvard Business School Case 101–067. Boston, MA.

———, and D. P. Norton. 2000. Having trouble with your strategy? Then map it. *Harvard Business Review* (September–October): 167–176.

———, and ———. 2001a. *The Strategy-Focused Organization: How Balanced Scorecard Companies Thrive in the New Business Environment.* Boston, MA: Harvard Business School Press.

———, and ———. 2001b. Transforming the Balanced Scorecard from performance measurement to strategic management, Part II. *Accounting Horizons.* (forthcoming).

Kiechel, W. 1982. Corporate strategists under fire. *Fortune* (December 27): 38.

Lebas, M. 1994. Managerial accounting in France: Overview of past tradition and current practice. *European Accounting Review* 3 (3): 471–487.

Lipe, M., and S. Salterio. 2000. The Balanced Scorecard: Judgmental effects of common and unique performance measures. *The Accounting Review* (July): 283–298.

Porter, M. E. 1992. Capital disadvantage: America's failing capital investment system. *Harvard Business Review* (September–October).

———. 1996. What is strategy? *Harvard Business Review* (November–December).

Treacy, F., and M. Wierserma. 1997. *The Wisdom of Market Leaders.* New York, NY: Perseus Books.

Webber, A. M. 2000. New math for a new economy. *Fast Company* (January–February).

ENDNOTES

1. For example, General Electric attempted a system of nonfinancial measurements in the 1950s (Greenwood 1974), and the French developed the Tableaux de Bord decades ago (Lebas 1994; Epstein and Manzoni 1998).

2. Brand names, which can be sold, are an exception.

3. Shareholder value can also be increased through managing the right-hand side of the balance sheet, such as by repurchasing shares and choosing the low-cost mix among debt and equity instruments to lower the cost of capital. In this paper, we focus only on improved management of the organization's assets (tangible and intangible).

4. Measurement of customer profitability (Kaplan and Cooper 1998, 181–201) provides one of the connections between the Balanced Scorecard and activity-based costing.

5. These observations indicate why attempts to "value" individual intangible assets almost surely is a quixotic search. The companies achieved breakthrough performance with essentially the same people, services, and technology that previously delivered dismal performance. The value creation came not from any individual asset—tangible or intangible. It came from the coherent combination and alignment of existing organizational resources.

Robert S. Kaplan is a professor at Harvard University and David P. Norton is founder and president of the Balanced Scorecard Collaborative in Lincoln, MA.

QUESTIONS

9.2a What is a strategy map?

9.2b According to Kaplan and Norton, what are the two basic approaches to increasing economic value?

9.3 Transforming the Balanced Scorecard from Performance Measurement to Strategic Management: Part II

by Robert S. Kaplan and David P. Norton*

In a previous paper (Kaplan and Norton 2001b), we described the role for strategy maps and Balanced Scorecards to develop performance objectives and measures linked to strategy. With this paper, we show how organizations use their scorecards to align key management processes and systems to the strategy. We also discuss the relationship of the Balanced Scorecard (BSC) to other financial and cost measurement initiatives, such as shareholder value metrics and activity-based costing, and quality programs. We conclude with suggestions about opportunities for additional research on measurement and management systems.

THE FIVE PRINCIPLES OF A STRATEGY-FOCUSED ORGANIZATION

When asked to describe how the Balanced Scorecard helped them achieve breakthrough performance, executives of adopting organizations continually referred to two words: *alignment* and *focus* (Kaplan and Norton 2001 a, Chapter 1). Although each organization achieved strategic alignment and focus in different ways, at different paces and in different sequences, each eventually used a common set of five principles, which we refer to as the Principles of a Strategy-Focused Organization, portrayed in Figure 1.

Principle #1: Translate The Strategy to Operational Terms. Organizations translate their strategy into the logical architecture of a strategy map and Balanced Scorecard to specify in detail the critical elements for their growth strategies (Kaplan and Norton 2001 b). These create a common and understandable point of reference for all organizational units and employees.

Principle #2: Align the Organization to the Strategy. Organizations consist of numerous sectors, business units, and specialized departments, each with its own operations and often its own strategy. Functional departments, such as finance, manufacturing, marketing, sales, engineering, and purchasing, have their own bodies of knowledge, language, and culture. Functional silos arise and become a major barrier to strategy implementation since most organizations have great difficulty communicating and coordinating across these specialty functions. For organizational performance to be more than the sum of its parts, individual strategies must be linked and integrated. The corporate role defines the linkages expected to create synergy and ensures that the linkages actually occur.

FIGURE 1. THE PRINCIPLES OF A STRATEGY-FOCUSED ORGANIZATION

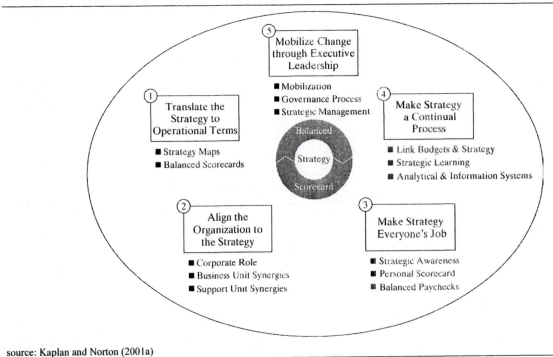

source: Kaplan and Norton (2001a)

* From: R. S. Kaplan and D. P. Norton. "Transforming the Balanced Scorecard from Performance Measurement to Strategic Management: Part II," *Accounting Horizons* (June 2001): 147–160.

Figure 2 shows the linkages at the Mobil North American Marketing and Refining division (NAM&R). The high-level strategic themes in #1 guide the development of the Balanced Scorecards in the business units in #2, which are either geographic regions or product lines, such as lubricants. Each unit formulates a strategy appropriate for its target market in light of the specific circumstances it faces—competitors, market opportunities, and critical processes—but that is consistent with the themes and priorities of NAM&R. The measures at the individual business-unit levels do not have to add to a divisional measure, unlike financial measures that aggregate easily from sub-units to departments to higher organizational levels. The business-unit managers choose local measures that *influence* but are not necessarily identical to the divisional scorecard measures.

Beyond aligning the business units, strategy-focused organizations must align their staff functions and shared service units, such as human resources, information technology, purchasing, environmental, and finance as in #3 of Figure 2. Often this alignment is accomplished with service agreements between each functional department and the business units. Management and cost accounting textbooks describe how to assign the costs of support departments to production departments and selling units. The scorecard approach is much more comprehensive. In addition to contracting on price or cost, the staff functions and the line business units agree to the menu of services to be provided, including their functionality, quality level, response time, and cost. This service agreement becomes the basis of the Balanced Scorecard constructed by the functional department. The department's customers are the internal business units, the value proposition is defined by the negotiated service agreement, and the financial objectives are derived from the negotiated budget for the department. Next, the department identifies the internal process and learning and growth objectives that drive its customer and financial objectives.

When this process is complete, all the organizational units—line business units and staff functions—have well-defined strategies that are articulated and measured by Balanced Scorecards and strategy maps. Because the local strategies are integrated, they reinforce each other. This alignment allows corporate-level synergies to emerge in which the whole exceeds the sum of the individual parts.

Linkages can also be established across corporate boundaries, as in #4 of Exhibit 2. Several companies constructed Balanced Scorecards to define their relationships with key suppliers, customers, outsourcing vendors, and joint ventures. Companies use such scorecards with external parties to be explicit about (1) the objectives of the relationship, and (2) how to measure the contribution and performance of each party to the relationship in ways other than just price or cost. Sometimes, particularly in governmental settings, scorecards are defined for high-level themes, such as salmon recovery in Washington State and economic development in the City of Charlotte, that encompass multiple departments and government agencies. No one department or agency has complete jurisdiction or ability to influence the desired outcomes. The scorecard for the high-level theme provides the mechanism that engages managers from multiple departments and agencies to discuss how they can contribute to achieving high-level strategic objectives.

FIGURE 2. ALIGNING THE ORGANIZATION TO ITS STRATEGY

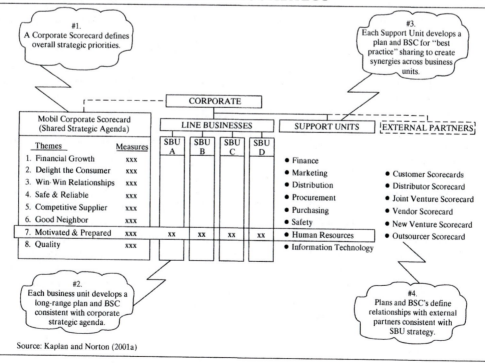

Source: Kaplan and Norton (2001a)

211

Principle #3: Make Strategy Everyone's Everyday Job. The CEOs and senior leadership teams of adopting organizations understood that they could not implement the new strategy by themselves. They wanted contributions—actions and ideas—from everyone in the organization. The third principle of strategy-focused organizations requires that all employees understand the strategy and conduct their day-to-day business in ways that contribute to the success of that strategy. This is not top-down *direction*. This is top-down *communication*. Senior managers understand that individuals far from corporate and regional headquarters can create considerable value by finding new and improved ways of doing business.

Executives start this process by using the Balanced Scorecard to *communicate* and *educate* the organization about the new strategy. Some observers are skeptical about communicating strategy to the entire organization, feeling that valuable information would be leaked to competitors. Mobil's Brian Baker's response was:

> Knowing our strategy will do them little good unless they can execute it. On the other hand, we have no chance of executing our strategy unless our people know it. It's a chance we'll have to take.

Companies can educate the employees about surprisingly sophisticated business concepts. To understand the scorecard, employees learn about customer segmentation, variable contribution margin, and database marketing. Instead of assuming that the workforce is incapable of understanding these ideas, managers make concerted efforts to educate employees at all levels of the organization about key strategic components.

Peter Drucker (1954) introduced management-by-objectives (MBO) nearly 50 years ago. But Drucker's excellent concept was implemented poorly in practice, leading to MBO in most organizations focusing on a myriad of local measures and initiatives not linked to high-level organizational objectives or coordinated with each other. The Balanced Scorecard enables personal objective setting to be integrated across the organization and linked to high-level strategic objectives.

Companies communicate their strategy and scorecard *holistically*. Instead of cascading objectives through the chain of command, as is normally done, they communicate the complete strategy down to individual employees. Individuals and departments at lower levels are challenged to develop their own objectives in light of the broader priorities; in some cases, personal scorecards are used to set *personal objectives*. Many pleasant surprises result from this process as individuals find new ways to do their jobs and identify areas outside their normal responsibilities to which they can contribute.

Finally, most organizations link *incentive compensation* to the Balanced Scorecard, typically after managing with the scorecard for a year. The executives must be confident that they are using sensible measures, have valid and reliable data collection processes to support the measures, and have measures not easily manipulated. Once they become confident about their measures and data, they turn the powerful compensation lever on. Brian Baker at Mobil declared:

> People got that scorecard out and did the calculations to see how much money they were going to get. We could not have gotten the same focus on the scorecard if we didn't have the link to pay.

Gerry Isom, CEO of Cigna Property and Casualty agreed:

> It would be hard to get people to accept a totally different way of measurement if you don't reinforce that change through incentive compensation.

A study of 214 companies reports that 88% of responding companies considered the use of Balanced Scorecard measures linked to reward systems to be effective (Mercer & Co. 1999).

Incentive systems based on the Balanced Scorecard vary widely. Some companies, such as Mobil, deploy a team-based incentive system, using business-unit and division scorecards as the basis for rewards. Others use a combination of business-unit, company, and individual performance rewards. Compensation can be based on up to 25 strategic measures. Instead of promoting confusion, as many fear, the scorecard compensation systems heighten the employees' interest in all components of the strategy and further their demand for knowledge and information about scorecard measures. Strategy becomes everyone's everyday job because employees now understand the strategy and are motivated to make it succeed.

Principle #4: Make Strategy A Continual Process. Most organizations build their management processes around the budget and operating plan. The monthly management meeting reviews performance vs. plan, discusses variances from past performance, and requests action plans for dealing with short-term variances. There is nothing wrong with this, *per se*. Tactical management is necessary. But in most organizations that's all there is. Besides the annual strategic-planning meeting, no meeting occurs where managers discuss strategy. We surveyed participants at conferences and learned that 85% of their management teams spend less than one hour per month discussing strategy.

The adopting BSC companies introduce a new "double-loop process" to manage strategy. The process integrates the management of tactics with the management of strategy, using three important processes, as depicted in Figure 3.

First, organizations *link strategy to the budgeting process*. They use the Balanced Scorecard as a screen to evaluate potential investments and initiatives. At Chemical Bank, where more than 70 different requests for funding were submitted, executives found that over 50% of the proposed initiatives had no impact on any scorecard measure. These were discarded as "nonstrategic." They also found that despite having more than three times as many proposed initiatives as scorecard measures, about 20% of the measures on the scorecard had no initiatives associated with improving them. A new process for managing strategic initiatives emerged that included authorizing funds for strategic initiatives within the annual budget process.

Companies usually have an *operational budget* that authorizes spending for producing and delivering existing products and services, and marketing and selling them to existing customers. They now introduce a *strategy budget* that enables them to develop entirely new capabilities, reach new customers and markets, and make radical improvements in existing processes and capabilities. This distinction is essential. Just as the Balanced Scorecard attempts to protect long-term objectives from short-term suboptimization, the budgeting process must protect the long-term initiatives from the pressures to deliver short-term financial performance.

The second step to make strategy a continual process introduces a *simple management meeting* to review strategy. As obvious as this step sounds, such meetings did not exist in the past. Now, management meetings are scheduled on a monthly or quarterly basis to discuss the Balanced Scorecard so that a broad spectrum of managers comes together to discuss the strategy. A new kind of energy is created. People use terms like "fun" and "exciting" to describe the meetings. One senior executive reported that the meetings became so popular, there was standing room only and he could have sold tickets to them.

Information feedback systems change to support the new management meetings. Initially, these systems are designed for the needs of the executive team. But organizations can go further by creating *open reporting* in which performance results are made available to everyone in the organization. Building upon the principle that "strategy is everyone's job," they empower "everyone" by giving them the knowledge needed to do their jobs. At Cigna Property & Casualty, a first-line underwriter sees performance reports before a direct-line executive if she happens to be monitoring the feedback system. This creates a set of cultural issues that revolutionize traditional, hierarchical approaches to information and power.

Finally, a *process for learning and adapting the strategy* evolves. The initial Balanced Scorecard represents hypotheses about the strategy; at time of formulation it is the best estimate of the actions expected to create long-term financial success. The scorecard design process makes the cause-and-effect linkages in the strategic hypotheses explicit. As the scorecard is put into action and feedback systems begin their reporting on actual results, an organization can test the hypotheses of its strategy. Some, like Brown & Root and Sears, did the testing formally, using statistical correlations between measures on the scorecard to determine whether, for example, employee empowerment programs were increasing customer satisfaction and improved processes. Others, like Chemical Bank, tested the hypotheses more qualitatively at meetings where managers validated and refined the programs being used to drive service quality and customer retention.

FIGURE 3. MAKING STRATEGY A CONTINUAL PROCESS

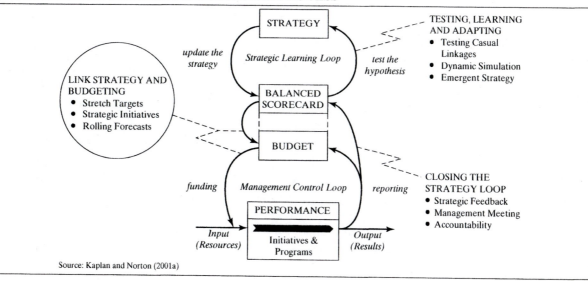

Source: Kaplan and Norton (2001a)

Still others use the meetings to search for new strategic opportunities that were not currently on their scorecard (see Mintzberg [1987] and Hamel [2000] for discussions of emergent strategy). Ideas and learning emerge continually from within the organization. Rather than waiting for next year's budget cycle, the priorities and the scorecards are updated immediately. Much like a navigator guiding a vessel on a long-term journey, constantly sensing the shifting winds and currents and constantly adapting the course, the executives of the successful companies use the ideas and learning generated by their organization to fine-tune their strategies. Instead of being an annual event, strategy formulation, testing, and revision became a continual process.

Using the Balanced Scorecard in this manner matches what Bob Simons (1995, Chapter 5; 2000, Chapter 10) describes as an interactive control system, characterized by four defining characteristics:

■ Information in the control system provides an important and recurring agenda for senior management.
■ The system demands frequent and regular attention from operating managers at all levels of the organization.
■ Date generated by the system are interpreted and discussed in face-to-face meetings of superiors, subordinates, and peers.
■ The system is a catalyst for the continual challenge and debate of underlying data, assumptions, and action plans.

Simons' research reveals how managers choose one system, such as the budget system, the revenue reporting system, or the project management system, and make it their interactive system. After that research was conducted, the Balanced Scorecard emerged to provide a general template for an organization's interactive system. Rather than having to choose one from the many existing systems, executives can design their own interactive system to focus intensely on strategy and its implementation. And the process of constructing their customized interactive system provides the additional benefit of team building and gaining coherence and commitment within the senior management team for the strategy. This leads naturally to the discussion of the fifth principle to create a strategy-focused organization.

Principle #5: Mobilize Leadership for Change. The first four principles focus on the Balanced Scorecard tool, framework, and the processes to support it. To become truly strategy-focused, however, requires more than processes and tools. Ownership and active involvement of the executive team is the single most important condition for success. Strategy requires change from virtually every part of the organization. Strategy requires teamwork to coordinate these changes. Strategy

implementation also requires continual focus on the change initiatives and on the performance against targeted outcomes. If those at the top are not energetic leaders of the process, change does not occur, strategy is not implemented, and the opportunity for breakthrough performance is lost.

A Balanced Scorecard program starts with the recognition that it is not a "metrics" project; it's a change project. Initially the focus is on *mobilization* and creating momentum, to get the process launched. Once mobilized, the focus shifts to *governance* to install the new performance model. Finally, and gradually over time, a new management system evolves, a *strategic management system* that institutionalizes the new cultural values and processes into a new system for managing. Convergence to the new management system can take two to three years.

In the mobilization phase, the leaders must make the organization understand why change is needed; the organization must be unfrozen. Kotter (1996) describes how transformational change begins at the top and with three discrete actions by the leaders: (1) establish a sense of urgency; (2) create the guiding coalition; and (3) develop a vision and a strategy. The leaders of successful Balanced Scorecard organizations clearly followed this mode. Several of the adopting companies were experiencing difficult times. The obvious threat of failure and loss of jobs was a motivator that created receptivity for change. But the role for the Balanced Scorecard to drive change and breakthrough performance is not limited to distressed or failing companies. Often, executives at companies currently doing well create stretch targets to ensure that the organization does not become complacent. They use the Balanced Scorecard to communicate a vision for dramatically better performance than the present. Executive leadership makes the need for change obvious to all.

Once the change process is launched, executives establish a *governance* process to guide the transition. This process defines, demonstrates, and reinforces the new cultural values to the organization. Breaking with traditional power-based structures is important. The creation of strategy teams, town hall meetings, and open communications are all components of the new management approach.

Embedding the new strategy and culture into a new management system, however, creates a risk that the organization fails to adapt to future shifts in opportunities and threats. Good executives recognize that strategies must continually evolve to reflect changes in the competitive landscape. The art of the leader is to delicately balance the tension between stability and change.

This concludes the summary of the five principles to become strategy-focused. We now turn to the relationship of the BSC to other improvement initiatives and to promising areas of future research.

RELATIONSHIP OF BSC TO OTHER ORGANIZATIONAL IMPROVEMENT INITIATIVES

The BSC emerged in the 1990s just as two other approaches—activity-based costing and shareholder value management—were being advocated as measurement systems to help managers improve organizational performance. The three approaches do not compete with each other; in fact they are highly compatible and while each can be implemented independently of the others, organizations will get the greatest benefit from integrating all three.

Shareholder Value Management. Shareholder value metrics, such as residual income, economic value-added, and shareholder value-added (Myers 1996, 1997), address two defects in traditional financial performance measurement: the overinvestment problem when only net income or earnings is used as the aggregate performance measure, and the underinvestment problem when a ratio—such as return-on-investment or return-on-equity—is used. We encourage managers who operate under a shareholder value discipline to use that metric as their overarching measure in the financial perspective. Within the financial perspective of the BSC, the shareholder value metric is decomposed into the subobjectives of cost reduction, improved asset productivity, and revenue growth (see strategy map template, Kaplan and Norton 2001b, Figure 2). Customer objectives define the strategy for revenue growth.

Managers operating only with shareholder value metrics, and without the more comprehensive BSC measurement framework, often take a low-risk and short-term path—reduce costs and dispose of underutilized assets—to achieve their financial improvements. Growing revenues typically takes longer, involves more risk, and requires more near-term spending to develop new products, services, and markets, enhance customer relationships, improve service, and increase employee capabilities. Nothing in shareholder value management is incompatible with revenue growth. But the financial metrics in a shareholder value approach cannot serve as a vehicle for articulating a revenue growth strategy and the complementary processes for achieving it. The BSC complements shareholder value management by defining the drivers of revenue growth—explicit objectives and measures for targeted customers, the differentiating customer value proposition, the internal business processes for innovation and enhanced customer relationships, and the needed infrastructure investments in people, systems, and organizational alignment. It also helps executives manage the trade-offs between short-term productivity improvements and long-term sustainable revenue growth.

Activity-Based Costing. Activity-based costing (ABC) was developed to correct another defect in financial systems—the inability of traditional costing systems to identify the drivers of indirect and support costs (Kaplan and Cooper 1998). ABC operates by relating organizational spending to activities and processes that support the design, production, marketing and delivery of products and services to customers.

Operational Linkage. The first linkage between ABC and the BSC occurs in the operational measures of the BSC's internal process perspective. Three parameters—cost, quality, and time—usually define the operating performance of any process. Quality and time are relatively easy to measure since they are based on physical measurements. Cost, however, is an analytic concept that cannot be measured by a stopwatch or a laser-gauging instrument. Only with an ABC model can organizational expenses be accurately traced to processes of product development, marketing and sales, manufacturing, distribution, and service delivery.

Customer Profitability Linkage. A second linkage occurs when an ABC model is used to measure the profitability of individual customers (Kaplan and Cooper 1998, Chapter 10). The BSC customer perspective typically includes customer outcome measures such as acquisition, satisfaction, retention, account share, and market share. But companies also need to measure whether their loyal, satisfied customers are profitable. Balancing measures such as customer profitability or percentage of unprofitable customers help managers ensure they are not improving their customer measures at the expense of high-level financial profitability measures.

Budgeting Linkage. A third linkage arises when the ABC model is used for activity-based budgeting: combining information on the forecasted volume and mix of products and services with anticipated activity and process efficiencies to construct a bottom-up budget for forthcoming periods (Kaplan and Cooper 1998, Chapter 15). With the BSC providing the management process for defining the strategic budget, and activity-based budgeting used to develop the operational budget (see discussion of these two budgets in Principle #4 above, "Making Strategy a Continual Process"), managers have powerful analytic tools for their budgeting processes.

ABC can also be combined with shareholder value management by applying ABC principles to assign assets to activities and then to cost objects. This enables capital costs and residual income to be calculated at the individual product and customer level.

Getting Started. Thus, shareholder value metrics, ABC, and the BSC play complementary roles. People often ask, "My organization has limited capacity for these major change initiatives. I can't do all three at the same time. Which should I do first?"

1. If the biggest problems facing an organization are large, growing indirect and support expenses, and inefficient processes, then implement ABC first. It gives managers a deep understanding of their cost structure, helps them to identify the most costly and nonvalue-added processes, and reveals how much of the growth in support resources can be reversed by taking appropriate actions with inefficient processes, complex products, or demanding customers.

2. If the organization has a low return on investment, a weak financial structure, a low sales-to-asset ratio, and high levels of working capital, then start with shareholder value management. The shareholder value approach highlights the inefficient use of capital and provides explicit incentives for managers to divest underperforming assets and increase the utilization of the remaining assets.

3. If the organization wishes to implement a major change in its strategy, or has just been restructured from a centralized, functional organization to a decentralized, customer-focused one, then start with the BSC. No other tool facilitates major changes in strategy better or faster.

Organizations ultimately benefit from all three measurement approaches: the financial and investment discipline that comes from adopting a shareholder value approach; the deep understanding of cost structure and cost drivers that activity-based costing provides; and the integrated framework for managing strategy, including value and revenue drivers, that the Balanced Scorecard delivers.

Total Quality Management. Many companies also engage in quality initiatives. The causal linkages in a BSC strategy map enhance quality programs by articulating the two ways that process improvements can link to strategic outcomes. First, quality improvements in the internal perspective should improve one or more outcome measures in the customer perspective; second, quality improvements can lead to cost reduction, an outcome in the financial perspective. The BSC enables managers to describe how they expect to translate quality improvements into higher revenues, fewer assets, less people, and lower spending.

The BSC process also guides organizations to redeploy their scarce resources of people and funds away from nonstrategic process improvements and toward those processes and initiatives most critical for implementing the strategy to achieve breakthrough customer and financial performance. In addition, building a Balanced Scorecard often reveals entirely new processes at which the organization must excel. Rather than just improving existing processes, the scorecard process focuses quality initiatives on improving the performance of these newly identified processes.

RESEARCH AGENDA ON ORGANIZATIONAL PERFORMANCE MANAGEMENT

During the past ten years, the Balanced Scorecard evolved from a performance measurement system to an organizing framework for successful strategy implementation. Changing what is measured profoundly affects the behavior of managers and employees, and helps organizations deliver dramatically improved performance. This is good news for accounting researchers. Accountants are in the measurement business and the experience of adopting companies reaffirms that *measurement matters*. Moreover, the experience affirms that *management control systems matter*. It's not just *what* is measured but *how* the measurements are used that determines organizational success. The impact of the scorecard is reinforced when it is used in a multiplicity of management processes: compensation (the most studied process by accounting researchers); alignment of diverse organizational units to a common strategy; communication and education; setting individual objectives; linking strategy, planning, resource allocation, and budgeting; setting targets; exploiting information technology for new reporting presentations; conducting management meetings interactively to promote testing, learning, and adaptation; and senior leadership's use of measurement to drive organizational change All these processes can be studied to assess their individual and collective effectiveness.

Some good empirical work tests the causal linkages that underlie the construction of strategy maps (Ittner and Larcker 1998; Banker et al. 2000). Interesting experimental work assesses how individuals respond to reports containing financial and nonfinancial data (Lipe and Salterio 2000; Swain et al. 1999). But these are only the beginning of promising research initiatives on performance measurement and management.

Analytic research can expand beyond contracting issues to address how synergies—nonlinear returns—are created when diverse individuals do their tasks in ways that are in phase with and reinforce each other. The successful BSC implementers did not hire new, more skilled employees. They did not work their employees harder or longer. They achieved the benefits by having their existing employees focus and align their efforts around a common strategy. Understanding how measurement yields nonlinear performance returns by coordinating and focusing employees' effort could be fertile ground for analytic modeling.

Empirical and experimental research can explore several important issues. How can targets with comparable degrees of difficulty be established across diverse business and shared service units? Mobil adopted a process they called "leveling" to put all units on a level playing field for rewards. It called for active involvement of senior staff specialists and managerial peers to review, challenge, and eventually ratify the targets proposed by decentralized units. The form of the reward is also of interest. Mobil's previous policy rewarded managers who achieved their targets, but gave zero rewards when performance fell short of targets. The new policy was a continuous reward function that increased with the degree of difficulty of the targets. As the CEO stated, "I prefer to give a better rating for a manager who stretches for a target and falls a little short, than to someone who beats an easy target." Just how to implement such a process in practice, of course, is a nontrivial task for which additional research could certainly be beneficial. Analytic schemes already exist for rewarding the achievement of stretch targets (Kaplan and Atkinson 1998, p. 773–780), but our experience with implementing these schemes in practice is quite limited.

The visibility of a manager's ability and effort is heightened when the BSC is used as an interactive control system. A Mobil senior executive claimed, "The process enables me to see how managers think, plan, and execute. I can see the gaps." Such increased observability of managers' performance allows companies to use subjective rewards based on ability and effort, not the second-best approach of rewarding only on results. Again, empirical and experimental research can investigate the effectiveness of subjective rewards based on such increased observability. How well are people making subjective evaluations and judgments? What kind of subjective judgments can we confidently allow individuals to make and in what circumstances?

Many organizations obtain substantial commitment and contributions from their employees without introducing incentive compensation based on BSC measures. Individuals want to be part of and contribute to a successful organization. Without the guidance of a BSC, however, employees are often just given a job to do, not an opportunity to find new and better ways to help the organization achieve its strategic objectives. Thus, research on the mix between intrinsic and extrinsic motivation can be effectively conducted with the communication and personal goal-setting processes of the BSC management system.

The multiplicity of management processes required to create strategic focus in an organization can be studied. Are all critical? Is success a multiplicative model in which the performance breakthroughs come from all processes being implemented effectively? Or can some processes be effective and deliver significant results without being reinforced by others? This research will likely require intense field research, probably by studying an implementation in a multi-unit organization, where different units adopted different aspects of the BSC management system. For example, some units might have implemented all five principles of a strategy-focused organization, while others did only one or two. How did this affect the resulting performance of all these units?

During the past ten years, many organizations of all types and in all geographic areas adopted performance management systems that use a mixture of financial and nonfinancial metrics. In these two papers, we present a framework that describes the measurement and management systems of successful organizations we observe in practice. With the widespread availability of organizational implementations and a framework to describe how the implementations were performed, accounting researchers can now begin a systematic research program, using multiple research methods, to explore the key factors in implementing more effective measurement and management systems. Such a systematic exploration provides a valuable complement to the individual case studies to be produced in the years ahead.

ENDNOTES

Banker, R., G. Potter, and D. Srinivasan. 2000. An empirical investigation of an incentive plan that includes nonfinancial performance measures. *The Accounting Review* (January): 65–92.

Drucker, P. 1954. *The Practice of Management*. New York, NY: HarperBusiness.

Hamel, G. 2000. *Leading the Revolution*. Boston, MA: HBS Press.

Ittner, C., and D. Larcker. 1998. Are nonfinancial measures leading indicators of financial performance? An analysis of customer satisfaction. *Journal of Accounting Research*: 1–35.

Kaplan, R. S., and A. A. Atkinson. 1998. *Advanced Management Accounting*. Third edition. Upper Saddle River, NJ: Prentice Hall.

— — —, and R. Cooper. 1998. *Cost & Effect: Using Integrated Cost Systems to Drive Profitability and Performance*. Boston, MA: HBS Press.

— — —, and D. P. Norton. 2001a. *The Strategy-Focused Organization*. Boston, MA: Harvard Business School Press.

— — —, and — — —. 2001b. Transforming the balanced scorecard from performance measurement to strategic management: Part I. *Accounting Horizons* (March): 87–104.

Kotter, J. 1996. *Leading Change*. Boston, MA: HBS Press.

Lipe, M., and S. Salterio. 2000. The balanced scorecard: Judgmental effects of common and unique performance measures. *The Accounting Review* (July): 283–298.

Mercer, William M. & Co. 1999. Rewarding employees: Balanced scorecard fax-back survey results. May 20. London, U.K.

Mintzberg, H. 1987. Crafting strategy. *Harvard Business Review* (July–August).

Myers. R. 1996. Metric wars. *CFO Magazine* (October).

— — —. 1997. Measure for measure. *CFO Magazine* (November).

Simons, R. 1995. *Levers of Control*. Boston, MA: HBS Press.

— — —. 2000. *Performance Measurement & Control Systems for Implementing Strategy*. Upper Saddle River, NJ: Prentice Hall.

Swain M., K. Krumwiede, and T. Eaton. 1999. Effects of balanced scorecard performance measures on decision process and design quality. Working paper, Brigham Young University.

Robert S. Kaplan is a Professor at Harvard University and David P. Norton is founder and president of the Balanced Scorecard Collaborative in Lincoln, MA.

QUESTION

9.3 Describe the five principles of a Strategy-Focused Organization.

9.4 Pitney Bowes Calls for New Metrics
The company used a balanced scorecard to manage performance and increase the bottom line.

*by Mark Green, Jeanine Garrity, Andra Gumbus, and Bridget Lyons**

The importance of measuring strategy and action plans is here to stay. Too often, mission statements are designed to sound good but are not linked to operational strategies and are seldom re-examined to see if they are working effectively. That's why savvy companies are using a scorecard.

Whether it's the balanced scorecard (BSC) or some other type of approach, using some kind of scorecard drives senior management to link the company's mission to strategy and then translate the strategy into operational objectives and measures. Employees can be evaluated in this context through metrics that measure progress toward stated objectives. This leads to an employee base, whether of five or 5,000, working toward the same goals.

Pitney Bowes Inc. (PBI) is one company that believes in the balanced scorecard. At PBI the basis is in place with a newly defined mission statement, individual objectives linked to the mission, and metrics designed to measure progress toward achieving those objectives. The company has been successful on several fronts. In fact, the balanced scorecard approach helped PBI to improve a process in its core business and ultimately saved the company millions. Headquartered in Stamford, Conn., PBI is a $4 billion global provider of integrated mail and document management solutions. The company serves more than two million businesses of all sizes through dealer and direct operations. A key implementation of the BSC methodology took place in the company's core business—Pitney Bowes Mailing System (PBMS), the worldwide leader in advanced mailing solutions. The company's mission is to provide customers high-quality solutions that allow documents to be mailed without shifting focus from core competencies.

DEEP ROOTS IN THE BSC

PBI has worked with a balanced scorecard since 1993 when the president of Pitney Bowes Mailing Systems made a request to create a concise, timely reporting tool that would provide accurate information on the business. The president originally assigned the project to the IT department, but it wasn't accomplished, so within that same year the CEO gave Finance the task to create the metrics and reporting system within a six-month time frame. The BSC's main purpose was to be used to assimilate data coming from a variety of sources, observe trends, and combine this data into one easy-to-use source for the decision makers to make quick, informed decisions. Mark Green, then director of financial planning, worked fulltime on the project and focused on the following criteria:

- **Cost**—Funds should be limited (the project cost $50,000 to implement).
- **Quality**—The CEO wanted user-friendly computer access to all pertinent information.
- **Speed**—The time frame for accomplishing the task was six months.

DESIGN AND IMPLEMENTATION

Three full-time staff members plus two to three part-time staff helped Green create the balanced scorecard. He sought input on measures and received requests for over 500 critical measures to assess performance of the business. Task forces of all employee levels worked to narrow the massive list to 55 key metrics that they rated on a Priority Worksheet using a 1–6 scale with some of the following criteria:

- Importance to the business,
- Electronically reportable,
- Routinely reported,
- Accurate,
- Critical to objectives.

---

* From: M. Green, J. Garrity, A. Gumbus, and B. Lyons, "Pitney Bowes Calls for New Metrics," *Strategic Finance* (May 2002): 30–35.

FIGURE 1: IMPLEMENTING CONTINUOUS IMPROVEMENT EFFORTS BY PERFORMING PERIODIC AND SYSTEMATIC STRATEGIC REVIEWS

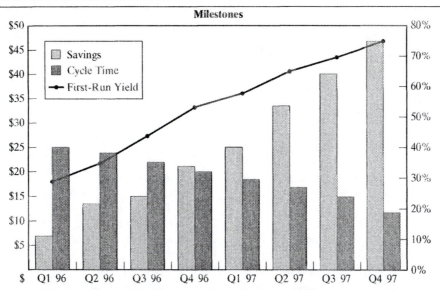

What resulted from Green's research was an Executive Information System that featured a user-friendly, picture icon-based tool enabling instant access to not only the 55 key metrics on the BSC but also the closing stock price and news about the company. It was organized by five objectives: business results, competitiveness, quality, employees, and carriers.

- **Business results metrics** are financial in nature, measuring key performance indicators (KPIs) related to revenue, net income, and cash flow.
- **Competitiveness** measures productivity and quality through items such as cycle time, first-run yield (FRY), turnover or revenue metrics, and performance relative to competitors. (Cycle time is the duration a given process takes as measured in minutes, hours, days, etc. For example, the cycle time to develop a new product might be 18 months with an objective to drive to less than one year. FRY measures the efficiency of a given operation. For instance, a process that takes place between two points and is 90% efficient would have a FRY of 81% (90% × 90%). The lower number of steps and more efficient, the higher the yield.) See Figure 1 for an example of a report.
- **Quality** measures include results of surveys relating to customer care, loyalty, and retention.
- **Employee metrics** include items that focus on people development and diversity.
- **The carrier objective** relates to activities of the various posts (such as Deutshe Post in Germany, Royal Mail in the UK, or LaPoste in France) or carriers (such as FedEx, UPS, or DHL) around the world.

The balanced scorecard changed the way the company measured areas within these five objectives. Take customer satisfaction within the quality objective as an example. Customer satisfaction metrics were historically gathered in two quality surveys, one for initial quality of new Pitney Bowes customers who had never purchased a particular piece of equipment and one for continuing quality for those who renewed their lease or had placed a service call. The resulting reports were so cumbersome that it was difficult for top management to act on the customer satisfaction data and to determine what the customer really wanted the company to improve.

To turn this around, Green and his staff uses SAS, a statistical software package, to analyze the 10 questions on the survey to determine which qualities were significantly correlated to high customer satisfaction. They further analyzed these qualities using a quadrant analysis to determine the importance to the customer as well as the company's measured performance. In this way, PBI prioritized the items that needed attention according to what was critical to their customers. The end result: a much more understandable, easier-to-use approach to determining customer satisfaction levels.

EVOLUTION OF THE BALANCED SCORECARD
In expanding its BSC to identify performance metrics for specific projects, such as identifying competitive cost structure, Pitney Bowes Mailing Systems compiled desired metrics from senior managers and objective criteria for the selection process, then used gap analysis to generate a list of targets and actions required to achieve those targets. The company compiled information, both internal financial and nonfinancial data, and obtained

similar information from sister companies and those with best practices in the industry. Comparing income statements, balance sheets, and ratios provided the company with an "income statement perspective" and gave insights to the division, or a rough idea, of how internally competitive it was with other PBI units. Then the company performed comparisons regarding sale, rental, and service business to provide a market perspective they could compare to other benchmarked companies. At the end of this exercise, a list of 30 to 35 issues identified competitive gaps. They grouped these issues into five broad categories, which were their core competencies: order management, integrated supply chain, sales, service, and manufacturing. These are the basic drivers or areas where their costs were concentrated, so after they identified and categorized the gaps, Green and his team quantified closing those gaps in dollar terms.

The gap analysis included a careful study of key processes and captured performance measures important to the key processes. Key measures emerged, which led to the next phase of BSC reporting. One specific initiative that emerged as a result of the gap analysis involved the order management process as one of five processes to analyze. The initiative improved the process of presenting product offerings and prices to customers, and, as a result, the company saved millions and achieved a twofold increase in the first-run yield of their order management process. Here's how the project unfolded.

The order management process at Pitney Bowes Mailing Systems focused on three types of orders: simple, complex, and compound. A simple order could take as few as eight days to process, a complex order as long as six months. Analysis showed that most orders are compound and take 25 days to process on average (eight to 10 days just to satisfy U.S. Postal Service postal license requirements) and entail a combination of more than 20,000 product variables the sales force had to sort and analyze in order to accurately post the order. Next, the sales force had to deliver the order to customer service to enter the order, and on the initial analysis of the first-run yield, only one out of three orders was fulfilled correctly from more than eight different process points.

The order management team spent four to five months analyzing the components of the process such as sales, call center, distribution, logistics, order pulling and packing, loading dock, customer service, and installation. The team decided to focus on the order-entry component since it triggered all other aspects of the workflow.

Many hands touched this complex order-entry process. Sales determined the combination of product codes from more than 20,000 options, and the call center personnel ultimately put the order through. Individual personalities and work styles came into play as well. For example, together the sales representative and the order-entry staff made subjective decisions about pricing to avoid repeated encounters with the customer that might reflect a larger quote than sales originally made. The result: lack of standardization, waste, confusion, errors, and much variation in the process.

The analysis also showed that compound orders have relatively few products that make up the majority of the orders. The team selected a solution to reduce this variation and decided to implement Smart Value Packages that bundled the products under one price and code to eliminate confusion. A pilot of salespeople around the country participated using laptops and watched their productivity soar as a result of selling the newly created packages.

With the help of IT support, the call center was automatically updated with standard pricing for the packages. Prior to this pilot the company didn't have a sales force automation tool, and many of the reps didn't have laptops. Thanks to the pilot, first-run yield increased to 75%, or three out of four orders processed perfectly, and cycle time was reduced from 25 to 19 days. Today Pitney Bowes Mailing Systems has supplied the entire sales force with Sales Force Automation tools, and most reps use laptops for order management.

SUCCESSES AND CHALLENGES

After seeing success in areas such as order management, a corporate initiative to develop a company-wide scorecard was begun in 2000. Approximately 200 performance metrics were identified for business units throughout PBI, and they fall into four categories: customer, financial, operational, and employee. These metrics encompassed some of the ones already used at the business unit level such as those identified for the Mailing System Unit. By the end of 2000, approximately 100 balanced scorecard metrics were accumulated and available through an internal website for management to use.

Presentation of the BSC on the Web is graphical—to identify trends—and numerical. A traffic light approach using red, yellow, and green is planned to identify metrics that are below, at, or above, targeted results. Financial analysts and managers at PBI are using the system to signal red flags earlier in the business cycle and to evaluate the quality of end-of-quarter and end-of-year forecasts so the company can implement corrective action plans if necessary.

Because of the information the balanced scorecard can supply, the nature of the monthly financial meetings changed from a focus on the five things PBI is doing well to the three things they need to improve, with emphasis on an appropriate action plan. The BSC also has helped the company focus on how to retain customers by conducting an analysis of who the top customers of PBI are and how they should be measured and managed.

The BSC has also been linked to the capital budgeting process. The capital budgeting process now requires a definition of how an expenditure relates to the company's strategy, how it will be measured, and what the return on investment will be.

The CFO plans to use an abbreviated version of the balanced scorecard to lead discussions with the top executive team and the board of directors. In addition, the BSC is used in meetings with investors, stockholders, and industry analysts to report timely financial information. Future challenges are to integrate strategic initiatives and company strategy into the BSC model.

LESSONS LEARNED

PBI employees have learned a great deal through implementing the BSC. Here are a few of the lessons:

- Remember that the BSC will never be 100% correct since it's a dynamic document under constant revision.
- Get the BSC done quickly, and start using it, even if it isn't perfect.
- Expert feedback from all levels, and ensure the system is flexible enough to make modifications.
- Get and maintain communication upward and downward in the organization during implementation.
- Stay flexible because the card will change, and don't take requested modifications personally.
- Accept the fact that some metrics are reported manually and aren't fully automated.
- Assign full-time staff to the BSC because it isn't a part-time endeavor or a rotational assignment.
- Ensure the project champion possesses a blend of many skills: accounting, finance, analytical, written, and verbal communication skills. Beyond these skills, this person must also be respected in the business as well as knowledgeable about the business.

PBI has a company culture that is process- and performance-measurement oriented, so the balanced scorecard is a natural in this environment. That's why it's continually updated and modified as a living document that reflects decisions about what the company wants to measure, how it will be measured, and at what frequency. Using the BSC, PBI can predict market trends and determine its future as this 80-year-old company looks forward to the next 80 years.

Mark Green is now the vice president and general manager of Mailcode Inc., a 57%-owned Pitney Bowes subsidiary headquartered in Lafayette, Ind.

Jeanine Garrity is project manager of finance in the financial planning and analysis group at Pitney Bowes in Stamford, Conn.

Andra Gumbus, Ed.D., is an assistant professor at Sacred Heart University in Fairfield, Conn. She was the former director of training and development at Philips Medical System North America.

Bridget Lyons, D.P.S., is assistant professor in the finance department at Sacred Heart University in Fairfield, Conn., and can be reached at (203) 365-7673 or lyonsb@sacredheart.edu.

QUESTION

9.4   What were the eight lessons that Pitney Bowes Inc. learned by implementing the Balanced Scorecard?

9.5 Measuring the Strategic Readiness of Intangible Assets

by Robert S. Kaplan and David P. Norton *

How VALUABLE IS A COMPANY culture that enables employees to understand and believe in their organization's mission, vision, and core values? What's the payoff from investing in a knowledge management system or in a new customer database? Is it more important to improve the skills of all employees or focus on those in just a few key positions?

Measuring the value of such intangible assets is the holy grail of accounting. Employees's skills. IT systems, and organizational cultures are worth far more to many companies than their tangibles assets. Unlike financial and physical ones, intangible assets are hard for competitors to imitate, which makes them a powerful source of

sustainable competitive advantage. If manages could find a way to estimate the value of their intangible assets, they could measure and manage their company's competitive position much more easily and accurately.

But that's simpler said than done. Unlike financial and physical assets, intangible assets are worth different things to different people. An oil well, for example, is almost as valuable to retail firm as it is to an oil exploration corporation because either company could sell it swiftly if necessary. But a workforce with a strong sense of customer service and satisfaction is worth far more to the retailer than it would be to the oil company. Also, unlike tangible assets, intangible assets almost never

---

create value by themselves. They need to be combined with other assets. Investments in IT, for example, have little value unless complemented with HR training and incentive programs. And, conversely, many HR training programs have little value unless complemented with modern technology tools. HR and IT investments must be integrated and aligned with corporate strategy if the organization is to realize their full potential. Indeed, when companies separate functions like HR and IT organizationally, they usually end up with competing silos of technical specialization. The HR department argues for increases in employee training, while the IT department lobbies for buying new hardware and software packages.

What's more, intangible assets seldom affect financial performance directly. Instead, they work indirectly through complex chains of cause and effect. Training employees in Total Quality Management and Six Sigma, for instance, should improve process quality. That improvement should then increase customer satisfaction and loyalty— and also create some excess resource capacity. But only if the company can transform that loyalty into improved sales and margins and eliminate or redeploy the excess resources will the investment in training pay off. By contrast, the impact of a new tangible asset is immediate: When a retailer develops a new site, it sees financial benefits from the sales in the newly opened outlet right away.

Although these characteristics make it impossible to value intangible assets on a freestanding basis, they also point the way to a new approach for quantifying how intangible assets add value to the company. By understanding the problems associated with valuing intangible assets, we learn that the measurement of the value they create is embedded in the context of the strategy the company is pursuing. Companies such as Dell, Wal-Mart, or McDonald's that are following a low-cost strategy derive value from Six Sigma and TQM training because their strategies are predicated on continuous process improvement. The strategy of offering customers integrated solutions (rather than discrete products) pursued by Goldman Sachs, IBM Consulting, and the like requires employees good at establishing and maintaining longterm customer relationships. An organization cannot possibly assign a meaningful financial value to an intangible asset like "a motivated and prepared workforce" in a vacuum because value can be derived only in the context of the strategy. What the company *can* measure, however, is whether its workforce is properly trained and motivated to pursue a particular goal.

Viewed in this light, it becomes clear that measuring the value of intangible assets is really about estimating how closely aligned those assets are to the company's strategy. If the company has a sound strategy and if the intangible assets are aligned with that strategy, then the assets will create value for the organization. If the assets are not aligned with the strategy or if the strategy is flawed, then intangible assets will create little value, even if large amounts have been spent on them.

In the following pages, we will draw on the concepts and tools of the Balanced Scorecard to present a way to systematically measure the alignment of the company's human, information, and organization capital – what we call its *strategic readiness* – without which even the best strategy cannot succeed.

THE STRATEGY MAP

The strategy map provides a framework for linking intangible assets to shareholder value creation through four interrelated perspectives. The *financial perspective* describes the tangible outcomes of the strategy in traditional financial terms, such as ROI, shareholder value, profitability, revenue growth, and lower unit costs. The *customer perspective* defines the value proposition the organization intends to use to generate sales and loyalty from targeted customers. This value proposition forms the context in which the intangible assets create value. The *internal process perspective* identifies the critical few processes that create and deliver the differentiating customer value proposition. At the foundation of the map, we have the *learning and growth perspective*, which identifies the intangible assets that are most important to the strategy. The objectives in this perspective identify which jobs (the human capital), which systems (the information capital), and what kind of climate (the organization capital) are required to support the value-creating internal processes. These intangible assets must be integrated and aligned with the critical internal processes.

DEFINING STRATEGIC READINESS

In developing the Balanced Scorecard more than a decade ago, we identified, in its Learning and Growth Perspective, three categories of intangible assets essential for implementing any strategy:

- **Human Capital:** the skills, talent, and knowledge that a company's employees possess.
- **Information Capital:** the company's databases, information systems, networks, and technology infrastructure.
- **Organization Capital:** the company's culture, its leadership, how aligned its people are with its strategic goals, and employees' ability to share knowledge.

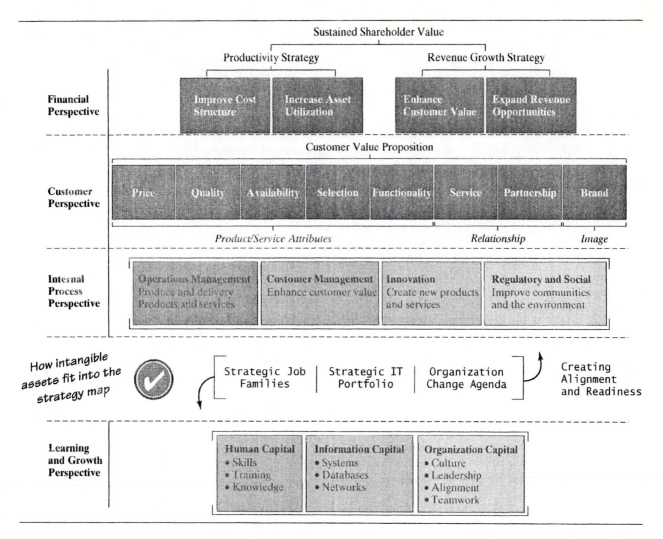

Sustained Shareholder Value

Productivity Strategy   Revenue Growth Strategy

Financial Perspective

| Improve Cost Structure | Increase Asset Utilization | Enhance Customer Value | Expand Revenue Opportunities |

Customer Perspective

Customer Value Proposition

| Price | Quality | Availability | Selection | Functionality | Service | Partnership | Brand |

Product/Service Attributes   *Relationship*   *Image*

Internal Process Perspective

| **Operations Management** Produce and delivery Products and services | **Customer Management** Enhance customer value | **Innovation** Create new products and services | **Regulatory and Social** Improve communities and the environment |

How intangible assets fit into the strategy map ✓ | Strategic Job Families | Strategic IT Portfolio | Organization Change Agenda | Creating Alignment and Readiness

Learning and Growth Perspective

| **Human Capital** • Skills • Training • Knowledge | **Information Capital** • Systems • Databases • Networks | **Organization Capital** • Culture • Leadership • Alignment • Teamwork |

To link these intangible assets to a company's strategy and performance, we developed a tool called the "strategy map," which we first introduced in our previous article for *Harvard Business Review*, "Having Trouble with Your Strategy? Then Map It" (September–October 2000). As the exhibit "The Strategy Map" shows, intangible assets influence a company's performance by enhancing the internal processes most critical to creating value for customers and shareholders. Companies build their strategy maps from the top down, starting with their long-term financial goals and then determining the value proposition that will deliver the revenue growth specified in those goals, identifying the processes most critical to creating and delivering that value proposition, and, finally, determining the human, information, and organization capital the processes require.

This article focuses on the bottom – the foundation – of the map and will show how intangible assets actually determine the performance of the critical internal processes. Once that link has been established, it becomes easy to trace the steps back up the map to see exactly how intangible assets relate to the company's strategy and performance. That, in turn, makes it possible to align those assets with the strategy and measure their contribution to it. The degree to which the current set of assets does – or does not–contribute to the performance of the critical internal processes determines the strategic readiness of those assets and thus their value to the organization. The strategic readiness of each type of intangible asset can be thought of as follows:

Human Capital (HC): In the case of human capital, strategic readiness is measured by whether employees have the right kind and level of skills to perform the critical internal processes on the strategy map. The first step in estimating HC readiness is to identify the *strategic job families*–the positions in which employees with the right skills, talent, and knowledge have the biggest impact on enhancing the organization's critical internal processes. The next step is to pinpoint the set of specific competencies needed to perform each of those strategic jobs. The difference between the requirements needed to carry out these jobs effectively and the company's current capabilities represents a "competency gap" that measures the organization's HC readiness.

Information Capital (IC): The strategic readiness of information capital is a measure of how well the

223

company's strategic IT portfolio of infrastructure and applications supports the critical internal processes. Infra-structure comprises hardware–such as central servers and communication networks – and the managerial expertise – such as standards, disaster planning, and security – required to effectively deliver and use applications. Two categories of applications, in turn, are built on this infra-structure: *Transaction-processing applications*, such as an ERP system, automate the basic repetitive transactions of the enterprise. *Analytic applications* promote analysis, interpretation, and sharing of information and knowledge. Either type may or may not be a *transformational application* – one that changes the prevailing business model of the enterprise. Levi's uses a transformational application to tailor jeans to individual customers. Home Shopping Network uses a transformational application to measure the "profits per second" being generated by currently offered merchandise. Transformational applications have the most potential impact on strategic objectives and require the greatest degree of organization change to deliver their benefits.

Organization Capital (OC): Organization capital is perhaps the least understood of the intangible assets, and the task of measuring it is correspondingly difficult. But in looking at the strategic priorities that companies in our database of Balanced Scorecard implementations used for their organization capital objectives, we found a consistent picture. Successful companies had a *culture* in which people were deeply aware of and internalized the mission, vision, and core values needed to execute the company's strategy. These companies strove for excellent *leadership* at all levels, leadership that could mobilize the organization toward its strategy. They strove for a clear *alignment* between the organization's strategic objectives and individual, team, and departmental goals and incentives. Finally, these companies promoted *teamwork*, especially the sharing of strategic knowledge throughout the organization. Determining OC readiness, we concluded, would involve first identifying the changes in organization capital required by the new strategy – what we call the "organization change agenda" – and then separately identifying and measuring the state of readiness of the company's cultural, leadership, alignment, and teamwork objectives.

Strategic readiness is related to the concept of liquidity, which accountants use to classify financial and physical assets on a company's balance sheet. Accountants divide a firm's assets into various categories, such as cash, accounts receivable, inventory, property, plant and equipment, and long-term investments. These are ordered hierarchically according to the ease and speed with which they can be converted to cash – in other words, according to the degree of their liquidity. Accounts receivable is more liquid than inventory, and both accounts receivable and inventory are classified as short-term assets since they typically convert to cash within 12 months, faster than the cash recovery cycle from such illiquid assets as plant and equipment. Strategic readiness does much the same for intangible assets – the higher their state of readiness, the faster they contribute to generating cash.

HUMAN CAPITAL READINESS AT CONSUMER BANK

Here we can see how human capital at our composite company, Consumer Bank, is linked to its critical strategic processes and how well the company scores in terms of the skills and capabilities it needs. The top row lists the internal processes the bank identified as critical to delivering its value proposition. The second row shows the jobs that have the greatest influence on those processes – the *strategic job families*. The third row lists the competencies needed for each job, and the fourth row specifies the number of people with those skills the company requires.

The bottom row shows how ready Consumer Bank's human capital is for its new strategy. Taken together, these internal assessments indicate the extent to which the bank actually has the capacity it needs. The bank is in excellent shape for its two operations management processes (100% and 90% readiness) but deficient for the two customer management processes (only 40% and 50% readiness) and for one of the innovation processes (20% readiness). The aggregate measure of 65% human capital readiness (in the red zone) is a weighted average of readiness scores for all seven strategic job families. In terms of human capital, this report tells executives how quickly they can implement their new strategy.

HUMAN CAPITAL READINESS

All jobs are important to the organization; otherwise, people wouldn't be hired and paid to perform them. Organizations may require truck drivers, computer operators, production supervisors, materials handlers, and call center operators and should make it clear that contributions from all these employees can improve organizational performance. But we have found that some jobs have a much greater impact on strategy than others. Managers must identify and focus on the critical few that have the greatest impact on successful strategy implementation.

	Operations Management		Customer Management		Innovation		Regulatory and Social	
Strategic Processes	Minimize problems	Provide rapid response	Cross-sell the product line	Shift to appropriate channel	Understand customer segments	Develop new products	Diversify workforce	
Strategic Job Families	Quality manager	Call center representative	certified financial planner	Telemarketer	Consumer marketer	Joint venture manager	Community recruiter	
Competency Profile	Six Sigma program Problem management system	Customer interaction center Problem management system Team building	Solutions selling Relationship management Product-line knowledge Professional certification	Phone selling Product line knowledge Older management system	Market research Market communication Cross business process	Relationship management Negotiation E-commerce know-how	Community roots Public relations Legal frameworks	**Overall Assessment of Human Capital Readiness**
Number Required	30	20	100	20	10	30	10	
Strategic Job Readiness	100%	90%	40%	50%	20%	70%	80%	65%
	✔	✔	✘	✘	✘	?	✔	✘

John Bronson, vice president of human resources at Williams-Sonoma, estimates that people in only five job families determine 80% of his company's strategic priorities. The executive team of a chemical company has identified eight job families critical to its strategy of offering customized innovative solutions. These job families employ, in aggregate, 100 individuals – less than 7% of the total workforce. Kimberlee Williams, vice president of human resources at Unicco, a large integrated facilities-services management company, says that three job families are key to its strategy: project managers, who oversee the operations in specific accounts; operations directors, who broaden the relationships within existing accounts; and business development executives, who help acquire new accounts. These three job families employ only 215 people, less than 4% of the workforce. By focusing human capital development activities on these critical few individuals, the chemical company, Unicco, and Williams-Sonoma can greatly leverage their human capital investments. It is sobering to think that strategic success in these three companies is determined by how well they develop competencies in less than 10% of their workforces.

Once a company identifies its strategic job families, it must define the requirements for these jobs in considerable detail, a task often referred to as "job profiling" or "competency profiling." A competency profile describes the knowledge, skills, and values required by successful occupants in the job family. Often, HR managers will interview individuals who best understand the job requirements to develop a competency profile they can use to recruit, hire, train, and develop people for that position. To see how this might be done, consider Consumer Bank, a composite example distilled from our experiences in working with about a dozen retail banks.

Consumer Bank was migrating from its historic strategy of promoting individual products to one offering complete financial solutions and one-stop shopping to targeted customers. The map for this new strategy identified seven critical internal processes, one of which was "crosssell the product line." Human resources and line executives then identified the financial planner as the job most important to the effective performance of this process. A planning workshop further identified four skills fundamental to the financial planner's job: solutions selling, relationship management, product-line knowledge, and professional certification. For each internal process on its strategy map, Consumer Bank replicated this approach, identifying the strategic job families and critical competencies each required. The results are summarized in the exhibit "Human Capital Readiness at Consumer Bank."

To take the next step–assessing the current capabilities and competencies of each of the employees in each strategic job family–companies can draw from a broad range of approaches. For example, employees can themselves assess how well their current capabilities fit the job requirements and then discuss those assessments with a mentor or career manager. Alternatively, an assessor can solicit 360-degree feedback on employees' performance from their supervisors, peers, and subordinates. From these assessments, employees get a clear understanding of their objectives, meaningful feedback on their current levels of skill and performance, and specific recommendations for future personal development.

Consumer Bank estimated that it needed 100 trained and skilled financial planners to execute the cross-selling process. But in assessing its recent targeted hiring, training, and development programs, the bank's HR group determined that only 40 of its financial planners had reached a high enough level of proficiency. The bank's human capital readiness for this piece of the strategy was, therefore, only 40%, as the exhibit shows. By replicating this analysis for all its strategic job families, the bank learned the state of its human capital readiness and thus whether the organization could move forward quickly with its new strategy.

INFORMATION CAPITAL READINESS

Executives must understand how to plan, set priorities for, and manage an information capital portfolio that supports their organization's strategy. As with human capital, the strategy map serves as a starting point for delineating a company's IC objectives. In the case of Consumer Bank, the chief information officer led an initiative to identify the specific information capital needs of each of the seven internal processes previously identified as critical to the bank's new value proposition.

For the customer management process "cross-sell the product line," the workshop team identified an application for customers to analyze and manage their portfolios by themselves (a customer portfolio self-management system) as a transformational application. The workshop team identified an analytical application for the same process (a customer profitability system) and a transaction-processing application (an integrated customer file). The internal process "understand customer segments" also needed a customer profitability system, as well as a separate customer feedback system to support market research. The process "shift to appropriate channel" required a strong foundation of transactional systems, including a packaged CRM software suite that included modules for lead management, order management, and sales force automation. For the operations process "provide rapid response," participants identified a transformational application (customer self-help) as well as an analytic application (a best-practice community knowledge management system) for sharing successful sales techniques among telemarketers. Finally, the "minimize problems" process required an analytical application (service quality analysis) to identify problems and two related transaction-level systems (one for incident tracking and another for problem management).

After defining its portfolio of IC applications, the project team identified several required components of IT infrastructure. Some applications needed a CRM transactions database. Others required that a Web-enabled infrastructure be integrated into the bank's overall Web site architecture. The team also learned about the need for an internal R&D project to develop a new interactive voice-response technology. All together, the bank's planning process defined an information capital portfolio made up of 14 unique applications (some of which supported more than one internal process) and four IT infrastructure projects. (See the exhibit "Information Capital Readiness at Consumer Bank.")

The team then turned to assessing the readiness of the bank's existing portfolio of IC infrastructure and applications, assigning a numerical indicator from 1 to 6 to each system. A score of 1 or 2 indicates that the system is already available and operating normally, perhaps needing only minor enhancements. A score of 3 or 4 indicates that the system has been identified and funded but is not yet installed or operational. In other words, current capability does not yet exist but development programs are under way to close the gap. A score of 5 or 6 signals that a new infrastructure or application is needed to support the strategy, but nothing has yet been done to create, fund, and deliver the capability. Managers responsible for the IC development programs provided the subjective judgments for this simple measurement system, and the CIO was responsible for assessing the integrity of the reported numbers. In the IC exhibit, we can also see that Consumer Bank aggregated the readiness measures of individual applications and infrastructure programs – designating them green, yellow, or red, based on the worst-case application in the category – to create a portfolio status report. With such a report, managers can see the strategic readiness of the organization's information capital at a glance, easily pinpointing the areas in which more resources are needed. It is an excellent tool for monitoring a portfolio of information capital development programs.

Information Capital Readiness at Consumer Bank

The first two rows of the information capital readiness report, like the human capital report, list the company's critical internal processes and its strategic job families. The remaining five rows specify the various items in the IC portfolio, assigning scores indicating how well developed each item is. In this example, Consumer Bank has the IC portfolio it needs to support innovation but is less able to support the job most critical to its customer management and operational excellence goals.

	Operations Management		Customer Management		Innovation	
Strategic Processes	Minimize Problems	Provide rapid response	Cross-sell the product line	Shift to appropriate channel	Understand customer segments	Develop new products
Strategic Job Families	Quality manager	Call center representative	Certified financial planner	Telemarketer	Consumer marketer	Joint Venture manager

Strategic Information Capital Portfolio

	Operations Management		Customer Management		Innovation	
Transformational Applications		Customer self-help 4	Customer portfolio self management 4			
Analytical Applications	Service quality analysis 2	Best practice community knowledge management system 3	Customer profitability 3	Best practice community knowledge management system 2	Customer profitability 3	Best practice community knowledge management system 2
Transaction-Processing Applications	Incident tracking 6 / Problem management 2	Workforce scheduling 3 / Problem management 2	Integrated customer file 3	CRM/lead management 6 / CRM/order management 6 / CRM/sales force automation 4	Customer feedback 2	Project management 2
Technology Infrastructure	Web enabled 3 / Computer telephony integration 4	Computer telephony integration 4 / Interactive voice response	CRM packaged software 2 / Web enabled 3	Web enabled 4 / Computer telephony integration 4	CRM packaged software 2	

Ratings

1 OK

2 Minor enhancements needed

3 New development under way

4 New development behind schedule

5 Major enhancements required

6 New application required

Combined Readiness Level

✗ ✗ ? ✗ ✓ ✓

Many sophisticated IT organizations already use more quantitative, objective assessments of their information capital portfolios than the subjective process we've just described for Consumer Bank. These organizations survey users to assess their satisfaction with each system. They perform financial analyses to determine the operating and maintenance costs of each application. Some conduct technical audits to assess the underlying quality of the code, ease of use, quality of documentation, and frequency of failure for each application. From this profile, an organization can build strategies for managing its portfolio of existing IC assets just as one would manage a collection of physical assets like machinery or a fleet of trucks. Applications with high levels of maintenance can be streamlined, for example, applications with high operating costs can be optimized, and applications with high levels of user dissatisfaction can be replaced. This more comprehensive approach can be effective for managing a portfolio of applications that are already operational.

ORGANIZATION CAPITAL READINESS

Success in performing the critical internal processes identified in an organization's strategy map invariably requires an organization to change in fundamental ways. Assessing OC readiness is essentially about assessing how well the company can mobilize and sustain the organization change agenda associated with its strategy. For instance, if the strategy involves focusing on the customer, the company needs to determine whether its existing culture is customer-centric, whether its leaders have the requisite skills to foster such a culture, whether employees are aware of the goal and are motivated to deliver exceptional customer service, and, finally, how well employees share with others their knowledge about the company's customers. Let's explore how companies can make these kinds of assessments for each of the four OC dimensions.

Culture. Of the four, culture is perhaps the most complex and difficult dimension to understand and describe because it encompasses a wider range of behavioral territory than the others. That's probably why "shaping the culture" is the most often-cited objective in the Learning and Growth section of our Balanced Scorecard database. Executives generally believe that changes in strategy require basic changes in the way business is conducted at all levels of the organization, which means, of course, that people will need to develop new attitudes and behaviors – in other words, change their culture.

Assessment of cultural readiness relies heavily on employee surveys. But in preparing surveys, companies need to distinguish clearly between the values that all employees share – the company's base culture – and the perceptions that employees have of their existing system – the climate. The concept of base culture has its roots in anthropology, which defines an organization's culture as the symbols, myths, and rituals embedded in the group consciousness (or subconscious). To describe a company's base culture, therefore, you have to uncover the organization's systems of shared meanings, assumptions, and values.

The concept of climate has its roots in social psychology and is determined by the way organizational influences – such as the incentive structure or the perceived warmth and support of superiors and peers – affect employees' motivation and behavior. The anthropological component reflects employees' shared attitudes and beliefs independent of the actual organizational infrastructure, while climate reflects their shared perception of existing organizational policies, practices, and procedures, both formal and informal.

Surveying perceptions of existing organizational policies and practices is a fairly straightforward task, but getting at the base culture requires a little more digging. Anthropologists usually rely on storytelling to identify shared beliefs and images, but that approach is inadequate for quantifying the alignment of culture to strategy. Organizational behavior scholars have developed measurement instruments, such as Charles O'Reilly and colleagues' Organizational Culture Profile, in which employees rank 54 value statements according to their perceived importance and relevance in the organization. Once ranked, an organization's culture can be described with a reasonable degree of reliability and validity. Then the organization can assess to what extent the existing culture is consistent with its strategy and what kinds of changes may be needed.

One caveat: Managers do need to be aware that some variations in culture are necessary and desirable in different operating units or functions. The culture of an R&D group, for example, should be different from the culture of a manufacturing unit; the culture of an emergent business unit should be different from the culture of a mature one. Executives should strive for agreement throughout the organization about corporatewide values such as integrity, respect, treatment of colleagues, and commitment to customer satisfaction. But some value statements in the survey instrument should refer to the culture of specific operating units. So, for example, surveys of the employees in operations and service-delivery units would include statements about quality and continuous improvement, whereas the R&D department survey might include statements about creativity and innovation. For employees involved in customer acquisition, statements might relate to retention and growth or to a deep understanding of individual customers' preferences and needs.

Leadership. If companies change their strategies, people will have to do some things differently as well. It is the responsibility of leaders at all levels of the organization – from the CEO of a retail chain down to the local store managers – to help employees identify and understand the changes needed and to motivate and guide them toward the new ways of working.

In researching the best practices in our Balanced Scorecard database, we were able to identify seven generic types of behavioral changes that build organization capital, and each fell into one of two categories: changes that support the creation of value – such as increasing people's focus on the customer – and those required to carry out the company's strategy – such as increasing accountability. The sidebar "Seven Behaviors for Transformation" describes these behavioral changes in more detail.

To ensure that it gets the kind of leaders it needs, a company should draw up a *leadership competency model* for each of its leadership positions. This is a kind of job profile that defines the competencies a leader is expected to have to be effective in carrying out the company's strategy. For example, one manufacturing company, attempting to create teams to solve customers' problems, identified and defined three competencies essential for people in team leadership positions:

- **Customer Focus** – Outstanding leaders understand their customers. They place themselves in the customers' minds and spend time with them to understand their current and future needs.
- **Fostering Teamwork** – Outstanding leaders work collaboratively with their own teams and across organizational and geographic boundaries. They empower their teams to achieve excellence.

ORGANIZATION CAPITAL READINESS REPORT

The various measures for organization capital readiness should be put together in a readiness report, which shows, for all the components of organization capital, where the company needs to introduce changes to its behaviors and policies. The report shown here is a simplified version of one prepared by a company in our Balanced Scorecard database.

Attribute	Strategic Objective	Strategic Measure	Target	Actual	
Culture	Foster awareness and internalization of the mission, vision, and core values needed to execute the strategy	Customer-focused (customer survey; percentage who understand the organization's mission)	80%	68%	✗
		Other core values (employee change readiness survey)	80%	52%	✗
Leadership	Develop leaders at all levels who can mobilize the organization toward its strategy	Leadership gap (percentage of key attributes in competency model rated above threshold)	90%	92%	✓
Alignment	Align goals and incentives with the strategy at all levels of the organization	Strategic awareness (percentage of staff who can identify organization's strategic priorities)	80%	75%	✗
		Strategic alignment (percentage of staff whose objectives and incentives link to Balanced Scorecard)	100%	60%	✗
Teamwork	Ensure that knowledge and staff assets that have strategic potential are shared	Sharing best practices (number of knowledge management system hits per employee)	5.0	6.1	✓

- **Open Communications** – Outstanding leaders tell the truth. They openly share information with peers, managers, and subordinates. They tell the whole story, not just how it looks from their position.

Often, organizations will measure leadership traits, such as those listed above, through employee surveys. A staff or external unit solicits information from subordinates, peers, and superiors about a leader's mastery of the critical skills. This personal feedback is used mainly for coaching and developing the leader, but the unit can also aggregate the detailed (and confidential) data from the individual reviews to create a status report on the readiness of key leadership competencies needed throughout the organization.

Alignment. An organization is aligned when all employees have a commonality of purpose, a shared vision, and an understanding of how their personal roles support the overall strategy. An aligned organization encourages behaviors such as innovation and risk taking because individuals' actions are directed toward achieving high-level objectives. Encouraging and empowering individual initiative in an unaligned organization leads to chaos, as the innovative risk takers pull the organization in contradictory directions.

Achieving alignment is a two-step process. First, managers communicate the high-level strategic objectives in ways that all employees can understand. This involves using a wide range of communication mechanisms: brochures, newsletters, town meetings, orientation and training programs, executive talks, company intranets, and bulletin boards. The goal of this step is to create intrinsic motivation, to inspire employees to internalize the organization's values and objectives so that they want to help the organization succeed. The next step uses extrinsic motivation. The organization has employees set explicit personal and team objectives aligned to the strategy and establishes incentives that reward employees when they meet personal, departmental, business unit, and corporate targets.

Measuring alignment readiness is relatively straightforward. Many survey instruments are already available for assessing how much employees know about and how well they understand high-level strategic objectives. It is also fairly easy to see whether or not individuals' personal objectives and the company's existing incentive schemes are consistent with the high-level strategy.

For example, a large property and casualty insurance company adopted a new strategy intended to reduce its underwriting losses by creating a tighter link between the underwriters, who decide whether to accept a new piece of business, and the claims agents, who deal with the consequences from poor underwriting decisions. Historically, these specialists lived in different parts of the organization, and their incentives were totally unrelated to each other, which clearly did little to foster cooperation between them or with the line business units they supported. To reflect the new strategy, the company changed to a team-based compensation system in which everyone's incentive pay was based on a common set of measures (their Balanced Scorecard). Underwriters and claims agents, who worked in service departments shared by the various business units, were now rewarded using the Balanced Scorecard measures related to the business units they supported. The company used a survey instrument to capture the employees' perceptions of the improved teamwork created by aligning the incentive systems.

Teamwork and Knowledge Sharing. There is no greater waste than a good idea used only once. Most organizations have to go through a cultural change to shift individuals from hoarding to sharing their local knowledge. No asset has greater potential for an organization than the collective knowledge possessed by all its employees. That's why many companies, hoping to generate, organize, develop, and distribute knowledge throughout the organization, have spent millions of dollars to purchase or create formal knowledge management systems.

The challenge in implementing such systems is motivating people to actually document their ideas and knowledge to make them available to others. Most organizations in our Balanced Scorecard database attempted to develop such motivation by selecting "teamwork" and "knowledge sharing" as strategic priorities in their Learning and Growth Perspective. Typical measures for these priorities included the number of best practice ideas the employees identified and used, the percentage of employees who transferred knowledge in a workout process, the number of people who actually used the knowledge management system, how often the system is used, the percentage of information in the knowledge management system that was updated, and how much was obsolete.

For knowledge sharing to matter, it must be aligned with the priorities of the strategy map. For example, one organization – a chemical company – created several best practice communities to complement the internal process objectives on its strategy map. The Improve Workplace Safety community consisted of the safety directors from every facility. They studied the best practices at the high-performing plants and created a best practice–sharing program. The company's output measure, "days away from work," dropped by 70%. In another example, a children's hospital was attempting to reduce costs without reducing the quality of patient care. Intensive discussions resulted in a top-ten list of best practices already being used somewhere in the hospital. The hospital then formed cross-functional medical practice teams of physicians, nurses, and administrators to implement as

many of these procedures as they practically could. It measured success, the output of this knowledge-sharing process, by the "number of best practices utilized." The effective implementation of best practices over the next three years led to dramatic improvements in organizational outcomes: Readmission rates dropped by 50%, cost per case and length of stay each declined by 25%, and both customer satisfaction and quality of care increased. In these and many other examples in our case files, organizations enhanced their performance by aligning the teamwork and knowledge-sharing component of their organization capital with their strategy.

To get an overview of organizational readiness, companies can put the information they obtain from their various surveys and assessments together in a report like the one shown in "Organization Capital Readiness Report." In this exhibit, the leadership measure, drawn from the leadership competency model, displays the company's estimate, based on employee surveys, of the degree to which the company possesses the key attributes for leadership. At 92%, the company is above target on its leadership objective and can be considered strategically ready in terms of this dimension. The company's OC with respect to teamwork and knowledge sharing is also in good shape. But the firm is performing inadequately in alignment and in developing the right culture, and these problems are lowering its overall level of organization capital readiness.

The intangible assets described in the Balanced Scorecard's Learning and Growth Perspective are the foundation of every organization's strategy, and the measures in this perspective are the ultimate lead indicators. Human capital becomes most valuable when it is concentrated in the relatively few strategic job families implementing the internal processes critical to the organization's strategy. Information capital creates the greatest value when it provides the requisite infrastructure and strategic applications that complement the human capital. Organizations introducing a new strategy must create a culture of corresponding values, a cadre of exceptional leaders who can lead the change agenda, and an informed workforce aligned to the strategy, working together, and sharing knowledge to help the strategy succeed.

Some managers shy away from measuring their intangible assets because these measures are usually "softer," or more subjective, than the financial measures they conventionally use to motivate and assess performance. The Balanced Scorecard movement has encouraged organizations to face the measurement challenge. Using the systematic approaches set out in this article, companies can now measure what they want, rather than wanting only what they can currently measure. Even if the measures are imprecise, the simple act of attempting to gauge the capabilities of employees, information systems, and organization capital communicates the importance of these drivers for value creation. In the course of our work, we have seen many companies find new ways to measure – and consequently new ways to enhance the value of–their intangible assets. The measurement and management of these assets played a prominent role in their transformation into successful, strategy-focused organizations.

*Robert S. Kaplan (rkaplan@hbs.edu) is the Marvin Bower Professor of Leadership Development at Harvard Business School in Boston. **David P. Norton** (dnorton@bscol.com) is the founder and president of the Balanced Scorecard Collaborative (www.bscol.com) in Lincoln, Massachusetts. This article is based on their book Strategy Maps: Converting Intangible Assets into Tangible Outcomes (Harvard Business School Press, 2004).*

QUESTION

9.5 Where and how do intangibles fit into the strategy map? Explain.

Chapter 10

Using Budgets to Achieve Organizational Objectives

Reading 10.1, *Continuous Budgeting at the HON Company*, by Drtina, Hoeger and Schaub illustrates this large furniture maker's approach to staying competitive with the help of its budgeting process. Unlike many companies, HON uses a continuous, quarterly, budgeting system. For each quarter a budget is prepared, which includes plans not only for that particular quarter but also for the next three quarters. As each new quarter arrives, the budgeting process is repeated. HON employees believe that the information generated is timely and comprehensive and provides them with information to respond quickly to their volatile environment. The article provides a detailed step-by-step approach to illustrate HON's method.

Reading 10.2, Christopher Bart's, *Budgeting Gamesmanship*, describes the games that managers play with their budgets. Bart defines budgeting gamesmanship as "the deliberate and premeditated manipulation of current year sales, cost and profit forecasts by product managers to project an overly conservative image into their product budgets." Using interview and company data from eight large diversified companies, Bart documents how, and why, managers pad their budgets. Two key factors for why such padding occurs are the fear that senior management will arbitrarily slash their submitted budgets, and the managers' own concerns about uncertainty in the competitive environment in which they work.

In *Budgeting Made Easy*, Reading 10.3, Steve Hornyak discusses the enormous amounts of time and energy devoted to traditional budgeting. Among the many difficulties are incompatible software programs, time delays that mount up based on the difficulty of hooking up remote-user participants, and the inaccessibility of historical data that many managers need to help them gauge what resources they will need for the coming time period. Hornyak suggests that organizations begin to consider e-budgeting as a way to overcome many of these problems. E-budgeting can completely automate the budgeting process and include participants from remote locations world-wide. Web-based budgeting also allows access to important budget data from anywhere increasing the flexibility for all concerned. Other benefits include reductions in administrative resources, an increase in employee participation (shown by research to be a determinant of employee satisfaction), and more time to focus on strategic aspects of the budgeting process rather than the minutia of the process.

Michael Jensen's thesis in Reading 10.4, *Corporate Budgeting is Broken – Let's Fix It*, is that traditional corporate budgeting is a joke. The process takes an inordinate amount of time and causes usually honest people to be dishonest as they strive to low-ball targets and inflate results. Jensen suggests that the root cause of this dysfunctional behavior is that many companies link the achievement of certain goals to their compensation. To overcome this problem, Jensen suggests that managers be rewarded using a linear bonus scheme rather than one that provides them with a bonus once they achieve a certain level of performance.

The article, "Beyond Budgeting," Reading 105 by Jeremy Hope and Robin Fraser us another strong critique of traditional budgeting. The authors discuss two new approaches to budgeting — devolution and strategic performance management. Devolution involves flattening organizational hierarchies, reengineering processes, and using teamwork more effectively. One problem with this approach is that while delegation of control occurs, it is often within the strict regime of coordination and accountability with budgets as the key tool for policing control. Strategic performance management involves the use for a wide-ranging system for controlling the business, driving management behavior, and rewarding results. Although these systems have been effective, they often do not square nicely with a company's budgeting system. The "Beyond Budgeting" approach combines effective devolution and effective performance management systems.

Richard Steele and Craig Albright in *Games Managers Play at Budget Time* (Reading 10.6), describe five archetypes of bad behavior that are used by managers to subvert the budgeting system for their own ends. This article is a very good companion to Reading 10.2 and fleshes out specific types of dysfunctional managerial budgeting behavior. The authors argue that managerial game playing occurs sometimes because of lack of the appropriate skills to get the job done, very clear self-interested behavior, lack of clarity about performance expectations, or a response to an organization's culture. While game playing will never go away, the authors offer some prescriptions for curbing dysfunctional behavior with the budget.

Readings
Chapter 10

10.1 Continuous Budgeting at the HON Company

This furniture manufacturer builds a solid competitive strategy with progressive quarterly budgets.

by Ralph Drtina, CPA; Steve Hoeger, CMA; and John Schaub, CMA*

Survival in today's competitive environment means that businesses must be flexible and innovative, largely through development of new products and services, while simultaneously improving productivity and customer service. But building the effects of innovation into the annual budget can be difficult because actions and outcomes often are evolutionary and only become known as the year progresses. Under these conditions it is understandable that the annual budget is not an effective control tool because revenue and spending targets are based on operating conditions different from those actually encountered.

Standard cost accounting systems are not helpful either when budgeting for continuous change because of built-in contradictions. One shortcoming of standard costs for companies seeking continuous improvement, for example, is that they presuppose the goal is to optimize efficiency within a given state of operating conditions rather than to strive for ongoing improvement. Consequently, when production processes undergo continuous change, standards developed annually for static conditions no longer offer meaningful targets for gauging their success.

The HON Company, the largest maker of mid-priced office furniture in the United States and Canada, has overcome these obstacles through use of a continuous three-month budget cycle. The budget has become the integral planning and control device for achieving two strategic objectives: ongoing new product and service development and rapid continuous improvement. The budget also serves as an important vehicle for ensuring that the corporate culture is unified in its understanding of—and commitment to—strategic objectives.

VOLATILE FURNITURE INDUSTRY
The largest of nine operating companies that compose HON Industries, the HON Company operates exclusively as a manufacturer of office furniture and accessories. Organized along functional lines, it has 14 production plants located throughout the United States and operates

as an independently run profit center with its operations tied to its parent through its strategic plan and budget.

Highly dependent on the overall economy's health, the office furniture industry is characterized by cyclical demand and uncertainties that make planning difficult, even in the short term. Furniture buyers often postpone purchases until their own business operations are profitable, and demand is normally seasonal with sales much higher in the second half of the calendar year.

Dominated by larger but fewer customers, the office furniture industry is faced with an increasing level of industry competition. As these customers continue to consolidate and grow, they put tremendous price pressure on their suppliers. Manufacturers that do win contracts often expand capacity to meet increased volume. As time passes, the large customers pressure suppliers to maintain or even lower prices, thereby disallowing cost increases incurred by suppliers to be passed on. Suppliers often find they are victims of their own success—their revenues increase, but profits are squeezed by rising costs. Yet they become captive suppliers to the large customers whose volume is needed to absorb the cost of expanded capacity. Given these highly uncertain industry conditions, considerable planning and coordination is needed to ensure that production capacity is used fully and unit costs are maintained or reduced.

DOVETAILING STRATEGY AND BUDGET
Managers at the HON Company communicate and coordinate operating plans through a process called continuous quarterly budgeting. All departments work together to produce an updated four-quarter budget at the beginning of each quarter. Thus, as shown in Figure 1, a budget prepared for the third quarter 1996 includes plans for the third and fourth quarters of 1996 and the first and second quarters of 1997. Each quarterly budget requires the next four quarters to be completely re-budgeted. By having a detailed quarterly budget that is up-to-date and comprehensive, managers and employees in all areas are prepared to deal with rapid change.

---

* From: R. Drtina, S. Hoeger, and J. Schaub, "Continuous Budgeting at the HON Company," *Management Accounting* (January 1996): 20–24. Reprinted with permission.

FIGURE 1. OVERVIEW OF CONTINUOUS QUARTERLY BUDGE

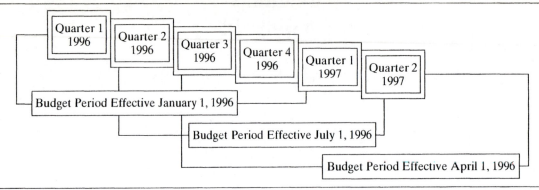

In the HON Company's aggressive but realistic budget philosophy, senior management expects each quarter's performance to exceed the previous one. New products and services drive company growth, and research to define and meet emerging customer demand is ongoing. In 1996, for example, the company expects to launch dozens of new product series in addition to introducing hundreds of variations to the size, shape, and features of existing models. Recognizing that service is critical, too, HON offers two- and three-week delivery for orders of any product size and combination. Competitors typically require four- to five-week lead time for single product orders.

Budget targets must be supported by action plans that coordinate operational improvements throughout the organization. For example, when the strategic plan calls for a specified increase in productivity (8% in 1995), all departments are expected to work together to bring about needed change. In manufacturing, production processes repeatedly are challenged and bottlenecks removed. Sales and marketing are expected to generate increased sales volume to make full use of capacity gained through manufacturing improvements. Distribution then must develop plans to handle increased deliveries while reducing the cost of delivery per sales dollar.

PREPARING THE BUDGET

The typical quarterly budget process is done in five basic steps over a six-week period. (See Figure 2.)

Step 1—Develop sales budget. Preparation of the sales budget begins with the territory sales managers when they submit quarterly sales budgets to the sales

department for consolidation. Then the sales budget is summarized by geographic territory and by distribution channel. At the same time the sales department is preparing territory budgets, the marketing department independently prepares a sales budget based on general product types and distribution channels. These two sales budget submissions typically differ, largely due to divergent perspectives and sources of information. While the sales department bases its estimates on historical patterns of existing products, marketing has more detailed information about new products and their introduction dates and about special promotion programs.

After the marketing and sales departments have made their separate sales forecasts, the two groups compare forecasts, analyze differences, and reach agreement on the final sales targets. If the two sales targets differ by a substantial amount, more detail about sales derivation and rationale is shared and discussed. Negotiations over acceptable targets continue until the two parties reach a consensus.

Once sales and marketing reach agreement, their sales targets are compared to the strategic plan at a top-level meeting attended by the president and senior staff. The purpose of the meeting is to identify major product group sales levels that appear too low or too high. As a result of discussions on the issues causing these discrepancies, changes are made to reconcile budgeted sales and market share with the strategic plan. Upon final approval, sales dollar targets are sent to production scheduling for conversion to production units and shipping volume.

FIGURE 2. QUARTERLY BUDGET PROCESS

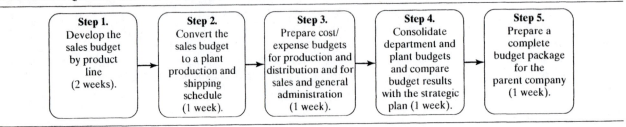

Step 2—Convert the sales budget to a plant production and shipping schedule. The scheduling group allocates production targets to the company's 14 plants to gain greatest production and distribution efficiencies. This group has one week to convert the sales budgets derived in Step 1 into unit production targets for each plant. Scheduling makes this conversion by analyzing the history of each product category and including such factors as product destination, delivery distance, and plant capabilities. It also takes into account current product inventories and adjusts or planned increases or decreases. After unit production targets are assigned, production managers begin budgeting their quarterly costs.

Step 3—Prepare cost/expense budgets. All the HON Company's functional areas are organized as either cost or expense centers. Separate budgets are prepared for research and development, SG&A, customer service, production, and distribution. In this step, area managers submit expense budgets that determine spending and efficiency targets for the upcoming quarter and year. Each area is expected to provide for improvements designated in the strategic plan. Managers have five working days to complete their expense budgets.

Preparation of a production plant's budget within one week requires widespread participation of department managers and employees and the full commitment of the plant accountant. The budget process pushes responsibility down to the lowest departmental levels within each plant. Department managers are expected to base their budgets on action plans that detail how improvements will be made. The plant accountant must prepare the direct and indirect salary budgets, consolidate department budgets into an overall plant budget, and prepare productivity performance measures. The plant manager helps to guide improvement efforts between departments and makes sure that overall outcomes agree with goals set forth in the strategic plan.

Company-wide productivity improvements begin with the production and distribution processes. Every department in these two areas is expected to initiate changes that allow more units to be processed without incurring added cost. For example, as unit sales increase, it is presumed that production plants will keep inventory levels constant by striving for a one-piece production flow through which products are processed, without interruption, from the time they are started to the point of being loaded on delivery trucks. Similarly distribution is expected to reduce average costs by increasing use of freight container capacity.

The strategic plan specifies an allowable sales percentage for R&D, for SG&A expenses broken down by functional area (general administration, marketing, selling), and for customer service. At the beginning of the budget process, area managers are given general expense guidelines based on past history. Here, as in production, budget responsibilities are pushed down to department levels where guideline targets are refined to take into account the effects of improvements and new programs.

As improvement projects are implemented, SG&A areas are expected to trade spending authority among themselves. For example, if marketing were to find that a new product was to be delayed for one quarter, it could push back its planned expense for printing new literature and for new product training. SG&A managers then would prioritize needs to find where these funds might best be used while still meeting the allowable spending targets for all of SG&A. They may agree, for instance, that MIS can best use the free resources to bring in temporary workers to help speed up completion of a current high-priority project, such as putting customers on electronic data interchange.

Step 4—Consolidate budgets and compare with strategic plan. After individual budgets are completed by functional areas, they are forwarded to the HON Company headquarters. At this point, the company accounting group has one week to review the budget for obvious errors and assemble the final budget package. The budget is analyzed to ensure that strategic plans are being accomplished and that the plants and the SG&A departments are focused on the correct efforts. For example, the budget for the first two quarters of the year—when seasonal activity is low—should include adequate provision for periodic maintenance. If budgeted maintenance expenditures are low, a production plant may have under-budgeted preventive maintenance or neglected special overhaul projects which would require further budget revision.

Step 5—Prepare a budget package for parent company. The company's controller department has one week to prepare a complete set of financial statements plus a host of comparative data: budgeted return on assets employed, productivity measures, budgeted sales attributable to new product introductions, major tooling expenditures, and an analysis of list prices to net sales. These data first are analyzed to ensure that the HON Company's performance trends satisfy the targets set forth in the strategic plan. Normally, any shortfalls already would have been identified and corrected prior to this point in the process. If additional deficiencies are identified, however, the company controller first must correct problem areas before proceeding further.

Then the completed budget is sent to the parent company, HON Industries, for approval. If the parent does not approve the budget, the HON Company controller must investigate needed changes, such as additional cost cuts. In these cases, the HON Company president normally has one additional week to assure the parent company that the budget is the best that is attainable, or, if such arguments fail, the budget is trimmed further. This type of approach has proven effective because the HON Company's philosophy is that a change in the budget is not simply a change in numbers, but rather it means that the company's action plans also must be changed.

BUDGETING FOR COMMITMENT AND ACTION

The HON Company's continuous budgeting system enables senior managers to inspire and motivate the achievement of corporate strategies. Employees at all levels and in all departments are kept informed of new product and process developments, and they in turn update their own performance targets accordingly. By planning in three-month time frames, managers and front-line employees can make a fair assessment of their work improvements and thus can set realistic targets. This interactive approach pushes decisions down to the production floor, and, as a result, helps to gain employee commitment and faster adoption of productivity improvements. It also ensures that standard costs and variance reports are meaningful, an important consideration for helping employees gain the satisfaction of short-term victories in their work.

Does quarterly budget preparation consume a disproportionate amount of company time? Experience has shown that managers improve their budgeting skills over time and need no more time to do quarterly budgets than would be needed for one annual budget. Information technology advances also have shortened budget preparation time. A highly integrated computer budgeting system supplies each department manager with four-quarter histories and four-quarter projections of budget line items. Driver codes for revenue and cost targets are set by default, and, thus, managers need only change budgets for line items on an exception basis. The budget system speeds up information flows to higher levels, too, because proposed targets are rolled up to the next level immediately where they can be reviewed and revised quickly by senior management.

Most important, the HON Company's process of continuous quarterly budgeting unites senior-level strategy with a committed corporate culture. Corporate management best understands where energies need to be focused to enhance the firm's competitive edge, but attaining strategic goals depends on a workforce that can translate corporate strategies into a well-coordinated action plan. Continuous budgeting is the vehicle for ensuring both understanding and ownership by front-line workers by communicating a corporate vision, empowering employees to act on the vision, and targeting and tracking short-term wins.

The result is an attitude among employees that ongoing improvement is a way of life.[1]

ENDNOTE

1. For more on this perspective, see John P. Kotter, "Why Transformation Efforts Fail," *Harvard Business Review*, March–April 1995, pp. 59–67.

Ralph Drtina, CPA, is professor of accounting and management, Crummer Graduate School of Business, Rollins College, Winter Park, Fla. He is a member of Mid-Florida Chapter, through which this article was submitted.

Steve Hoeger, CMA, CPA, is manager of financial analysis, Speed Queen, a Raytheon Company, Ripon, Wis. He is a member of Illowa (Wis.) Chapter.

John Schaub, CMA, is assistant controller, the HON Company, Muscatine, Iowa. He is a member of Illowa Chapter.

QUESTIONS

10.1a Is HON's budgeting philosophy an aggressive one? Is there a downside to this philosophy? Explain.

10.1b How are HON managers able to develop their budgets without the process taking all of their time? Explain.

10.2 Budgeting Gamesmanship

by Christopher K. Bart*

While most managers dislike having to deal with them, budgets are nevertheless essential to the management and control of an organization. Indeed, budgets are one of the most important tools management has for leading an organization toward its goals. As viewed in the literature, budgets are required to "institutionalize" a firm's goals, monitor the performance and progress of both the business and individual products, and measure the performance of managers.[1] While not all firms have five- or ten-year financial forecasts, practically all firms (beyond a certain maturity and size) have budgets.[2]

Given their unique role and importance in the overall planning process, it may seem superfluous to state that— budgets need to be rooted in reality. In fact, one of budgeting's main principles is that the budget numbers be challenging (yet realistic), honest, and accurate—given

---

* From: C. Bart, Budgeting Gamesmanship," *Academy of Management Executive* (1988): 285–294. Reprinted with permission.

the best information available.[3] Otherwise, both the purpose of strategic planning in general and manager motivation in particular is destroyed.

The translation of strategic plans into measurable financial standards and goals for an organization, however, is not a precise science.[4] In the first place, there is always uncertainty in the business environment. Consequently, making precise predictions as to a firm's performance and position vis-à-vis the competition can be problematic. Second, it is generally assumed that lower-level managers are wont to "play games" in preparing their budget forecasts—resulting in distorted and even falsified information for those to whom it is reported.[5] Consequently, this "budgeting gamesmanship" is generally considered a form of dysfunctional behavior in that it frustrates both the planning process and the accuracy of business and manager evaluations. It is, therefore, typically recommended that senior managers actively strive to discourage and eliminate budgeting gamesmanship.[6]

PRIOR RESEARCH AND THEORY

The games that managers play with their budgets is a topic that has received only limited attention from business writers and academics. In addition, budgeting gamesmanship activities have been reported largely by way of anecdotal reference in qualitative and very limited studies.[7] What research there has been has tended to confirm the general notion that when budgets are used to evaluate managerial performance, they influence the attitude of managers toward accounting information. Some of the budget-related variables that researchers have investigated to determine their impact on managerial behavior include the degree of budget participation, the level of budget difficulty, and the frequency of budget feedback.[8]

Despite these efforts, the topic of budgeting games has generally remained an area of speculation among budgeting researchers and academics.[9] The nature and extent of budget games are still relatively unknown; most managers, therefore, do not know how widespread budgeting gamesmanship is within their organization. Unfortunately, some previous studies have also tended to confuse faulty accounting systems with the way that managers use the information provided by those systems.[10] Thus, while budgeting gamesmanship is of interest, it remains understudied and misunderstood.[11]

Relatively little is known about how budgeting activities operate at the product level within large, multiproduct firms. The business policy literature on the strategy formulation process and its associated budgeting activities has generally confined itself to the corporate level.[12] Fortunately, research at the product level is becoming more common.[13] However, given the diversification trend among firms generally and the widespread use of product managers by firms to manage their multiproduct circumstances,[14] it is important that

"strategic processes and their related practices at the product level" be further explored.[15]

This article presents findings from some recently conducted clinical research that investigated budgeting gamesmanship at the product level in several large, diversified companies.

RESEARCH FINDINGS

Budgeting gamesmanship was found to be a widespread practice in six of the eight firms we examined—specifically, at the companies we will call Alpha, Beta, Delta, Kappa, Omega, and Phi. The types of games that product managers play in these firms; the size of the games; and the factors motivating, facilitating, and constraining the playing of games are examined in the following sections. Thereafter, the two firms where budgeting games were not found to exist (which we will call Gamma and Sigma) are discussed.

THE FIRMS WITH GAMES: THE CASES OF ALPHA, BETA, DELTA, KAPPA, OMEGA, AND PHI

The Games that Product Managers Play. Although they never referred to them as "games" per se, the product managers interviewed were not wanting for a rather extensive lexicon to describe their budgeting manipulations. "Cushion," "slush fund," "hedge," "flexibility," "cookie jar," "hip/back pocket," "pad," "kitty," "secret reserve," "war chest," and "contingency" were just some of the colorful terms used to label the games that managers played with their financial forecasts and budgets. For the most part, however, all of these terms could be used interchangeably.

We asked the product managers to expand on the specific types of games that were played with their budgets. A list of these games and their frequency of mention is provided in Exhibit 1. The responses show that the potential for budget games exists wherever a product manager is asked to make an estimate of his or her plans—in other words, practically anywhere. Their responses also suggest that some games are played more often than others (see rankings in Exhibit 1).

The Size of the Games. Product managers were asked to state the exact amount of "cushions and hedges" that they had built into their plans. The relevant statistics are displayed in Exhibit 2. As the exhibit shows, the size of the games can be quite substantial in absolute dollar terms and in relative terms as a percentage of sales. In some cases, the games could be said to have a material impact on overall company profitability. The overall average also appeared to be fairly large.

Facilitating Factors in Budgeting Gamesmanship. Product managers were quick to identify how certain situations facilitated—even encouraged—budgeting games in their strategic plans. The consensus was that the bigger the promotional budget, the greater the opportunity.

EXHIBIT 1. PRODUCT MANAGERS' BUDGET GAMES

Type of Game	Frequency of Mention	Rank
Understating volume estimates	48.5%	1
Undeclared/understated price increases	39.4%	3
Undeclared/understated cost reduction programs	36.4%	4
Overstated expenses		
—Advertising	48.5%	1
—Consumer promotions	45.5%	2
—Trade-related	33.3%	5
—Market research	27.3%	6
Undeclared line extensions	33.3%	5

Product history was another factor identified as facilitating cushions. New products, in particular, seemed to provide greater latitude in negotiating volume estimates as the firm had no prior experience with the product.

Other managers claimed, however, that even among products with fairly long histories, the opportunity for budget games was there—though greater for some products than for others. Opportunity seemed to vary with the *strategic posture* of the product. For example, in the case of "growth" postured products, managers stated that the amount of competitive activity was higher than normal and that prices tended to be unstable. Senior management was seen as being committed in terms of spending money. It was, therefore, deemed easier to convince top management of the need for "spending even more."

Products with a "harvest" strategic posture, on the other hand, were said to be characterized by less environmental uncertainty and usually smaller promotional budgets. The "cushionability" of these products was consequently seen to be reduced considerably.

Another condition identified as facilitating budgeting games was the time constraints imposed on senior managers during the product plan review period. As one manager put it:

"Senior management just doesn't have the time for checking every number you put into your plans .... So one strategy is to 'pad' everything. If you're lucky, you'll still have 50% of your cushions after the plan reviews."

Finally, product managers claimed that the less knowledgeable a group manager was about a product and the less experience he or she had, the less able he or she was at finding where the cushions were. One product manager was particularly candid in describing how his group manager's lack of experience was capitalized on:

"We've got this new group manager this year who came to us from a consumer promotion house. This just means that I'll have to be especially careful in

estimating the costs for my brands' consumer promotions. But I know that I'll be able to 'get him' when it comes to my advertising and trade promotion forecasts."

Factors That Constrain Budget Games. Several factors appeared to aid senior managers in the detection of budget games. One was the historical promotional spending pattern of the products. If current promotional expenses—calculated as a percentage of sales—were significantly out of line with earlier figures, they would be closely examined by senior management. Surprisingly, not all firms required these calculations and, where they did, a few product managers actually admitted to manipulating them to avoid calling attention to their current budget numbers. Some also stated that they would take advantage of "rounding out effects" in their calculations to accomplish the same purpose.

Interestingly, while all the product managers recognized that glaring, obvious, or ridiculous cushions invited their detection, many claimed that their selective use sometimes served a purpose. As one manager pointed out:

"It doesn't hurt to have a few things that 'stick out.' Management thinks that you're hiding something, so it's good if you give them some things to find. Sometimes they're happy with it. Other times, they come back and ask you for still more [profit]."

Another factor contributing to the discovery—and often the elimination—of product managers' budgeting games was the practice among senior managers of telling product managers what their total assignment profit target had to be. In such circumstances, if a product manager were unlucky, his or her cushions would be wiped out instantly. A variation of this practice was for the group product manager simply to demand that he or she be informed of where the hedges were. Few of the product managers who had experienced this latter situation, however, admitted to "telling all."

EXHIBIT 2. THE SIZE OF THE BUDGET GAMES ($ IN 000)[a]

Company	Mean ($)	Range ($)	Mean (% of sales)	Range (% of sales)
Alpha	$83.2	$11–210	0.3%	0.2–1.5%
Beta	175.0	50–500	1.5	0.5–3.0
Gamma	0.0	0–0	0.0	0.0–0.0
Delta	93.3	80–100	1.2	1.0–1.7
Kappa	640.0	100–1,400	1.9	0.4–3.2
Omega	298.8	44–750	0.8	0.6–1.5
Phi	940.0	100–2,460	2.1	0.5–5.0
Sigma	0.0	0–0	0.0	0.0–0.0
Average[b]	$364.3	n.a.	1.4%	n.a.

[a] Calculations are per product manager or per product assignment.

[b] Overall average calculations exclude Gamma and Sigma because product managers in these firms did not have any cushions in their budgets.

Most product managers expressed the view that the greater the profit pressures on the company, the more the marketing vice-president and group product managers would be driven to "ferret out the cushions." And, as previously mentioned, many managers said that for products with a harvest strategic posture, it was much more difficult to play budgeting games. Several remarked, however, that because the environment for harvest-postured products was relatively stable, there was less need for cushions to begin with.

Why Product Managers Play Games with Their Budgets. There were a number of factors motivating product managers to play games with their budgets. The first involved the objective setting process itself. One product manager described the problem as follows:

"When a product manager puts together his plans, he usually has a fairly good idea of what he thinks his business can do next year in both volume and profit terms. However, most managers here know that when their forecasts and budgets are submitted, invariably they will be changed by senior management—often with the simple 'stroke of a pen.' Consequently, if a manager were to give a realistic 'call' on his numbers, he could wind up with an even higher volume target and also [fewer] promotional dollars to achieve it. In the end, the product manager would have a profit target that everyone tells him 'he set' but that he would be hard pressed to deliver. So, you have to learn how to play the game."

Along similar lines, many managers commented that arbitrary budget cuts by senior management during the year also prompted the necessity of hedges. And several product managers blamed the budgeting gamesmanship within their firms on senior management's request for forecasts so early in the planning process.

A second major factor motivating managers to put hedges into their plans was market uncertainty. If "unanticipated competitive activities" threatened a product's volume forecast—and if additional funds were not available to counter the attack—a product manager would use his or her hedge (for example, cancel some "approved" but "not intended to be used" marketing program) in order to meet his original profit commitments.

The main reason motivating product managers to play games with their plans, however, was the drive to achieve their product's profit targets. This drive was, in turn, nurtured by one of two factors:

1. *formal company systems that specified the performance evaluation criteria for product manager salary adjustments and/or bonus payments; and*

2. *informal company practices that led product managers to perceive what the real performance evaluation criteria were within the organization.*

At Beta, for example, product managers were rewarded with a bonus payment that was determined, in part, on their products' profit performance compared with the "original plan." Cushions were, therefore, considered a form of insurance for product managers in meeting their profit targets—and thus earning their bonus. As one product manager put it:

"Some of the more successful managers here last year were the ones that really got their profit targets as low as possible and then 'exceeded plans' in terms of results. Unfortunately, last year I called my numbers realistically and am now being penalized in terms of my bonus. You might say, though, that last year I was young and innocent. This year I'm older and wiser!"

In two of the other firms, Alpha and Delta, either the product manager's formal job description or his or her formally contracted salary performance evaluation criteria was used to reinforce the notion of profit responsibility. Consequently, product managers in both these firms placed a very high premium on achieving their products' profit objectives.

There were other firms, however, where such formal mechanisms were not used (Kappa, Omega, and Phi) and still product managers were strongly motivated to achieve their profit targets. In other words, product managers somehow perceived that it was incumbent on them to deliver their products' budgeted profit targets. As one of them expressed it:

"Sure, I don't have anyone telling me that I have to meet my targets but I know that it's the first thing that the boss looks at before he considers my performance appraisal. After all, that's what I'm really being paid to do. He may not even bring up the fact that I missed my targets in some areas but I just know he takes that fact into account when he tells me my salary increase—or worse!"

Interestingly, the method by which reward criteria were conveyed (formal/explicit or informal/implicit) did not appear to have any influence on the degree of product manager gamesmanship as shown in Exhibit 3. Consequently, it does not seem to follow that the more explicitly rewards (such as pay, promotion, and incentives) are tied to goal achievement, the more product managers will try to pad their budgets.

Senior Management Attitudes. Senior managers in the firms where product managers played budget games acknowledged that they were aware of such practices among their subordinates. But there were important differences in term of their acceptance of it. Two dominant attitudes seemed to prevail.

The situation at Alpha, Delta, and Omega. For the most part, the senior executives in these firms did not seem to be overly concerned that game playing at lower levels existed. The attitude frequently expressed was: "I like to know that my product managers have some flexibility built into their plans." Their reasoning seemed to parallel that of their subordinates—that is, senior executives want to feel assured that if a product manager's market environment does not turn out as forecasted, he or she will be able to cancel certain programs and still be able to deliver the "bottom line." This tacit acceptance, in turn, enabled senior executives to feel more confident about meeting their more macro targets.

There was much more concern expressed, however about knowing the actual size of the product managers cushions. In fact, this was a traditional area of debate and negotiation among the various levels as senior managers tried to pinpoint just how much flexibility existed one level down. Top management's rationale in wanting to know was quite simple: "We've got to know so we can judge whether those guys down below have gone too wild—and in the process screwed up our inventory and capacity planning—or whether there is not enough slack built in." Given their profit responsibilities, however, it did not seem unusual that product managers were reluctant to disclose the scope of their game playing

activities. After all, disclosure of the cushions could mean their reduction or removal.

The situation at Beta, Kappa, and Phi. The senior managers in these firms, however, were not so relaxed about allowing their product managers to build cushions into their plans. The attitude in these firms was that senior management should be the custodian of the company's cushions, not lower-level managers; that it was top management's job to balance the portfolio of products, not individual product managers and that it was senior management's prerogative to decide which—if any—product managers were to be excused for not meeting their profit targets. The view was frequently expressed that giving lower-level managers "tight numbers" enabled senior managers to "see what stuff [the product managers] were made of"; and that holding all cushions at the corporate level put pressure on product managers which produced higher creativity and energy than would otherwise be achievable. The role of product managers at these firms, in turn, was to present their best profit forecasts and then "work like hell" to achieve them since they knew (as in the case of Beta) or strongly suspected (as in the case of Kappa and Phi) that they were going to be held responsible for their product assignment's profit target.

Attitudes, Cushion Size, and Performance. Unfortunately, results did not match expectations in the cases of those firms where senior managers opposed product manager game playing. In fact, their opposition seemed to have the opposite effect as product managers at these firms appeared to be more determined than managers elsewhere to have cushions. As Exhibit 4 shows, Beta, Kappa, and Phi have much higher cushioning levels, on average, than firms where product manager game playing is not so actively discouraged (Alpha, Delta, and Omega).

Senior management attitude also seemed to be related to company performance in a number of ways. For example, Exhibit 4 shows that firms where senior managers tolerate the reasonable use of cushions by lower-level managers (Alpha, Delta, and Omega), out-perform the companies where game playing is discouraged—both in terms of profits as a percentage of sales and profits as a percentage of assets. It is also our impression that in the firms where senior managers were at odds with their subordinates on the use of cushions, there were both more morale problems and higher turnaround than in the companies where senior management and product managers were more of one mind on the issue.

FIRMS WITHOUT GAMES: THE CASES OF GAMMA AND SIGMA

In two of the firms examined (Gamma and Sigma), product managers were found not to use cushions in their budgets. There were a number of factors to explain this occurrence.

EXHIBIT 3. EXPLICITNESS OF REWARD CRITERIA AND BUDGETING GAMESMANSHIP ACTIVITIES

Company	Reward Criteria Explicitness	Budget Games (mean % of sales)	Return on sales (%)	Return on assets (%)
Alpha	Job Description	0. 3%	3.4%	8.8%
Beta	Bonus criteria	1.5	3.5	5.7
Delta	Merit criteria	1.2	8.2	12.2
Kappa	Perceived/implicit	1.9	5.1	7.2
Omega	Perceived/implicit	0.8	3.9	9.5
Phi	Perceived/implicit	2.1	2.4	7.0

EXHIBIT 4. SENIOR MANAGEMENT ATTITUDES, BUDGETING GAMESMANSHIP ACTIVITIES, AND PERFORMANCE

Company	Senior Management Attitudes	Budget Games (mean % of sales)	Return on sales (%)	Return on assets (%)
Alpha	Tolerate games	0.3%	3.4%	8.8%
Delta	Tolerate games	1.2	8.2	12.2
Omega	Tolerate games	0.8	3.9	9.5
Beta	Discourage games	1.5	3.5	5.7
Kappa	Discourage games	1.9	5.1	7.2
Phi	Discourage games	2.1	2.4	7.0

First, senior managers at these companies did not encourage product managers to pursue budgeting activities. But unlike their counterparts at Beta, Kappa, and Phi (who were prodded into disobeying their superiors because of the reward criteria), product managers at Gamma and Sigma were not formally or informally held responsible for their products' profit performance, nor did they perceive such responsibility. Instead, product managers in these firms stated that their performance evaluations tended to focus on three-areas: (1) personal development, (2) training of assistants, and (3) overall management of their products. Thus, there appeared to be no formal or informal signals prompting product managers to play games with their budgets. This does not mean, however, that the product managers at Gamma and Sigma did not strive to achieve their products' profit targets, because they did. The difference—as the product managers themselves explained—as that of being "profit conscious" as opposed to being "profit responsible":

"You have to ask yourself: Why is the product manager here? He is the person responsible for formulating and executing the objectives and strategies of the brands in his assignment. It's expected, then, that he's going to work toward— strive—to achieve the financial targets in his plans. You don't have to tell him what his job is—he already knows. The key point is that the product manager has to take his assignment and job personally. If he does then, naturally, he'll have high commitment to seeing his brands' financial objectives realized."

But profit consciousness without game playing also depended on one critical assumption. This product manager put it most succinctly:

"You have to believe that your boss isn't going to hurt you at performance evaluation time when you did everything humanly possible to hit your targets but still you missed them."

Thus it appeared that in the firms without budgeting gamesmanship, there was a good deal of trust between senior management and product managers. Senior managers trusted their subordinates to report honestly and to work ambitiously. Product managers, on the other hand, relied on their superiors to treat and judge them with fairness and understanding.

But how does this climate of trust maintain its balance? Why should product managers trust their bosses? Why shouldn't product managers in these firms try to put cushions into their plans and succeed? And why should they rely on their bosses not to betray them at performance evaluation time?

Essentially, the relationship of trust seemed to be sustained largely as a result of senior management effort. Senior managers at both Gamma and Sigma stated that they worked hard to maintain the climate of trust, that trust smoothed the relationship between superiors and subordinates; and that betraying the trust of lower-level managers had serious implications for both the prosperity of the firm and their own career paths. As one group product manager put it:

"The moment I betray my product manager, I've had it in this company. My bosses will be angry with me for being unfair. And my subordinates will never take my word at face value again. They'll start to play games with me and I'll have to try and catch them … and that sure can waste a lot of time!"

ATTITUDES, REWARD CRITERIA, AND PERFORMANCE

Throughout our study, the attitude of senior managers in conjunction with the product managers' reward criteria seemed to be related to both the scope of the games product managers played and the performance of the firm as a whole. Referring to Exhibit 5, the firms with the highest amount of game playing and the lowest performance were those firms in which the senior managers actively opposed budgeting games at lower levels and where the product managers felt that they had "profit responsibility" (at Beta, Kappa, and Phi). Lower levels of budgeting gamesmanship and higher company performance, on the other hand, were associated with two different situations. In one situation (Gamma and Sigma), senior managers opposed budgeting games at lower levels but also took the steps necessary to ensure that product managers did not feel they had to play them for rewards. In the other situation (Alpha, Delta, and Omega), senior managers did not discourage game playing—they even tacitly encouraged it—but product managers were either formally or informally held responsible for their products' profits. It appears, therefore, that where budgeting games are concerned, as long as that attitudes of senior managers are consistent with the product managers' reward system, superior performance may result. And because game playing was found to occur in both high- and low-performing firms, it cannot be automatically, regarded as dysfunctional behavior among product managers.

SUMMARY AND CONCLUSIONS

The findings presented in this article attempt to shed light into the games that product managers play in the course of preparing their products' budgets. Our study has shown that product managers do indeed play games in their budgets, that the games are many and varied, that some games are preferred to others, and that the actual size of the budgeting games appears to be quite large on average. The study has also identified the factors that contribute to and facilitate the playing of budgeting games and those that frustrate and constrain their occurrence.

Four of the findings, however, deserve highlighting. First, the data suggest that formal and explicit performance evaluation criteria are no more likely to result in higher levels of budgeting gamesmanship than less formal and more implicit reward criteria. Second, the firm's reward system seems to have a greater influence over the behavior of product managers (insofar as budgeting games are concerned) than the verbal dictates of senior managers. In other words, lower-level managers will ignore the orders of superiors not to play budgeting games if they perceive that their performance evaluation will be based on whether they achieve their budget target. Third, the attitudes of senior managers in

conjunction with the product managers' reward systems seem to be related to both the scope of the games that product managers play and the performance of the firm as a whole. Finally, the findings suggest that budgetary game playing by product managers does not necessarily constitute dysfunctional behavior as it is conventionally viewed in the management literature. Instead, budgeting games may simply be a form of tactical maneuver that product managers deploy to survive in what they consider to be a hostile environment.

RESEARCH METHODOLOGY

Budgeting Gamesmanship. This term is defined as the deliberate and premeditated manipulation of current year sales, cost, and profit forecasts by product managers to project an overly conservative image into their product budgets. To measure this variable, product managers in the study were simply asked whether they "played games" in their budgets. While most managers initially expressed reluctance to discuss such a sensitive matter, all eventually spoke candidly—on the understanding that individual identities would be kept strictly confidential.

Sample Selection and Size. The study was based on indepth interviews with product managers in eight large diversified firms. Firms engaged in diverse activities were selected to ensure a wide variety of situations and circumstances. Six of the firms (Alpha, Beta, Gamma, Delta, Kappa, and Omega) were wholly owned subsidiary divisions of major U.S.-based firms. The remaining two firms (Phi and Sigma) were single-division, stand-alone companies. A summary of key financial and operating performance statistics for the units is presented in the accompanying exhibit.

The unit of analysis was the individual product manager. The budgeting system in each firm was also mature.

Research Instrument. The following list of questions constituted the research instrument for the study on which this article is based:

- Do product-level managers play games with their budgets? If yes, why?
- How widespread are budgeting games among product managers?
- What exactly are the types and scope of budget games that product managers play?
- Are there preferred games?
- Is there a relationship between budgeting gamesmanship and different product strategies?
- What factors contribute to the detection of product managers' budget games by senior managers and what factors allow them to go undetected?
- How does the product managers' performance evaluation system influence budgetary game playing?

EXHIBIT 5. SENIOR MANAGEMENT ATTITUDES, PRODUCT MANAGER SALES/PROFIT RESPONSIBILITY, BUDGETING GAMESMANSHIP, AND PERFORMANCE

Company	Senior Management Attitudes	Sales/profit Responsibility	Budget Games (mean % of sales)	Return on sales/assets (%)
Beta	Discourage games	Yes	1.5%	3.5/5.7%
Kappa	Discourage games	Yes	1.9	5.1/7.2
Phi	Discourage games	Yes	2.1	2.4/7.0
Gamma	Discourage games	No	0.0	9.5/44.3
Sigma	Discourage games	No	0.0	9.3/9.4
Alpha	Tolerate games	Yes	0.3	3.4/8.8
Delta	Tolerate games	Yes	1.2	8.2/12.2
Omega	Tolerate games	Yes	0.8	3.9/9.5

PERFORMANCE AND OPERATING STATISTICS FOR THE EIGHT RESEARCH FIRMS[a] (IN MILLIONS OF DOLLARS)

	Alpha	Beta	Gamma	Delta	Kappa	Omega	Phi	Sigma	Avg.
Sales	$110	$267	$94	$87	$201	$300	$1,900	$2,100	$632
Profit									
Percentage of sales	3.4%	3.5%	9.5%	8.2%	5.1%	3.9%	2.4%	9.3%	5.8%
Percentage of assets	8.8%	5.7%	44.3%	12.2%	7.2%	9.5%	7.0%	9.4%	8.9%
Total number of products	23	24	16	33	25	40	12	24	24.6
Number of "growth" products	9	9	8	11	10	22	4	8	10.1
Number of "harvest" products	14	15	8	22	15	18	8	16	14.5
Number of product managers/product assignments	5	9	4	9	7	9	10	4	7.1
Average product assignment size									
Number of products	4.6	2.7	4.0	3.7	3.6	4.4	1.2	6.0	3.5
Sales volume	$21.6	$15.9	$5.4	$5.1	$25.7	$30.0	$106.0	$375.0	$58.4
Product concentration	Food	Food	Health & Beauty Aids	Home & Beauty Aids	Food	Food	Beverages	Commodity Metals	

[a] Adapted from company data. Absolute numbers have been disguised. Key ratios, however, have been preserved.

- Do senior managers encourage or discourage budget gamesmanship by their product managers?
- Do product manager budgeting games represent a form of dysfunctional behavior?

Data Collection. The point of entry into each company was the president or a divisional general manager. Data on the management of products were gathered by on-site interviews with product, product group, and corporate-level managers and by physical inspection of company documents (such as individual product plans). In total, 113 managers (including 41 of the firms' 57 product managers) were interviewed over a period of 151 hours.

Limitations. The research method restricted the sample size. The sample selection method (judgmental) and the sample size also limited the generalizability of the findings. The high response rate by company managers, however, gives the results high validity in spite of the small number of firms sampled. It should also be noted that the exploratory nature of this study precluded the testing of all possible variables.

ENDNOTES

The author wishes to express his appreciation to the Social Sciences and Humanities Research Council of Canada for funding this research study. The author is also indebted to Professors Robert Cooper, Peter Banting, Julie Desjardins, Wayne Taylor, and Frank Tyaack of McMaster University for their comments and suggestions on earlier versions of this article.

1. J. Bower, *Maintaining the Resource Allocation Process: A Study of Corporate Investment Planning*, Boston: Graduate School of Business, Harvard University, 1970; W. J. Bruns and D. T. DeCoster, *Accounting and Its Behavioral Implications*, New York: McGraw-Hill. 1969; A. Hopwood, *Accounting and Human Behavior*, Englewood Cliffs, NJ:

Prentice-Hall, 1977; H. Koontz and C. O'Donnell, *Principles of Management: An Analysis of Managerial Functions*, New York: McGraw-Hill, 1964; P. Lorange and R. F. Vancil, *Strategic Planning Systems*, Englewood Cliffs, NJ: Prentice-Hall, 1977; G. A. Steiner, *Strategic Planning: What Every Manager Must Know*, New York: The Free Press, 1979; and G. A. Welsch, *Budgeting: Profit Planning and Control*, Englewood Cliffs, NJ: Prentice-Hall, 1976.

2. See W. J. Bruns and D. T. DeCoster. Endnote 1.

3. See W. J. Bruns and D. T. DeCoster, H. Koontz and C. O'Donnell, Steiner, and Welsch, Endnote 1.

4. See A. Hopwood. Endnote 1.

5. C. Argyris, *Impact of Budgets on People*, New York: Controllership Foundation, 1952; J. Cherrington and D. J. Cherrington. "Budget Games for Fun and Frustration," *Management Accounting*, January 1976, 28–32; F. Collins, "The Interaction of Budget Characteristics and Personality Variables with Budgetary Response Attitudes," *Accounting Review*, April 1978, 324–335; and H. Simon, H. Guetzkow, G. Kozmetsky, and C. Lyndall, *Centralization vs. Decentralization of the Controller's Department*, New York: Controllership Foundation, 1954.

6. See G. H. Hofstede's *The Games of Budget Control*, London: Tavistock Publications, 1968: Hopwood, Steiner, and Welsch, Endnote 1.

7. See C. Argyris. D. J. Cherrington et al., F. Collins, and H. Simon et al., Endnote 5: and P. Munter, F. Collins, and D. Finn, *Gameplay in Budgeting*, Oxford, OH: Planning Executives Institute, 1983.

8. S. Becker and D. Green, "Budgeting and Employee Behavior," *Journal of Business*, Vol. 35, October 1962, 392–402; W. J. Bruns and D. J. DeCoster, and A. Hopwood, Endnote 1; F. Collins, Endnote 5; D. Searfoss and R. Monczka, "Perceived Participation in the Budget Process," *Academy of Management Journal*, December 1973: and R. Sapp and R. Seiler. "Accounting for Performance: Stressful But Satisfying," *Management Accounting*, August 1980, 29–35.

9. P. Munter et al., Endnote 7.

10. A. Hopwood. "An Empirical Study of the Role of Accounting Data in Performance Evaluation," *Empirical Research in Accounting: Selected Studies*, 1972, supplement to the *Journal of Accounting Research*. Vol. 10, 156–182; R. Dew and K. Gee, *Management Control and Information*, New York: Macmillan, 1973.

11. P. Munter et al., Endnote 7.

12. D. E. Schendel and C. W. Hofer, *Strategic Management: A New View of Business Policy and Planning.* Boston: Little, Brown, 1979.

13. C. K. Bart, "Product Strategy and Formal Structure," *Strategic Management Journal*, 7, 1986, 293–312. J. Bower, Endnote 1.

14. *Current Advertising Practices: Opinions as to Future Trends*, New York: Association of National Advertisers, 1974.

15. T. J. Peters and R. H. Waterman, *In Search of Excellence: Lessons from America's Best Run Companies*, New York: Harper & Row, 1982.

Dr. Christopher K. Bart is a recognized expert in the areas of corporate strategic planning for turnaround situations, planning for performance, strategy implementation, and new venture management. He has a unique expertise in helping firms organize their internal structure better to achieve their goals. Dr Bart has been involved in examining the issues and problems associated with managing multibusiness firms in the consumer products industry. Currently, he is investigating the organizational practices that large, diversified firms use to manage and control product innovation.

Dr. Bart is an associate professor of business policy at the Faculty of Business, McMaster University, in Hamilton, Ontario, Canada. He has also recently been a Research Fellow at the newly created National Centre for Management Research and Development in London, Ontario, Canada. Professor Bart holds degrees in business administration from York University (MBA, 1975) and the University of Western Ontario (Ph.D., 1982). A highly regarded lecturer, he has been named both "Outstanding Undergraduate Business Professor" and "MBA Professor of the Year," He has also received many academic awards and honors.

Among his other qualifications. Dr. Bart is a chartered accountant. He is a past director of the Planning Executives Institute and a member of numerous boards of directors and professional organizations.

QUESTION

10.2 What are some of the factors that constrain the budget games discussed by Christopher Bart? Explain.

10.3 Budgeting Made Easy

by Steve Hornyak*

It's budget time!

In most companies, these three words strike fear in employees' hearts. Financial officers and management accountants brace themselves for reconciling ream of spreadsheets that may reveal wildly disparate data depending on order and configuration. Nonfinance employees in various divisions scurry to understand their role in the process and struggle to pull together the facts and figures they hope will appear attractive to management. And fast-approaching budget deadlines invariably will result in weeks of all-night numbers crunching if the process proves to be as bumpy as usual.

Managers in the modem mid- to large-sized company want to work a different way, and a number of additional factors are prompting a change in their philosophy regarding budgeting and planning. Many of these organizations are expanding rapidly, prompting managers to demand precise resource allocation to support growth plans. Operational managers are heavily involved in preparing the company's budget. A tight management plan is contingent upon a comprehensive and accurate budget. A company's officers want the budget completed on time and correct on the first round. And people in various departments want to know how their piece of the budget affects overall corporate operations so they can do some "what if" scenarios and modeling.

Fortunately, new technology solutions are taking the toil, guesswork, and disparity out of the budgeting process. Enterprisewide budgeting and planning over the Internet ("e-budgeting") is a corporate service application that supports an organization's operations and efficiency. The "e" in e-budgeting refers to both "electronic" and "enterprisewide" and it represents a revolutionary new way for companies to plan for the future. Companies can implement a budgeting system that scales to the entire enterprise, and they can harness the power of the Internet from any location in the world to budget effectively. Some significant benefits e-budgeting offers an organization include:

- Reducing administrative costs and tasks.
- Increasing service levels to employees.
- Freeing the finance department to focus on strategy, not spreadsheets.

As financial managers and management accountants, you can help steer your company toward these new, Internet-based applications that can deliver immediate benefits, especially the streamlining of a previously cumbersome process. By discovering ways new e-budgeting technology can deliver business solutions, you can transform the budgeting and planning process from a chore of drudgery to a strategic luxury for your organization.

PITFALLS OF TRADITIONAL BUDGETING

First, let's look at the traditional budgeting process. Whether manual or performed via spreadsheets, in the past, the budgeting process has depended on the notion that everyone involved in the planning phase comes equipped with a baseline knowledge of accounting. This is rarely the case. Although few will admit it, many nonfinance participants in the budgeting process often don't know where to begin. They understand their jobs thoroughly—and how those functions fit into overall operations—but they have not been trained in any kind of budgeting procedures. And they have been told that all the tools anyone needs to develop a specific slice of a company's budget are a spreadsheet and a deadline. But a lack of guidance and knowledge of appropriate budgeting tools for nonfinance participants can hinder them when they try to develop a meaningful contribution to their company's master plan.

Another stumbling block results when different departments use a variety of spreadsheet or software program to pull together their part of the budget information. The finance department has to compile all the spreadsheets—that usually are not interpretable—and management accountants must weed through the resultant paperwork that has been generated in these disparate systems. It's an intensive, unnecessary extra step that begins to slow down the process.

The budgeting process also is prolonged because the finance department must account for any time lag in this input from remote-user participants. Management accountants and financial managers watch deadlines disappear while they wait for copies of spreadsheets via e-mail and "snail mail." Gridlock results. Waiting on the "latest and greatest" version of a manager's budget component and then trying to reconcile disparate numbers with others in the system can be a financial manager's worst nightmare. Never mind that numbers may have to be rekeyed every time a change is made because the data in different systems don't affect each other.

The biggest drawback of traditional budgeting systems is the inability of participating individuals to access and use historical data during the budgeting and planning process. In fact, employees or managers

---

* From: S. Hornyak, "Budgeting Made Easy," *Management Accounting* (October 1998): 18–23. Reprinted with permission.

attempting to allocate their sliver of the company funds often work in a vacuum. Without access to historical budgeting information, creating a budget from the ground up or making alterations to the existing budget may become tedious—and sometimes futile—tasks for nonfinance users.

HOW E-BUDGETING WORKS

Although a company can use e-budgeting programs as stand-alone applications, they are most effective when integrated with financial systems, particularly with a general ledger application, so budgeters can "close the loop." Participants in the budgeting process can link back to past data, validate assumptions implicit in their budget area, and, at some levels, see how their numbers will affect others.

An e-budgeting solution completely automates the development of an organization's budget and forecast. From anywhere in the world, at all times, participants in the process can log on through the Internet to access their budget and any pertinent related information so they can work on their plans. Web-based enterprise budgeting systems offer a centrally administered system that provides easy-to-use, flexible tools for the end users who are responsible for budgeting. The Web functionality of these applications allows constant monitoring, updates, and modeling.

Pushing the initial phase of the budget process from the back office to corporate managers and front-fine employees frees up the finance department to focus on more strategic issues such as "what if" modeling, sales, and fiscal objectives. In fact, corporate service applications such as e-budgeting bolster employee productivity by reducing administrative tasks and supporting the day-to-day operation of an organization.

Although Web-based enterprisewide budgeting and planning solutions facilitate participation by a wide range of users, they rely on the finance department to maintain ultimate control. It's the management accountants and financial managers who will monitor the process continually from inception to the final working budget.

E-budgeting provides the flexibility demanded by modem organizations. For example, the finance department can request across-the-board reallocations of expenditures and model the result immediately. No longer do financial managers and management accountants have to go back and forth with other managers, reinputing data and retallying results. E-budgeting can eliminate the cumbersome accounting tasks of pulling numbers from disparate files, cutting and pasting, entering and uploading, and constantly performing reconciliation. Financial managers don't want to scroll through hundreds of spreadsheets; they simply want to see if the company is making money, how much it's making, and if actual income and expenditures are on track with budget projections. Web-based solutions bring everyone to "the same page" and free up the finance department for strategic decision making rather than paper pushing.

Also, a Web-based budgeting application lets managers access data from the office, home, or even the airport—wherever they happen to be working. It broadens the system's availability to the user community. With Web deployment and distributed capabilities, new systems are accessible to users regardless of the technology at their workstations.

For maximum control, e-budgeting incorporates an automated "check-out/cheek-in" process that provides flexibility for highly distributed users (those famous road warriors) while maintaining strict security to sensitive information. All activity is logged and recorded to provide a complete audit trail, which allows the finance department to maintain ultimate control.

Because many employees outside finance may have little finance and budgeting experience, e-budgeting applications take into consideration the needs of various users and the types of budgets for which they are responsible. For example, a customer service manager needs to be able to do workforce planning. He needs the application to help him conduct detailed planning by individual employee, not just at the salary account level. He needs to be able to decide when each person on his team will get a salary increase and what that increase percentage will be. In addition to tabulating bonuses and overtime, an e-budgeting system will automatically calculate all related benefits percentages for his department behind the scenes.

Similarly, an IT director who makes important capital planning decisions for the company needs an easy tool that allows her to plan for new networks, new servers, and new PCs. With an e-budgeting system, she can easily ascertain which periods of the year capital additions will be needed and can plan for capital acquisitions by major category or even down to specific models of PCs. Also, e-budgeting automatically calculates the related depreciation expense associated with each type of capital item. It's just one more piece of the overall plan that is required to derive a realistic budget from which to manage. In all cases, companies can use an e-budgeting system to help build these diverse types of budgets—capital, expense, human resources, and revenue—with ease and flexibility.

E-budgeting solutions also facilitate flexible planning with their "what-if" modeling capabilities. For example, a controller could propose, "What would happen if we increase revenue by 10% or cut R & D by 2%?" The application would model the result. E-budgeting technologies also are capable of supporting mass updates and changes through top-down and bottom-up revisions, so individuals can quickly forecast a wide array of budgetary possibilities before deriving an accurate final projection.

BUDGETING FOR "OUR CORNER OF THE WORLD"

The intuitive interface of Web-based budgeting solutions recognizes that most users are nonaccountants who may prepare a budget only once a year. These users may not know how to develop a plan, or they may be proficient with planning but may not want to know the intricacies of how a budget system works. Take, for instance, a CIO (chief information officer) who is responsible for a considerable amount of a company's budget. He or she has control over investments in technology and is therefore accountable for the technology budget. The CIO does not necessarily want to be accounting savvy, but because this executive's department will be spending money from the annual budget, he or she is in charge of developing a budget forecast.

Now the CIO can use an intuitive e-budgeting application to submit his/her segment of the total corporate budget and save the aggravation of performing manual input. Members of the MIS department also can submit subsets of their collective budget through a standardized system. Other individuals, who are experts in their areas of the company's operations but who may not have an accounting background, can participate strategically whether they are in charge of workstation upgrades, new software, or the online services budget.

As you can see, an intuitive e-budgeting solution, which is based on artificial intelligence and business rules programmed into the software, integrates all the individual "pieces" into a well-developed composite of the corporate budget. Quite simply, it gives budgeters the necessary tools to plan accurately and efficiently and the finance department the mechanism to integrate all components into a streamlined "big picture" of how the company is expected to spend its money.

BENEFITS OF E-BUDGETING

Chief among the benefits of Web-based enterprisewide budgeting and planning are a dramatic reduction of administrative resources devoted to tasks and transactions, an overall increase in employee participation, and a significantly more strategic focus for the finance department. New e-budgeting solutions reduce the number of administrative tasks and the associated time and cost necessary to carry out the budgeting and planning process. By slashing the need for hundreds of spreadsheets and by eliminating the monotonous task of reconciliation, the e-budgeting process uses a variety of creative techniques to cut down the paperwork trail and save time for the finance department and other budget participants. Administrative costs and tasks are curtailed because fewer handoffs are required. E-budgeting provides check-out/check-in management and top-down/bottom-up revisions, so budgeters can fill out, print out, and exchange fewer reports. Everything is online. E-budgeting also offers analysis and reporting capabilities with the ability to drill down to details. This process provides automated consolidations and a clean audit trail.

E-budgeting also extends the budgeting process to a wider range of users. Corporate managers and employees with budget responsibility gain easy access and an intuitive interface via the Internet. For example, an employee can "check out" the budget on a laptop (like you check out books with your library card) and work on it while traveling on a plane. When finished with the changes, he or she can log back into the application via the Web and upload the changes to the application database. The new figures the employee inputs into the budget will immediately affect and be affected by other budget components when the employee "checks in" (returns) the information via the Internet. Web access with distributed/disconnected capabilities is a key enabler for this flexibility.

Now more than ever, companies are following strict budgets, and managers are being held accountable for their budget plans. Many companies actually base compensation plans on budgeting. Organizations often award merit pay increases or base promotions on a manager's ability to develop, implement, and meet budgets. E-budgeting systems provide these managers with the right tools to budget accurately and effectively.

All budgeting participants benefit from a user-definable interface that is customized to an employee's skill sets. E-budgeting systems also provide the historical data necessary for current budgeters in any department to make crucial decisions and allocations based on past forecasts and trends.

New e-budgeting solutions provide the tools for a variety of employees to help build different types of budgets, whether they are expense, capital, or payroll/HR. A corporate human resources executive planning a budget can take a close look at "the people costs" for each individual in the company, not just from the perspective of salary, but also taking into account other line item information such as forecasted bonuses and raises.

Most important, e-budgeting allows an organization's finance department to focus on more strategic activities instead of managing spreadsheet consolidations. They can shift their attention to business analysis and more proactive efforts to monitor critical issues in a company's growth cycle. For example, they can research how expanding a particular service in a geographic region would affect the revenue forecast and the associated expenses that would offset that effect. Or they can easily do top-down adjustments and take a look at the bottom line if expenses are reduced for each department by 5% or 10%. This "what-if?" modeling will help budgeters ascertain the impact of changes to the budget and make informed decisions about the status of the budget.

A STRATEGIC SOLUTION FOR THE ENTERPRISE

Organizations put a huge amount of time and energy into budgeting, but the process often is so labor intensive that the finance department gets bogged down in data consolidation and verification rather than planning and analysis. The major value of new e-budgeting solutions is that they turn budgeting into a management tool instead of an accounting chore. These powerful applications dramatically change how an organization's employees develop strategic budgets and plans.

E-budgeting solutions streamline and transform the strategic budgeting process for nonfinancial users. The applications empower front-line employees and corporate managers to participate in areas in which they have expertise and allow the finance department to perform its vital role of fusing information into strategic goals and objectives. New e-budgeting solutions can eliminate literally hundreds of spreadsheets and staff-hours from the budget process.

Budgeting should never be a full-time job, but many companies are moving toward "continuous budgeting" and away from an annual or quarterly plan. That means someone will be accessing budget data almost every day in some shape or form, especially when the potential for new business or products arises. A Web-based solution for the entire enterprise will let executives produce a more accurate and strategically sound budget than ever before.

CANADIAN COMPANY ADOPTS WEB-BASED BUDGETING PROGRAM

Last year Toronto Dominion Bank decided to use the World Wide Web to advance its business objectives. Since then more than 200,000 bank customers have used TD Access Web and PC Banking in Canada. In addition, the company launched TD Access Web Business, a comprehensive, secure, and easy-to-use Internet banking service for its Main Street Banking small business customers, and it introduced TD Access WebFunds, an Internet-based mutual fund trading service.

When executives at Toronto-Dominion Bank were searching for a new solution capable of handling the bank's enterprisewide budgeting and planning function, they once again turned to the Internet. The company selected Clarus Corporation's Web-deployed, enterprisewide Clarus™ Budget solution.

"In the past, we have compiled our business plan using hundreds of spreadsheets, and our analysts have spent a disproportionate amount of their time compiling and verifying data from multiple sources," said David Bickley, associate vice president and controller of Toronto-Dominion Bank's Corporate & Investment Banking Group. "Implementing a Web-based, enterprisewide budgeting solution will help us develop business plans and allow our analysts to be proactive in monitoring quarterly results."

Clarus Budget combines operating, capital, and personnel budgeting in one distributed application. Through reducing paperwork and pencil pushing associated with administrative tasks, providing intuitive tools to participants in the budget process, and enabling its finance department to focus squarely on strategy, Claris Budget is expected to provide a significant business payback for Toronto-Dominion Bank.

Steve Hornyak is vice president, marketing, for Clarus Corp. (formerly SQL Financials International, Inc.). He joined the company in 1994. Prior to joining Clarus Corp., he worked for Oracle Corporation and for Price Waterhouse LLP (now PricewaterhouseCoopers) in its Management Consulting Services Group. He can be reached at 770-291-3900 or via e-mail at hornyak@ claruscorp.com.

QUESTIONS

10.3a What are four of the pitfalls of traditional budgeting according to Steve Hornyak?

10.3b What are the major benefits that Hornyak envisions for e-budgeting?

10.4 Corporate Budgeting is Broken—Let's Fix It

Traditional budgeting processes waste time, distort decisions, and turn honest managers into schemers. It doesn't have to be that way—if you're willing to sever the ties between budgets and compensation.

by Michael C. Jensen*

Corporate budgeting is a joke, and everyone knows it. It consumes a huge amount of executives' time, forcing them into endless rounds of dull meetings and tense negotiations. It encourages managers to lie and cheat, lowballing targets and inflating results, and it penalizes them for telling the truth. It turns business decisions into elaborate exercises in gaming. It sets colleague against colleague, creating distrust and ill will. And it distorts incentives, motivating people to act in ways that run counter to the best interests of their companies.

Consider just two examples. At one international heavy-equipment manufacturer, managers were so set on hitting their quarterly revenue target that they shipped unfinished products from their plant in England all the way to a warehouse in the Netherlands, near the customer, for final assembly. By shipping the incomplete products, they were able to realize the sales before the end of the quarter and thus fulfill their budget goal and make their bonuses. But the high cost of assembling the goods at a distant location—it required not only the rental of the warehouse but also additional labor—ended up reducing the company's overall profit.

Then there's the recent debacle involving a big beverage company. The vice president of sales for one of the company's largest regions dramatically, underpredicted demand for an upcoming major holiday. His motivation was simple—he wanted to ensure a low revenue target that he could be certain of exceeding. But the price for his little white lie was extremely high: The company based its demand planning on his sales forecast and consequently ran out of its core product in one of its largest markets at the height of the holiday selling season.

Such cases of distorted decision making are legion in business. No doubt, you could list similar instances that you've observed—or perhaps even instigated—at your own company The sad thing is, these shenanigans have become so common that they're almost invisible. The budgeting process is so deeply embedded in corporate life that the attendant lies and games are simply accepted as business as usual, no matter how destructive they are.

But it doesn't have to be that way. Even if you grant that budgeting, like death and taxes, will always be with us, deceitful behavior doesn't have to be. That's because the budget process itself isn't the root cause of the counterproductive actions; rather, it's the use of budget targets to determine compensation. When managers are told they'll get bonuses if they reach specific performance goals, two things inevitably happen. First, they attempt to set low targets that are easily achievable. Then, once the targets are in place, they do whatever it takes to see that they hit them, even if the company suffers as a result.

Only by severing the link between budgets and bonuses—by rewarding people purely for their accomplishments, not for their ability to hit targets—will we take away the incentive to cheat. Only then will we eliminate the budgeting incentives that drive individuals to act in ways that destroy corporate value.

CHEATERS PROSPER

Let's look more carefully at how budgets drive compensation and, in turn, behavior. In a traditional pay-for-performance incentive system, a manager's total cash compensation (salary plus bonus) is constant until a minimum performance hurdle is reached—commonly 80% of a budgeted target. (The target might be expressed as profits, sales, output, or any number of things; for our purposes, it doesn't matter what's being measured.) When the manager exceeds that hurdle, she receives a bonus—often a substantial one. The bonus then increases as performance mounts above the hurdle until the bonus is capped at some maximum level—120% of the target is usual. This system is illustrated in Exhibit 1 "A Typical Executive Compensation Plan."

EXHIBIT 1. A TYPICAL EXECUTIVE COMPENSATION PLAN

In a traditional pay-for-performance compensation plan, a manager earns a hurdle bonus when performance reaches a certain level (A). The bonus increases with performance until it hits a maximum cap (B). The kinks in the pay-for-performance line create incentives to game the system. When performance approaches the hurdle target, a manager has a strong incentive to accelerate the realization of revenue and profit. When performance hits the cap, the manager has a strong incentive to push revenue and profit into the next year.

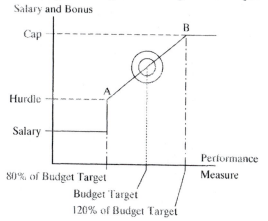

The kinks in the pay-for-performance line—caused by the minimum hurdle bonus and the maximum cap—create strong incentives to game the system. As long as the manager believes she can make the minimum hurdle, she will naturally try her best to increase performance—by legitimate means or, if push comes to shove, by illegitimate ones. If the measure is profits, for instance, she will have a strong incentive to increase the current year's earnings at the expense of next year's, either by pushing expenses into the future (delaying purchases or hires, for example) or by moving future revenues to the present (booking orders early or offering special discounts to customers, for example).

If, on the other hand, the manager concludes that she can't make the minimum hurdle, her incentives flip 180 degrees. Now her goal is to move earnings from the present to the future. After all, her compensation doesn't change whether she misses the target by a little or a lot; she still gets her full salary (assuming she doesn't get fired, of course). But by shifting profits forward—by prepaying expenses, taking write-offs, or delaying the realization of revenues—she increases her chances of getting a large bonus the following year. This is a variation on the "big bath" theory of corporate financial reporting: If you're going to take a loss, take as big a loss as possible.

Finally, if the manager is having a great year and her performance is nearing the budget cap, she again has an incentive to push profits into the future. Because she's not going to get any additional compensation if performance exceeds the level at which the cap is set, accelerating expenses or postponing sales will have no negative impact on her current earnings, but it will raise the odds that she'll reap a high bonus next year as well. This perverse incentive becomes even stronger if her current year's performance is used in setting the following year's targets, as is often the case.

When these kinds of subterfuge simply move profits from one year to another—by changing accruals, for example—the adverse impact on company value is probably small. But rarely is the activity so benign. Usually, the shuffling of dollars results from decisions that change the operating characteristics of a company, and it generates high, if sometimes hidden, costs that erode the total value of the company. We saw such erosion in the two examples presented earlier. We see it as well in the common practice of channel stuffing—when managers ship loads of products to distributors to meet immediate sales goals, even though they know many of the goods will soon come back as returns. And we see it in distorted pricing decisions. The managers of one durable-goods manufacturer, struggling to meet their minimum bonus hurdles, announced late one year that they would be raising prices 10% across the board on January 2. The managers made the price hikes because they wanted to encourage customers to place orders by year-end so they could hit their annual sales goals. But the price increase was out of line with the competition and undoubtedly ended up costing the company sales and market share.

Even more insidious effects are common. One of the main reasons that big companies have budgets in the first place is to help coordinate the disparate parts of their businesses. By openly sharing accurate information and basing decisions on a common set of numbers, the thinking goes, you ensure harmonious interactions among units, leading to efficient processes, high-quality products, low inventories, and satisfied customers. But as soon as you start motivating unit and department heads to falsify forecasts and otherwise hide or manipulate critical information, you undermine the salutary effects of budgeting. Indeed, the whole effort backfires. You end up with uncoordinated, chaotic interactions as people make decisions on the basis of distorted information they receive from other units and from headquarters. Moreover, since managers are well aware that everyone is attempting to game the system for personal reasons, you create an organization rife with cynicism, suspicion, and mistrust.

When the manipulation of budget targets becomes routine, moreover, it can undermine the integrity of an entire organization. Once managers see that it's okay to lie and conceal information to enrich themselves or simply to hold on to their jobs, they soon begin to extend their dishonest behavior to all parts of the company's management system and even to its relationships with outside parties. Managers start to feed misleading information to customers, suppliers, and employees, and the CEO and CFO begin to "manage the numbers" to influence the perceptions of board members and Wall Street analysts. Even boards of directors are drawn into the fray, as they end up endorsing deceptive reports to shareholders. Sometimes, outright fraud ensues, as we've seen recently in high-profile cases involving companies such as Informix, Sabratek, and Lernout & Hauspie.

The damage can go well beyond the walls of individual companies. Think about what happens, for example, during a boom. As financial analysts and investors raise expectations for growth beyond the capability of companies, many managers begin to borrow from the future to satisfy the present demands. This results in an overstatement of earnings and cash flows for many companies and an exaggeration of the extent of the good times. Conversely, during the early stages of an economic slowdown, as demand falls below predicted levels and inventories build up, managers often find themselves falling short of their bonus targets. When they and their companies all react in the same, predictable way—taking big baths by maximizing the bad news—the cumulative effect is to exaggerate economic weakness, perhaps deepening or extending the recession. Macroeconomic statistics and even public policy are likely distorted in the process.[1]

GETTING THE KINKS OUT

The only way to solve the problem is to remove all the kinks from the pay-for-performance line—to adopt a purely linear bonus schedule, as shown in Exhibit 2 "A Linear Compensation Plan." Managers are still rewarded for good performance, but the rewards are independent of budget targets: The bonus a manager received for a given level of performance remains the same whether the budget goal is set at Target 1 (below actual performance) or at Target 2 (above actual performance). The linear bonus schedule, in other words, rewards people for what they actually do, not for what they do relative to what they say they can do.

That removes the incentives to game the system. Because unit managers no longer get a pile of cash for exceeding a target, they have no motivation to feed falsified information into the budgeting process in order to lowball their goals. As a result, senior management receives unbiased estimates of what can be accomplished in the future, and the quality of planning and coordination improves considerably. At the other end of the process, managers are no longer rewarded for moving revenues and expenses around when the end of a budget period approaches. Because their bonuses are always determined by their actual performance, an extra dollar of revenue or profit (or whatever measure is used) will generate the same bonus this year as it will next year. Not only will this remove the costs of gaming, it will also free managers from all the time they traditionally had to devote to it. They can dedicate that time to their real jobs: maximizing the performance and value of their businesses.

Two additional points should be made here. First, nonmonetary rewards also have to be independent of budget targets. Handing out promotions or public accolades based on the ability to hit budget numbers, for example, will provide a continued incentive for gaming. That practice has to stop. All rewards must be based purely on actual performance.[2] Second, since pay will still go up as performance improves, dishonest managers may continue to lie about their numbers in order to increase their bonuses. That, of course, is a risk that companies have always had to watch out for. A linear bonus schedule does not reduce the need for good control systems and attentive executives.

Removing the kinks from the compensation system allows the budgeting process to do what it's intended to do: provide the basis for good business decisions and enable the effective coordination of disparate units. But many managers will reflexively object to this proposal. Yes, they'll say, a linear bonus schedule will remove the incentive to game the system, but won't it also remove the motivational effects of performance targets? It's a legitimate question, and it's one that is difficult to answer with hard numbers. Empirical evidence shows that tying goals to rewards does enhance performance. A recent survey of more than 500 studies, for example, indicates that performance increases by an average of approximately 16% in companies that establish targets.[3] But even if we assume such findings are accurate, we don't know whether the performance increase is itself a result of gaming, as managers rush to overstate their results to meet the new targets.

EXHIBIT 2. A LINEAR COMPENSATION PLAN

The solution to the budget gaming problem: Adopt a purely linear pay-for-performance system that rewards actual performance, independent of budget targets. A manager receives the same bonus for a given level of performance whether the budget goal happens to be set beneath that level (Budget Target 1) or above it (Budget Target 2). Removing the kinks eliminates the incentives for managers to game the process.

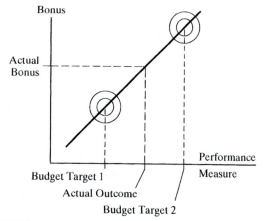

251

Nor do we know definitively the long-term costs of gaming. No comprehensive study has been done, and such a study would be hard to carry out, given how pervasive and well-hidden these costs are. However, Donald Roy conducted a landmark study, published in the *American Journal of Sociology* in 1952, of an analogous situation: the use of piecework targets to determine the bonuses of factory workers. Based on his findings, Roy estimated that productivity in the factory he studied would increase by 33% to 150% if the targets were discontinued. Based on that research, as well as my own observations of the widespread, destructive effects of gaming, I conclude that the costs of budget-based bonuses far outweigh the benefits in most, if not all, situations.

Finally, it's important to note that setting extremely aggressive stretch goals, as is so common in business today, can itself have damaging repercussions. By establishing the expectation that managers will constantly push to exceed reasonable growth and profitability targets, senior executives can end up creating a dysfunctional organizational culture in which all the problems I've described are amplified. That's what happened recently at one prominent multinational corporation. A new CEO came in, and he suspected that unit heads were routinely lowballing their budget targets and then delivering mediocre results. He quickly reorganized the company to establish clearer accountability down the line, and then he launched an intensive campaign to get everyone to set stretch goals for the coming year, with their bonuses hanging in the balance. The effort blew up in the CEO's face.

The budget-setting process became a year-long exercise in internecine warfare. Knowing that their bonuses hinged on their ability to hit the new targets, line managers battled over the way the overall corporate stretch goals for revenues and profits should be allocated among the business units. Each, of course, tried to reduce his or her unit's target. Every time revised goals were circulated, new arguments broke out. And when the targets were eventually finalized, things got even worse. Within months, most unit heads realized they wouldn't be able to reach their stretch goals, and they let the year fall into the tank in a way that is consistent with pushing revenues and profits out to the future. They were clearly hoping that by taking a bath this year they would be given lower targets next year. Needless to say, the CEO's tenure was short.

MAKING THE SWITCH

It's not going to be easy for companies to adopt a linear compensation system. Target-based bonuses are deeply ingrained in the minds of managers and in the managerial codes of most organizations. Getting managers to give them up will be tough, and getting them to give up promotions or reputational rewards for "beating budget" will be even tougher. Most difficult of all, though, will be getting them to break free of the cynicism that surrounds the entire budgeting and bonus-paying system. But the benefits are so great—in terms of a company's long-run economic and organizational health—that the journey will be well worth the time and effort. And there are some guidelines that can help the transition proceed more smoothly.

Get the details right. The design of compensation programs lies outside the scope of this article. But it is important to emphasize that the success of a linear bonus program, like that of any pay system, hinges on its details. There are three key considerations: the performance measures used, the positioning and slope of the bonus line, and the establishment of minimum and maximum compensation levels.

In establishing performance measures, executives run the risk of distorting managerial decisions, even under a linear bonus system. One example is the use of multiple measures of performance. This practice can motivate managers to think more broadly and carefully about the operating and economic drivers of business success. But it also adds complexity to the system in a way that can impede decision making. Suppose, for example, a manager is told to increase both profits and market share in the coming year. If, after some point, market share can be increased only by cutting prices, and thus profits, the manager no longer has a basis for making reasoned decisions. The conflicting goals eliminate his ability to act purposefully. When using multiple performance measures for individual managers, companies should be careful to establish a single, clearly defined measure of overall business success, such as economic value added. That will give managers a basis for making trade-offs among performance measures when they come into conflict.[4]

A second example is the use of ratios as performance measures. Here I can be blunt: Don't do it. Using ratios, such as sales margin or return on assets, inevitably produces gaming. That's because managers can increase the measure in two ways: by increasing the numerator or decreasing the denominator. If, for example, a company tracks performance according to margin as a percentage of sales, managers can increase their pay by simply cutting back sales (selling only the highest margin products) instead of working to increase the margins on all products. The result: Total dollars of profit fall, and company value erodes.

The positioning and slope of the bonus line work in tandem to determine the amount of money a manager received for a given level of performance. Moving the line to the right on the performance scale, for instance, makes it harder to get an additional dollar of bonus, while providing a steeper slope makes it easier to get that dollar. In setting the line, executives have a tendency to focus on the short term. In particular, they often position the line based on the prior year's performance. That reduces the risk that managers will be overcompensated for overly conservative projections of performance (a high bonus in one year makes it harder to get a high bonus the next year), but it also reduces incentives for increasing performance. Because managers know that an increase in performance this year will result in higher targets for succeeding years, the motivation to make the extra effort is dampened—unless the current year's bonus is extraordinarily large. A better way is to look further into the future, setting bonus lines for a number of years out based on longer-term projections for growth and profitability. This is harder to do, but it reduces the potential for manipulation.

In general, it is extremely important that companies model the economic impacts of different positionings and slopes for their bonus lines. As in any compensation system, the right balance must be struck between the rewards delivered to employees for incentive purposes and the capital retained for reinvestment or for distribution to investors or other owners.

Finally, there's the issue of limits on compensation. Ideally, you wouldn't have any—all pay would be directly related to actual performance. But there are strong pressures to limit both the upside and the downside for employees and managers. Most companies have to pay salaries in order to attract and retain employees (thus defining the lower bound of compensation), and most feel compelled to set some upper limit to bonuses. What's important is to try to set the upper and lower limits outside the range of likely outcomes to minimize their potential for setting off gaming. In many cases, this will require companies to raise bonus caps well above traditional levels, which is sure to create organizational discomfort. For example, a manager will inevitably end up paying certain high-performing subordinates more than he himself makes. Also, some managers may complain that certain people are being paid inordinately large amounts just because they happened to get lucky. (Of course, luck is extremely hard to distinguish from talent, and much of the griping will simply be a sign of jealousy.) Managing such conflicts—by clearly articulating the philosophy underlying the pay plan, for example—is one of the difficult but necessary challenges in moving to a more rational compensation scheme.

Don't backtrack. Even after managers become intellectually convinced that a linear bonus schedule is desirable, they may still argue for a compromise plan that again allows budget targets to influence compensation. In a number of companies I have worked with, executives have, for instance, proposed replacing the new linear schedule with a curvilinear one. By making the pay-for-performance line curve upward more steeply after the budget goal is reached (and less steeply before it is

reached), bonuses begin to increase more rapidly for every incremental improvement in performance beyond the target. That may appear to fulfill the psychological need of many managers to "get something more" after surpassing a goal, without putting any obvious kinks back into the system. But, in fact, curvilinear schedules reintroduce a strong incentive for gaming.

To see why, look at Exhibit 3 "The Impact of a Curvilinear Compensation Plan." In the example portrayed here, a manager whose profit performance in two succeeding years exactly matched the budget goal would receive a bonus of $12,000 in each year, for a total of $24,000. But if she could manipulate that same amount of profit so that she hit 80% of the goal in one year and 120% in the next, she would receive $10,000 in one year and $20,000 in the other, for a total of $30,000. The curvilinear plan, in other words, has given her a strong monetary incentive to start fudging the numbers again, and, in this case, she would be rewarded for increasing the variability of performance. What's more, she would be willing to do this even if it lowered overall performance within some range. In contrast, under a truly linear scheme, the manager would receive the same total ($30,000) in both scenarios.

Last January, Chrysler Motors introduced a new dealer-incentive plan that was based on a curvilinear pay-for-performance scale. The plan paid dealers a monthly bonus ranging from zero (for those who achieved less than 75% of their sales targets) to $500 per car sold (for those who achieved more than 110% of the target). When car sales began to slow in April, many Chrysler dealers realized that they were unlikely to exceed the targets for the month and therefore they reduced inventories, shifting sales of cars from April to May, when they could be much more certain to earn the $500 per car bonus. In the end, Chrysler's CEO had to announce that company sales fell 18% in April as a result of its dealer bonus program, while overall industry sales were down only 10%.

Lead from the top. Given the complexity of designing a new pay system, as well as the controversy it inevitably sets off, CEOs will feel a natural desire to hand off responsibility for the effort to the human resources department. That would be a mistake, probably a fatal one. HR has neither the standing nor the influence to make a fundamental business change that will have a profound impact on the decisions of line managers. And that's exactly the kind of change that I'm talking about: All members in the organization will have to shift their thinking about the role and use of both budgets and incentives. Performance measures will have to be changed, and bonus levels will have to be recalculated. Since these issues are as sensitive as any within a company, strong leadership is essential. Only the CEO has the credibility to make the business case for the changes and to rally the troops behind them.

EXHIBIT 3. THE IMPACT OF A CURVILINEAR COMPENSATION PLAN

Curvilinear pay-for-performance plans are no cure for gaming. They encourage managers to increase the variability of year-to-year performance measures. In this example, a manager makes more by achieving 80% of a budget target one year and 120% the next than by hitting the target both years. Under the linear plan, by contrast, the manager would earn the same in both scenarios.

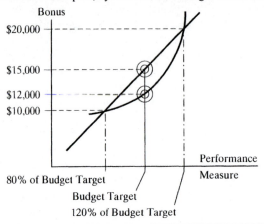

The CEO should recognize that the new plan will meet with intense resistance, even at the highest reaches of the organization. Some of the strongest objections, I have found, tend to come from CFOs and their teams. Finance executives naturally fear that reducing the importance of budget targets in motivating line managers will make it more difficult to control results and avoid surprises. It will be the CEO's responsibility to make sure the CFO, not to mention Wall Street analysts, understands that the new approach will improve the quality of both the information provided and the incentives paid to managers. And better information and better incentives will lead to better results. Yes, there may be greater uncertainty in quarter-to-quarter results—as there will no longer be any motivation to set artificially low targets and then do everything possible to meet them—but the long-run profits will be superior.

Finally, every line manager will have to understand the new system and the theory behind it and be prepared to explain it and defend it against opposition and opportunism from the ranks. There are no shortcuts through the education process. Organizations don't change overnight, particularly when the very frame through which we see the business is involved. Remember, it has taken many years to weave lying and deceit into the fabric of our business; cleansing the fabric will take time as well.

ENDNOTES

1. See M. C. Jensen, "Paying People to Lie: The Truth About the Budgeting Process," working paper (Harvard Business School, April 2001). Available on-line at http://ssrn.com/paper=267651.
2. To read more on how goals can distort behavior, even in the absence of ties to tangible rewards, see M. Schweitzer, L. Ordonez, and B. Douma, "The Dark Side of Goal Setting: The Role of Goals in Motivating Unethical Behavior," working paper (Wharton School, University of Pennsylvania, 2001).
3. See Edwin A. Locke, "Motivation by Goal Setting," in *Handbook of Organizational Behavior*, ed. Robert T. Golembiewski (Marcel Dekker, 2001). Also see Edwin A. Locke and Gary P. Latham, *A Theory of Goal Setting and Task Performance* (Prentice Hall, 1990).
4. See Michael C. Jensen, "Value Maximization, Stake-holder Theory, and the Corporate Objective Function," *Business Ethics Quarterly*, January 2001. Available on-line at http://ssrn.com/paper=220671.

The author thanks Joseph Fuller, Michael Gibbs, Jennifer Lacks-Kaplan, and Edwin Locke for their contributions to this article.

To further explore the topic of this article, go to www.hbr.org/explore.

Michael C. Jensen, the Jesse Isidor Straus Professor of Business Administration, Emeritus, at Harvard Business School in Boston, is the managing director of the organizational strategy practice of the Monitor Group, a collection of global professional services firms with headquarters in Cambridge, MA.

QUESTION

10.4 Discuss the typical executive compensation plan, the linear compensation plan, and the curvilinear compensation plan. According to the author, which of these plans *solves* the budget gaming problem?

10.5 Beyond Budgeting

The traditional performance management model is too rigid to reflect today's fast-moving economy. Two new approaches—devolution and strategic performance management—have risen in popularity, but they are equally frustrated by unyielding budgeting systems.

by Jeremy Hope and Robin Fraser*

In an age of discontinuous change, unpredictable competition, and fickle customers, few companies can plan ahead with any confidence—yet most organizations remain locked into a "plan-make-and-sell" business model that involves a protracted annual budgeting process based on negotiated targets and resources and that assumes that customers will buy what the company decides to make. But such assumptions are no longer valid in age when customers can switch loyalties at the click of a mouse.

Organizations need to find a new model that effectively empowers front-line managers to make fast decisions based on current information. The "Beyond Budgeting" model represents a set of information-age best practices—from organization design and devolution of authority to planning and performance management—that leading-edge companies are now using to respond much faster to customer demands. Understanding what these practices are and what you need to do to adopt them is increasingly likely to determine whether or not your company is able to compete effectively in the new economy.

Such companies as Svenska Handelsbanken (see Exhibit 1), Volvo Cars, IKEA, Borealis, Fokus Bank, and Boots have all abandoned the budgeting model in one form or another in recent years. And the momentum is gathering pace. Ericsson, Diageo, and British cider maker Bulmers are among the latest companies to see the light. Such is the current interest that in 1998 a Consortium for Advanced Manufacturing-International (CAM-I) research forum known as the Beyond Budgeting Round Table (BBRT) was established to understand and report on these developments.

After two years' research and numerous case visits, the BBRT has concluded that not only do firms need more effective strategic management, but they also need to redesign their organizations to devolve authority more effectively to the front line. Crucial to success, however, is the recognition that these two elements of the beyond budgeting model must be given equal attention.

EXHIBIT 1. SVENSKA HANDELSBANKEN—A MODEL FOR THE NEW ECONOMY

Since 1972, annual contributions to the Handelsbanken groupwide profit-sharing fund have been based on the margin by which it beats the average return on capital of all its Nordic rivals, and, apart from 1973, it has always made significant contributions. **Yet inside the firm there is no annual budget or target-setting process.** The bank and its constituent parts are all continuously striving to improve their place in a series of performance league tables geared to key measures such as return on capital, cost-to-income ratio, and profit per employee. It is these league tables and their constituent measures, underpinned by intense peer pressure, that drive continuous improvement at local and regional levels. Beating the competition rather than some negotiated budget goes to the heart of the Handelsbanken model.

Branch managers run their own business with high levels of freedom and responsibility. This means deciding which products to offer individual customers (there are no centrally imposed targets), which central services to use (services and prices are negotiated), and how many staff are needed. This freedom to act is supported by the capability to act. For example, there is a fast and open information system geared to measuring customer acquisitions and defections, work productivity, and customer and branch profitability. Information is online and is seen by local, regional, and group managers at the same time, but it is *how they use it* that's important. **Managers are empowered to make decisions and to fix mistakes** (higher-level managers only interfere when absolutely necessary). The result is a very flat organization with a multitude of semi-autonomous work units (600 for the whole bank) with peer pressure (using performance league tables) driving performance improvement.

The benefits are evident everywhere you look. Employee turnover is extremely low, reflecting high levels of satisfaction (redundancies are unknown). Talented graduates want to join Handelsbanken more than any other financial services company in Sweden, not because it offers the highest salaries and benefits but because young managers are given exceptional levels of responsibility within a radically decentralized structure. It is perhaps because **branches "own" their customers** (no matter where transactions take place), make fast decisions, and provide flexible products and services that Handelsbanken has the lowest number of complaints in its sector and consistently tops the customer satisfaction charts in Sweden. Costs are also the lowest in the industry (half the level of the European average taken as a percentage of assets). One reason is that costs are constantly challenged (rather than protected by the budgeting system); another is that bad debts are exceptionally low, largely due to the company's policy of devolving credit responsibility to front-line people who know the customer.

* From: J. Hope and R. Fraser, "Beyond Budgeting" *Strategic Finance* (October 2000): 30–35. Reprinted with permission.

ORGANIZATION DESIGN AND DEVOLUTION

Most attempts at redesigning organizations and devolving decisions making have focused on flattening hierarchies, reengineering processes, and introducing team working. Invariably, such approaches simply lead to the delegation of control within a strict regime of coordination and accountability, with budgets as the primary weapon for policing this control.

Delegation and coordination don't make comfortable bedfellows. A constant battle is being waged in most large organizations between the forces of decentralized initiative (usually the losers) and the forces of centralized coordination (invariably the winners). The difference is the centralizing power of the budgeting system that emphasizes coercion rather than coordination (you *will* cooperate, *won't you?*), focuses on cost reduction rather than value creation, stifles initiative, and keeps planning and execution apart, thus reinforcing the separation between thinkers and doers. Other symptoms of failure include cost allocations that are nonnegotiable and middle managers who remain "commanders and controllers."

In the information economy, it's not so much decentralization that's required but *autonomy within boundaries*. Autonomy is much more than decentralization and a few steps beyond empowerment. Autonomy is a Greek word meaning self-governance. It means the freedom to act *and* the capability to act. The key to autonomy isn't to try to empower cost centers (it doesn't work) but to give more responsibility and accountability to a greater number of business units for value creation. Effective devolution is tough, and it takes many years of painstaking effort to hold back the forces of centralization, but such efforts usually prove worthwhile as they lead to a self-renewing organization with strong values, dispersed responsibilities, and a performance culture that no longer depends on one or two inspirational leaders at the top. Its features include:

- *Governing through shared values and clear boundaries*, enabling local managers to make fast decisions knowing that they are within agreed parameters.
- *Creating as many autonomous profit centers as possible*, providing enterprising people with the opportunity to "run their own business."
- *Coordinating the organization through market forces*, thus, for example, creating an "internal market" in which central services units see operating units as internal customers that must be serviced and satisfied.
- *Providing front-line managers with fast and open information networks* that convey up-to-the-minute knowledge about critical issues. Because everyone receives important information at the same time, controls are distributed (making them stronger) and bad news is shared immediately.

- *Giving managers the freedom to act and the responsibility to deliver results*, placing the onus of responsibility on front-line people to perform.
- *Giving managers the training and tools to think and act decisively*, providing managers with the capability to make fast decisions at the point of contact with the customer.

PERFORMANCE MANAGEMENT

In the latter decades of the twentieth century the role of budgets mutated from a set of coordinated financial plans to a wide-ranging management system for controlling the business, driving management behavior, and rewarding performance. As Figure 1 illustrates, the underlying thread was one of *control*. The vision of the chief executive was translated into the strategic plan by the planners and handed down the hierarchy to operational managers who prepared their budgets. Once these were agreed, all that was demanded was adherence to the plan. The head office didn't like surprises. Control reports were constantly fed back up the line, and if they showed that performance was veering off track, new directives would be issued from the head office. It isn't hard to see why the budgeting system became essential to success. It was the core management process and provided much needed stability and continuity in an increasingly competitive business world.

But despite attempts to fine-tune this model by introducing zero-base or faster (for example, quarterly) budgeting (neither of which takes the firm toward more effective devolution or strategic performance), such a model is now out of kilter with a fast-changing business world. A number of new approaches have been promoted over the past 10 years to overhaul the traditional model and build performance management processes that enable managers to steer their firms toward clear strategic goals.

But despite the undoubted success of tools such as the Balanced Scorecard, there is often such a gulf between theory and practice that relatively few companies sustain their interest at the highest level. Most collide rather than connect with the budgeting process. The group finance people are often to blame. They see themselves as the guardians of the budget, and if a business unit or division is veering off its agreed performance track, then corrective action must be taken, and they are the ones that must enforce such action. This may well involve directives aimed at (unplanned) cost reductions. Of course, the first costs to be cut tend to be so-called discretionary investments in, for example, employee skills and management training, customer satisfaction programs, and "special" projects such as those that improve quality and increase the speed of operations. The trouble is that these are also the very investments that underpin the success of the medium-term strategy as laid down in the Balanced Scorecard. Other pitfalls await the inexperienced scorecard user.

For example, if the planning process remains locked into an annual cycle with a highly deterministic approach to strategy, then much of the promise from so-called strategic management will be unfulfilled. A "take that hill" strategy (to use a military metaphor) is of little value if the hill itself has moved in the meantime. Incentive schemes too heavily weighted toward achieving the fixed plan reinforce this inflexibility. Moreover, there's a fine line between "alignment" and "control," and there's a real danger of using the scorecard (wittingly or unwittingly) for top-down control (in the same way as a budget with some nonfinancial measures).

In the beyond budgeting model, an effective performance management system should be aimed at supporting self-governing business units (see Figure 1). Its principal features should include:

- **Targets** that are relative to the competition (internal or external) and thus are always self-adjusting and stretching the performance of the business unit.
- **Effective anticipatory management systems (including rolling forecasts)** that enable managers to continuously adjust strategy and manage investments and shareholder expectations.
- **A rolling strategy process** (with appropriate cycles) that is devolved to business unit teams and that operates within clear boundaries and values.
- **An investment management process** that forces managers to build flexibility and "exit routes" into their forecasts and in which execution is made at the latest possible time.

- **Distributed controls aimed at supporting front-line managers** and keeping senior managers informed (by exception).
- **Rewards based on relative performance** at a business unit or company level that encourage team performance and cross-company sharing at various levels.

THE BEYOND BUDGETING MODEL—MORE THAN THE SUM OF THE PARTS

To create new wealth, firms need both the benefits of effective devolution (such as fast decision making) and the benefits of effective performance management (such as fast, open, and relevant information). The power of this dual approach was recognized more than 25 years ago by Dr. Jan Wallander, the architect of the Svenska Handelsbanken business model.

Management books and journals are replete with success stories that support one management model or another, but how many can point to companies that have consistently beaten their rivals for almost 30 years without having a dominant market position (Handelsbanken only has 15% of the highly deregulated Swedish market)?

What's the reason for this sustained success? It's the combination of effective devolution and effective performance management that makes the Handelsbanken case so special and has pointed many more companies in the right direction. It paves the way for companies to simplify their performance management processes, reduce the cost and complexity of the organization, and create a firm that is strategically focused and much more innovative and responsive.

FIGURE 1.

THE BUDGETING MODEL

Vision → Strategic plan → Annual budget → "Keeping on track" → Control (vs. budget) → Incentives (vs. budget)

Culture: "Contract, compliance, and control"

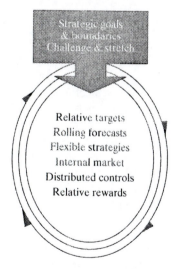

THE BEYOND BUDGETING MODEL

Strategic goals & boundaries Challenge & stretch

Relative targets
Rolling forecasts
Flexible strategies
Internal market
Distributed controls
Relative rewards

Culture: "Responsibility, enterprise, and learning"

Yet the gravitational force of the budgeting system makes it extremely difficult for most firms to escape the world of compliance and control. This is *not* a comfortable message for a measurement industry that believes it alone has the power to drag the traditional model kicking and screaming into the information age. Only by over-coming the constraints of the traditional budgeting approach can managers build a business model that operates at high speed; is self-questioning, self-renewing, and self-controlling; and rewards innovation and learning.

The authors are program directors on the CAM-1 Beyond Budgeting Round Table. Jeremy Hope is coauthor of Transforming the Bottom Line *and* Competing in the Third Wave, *both published by Harvard Business School Press. You can reach him at lh23@dial.pipex.com. Robin*

Fraser was until recently a management consulting partner in PricewaterhouseCoopers and led the development of their Priority base Budgeting and ABM practices in the UK. You can reach Robin at:
RobinFraser@Compuserve.com.

CAM-I Inc. is a not-for-profit international research consortium. To download a white paper or find out about joining the BBRT visit www.beyondbudgeting.org *or contact Peter Bunce by phone: +44 (0)1202-670717, fax: +44 (0)1202-680698, or e-mail:*
Peter@cam-i.demon.co.uk.

QUESTION

10.5   What are the principle features of the "Beyond Budgeting Model"?

10.6 Games Managers Play at Budget Time

*by Richard Steele and Craig Albright**

One of the most thoroughly studied questions in business is how, at budgeting time, large corporations should choose among investment opportunities. In-house economists, management advisors and even Nobel laureates have worked on this problem and come up with an impressive array of quantitative and process-oriented resource allocation systems. Why, then, are so many senior executives frustrated with the process and convinced that their companies' capital is not being invested as well as it could be?

One reason is that even the best-designed systems can be trumped by the power of personality. A forceful appeal sometimes carries more weight than even the most objectively accurate financial analysis built on highly reliable facts. It is now commonplace, in fact, for talented and charismatic managers to spin, manipulate and otherwise cajole senior management into funding their business ideas — often in the face of numbers that would, on their own, dictate a negative decision. Put another way, when people are economical with the truth during capital budgeting, the underlying economics get lost.

Having guided dozens of major corporations through the budgeting process and watched hundreds of presentations by line managers asking for capital, we have profiled five archetypes of bad behavior commonly used by managers to subvert decision-making standards and win resources. It is not uncommon for a manager to adopt more than one type, depending on how his or her plan is faring relative to others in the planning and budgeting process. Fortunately, there are ways for senior management teams to counteract such behavior directly during budgeting discussions and, over time, to instill values that lead to better use of investment capital.

THE SANDBAGGER
"There is no way that we, or anyone else, can grow by 10%."
Managers are sandbagging when they routinely come to the table with a business plan that is less ambitious than one they know they could probably fulfill. Sandbaggers argue that the market is so tough, the best the company could hope for is slight incremental improvement even with additional resources or the most heroic leadership. Of course, when such managers exceed their targets, as they usually do, they appear to be heroes themselves.

The president of a successful $700 million North American brokerage business, for example, was reluctant to commit to an earnings-growth target that the company's CEO had proposed. While the president thought the business had the potential to achieve the CEO's target, he did not want to risk missing the target and lose his group's bonuses. Instead of turning to his team for ideas on how to reach the goals, however, he dug his heels in and insisted that the business really could not meet them; he eventually negotiated a lower target. At the end of the year, the brokerage division announced earnings growth that was just above the reduced target.

Later, during the president's performance review, the CEO pointed to the repeated sandbagging and the time spent debating performance targets in the planning process as a serious problem. It was preventing the CEO

---

* From: R. Steele and C. Albright, "Games Managers Play at Budget Time," *MIT Sloan Management Review* (Spring 2004): 81–84. Reprinted with permission.

and his team from spending time where they needed to most — with their employees and customers.

Sandbagging costs more than time, however: It also creates energy-sapping internal debate and, worse still, leads to people being overpaid for their performance as bonuses kick in even when low budget targets are met.

THE MAGICIAN

"There really are no weak spots in our business right now."
Sometimes division managers know things about their business that do not show up in the budget figures. They may have heard that a large customer was intending to defect, that a key manager was on her way out, or that market share numbers were starting to slip. But at budget time, magicians cover up faults in the business by conveniently leaving out uncomfortable facts and diverting attention to more positive aspects of the operation.

For instance, the manager of a European beverage company was taken aback when her colleagues noted several weaknesses in her plan for the core business. In response, she diverted their attention to a speculative new idea to launch store-branded products for discount retailers. A true magician, she alternately pointed to growth rates and customer surveys in that channel to support her claims that the new plan would significantly boost the company's top line. After several months of debate, the top management team remained hopelessly deadlocked and frustrated at their inability to come to an agreement on the proposed new line of business. Meanwhile, the core business's performance was declining.

There should be no magic to the budget process, but some managers try to cast a spell rather than answer legitimate challenges to their proposals. If they are not brought back to reality, the inconvenient details they've forgotten to mention will reappear and expose what may turn out to have been disastrous decisions.

THE LONE AGENT

"Yes, but that principle does not apply to our business."
Some managers contend that their business cannot conform to corporate-budgeting conventions because of its supposedly unique character. In comparison with competitors, they say, it may be much bigger or much smaller, more international or more domestic, more high-tech or more low-tech. Driven by their fear of being managed to the norm, lone agents stonewall during meetings ("Yes, but …") and expect special treatment. They demand different standards for goals and performance that undermine trust and teamwork and make performance management across a company's businesses difficult.

The group executive of a Latin American wholesale bank, a unit of a financial services company, lost his temper when he was asked by the executive committee to cut operating costs by 5% as part of a groupwide exercise to identify funds that could be reinvested in new businesses. Believing the target to be at odds with the right strategy for the bank — its location in a developing market made it different from other units, he contended — the executive would not agree to the request. Rather than open his thinking to alternatives, he lashed out at those who had proposed the cost targets and any other executive who appeared to support them. Other top executives, in turn, saw the executive's behavior as divisive and an attempt to gain unfair privilege.

By claiming to merit special consideration, lone agents sow mistrust among their peers and superiors and, in the process, damage the top team's ability to debate the key strategic issues it faces in a mature and disciplined way.

THE VISIONARY

"I can't say exactly when, but this is going to be big — really big."
Managers who don't have the numbers on their side often appeal to emotions. Visionaries harp repeatedly on the "breakthrough" technology or service that will "revolutionize" the industry and remain on the "cutting edge" for years to come. The core of the argument often goes like this: "Given the enormous upside, which at this point cannot be quantified because it is 5 to 10 years out, it will be worth putting up with poor short-term performance."

For example, an ambitious director of business development for an insurance company proposed a plan that would allow consumers to buy term life insurance directly from the company, rather than through agents. His boss told the director that while the vision was compelling, he was troubled by the deep investment required throughout the planning horizon in order to set up the technology, change processes, educate consumers and so on. The fact was, the director had very little to say about near- or medium-term performance and tried to meet objections by going back to the long-term opportunity his vision represented. The end result in this case was a stalemate among the top executives, although visionaries often do win the resources they need — at least for a year or two, until top management and stockholders, frustrated by the lack of results, raise questions that lead to the plan's termination.

Companies need visionaries, to be sure. But visionaries should be standing on solid factual ground when they look to the future, not floating in the clouds. The challenge, then, is to find a way to marry the vision with a genuine commitment to delivering short-term performance.

THE HOSTAGE TAKER

"If we don't invest big right now, we'll be left on the sidelines."

Sometimes managers claim that they can deliver significant and immediate performance improvements if they are given a huge proportion of the available corporate capital. Hostage takers act as if the decision-making obstacle is not the management team but the chief executive, who in their view should be prepared to bet the company on their brilliant plan.

The managing director for a U.K. Internet company wanted to turn his business into a full-service Web-hosting service provider — a radical proposal that would require a huge investment in a risky market and direct resources away from other profitable lines of business. Although the chief executive respected the managing director's strategic and financial acumen, she was not convinced that the plan reflected the best use of the company's capital. Rather than force a broader discussion of options and alternatives, however, she allowed her attention to be captured by the hostage taker's ultimatum.

Consequently, the company invested hundreds of millions of pounds behind his growth plan and continued to do so for each of the next three years, even as the markets proved much more difficult than initially forecast. Other growth options were starved of investment during this time, leaving the company overexposed to a single high-risk opportunity.

Like lone agents, hostage takers want special treatment and, like visionaries, they appeal to emotions. But because of the percentage of corporate investment that they seek, they have the potential to do the most damage to the company's future if their plans do not turn out as projected.

WHY DO MANAGERS PLAY GAMES?

It is one thing to be able to identify the games managers play and quite another to be able to do something about them. Each of the six archetypes reflects organizational or individual shortcomings — be it a lack of critical thinking, a misalignment in ambition and purpose, a breakdown in corporate culture or poor incentives.

First, managerial game playing sometimes reflects a lack of skills and know-how rather than Machiavellian intentions. For example, managers may be weak strategic thinkers, have poor planning skills, or be inexperienced in valuing investment opportunities correctly. In such situations, the remedy would include training, coaching and other forms of management education.

Second, bad behavior can be a matter of deeper flaws. Some managers know full well what they are doing and are simply not team players; others lack a proper focus on short-term performance. These deficiencies require a firmer hand.

Third, managerial stratagems at budget time can also reflect a lack of clarity about performance goals and expectations. It is not always easy to get the executive team and business-unit management to agree on specific performance targets. More often than not, misunderstandings arise over the pace at which goals are to be met: Executive teams usually have a much shorter time frame in mind when it comes to most performance targets. The end result is that business-unit managers feel they have to tap dance their way through uncomfortable meetings. While this gap may never be fully closed, its existence should be acknowledged by top management in order to minimize inefficient behavior.

Finally, managerial antics may be a response to the environment — the corporate culture, incentives and values that shape the workplace. For example, if the company tends to promote hard-charging, sales-oriented types into senior management positions, the company may produce a surplus of lone agents and hostage takers. If the company's general managers came up through the finance function, there may be a tendency to produce sandbaggers and magicians — people who know how to manipulate financial data to their own advantage. In either case, senior management will have to use all the tools at its disposal — mission statements, compensation, promotions and training — to develop a more cooperative, forward-looking and results-oriented system within the company.

CHANGING THE RULES

Even in the most perfectly designed organization, managers are going to play the system, and executives need to be ready to deal with disruptive behavior when it arises. While this is clearly a long-term, complex issue, there are actions that senior management can take in the short term to reduce the tax that bad behaviors can levy on a company's capital. It's important to take action quickly, however, because managers who are successful game players will continue their behavior until it is checked — a sandbagger who gets his bonus one year will come up with new reasons for being unable to meet corporate targets the next time around.

1. **Get It on the Table.** Openly acknowledge at the beginning of each budgeting meeting — in a lighthearted way — the human tendency to twist the facts to one's favor. That will help diffuse tension and make it clear that the criteria for investment approval will be not only the hard numbers that make up the proposal but also the overall integrity with which the numbers are presented. Even if a business plan comes in with the highest internal rate of return of all the proposals, for example, it may not receive funding if the investment committee sees games being played that undermine the credibility of the analysis.

NEUTRALIZING DISRUPTIVE BEHAVIORS

For a variety of organizational and personal reasons, many managers will come to budgeting discussions with less than optimal proposals. But their discussions of these proposals can be disruptive, with repercussions for both employee and company performance. Top management needs to rein in such behavior, but angry criticisms are not the way to go about that task. Instead, top executives should neutralize the behavior with unemotional responses.

Disruptive Behavior	Inflammatory Response	Neutralizing Action
Sandbagger	Criticize the manager's lack of ambition	Refer to and enforce top-down corporate goals
Magician	Berate the manager for failing to reconcile conflicting datas	Refocus the manager's attention on trends in the core business
Lone Agent	Accuse the manager of failing to be a team player	Reinforce group standards as the price of a seat at the table
Visionary	Belabor the missing details in the manager's plan	Require the manager to demonstrate how and when the vision will be economically attractive
Hostage Taker	Claim that capital constraints rule out the proposal	Require the manager to develop several credible alternatives and to make trade-offs transparent

2. **Paint a Picture of the Ideal.** Create a profile of the behaviors and values that managers ought to reflect when presenting budgets for approval. Examples might include the ability to meet short- and long-term expectations, the ability to be candid about the condition of the business, the ability to make and reach stretch targets and so on. The development of such skills can be made a part of corporate training programs. At Cadbury Schweppes Plc, 150 top managers learned about the behaviors and capabilities necessary for success at the company by participating in simulated dialogues focused on resource allocation. To put some bite into the program, even the CEO took part, role playing both good and bad behaviors and making it clear that failure to meet the required standards could cost a manager his or her seat at the top table.

3. **Deal Positively With Disruptive Behavior.** Be willing and ready to respond to disruptive game playing during budget meetings. For each type of manipulation, there is both an inflammatory and a productive way to respond. (See "Neutralizing Disruptive Behaviors.") For example, when lone agents are demanding that a different set of rules be applied to their budgets, reemphasize the company's well-publicized decision-making standards. And when managers are sandbagging, point to the existence of top-down goals, known to the sandbaggers well ahead of time.

4. **Put Peer Pressure to Work.** Require that all business-unit and general managers be present for key business reviews — and that they participate in the question-and-answer phase. General managers from other businesses may have firsthand knowledge that will lead them to raise questions that executives may not have thought of. For example, a general manager who has seen business-unit magicians perform before may be able to redirect the meeting's attention away from the dazzle of a new market and ask whether the company really has the organization in place to compete within it.

Executives with their hands on the till need to keep one eye on the numbers and the other on the psychology of their managers — and be ready to respond in real time to disruptive behavior. Taking the veil off of bad behaviors, however, does more than just make budgeting discussions more productive. It also lays the foundation for addressing two larger and longer-term challenges. By taking the time to define which competencies and behaviors are required to make the capital-budgeting process more effective and efficient, senior executives create organizational discipline and a concrete way of establishing the highly sought-after performance-oriented culture. And by linking behaviors and values to strategy and capital-allocation decisions, senior executives tap into a proven way of delivering better performance. In the end, everyone wins when the means and the ends of delivering performance are aligned.

Richard Steele is a London-based partner with Marakon Associates, an international strategy-consulting firm. He can be reached at rsteele@marakon.com. Craig Albright was formerly with Marakon in New York City. He can be reached at craig489@optonline.net.

QUESTION

10.6 What are the 5 archetypes of bad budgeting behavior?

Chapter 11

Capital Budgeting

Reading 11.1 is Steve Coburn, Hugh Grove and Tom Cook's article on *How ABC was used in Capital Budgeting*. The article provides a good contrast between a more traditional business case forecast approach to a major capital budgeting decision and a more detailed look using an ABC model and benchmarking data. The context of the comparison is in a division of a Fortune 500 company that was established to make decisions regarding new opportunities in the electronic (broadband) marketplace of interactive television. The first project proposal was whether to develop a "cybermall" that would bring sellers and buyers together in the interactive television context. As a result of the ABC analysis, which showed that market share and revenues would not occur quickly enough and that the investment costs were too large, plans were halted to invest in the cybermall.

Kalagnanam and Schmidt's *Analyzing Capital Investments in New Products* (Reading 11.2), presents a case study of a biotechnology firm, Cyto Technologies. The company manufacturers hundreds of products such as enzymes and biochemical reagents, and its R&D scientists also are involved in developing scientific techniques to aid others in conducting experiments. Historically, Cyto used rough financial methods to determine whether a new product or technique should be developed. Due to external competition and the high cost of capital, Cyto has developed a much more rigorous four-phase process to determine whether a project should be funded. The article discusses the four phases as well as the reactions of R&D scientists to this new form of project evaluation.

Readings
Chapter 11

11.1 How ABC Was Used in Capital Budgeting

by Steve Coburn, CPA; Hugh Grove, CPA; and Tom Cook*

How do you estimate cash flows for capital expenditure projects in your company? Many firms use broad strategic approaches for estimating cash flows that are not closely tied to detailed tactical assumptions about future operations. These forecasts may not be very reliable because cash flow projections of new products can have a 30% to 40% margin of error.

A new division of a Fortune 500 company was established to analyze new business opportunities in the electronic (broadband) marketplace of interactive television. The company and data have been disguised here for confidentiality purposes. The initial investment proposal was to develop a "cybermall," similar to the way marketing service organizations bring together sellers and buyers in the traditional television marketplace. At the time, this cybermall proposal was a new idea without any close counterparts in this emerging electronic marketplace.

Senior management of this new division initially had focused upon the marketing strategy of "speed to market" for this cybermall project. Thus, the business case forecast was done at a broad strategic level with few supporting details. A consulting firm provided general forecasts of the electronic market size and market share, which it converted into aggregate forecasts of revenue, operating costs, and capital costs. Driven by this "speed-to-market" strategy, senior management was willing to commit $50 million to this cybermall project, based upon the business case forecast.

The chief financial officer (CFO) of this new division, however, successfully argued for a tactical translation of the business case's broad strategic view into a detailed analysis of the cybermall's projected business processes and activities. Senior management approved the CFO's proposal because it still had concerns about how the technical development and deployment of the electronic marketplace would impact the cybermall financial forecasts. The CFO's proposal became an activity-based cost (ABC) model (with benchmarking) that created a pro forma process engineering approach for analyzing this business opportunity.

Process analysis typically has been used for reengineering existing—not pro forma—processes.[1] In contrast, this business opportunity related to an emerging industry with new processes. Also, ABC has been advocated for use in annual, not capital, budgeting.[2] Using ABC for capital budgeting analysis of this cybermall project created an example of activity based management (ABM), which has been defined as providing economic information for management decision making.[3]

The ABC model (with benchmarking) forecasted business processes, activities, revenues, operating costs, and capital costs for this cybermall project. This tactical ABC approach generated forecasts that differed significantly from the forecasts of the strategic business case. For example, the ABC model forecasted that an additional $10 million of capital costs would be needed. Also, revenue forecasts were slowed down and startup cost forecasts were increased. Senior management used these ABC results to reverse its initial decision to go ahead with this cybermall project. Thus, the CFO provided strategic ABM information and became part of the business decision-making process. Senior management also has decided to use this ABC approach for evaluating future business opportunities. Such a strategic role has been advocated as the most important goal for a CFO's mission statement and the future of management accounting.[4]

The ABC analysis provided an understanding of projected business processes and activities that allowed senior management to have more confidence in the detailed tactical ABC forecasts, rather than the initial, broad strategic forecasts. This pro forma ABC approach also is a logical next step for companies currently using ABC and benchmarking to understand existing business processes and activities.

We describe here an overview of the business case and the ABC model approaches; then a description of the ABC approach for analyzing this cybermall project is provided. Finally, the forecasts from both approaches are compared.

BUSINESS CASE VS. ABC MODEL APPROACHES
Figure 1 provides an overview of the business case approach to capital budgeting for this cybermall project. The strategic business case forecasts started with broad market assumptions concerning electronic market size and share provided by a consulting firm. These consultants then converted this market data into general projections of revenues with few supporting details. They

---

* From: S. Coburn, H. Grove, and T. Cook, "How ABC Was Used in Capital Budgeting," *Management Accounting* (May 1997): 38–46. Reprinted with permission.

also used general cost assumptions to project variable and fixed expenses without any detailed cost analyses.

For example, the budget line items of technology development, video production, and network operations were mainly aggregate fixed cost forecasts. The few variable cost forecasts were based upon general revenue projections, such as distribution access as a flat fee per subscriber and order processing as a specified amount per customer. A key capital infrastructure forecast used just one type of client/server technology for all interactive television markets although four different types of client/server technology were being deployed by cable system operators.

The business case provided general revenue and expense projections and pro forma financial statements. Also, the business case provided senior management with capital budgeting information for the decision criteria of net present value (NPV), internal rate of return (IRR), and payback.

Figure 2 provides an overview of the ABC approach to capital budgeting for this cybermall project. The tactical ABC model forecasts were based upon detailed benchmarked data from the cybermall business process analyses provided by the CFO. Using benchmark assumptions, the ABC approach developed a broadband deployment or buildout schedule of the electronic marketplace for potential interactive television subscribers. It also developed a transaction volume schedule for potential cybermall customers. Both schedules were used to help generate the revenue, cost, and capital assumptions and projections of the ABC model.

The ABC model created a broadband network deployment schedule by benchmarking with external parties to obtain detailed data concerning the build-out of the broadband infrastructure for the electronic marketplace. The ten largest cable or multi-system operators (MSOs) were projected to build or deploy broadband infrastructures over five years, starting in 1996, and all other MSOs to deploy over seven years, starting in 1997. This deployment was projected to start in the 50 largest cities or suburbs named as areas of dominant influence (ADI).

Using this deployment schedule as a starting point, the ABC model created a detailed transaction volume schedule by benchmarking shopping participation, purchase frequency, and average spending for this cybermall project. Because no interactive television operators existed for this emerging market, the traditional television marketing operators, Home Shopping Network (HSN) and the QVC system, were used as indirect or "out of market" benchmarks. For example, HSN had about five million active shoppers representing 8.3% of the homes reached, and QVC had four million shoppers representing 8.0% of the homes reached. Also, HSN repeat customers had made purchases between five and seven times a year. Average spending per shopping household for repeat customers was about $300 for HSN and about $500 for QVC.

The tactical ABC model used detailed revenue assumptions and forecasts for this cybermall project, as opposed to the general ones of the strategic business case. The ABC model forecasted slower access to cybermall customers, primarily due to delays in developing and provisioning the broadband network. Accordingly, the revenue forecasts for the early years were lower than in the business case.

FIGURE 1. BUSINESS CASE MODEL

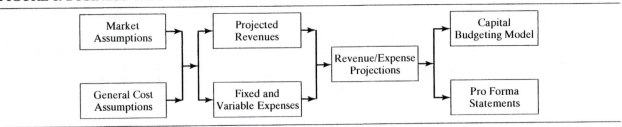

FIGURE 2. ABC/BENCHMARKING MODEL

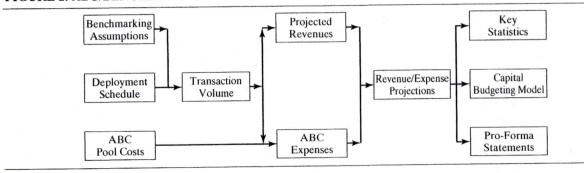

Concerning the ABC pool costs, the ABC model used a pro forma process engineering approach to construct activity resource consumption profiles and transaction (cost) drivers that were multiplied together to derive the ABC expense projections. A cybermall value chain of workflow or business processes was specified with key activities and cost drivers. This pro forma process engineering approach is described below.

PRO FORMA PROCESS ENGINEERING

A pro forma process engineering approach was used by the ABC model to forecast operating and capital costs for the cybermall project. A cybermall value chain was created with six sequential workflows or business processes as shown in Table 1. First, cybermall seller relationships must be developed to provide the goods and services available for purchase on this interactive television system. Second, the system to operate interactive television applications must be developed. Third, content programs must be purchased or produced. Fourth, the ongoing operations of this interactive television system must be performed, especially the processing of cybermall buyers' orders. Fifth, the marketing of the cybermall must be done. Sixth, the network distributors and access fees must be managed.

Major activities were identified for each of these six business processes in the cybermall value chain. Resource consumption profiles and cost drivers were identified for the major activities. Cost pool rates were calculated and multiplied by the number of cost drivers needed at various transaction volumes to project the ABC process expenses as summarized in Table 1.

Detailed capital costs also were forecasted for various levels of activities. The $2 million total capital costs in Table 1 represented four initial broadband deployments. Each deployment used a different type of client/server, and each server type was estimated to require $0.5 million in capital costs. Over the initial 10-year period of this cybermall project, 120 network deployments were estimated for total capital costs of $60 million, which was $10 million or 20% higher than the business case estimate of $50 million, as shown in Table 2.

TABLE 1. KEY ACTIVITIES, DRIVERS, AND COSTS IN THE CYBERMALL VALUE CHAIN

Business Processes	Major Activities	Cost Drivers	Process Expenses	Capital (000,000)
Seller Relationship	Acquire sellers	No. of sellers	Selling	$0
	Do promotions	No. of direct mailings	Selling	0
	Manage seller relationships	Annual staffing	Selling	0
Application Development	Product concept	No. of product start-ups	Product R&D	$.4
	Design application:	No. of product Start-ups	Product R&D	
	Asset mgt. system			$.1
	Order process sys.			$.1
	Develop database	No. of product Start-ups	Product R&D	$.3
	Technology:			
	Planning	Annual staffing	Product R&D	0
	Deployment	No. of client server types	Product R&D	$.4
Content Production	Brokerage of Program purchase	No. of programs	Content production	0
	Program production	No. of programs	Content production	0
	Post production guidelines	Annual staffing	Content production	0
Operations	Order processing	No. of orders	Operations	$.1
	Customer Service	No. of network head-ends	Operations	$.1
	Provision network	No. of fiber loops	Operations	$.5
	Seller interface	Annual staff	Operations	0
MARKETING	Buyer acquisition	No. of buyers	Marketing	0
	Advertising	No. of ads	Marketing	0
	Public Relations	Annual staffing	Marketing	0
	Buyer maintenance	Revenue Percent	Marketing	0
NETWORK DISTRIBUTION	Distributor Relationships	Annual staffing	Distribution	0
	Access Fee	No. of buyers	Distribution	0

Capital Costs in Table 2: 4 Types of Deployment $.5 = $2.0
Total Capital Costs in Table 1: 120 Deployments $.5 = $60.0

TABLE 2. COMPARISONS OF ABC VS. BUSINESS CASE (IN MILLIONS AND 10-YEAR TOTALS)

Panel A: Key projections

	Business Case	ABC Model	Variances Increase Amount	(Decrease) Percent
Total revenues	$1,650	$1,480	($170)	(10%)
Total cash operations expenses	$1,000	$950	($50)	(5%)
Total net income after tax	$250	$175	($75)	(30%)
Total capital expenditures	$50	$60	$10	20%
Total net cash flow (without residual value)	$400	$320	($80)	(20%)

Panel B: Key Decision Criteria:

	Business Case	ABC Model	Increase Amount	(Decrease) Percent
1. Without Residual Value:				
Internal rate of return Net present values:	43%	33%	(10%)	(23%)
@ 20%	$60	$35	($25)	(42%)
@ 30%	$20	$4	($16)	(80%)
@ 40%	$3	($8)	($11)	N/A
Discounted payback @ 20% in yrs.	7	9	2	29%
2. With Residual Value:				
Internal rate of return	61%	50%	(11%)	(18%)
Not present values:				
@ 20%	$225	$190	($35)	(16%)
@ 30%	$100	$80	($20)	(20%)
@ 40%	$40	$25	($15)	(38%)

Also, three types of external parties were identified because they were needed to perform critical activities in various business processes for this cybermall project to become operational. First, cybermall sellers were needed to do core programming in the content production process. They also were needed in the operations process for selling, shipping, billing, and collecting the cybermall goods and revenues. Second, software vendors were needed to develop and test network applications, video content programs, and network operations for the cybermall. Third, distributors were needed to develop, operate, and deploy the interactive broadband network where the cybermall will be located.

Seller relationship process. The seller relationship business process for the cybermall has three major activities. First, for the activity of acquiring cybermall sellers, account managers are needed to obtain and maintain sellers of goods and services. One full-time equivalent (FTE) manager and one secretary are projected for 1995, increasing to a cap of seven FTEs by 1997. Second, for the promotion activity, the cybermall will be publicized with an annual budget for promotional mailings to potential sellers and distributors. Third, a general manager is needed for managing seller relationships. One half-time position is needed in 1995, increasing to a cap of two FTEs by 1997.

Application development process. The application development business process for the cybermall has four major activities. First, product concepts will be defined and evaluated with product research, product specifications, and simulated operations. Capital costs of $350,000 are needed for simulation equipment, a

client/server, work-stations, and personal computers. Second, two key types of design application activities are needed. An asset management system will be developed with a simulated startup for this cybermall. Capital costs of $150,000 are needed for video equipment, software, and production workstations. Also, an automated order processing system for cybermall customers will be developed with $100,000 of capital costs.

Third, for the database activity, a database operations center will be developed. Capital costs of $300,000 are needed for the central hardware to coordinate the work-stations. Fourth, two key types of technology activities are needed. For the planning activity, three technical employees and $50,000 for test equipment each year are needed to maintain technical core competency and to update technical strategy continuously. For the deployment activity, this cybermall project will be adapted to four technology types of client/servers and will cost $100,000 for each type of server. Thus, capital costs of $400,000 are needed initially to provision four servers (one for each server type).

Content production process. The content production business process for the cybermall has three major activities. First, for the brokerage of program purchases, rights to use existing programming will be purchased when appropriate for this cybermall. Estimated annual costs are $100,000 in 1995, increasing to a $700,000 cap by 2000. Second, for the program production activity, programs for video content describing the cybermall sellers will be produced in-house or outsourced. It is assumed that the company and the sellers will split these costs equally, which are similar to the brokerage program costs. Third, concerning post-production guidelines, costs to monitor and manage programming and production are estimated as one technical employee in 1995, increasing to a cap of four FTEs by 1997.

Operations process. The operations process has four major activities. First, for the order processing activity, there will be two cost structures. Manual processing will be used from 1995 through 1997 until higher cybermall shopper volume is obtained. Thereafter, automated processing will be used with capital costs of $100,000. Second, concerning customer service, employee costs are estimated at one-third FTE for each network head-end. Capital costs of $100,000 are estimated for workstations and software.

Third, to provision an interactive (broadband) television network, this cybermall project must be deployed on fiber loops, requiring video server equipment. Each server may feed up to four head-end networks and up to 500,000 interactively passed homes. Capital costs of $500,000 are estimated for the video servers, storage units, and personal computer systems to interface with the fiber loops. Fourth, for cybermall seller interfacing, one manager and three technical employees are needed for the post-production functions of program content and network operations.

Marketing process. The marketing process has four major activities. First, for the buyer acquisition activity, salespersons are needed to obtain cybermall shoppers or buyers. Related selling costs also are included. Such buyer acquisition costs are estimated to decrease over time. Second, advertising primarily via television and radio promotions is necessary. Costs for preparation of such advertisements are budgeted for $200,000 in 1996, increasing up to a $500,000 cap by 1999. Third, public relations activities included marketing management. Personnel are estimated at two FTEs in 1995, four FTEs in 1996, and eight FTEs thereafter. Fourth, concerning buyer maintenance, costs to maintain cybermall shoppers are estimated as a percentage of total revenue.

Network distribution process. The network distribution process has two major activities. First, account managers are needed to manage relationships with the distribution networks used by this cybermall. Personnel are estimated at one half time position in 1995, increasing to a cap of two FTEs by 1998. Second, concerning network access fees from 1995 through 1997, charges are based upon the number of cybermall shoppers making purchases and are paid monthly to the network provider. Thereafter, the charges will be based upon a percentage of total shopping purchases.

In summary, the tactical ABC model engineered pro forma business processes, activities, and cost drivers to calculate detailed revenue and resource consumption patterns, as opposed to the general assumptions of the strategic business case approach. Also, to help senior management make this capital budgeting decision, key

operating statistics were compiled by the ABC model. Such statistics were not provided by the business case because it was done without detailed analyses. These statistics were classified by four types of metrics: buyers, sellers, networks, and infrastructure, as shown in Table 3.

If comparisons had been available, the ABC model generally would have provided less optimistic forecasts of operating statistics because its related revenue forecasts were lower and startup cost forecasts higher than the business case. For example, the acquisition cost per buyer would have been higher and the revenue per seller, lower. In the network and infrastructure metrics, the access costs and the cost per minute/content both would have been higher.

If the cost drivers were not already represented in the benchmarked transaction file, they were added to these existing transaction volumes. For example, a new cost driver for the number of client/servers was measured by the interactive television deployment sequence under the cybermall revenue assumptions. From the pro forma engineering analysis, an activity resource consumption profile was established to measure the cost of a client/server. Then, the number and cost of the client/servers were multiplied together to project the ABC expenses at various levels of interactive television deployment.

Thus, detailed resource consumption patterns and transaction (cost) drivers were used to generate the ABC expense and capital forecasts, as opposed to general assumptions in the business case forecasts. For example, the application development and design costs were forecasted using the number of product startups as the cost driver. (A fixed cost was used throughout the business case.) For another example, manual order processing initially was assumed due to low customer volume in the startup phase. Subsequently, automated order processing was assumed. (A variable cost per customer was used throughout the business case.) The ABC model forecasted specific network operating costs using the cost drivers of network headends and fiber loops. (Aggregate amounts of fixed costs were used in the business case.) The ABC model forecasted capital costs that represented four types of broadband deployments, one for each of the actual types of client/servers being deployed by cable television operators. (Only one client/server type was used in the business case.)

The ABC model calculated key operating statistics and differences between the ABC and the business case dollar projections and NPV, IRR, and payback results. The operating statistics are described in Table 3. The ABC model also generated pro forma financial statements. All this information was provided to help senior management make its final decision on this cybermall project. The ten different categories of the ABC model in Figure 2 were linked together as a series of related Excel spreadsheets to facilitate risk analysis. The final ABC model used six megabytes of random access memory.

TABLE 3. KEY OPERATING STATISTICS

Buyers:	Networks:	Infrastructure:	Sellers:
No. of shoppers	Homes passed	Programming shelf life	Items per view hour
Purchases per year	Access cost percent of revenue	Cost per minute/content	Number of sellers
Return percent	ADI coverage percent	Connect time	Revenue per seller
Browser time	Network profitability	Percent automatic fulfillment	Transactions per month
Repeat time	Number of platforms supported	Cost per transaction	Percent ship date target
Acquisition cost per buyer	Number of shopping applications	Transaction response time	Seller renewal rate

COMPARISONS OF FORECASTS

For this cybermall project, 10-year financial forecasts are summarized in Table 2. Panel A has comparisons of key dollar projections for the business case and the ABC model. Panel B has comparisons of key capital budgeting forecasts for the business case and the ABC model. In Table 2, the residual value for this cybermall project represented the net present value of its sales price in year 10. The ABC spreadsheet model calculated both dollar and percent variances between the two approaches as shown in Table 2.

Key projections of 10-year financial amounts for both approaches were summarized in Panel A of Table 2. For the business case, key dollar projections were (in millions): $1,650 revenues; $1,000 cash operating expenses; $250 net income after taxes; $50 capital expenditures; and $400 net cash flow without residual value. For the ABC model, key dollar projections were (in millions): $1,480 revenues; $950 cash operating expenses; $175 net income after taxes; $60 capital expenditures; and $320 net cash flow without residual value. Concerning the variances, all the business case forecasts were from 5% to 30% higher than the ABC model forecasts, except for capital expenditures, which were 20% ($10 million) lower. Consequently, the ABC dollar projections, especially the 20% reduction in net cash flow, generated lower capital budgeting forecasts than in the business case.

Capital budgeting forecasts for both approaches are summarized in Panel B of Table 2. For the business case, the internal rates of return were 43% without any residual value and 61% with the residual value. The net present values were $60 million, $20 million, and $3 million, using cost-of-capital rates of 20%, 30%, and 40%, respectively, without any residual value. With the residual value, the net present values were much larger at $225 million, $100 million, and $40 million, respectively. The discounted cash flow payback was seven years, using a 20% cost of capital rate.

For the ABC model, the internal rates of return were 33% without any residual value and 50% with the residual value. The net present values were $35 million, $4 million, and negative $8 million, using cost of capital rates of 20%, 30%, and 40%, respectively, without any residual value. With the residual value, the net present values were much larger at $190 million, $80 million, and $25 million, respectively. The discounted cash flow payback was nine years, using a 20% cost-of-capital rate.

The variances for the capital budgeting forecasts showed that the ABC model results were significantly lower than the business case results. The internal rates of return decreased by 23% and 18%, without and with the residual values, respectively. The net present values were reduced from 16% to 80%, depending upon which cost of capital rate was used. The discounted cash flow payback was increased by two years or 29%. With higher capital forecasts and lower revenue and cash flow forecasts, the ABC capital budgeting forecasts were less favorable for this cybermall project than the business case forecasts.

From the ABC analysis, the electronic marketplace deployment and resulting market share and revenues were too slow while the startup and investment costs were too big and too early to justify the cybermall project at this time. Also, the operating leverage for profit growth did not become favorable until the mid-life point of this cybermall project, as opposed to an earlier prediction in the business case.

ABC PROVIDES TACTICAL APPROACH

The ABC model provided a methodology to analyze future business opportunities concerning new types of products and services in emerging markets. The additional level of detail was the key difference from the business case approach for this cybermall project. The pro forma analysis of the business processes and activities with linkages to revenue and cost structures provided critical information for the final decision on this cybermall project.

This approach appears to be applicable to all types of capital budgeting decisions and should provide a unique opportunity for senior management to understand how business processes and activities impact revenue and cost forecasts. As in this cybermall project, the business case approach typically analyzes the symptoms of changes using various levels of market shares, revenues, and costs, but no clear analyses of the causes or drivers of these changes are provided. By contrast, such causal analyses *are* provided by this ABC approach which attempts to understand how changes in business processes and activities impact market share, revenues, and costs.

The ABC information provided a better understanding of the cybermall business processes and activities.

This additional knowledge allowed senior management to have more confidence in its strategic decision making for this project. Senior management agreed that the additional costs spent on the ABC and benchmarking analyses were justified by the benefits of more detailed operating and financial information.

For example, the following key uses of this ABC model were identified for this cybermall project in the emerging electronic marketplace:

- Establishing linkages between technology (the electronic market deployment and distribution of interactive services) and financial forecasts,
- Using indirect or "out of market" benchmarks for revenue and cost forecasts,
- Creating a dynamic model that showed how unitized ABC costs behaved and changed over time in providing interactive services, and
- Specifying operating leverage more precisely with different step-cost functions at different levels of volume.

These key uses also helped clarify marketing strategies for this emerging industry, i.e., broad market coverage versus narrow or niche market development of interactive services.

As shown by the comparisons in Table 2, the tactical ABC model produced less favorable forecasts for the capital budgeting decision criteria than the strategic business case. Thus, senior management decided not to do this project at this time. Because the ABC model also was a working spreadsheet model, sensitivity and "what-if" risk analyses were performed but the final decision was to reject the project. Senior management decided not to be a first or early entrant into this emerging electronic market.

This ABC model provided a detailed tactical methodology to analyze business opportunities in emerging markets, as opposed to the general strategic view of the business case approach. The initial "speed-to-market" strategy in the business case was tempered by the tactical ABC analysis of the cybermall project's feasibility. Forecasts of the ABC model created more confidence in making this cybermall decision; therefore, senior management has decided to use this ABC model for analyzing subsequent business opportunities in the electronic marketplace. Thus, by using this ABC and benchmarking methodology to provide strategic information, the CFO became part of the strategic decision-making process in accordance with the key goal for a CFO's mission statement and the future of management accounting.

ENDNOTES

1. Refer to M. Hammer and J. Champy, *Reengineering the Corporation*, Harper Business, New York, 1993.
2. Refer to J. Schmidt, "Is It Time to Replace Traditional Budgeting?", *Journal of Accountancy*, November 1992, pp. 103–107.
3. Refer to R. Kaplan, "In Defense of Activity-Based Cost Management," MANAGEMENT ACCOUNTING ®, November 1992, pp. 58–63.
4. Refer to A. Pipkin, "The Twenty-First Century Controller," MANAGEMENT ACCOUNTING, February 1989, pp. 21–25; and W. Birkett, "Management Accounting and Knowledge Management," MANAGEMENT ACCOUNTING, November 1995, pp. 44–48.

Steve Coburn, CPA, is chief financial officer, Teletech Corporation, Denver, Colo.

Hugh Grove, CPA, is professor, School of Accountancy, University of Denver, Denver, Colo., and a member of the Denver Chapter, through which this article was submitted.

Tom Cook is associate professor of finance, Daniels College of Business, University of Denver, Denver, Colo.

QUESTION

11.1 Contrast the business case model (Figure 1) and the ABC/benchmarking model (Figure 2). What are the main differences?

11.2 Analyzing Capital Investments in New Products

by Suresh Kalagnanam and Suzanne K. Schmidt*

To succeed in the rapidly growing, highly competitive biotechnology industry, companies will have to develop innovative products, processes, or technologies that can be realized within reasonably short time periods. Playing an important part is the high cost of capital. Because capital has to be used wisely to generate sufficient returns, companies investing large sums of money in research and development (R&D) are compelled to conduct rigorous *a priori* financial analyses to evaluate their new projects.

* From: S. Kalagnanam and S. K. Schmidt, "Analyzing Capital Investments in New Products," *Management Accounting* (January 1996): 31–36. Reprinted with permission.

To see the effect of this development, we followed the experiences of a biotechnology company that placed increased emphasis on the financial performance of its new projects. In particular, we addressed the issues of the accuracy of the financial numbers and the behavioral implications of this recent financial emphasis. We collected information through discussions and interviews with several employees in the marketing, R&D, and accounting departments and from documentary evidence.

THE PROJECT DEVELOPMENT AND EVALUATION PROCESS

Cyto Technologies,[1] which started approximately 15 years ago, is a rapidly growing biotechnology company with manufacturing operations in the United States and sales operations there and abroad. Cyto manufactures and sells hundreds of products in seven major product areas: enzymes, nucleic acid, molecular biology, cellular regulation, eukaryotic transcription, protein translation, and biochemical reagents. Two typical uses for the company's products are providing life science researchers with materials and techniques for their experiments and providing private and government-supported testing laboratories with materials and techniques for use in DNA and food testing.

In the past, the project selection process at Cyto lacked a structured approach. Projects were selected with just sketchy ideas about financial numbers and rough ideas of payback periods. Increasing competition and the higher cost of capital have forced Cyto to change its approach. A project approval team (PAT) was set up three years ago to provide structure for the project development and evaluation process. The PAT consists of five constant members (the heads of manufacturing, quality assurance, finance and accounting, research and development, and marketing) and two rotating members (one each from marketing and R&D). This team oversees the allocation of resources to new projects in alignment with the company's objectives.

The current project development and evaluation process consists of four phases: idea-initial screening, product design, product development, and launch.[2] See Figure 1 for an example.

Phase 1, idea, consists of two stages: idea generation and investigation. In the generation stage, any R&D scientist with an idea for a new product or technique is granted a certain (small) sum of money to conduct a literature search or preliminary laboratory research. The idea, which is documented in an idea evaluation report, is screened by the marketing and R&D (or manufacturing) co-chairs. If the idea appears promising, it enters the investigation stage. An additional sum (usually three times the initial amount) is allocated to the project, an identification number is assigned to it, and all time is charged to that number. The investigation stage results in a report that contains a proposal for a feasibility study or product development, and that report is reviewed by members of the project approval team.

Phase 2, product design, consists of a feasibility study. The study results in a report on the final definition of the product—image, specifications, marketing potential, and initial return on investment (ROI) or internal rate of return (IRR) estimates. Once again this report is reviewed by the project approval team. A favorable review moves the project into the next phase.

Phase 3, product development, consists of two stages: specifications and final optimization. The specifications stage establishes product definitions (in terms of the components), packaging and fitness testing, and hazard and stability evaluation. Production cost estimates also are figured, and marketing personnel determine the final sales forecasts. Then the final estimate of IRR is computed, and test marketing is conducted. At this point, the PAT once again reviews the project, which, if approved, enters the next stage. In the final optimization stage, the first batch is made, documentation is completed, quality assurance specifications are detailed, regulatory compliance's are met, and the final design is demonstrated. The marketing personnel are involved in planning product promotion and advertising campaigns. Finally, in Phase 4, the product is launched.

PROJECT SELECTION CRITERIA

The project approval team uses nine criteria to evaluate projects (see sidebar). Financial performance is only one of the nine, so a project may be approved even if it performs relatively poorly on that test. For example, the first criterion, potential for proprietary position (patent and technical strength), is very important in this industry. Once a company has a patent, it can gain market advantage by forcing competitors to stop pursuing that line of products. Also, patents enhance the reputation of the company and of its scientists. In such situations, Cyto may be willing to accept short-term losses in exchange for future benefits, but it will not accept projects that are totally without financial promise.

In recent years, Cyto has decided to increase the importance of financial returns for three reasons. First, the company has been growing rapidly, so total costs have multiplied. It has a larger workforce, more sophisticated equipment, greater workspace, and bigger and more expensive buildings (costlier infrastructure). Cyto must invest wisely to maintain this infrastructure.

Second, there are more ideas than funds available. One product team that brainstormed on new project ideas two years ago came up with almost 25. Unfortunately, only five could be selected for further research because the allocation of funds among multiple project ideas necessitates capital rationing. Thus, financial analysis can help in the earlier stages of the evaluation process.

FIGURE 1. PROJECT DEVELOPMENT PROCESS AT CYTO

Phase 1			Phase 2			Phase 3			Phase 4
Idea	Initial screening by marketing and Research & Development co-chairs	Investigation	PAT Review	Review Technological and Marketing Feasibility	PAT Review	Specifications (inlcuding financial analysis)	PAT Review	Final Optimization	Launch

Third, increased competition and a higher cost of capital also have compelled Cyto to be wise about its investments.

CURRENT FINANCIAL ANALYSIS

Cyto conducts a capital investment analysis (which it calls ROI analysis) during the product development phase. The analysis involves computing the payback period (PBP), net present value (NPV), and the internal rate of return of a project. R&D scientists track their time for conducting literature searches, preliminary laboratory testing, and so on, on time sheets, by project numbers as soon as a project receives a number. This result represents the direct labor cost of the R&D department. All of the other costs incurred by R&D, and costs allocated to R&D from three service departments,[3] are classified as overhead costs. The total R&D cost is divided by the number of direct R&D labor hours in order to determine a burden rate for allocating the R&D costs to various projects on the basis of the direct labor hours consumed.

The above R&D cost allocated to each project, plus any initial marketing costs, represent the investment in the project (cash flow at time zero). Cyto uses a three-year time horizon in its investment analysis, and the cash flows for periods one to three are the estimated after-tax earnings adjusted for accruals. The computer model allows the project team to conduct a sensitivity analysis by varying some of its parameters. Although payback period, net present value, and internal rate of return are computed, IRR appears to be the most easily understood number and forms the basis of analysis.

PROBLEMS WITH THE NEW EMPHASIS

Cyto's employees had five major concerns about the increased emphasis on financial performance: (1) cost accuracy, (2) cost specification, (3) timing, (4) evaluation criteria, and (5) behavioral implications. They also had suggestions for dealing with the problems.

Cost accuracy. Any financial analysis can be only as good as the data used. In our interviews, employees raised two important concerns regarding the accuracy of the numbers used in the analysis—the allocation of R&D overhead costs and costs that differ for different products.

Overhead costs account for more than 58% of the total R&D costs. Currently they are assigned to projects on the basis of direct R&D labor, even though many overhead items are unrelated to direct labor. Activity-based costing (ABC), however, suggests that the sole use of direct labor allocation can lead to potentially inaccurate costs. Further analysis would be required to determine if the use of ABC or any other allocation method would be better than the current setup.

The management at Cyto also wants a clearer picture of R&D cost behavior (fixed versus variable cost). The single, predetermined overhead rate does not allow a separation of these costs.

The suggestion from the employees concerning this situation is to use multiple drivers to increase accuracy. For example, the current allocation procedure could be modified by computing separate rates for the fixed and variable portions of the total overhead.

Further analysis would be required to determine the extent of modification that would be cost beneficial.

The use of one overhead cost driver implies that all products use resources in the same proportions. Our discussions with several Cyto employees revealed two separate types of products, innovative and "me-too," that use resources in different quantities. An innovative product is defined as one that offers new features or is produced in a totally new way. A "me-too" product does not offer any new features compared to competing products. On the average, Cyto produces approximately 50% innovative and 50% "me-too" products.

It can be argued that the two product types have different cost structures. The R&D and marketing costs associated with each type of product can be quite different. Innovative products require more time because new markets have to be developed, and the marketing personnel have little idea of the characteristics of these new markets and so must do more market research. R&D personnel may need to do more extensive reading and laboratory work. The outlay costs for innovative products are likely to be higher than those for "me-too" products. Employees have suggested that more in-depth analysis of the differences in the resource consumption of the two types of products is required.

Cost specification. Cyto does not distinguish between pre-launch and post-launch costs. For example, although marketing, quality assurance, and process development personnel are involved in pre-launch activities, their times are not captured in the initial investment amount. The costs associated with their activities typically are classified as post-launch costs; they are a part of the cost of goods sold—COGS.

With respect to marketing, the directors spend considerable time on new products, conducting market research and competitor analysis—both pre-launch activities. The costs of these activities are included in the marketing and administration costs and are allocated to the COGS using a formula based on historical data. It is clear that this allocation to COGS is partially incorrect. Some of the marketing and administration costs should be classified as pre-launch costs.

Although Cyto's system could result in some distortion in the capital investment analysis, the company uses it with the idea that more accuracy may not be cost beneficial. Additional resources would be required to track the time spent by non-R&D personnel on new projects. Employees suggested including a few additional steps to capture more accurate time allocation in the marketing department. In order to capture the more routine (post-launch) activities, the relevant personnel could maintain log books to record activities and times. The times for the nonstandard (pre-launch) activities performed by more senior employees, however, are relatively difficult to capture. These activities can be measured "... by asking these employees to estimate the percentages of their time available to spend on each defined activity."[4]

A logical approach would be to develop a survey to gather information such as: (1) the factors that influence the amount of time marketing personnel spend on their activities, (2) an estimate of the time spent on these activities based on past experience, and (3) the proportion of time spent on pre-launch activities versus post-launch activities. This information, if possible, should be obtained based on project categories ranked on a scale from innovative to "me-too" (see Table 1 for the characteristics of the possible product categories).

Timing. Cyto evaluates projects over a three-year period, yet the typical life cycle of a product is five to seven years. Omitting the cash flow data for the additional years may result in misleading NPV and IRR estimates, especially for products that do well in the later years. On the other hand, one can argue that any cash flow data (especially sales revenues) pertaining to years five and beyond are just fuzzy estimates (especially for products selling in new markets).

Scientists at Cyto say that using a three-year time horizon may be inappropriate. Cyto could consider conducting analyses using more than one time horizon. Additional suggestions include investigating the life spans of innovative and "me-too" products and examining the life spans of previous similar products. This information would allow Cyto to develop norms for time horizons to be used in the financial analyses of different products.

Financial analysis is performed only during phase three of the development process. Several Cyto employees expressed concern that the analysis is conducted too late in the process. Although it would be ideal to conduct a financial analysis sooner, it is not possible because sales estimates are finalized only in phase three, and more accurate COGS numbers also are available only in this phase (after the first batch has been made). This means that projects must be evaluated more carefully during phases one and two, based on market research, product design, and technological development.

Additional concerns were raised about the likelihood of terminating financially unsatisfactory projects at such a late step in the evaluation process. At this point in the process, a significant amount of money (as much as $100,000) already has been invested. Employees and management were concerned that such a decision would come too late, creating a potential for significant losses. Because this amount is a sunk cost, the crucial decision would be whether to proceed with minimum additional investment and recover the money if the project comes in or to abort and accept the loss. This decision involves evaluating a tradeoff between possible future returns from the current project and the cost of starting a new project.

Evaluation criteria. Cyto has not established an *a priori* cut-off internal rate of return. One PAT member noted, "..... I don't think we have ... a cut-off, that ... [below a certain IRR] we are not going to consider [a project] ...." This lack of an appropriate hurdle rate sometimes is beneficial but at other times poses a problem. On one hand, members of a PAT will not reject projects outright because they do not meet "acceptable" financial criteria, but, on the other hand, they also do not have objective financial criteria upon which to make project approval decisions.

Possible changes that have been suggested to correct this problem include the use of a minimum acceptable IRR based on historical returns and the use of different cut-off rates for the innovative and "me-too" products. Higher cut-off rates of return could be used for innovative products especially "when ... new [markets are] being created, [because] the investment requirements and the corresponding risks are ... large."[5]

Behavioral implications. The scientists at Cyto may resist the changes caused by the increased importance of financial performance because it may impact the way their performance is measured, and there could be problems of deskilling (a reduction in the number and kind of tasks performed), alienation (from new work that employees may find unsuitable), and sabotage (tampering with the new system).[6]

TABLE 1. POSSIBLE PRODUCT CATEGORIES

Application	Technology	Market	Competition	Category	Category Rank
New	New	New	No	Highly innovative	1
New	New	Existing	No		2
New	Existing	New	No		3
New	Existing	Existing	No		A
Existing	New	New	No		5
Existing	New	New	Yes		6
Existing	New	Existing	No		7
Existing	New	Existing	Yes		8
Existing	Existing	New	No		9
Existing	Existing	New	Yes		10
Existing	Existing	Existing	No		11
Existing	Existing	Existing	Yes	Me-too	12

Note: An innovative product is defined as one that is revolutionary in that it offers new features to the customer or is produced in a totally new way. A "me-too" product does not offer any new features compared to the competing products that are available.

Currently, the R&D scientists are not evaluated on the basis of strict, objective guidelines. With more emphasis on the financial performance of projects, however, these scientists may perceive that increasingly they are being evaluated on how well their projects do financially. This belief could have both positive and negative repercussions. Some scientists probably will be more careful about designing and developing their products and consciously will work toward developing products that add value to the company. Others may attempt to get around the problem by fudging the numbers so that pet projects show favorable results. Two obvious tactics to get around the numbers would be to log fewer hours or to change the time horizon.

A change in the evaluation criteria for new projects may cause scientists emotional conflict. The creativity and reputation of a scientist in the biotechnology industry is important for his or her career survival. Management must provide some flexibility in how these scientists function. Overemphasis on financial performance could stifle their creativity, and they may be encouraged to develop more "me-too" rather than innovative products. As a result, the challenges of the tasks that the scientists perform may diminish, resulting in de-skilling.

The overemphasis on financial performance also has the potential to create an atmosphere of fear. One scientist remarked that he would be able to sleep the night before his presentation to the PAT because of the possible rejection of his project. These consequences can demoralize the scientists, leading to acts of sabotage such as logging fewer hours, not including certain costs, and so on. Emphasis on both financial and nonfinancial criteria, however, should alleviate a scientist's fear about the consequences of a project's poor financial performance. Thus the scientist will be confident that his or her project will not be rejected strictly on poor financial performance.

Increased emphasis on financial performance also can lead to decreased motivation and eventually alienation if the change is not handled appropriately. Cyto scientists felt they would be less motivated because their opinions on projects would be less valued. The danger is that unhappy employees could lead a migration out of Cyto over to a competitor. This point is very relevant to the biotechnology industry because losing creative scientists, who are key resources, can be very damaging.

What could Cyto do to reduce the negative impact of change? The controller, with the leader of the R&D team, could educate the scientists about the level of competition Cyto is facing, providing the rationale for emphasizing financial performance. The company could stress the fact that IRR is only one of the nine project evaluation criteria and that financially marginal projects could still be accepted based on the other criteria. In addition, Cyto could involve more of its employees (scientists, marketing personnel, production personnel) in the development and continual revising of the guidelines for the project development and evaluation process.

CHANGES HAVE OCCURRED

Several important changes affecting the project development and evaluation process have taken place at Cyto since we concluded our data collection in October 1993.

Four important system changes now allow communication regarding individual projects to be online rather than on paper. First, each project's status is monitored on the computer, and project progress reports are readily available, so any changes to the project are relayed quickly. Second, R&D personnel maintain their time sheets online, so data are available for analysis. Third, Cyto has installed its new cost accounting System (called BPICS). The system allows more accurate tracking of product manufacturing costs. As a result, more accurate COGS numbers are available to perform capital investment analyses. In addition, costs of product and sales support are available online. Fourth, the initial project identification numbers, assigned during phase one, are tied to the final catalog numbers so that actual sales information can be compared to the forecasts made before the product was launched. This before-and-after comparison of returns lets Cyto identify which projects did or did not generate the expected returns and why.

With the increased emphasis on financial performance, Cyto saw the need for more training for R&D scientists in product cost terminology and the costing issues involved. The controller and his staff made several presentations to the R&D staff regarding the importance of a detailed financial analysis along with other criteria. The R&D scientists also were taught the basics of the BPICS system so they could understand the variables of the system.

Now Cyto is addressing the issue of the effectiveness of the project development and evaluation process under the project approval team. The company has developed a brief survey designed to obtain employees' opinions regarding the PAT process. It also seeks insight into what can be done to improve the process, so Cyto is involving its employees in a redesign. The vice president of R&D says that R&D personnel and other employees are more amenable to the idea of PAT today than even a year ago. She also feels that the increased emphasis on financial performance has resulted in cost consciousness among the R&D scientists.

The core issue in dealing with the PAT process involves a cost-benefit trade-off. Cyto is expending greater effort, and significant sums of money to track activities and costs more accurately. More accurate cost information will allow Cyto to make more informed decisions and to maintain a competitive edge. Moreover, Cyto is finding ways to deal with possible dysfunctional behavior among the scientists. Management firmly believes that an increased emphasis on financial performance will result in the scientists' developing more cost-effective products that will enhance the future performance of the company.

NOTES

This project was conducted under the guidance of Prof. Ella Mae Matsumura; we thank her for her contribution to this project. We also thank Marilyn Sagrillo for her comments, and the individuals of the case study firm for contributing their time to this research project.

PROJECT EVALUATION CRITERIA
1. Potential for proprietary position.
2. Balance between short-term and long-term projects and payoffs.
3. Potential for collaborations and outside funding.

4. Return on investment.
5. Need to establish competency in an area.
6. Potential for spin-off products.
7. Strategic fit with the corporations planned and existing technology, manufacturing capabilities, marketing and distribution systems.
8. Impact on long-term corporate positioning.
9. Probability of technical success.

ENDNOTES
1. The company name has been changed at the request of management.
2. We conducted this study between February and October 1993. The details in this Section are taken from Cyto's following document: "Idea to New Product Guidelines," dated September 1992. The project development process used at Cyto resembles the Stage-Gate model for moving a new product from idea to launch. See R. G. Cooper. "Stage-Gate Systems: A New Tool for Managing New Products," *Business Horizons*, May–June 1990, pp. 44–54, for details.
3. The three service departments are immunological services, scientific support, and purchasing.
4. R. Cooper and R. S. Kaplan, *The Design of Cost Management Systems*, Prentice-Hall, Inc., Englewood Cliffs. N.J., 1991, p. 468.
5. G. S. Day, *Market Driven Strategy: Processes for Creating Value*, The Free Press, New York. N.Y. p. 31.
6. M. D. Shields and S. M. Young, "A Behavioral Model for Implementing Cost Management Systems," *Journal of Cost Management*, Winter 1989. pp. 17–27.

Suresh S. Kalagnanam is an associate professor at accounting at the University of Saskatchewan, Sasketoon, Canada. He is a member of IMA's Madison (Wis.) Chapter and can be reached at (306) 966-8453. He holds M.S. and MBA degrees from the University of Saskatchewan and is completing his doctorate studies at the University of Wisconsin-Madison.

Suzanne K. Schmidt is a bookkeeper at Kohl's Food Stores. She has an MACC degree from the University of Wisconsin-Madison and can be reached at (608) 244-7596.

QUESTION
11.2 What are some of the negative behavioral implications of evaluating the work of R&D scientists with Cyto's new method? Can these be overcome? If so, how?

Chapter 12

Responsibility Centers and Financial Control

In Reading 12.1, *Transfer Pricing with ABC*, Robert Kaplan, Dan Weiss and Eyal Desheh, trace Teva Pharmaceutical Industries history in arriving at a transfer price that would satisfy senior management, division managers and the financial staff. After considering numerous traditional approaches, they decided to follow an ABC approach. ABC allowed them to uncover numerous inefficiencies and misallocation of costs to products. Not only was the ABC based transfer pricing system successful from a technical point of view, but there was a dramatic reduction in conflicts among marketing and manufacturing managers.

In Reading 12.2, *What is EVA, and How Can It Help Your Company*, Paul Dierks and Ajay Patel present a primer on EVA and MVA. One of the benefits of this article is that the authors walk readers through the mechanics of calculating both EVA and MVA. Readers should work through the example given in Table 2 to obtain insight into how MVA and EVA are calculated from financial statement. The authors also discuss criticisms of both concepts, contrast them with other performance metrics, and present the benefits of EVA-based incentive plans.

M. Epstein and S. D. Young's, *'Greening' with EVA* (Reading 12.3), complements Reading 12.2 by presenting a checklist of what must considered before EVA is implemented. The checklist includes behavioral factors such as the buy-in of the board and senior management as well as technical factors such as how EVA will be tied to critical functions in the organization such as compensation, strategic planning and budgeting. The authors also discuss how Georgia-Pacific tied EVA to environmental responsibility. One senior executive is quoted as saying that the tie between the two concepts means, "integrating society's desire for a clean environment and shareholder expectations with financial concerns." Instructors might refer back to the material in chapter 7 on environmental issues and Chapter 11 on capital budgeting.

Reading 12.4 is *Evaluating Internal Operations and Supply Chain Performance Using EVA and ABC* by Terrance Pohlen and B. Jay Coleman. The authors provide a very clear dyadic linkage between the methods of ABC and EVA as applied to supply chain management. EVA is used to evaluate how process changes drive value in each firm and develops measures that align operations performance with supply chain objectives. ABC is used to determine what drives costs and performance and translates non financial performance into activity costs and financial measures. A number of examples are used to illustrate how the two methods work together to provide a more integrated way to understand the entire supply chain of the organization.

Readings
Chapter 12

12.1 Transfer Pricing With ABC

Here's the story of how a multinational pharmaceutical company solved its transfer pricing problems by using activity-based costing.

by Robert S. Kaplan, Dan Weiss, and Eyal Desheh*

In the mid-1980s, Teva Pharmaceutical Industries Ltd. decided to enter the generic drug market. Already a successful worldwide manufacturer of proprietary drugs, the Israel-based company wanted to vie globally in this competitive new market, particularly in the United States. The move has proved lucrative so far, as sales have been increasing at an annual rate of nearly 20%. In 1996, Teva's worldwide sales were $954 million and its after-tax net income, $73 million.

As part of its new strategy, Teva reorganized its pharmaceutical operations into decentralized cost and profit centers consisting of one operations division and three marketing divisions. The operations division is made up of four manufacturing plants in Israel, which are organized as cost centers because plant managers have no control over product mix or pricing. The plants produce to the orders placed by the marketing divisions, and plant managers are responsible for operational efficiency, quality, cost performance, and capacity management.

The marketing divisions are organized into the U.S. market (through Teva's Lemmon subsidiary), the local market (Israel), and the rest of the world. All three have substantially different sales characteristics. The Lemmon USA division handles about 30 products, each sold in large quantities. The Israel division handles 1,200 products in different packages and dosage forms, with many being sold in quite small quantities. The division handling sales to the rest of the world works on the basis of specific orders and tenders [a request from a customer for a price/bid to deliver a specified product or service], some of which are for relatively small quantities. All three divisions order and acquire most of their products from the operations division, although occasionally they turn to local suppliers. The marketing divisions are responsible for decisions about sales, product mix, pricing, and customer relationships.

Until the late 1980s, the marketing divisions were treated as revenue centers and were evaluated by sales, not profit, performance. Manufacturing plants in the operations division were measured by how well they met expense budgets and delivered the right orders on time.

The company's cost system emphasized variable costs, principally materials expenses—ingredients and packaging—and direct labor. All other manufacturing costs were considered fixed.

Teva's managers decided to introduce a transfer pricing system, which they hoped would enhance profit consciousness and improve coordination between operations and marketing. They were concerned with excessive proliferation of the product line, acceptance of many low-volume orders, and associated large consumption of production capacity for changeovers. They proposed a transfer pricing system based on marginal costs, defined to be just materials cost. Direct labor would not be included in the transfer price because the company was not expecting to hire or fire employees based on short-term marketing decisions. High costs were associated with laying off workers in Israel, and, more important, pharmaceutical workers were highly skilled. With Teva's rapid growth, managers were reluctant to lay off workers during short-term volume declines because if new employees had to be hired later, they would need up to two years of training before they acquired the skills of the laid-off workers.

But the proposed transfer pricing system generated a storm of controversy. First, some executives observed that the marketing divisions would report extremely high profits because they were being charged for the materials costs only. Second, the operations division would get "credit" only for the expenses of purchased materials. There would be little pressure and motivation to control labor expenses and other so-called fixed expenses or for improving operational efficiency. Third, if Teva's plants were less efficient than outside manufacturers of the pharmaceutical products, the marginal cost transfer price would give the marketing divisions no incentive to shift their source of supply. Finally, the executives concluded that using only a short-run contribution margin approach would not solve the problems caused by treating the marketing divisions as revenue centers. Measuring profits as price less materials cost would continue to allow marketing and sales-decisions to be made without regard

---

* From R. S. Kaplan, D. Weiss, and E. Desheh, "Transfer Pricing with ABC," Management Accounting (May 1997): 21–28. Reprinted with permission.

to their implications for production capacity and long-run costs. An alternative approach had to be found.

WHAT EVERYONE WANTED

Teva senior management wanted a new transfer pricing system that would satisfy several important characteristics:

1. The system should encourage the marketing divisions to make decisions consistent with long-run profit maximization. The transfer price should not encourage actions that improved the profit or cost performance of a division at the expense of Teva's overall profitability.
2. The system should be transparent enough so that managers could distinguish costs relevant for short-run decisions—such as incremental occasional bids for orders—from long-term decisions—such as acquiring a new product line, deleting product lines, and adding to existing product lines.
3. The transfer prices could be used to support decisions in both marketing and operating divisions, including:

Marketing	Operations
■ Product mix	■ Inventory levels
■ New product introduction	■ Batch sizes
■ Product deletion	■ Process improvements
■ Pricing	■ Capacity management
	■ Outsourcing: make vs. buy

Division managers wanted a transfer pricing system with the following characteristics:

1. The transfer prices would report the financial performance of their divisions fairly.
2. Managers could influence the reported performance of their divisions by making business decisions within their scope of authority. That is, the reported performance should reflect changes in product mix, improved efficiency, investments in new equipment, and organizational changes.
3. The decisions made by managers of marketing divisions would reflect both sales revenue and associated expenses incurred in the operations division.
4. The system must anticipate that division managers would examine, in depth, the method for calculating transfer prices and would take actions that maximized the reported performance of their divisions.

Finally, the financial staff wanted a transfer pricing system such that:

1. The transfer prices and financial reports derived from them would be credible and could be relied upon for decision making at all levels of the organization without excessive arguments and controversy.

2. The transfer pricing system would be clear, easy to explain, and easy to use. Updating transfer prices should be easy, and the components of the transfer price calculation should promote good understanding of the underlying factors driving costs.
3. The system would be used for internal charging of costs from the operations division to the marketing divisions.

TRADITIONAL TRANSFER PRICE APPROACHES WOULDN'T WORK

Teva's managers considered but rejected several traditional methods for establishing a new transfer pricing system: market price, full cost, marginal cost, and negotiated price. Market price for the transferred product was not feasible because no market existed for Teva's manufactured and packaged pharmaceutical products that had not been distributed or marketed to customers. A full cost calculation including materials, labor, and manufacturing overhead was rejected because the traditional methods for allocating overhead (labor or machine hours) did not capture the actual cost structure in Teva's plants. Also, the accumulation of all factory costs into average overhead rates could encourage local optimization by each division that would lower Teva's overall profit. For example, manufacturing plants would be encouraged to overproduce in order to absorb more factory overhead into inventory, while marketing divisions might be discouraged from bidding aggressively for high-volume orders and encouraged to accept more low volume custom orders. Also, this system would not reveal the incremental costs associated with short-run decisions or the relative use of capacity by different products and different order sizes.

Using short-run marginal cost, covering only ingredients and packaging materials, was the system proposed initially, which the managers already knew was inadequate for their purposes. And, finally, senior executives believed strongly that negotiated transfer prices would lead to endless arguments among managers in the different divisions, which would consume excessive time on nonproductive discussions.

ACTIVITY-BASED COSTING IS THE ANSWER

In December 1989, Teva's senior management attended a presentation on the fundamentals of activity-based costing and decided to implement ABC in its largest production plant. They wanted to investigate the use of ABC for calculating transfer prices between that plant and the marketing divisions. Teva put together a multidisciplinary project team consisting of managers from the production, finance, and marketing divisions. The team worked for about six months to develop an activity dictionary, drive factory costs to activities, identify cost drivers for each activity, collect data, and calculate ABC based product costs. It took the team several more weeks to analyze the results. Table 1 shows a sample calculation (updated to reflect 1996 data) of the costs to produce 10 tablets of a pain reliever. With this information, managers believed they now had a defensible, quantifiable answer to a question about how much it cost to manufacture a special small batch for a customer.

After seeing how ABC worked at the first plant, in subsequent years the project team rolled out the ABC analysis to the remaining production plants. The ABC models were retrospective, calculating the activity costs, activity cost driver rates, and product costs for the prior year. By the end of 1993, senior managers wanted to use ABC prospectively, to calculate transfer prices for the coming year. In November, Teva built its ABC production cost model for 1994 using data from the first three quarters of 1993. But managers objected to calculating costs for 1994 based on 1993 historical data. The numbers would not incorporate the impact of new products, new machines, and expected changes in production processes. Also, the historical data contained volume and spending variances that occurred in 1993 but that were not expected to be representative of production operations in 1994.

TABLE 1. PAIN RELIEVER 10 TABLETS, 250 MG

Annual Sales 1996—$2.1 million	
ABC Cost per package	
Material use	$1.50
Production costs	2.10
(The traditional production costs per package were only $1.50, 40% difference)	
Total:	$3.60
Production Cost Analysis:	
Resources	
Salaries	$0.86
Energy	0.27
Utilities	0.34
Deprecation	0.41
Administrative	0.22
Total	$2.10
Main Activities	
Storage	$0.25
Manufacturing	0.61
Packaging	0.71
Q.A.	0.42
Logistics	0.11
Total	$2.10
Cost Drivers	
Number of materials	$0.55
Batches	0.24
Labor hours	0.71
Machine hours	0.47
Samples	0.13
Total	$2.10

The project team took this issue to the company's Financial Control Forum where representatives from the operations and marketing divisions and company headquarters met to discuss costing and financial reporting methodologies. After several meetings, the group decided to use the next year's (1994) forecasted costs—based on budgeted expense data, forecasted volume and mix of sales, and projected process utilization and efficiencies—to calculate the transfer prices.

THE ABC TRANSFER PRICE MODEL STRUCTURE

The structure of the early retrospective ABC models and the current prospective model recognizes the ABC hierarchy of unit, batch, product sustaining, and plant-level costs.[1] Unit liable costs represent all the direct expenses associated with producing individual product units such as tablets, capsules, and ampoules. These expenses principally include the cost of raw materials, packaging materials, and direct wages paid to production workers.

Batch-level costs include the expenses of resources used for each production or packaging batch, mainly the costs of preparation, setup, cleaning, quality control, laboratory testing, and computer and production management. The lot sizes for pharmaceutical production usually are predetermined based on the capacity of containers in the production line,[2] but a second batch process, determined by customer orders, occurs for packaging the tablets or syrup. The costs of a production or a packaging batch can vary among different products and, of course, among different plants. For example, a small customer order can trigger the production of a large batch of tablets or syrup of which only a small portion may be packaged for the particular customer order.[3] Thus, the batch costs assigned to a particular order include two components: a pro-rata share of the batch cost of the production setup and the full batch cost of the packaging setup. The calculation of batch-level costs for several different types of customer orders is shown in Table 2.

Product-specific costs include the expenses incurred in registering the products,[4] making changes to a product's production processes, and designing the package. Plant-level costs represent the cost of maintaining the capacity of production lines including depreciation, cost of safety inspections, and insurance, as well as the general expenses of the plant such as security and landscaping. In many ABC applications, machine depreciation would be included in the unit and batch costs associated with producing products and changing from one product to another. Teva decided to treat equipment depreciation as a plant-level cost so the calculated unit and batch costs could be used to estimate more closely the marginal costs associated with producing one more unit or batch of a product.

TABLE 2. BATCH-LEVEL TRANSFER PRICE

The batch-level transfer price has two components, the production setup and the packing setup. Consider the production and packaging process for a cough syrup. In the production process, the active ingredients, a syrup simplex, and flavors, are mixed together in a 600-liter container to produce the syrup solution. The cost of setup—labor, cleaning, maintenance, and quality control resources is $300. The setup cost is assigned proportionally to the entire output.

Subsequently, bottles are filled with the syrup solution and packed into cardboard boxes. The entire packaging process is performed on an automated filling and packing line. The setup of the line costs $500, which includes the cost of a skilled technician, cleaning, maintenance and quality control. Packing the same syrup into two different presentations such as different sized bottles (50 ml and 100 ml) or different packaging materials, requires two different setups.

The batch-level transfer price consists of the pro-rata share of the production setup and the full cost of the packaging setup. We illustrate the approach with three numerical examples:

Produce a full batch of 6,000 bottles of 100 ml syrup for a large order from a customer in the local market

$$[\$300/6,000] + [\$500/6,000] = \$.05 + \$.083 = \$.133/bottle$$
$$\text{mixing} \qquad \text{packing}$$

Produce a small order of 1,000 bottles of 100 ml syrup, packed in special boxes, for a special tender in South America

$$[\$300/\$6,000] + [\$500/1,000] = \$.05 + \$.50 = \$.55/bottle$$
$$\text{mixing} \qquad \text{packing}$$

Produce a full batch of 12,000 bottles of 50 ml syrup for a large order from a customer in the local market

$$[\$300/12,000] + [\$500/12,000] = \$.025 + \$.042 = \$.067/bottle$$
$$\text{mixing} \qquad \text{packing}$$

USING ABC COSTS FOR TRANSFER PRICING

Teva bases its transfer price system on a prospective ABC calculation. Prices are set for the coming year based on budgeted data. The company calculates standard activity cost driver rates for each activity. During the year, these costs get charged to products based on the actual quantity of activities demanded during the year. The use of standard activity cost driver rates enables product costs to be calculated in a predictable manner throughout the year. It also eliminates monthly or quarterly fluctuations in product costs caused by variations in actual spending, resource usage, and activity levels.

Transfer prices are calculated in two different procedures. The first one assigns unit and batch-level costs, and the second assigns product specific and plant-level costs. The marketing divisions are charged for unit-level costs (principally materials and labor) based on the actual quantities of each individual product they acquire. In addition, they are charged batch-level costs based on the actual number of production and packaging batches of each product they order (see examples in Table 2). Now that Teva has the ability to analyze the costs of different presentations, the trend of having a large number of presentations for each product has slowed, For example, the marketing divisions realized that producing special sample packages of six tablets was very expensive and that it was cheaper to give physicians the regular packages of 20 tablets. In general, the procedure has given marketing managers the flexibility to decide when to accept a small order from a customer or how much of a discount to grant for large orders. Table 3 shows a sample calculation of the monthly unit and batch-level charges from a plant to a marketing division.

The product-specific and plant-level expenses are charged to marketing divisions annually based on budgeted information (see Table 4). The product-specific costs are easy to assign because each marketing division has specific products for its own markets. No individual product is sold to more than one marketing division. The plant-level (capacity-sustaining) expenses are charged to each marketing division based on the budgeted use of the capacity of the four manufacturing facilities.

Activity cost driver rates are calculated based on the practical capacity of each of the four plants. In this way, the rates reflect the underlying efficiency and productivity of the plants without being influenced by fluctuations in forecasted or actual usage. Analysts estimated the practical capacity by noting the maximum production quantities during past peak periods.

What about unused capacity? Unused capacity arises from two sources: (1) declines in demand for products manufactured on an existing line, and (2) partial usage when a new production line is added because existing production lines cannot produce the additional quantities requested by one of the marketing divisions. To foster a sense of responsibility among marketing managers for the cost of supplying capacity resources, Teva charges the marketing division that experienced the decline in demand a lump-sum assignment (see Table 4) for the cost of maintaining the unused production capacity in an existing line. When a marketing division initiates an increment in production capacity or manufacturing technology, it bears the costs of all the additional resources supplied unless or until the increment begins to be used by one of the other marketing divisions. At that point, each marketing division would be charged based on its percentage of practical capacity used.

TABLE 3. MONTHLY DEBIT MAY 1995

Product	Quantity Produced	Material (per package)	From Plant A to Local Market Division Unit Based Costs (Per Package)	Batch Based Costs (Per Package)	Total Costs† (Per Package)	Total Debit‡
Pain reliever 20 tablets, 500 mg.	1,000,000	$2.10	$0.22	$0.41	$2.73	$2,730,000
Pain reliever 30 capsules	1,200,000	1.60	0.20	0.32	2.12	2,544,000
Syrup 200 c.c.	200,000	0.81	0.43	0.11	1.35	270,000
•	•					•
•	•					•
•	•					•
Total						$15,100,200

† Total costs = material + unit based cost + batch based costs

‡ Total debit = total costs per package × quantity produced

TABLE 4. ANNUAL DEBIT—1995

Product	From Plant A to Lemmon Marketing Division (USA) Annual Budgeted Quantity	Product Based Costs (Per Package)	Plant Based Costs (Per Package)	Total Costs† (Per Package)	Total Debit‡
Pain reliever 20 tablets, 500 mg.	12,000,000	$0.10	$0.21	$0.31	$3,720,000
Pain reliever 30 capsules	20,000,000	0.12	0.20	0.32	6,400,000
Syrup 200 c.c.	3,500,000	0.14	0.12	0.26	860,000
•	•				•
•	•				•
•	•				•
Cost of used capacity					141,900,000
Cost of unused capacity					1,300,000
Total					$143,200,000

† Total cost = production based costs + plant based costs

‡ Total debit = total cost per package × annual budgeted quantity

The assignment of the plant-level costs (still referred to as "fixed costs" at Teva because of its long history with the marginal costing approach) receives much attention, particularly from the managers of the marketing divisions. They want to verify that these costs do indeed stay "fixed" and don't creep upward each period. By separating the unit and batch level costs from the product-sustaining and plant-level costs, the marketing managers can monitor closely the costs incurred in the manufacturing plants. In particular, the marketing managers make sure that increases in plant-level costs occur only when one or more of them requests a change in production capacity. The responsibility for the fixed cost increment is then clearly assignable to the requesting division.

The integrated budget process lets marketing managers plan their product mix with knowledge of the cost impact of their decisions. When they propose increases in variety and complexity, they know the added costs they will be charged because of their increased demands on manufacturing facilities. Active discussions occur between marketing and operations personnel about the impact of product mix and batch sizes.

Marketing managers now distinguish between products that cover all manufacturing costs versus those that cover only the unit and batch-level expenses but not their annual product-sustaining and plant-level expenses. Because of the assignment of unused capacity expenses to the responsible marketing division, the marketing managers incorporate information about available capacity when they make decisions about pricing, product mix, and product introduction.

One example illustrates the value of assigning product-sustaining and plant-level expenses to individual products in the new transfer pricing system. The initial and subsequent ABC analyses revealed that quite a few of Teva's products were unprofitable; that is, the revenues they earned were below the cost of the unit, batch, and product and plant-sustaining expenses associated with these products. But managers were reluctant to drop these products because many of the expenses assigned to them, including direct labor, would remain for some time even if production of the unprofitable products were to cease.

In the early 1990's, however, Teva's growing sales volume led to shortages in capacity. Teva eventually decided to sell 30 low volume products to another company. These products were not central to Teva's strategy, yet they consumed a great number of resources and managers' attention. By shifting the product mix away from the unprofitable products, Teva was able to use the freed-up capacity of people, machines, and facilities to handle the production of newly introduced products and the expanded sales of existing profitable products. While the debate about selling off the 30 products lasted three years, the ABC system contributed to the final decision by revealing that the cheapest source of new capacity was the capacity released by reducing the production and sales of currently unprofitable products.

ONGOING BENEFITS FROM ABC TRANSFER PRICING SYSTEM

With Teva's continued growth, requests for investments in new production capacity arise continually. ABC's high-lighting of unused capacity often reveals where production can be expanded without spending additional money. A second source is the capacity released by ceasing production of unprofitable products—when feasible without disrupting customer relations. Beyond these two sources, investments in a new production line can be assessed by simulating production costs if the line were to be installed. For example, a new line can reduce batch level costs because of less need for changeovers on both the existing and the proposed production lines. These cost reductions could provide the justification for the investment decision. In addition, the investment decision for a new production line explicitly incorporates the cost and assignment of responsibility for the unused capacity in the early periods while market demand has not yet built to long-term expected levels. Teva executives say that the discipline of recognizing and assigning unused capacity costs of new production lines provides valuable realism to the demand forecasts provided by the marketing divisions.

The transfer pricing system also motivates cost reduction and production efficiencies in the manufacturing plants. Managers in the different divisions now work together to identify ways to reduce unit and batch-level expenses. Manufacturing, purchasing, and marketing employees conduct common searches for lower-cost, more reliable, and higher-quality suppliers to reduce variable materials costs. Marketing managers compare Teva's production costs with those of alternative suppliers around the world. They share this information with manufacturing managers who learn where process improvements are required and may concur with a decision

to outsource products where the external suppliers' costs are lower than Teva could achieve in the foreseeable future. These actions contribute to increasing Teva's long-term profitability.

The activity-based cost information also helps managers determine which manufacturing facility is appropriate for different types of products. For example (see Figure 1), Plant A has a relatively inflexible (high capital-intensive) cost structure with a high percentage of plant-level costs and a low percentage of unit costs. This plant is most appropriate for high-volume production of standard products. Plant B, with a significantly lower percentage of plant-level costs and a relatively high percentage of unit costs, is much more flexible and is appropriate for producing small batch sizes and test runs of newly introduced products. Thus, ABC information also is being used to determine operating strategy.

THE BEST NEWS: HARMONY IS GROWING

An unexpected benefit of the activity-based transfer price system is the ability to measure profit performance under changing organizational structures. Teva, like many other pharmaceutical companies, undergoes periodic organizational changes. By understanding cost behavior at the activity and product level, financial managers can forecast the potential performance of newly created profit centers and reconstruct what the past profit performance history would have been, assuming that the proposed profit center reorganization had existed for the past several years. The ABC system also enables senior executives to measure profit performance across organizational—cost and profit center—boundaries. For example, Table 5 shows the profitability of a significant product family whose individual products are manufactured in different plants and are sold by more than one marketing division.

TABLE 5.10 PRODUCTS (SEGMENT A): 1995

	$ Million
Sales Revenue	50
Marketing expense	
USA Lemmon division	10
Local market division	9
Other export division	
Total	19
Manufacturing expenses	
Plant A	11
Plant B	
Plant C	9
Plant D	
Total	20
Total expenses	39
Profit	11

FIGURE 1. STRUCTURE OF COSTS IN PLANT "A" AND PLANT "B"

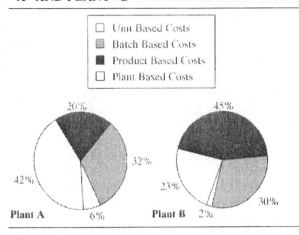

Jacob Winter, Teva's vice president of pharmaceutical operations, commented on the benefits derived from the ABC transfer price system:

In our changing environment, it is important for us to be able to understand and forecast our cost behavior. Some products remain in certain stages of production for a long time. These stages require resources of professional production and quality assurance staff, even when no direct labor is involved. On the other hand, since the supply of these resources is relatively fixed in the short run, we understand that we can use their capabilities for several small batch runs.

He also recognized that activity-based costs are not the primary information used for short-term operational decision making:

The ABC data provide an indication that must be supported by other information and facts. One cannot rely only on costing information when making operational decisions. Our short-term operational decisions focus on current bottlenecks and lead-time considerations. ABC provides guidance and insights about where we should be looking, but it is not the primary data for operational decisions.

Perhaps most important, the introduction of ABC-based transfer prices has led to a dramatic reduction in the conflicts among marketing and manufacturing managers. The managers now have confidence in the production cost economics reported by the transfer price system. Manufacturing managers who "sell" the product and marketing managers who "buy,' the product concur with the reasonableness of the calculated transfer prices. Teva's senior executives interpret the sharp reduction in intraorganizational conflicts as one of the most important signs that the use of activity-based transfer prices is succeeding.

ENDNOTES

1. R. Cooper, "Cost Classification in Unit-Based and Activity-Based Manufacturing Cost Systems." *Journal of Cost Management*, Fall 1990, pp. 4–14.
2. Production lot sizes can be expanded, if demand increases to a higher, sustainable level, by making technical changes to the production process and performing a quality control procedure to verify and validate that the product characteristics and quality have not been altered by the larger production batch.
3. At present, the Teva transfer price system does not charge the customer order for the full cost of setting up the production batch nor for the inventory carrying cost of the unused tablets or syrup. This is a refinement that could be added to the system in future years.
4. Registration costs include the costs of gaining and maintaining approval from governmental agencies for the right to manufacture each product.

Robert S. Kaplan is the Marvin Bower Professor of Leadership Development at the Harvard Business School. Dan Weiss is an instructor in the Industrial Engineering and Management Department of the Technion (Israel Institute of Technology) and partner, OIC Technologies Consulting Group. Eyal Desheh, formerly deputy chief financial officer at Teva Pharmaceuticals, is currently vice president and CFO of Scitex Corporation. Comments can be addressed to rkaplan@hba.edu.

QUESTIONS

12.1a Why wouldn't the traditional transfer-pricing approaches work at TEVA?

12.1b How did the new ABC transfer-pricing system affect the Marketing Division? Explain.

12.2 What Is EVA, and How Can It Help Your Company?

Economic value added (EVA) and market value added (MVA) arenot just performance metrics used to rank companies for investors—they can be used to manage your company better.

by Paul A. Dierks, CPA; and Ajay Patel*

Economic Value Added, or EVA, is a measure of financial performance that combines the familiar concept of residual income with principles of modem corporate finance—specifically, that all capital has a cost and that earning more than the cost of capital creates value for shareholders. EVA is after-tax net operating profit—NOPAT—minus a capital charge. If a company's return on capital exceeds its cost of capital, it is creating true value for the shareholder. Companies consistently generating high EVAs are top performers that are valued highly by shareholders.

Both EVA and MVA (Market Value Added) have been highly publicized in leading business magazines, but the focus usually is on what EVA and MVA are and how they are used externally to rank companies. Little detail is given on how the numbers in an EVA calculation actually are determined—which we propose to do here. Further, we demonstrate that these techniques have utility within a company in managing a company's operations, in guiding its strategy, and in providing incentives to its employees.

Key components of EVA are NOPAT and the capital charge—the amount of capital times the cost of capital. NOPAT is profits derived from a company's operations after taxes but before financing costs and noncash-bookkeeping entries. It is the total pool of profits available to provide a cash return to those who provided capital to the firm. Capital is the amount of cash invested in the business, net of depreciation. It can be calculated as the sum of interest-bearing debt and equity or as the sum of net assets less noninterest-bearing current liabilities.[1]

The capital charge is the cash flow required to compensate investors for the riskiness of the business given the amount of capital invested. Reducing the amount of working capital or fixed assets required to run the business while holding profits steady increases EVA.

The cost of capital is the minimum rate of return on capital required to compensate debt and equity investors for bearing risk, e.g., cut-off rate to create value.

In formula form,

$$EVA = (r - c^*) \times capital;$$
where r = rate of return;and
c^* = cost of capital, or the weighted average cost of capital

Then, $EVA = (r \times capital) - (c^* \times capital);$
$$EVA = NOPAT - c^* \times capital ; and$$
$$EVA = operating\ profits - a\ capital\ charge$$

Another perspective on EVA can be gained by looking at a firm's RONA—Return on Net Assets. For a firm, RONA is a ratio that is calculated by dividing its NOPAT by the amount of capital it employs (RONA = NOPAT/Capital) after making the necessary adjustments of the data reported by a conventional financial accounting system.

A convenient formulation of EVA is obtained by multiplying the total amount of net assets tied up by the spread between RONA and a threshold or minimum rate of return such as the cost of capital. Thus:

$$EVA = net\ investments \times$$
$$(RONA - required\ minimum\ return)$$
If RONA is above the threshold rate, EVA is positive.

Gains in shareholder wealth are driven by gains in EVA. The market price of a stock incorporates the current level of EVA and the expectation of future EVA. To increase the stock price, management must increase the current level of EVA and change the market's expectations of growth in future EVA.

In summary, EVA is really just another definition of earnings—sales less operating expenses—with one more item subtracted, a charge for the use of the capital involved. It is true economic profit consisting of all costs including the cost of capital.

WHAT IS MARKET VALUE ADDED (MVA)?

Market Value Added, or MVA, is a measure of the wealth a company has created for its investors. In effect, MVA shows the difference between what investors put in and what they can take out. EVA is the fuel that fires up a company's MVA. A company that has a positive EVA year after year will see its MVA rise, while negative EVA year in and year out will drag down MVA as the market loses faith that the company will ever provide a decent return on invested capital.

MVA is a cumulative measure of corporate performance that looks at how much a company's stock has

* From P. A. Dierks and A. Patel, "What Is EVA, and How Can It Help Your Company? *Management Accounting* (November 1997): 52–58. Reprinted with permission.

added to (or taken out of) investors' pocketbooks over its life and compares it with the capital those same investors put into the firm. If MVA is a positive number, the company has made its shareholders richer. A negative MVA indicates how much shareholder wealth has been destroyed. Maximizing MVA should be the primary objective for any company that is concerned about its shareholders' welfare.

How is MVA calculated? First, all the capital a company took in over its span of existence is identified including equity and debt offerings, bank loans, and retained earnings, and the amounts are added up. Then, some "adjustments" are made that capitalize certain past expenditures, like R&D spending, as an investment in future earnings. This adjusted capital amount is compared to a firm's total market value, which is the current value of a company's stock and debt to get MVA or the difference between what the investors can take out (total market value) and the amount investors put in (invested capital). In formula form, MVA is calculated as follows:

MVA = [(shares outstanding × stock price) + market value of preferred stock + market value of debt] – total capital

MVA tends to move in tandem with the firm's stock market value. Stern Stewart, the consulting firm that developed and promoted EVA in the business community, contends that EVA is the sole measurement method that can be correlated with a firm's stock price. Many interesting movements of firms, some counter to one's expectations, can be seen in the Stern Stewart rankings of the top 1,000 firms in Lieber's, Fisher's, and Tully's *Fortune* articles.[2]

CALCULATING EVA AND MVA
As indicated earlier, EVA and MVA can be calculated using some very simplistic formulas, but the simplicity of these calculations can be misleading because the after-tax operating profit, NOPAT, and the amount used for capital are not readily available—that is, they don't come directly off the financial statements. The amount of equity equivalent reserves for certain accounts must be determined first, and the footnotes to the financial statements are the primary source for this information.

In The Quest for Value, G. Bennett Stewart calculates a firm's EVA in two ways: an Operating Approach and a Financing Approach.[3] These two approaches then are reconciled in a summary report. To understand how these approaches work, we first must understand the concepts of equity equivalent reserves or EEs.

Equity equivalents are adjustments that turn a firm's accounting book value into "economic book value, which is a truer measure of the cash that investors have put at risk in the firm and upon which they expect to accrue some returns."[4] In this way, capital-related items are turned into a more accurate measure of capital that better reflects the financial base on which investors expect to accrue their returns. Also, revenue- and expense-related equity equivalent adjustments are included in NOPAT— Net Operating Profit After Taxes—which is a more realistic measure of the actual cash yield generated for investors from recurring business activities.

Stern Stewart has identified a total of 164 equity equivalent reserve adjustments; however, only about 20 to 25 have to be addressed in detail, and only a portion of these actually may be made in practice. "In our published rankings and illustrations, we have chosen to make only a handful of such adjustments in the calculation of EVA and MVA—typically those which can be made with information contained in the Compustat database and easily explained to the general business reader."[5] It recommends making an adjustment only in cases that pass four tests:

- Is it likely to have a material impact on EVA?
- Can the managers influence the outcome?
- Can the operating people readily grasp it?
- Is the required information relatively easy to track and derive?[6]

An example of an equity equivalent adjustment occurs with R&D expenditures. Under accounting conventions, outlays for R&D are charged off in the period when they are incurred. These immediate charge-offs as operating expenses say there is no future value to be derived from R&D. As a result, the company's profits are reduced, and its capital is undervalued. For EVA purposes, all outlays over the life of successful R&D projects should be removed from the income statement, be capitalized into the balance sheet, and amortized against earnings over the period benefiting from the successful R&D efforts. Thus, in calculating EVA, R&D is seen as an investment, and amounts spent for it must be included in a firm's capital base to reflect accurately the true amount of capital employed. Only the portion of the R&D that no longer has future value should be charged to the income statement in order to properly reflect the costs (and profit) of a period.

Other examples of EEs are the LIFO and Deferred Income Tax Reserves. In periods of rising prices, companies save taxes by using a LIFO basis of inventory costing. Under LIFO, recently acquired goods are expensed, and the costs of prior periods are accumulated in inventory resulting in an understatement of inventory and equity. A LIFO reserve account captures the difference between the LIFO and FIFO value of the inventory and indicates the extent that the LIFO inventories are understated in value. Adding the LIFO reserve to capital as an equity equivalent converts inventories from a LIFO to a FIFO basis of valuation, which is a better approximation of current replacement cost. Also, adjusting NOPAT for the change in the LIFO reserve brings into earnings the current period effect of unrealized gain attributable to holding inventories that appreciated in value. Action(s) to be taken for an equity equivalent adjustment for a LIFO reserve are:

Add to capital: amount of the LIFO reserve
Add to (deduct from) NOPAT: the amount of increase (decrease) in the LIFO reserve

Changes in the LIFO reserve also can be viewed as a difference between LIFO and FIFO cost of goods sold. Including this change in reported profits converts a LIFO cost of goods sold expense to FIFO but LIFO's tax benefit is retained. Thus, the overall effect of treating a LIFO reserve as an equity equivalent is to produce a FIFO balance sheet and income statement but preserve the LIFO tax benefit.

Deferred taxes arise from a difference in the timing when revenues and expenses are recognized for financial reporting versus when they are reported for tax purposes. The difference between the accounting provision for taxes and the tax amount paid is accumulated in the reserve for deferred income taxes account. If long-term assets that give rise to tax deferrals are replenished, a company's deferred tax reserve increases, which is the equivalent of permanent equity. Adjusting NOPAT for the change in the deferred tax reserve results in NOPAT being charged only with the taxes actually paid instead of the accounting tax provision. This calculation provides a clearer picture of the true cash-on-cash yield actually being earned in the business. Action(s) to be taken for an equity equivalent adjustment for a deferred tax reserve are:

Add to capital: amount of the deferred tax reserve
Add to (deduct from) NOPAT amount of increase (decrease) in the deferred tax reserve

See Table 1 for additional examples of equity equivalents and their effect on capital and NOPAT.

As noted, Stewart recommends two methods of calculating a firm's EVA: an Operating Approach and a Financing Approach. The Financing Approach builds up to the rate of return on capital from the standard return on equity in three steps: eliminating financial leverage, eliminating financing distortions, and eliminating accounting distortions. As a result of the first two steps, NOPAT is a sum of the returns attributable to all providers of funds to the company, and the NOPAT return is completely unaffected by the financial composition of capital. What matters is simply the productivity of capital employed in the business, no matter the financial form in which the capital has been obtained.

The Operating Approach starts by deducting operating expenses—including depreciation—from sales, but other noncash-bookkeeping entries are ignored. Next, EE reserve adjustments are made. Interest expense, because it is a financing charge, is ignored, but other (operating) income is added to get pretax economic profits or Net Operating Profit Before Taxes (NOPBT). In the final step, an estimate of the taxes payable in cash on these operating profits is subtracted leaving NOPAT at the same amount as in the financing approach. (See Table 2—Calculating EVA and MVA.)

CRITICISMS OF EVA AND MVA

A problem with EVA is that it does not account for real options (growth opportunities) inherent in investment decisions. The market value of a firm's securities reflects the market's perception of the value of those growth opportunities. But EVA does not reflect this information. Therefore, when using EVA to analyze the financial performance of a company, analysts should keep in mind that focusing on year-to-year changes in EVA will be better for firms with substantial assets in place in mature industries with few growth opportunities (public utilities for instance). For firms with fewer assets in place and substantial growth opportunities, however, year-to-year changes in EVA are less likely to explain changes in firm value. Firms in the technology and biotech sectors, for instance, would fall into the latter category. This problem can be avoided by refocusing the firm on the present value of expected future EVA instead of on year-to-year changes in EVA. But doing so would eliminate the essential factors (simplicity and ease of use) that caused EVA to be preferred to NPV.

TABLE 1. EQUITY EQUIVALENT ADJUSTMENTS FOR CALCULATING EVA

Add Equity Equivalents to Capital for:	Add Increases in Equity Equivalents to NOPAT for:
Cumulative goodwill amortization	Goodwill amortization
Unrecorded goodwill	Increase in (not) capitalized intangibles
(Net) capitalized intangibles	Increase in full-cost reserve
Full-cost reserve	Unusual loss (gain) after taxes
Cumulative unusual loss (gain) after taxes	Increase in other reserves
Other reserves for such things as bad debts, inventory obsolescence, and warranties	

This list is taken from Stewart, *The Quest for Value*, p. 112.

TABLE 2. CALCULATE EVA AND MVA

1997 Balance Sheet—*Dollars in Thousands*		1997 Capital—*Dollars in Thousands*		1997 Capital—*Dollars in Thousands*	
Assets		**Operating Approach**		**Financing Approach**	
Cash	$35	Cash	$ 35	Short-term debt (10%)	$100
Receivables (net)	190	Receivable (net)	190	Long-term debt (8%)	150
Inventory	190	Inventory	190	Present value of noncapital leases	50
Other current assets	95	LIFO reserve	10	Other long-term liabilities	120
Total current assets	510	Other current assets	95	Total debt and leases	420
		Current assets	520	Common equity	425
Property, plant and equipment (net)	530	Accounts payable	150	Plus: equity equivalents	
Goodwill	75	Income taxes payable	20	Accumulated goodwill	
Other long-term assets	120	Other current liabilities	200	amortization	50
Total assets	$1,235	NIBCLs	370	LIFO reserve	10
		Net working capital	150	Deferred income taxes	70
Liabilities and Net Worth		Property, plant and equipment (net)	530	Sum of equity equivalents	130
Short-term debt (10%)	$ 100	Present value of noncapital losses	50	Adjusted common equity capital	555
Accounts payable	150	Adjusted property, plant and equipment	580		
Income taxes payable	20	Goodwill	75		
Other current liabilities	200	Accumulated goodwill amortization	50		
Total current liabilities	470	Adjusted goodwill	125		
Long-term debt (8%)	150	Other long-term assets	120		
Other long-term liabilities	120	Capital (operating approach)	$975	Capital (financing approach)	$975
Total liabilities	270				
Deferred income taxes	70				
Common equity	425				
Total liabilities and net worth	$1,235				

1997 Income Statement - *Dollars in Thousands*		EVA NOPAT via Operating Approach		EVA NOPAT via Financing Approach	
Net sales	$2,000	Net sales	$2,000	Income available to common	$30
Cost of goods sold	1,670	Cost of goods sold	1,670	Plus, equity equivalent adjustments	
Gross profit	330	Gross profit	330	Increase deferred Wet;	5
		Less: selling general & administration	185	Goodwill amortization	14
Less: selling, general & administration	185	Other operating expenses	50	Increase LIFO reserve	2
Depreciation	20	Increase LIFO reserve	2	Sum of equity equivalents	21
Goodwill amortization	15	Interest expense noncapital leases	4	Adjusted income to common	51
Other operating expenses	50	Net operating profit	101	Interest expense	22
Total operating expenses	270	Interest expense	22	Interest expense noncapital leases	4
Net operating profit	60	Other income	12		26
Interest expense	22	NOPBT	91	Tax savings on interest expense	10
Other income	12	Income tax provision	20	Interest expense after taxes	16
Income before taxes	50	Less increase in deferred taxes	5		
Less: axes (40%)	20	Plus tax savings on interest expense	10		
Net profit after taxes	$30	Cash operating taxes	25		
		EVA NOPAT via operating approach	$66	EVA NOPAT via financing approach	$66

1. Calculate Market Value Added (MVA)

	Share Price	#Shares		
Market:	$25.00	50,000	$1,250,000	Equity market value
Book value:	$11.10	50,000	$ 555,000	Economic book value*
Market Value Added (MVA) =			$ 695,000	

* Sum of Common Equity and Equity Equivalents

2. Calculate Economic Value Added (EVA)

a. After-tax operating profit $ 66

b. Less: cost of capital (CDC)

Weighted Average COC

	Amount	Weight	Percent
LT Debt	$270	17.8%	4.8%
Equity:	$1,250	82.2%	12.0%
		COC =	10.7%

Times: amount of capital = $975 $105

c. Equals: Economic Value Added (EVA)   ($ 39)

To capture the growth opportunities inherent in companies, managers also should focus on MVA. Because MVA is constructed off the market value of a firm's securities, it reflects the market's expectations of future opportunities for the firm. Using both EVA and MVA to evaluate performance allows companies to account for both the year-to-year and long-term changes in value.

The empirical research of academics to date has been limited, and the results have been inconclusive. In a study of 241 firms over the period of 1987 to 1993, Kenneth Lehn and Anil Makhija found "that EVA and MVA are significantly positively correlated with stock price performance attesting to their effectiveness as performance measures."[7] But a sidebar to a CFO article reports on a study by three University of Washington professors who found that "while EVA may add incremental information in some settings, as a performance measure it can't even outperform basic income before extraordinary items."[8] The James Dodd and Shimin Chen study of 566 companies for the years 1983–1992 showed that stock returns were correlated with EVA, but "the alignment is not nearly as perfect as suggested by recent articles." These authors also observed that residual income (RI) explained about the same variation as EVA and, thus, similar stock returns will result from performance measurement systems using EVA and RI performance measurements. They then concluded, "Therefore, the off-line adjustments to operating income necessary to calculate EVA may not pass a prudent cost-benefit analysis."[9]

OTHER PERFORMANCE METRICS
Although we focus here on EVA, other performance metrics exist—such as NPV, CFROI, and RI. CFROI (cash flow return on investment) is a rate of return measure calculated by dividing inflation-adjusted cash flow from the investment by the inflation-adjusted amount of the cash investment. While CFROI does adjust for inflation, it fails to account for risk and the appropriate required return on the project. In a sense, CFROI is similar to the internal rate of return (IRR), hence it measures the investment's return as opposed to the wealth created or destroyed by the investment.

EVA comes closest in theory and construct to net present value (NPV). The information requirements for both techniques are the same. For both techniques you need an appropriate risk-adjusted cost of capital. To determine the NPV of an investment decision, you need estimates of expected future cash flow. Similarly, to determine the economic value of the decision, you need the present value of expected future EVAs that are based on expected future cash flows of the firm. In other words, the NPV of an asset is simply the present value of the expected future EVA from the asset. Therefore the notion of increasing or maximizing EVA each year is consistent with the goal of shareholder wealth maximization.

USING EVA AND MVA WITHIN A COMPANY
All managers are basically in the same business—putting scarce capital to its most promising uses. To increase their company's stock price, managers must perform better than those with whom they compete for capital. Then, once they get the capital, they must earn rates of return on it that exceed the return offered by other equally risky-seekers of capital funds. If they accomplish this goal, value will have been added to the capital that their firm's investors placed at their disposal. If they don't accomplish that goal, there will be a misallocation of capital, and the company's stock will sell at a price that discounts the sum total of the resources employed.

EVA is a financial management system that is well adapted to this kind of a situation because it focuses on creating shareholder value. In using the system, managers and employees focus on how capital is used and on the cash flow generated from it. It runs counter to the notion that long-term stock appreciation comes from earnings.

Focusing on EVA growth provides two benefits: Management's attention is focused more toward its primary responsibility increasing investor wealth—and, two, distortions caused by using historical cost accounting data are reduced or eliminated. As a result, managers spend their time finding ways to increase EVA rather than debating the intricacies of the fluctuations in their accounting for reported earnings.

EVA measures the amount of value a firm creates during a defined period through operating decisions it makes to increase margins, improve working capital management, efficiently use its production facilities, and redeploy underutilized assets. Thus, EVA can be used to hold management accountable for all economic outlays whether they appear in the income statement, on the balance sheet, or in the financial statement's footnotes. EVA creates one financial statement that includes all the costs of being in business, including the carrying cost of capital. The EVA financial statement gives managers a complete picture of the connections among capital, margin, and EVA. It makes managers conscious of every dollar they spend whether that dollar is spent on or off the income statement or on operating costs or the carrying cost of working capital and fixed assets.

Another very subtle benefit to a company that adopts EVA is that it creates a common language for making decisions, especially long-term decisions; resolving budgeting issues; evaluating the performance of its organizational units and its managers; and measuring the value-creating potential of its strategic options. An outgrowth of such an environment is that the quality of management also improves as managers begin to think like owners and adopt a longer horizon view.

EVA should not be viewed as "the" answer to all things. By itself, EVA doesn't solve business problems; managers must solve them. But having access to such a meaningful measure that is linked strongly to share price performance clarifies a manager's options and, in conjunction with MVA, provides a meaningful target to pursue for both internally and externally oriented decisions.

USING EVA TO FACILITATE THE MANAGEMENT OF THE COMPANY

Managers of EVA-adopting firms know their stock's price is tied to investors' expectations of the company's long-term cash flows; therefore, they will explicitly use value-added measures in guiding their firm's activities. In this way, greater emphasis will be placed on the operating profit needed to justify capital expenditures—or any expenditure, for that matter. It is this increased awareness of the efficient use of capital that eventually will produce additional shareholder value.

Value-added measures can be particularly effective for gauging the performance of subsidiaries, divisions, and other business units when a stock price measure is unavailable. By using value-added measures at the business unit level, companies can determine where capital will be invested most productively and the contribution each unit makes to the market value of the company. Unit managers then can be compensated on the basis of those contributions.

Under the aegis of "what gets measured gets managed": EVA concepts can lead to improvements in the overall management of a firm's everyday operations. Incorporating EVAs metrics into formal performance measurement systems facilitates both the use of measurements in areas that have been difficult to monitor and adds a degree of precision to measurements that previously have been taken and reported.

With a focus on EVA, managers can do a better job of asset management, which can free up cash for use in other areas of the business. For example, a good way to boost EVA is to increase inventory turns, which reduces the amount of cash tied up in raw materials. Also, the effects of increasing inventory turns can be readily evaluated against the costs of running out of materials, shipping products late, or otherwise failing to satisfy the customer. On a more microlevel, manufacturing employees will readily comprehend that by reducing waste they help create economic value.

Companies that have adopted EVA find they use it as a basis for decision making at all levels—whether it is at the strategic level of acquisitions, a new market entry, or even in thinking about day-to-day trade-offs in their business. In these situations, EVA provides a rather simplistic means of assessing the alternatives under review because there are only three basic means of raising a company's EVA:

1. Raise profit levels without raising the amount of capital spent—most obvious method is cost cutting, but imaginative man will always look for other methods.
2. Use less capital. That means looking for improvements in the way a business is run such as streamlining operations.
3. Invest capital in high-return projects. Any project should meet the minimum criterion of earning more than the cost of capital invested.[10]

EVA also has been found to be a worthy adjunct to other management change programs such as total quality management, quick response, and total customer development. Rather than being at odds with the aims of those efforts, EVA's quantification of results in financial terms helps to energize them by demanding and getting continuous financial improvement.

With a company-wide adoption and use of EVA concepts, all employees begin to think like, act like, and be paid like owners and feel responsible for and take part in the economic value of the firm. Teamwork will be fostered, and everyone will "care" about what is going on and how business is progressing on a daily basis.

BENEFITS OF EVA INCENTIVE PLANS

To this point, the emphasis has been on how focusing on EVA may help managers increase shareholder wealth. For the metric to help in creating shareholder wealth, however, managers must behave in a manner consistent with wealth creation. One powerful way to align managers' interests with those of the shareholders is to tie their compensation to output from the EVA metric. In fact, it is not just for managers but may be used for *all* employees. When implemented correctly, the basic notion of increasing shareholder value will permeate the entire organization, and employees at all levels, will begin to act in concert with upper levels of management.

Implementing an EVA-based incentive plan is fundamentally a process of empowerment—getting employees to be entrepreneurial, to think and act as owners; getting them to run the business as if they owned it; and giving them a stake in the results they achieve.

The overall, company-wide objective is to generate a persistent increase in EVA. To achieve that, employees must understand the role they play in increasing a firm's EVA. A key factor in sustaining a continuing interest in EVA, and in making it work, is to revise the compensation system to focus on creating value. It has been shown that one of the critical components in successfully using EVA to improve a company's MVA is tying it to bonuses and pay schemes. Designing an incentive compensation system that pays people for sustainable improvements in EVA, in concert with an understanding of what drives EVA and what drives economic returns, is what transforms behavior within a company.

A good way to get started quickly is to increase insider ownership of the firm's stock. One way to do this is to turn old profit-sharing plans into employee stock ownership plans.

If an incentive system is to work, it must have certain distinctive properties:

1. An objective measure of performance—one that cannot be manipulated by one of the parties who may benefit. For example, in many existing plans, the budget is a commonly used target for performance, but the manager usually is heavily involved in negotiating that budget. If the manager negotiates well, the budget target can be easily "beatable."
2. It must be simple so even employees far down in the organization will understand how EVA is tied to economic value so they can follow it well.
3. Bonus amounts have to be significant enough in amount for employees to alter their behaviors.
4. It must be definitive—which means the target stays fixed and the goalpost won't be moved after the plan gets under way.

Other conditions that are suggested strongly by members of the Stern Stewart organization are:

5. There should be no limits (caps) placed on the plan. The sky is the limit. Having caps will develop into operating a seasonal business—when the target is reached, slow down.
6. Seek sustainable performance by not paying the full bonus amount in one year. This procedure would entail setting up an incentive plan bank account where the entire bonus is deposited, but some (smaller) portion is paid now, and a larger portion is paid later—and the amount to be paid out later can be subject to a loss. The objective is to keep EVA positive and not have the focus on achieving that goal only one time. Anyone can do it once.
7. Include a cancellation clause. If a person resigns, the banked bonus is lost. But if he or she retires, the balance is converted into a deferred bonus account.

For middle and senior people, take a certain amount of each year's cash payment, pay most of it in cash (say, 80%) and the rest in stock options (to get an equity interest). In establishing the ground rules for the plan, the pay-for-performance ratio should be steeply sloped—meaning that a manager's reward is higher on the upside of performance.

Incorporating a long-term perspective into an incentive plan is another important feature to consider. To get managers to focus on creating real value for the shareholders, a portion of the stock options available to managers can be priced at a premium over the market price on the date of the grant, Thus, managers first must earn the hurdle rate for the shareholders before they can exercise their own options for a gain. Therefore, the managers' financial incentives are aligned with the shareholders', resulting in the impetus needed to get managers to think aggressively and long term.

Finally, the structure of the incentive system should be team based to focus more on individual or small work group results and should still capture a larger, longer-term perspective based on the company's performance. The proper weighting of these elements can provide different motivation to different people depending on their ability to influence the item being measured.

IMPLEMENTING EVA

Transitioning to value-added measures is an extensive (and expensive) process. It can require a year or more of planning by internal and external financial and compensation experts. Advocates of value-added measures justify the substantial costs by pointing to the benefits of optimizing the company's strategy for value creation.

A transition to value-added performance measurement must start with a serious commitment of the board of directors and senior executives to use these measures to manage the business. The interests of lower-level managers and the employees they supervise must be cultivated carefully so they "buy in."

Success with value-added performance measures also requires a massive education and communication effort directed at executives, line managers, and hourly employees. Although it probably will require a great deal of training time and money to educate everyone on the basic theory underlying the notion of creating economic value, doing it in a structured, unhurried manner probably will be the most productive way in the long run.[11]

ENDNOTES

1. The latter item, given the acronym NIBCLS, appears in an EVA financial statement prepared under an Operating Approach. See G. Bennett Stewart III, *The Quest for Value*, HarperCollins Publishers, Inc., 1991, pp. 92, 100.
2. Ronald B. Lieber, "Who Are the Real Wealth Creators?" *Fortune*, December 9, 1996; Shawn Tully, "The Real Key to Creating Wealth," *Fortune*, September 20, 1993; Anne Fisher, "Creating Stockholder Wealth," *Fortune*, February 5, 1996.
3. These approaches are very detailed, and the reader is referred to G. Bennett Stewart's book for a more thorough coverage of them. See G. B. Stewart, pp. 87–110.
4. G. B. Stewart, p. 91.
5. G. Bennett Stewart III, "EVA: Fact and Fantasy," *Journal of Applied Corporate Finance*, pp. 73–74.
6. *Ibid.*, p. 74.
7. Kenneth Lehn and Anil K. Makhija, "EVA & MVA as Performance Measures and Signals for Strategic

Change," *Strategy & Leadership Magazine*, May/June 1996, pp. 34–38.

8. Randy Myers, "Metric Wars," *CFO*, October 1996, p. 44.
9. James L. Dodd and Shimin Chen, "EVA: A New Panacea?" *B&E* Review, July/September 1996, pp. 26–28.
10. Shawn Tully, "The Real Key to Creating Wealth," *Fortune*, September 20, 1993, p. 50.
11. An excellent "how to" article on implementing EVA, including several specific steps and rules to follow, titled "How to Implement EVA and Make Share Prices Rise: Economic Value Added" by Mark Gressle, was published in *Cashflow Magazine*, March 1996, p. 28.

Paul A. Dierks, CPA, is an associate professor of management in the Babcock Graduate School of Management at Wake Forest University. He is a member of the Piedmont Winston-Salem Chapter, through which this article was submitted. He can be reached by phone at (910) 759-4579 or e-mail at paul_dierks@ mail.mba.wfa.edu. Ajay Patel is an assistant professor of management at the Babcock Graduate School of Management at Wake Forest University.

QUESTIONS

12.2a What exactly is EVA? Can it be labeled "true economic profit?"
12.2b Define MVA. What is the relation between MVA and EVA?

12.3 "Greening" With EVA
Now you can use Economic Value Added and other shareholder value measures to improve your corporate capital investment decisions.

by Marc J. Epstein and S. David Young*

Many companies are spending hundreds of millions of dollars a year on environmentally related operating costs and capital investments. But their accounting, costing, and capital investment systems don't identify and measure environmental costs properly. Instead, they hide these costs in various administrative and overhead accounts. Further, well-developed capital investment tools that companies use throughout their organizations are rarely employed for environmental capital investments. If used properly, shareholder value measures such as economic value added (EVA®), an increasingly popular performance metric, can significantly improve corporate decision making in the realm of environmental management and can improve both environmental and general capital investment decisions.[1]

Companies often make their investment decisions about environmentally-related projects based on incomplete data and incomplete analysis. If companies undertake the projects because they have to comply with an environmental regulation, they usually don't scrutinize them as much as they do capital projects. The main reason is the lack of financial expertise in environmental health and safety (EH&S) departments and the attitude, shared by managers throughout the corporate world, that they have no choice because they must comply with the regulations. We think this attitude produces substantially inferior decisions and compromises efforts to design, implement, and manage a corporate environmental

strategy. It continues to foster reactive approaches to environmental management and inhibits the development of proactive approaches that can lead to substantially reduced environmental impacts and dramatic improvements in long-term corporate profitability.

WHAT ARE THE USUAL PROCEDURES?
While discounted cash flow (DCF) analysis is common in most corporate capital investment projects, companies approve many environmental projects with only a simple payback analysis. Lack of financial expertise encourages the use of payback, and some finance departments believe DCF analysis isn't necessary in regulatory projects because the projects must be completed without regard to whether they are financially sound.

The result is that companies do not identify or analyze the impacts of such projects. Not only is this approach common for projects driven by regulatory mandate, but it often is applied to voluntary projects. Further, companies typically require payback periods that are substantially shorter than for other capital investments and don't subject the projects to the rigorous analysis the capital investment process usually entails. One study of environmental capital investments found that "payback periods were short; in nearly two-thirds of the activities, companies recouped their investments in six months or less."[2] By requiring extremely short payback periods; by avoiding the typical corporate technical,

* From: M. Epstein and S. David Young, "Greening with EVA," *Management Accounting* (January 1999): 45–49. Reprinted with permission.

environmental, and financial screens; and by ignoring a full understanding of future costs and benefits, companies often make improper capital investment decisions.[3]

But when they complete a DCF analysis that considers all the impacts of a project on the company through the entire life cycle, they are encouraged to think through the impacts and possibly examine process and product redesign. They can accomplish this task through cross-functional groups that examine all of the impacts and consider likely changes in regulations, technology, cost of technology, consumer demand, and the impacts of those changes on the proposed capital investment.[4] Financial professionals should use the same techniques they use to forecast cash inflows and outflows for traditional investment projects to estimate the likely future cash flows related to the environmental impacts of general corporate capital investments, plant sitings, and both voluntary and regulatory environmental capital investments.

Obviously, the decision process for regulatory projects and voluntary projects should be different, but the analysis of alternatives and impacts should not. Too often, companies focus only on minimizing costs instead of maximizing net benefits. Too often, they calculate only the payback period without considering the time value of money, the broad array of constituencies affected, or the significant future benefits and costs likely to arise from environmentally related capital projects. Choosing projects based only on the shortest payback period will not yield the best choices.

EVA, which can show the contribution of environmental investments to shareholder value and can be tied to compensation and long-term divisional improvement, is one way to go.

WHAT IS EVA AND HOW IS IT CALCULATED?

EVA is similar to conventional measures of profit but with two important differences: EVA considers the cost of all capital, and it is not constrained by the generally accepted accounting principles (GAAP) that govern corporate financial reporting. The net income figures reported in company income statements consider only the most visible type of capital cost—interest—while ignoring the cost of equity finance. Financial accountants do not measure the cost of finance provided by the company's shareholders because these costs, like all opportunity costs, can't be observed directly. But they are real, nonetheless. Although estimating the cost of equity is a highly subjective exercise, measures of performance that ignore such costs can't reveal how successful a company has been in creating value for its owners. One way to describe EVA is that it represents a company's profits net of the cost of both debt and equity capital. It is economic profit or residual income. But EVA doesn't stop there. It also corrects for potential distortions caused by GAAP. Very simply, the user of EVA

can abandon any accounting principles that are viewed as distorting the measurement of wealth creation.

To understand EVA, you need to understand Market Value Added (MVA).[5] MVA is the difference between the market value of the firm and its invested capital (including equity and debt) contributed to the firm:

$$MVA = Market\ value - Invested\ capital$$

Managers want to maximize MVA, not the value of the firm, which is accomplished easily enough by investing ever-increasing amounts of capital. For example, if a company raises $20 million in capital and invests it in projects that are expected to earn the cost of capital, both total value and total capital have increased by $20 million, and MVA is unchanged. MVA increases only when invested capital earns a rate of return greater than the cost of capital. When a company invests newly raised capital in value-creating projects—those with a positive net present value—MVA increases. When that capital is invested in value-destroying projects (those with a negative net present value), MVA decreases. So how does EVA relate to MVA? MVA is the present value of the firm's expected future EVAs. EVA generates more attention than MVA because, as we will explain later, it is more amenable to periodic performance measurement. EVA is calculated as follows:

	Net sales
–	Operating expenses
=	Operating profit
–	Taxes
=	Not operating profit
–	Capital charges
=	EVA

Capital charges equal a company's "invested capital" (or "capital employed") times the weighted-average cost of capital. Invested capital is the sum of all the company's financing apart from noninterest-bearing short-term liabilities, such as accounts payable, accrued wages, and accrued taxes.

If GAAP distorts the measurement of capital or operating income, it can be adjusted as necessary. Most of the adjustments are in the form of "equity equivalents." The logic behind these adjustments is that when companies apply GAAP, certain items are charged to income, such as provisions, deferred taxes, and goodwill, which artificially—and misleadingly—reduce stated capital. Unless these charges are restored to equity, capital charges will be understated, and operating income will be misstated.

The potential number of adjustments is practically limitless. EVA consultants have already identified more than 150 changes that can be made to operating profit and invested capital. But most companies that use EVA or similar measures make fewer than five adjustments (and many make none at all) for fear that the evaluation and reward system based on EVA would become impossibly complicated.

IMPLEMENTING EVA

Although the idea of using EVA is often proposed by the CFO or the corporate controller, the implementation process begins with the board and the CEO. The CFO's office may spearhead implementation, but the profound attitude shifts that are possible from value-based management practices require commitment at the highest levels. Why expect employees to accept EVA and all that goes with it if the CEO doesn't appear totally committed to the concept?

As shown in Table 1, after the board, the CEO, and other top managers have accepted value-based management and the use of EVA, a steering committee must be established to make the important strategic decisions regarding program design. The members of this committee should include the CFO, at least one senior level operating manager other than the CEO, and the corporate head of human resources. Other candidates might include a senior strategic business unit or product line manager, the corporate controller, and the head of investor relations. This committee will be tasked with determining, subject to board approval:

- Which corporate activities will be driven expressly by value-based management and which activities will be tied to EVA. A fully committed company incorporates value-based management into its strategic planning, capital allocation, operating budget, and compensation processes and systems. Investor relations also will be affected.
- How far down in the organizational hierarchy EVA will be calculated. The general rule of thumb is to continue until the arbitrariness of transfer pricing and/or overhead allocation policies offset the advantages of improving line of sight through the direct measurement of EVA for lower-level managers.
- EVA (or value) drivers will be used for levels in the hierarchy below those for which EVA is calculated and how they will be identified. The balanced scorecard is a popular approach for this purpose.
- How EVA will be calculated.
- If a single cost of capital figure will be used to calculate capital charges or if the cost of capital will be calculated separately for each division.
- Which managers and employees will have bonuses linked to EVA and how the bonus plan will work.

TABLE 1. A CHECKLIST FOR IMPLEMENTING EVA

Step 1:	Establish buy-in at the board and top management levels.
Step 2:	Set up a steering committee that will make the major strategic decisions on the EVA program (subject to board approval).
Step 3:	The steering committee formulates a strategy. What functions will be tied to EVA? Compensation Strategic planning Operating budgets Capital budgets Investor relations How far down the hierarchy will EVA be calculated? How will EVA be calculated? Management compensation Who will be covered? How will the bonus plan work? Relation to nonfinancial measures
Step 4:	The steering committee appoints a working committee to implement the strategy.
Step 5:	Set up a training program.

A working committee also should be appointed. This committee will implement the strategy set forth by the steering committee and approved by the board. The members of this committee should include, at a minimum, a senior representative from the CFO's office (probably an accountant), a human resources professional (with extensive experience in management training), and a senior-level line manager (but below the executive board level). For medium-sized and smaller companies, a single committee may be tasked with both the key strategic issues in EVA program design and with implementation of the program. Large, global companies are more likely to separate these tasks into two committees.

Whether performed by the steering committee or a working committee, one of the most delicate tasks in EVA implementation is designing a training program that draws genuine commitment to value creation from the company's employees.

EVA AND FINANCIAL MANAGEMENT

EVA is innovative in three important ways. First, because it is not bound by GAAP, its users are willing to make whatever adjustments are needed to produce more economically valid numbers. Second, proponents have been pushing companies to bring EVA into lower levels of the organization on the assumption that all employees, not just senior managers, must undertake their tasks with the overriding goal of creating shareholder value. Third, EVA offers a means of measuring and communicating performance that can be used in the capital markets, for capital investment appraisal, and in the evaluation and compensation of managerial performance. Instead of using, say, earnings per-share to communicate with security analysts, internal rates of return for capital investment appraisal, and return on net assets for the evaluation of managerial performance, companies can use EVA for all three.

Consider a typical capital investment. We undertake the investment when the net present value is positive and reject it when the NPV is negative. NPV is calculated by subtracting the capital to be invested from the present value of the net cash flows, or

$$NPV_{project} = Present\ Value_{project} - Capital_{project}$$

Now, consider the formula for MVA:

$$MVA = Total\ Value - Total\ Capital$$

In effect, MVA is equivalent to the present value of the cash flows to all capital providers (the value of the firm) net of the capital invested in the firm. Or it is the net present value for the entire firm. Remember that MVA, whether for the entire firm or just a single capital investment project, equals the present value of future EVAs.

When you view it in this way, you can see that firms can use EVA/MVA to evaluate capital investment proposals because these measurement tools will yield the same answer as NPV. That means the same terminology that companies use to communicate with shareholders can also be used internally for decision making. For capital budgeting proposals, nothing is lost by using EVA instead of discounted cash flow approaches because EVA produces equivalent results.

If the discounted present value of future EVAs yields the same answer as NPV, what does EVA offer that NPV doesn't? From a valuation standpoint, nothing. But EVA does have an important advantage. The problem with NPV (and MVA, for that matter) is that it is what economists call a "stock" or "wealth" measure; it is not a "flow." It measures the total amount of wealth that is expected to be created from undertaking an investment or activity, not performance. Managerial performance is evaluated over periods of time, say, three months, six months, or a year, not at a point in time. Because NPV and MVA are equivalent, and MVA is the present value of future EVAs, EVA becomes the means by which we can convert the stock measure of NPV (or MVA) into a flow. By linking management bonuses to EVA, companies reward managers for undertaking positive net present value projects, which is exactly what they want them to do.

EVA, CAPITAL INVESTMENT DECISIONS, AND ENVIRONMENTAL IMPACTS

To improve the quality of capital investment decisions, companies must be careful to consider the impacts of their products, services, and activities on their constituents over the life of the investment. Many companies make capital investment decisions on both environmental issues and general capital investments without considering the broad lifecycle impacts that will affect long-term corporate profitability. If companies want to improve capital investment decisions, they need to estimate future costs and benefits that probably will be internalized.[6] One such example is the cost of product take back. Already common in Europe and globally in some industries, these are costs that corporations incur when they take back and dispose of products they produced after consumers use them. Such costs should be included in both product costing and capital investment decisions.[7]

Once a company completes its analysis of future financial impacts, it should include those results in an NPV or EVA analysis. Corporate environmental health and safety managers often complain that the analysis of EH&S investments, both mandated and voluntary, are incomplete because they don't include a broad integration of impacts. But they also find that senior corporate managers don't see the value of these investments and, for this reason, often reject them.

This dilemma can be resolved through EVA because it can communicate the potential contribution of a project in language that is consistent with what many consider to be the most important of all corporate concerns: maximizing shareholder value.

BARRIERS AND CHALLENGES TO EVA IMPLEMENTATION

Companies adopt EVA because it can encourage managers to think and act more like owners. When managers are paid based on metrics other than EVA or similar value-based measures, there is a substantial risk that they will undertake activities, such as growth for its own sake, which might increase their own compensation at the expense of shareholder wealth creation. When companies link pay to EVA, and especially to improvements in EVA, managers soon learn that the surest way to high pay and advancement is creating as much wealth as possible for shareholders over the long term. But while the idea is simple enough, implementation is often complicated and frustrating.

Successful implementation of EVA requires:

- A full commitment from top management, especially the CEO. Not only must the value creation philosophy be integrated with all of the company's key systems—including strategic planning, capital budgeting, and management compensation—it must constantly be reinforced in management meetings, training seminars, company newsletters, performance reviews, and in communications with external parties such as security analysts and the financial press.

- A decision on which, if any, adjustments are to be made to the GAAP-based accounting numbers. Companies have a delicate balancing act to perform, managing the increased precision that comes from making more and more adjustments against the need to keep the measurement system easy and understandable.

- A careful consideration of transfer pricing and overhead allocation policies and their impact on EVA calculations. These issues are crucial because they can interfere with one of EVA's most potent advantages: its ability to get all managers, not just the most senior ones, to think more like owners. The power of EVA to accomplish this mission depends largely on the calculation of divisional EVA. But as any management accountant knows, different transfer pricing and overhead allocation policies can lead to wildly different divisional performance numbers. These issues are especially troublesome when large portions of managerial pay are linked to these numbers. Companies can sidestep the problem by calculating EVA only at the group level or for large stand-alone units. Unfortunately, when bonuses are linked to EVA at the corporate level, the compensation system becomes little better than conventional profit-sharing plans. Its ability to act as a motivator for employees at all levels becomes seriously blunted because, for all but the most senior managers, corporate EVA is too remote from their day-to-day activities.

- Intensive training for any manager or employee whose bonuses will be linked to EVA. In addition to explaining the imperative of value creation, and why it must go to the top of the corporate agenda, employees must understand how their unit EVAs will be calculated and how, in detail, the EVA numbers will be linked to compensation.

Management accountants and financial managers can make a major contribution to corporate profits by using their skills in measurement and analysis to improve capital investment decisions. On the environmental front, that includes identification and measurement of impacts related to a broader set of constituencies and a broader set of impacts than most companies now consider. It also means communicating this information effectively throughout the organization and demonstrating the relationship of the various impacts on shareholder value. EVA can be an important tool in this effort.

ENDNOTES

1. EVA is a registered trademark of Stern Stewart & Company.
2. Mark H. Dorfman, Warren R. Muir, and Catherine G. Miller, *Environmental Dividends: Cutting More Chemical Wastes*, Inform, 1992.
3. An extensive discussion of this topic can be found in Marc J. Epstein and Marie-Josee Roy, "Integrating Environmental Impacts into Capital Investment Decisions," *Greener Management International: The Journal of Corporate Environmental Strategy and Practice*, Spring 1997, pp. 69–87.
4. See, for example, Srikant Datar, Marc J. Epstein, and Karen White, "Bristol-Myers Squibb: The Matrix Essentials Product Life Cycle Review," *Stanford Business School Case*, 1997.
5. This section is largely adapted from Economic Value Added, INSEAD technical note 01/98-4667, and "Economic Value Added: A Primer for European Managers," *European Management Journal*, August 1997, both by S. David Young.
6. Additional details on incorporating life-cycle costing and total stakeholder analysis in product and project analysis (PPA) can be found in Marc J. Epstein, *Measuring Corporate Environmental Performance: Best Practices for Costing and Managing an Effective Environmental Strategy*, 1996.
7. Marc J. Epstein, "Accounting for Product Take Back," *Management Accounting*, August 1996.

Marc J. Epstein is visiting professor in the Jones Graduate School of Management at Rice University in Houston. Formerly a professor at Harvard and Stanford Business Schools, he has written extensively for Management Accounting *and is the author of the award-winning IMA book,* Measuring Corporate Environmental Performance: Best Practices for Costing and Managing an Effective Environmental Strategy. *His latest book,* Counting What Counts: Turning Accountability to Competitive Advantage, *will be released in April. He can be reached at epatein@rice.edu.*

S. David Young is professor of accounting at INSEAD. His research focuses on performance measurement and value based management. He is now writing a book on measuring and implementing Economic Value Added and can be reached by e-mail at david.young@insead.fr.

QUESTION

12.3 What factors must be considered before implementing EVA?

GEORGIA-PACIFIC'S EXPERIENCE

Georgia-Pacific, a large forest products company, has embraced both EVA and environmental responsibility. This requires, according to Susan Moore, Georgia-Pacific's vice president of environmental affairs, "integrating society's desire for a clean environment and shareholder expectations for financial returns."

Environmental projects at Georgia-Pacific are evaluated using EVA, and the environmental affairs department is evaluated like other departments using EVA, so employees are challenged to "come up with ideas that generate savings or, at a minimum, do not destroy value." Each environmental investment is evaluated by how it will "reduce consulting fees; lower capital costs; maximize revenues; reduce fines; or reduce sales, general, and administrative (SG &A) expenses."

Among the projects Georgia-Pacific has adopted are:

An aerator optimization project that reduced energy usage and generated $106,000 EVA. (continued)

An internal consulting team to be used for complex environmental permitting issues. It reduced the need for external consultants, speeded up the permitting process, and allowed more timely completion of construction projects, generating an EVA of $2.1 million.

A beneficial use for boiler fly ash generated at the plants reduced transportation and landfilling costs and created a valuable product, generating an EVA of $800,000.

In all cases, the analysis could have been completed with discounted cash flow analysis. But EVA has the advantage that it can be aligned with strategy throughout the organization and all employees can see how their actions can affect corporate profitability. In environmental affairs, the employees can see how these investments also improve the environment.[†]

Whether a company uses EVA or DCF, stakeholders must be defined broadly and the impacts of investments (along with all corporate products, services, and activities) must be evaluated and included in the investment analysis. An advantage of using EVA is that some departments—like environmental affairs—that are often seen as service departments or responding primarily to regulatory requirements can justify their expenditures in the language of the CFO. If defined broadly, including the impact on reputation, future revenues, long-term corporate costs, community interests, local regulation and enforcement, and so forth, investments in reducing environmental impacts often have big payoffs. Environmental affairs officers have just not had the tools or the language to evaluate or communicate these payoffs. If used broadly and properly, EVA can be an important part of the desire to improve corporate profitability and environmental responsibility simultaneously. When production processes yield only 85% of the raw material input, waste of 15% is created. The inefficiency is expensive in the loss of raw material, and the cost increases when companies must spend specifically to clean up the waste. When environmental investments can be made to reduce the waste and improve efficiency, both corporate profitability and the environment win. When water consumption in factories can be reduced through environmental investments in waste water cleansing and recycling equipment (and many companies report recent reductions of 75%–90% of water use) both the environment and company are improved. By considering long-term environmental and corporate impacts, an EVA analysis can align strategy and improve both decisions and communication.

[†] S. F. Moore, "Aligning Environmental Decision Making with Business Strategy: Georgia-Pacific's Economic Value Added Approach." *Strategic Environmental Management,* Volume 1, Number 1, 1998, pp, 69–76.

12.4 Evaluating Internal Operations and Supply Chain Performance Using EVA and ABC

Terrance L. Pohlen, *University of North Texas*
B. Jay Coleman, *University of North Florida**

INTRODUCTION

Firms cannot exist in isolation and must rely on other firms to perform a complex chain of interdependent activities from source-of-supply to the end-user. One company rarely controls an entire supply chain, and success depends on how well the combined capabilities of these firms can be integrated to achieve a competitive market-place advantage (Cook, DeBree, and Feroleto, 2001). Managers must extend their "line of sight" to understand system-wide performance and the contribution of each firm (Lummus and Vokurka, 1999). They subsequently need to develop measures for on meeting end-user requirements and aligning firm behavior with supply chain objectives. The ability to develop such measures is a major challenge to supply chain management (Pohlen, 2003).

Performance measures are critical to the success of the supply chain (Deloitte, 1999). Companies can no longer focus on optimizing their own operations to the exclusion of their suppliers' and customers' operations (Lummus, Vokurka, and Alber, 1999). By tying manufacturing and supply chain activities to performance outcomes, operations managers and senior executives can make more informed decisions regarding the allocation of scarce resources and the initiatives and partners that are best for the overall supply chain. Managers across an entire supply chain must collaborate to improve performance and obtain the greatest mutual benefit. Performance measures are needed to keep the trading partners aligned with the enterprise-wide goals so supply chain performance can be optimized.

Effective supply chain management requires measures capable of capturing inter-firm performance (van Hoek, 1998) and integrating the results to depict overall supply chain performance (McAdam and McCormack, 2001). Performance must be measured simultaneously across multiple firms, and the measures must demonstrate how each firm's behavior affects the others and the value delivered to the end-user. Supply chain performance measures must translate nonfinancial performance into financial terms and shareholder value (Ellram and Liu, 2002). Supply chain management will affect more than costs, and managers must be able to sell the value created to senior executives, trading partners, and shareholders. Although most managers acknowledge the importance of designing metrics and rewards, they lack an adequate framework for developing suitable performance measures (Kallio, 2000, Simatupang and Sridharan, 2002).

Few firms have measures capable of capturing performance across multiple companies (Keebler, 1999, Lambert and Pohlen, 2001, Lee and Billington, 1992, McAdam and McCormack, 2001, and Simatupang and Sridharan, 2002), and most are not satisfied with the measures they currently use for supply chain performance (Deloitte, 1999). In many instances, the measures identified as supply chain metrics are actually measures of internal operations or logistics performance (Lambert and Pohlen, 2001). Other approaches, such as the total cost of ownership (TCO) or the supply chain operations reference (SCOR) model, measure the effect of suppliers or other trading partners on performance within the firm. They do not measure performance across multiple firms or the overall supply chain.

In an effort to address this shortcoming, we apply a general framework introduced by Lambert and Pohlen (2001) to show how operations performance can be evaluated with a multi-firm, supply chain perspective. The framework can help operations managers achieve supply chain objectives such as "increased shareholder value" and "improved customer service" by providing a concrete roadmap. The focus is on increasing shareholder value for each firm in the supply chain by establishing within-company and cross-company links between actions (i.e., prospective value drivers) and profits. Senior executives can use the framework to determine whether operational-level actions did, indeed, create value, to demonstrate what requires measurement, to focus attention, and to align behavior within each firm with supply chain objectives. The framework differs from other approaches by simultaneously measuring and analyzing interfirm performance and linking operational performance measures directly to the drivers of shareholder value.

APPLYING THE FRAMEWORK

The framework employs a dyadic economic value added (EVA) analysis and activity-based costing (ABC). The dyadic EVA analysis 1) evaluates how process changes simultaneously drive value in each firm, and 2) develops measures that align operations performance with supply chain objectives. ABC determines what drives costs and

---

* From: R. L. Pohlen and B. J. Coleman, "Evaluating Internal Operations and Supply Chain Performance Using EVA and ABC," *S. A. M. Advanced Management Journal* (Spring 2005): 45–58. Reprinted with permission.

performance (Krumwiede and Roth, 1997, Buckingham and Loomba, 2001) and also translates nonfinancial performance into activity costs and financial measures. EVA and ABC enable managers to optimize and better coordinate the performance of activities across the entire supply chain (Dekker and Van Goor). The framework was adapted for an operational environment by developing five steps, each of which is performed by operations management personnel:

- Establish strategic objectives for the supply chain.
- Map the firms composing the supply chain.
- Examine operational decisions (i.e., potential value creators) using a dyadic EVA analysis.
- Translate process objectives into costs and operational performance measures using ABC.
- Measure and extend analysis to other trading partners.

1. *Establish strategic objectives for the supply chain*
The corporate strategy of the firm demonstrating the greatest leadership and power provides the most likely starting point for establishing supply chain objectives. Operations managers should look first at strategy when setting objectives and determining what to measure (Neely et al, 2000; Keegan et al, 1989; and Wisner and Fawcett, 1991). The corporate strategy reflects management's choices and trade-offs in its drive to achieve a unique competitive position and maximize shareholder value (Rappaport, 1987). Supply chain strategy flows directly from corporate strategy and the selected target markets by determining the configuration of the processes and companies that best meet end-user requirements and provide the greatest competitive advantage (Lummus, Vokurka, and Alber, 1999). Beginning with the consumer, management works backwards through the supply chain to consider what combination of trading partners best serves the target markets.

During this stage, operations managers perform a competitive analysis of the attractiveness of their industry and their position relative to their competitors. They seek to understand how alternative manufacturing strategies affect the firm's competitive position and the value created. The analysis leads to the selection of strategies that should best achieve corporate objectives and increase shareholder value. The resulting strategic plan and the company's mission statement provide direction and control for subsequent tactical planning and management of daily operations (Stock and Lambert, 2001).

2. *Map the firms composing the supply chain*
Mapping identifies the companies composing the supply chain from end-users to the raw material suppliers, after step 1 is completed and the most appropriate processes and strategic partners are identified (Stock and Lambert, 2001). Supply chain maps typically appear as a complex web like the branches and roots of an uprooted tree (Lambert and Pohlen, 2001). They rarely resemble the linear pipeline diagrams in most illustrations. This complexity makes it extremely difficult to understand what is actually happening and to communicate objectives across a supply chain (Keebler, 1999, McAdam and McCormack, 2001). Mapping enables managers to better understand their supply chains; however, few firms actually map them (Gardner and Cooper, 2003). Managers use the maps to achieve a competitive advantage — determining which branches or roots generate the most profit, pose the greatest risk, incur unnecessary cost and time, and require focused attention. The maps frequently reveal, previously undetected opportunities. For example, several tier-one suppliers may purchase critical components from the same tier-two supplier. Operations managers can leverage this information and negotiate a single ordering agreement with the tier-two supplier on behalf of their tier-one suppliers. They may also discover opportunities to reduce set-up times, eliminate waste, remove unnecessary intermediaries, and cut cycle times. Analyzing each link in the chain identifies many opportunities for improvement (Lummus, Vokurka, and Alber, 1998), but the value created by these opportunities must be demonstrated and sold to executives in the other firms to secure their buy-in and to align behavior with supply chain objectives.

3. *Examine operational decisions (potential value creators) using a dyadic EVA analysis *
Several processes span each link in the supply chain (Croxton, 2001), and a dyadic EVA analysis shows simultaneously how process changes drive value in multiple firms (Lambert and Pohlen, 2001). EVA has the advantage of providing "...a measure of wealth creation that aligns the goals of divisional or plant managers with the goals of the entire company" (Brewer, 1999). A dyadic EVA takes this a step further by measuring value creation across multiple companies and aligning management decisions with the objectives of the supply chain (Pohlen and Goldsby, 2003). A value-based approach expands the analysis beyond a simple "cost-cost" analysis by examining the effect on revenues, cost-of-goods sold, expenses, and assets. In many instances, a process change will affect activities in multiple companies. A dyadic analysis provides the capability to simultaneously determine the effect of any changes from the supplier's and customer's perspectives (Figure 1).

To illustrate how the value of an operational decision can be assessed within and across firms in the supply chain, consider a manufacturer who is attempting to implement a new manufacturing strategy or production initiative, such as lean production. As part of lean production, the manufacturer must reduce waste or, according to lean production doctrine, nonvalue-added items such as inventory, over-production (producing more units than needed to fill current orders), correction or rework (due to quality defects), the waiting of product during the production process, and overly long processing times. The lean focus also requires the manufacturer to increase its production flexibility.

In partial response to these needs, suppose the manufacturer decides to implement procedures to reduce production setup time. This will reduce setup costs, which are largely a function of production downtime caused by the setup, and thereby reduce production run sizes (i.e., less overproduction). With lower production quantities, average inventory levels will naturally go down as well, since order quantities directly influence the size of cycle stock, thus reducing that element of waste. These smaller production runs will also generate shorter order cycles (or time between orders) for the manufacturer. The shorter cycles, in turn, increase manufacturing flexibility, with a direct benefit for downstream customers. If a particular item is out-of-stock when ordered by a customer, the manufacturer will be able to launch a job to produce the needed item much sooner than if the manufacturer were tied to long production runs. The manufacturer can also afford to implement *heijunka* (Coleman and Vaghefi, 1994) – that is, the ability to make a little bit of everything every day, as opposed to making only one thing for a while before changing over to make something else. As a result, production plans can be set to make workloads much smoother across departments or work centers, and across time periods.

Wastes associated with waiting, processing, and correction also are improved. With shorter setup times and cycles, the likely waiting time for customer orders entering the production process is also reduced, as is the waiting time of work-in-process as it enters production queues. Also, reduced setup times will mean more time available for production, meaning the firm may be able to produce more during a given period, and possibly meet demand it is currently missing. With better designed setups, the scrap generated during and immediately after setups (due to testing) will be reduced. In sum, the potential benefits of a program to reduce setup times are substantial and permeate nearly all of the objectives of a lean production program.

However, note that the preceding concentrates on nonfinancial measures of performance. Ultimately, the performance changes should affect traditional financial measures within the firm. To illustrate, Figure 2 takes the supplier's perspective (the left half of Figure 1), and details the value drivers box. Also added is a box listing many aforementioned effects on various operational measures associated with reduced setup time and how they align with the firm's value drivers and financial metrics. As shown, setup time reduction should lead to a commensurate reduction in many of the expenses associated with inventory, including insurance; utilities; personnel directly associated with handling, maintaining, and auditing the inventory; interest (on any borrowing done to finance inventory); write-offs associated with inventory shrinkage due to damage, theft, or obsolescence; and scrap loss formerly experienced during and immediately following inefficient setups, etc. (Courtis, 1995). As a result, cost of goods sold and total expenses should decrease for the manufacturer, leading to a higher gross margin and net profit, respectively, and therefore a higher net operating profit after taxes (NOPAT). These effects are illustrated in the top half of Figure 2.

These benefits typically do not come without a price. In the short term, an investment in personnel time may be required to study setup practices and recommend changes. If a team approach is chosen for major setups, there may be an associated increase in personnel expenses and more employee training may be involved. Improved setups also may require modification of the product design itself to facilitate changeovers, which entails its own set of expenses. These and other costs will to some extent offset the previously noted improvements and will thereby affect the gross margin, net profit, and NOPAT, as shown in Figure 2.

But restricting the analysis to costs wouldn't be appropriate. As Courtis (1995) also notes, the reduction in time and expense, along with the increase in flexibility, should also benefit the revenue side. If cost savings are translated into lower prices for customers, sales volume and total revenue may increase. As noted, an increase in total output by converting setup time to productive time may allow the firm to meet demand it might not otherwise meet, and customer backorders may be reduced or eliminated. The gains in manufacturing flexibility and response time may generate increased business. In addition, the manufacturer may be able to reduce previously imposed minimum order quantities, thereby gaining a wider range of customers. As a result, the firm will see beneficial effects on sales revenue, gross margin, net profit, and NOPAT, over and above those associated with cost improvement (see Figure 2).

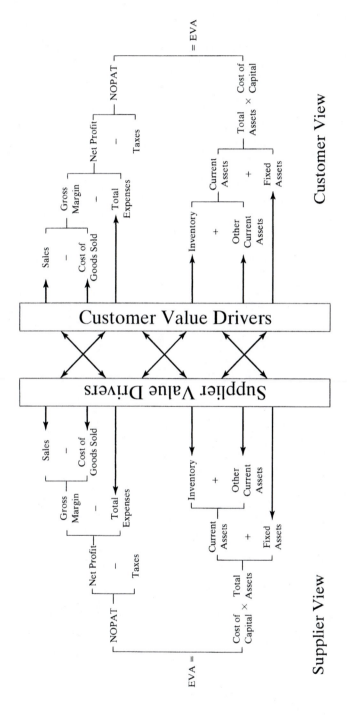

Supplier View

Customer View

Adapted from Stern, Joel M. and John S. Shiely with Irwin Ross, *The EVA Challenge*, New York: John Wiley & Sons, Inc., 2001, Figure 7.2, p. 120 and Pohlen, T. L. and Goldsby, t. J. (2003), "VMI and SMI Programs: How Economic Value Added Can Help Sell the Change," *International Journal of Physical Distribution and Logistics Management, 33*(7), 565-581.

Figure 1: Using Dyadic EVA Analysis to Demonstrate the Effect of Collaborative Action on Value Drivers in the Supplier and Customer Firms

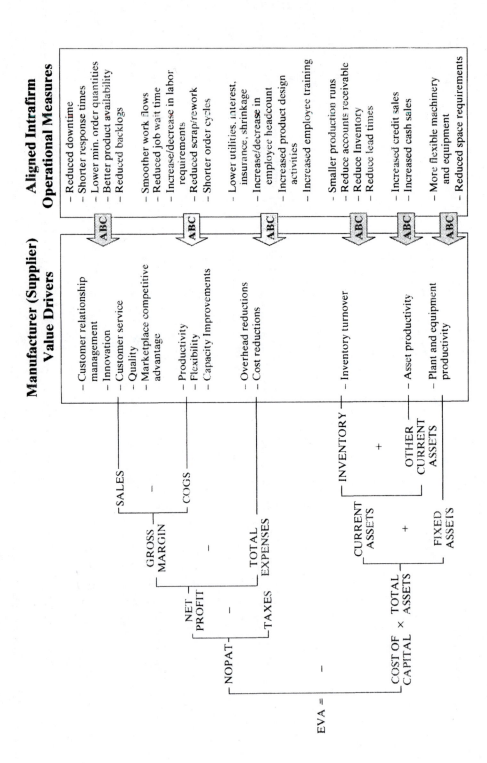

Figure 2: Evaluating the Manufacturer's Value Propositions of Reduced Setup Time

Again, however, the analysis shouldn't stop there. Restricting the analysis to revenues versus expenses ignores the impact on a firm's fixed and current assets. Although major investment is not necessarily required to improve setups (Shingo, 1985), this initiative may well require additional investment in fixed assets, such as newer and more flexible equipment (Courtis, 1995) and machinery that can be changed over more easily. Current assets will also be affected; the primary benefit will be the reduction in inventory already documented. However, this will likely be offset somewhat — and, according to Courtis (1995), perhaps completely — by higher cash balances and accounts receivable.

So, how does the firm factor in the classical profit and loss financial information with the changes in total assets? That is the advantage of opting for an EVA approach to see whether the setup reduction initiative generates value for the firm. As illustrated in Figures 1 and 2, the change in total assets is multiplied by the firm's weighted average cost of capital to determine the necessary benchmark return for the assets invested in the venture. If the changes in NOPAT exceed this benchmark, then the initiative creates economic value for the manufacturer.

However, stopping at the firm level would fail to account for the true influence on the manufacturer's supply chain partners and would likely not appropriately capture the total value of the initiative. Consider the corresponding view of one of the manufacturer's key retail customers, and the "mirror image" of Figure 2 that determines the retailer's own value propositions (in Figure 3). Recall that one of the benefits of setup savings is the possible reduction in prices that the retail customer must pay the manufacturer. When translated into the retailer's EVA analysis, the lower prices result in decreased costs of good sold, and a corresponding increase in gross margin, net profit, and NOPAT. Moreover, the manufacturer's faster production capabilities generated through more production uptime and increased flexibility translates into greater on-shelf availability for the retailer and a possible corresponding increase in retail sales and market share. The resulting increase in sales positively affects all profit measures as well.

There are also effects on the retailer's asset base. Suppose that as a result of the setup time savings the manufacturer can ship finished products more frequently and, in smaller quantities. (Perhaps the manufacturer had been requiring large minimum orders, which can now be greatly reduced). With smaller order quantities, the retailer's own cycle stock is reduced. Furthermore, the retailer's safety stock levels potentially could be reduced, since these are partially a function of lead time from the manufacturer.

With better manufacturing response times and reduced backlogs, safety stocks for the retailer can be lowered. The reduction in storage space requirements for the retailer also lowers the percentage of distribution center space allocated to the manufacturer's product. If significant enough, the retailer might even be able to eliminate distribution centers. All of this would have a positive impact on the retailer's total assets. When simultaneously evaluated against the retailer's changes in its own NOPAT, the change in EVA for the retailer can be estimated.

There are tangible benefits for the manufacturer associated with extending the analysis to its trading partner in the manner described. Suppose the manufacturer believes that an increase in selling price is needed to partially justify the investment in setup reduction. This obviously would run counter to the potential price reduction advantages to the retailer mentioned earlier in the section. However, a complete analysis of advantages to the retailer associated with the manufacturers' changes (e.g., in on-shelf availability and improved sales prospects), along with an illustration of the total asset reductions and corresponding increase in EVA for the retailer, could go a long way in selling the price increases to the retailer. It would also avoid the strict cost-versus-cost discussions that classically take place between supply chain partners.

Similar scenarios could also arise in which a member of the supply chain needs inter-firm visibility to make appropriate decisions or to sell trading partners on new initiatives. Suppose the manufacturer, as part of the lean initiative, wants to increase standardization (another lean production concept) by reducing the number or variety of products in its product line. Such a move would make it easier for the manufacturer to deal with the setup issues but would reduce the variety of product offered to the retailer. The retailer will typically view such a move negatively, as it would tend to imply reduced sales volume at the retail level. However, suppose the manufacturer promises a corresponding price decrease, as well as a minimum order reduction. Using the dyadic EVA analysis described, both parties can identify whether the reduction in the product line will pay off.

The dyadic EVA analysis demonstrates how working together to achieve supply chain objectives drives value in both firms. A holistic view of the supply chain facilitates communication and enables problems to be identified more easily (Cook, 2001). By incorporating all of the drivers of shareholder value, managers can move beyond cost-cost discussions, where one firm "loses" and another "wins," to identifying interfirm opportunities that create value for both firms and the entire supply chain.

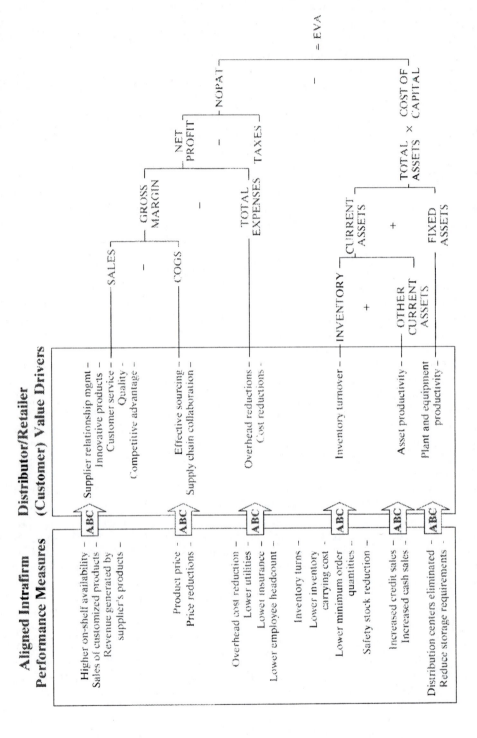

Figure 3: Evaluating the Retailer's Value Propositions of Reduced Setup Time by its Supplier

However, successful inter-firm collaboration will directly depend on the ability to accurately measure and assign any resulting cost changes by product, customer, supplier, or supply chain (Zank and Vokurka, 2003) and on the development of measures that align internal performance with supply chain objectives. This is the role and contribution to the framework performed by activity-based costing.

4. *Translate process objectives into costs and operational performance measures using ABC*

The financial and performance views of ABC support accurate costing and the development of supporting operational performance measures (Turney, 1991). The cost assignment, or vertical view, of ABC (Figure 4) assigns costs to the activities performed within an organization. An activity-based approach uses multiple drivers to reflect how resources and activities are actually consumed. The use of multiple drivers provides a more accurate assignment of costs than traditional cost systems that typically rely on a limited number of volume-based measures, such as direct labor hours or sales volume (Krumwiede and Roth, 1997). Operations managers can use this view to determine the costs of activities composing their firm's supply chain processes. ABC assigns the costs to the customers, suppliers, products, and supply chains involved in these activities. This cost information can be inserted directly into the dyadic EVA analysis when assessing performance and value resulting from conducting business with a specific customer.

Activity-based management (ABM), or the process view of ABC (Figure 5), decomposes supply chain processes into the specific activities performed within each firm. Operations managers can use this view to develop and align intrafirm performance measures that support the supply chain objectives. The horizontal perspective increases management understanding of activity performance by breaking down activities into measurable tasks, developing nonfinancial performance measures, and identifying the factors driving activity performance and cost. Management can act on this information to improve activity cost and performance.

An activity-based approach is essential for determining the inputs into the dyadic EVA framework. Reconfiguration of internal operational processes (such as setup time reduction) will drive changes in activities within the firm. ABC captures the effect of these changes in nonfinancial performance, translates the changes into costs, and updates the changes into financial performance and statements. The firm's impact on supply chain partners is also captured through ABC. Changes in performance are translated into assignable cost information that can be applied to the particular partner being

studied. Additionally, the determination of assignable nonfinancial performance information helps the firm identify the effect of an activity on factors that cross the supply chain, such as quality, cost, flexibility, dependability, and innovation (Wisner and Fawcett, 1991).

ABC provides the necessary mechanism to link operational measures (shown in the performance measure column) in Figures 2 and 3 with the associated value drivers and financial measures shown in those figures. The measures and cost information obtained through ABC are traced to each of the value drivers, as illustrated by the large arrows. The linkage demonstrates how improved performance at the activity level leads to value creation and increased profitability at the corporate level. The cascading of objectives to value drivers to operational measures ensures the alignment of intrafirm performance with interfirm strategy. It also promotes more effective communication by identifying exactly what each individual must accomplish to meet corporate and supply chain objectives. The framework enables operations managers to work backwards from the objective to reconfigure processes, redistribute activities, align performance, measure progress, and demonstrate improvement in profitability.

5. *Measure and expand analysis to other trading partners*

Expanding the dyadic EVA analysis from the supplier-customer relationship to include trading partners across the entire supply chain enables management to see how each firm contributes to achieving supply chain objectives and whether corporate behavior is properly aligned to improve performance and generate additional value. A dyadic upstream and downstream view is necessary to allow the manufacturer's leadership team to fully evaluate initiatives or proposals. For example, suppose the manufacturer is asking a tier 1 supplier for reductions in delivery quantities and quicker response to synchronize with the manufacturer's objective of smaller production quantities. The tier 1 supplier maintains that comply a significant investment is required to move distribution centers closer to the manufacturer. This will entail an associated price increase. If viewed myopically, the manufacturer simply could not capture the true value of a new arrangement, nor could they determine what a reasonable price increase would be. Using a dyadic EVA analysis, the manufacturer could assess the impact of the investment for the supplier, could examine the value drivers (e.g., lower raw material inventory) generated for itself by the results of that investment, assess the resulting EVA changes, and in the process assess the EVA impact that would be passed along to its own customers. Only then could an appropriate decision be made.

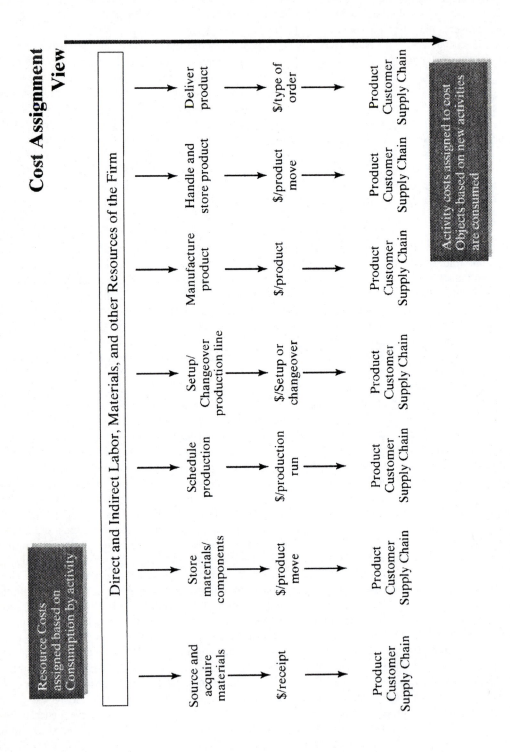

Figure 4: Vertical, or Cost Assignment, View of Activity-Based Costing

Adapted from Turney, P. B. B. (1991), *Common Cents*, Hillsboro, OR: Cost Technology and Kaplan, R. S. (2001), "Integrating Shareholder Value with Activity-Based Costing with the Balanced Scorecard," *Balanced Scorecard Report*, 3(1), 3-6

Process View →

Cost Drivers	Activities	Performance Measures
Vendor performance Component quality Inventory visibility	Source and acquire materials	Quality Cost Leadtime
Order frequency Minimum lot size Forecast accuracy	Store materials/ components	Inventory turns Inventory carrying cost Storage requirements
Equipment availability Changeover cost Lot size	Schedule production	Production run size Response time Backlogs
Equipment flexibility Product design Employee training	Setup/ changeover production line	Changeover time Reduced job wait time Employees trained/qualified
Component quality Product design Equipment maintenance	Manufacture product	Throughout rate/time Reduced scrap/rework Lower minimum quantity Employee headcount
Forecast accuracy Demand visibility Leadtimes Product run size	Handle and store product	Finished inventory turns Storage space requirement Inventory carrying cost
Product design Demand visibility Customer service Transp equipment availability	Deliver product	Shorter order cycles Reduce accounts receivable Better product availability

Adapted from Turney, P. B. B. (1991), *Common Cents*, Hillsboro, OR: Cost Technology

Figure 5: Activity-Based Management—the Horizontal, or Process View, of Activity-Based Costing.

Extending the dyadic EVA analysis beyond the supplier-customer dyad to include multiple trading partners provides several benefits. Managers can measure how effectively each firm has implemented the strategy and the supply chain's effect on shareholder value. Operations managers across multiple companies can identify opportunities where collaborative action could increase sales, eliminate duplicating or non-value-added activities, and reduce inventories. Executives obtain a better understanding of how their decisions affect upstream or downstream performance and costs. The focus shifts from negotiating lower prices and driving cost reductions to how to increase value for the end-user and the entire supply chain. An extended analysis also provides a more appropriate vehicle for assessing whether an equitable allocation of costs and benefits has occurred across the supply chain.

Although the previous discussion illustrates the effects of implementing one type of operations initiative within a supply chain, a similar process could be followed to analyze any operational changes made by any trading partner, including just-in-time (JIT), quick response (QR), flexible manufacturing systems (FMS), distribution requirements planning (DRP), material requirements planning (MRP), Six-Sigma, statistical process control (SPC), zero quality control (Shingo, 1986), collaborative planning, forecasting, and replenishment (CPFR), vendor managed inventory (VMI), sole/single sourcing, or concurrent engineering (CE, involving the supplier in product development). This is particularly recommended for initiatives that span the boundaries of multiple firms, as do JIT, QR, VMI, CPFR, and CE.

Working collaboratively with suppliers and customers on any of these will result at a minimum in ripple effects on EVA across a supplier-customer dyad and likely beyond to further branches of the supply chain. Quality improvement initiatives like CE, SPC, Six-Sigma, or zero quality control improve the ability to deploy new, innovative, higher-quality products faster than the competition. The customer's sales rise with increased market share and penetration into new markets resulting from the sale of new or better products, thereby producing additional sales revenue for the supplier. The exchange of information associated with CPFR will reduce cost-of-goods sold for a supplier through better production planning, ordering of materials, and workforce utilization. The customer's cost-of-goods sold can also decline as the supplier passes along cost savings. The supplier's current assets decrease as it holds less inventory due to improved forecasting and production scheduling. Accounts receivable may also decrease as the customer agrees to faster, electronic payments in return for off-setting cost reductions. Fixed assets decline due to improved scheduling and better utilization of plant, equipment, and warehouse assets. In VMI, expenses

decrease as the supplier eliminates non-value-added activities between the two firms: sales people no longer call on purchasing, orders are received electronically, shipments are scheduled to maximize truckload rates and leverage cross-docking opportunities, and warehousing and handling of finished goods inventories are reduced (Pohlen and Goldsby, 2003). The customer's current assets drop as the supplier assumes inventory ownership, and the customer's fixed assets drop through eliminating distribution centers and material handling equipment. Some customer expenses may increase if the supplier must be paid more quickly, or if it must purchase technology necessary for communicating with the supplier.

IMPLEMENTATION ISSUES

Several issues will confront managers attempting to implement the dyadic EVA and ABC framework. For example, other trading partners may be unwilling or unable to exchange the information needed to support the implementation of supply chain initiatives. However, this can be overcome by identifying common goals and providing objective information to a reluctant trading partner. In a value chain analysis examining interfirm relationships, Dekker (2003) found that improved discussion of outcomes and possible courses of action increased the interaction between trading partners. The objective nature of cost information eased communications and negotiations. As the consequences of changes in supply chain operations became more transparent, the trading partners perceived less risk that they would end up with inequitable outcomes or having their shares of the benefits appropriated. This approach applies even when the firms do not exchange financial information (Dekker and Van Goor, 2001). The ability to demonstrate the direction and magnitude of value creation provides a compelling argument for change. The dyadic EVA analysis does this by identifying mutually desirable objectives for the supply chain and providing objective information regarding the effects of changes in cost and performance on the affected trading partners.

The need to generate immediate results may preclude managers from investing in supply chain initiatives when there is a lag between investment and the subsequent benefits, even for changes with high payback. EVA overemphasizes the need to generate immediate results (Brewer, 1999), and increasing investments in assets has a negative effect on EVA-based metrics. The costs and expenses associated with any initiative are recognized when incurred; however, the associated benefits may not be realized for several years. The inability of some firms to accurately assign the benefits and costs to a specific supply chain initiative further exacerbates the situation. Managers can partially overcome this issue by using the framework to demonstrate how, over the long-run, supply chain investments will create value for the firm. However, without a balanced set of metrics that emphasize and reward investment in innovation and process improvement, EVA-based measures could act as a disincentive to managers weighing projects that do not provide immediate returns (Brewer, 1999).

The dyadic EVA and ABC approach may also produce a bias toward the development of financial and cost-based performance measures. The integration of EVA and ABC with the balanced scorecard (BSC) can overcome this situation. The BSC overcomes the limitations of managing only with financial measures (Davig, Elbert, and Brown, 2004). The BSC framework ensures a balanced set of measures by viewing performance from four perspectives: financial, customer, internal processes, and innovation and learning (Kaplan and Norton, 1992).

Robert Kaplan (2001), one of the principal architects of the BSC, argues that the BSC, EVA, and ABC are highly compatible and that organizations can greatly benefit from their integration. EVA takes into account the quantity of capital used to generate financial returns and can be used to organize the financial perspective of the BSC. However, EVA must be combined with other approaches, such as ABC, that can analyze activities and translate non-financial into financial performance. The first stage of ABC assigns the resources consumed in performing the activities and processes within an organization. Kaplan suggests the activity costs can be directly linked to the internal processes perspective in the BSC. The activity-based information demonstrates how reducing setup time and employing flexible manufacturing affects costs and process performance. The subsequent assignment of activity costs to determine cost-to-serve, supply chain profitability, or customer profitability, provides a linkage to the customer and financial perspectives of the BSC. ABM provides the link to the fourth perspective, innovation and learning, by identifying the factors that drive activity costs such as product design, employee training, and new product development, and the measures for assessing activity performance: percent of employees qualified/trained, change-over time, quality, and number of new product introductions. The BSC can integrate ABC, EVA, and ABM into a single framework that provides a balanced perspective between financial and nonfinancial results as well as long-term versus short-term performance. However, the BSC has been used only to integrate intrafirm performance measures, and its application across multiple firms requires further research.

CONCLUSION

Successful supply chain management ultimately comes down to the ability to create more value than the competition. The configuration of firms, processes, and activities composing the supply chain drives value creation. Operations managers and senior executives confront the problem of determining the configuration yielding the greatest value for the end-user and each trading partner. They need to evaluate how the operational capabilities of each firm contribute to attaining supply chain objectives and the level of value created. The value of collaborative action must be measured and sold across each link to obtain trading partner buy-in and to align intrafirm performance with supply chain objectives. Despite the need to measure and align performance across multiple firms, most managers view performance from an internal perspective, or at best, how it is affected by their immediate upstream or downstream trading partners. Complexity and the interdependent nature of the supply chain make interfirm performance measurement extremely difficult; however, firms that act first to apply interfirm measures and align their performance with supply chain value objectives will achieve a sustainable advantage their competitors may be unable to emulate.

Dr. Pohlen, who retired from the U.S. Air Force with over 20 years of logistics experience, has published in leading logistics journals. His articles focus on the costing and financial management of logistics and supply chain performance measurement. Dr. Coleman is actively involved in research on the mathematical modeling of managerial decisions and has published over 40 articles.

REFERENCES

Brewer, P. C., Chandra, G., and Hock, C. A. (1999). Economic value added (EVA): Its uses and limitations. *SAM Advanced Management Journal, 64*(2), 4–11.

Buckingham, M., and Loomba A. (2001). Advantageous cost structure: A Strategic costing case study. *Production and Inventory Management Journal, 42*(1), 12–18.

Coleman, B. J., and Vaghefi, R. M. (1994). Heijunka (?): A key to the Toyota production system. *Production and Inventory Management Journal, 35*(4), 31–35.

Cook, J. S., DeBree, K., and Feroleto, A. (2001). From raw materials to customers: Supply chain management in the service industry. *SAM Advanced Management Journal, 66*(4), 14–21.

Courtis, J. K. (1995). JIT's impact on a firm's financial statements. *International Journal of Purchasing and Materials Management, 3*(1), 46–50.

Croxton, K. L., García-Dastugue, S. J., Lambert, D. M., and Rogers, D. S. (2001). The supply chain management processes. *International Journal of Logistics Management, 12*(2), 13–36.

Davig, W., Elbert, N., and Brown, S. (2004). Implementing a strategic planning model for small manufacturing firms: An adaptation of the balanced scorecard. *SAM Advanced Management Journal, 69*(1), 18–24.

Dekker, H. C. (2003). Value chain analysis in interfirm relationships: A field study. *Management Accounting Research, 14*(1), 1–23.

Dekker, H. C., and Van Goor, A. R. (2003). Supply chain management and management accounting: A case study of activity-based costing. *International Journal of Logistics: Research and Applications, 3*(1), 41–52.

Deloitte Consulting. (1999). Energizing the supply chain: Trends and issues in supply chain management. Retrieved June 21, 2004 from http://www.deloitte.com/dtt/research/0,2310,sid%253D2222%2526cid%253D35758,00.html

Ellram, L. M., and Liu, B. (2002). The financial impact of supply management. *Supply Chain Management Review, 6*(6), 30–37.

Gardner, J. T., and Cooper, M. C. (2003). Strategic supply chain mapping approaches. *Journal of Business Logistics, 24*(2), 37–64.

Holmberg, S. (2000). A systems perspective on supply chain measurements. *International Journal of Physical Distribution and Logistics Management, 30*(10), 847–868.

Kaplan, R. S. (2001). Integrating shareholder value and activity-based costing with the balanced scorecard. *Balanced Scorecard Report, 3*(1), 3–6.

Kaplan, R. S., and Norton, D. P. (1992). The balanced scorecard—measures that drive performance. *Harvard Business Review, 70*(1), 71–79.

Keebler, J. S., Manrodt, K. B., Durtsche, D. A., and Ledyard, D. M. (1999). *Keeping score.* Oakbrook, IL: Council of Logistics Management.

Kallio, J., Saarinen, T., Tinnila, M. and Vepsalainen, A. P. J. (2000). Measuring delivery process performance. *International Journal of Logistics Management, 11*(1), 75–87.

Kaplan, R. S., and Norton, D. P. (1996). *The balanced scorecard.* Boston, MA: Harvard Business School Press.

Keegan, D. P., Eiler, R.G., and Jones, C.R. (1989, June). Are your performance measures obsolete? *Management Accounting,* 45–50.

Krumwiede, K. R., and Roth, H. P. (1997). Implementing Information technology innovations: The activity-based costing example. *SAM Advanced Management Journal, 62*(4), 4–12.

La Londe, B. J., and Pohlen, T. L. (1996). Issues in supply chain costing. *International Journal of Logistics Management, 7*(1), 1–12.

Lambert, D. M., and Pohlen, T. L. (2001). Supply chain metrics. *International Journal of Logistics Management, 12*(1), 1–19.

Lee, H. L., and Billington, C. (1992, Spring). Managing supply chain inventory: Pitfalls and opportunities. *Sloan Management Review, 33*(3), 65–73.

Lummus, R. R., and Vokurka, R. J. (1999). Managing the demand chain through managing the information flow: Capturing moments of information. *Production and Inventory Management Journal, 40*(1), 16–20.

Lummus, R. R., Vokurka, R. J., and Alber, K. L. (1998). Strategic supply chain planning. *Production and Inventory Management Journal, 39*(3), 49–58.

Neely, A., Mills, J., Platts, K., Richards, H., Gregory, M., Bourne, M., and Kennerly, M. (2000). Performance measurement system design: Developing and testing a process-based approach. *International Journal of Operations and Production Management, 20*(10), 1119–1145.

McAdam, R., and McCormack, D. J. (2001). Integrating business processes for global alignment and supply chain management. *Business Process Management Journal, 7*(2), 113–130.

Pohlen, T. L. (2003). A framework for evaluating supply chain performance. *Journal of Transportation Management, 14*(2), 1–21.

Pohlen, T. L., and Goldsby, T. J. (2003). VMI and SMI programs: How economic value added can help sell the change. *International Journal of Physical Distribution and Logistics Management, 33*(7), 565–581.

Rappaport, A. (1987). Linking competitive strategy and shareholder value analysis. *The Journal of Business Strategy, 7*(4), 58–67.

Shingo, S. (1986). *Zero quality control: Source inspection and the poka-yoke system.* Stamford, Conn.: Productivity Press.

Shingo, S. (1985). *A revolution in manufacturing: The SMED system.* Stamford, Conn.: Productivity Press.

Simatupang, T. M., and Sridharan, R. (2002). The collaborative supply chain. *International Journal of Logistics Management, 13*(2), 15–30.

Stock, J. R., and Lambert, D. M. (2001). *Strategic logistics management,* 4th Ed, New York: McGraw-Hill Irwin, 684.

Turney, P. B. B. (1991). *Common cents.* Hillsboro, OR: Cost Technology.

van Hoek, R. I. (1998). Measuring the unmeasureable—measuring and improving performance in the supply chain. *Supply Chain Management, 3*(4), 187–192.

Wisner, J. D., and Fawcett, S. E. (1991). Linking firm strategy to operating decisions through performance measurement. *Production and Inventory Management Journal, 32*(3), 5–11.

Zank, G. M., and Vokurka, R. J. (2003). The Internet: Motivations, deterrents, and impact on supply chain relationships. *SAM Advanced Management Journal, 68*(2), 33–40.